1 MONTH OF
FREE
READING

at

www.ForgottenBooks.com

By purchasing this book you are eligible for one month membership to ForgottenBooks.com, giving you unlimited access to our entire collection of over 1,000,000 titles via our web site and mobile apps.

To claim your free month visit:

www.forgottenbooks.com/free57605

ISBN 978-1-5284-6420-8
PIBN 10057605

This book is a reproduction of an important historical work. Forgotten Books uses
state-of-the-art technology to digitally reconstruct the work, preserving the original format
whilst repairing imperfections present in the aged copy. In rare cases, an imperfection in
the original, such as a blemish or missing page, may be replicated in our edition. We do,
however, repair the vast majority of imperfections successfully; any imperfections that
remain are intentionally left to preserve the state of such historical works.

SOME ACCOUNT

OF THE WORK OF

STEPHEN J. FIELD

AS A

LEGISLATOR, STATE JUDGE, AND JUDGE OF THE SUPREME COURT OF THE UNITED STATES.

WITH AN

INTRODUCTORY SKETCH

BY

JOHN NORTON POMEROY, LL.D.,

PROFESSOR OF LAW IN THE HASTINGS LAW DEPARTMENT OF
THE UNIVERSITY OF CALIFORNIA.

1881.

Copyright, 1882, by S. B. Smith.

INDEX.

APPENDIX.

INTRODUCTORY SKETCH.

I purpose to analyze and describe the work and its results of one who, to an extraordinary degree, has impressed his own conceptions upon the jurisprudence of the country—as much so, perhaps, as any living jurist of America. To those who are informed as to the extent and variety of his official labors, this will not appear an extravagant opinion; and its correctness will be demonstrated by the facts which I shall produce.

The subject of this memoir belongs to a remarkable family—a family which well illustrates the effects of American civilization and institutions working upon the best New England character. Commencing their careers with no advantages except the early training of God-fearing parents, and the education afforded by the country academy and college, the living members of the family, consisting of the brothers David Dudley Field, Cyrus West Field, Stephen Johnson Field, and Henry Martyn Field, have all risen to distinction. Of the first two named brothers the reputation is world-wide; in fact, David Dudley Field and Cyrus W. Field are even better known and more honored throughout Europe than in their own country. If the fourth brother has attained to a less extensive fame, it is because as a clergyman he has confined his activities to an American church, within which he has a high position and has long wielded a powerful influence as the editor of one of the leading religious papers of the country. Of David Dudley Field and Cyrus W. Field it is unnecessary to speak. The former, by his reforming measures in the systems of procedure in the courts, has revolutionized the modes of administering justice, and placed them upon a foundation of simplicity and truth in all those nations and regions of the world where the English common law has been adopted. The latter, by his far-seeing sagacity, untiring energy, and deep enthusiasm, has been the leader in accomplishing that triumph of science and commerce combined by which all parts of the world are united, time and space are annihilated, nations are made one, and the vast world-wide movements and transactions of business, trade, and commerce are controlled. The work of the third brother, who is the subject of this sketch, has been restricted to the legislation and jurisprudence of his own country, but in some respects it is equal in importance and variety to that accomplished by either of his brothers.

Stephen Johnson Field was born in Haddam, Connecticut, on the 4th of November, 1816. His grandfathers on both his paternal and maternal sides served as officers in the Revolutionary War, and were descended from a Puritan stock, their ancestors being among the earliest settlers of New England. In 1819, when he was about three years old, his father, who was a Congregational clergyman, removed to Stockbridge, Massachusetts, and Stephen's childhood and early youth were there passed in what has become one of the most famous and classic spots of New England. At the age of thirteen, a step was taken by him which undoubtedly produced a deep and lasting impression upon his intellectual and moral character, although its effects upon his external life were temporary and trifling. In 1829 an elder sister married the Rev. Josiah Brewer. Mr. and Mrs. Brewer, acting under the auspices of The Ladies' Greek Association in New Haven, soon afterwards sailed for the Levant, with the intention

of establishing schools in Greece for the education of females. They invited Stephen to accompany them. His
brother, David Dudley, who as the eldest of the family
took a deep and active interest in promoting the welfare
of the younger members, advised his going for the purpose of studying the Oriental languages, thinking that
he could thereby qualify himself for a professorship of
Oriental languages and literature in an American University. With this design he accompanied his sister
and brother-in-law. They sailed December 10th, 1829,
and arrived at Smyrna, February 5, 1830. Mr. Brewer
there changed his original plan and established a school at
Smyrna. Stephen remained in the Levant two and a half
years. In addition to the time spent in Smyrna he visited
many of the islands of the Grecian Archipelago, and famous cities of Asia Minor, and passed one winter in
Athens in the family of the Rev. John Hill, the well-
known American missionary of the Episcopal Church.
Mr. and Mrs. Hill had been on a visit to Smyrna, and Mr.
Hill being detained by some matters of business, Mrs. Hill
returned to Athens without him. Stephen accompanied
her as her escort and remained at Athens until Mr. Hill's
return. During this residence in the East, Stephen learned
the modern Greek so that he was able to write and to
speak it with ease, and acquired some knowledge of the
French, Italian, and Turkish. But the most important and
lasting result of the time thus spent in the East during
the plastic period of his youth, was a moral one; and the
lesson which he there learned was that of religious tol-
eration. He had been brought up as a boy in the strictest tenets of Calvinism. As he says of himself, "he had
been taught to believe that the New England Puritans
possessed about all the good there was in the religious
world," and to look with distrust upon all the great historical churches which they, with one sweeping condemnation, called Nominal Christians. During his Eastern life
he was thrown into close contact with Roman Catholics,

B

members of the Greek Church, and Armenians, as well as with Mahometans; he saw examples of faith, devotion, piety, and virtue among them all, and was profoundly impressed by them. Indeed, his views underwent an entire revolution; and there was laid the foundation of that broad tolerance which has ever since been a distinguishing element of his character.*

He returned to the United States during the winter of 1832-3; entered Williams College in the fall of 1833, and was graduated in 1837, having obtained the highest honors of his class—the Greek oration at the Junior Exhibition, and the valedictory oration at the Commencement. He entered upon the study of the law during the Spring of 1838, in the office of his brother, David Dudley, in New York City, and was admitted to the Bar in 1841. A portion of this interval he spent in Albany, giving instruction to classes of the Albany Female Academy, and pursuing his

---

*Stephen was in Smyrna when the dreaded plague visited the city in the spring of 1831. Every one then avoided his neighbor as if contagion would follow the slightest touch. Says a writer describing the scenes: "If two men met in the street, each drew away from the other, as if contact were death. Sometimes they hugged the walls of the houses, with canes in their hands ready to strike down any one who should approach. All papers and letters coming through the mails were smoked and dipped in vinegar before they were delivered, lest they might communicate infection. Even vegetables were passed through water before they were taken from the hands of the seller. Terrible tales were told of scenes when guests were carried away dead from the table, and servants dropped down while waiting upon it. On every countenance was depicted an expression of terror." Mr. Brewer remained in the city for two or three weeks, and then left with his family in a vessel.

In the Fall of the same year Smyrna was visited with the Asiatic cholera. Hundreds died every day from its attacks, and thousands left the city and camped in the fields. Mr. Brewer gave his time to administering to the sick and dying. With his pockets filled with medicines he went through the lanes and alleys of the city on his errand of mercy. Stephen, with his pockets filled in the same way, accompanied him in all his rounds. Commodore J. E. DeKay, in a work entitled "Turkey in '31 and '32," thus speaks of the heroic devotion of Mr. Brewer in those terrible scenes, as follows:

"The efforts of the physicians at Smyrna during the fearful season of cholera, were nobly seconded by many of the foreign missionaries. Among these I heard the labors of Mr. Brewer everywhere spoken of in terms of admiration. Furnished with all the requisite remedies, he scoured every lane and alley, proclaiming his benevolent intentions, and distributing even food to the needy. Let history, when it repeats the story of the good Bishop of Marseilles—who, after all, was merely a soldier at his post—also record the benevolence and the proud contempt of danger and of death evinced by an American stranger within the pestilential walls of Smyrna."

studies in the office of John Van Buren, then the Attorney-General of the State, and at the summit of his brilliant but disappointing career. On being admitted to the Bar, he was taken into partnership by his brother in New York City, which continued until the year 1848. On the breaking out of the Mexican war, and again at its close, his brother advised him to remove to California, making generous offers of pecuniary means for investment in the purchase of land, but Stephen had a strong desire to visit Europe, and declined the proposal. He sailed for Europe in June, 1848, with the design of making an extensive tour. While in Paris, the following winter, he read the annual message of President Polk to Congress, which officially announced the discovery of gold in California. He then felt some regrets that he had not acted upon the advice of his brother, but nevertheless concluded to visit the most interesting parts of Europe before returning. He did so, and returned to New York in the Fall of 1849, arriving on the 1st of October. Soon afterwards he left for California.

As I do not intend to write a life of Judge Field, I shall not attempt to describe the incidents and adventures of his California career. It will be sufficient to mention the most important events, so as to exhibit the more clearly his public and official labors, and to fix the date of the successive steps which he took until he reached his present high position as a member of the Supreme Court of the United States.

He arrived in San Francisco on the 28th of December, 1849, with hardly any funds, and with no resources except untiring energy and capacity for work, great intellectual ability, natural and cultivated, the well-laid foundation of legal learning, and the high hopes of opening manhood. In January, 1850, he removed to a settlement just commenced which became the important inland city of Marysville. Here he established himself, and the place continued to be his home during the whole of his professional life in California, until 1857. He was at once elected the first alcalde of the new town, and held the office until the organization of the State government, and the introduction of American institutions. In the Fall of 1850, he was elected a member of the Assembly, the popular branch of the State Legislature, from the county in which Marysville was situated. This Legislature commenced its session on the first Monday of January, 1851, and he was confessedly the leading and most efficient member of the body; many of its most important and permanent acts were planned, proposed, and adopted through his agency. At the expiration of the session he returned to Marysville, resumed the practice of his profession, and soon attained the recognized position of one of the foremost lawyers in the State, and so continued until, in the Fall of 1857, he was elected a Justice of the State Supreme Court for the term of six years, commencing on the first of January, 1858. At this election 93,228 votes in all were cast; of these he had 55,216, one of his competitors, 18,944, and the other, 19,068, so that he received a majority of more than 36,000 over each of the other candidates, and of 17,204 over both combined. A vacancy occurring on the Bench through the death of one of the justices, he was appointed by the Governor for the unexpired term, and took his seat on the 13th of October, 1857. On the resignation of Chief Justice Terry, in September, 1859, he became Chief Justice. He remained in this high office until, in 1863, he was removed to the still higher position—a seat in the Supreme Court of the United States. On March 3d, 1863, a statute of Congress was approved by the President providing for an additional justice of the Supreme Court, and making the States on the Pacific Coast a new circuit. On the recommendation of the entire delegation in Congress from those States, consisting of four Senators and four Representatives,—of whom five were Democrats and three Republicans, and all Union men,—Judge Field was nominated by President

Lincoln, and his nomination was unanimously confirmed by the Senate. He resigned the State judgeship, and took the oath of office as judge of the United States Supreme Court on the 20th of May, 1863. His commission was issued March 10th, but he gave the following explanation of his selection of May 20th, for entering upon the duties of the office. It was necessary that he should postpone his retirement from the State Bench for a while, in order that the Court might decide the causes which had already been argued and submitted for decision, so that the parties need not be put to the delay and expense of re-arguments. He chose the 20th of May because he believed the causes argued would be by that time decided, and because it was the birthday of his father; he thought that his father would be gratified to learn that on the 82d anniversary of his own birth, his son had become a Justice of the Supreme Court of the United States.

Having thus mentioned the most important events of Judge Field's life, I shall analyze and describe his work (1) as a Legislator in the early days of California; (2) as a Judge of the California Supreme Court; and (3) as a Justice of the Supreme Court of the United States.

I.—*Judge Field's work as a Legislator.*

In order to appreciate the extent and importance of Judge Field's legislative work during his single term of office, and the lasting effect which it has produced not only upon California, but upon other and especially the mining States, the anomalous condition of the State at that early day must be fully understood. I shall make no attempt to describe the mere social features of California during the years succeeding the discovery of gold; they have been often portrayed by masters in the art of word-painting. I shall refer to the condition of the State so far only as relates to the law, and the special property interests which then existed.

The discovery of gold, as is well known, brought a rush of emigrants from all parts of the United States, from European countries, from Australia, and even from the Pacific Islands and China. In addition to this heterogeneous mixture of all nationalities was the element of native Mexican or Californian population. Among these early comers, some were men of high character, intelligence, and culture, well fitted to be leaders in the community. A larger number were of less education and culture, but still were full of energy, and, coming from the United States, were inclined to be law-abiding, possessing at least some of the American feeling of respect for the law and love of justice. A third, and it must be confessed, a large class, consisted of the worst characters of the older communities, rogues, knaves, gamblers, and professional criminals, acknowledging no law, and defying all law.

The law itself of the country was unsettled. The civil law, as formulated in Spanish codes and applied to Spanish colonies, modified in few particulars by Mexican legislation, prevailed prior to the cession of California to the United States. Large tracts of land were held by grantees under concessions from Spain or Mexico; and the law in force contained provisions unlike any doctrines of the common law, concerning the organization of " pueblos" or towns, which were the basis of proprietary and municipal rights of enormous value; and it prescribed regulations for mining, and for the occupation of mineral land different from the common-law rules applicable to the same subjects.

The stream of immigrants which poured into the State brought along with them their own customs, opinions, and preferences. At home they had been familiar with a great variety of laws, and they naturally preferred to follow those legal rules to which they had been accustomed. The Eastern States had mostly been settled by a homogeneous population, all familiar with the common law, and they adopted it without a question. The same was true with respect to the States of the Ohio and Mississippi Valleys. But such was not the case with California; no such homogeneity existed among its people. And it was perceived by intelligent and thoughtful men, that the common law of England, adopted by the first Legislature as a rule of decision in the courts, when not repugnant to the constitution and laws of the State, did not meet the exigencies and conditions of the country. Many of its most characteristic and fundamental principles and doctrines were unfitted for the new commonwealth, partly from the anomalous condition of society, partly from the effect of the pre-existing system of Spanish-Mexico, and partly from a great variety of most important proprietary interests, which had not existed in countries where the common law prevailed, or had existed under conditions essentially different from those presented by California.

The proprietary rights to which I refer, and which at that time surpassed in value all others within the State, were those growing out of the mining industries, the claims of miners to occupy portions of the public mineral land, and to extract the mineral, the works constructed by them to aid in opening and developing the mines, and the appropriation of water in the mining region for that and other beneficial purposes. No legislation, either State or national, had yet been enacted concerning these subjects. And the intricate and restrictive system of the Spanish-Mexican codes was as inapplicable as the doctrines of the common law. The seekers for gold, who had been drawn from all parts of the earth, were thus left to adjust their respective rights and claims as best they might.

The mineral lands, as a whole, belonged to the United States, as a part of the public domain; but different opinions prevailed with respect to the ownership of the minerals themselves while still remaining in the soil. Some persons maintained that they belonged to the United States, others that they were owned by the State, but the
.ns.

conviction was universal that neither the national nor the State government should assert any right of ownership, and that its assertion would greatly impair the development of the mineral wealth of the country. The immigrants had poured over the mineral regions, settled down in every direction, appropriated parcels of the territory to their own use, and were prospecting and mining in every mode rendered possible by their own resources, under no municipal law, and with no restraint except the danger of conflict with other and more powerful parties who could wield a greater physical force. As justly observed by one who, at the time, was observant of the conduct of the miners, " the situation was a grave one, and it demanded statesmanlike treatment. To do nothing was to leave the peace of the State at the mercy of those whose fierce thirst for gold might outrun their respect for fair dealing. Honest misunderstandings as to facts were oftenest settled by immediate appeal to brute force. The world has probably never seen a similar spectacle—that of extensive gold-fields suddenly peopled by masses of men from all States and countries, restrained by no law, and not agreed as to whence the laws ought to emanate by which they would consent to be bound."

In this condition of the country the miners had taken some most important steps, which illustrate in the clearest manner the love of order and justice, and respect for law which characterize American-born citizens of all classes, and which prevented the destructive consequences, that otherwise would have resulted from the absence of any municipal law. They were scattered over the territory in larger or smaller groups, located at different places, technically known as " camps," " bars," or " diggings." In each mining district they had held meetings and had enacted rules and regulations by which they agreed to be governed in that district. These rules were simple, but ullated to the most important questions of property, to it w.

priority in claims, and the extent of ground which one person could appropriate. The rules once adopted were enforced with rigor upon all settlers in the particular camp. This voluntary, self-imposed legislation originated with the American immigrants, and they were ordinarily so superior in numbers that they could compel obedience by the less law-abiding foreigners. The rules they adopted governed the extent of each individual claim at the particular locality, and prescribed the acts necessary to constitute such an appropriation of a parcel of mineral land or portion of a stream as should give the claimant a prior right against all others, the amount of work which should entitle him to continued possession and enjoyment, what should constitute an abandonment, and like fundamental conditions to the acquisition and use of their respective claims. These rules differed in their details in the various camps, but there was still a general similarity among them all.

In this condition the Legislature of 1851 was called upon to act. Mr. Field, as the result of accurate knowledge and careful study, determined upon a legislative policy. He understood the material upon which any legislation must work; he was familiar with the miners as a class, and knew their habits and peculiarities, their common sense and general love for fair play, coupled with strong will and occasional violence. He saw at a glance that the Legislature could not enact any complicated system of mining law that would not interfere with the regulations which they themselves had established, and under which their claims were protected. The plan which he finally concluded to propose, and, if possible, procure to be adopted, was simple, and its very simplicity may, at first blush, tend to obscure its wisdom ; but all possible doubts in that respect have long since been settled by its complete success. The root idea of this plan was that the rules voluntarily imposed upon themselves by the miners should receive the sanction of the law, and as laws should be enforced by the courts in adjudicating upon mining rights and claims.

He, therefore, drew up and offered to the Legislature the following provision, which, through his advocacy, was adopted and incorporated into a general statute regulating proceedings in civil cases in the courts of the State:

"In actions respecting mining claims, proof shall be admitted of the customs, usages, or regulations established and in force at the bar or diggings embracing said claims, and such customs, usages, or regulations, when not in conflict with the constitution and laws of this State, shall govern the decision of the action."

The far-sighted sagacity, expediency, and wisdom of this provision have been conclusively established by the experience of thirty years throughout all the Pacific Mining States and Territories. The same fundamental principle of recognizing and giving the force of law to the local customs and rules of the miners has been continued without change in the subsequent legislation of California, and has been incorporated into the statutes of the other Mining States. It has also been accepted by Congress; and with some modifications in detail, and especially with the addition of a more certain and uniform specification as to the extent of each mining claim and the modes of location and appropriation, it has been made the basis of the laws enacted for the government of the public mineral lands. I therefore venture the opinion, and think that its correctness cannot be questioned, that no single act of creative legislation, dealing with property rights and private interests, has exceeded this one in importance and in its effects in developing the industrial resources of the country. The causes which led to its enactment, its simple but efficient nature, and its beneficial consequences, cannot be better described than in the language of Judge Field himself, in an opinion delivered many years afterwards in the Supreme Court of the United States, in the case of Jennison vs. Kirk, an extract from which is given on pages 6, 7, and 8 of the accompanying volume.

This enactment gave the force of law to an equitable system of mining and water regulations, and has been the direct means of promoting and protecting an industry which has secured and added an untold amount to the total wealth and resources of the country. I cannot leave this subject without a brief comment upon the social events themselves which I have been describing—events unexampled, I think, in the history of any other people. The whole conduct of the miners, their voluntary adoption, in the absence of all municipal law, of regulations so just, wise, and equitable that neither the State nor the national government has attempted to improve them, exhibits in the most striking manner those qualities which lie at the basis of the American character. So long as these qualities last, so long as American citizens, individually or collected into communities, possess and act upon these conservative tendencies, the liberties, safety, and perpetuity of the nation rest upon a certain and immovable foundation.

In addition to the provision concerning mining claims, Mr. Field was also the author of many other measures of the greatest importance to the State, which was then just commencing its wonderful course of development. As most of these enactments relate to the internal affairs of California, and have been confined in their operation to that commonwealth, I shall merely enumerate them, with such brief description as will serve to indicate their purpose and character. Being a member of the Judiciary Committee, Mr. Field's work naturally related, in the main, to the administration of justice. Among the most important of these measures, planned and drawn up by him, was a bill concerning the Judiciary of the State. This act was general, dealing with the whole judicial system, and requiring great labor in its preparation. It completely reorganized the judiciary, and defined and allotted the jurisdiction, power, and duties of all the grades of courts and judicial officers. An act passed in the subsequent session of 1853, revising and amending in its details the original statute of 1851, was also drawn up by Mr. Field, although he was not then a member of the Legislature. The system then

planned and established in 1851, and improved in 1853,
and again in 1862, to conform to the constitutional amendments of the previous year, was substantially adopted in
the codes of 1872, and continued in operation until it was
displaced by the revolutionary changes made in the new
constitution of 1879-80. In connection with this legislation affecting the judiciary, Mr. Field also drafted and
procured the passage of an act concerning county sheriffs,
defining all their official functions and duties; an act concerning county recorders, creating the entire system of
registry which has since remained substantially unaltered;
and an act concerning attorneys and counsellors at law, by
which their duties were declared and their rights were protected against arbitrary proceedings by hostile judges.

He also prepared and introduced two separate bills to
regulate the civil and criminal practice. These acts were
based upon the Code of Civil Procedure, and the Code of
Criminal Procedure proposed by the New York commissioners, but they contained a great number of changes and
additions made necessary by the provisions of the California constitution. and by the peculiar social condition and
habits of the people. They were by no means bare copies
taken from the New York Codes, since Mr. Field altered
and reconstructed more than three hundred sections and
added over one hundred new sections. The two measures
were generally designated as the Civil and the Criminal
Practice Acts. They were subsequently adopted by the
other States and Territories west of the Rocky Mountains.
They continued with occasional amendments in force in
California until the present system of more elaborate codes
was substituted for them in 1872; and even this change
was more in name than in substance, since all their provisions substantially reappear in some one of these codes.

In the Civil Practice Act he incorporated the provision
above mentioned respecting mining claims. He also incorporated into it another provision, which has become a
permanent feature of the legislative policy of California,

and has proved of inestimable benefit to its population—
the provision exempting certain articles of property of
judgment debtors from seizure and sale upon execution.
Some exemption has long been found in the statute-
books of every State, but it has ordinarily been small in
amount and value, restricted to householders, and extending only to a few articles of absolute necessity for the existence of a family—such as a little kitchen and bed-room
furniture, bedding, clothing, and a few other similar articles. Mr. Field justly thought that the scheme of exemption should, especially in a new State, be planned
after another policy,—a policy of generosity as well as of
strict justice, believing that even the strictest justice and
the claims of creditors would be better subserved thereby.
The fundamental principle of the plan proposed by him
was, that every person, in addition to those articles necessary for individual preservation, such as clothing, reason-
·able household furniture and effects, and the like, should
be secured in the possession and use of those things by
which, as necessary means and instruments, he pursues his
profession, trade, business, or calling, whatever it may be,
and acquires the ability of paying the demands of his creditors. This law, therefore, exempts, not only household furniture and the like, but the implements, wagons, and teams
of a farmer, the tools of a mechanic, the instruments of a
surveyor, surgeon, and dentist, the professional library of a
lawyer and a physician, the articles used by the miner, the
laborer, etc. In this connection it should also be stated,
that, though not its author, Mr. Field was a most strenuous
supporter of the Homestead Bill, which finally passed after
a severe struggle. At that time there was no exemption
whatever of personal property in California, and none
equally extensive to be found in the previous legislation
of any State of the Union. It is understood by those who
are familiar with Judge Field, that he looks back with
greater satisfaction upon the exemption system which he
thus created than upon any other of his legislative work.

It lifted a heavy load from debtors, enabled them to pursue their callings with freedom, and instead of defeating the ends of justice by preventing the collection of debts, it has actually operated in favor of creditors, by securing the means whereby debts can be paid.

Mr. Field also drew a bill creating the Counties of Nevada and Klamath. As there was much complaint at the boundary lines of several counties in the State, various bills for their correction had been presented. These being referred to him, he reported a general bill revising and amending the bill of the previous year, dividing the entire State into counties, and establishing the seats of justice in them, in which the provisions for the new counties were incorporated; and the bill passed. He also drew the charters of Marysville, Nevada, and Monterey; and the bill regulating divorces and defining the causes for which marriages may be annulled and absolute divorces granted.

The foregoing summary shows an enormous and, I venture to say, an altogether unprecedented amount of legislative work, conceived, prepared, perfected, and accomplished by one man in a single session of only a few months in duration. The influence of this legislation upon the people and the material prosperity of California has been simply immeasurable; but it has not been confined to the limits of a single State; it has extended over the entire Pacific Slope, and especially through all the mining regions.

II.—*His work as a Member of the California Supreme Court.*

The direct effects of Judge Field's work on the State Bench, various and important as it was, have, of course, been confined to the State of California; and it is little to say that he has contributed more than any other of the judges to settle the jurisprudence of that State upon a broad and scientific basis of justice and equity.

As a student of the California law, I venture the opinion that wherever the present codes have departed from the rules laid down by him in his decisions, or in statutes of which he was the author, it will be found that the change has been for the worse—that it has produced inconvenience and sometimes injustice.

The *indirect* effects of his work have extended throughout the whole country, in two distinct forms: *First.* Many particular conclusions arrived at by the Court through his influence, and embodied in positive rules for the State of California, and, in some instances, incorporated into its statutory legislation, have been borrowed by the Courts and Legislatures of other commonwealths; and thus, while directly constructing the law for one State, he has actually performed the same labor for other States of the Union. *Secondly.* The general doctrines which he as a judge, or the Court under his lead, has discussed, expounded, and declared in judicial opinions, have exerted a powerful influence in aiding the decisions of other tribunals and in shaping the development of legal and equitable principles in other parts of the United States.

In the examination which I shall now make of his work in the State Supreme Court, I shall not attempt to describe in detail any causes in the decision of which he took a part, nor to quote from his legal opinions, nor to narrate the legal controversies which he aided in adjusting, nor even to discuss the legal principles and doctrines which he determined. The most important of these causes, opinions, controversies, and doctrines may be found, set forth at sufficient length and fully explained, in the printed volume to which this sketch is designed as an introduction. It would be a useless expenditure of time and labor for me to recapitulate in a condensed form the matters of fact which are there more elaborately displayed. For this account in all its completeness of detail I simply refer to that section of the volume which deals with his labors while a judge of the Supreme Court of California. The single purpose of this second division will be to portray his character as a judge; to describe the general nature of his State judicial work as a whole, and to enumerate the most important legal principles and branches of the State jurisprudence which were determined and established by him, and by the Court through his influence.

In order to form any adequate conception of his judicial character, the nature and extent of his judicial work, and the vast results which it accomplished, it is necessary to understand and to appreciate clearly the remarkable and wholly anomalous condition of the law at the time when he took his seat in the court. I have already spoken of this condition in general terms. California was utterly unlike any of the other States at their early settlement. From the heterogeneous mass of immigrants, every variety of legal notions, habits, customs, and national systems was represented among the population. The common law was not accepted as a whole, and how far its principles should prevail as the foundation of the State jurisprudence was not determined. The civil law, modified and adulterated by passing through the Spanish-Mexican Codes, was acknowledged as furnishing the rules controlling many of the older land titles.

In the absence of positive law, the various settlements and collections of miners had adopted local regulations concerning mining and water privileges, which were treated as having the force and effect of law. The greatest amount, however, of embarrassment and difficulty presented arose from the vast number of peculiar interests, industries, and proprietary rights and claims, wholly unlike anything to be found elsewhere in this country, and for which the principles of the common law and of equity, and the statutes of England and of the other States, furnished few, if any, analogies. Among these were the mines and all mining operations, water claims, ditches, irrigating canals, the titles to minerals in the soil, and the Mexican titles to land grants. In fact, the California judge was obliged to perform his work with little help

from his previous knowledge of the law in the settlement
of these and similar questions—questions entirely different from those which had been presented to other courts,
American or English. He was required to frame a State
jurisprudence *de novo*—to create a system out of what was
at the time a mere chaos. Three distinct matters furnished the material for the most important as well as violent controversies, involving legal questions of the utmost
difficulty and magnitude, affecting pecuniary interests to
an incalculable amount, and provoking most bitter animosities among the opposing parties—which animosities
were often directed against the judges when the unjust
and illegal claims of individuals or communities were defeated. These matters were: 1st. The immense extent
and indefinite boundaries of the Mexican land grants.
2d. The occupation by settlers of the public lands belonging to the United States, before the government had taken
any steps to provide regulations for their use and sale.
3d. The mineral resources, the mining and water rights,
and the claim of California to own the gold and silver
found in any lands situated within the State.

Added to this unprecedented condition of the law was
the equally unprecedented condition of all business relations subsisting between individuals, which cannot be better portrayed than by quoting the language of an associate
with Judge Field upon the Supreme Court Bench of the
State:

"When, in addition, it is considered that an unexampled number of contracts, and an amount of business
without parallel, had been made and done in hot haste,
with the utmost carelessness; that legislation was accomplished in the same way, and presented the crudest and
most incongruous materials for judicial construction; and
that the whole scheme and organization of the government,
and the relation of the departments to each other, had to
be adjusted by judicial interpretation,—it may well be conceived what task even the ablest jurist would take upon
himself when he assumed this office."

c

On the whole, the California judges were confronted by a task enormous in its difficulty and importance; wholly unprecedented in the legal and judicial history of the country; with little aid from the doctrines of jurisprudence prevailing in other States; and requiring to be grappled with, adjusted, and settled without delay, upon a just and solid basis. Their difficulties were still further enhanced by the character and dispositions of a large portion of the population. As was inevitable, the absence of legal and social restraints had induced great numbers of persons to engage in the most extensive schemes of fraudulent acquisition, of grasping and accumulating property through an open disregard of others' rights, of asserting the most unscrupulous and unfounded claims, of overriding law, order, equity, and justice in every possible manner, having the semblance of legal sanction. These persons were often influential, and could control the newspapers and other organs of temporary popular opinion. When their projects were thwarted by judicial decisions, they attempted to coerce the Court by public attacks of the most bitter nature upon individual judges, attacks such as have never been known, and would never for a moment be tolerated in the Eastern States, but which the Court was powerless either to prevent or to punish. The most able and upright members of the Court were made the objects of virulent abuse, the extent and fierceness of which we can hardly realize at the present day. It is true, that in the course of time, the truth gradually asserted its power, the public mind appreciated the justice and integrity of the decisions, perceived their wisdom, and acknowledged their beneficial results. Notwithstanding this complete change in the popular opinion, now at the present day the old abuse is occasionally revived; individuals whose schemes were defeated still pursue the court with their hostile criticisms. As Judge Field stood pre-eminent among his associates in the fearless discharge of duty, he has been the especial object of these persistent libels.

Such being the problem presented to the California Supreme Court, it should be added, in forming a just estimate of Judge Field's work, that up to the time when he was placed upon the Bench, much less had been done towards its permanent solution than the public had a right to expect. The Court, in its early years, had not always commanded that entire confidence and respect of the public which are essential to any tribunal, if its judgments are to have moral weight in a community in settling disputed questions and putting controversies at rest. While some of its members were men of great ability and learning, and would have added to the strength of any Court, some of them had not had much experience at the bar, and were not possessed of the requisite acquirements for their position. And it must be confessed also that some of them, by their habits, had subjected themselves to unpleasant comment, and the Court had thus suffered in public estimation. It would subserve no useful purpose to enter into any particulars. The distinguished members of the Court of those days now living are the most ready to admit and deplore the truth of this statement. Their usefulness was greatly impaired by the circumstances mentioned, of which no one was more forcibly impressed than themselves.

The most important work of Judge Field was done after Judges Baldwin and Cope had become his associates on the Bench. They were able and learned judges, and fully bore their share of the labors of the Court. Some of their opinions were admirable specimens of judicial reasoning. Yet it is admitted by all who were personally acquainted, as contemporaries and participants, with the judicial history of the State, and it is a truth patent to all who have obtained their only knowledge from the reports of decisions during his term of office, that he assumed and maintained the position of leadership. In the fundamental principles adopted by the Court, in the doctrines which it announced, in the whole system which it constructed for the adjustment of the great questions hereinbefore described, his controlling influence was apparent; his creative force impressed itself upon his associates, guided their decisions, shaped and determined their work. The pre-eminence which he thus attained was universally recognized.

Many of the decisions of the Court, however, though exhibiting great ability and learning, were of local interest alone, dealing with matters confined to California, or, at most, to the Pacific Coast. But in its dealings with matters of general interest, with the principles and doctrines of common law and of equity, with municipal and private corporations, and with constitutional law, it rapidly rose in the estimation of the profession, until it reached a position of authority with the Bench and Bar of the country second to no other State tribunal.*

It would be a comparatively easy task for one who was personally a stranger to Judge Field, and was only acquainted with him through his reported decisions, to form a correct estimate of his judicial character. Its important elements, those which distinguish him from the other judges, and which constitute the special grounds of his success and of his power, stand out in clear-cut lines upon all the creations of his official labors. He has stamped himself—his intellectual and moral features—deeply into all the work which he has done. From my own personal acquaintance with him, but chiefly from a careful study

---

* About four years ago I was told by a gentleman, who for many years had been employed by a leading law publishing house of Boston as its travelling agent through all the States of the Mississippi and Ohio Valleys, that when he first began his work the New York reports were universally sought for in every State, but that of late years the demand had changed from the New York to the California reports. Everywhere through the Western and Northwestern States, he said, the profession generally wished to obtain the California reports as next in authority after those of their own States. This fact alone speaks volumes.

of all his important judgments rendered both while a member of the State Court, and after his transfer to the National Judiciary, I have arrived at the following conclusions, which I unhesitatingly submit as the most striking and distinctive elements of his judicial character and work. They are undoubtedly the very qualities which, in our system of jurisprudence, steadily developing through the creative functions of the courts, mark the ideal judge;—the qualities which have been held by, and which admit him to be ranked with, the very foremost class of jurists who have sat upon the English and American Bench,—the class which embraces among others the names of Hardwicke, Mansfield, Cottenham, and Cockburn, in England, and Marshall, Kent, Story, Shaw, and Denio, in America.

In the first and lowest place, he possesses an ample legal learning. It cannot be pretended that he has that exact knowledge of technical common-law dogmas which distinguished such a judge as Lord Kenyon or Baron Parke, or of the intricate minutiæ of real estate and conveyancing law which alone gave Lord Eldon his pre-eminence among English chancellors,—a sort of knowledge which with a certain pedantic school has passed for the highest legal learning, but which is worse than useless rubbish for the American judge of to-day. Judge Field's learning, as a distinctive feature of his intellect, is rather the capacity in an extraordinary degree to acquire the new knowledge made necessary by the demands of his position;—the capacity to investigate sources and systems of jurisprudence hitherto unknown, to sift truth from error, to extract whatever there is of living principle, and to appropriate and to assimilate the materials thus obtained with the State or national law which he is administering. He brought to the Bench a mind stored with the doctrines of the common law and of equity, great intellectual vigor, and a most remarkable capacity for rapid and sustained mental labor. The exigencies of his position required him to investigate the Spanish-Mexican Codes, which furnished the authoritative rules concerning " pueblos," with all the municipal and proprietary rights flowing therefrom, and concerning the Mexican Govermental grants to private owners, and also to create general principles and doctrines for which the common law and equity of England and the United States afforded very few if any analogies. It is enough to say that his learning, his intellectual power, and his thorough and accurate study of foreign systems, were always adequate to meet the requirements of the occasion. Still, I regard Judge Field's mere technical legal knowledge—the facts which he has acquired in a concrete form and stored up in his memory—as a very subordinate element in his judicial character. In this mere learning he is undoubtedly surpassed by many judges who are not only otherwise his inferiors, but who have never even attained to any comparative distinction in their own States. But in the high intellectual power, which I have attempted to describe, the power to analyze, to sift, to select, to appropriate truths, principles, and doctrines, and to assimilate them with the jurisprudence already established, and above all, to create where there was no material from which to borrow, he has been equalled by few, and, in my opinion, surpassed by none of the modern American judges.

The second and much more important element which I shall notice, is his devotion to principle;—that quality of intellect which leads him, on all judicial occasions, to seek for, apprehend, and appreciate principles, rather than to rest satisfied with mere rules, although sustained by precedent, and to apply firmly these principles where found in all their relations and consequences ;—to place his decisions upon the solid basis of fundamental and universal principles, rather than upon arbitrary dogmas. This quality gives a most marked unity, consistency, and universality to his decisions, not only to those connected with some single branch of the law, but to those belonging to any and all departments. His adjudications generally will thus be found related to each other, harmonious, corresponding parts of one completed system. This method of adhering to principle as the sure and constant guide in ascertaining, interpreting, and applying the law, is the immediate and efficient cause of that most remarkable consistency which runs through all his judicial utterances. I shall have occasion to speak more in detail of this special feature of consistency, when describing his judgments upon questions of constitutional law ; and although it appears, perhaps in the most striking manner, in that class of cases, it is still a distinguishing mark of all his work. √The power of discovering, apprehending, and applying principles, is the highest *intellectual* faculty of the ideal judge ; it takes the place of, and is universally superior to, any amount of mere learning ; it is the very essence of the best learning which can be employed in the judicial station. In fact great learning alone, with a total absence of the power to comprehend, combine, and enforce the general truths of jurisprudence, would undoubtedly be more dangerous on the Bench, more liable to produce injustice, than comparative ignorance. This intellectual quality of appreciating and applying principles, of discovering their mutual relations, of following them to their legitimate consequences, and of applying them in the deduction of particular rules, which Judge Field possesses in such a high degree, has rendered his opinions exceedingly useful to text-writers, who have frequently spoken of them in the highest terms of praise. As has already been said, many of his judgments, pronounced while in the State Court, relate to matters of purely local interest, such as the peculiar land titles of California, the Mexican pueblos, the ownership of gold and silver *in situ*, mining and water rights, etc.; and this class of cases undoubtedly required for their decision the greatest amount of original investigation, tracing of obscure analogies, and creative power,—an expenditure of intellectual force which can hardly be appreciated by the profession in other parts of the country who are unfamiliar with the intricate questions involved. On the other hand, many of his opinions deal with subjects of universal interest, as for example, the powers and liabilities of municipal and of private corporations, the nature of mortgages, the validity of Sunday laws, etc. These judgments have uniformly been regarded by the profession and courts of other States, and by text writers, as having the highest authority. They have been quoted with the strongest language of approval by such authors as Washburn and Dillon ; and their clear and accurate statement of principles renders them peculiarly instructive to students of the law in all parts of the Union.

The third distinctive element requiring special notice is what may appropriately be called his *creative power*. By this designation I mean his ability in developing, enlarging, and improving the law, by additions of new material, whether this material be borrowed from foreign sources or created by means of the legislative function belonging to all Superior Courts. The intellectual attributes referred to in this and in the preceding head are entirely distinct; they may co-exist in the same individual, or the first may be possessed in a high degree without the other. The first deals with the jurisprudence as it has already been established, investigating, examining, and expounding or applying its settled principles and doctrines; the other is creative and legislative, employed in constructing new law, or reforming and expanding that which already exists. Many judges of great and well-deserved reputation have possessed the first quality to a remarkable extent, without any of the second—of which class, I think, Judge Story was an example. Judge Field's peculiar talent as a legal reformer was shown in his purely legislative work done while a member of the State Assembly, and described in a previous division of this essay. He exhibited the same power and tendency upon the Bench. They were shown in his constant rejection of ancient common-law dogmas, no matter how firmly settled upon authority, which had become outgrown, obsolete, and unfitted for the present condition of society, and in the substitution of more just, consistent, and practical doctrines adapted to the needs of our own country and people. I merely mention, as sufficient examples of this class, his decisions upon the nature and effect of mortgages, and those concerning the ownership of gold and silver while in the soil, by which he boldly swept away the common-law rules on the subject, with all the absurd reasoning upon which they had been founded. The same power and tendency were shown in his accurate perception of those principles and rules contained in foreign systems of jurisprudence which should be borrowed and incorporated into the judicial legislation of the State, both for the purpose of protecting many peculiar rights of property and special interests, and of regulating social relations, existing in California but unknown in nearly all the other States. Illustrations of the first kind may be found in his series of most important decisions concerning " pueblos " and the municipal and proprietary rights belonging to them; and concerning Mexican land-grants, in which the rules were borrowed from the Spanish-Mexican codes; and in those concerning the occupation of public lands and mining and water rights. A most illustrative example of the other kind is seen in his decisions relating to the community property of husband and wife,—an incident of the marriage relation derived from the Spanish-Mexican jurisprudence,— which placed the rights of the two spouses in that unique species of property upon a firm and equitable foundation. The same power and tendency are shown in his decisions concerning procedure, in which he more ably and consistently, perhaps, than any other judge, has carried into operation the true spirit and intent of the reformed American procedure.

The fourth element of his judicial character is his fearlessness. As the power to apprehend and apply principles is the highest *intellectual* quality, so is a true fearlessness the highest *moral* attribute of the ideal judge. No other American judge has so often been called upon to face popular opposition in the decision of controversies involving important legal questions, in which large masses of the population were interested, and on one side of which all their passions, prejudices, and selfish motives were fully aroused, and often were raging in the fiercest manner; and no other judge has more frequently and faithfully discharged his sacred duty of deciding according to his own enlightened convictions of law and justice, in complete oblivion of all external forces, and in absolute fearlessness of the consequences. He has neither courted personal popularity nor shrunk from unpopularity by means of his decisions. He could well apply to himself the memorable and noble language which Lord Mansfield used from the Bench when made the object of a violent clamor on account of his decisions:

" I will do my duty unawed. What am I to fear? The lies of calumny carry no terror to me. I trust that my temper of mind, and the color and conduct of my life, have given me a suit of armor against these arrows. . . . I wish popularity, but it is that popularity which follows, not that which is run after; it is that popularity which, sooner or later, never fails to do justice to the pursuit of noble ends by noble means. I will not do that which my conscience tells me is wrong upon this occasion, to gain the huzzas of thousands, or the daily praise of all the papers which come from the press; I will not avoid doing what I think is right, though it should draw on me the whole artillery of libels,—all that falsehood and malice can invent, or the credulity of a deluded populace can swallow. I can say, with a great magistrate, upon an occasion and under circumstances not unlike, ' Ego hoc animo semper fui, ut invidiam virtute partam, gloriam, non invidiam, putarem.' "

No friend of Judge Field can estimate his intellectual and moral fearlessness too highly; no enemy can deny, or ever has denied that he possessed it. He has repeatedly

encountered, and been compelled to endure, the bitter hostility of extreme partisans belonging to the most opposite
schools of opinion; of extreme Republicans and extreme
Democrats; of those who maintain the dogma of State sovereignty, and of those who assert the absolute legislative
power of the national government; of ignorant and prejudiced masses, and of scheming speculators who would disregard all law and right in order to accomplish their purposes. All these outbursts of opposition have, however,
died away; the justice and wisdom, as well as the law, of
his decisions are vindicated. That true popularity has
succeeded among all intelligent persons, which, in the
words of Lord Mansfield, " never fails to do justice to the
pursuit of noble ends by noble means." From the very
commencement of his career on the State Bench, and
through all the following years, opportunities have frequently been presented to him, in the regular discharge of
his official functions, by which, without any plain surrender of right, any obvious transgression of duty, by the
mere adoption of a different line of argument leading to a
different conclusion,—and even sometimes when that line
of argument and that conclusion were, upon a surface view,
correct, and were approved by a majority of the legal profession,—opportunities, I say, by which, in this manner, he
might have obtained an immediate and even an enthusias-
tic popularity; but in which, by following the voice of conscience and duty, and the dictates of his own matured
judgment, he was certain to encounter a storm of hostile
criticism, and even malignant hatred. On no occasion
was he ever influenced by either of these considerations;
on no occasion did he ever swerve from his duty and surrender his own conscience and enlightened judgment.
My space will not permit me to review these events in
his life. Any correct account of the decisions made
in the State Supreme Court concerning the pueblo of
San Francisco and the titles derived from the municipality, concerning the occupation of public lands, con-

cerning the State ownership of gold and silver, and the claims of miners to enter upon all lands, private as well as public, in search for the precious metals, concerning the rights of Mexican grantees and the intruders upon their lands, and concerning the validity of certain acts done by the municipal government of San Francisco, will exhibit in the clearest manner the quality of rectitude and fearlessness which is such a distinctive element of his character.* In many of the decisions rendered in the United States Supreme Court, indirectly growing out of the civil war, and directly out of congressional legislation enacted in consequence of the war, including those dealing with the validity of test-oaths, the extent and limitations of martial law, the trial of civilians by military tribunals, the suspension of the writ of habeas corpus, and similar questions affecting the very foundations of our political institutions and of our civil liberties,—the same quality was exhibited from a higher station and in the presence of the whole nation. In addition to other instances, there is one of later occurrence which is still more illustrative. It may be affirmed, I think, without any real doubt as to its correctness, that during the past year, by his deliberate and fearless discharge of duty, by following his own convictions as to the law, and by rendering a decision in the now memorable Chinese Queue Case, which, however righteous and in accordance with the fundamental principles of constitutional law, awoke a storm of fierce opposition and hatred among all the lowest and most ignorant classes of the political party with which he is connected, Judge Field lost—nay, sacrificed—his chances, otherwise good, of a nomination by his party for the Presidency. It can be certainly shown that scheming politicians, anxious only for their own personal advancement, working upon this temporary unpopularity among the Democratic masses of California, prevented him

---

* See "Personal Reminiscences of Early Days in California," pages 137 to 171, inclusive.

from obtaining the support of his own State, and thus rendered his nomination by the National Convention impossible. As a moderate Republican, knowing the opinions of that large division of the party commonly called "Liberal Republicans," I do not hesitate to express the strong conviction that if Judge Field had received the nomination from the Democratic party, he would certainly have been elected. The decision as to the validity of a miserable city ordinance requiring the queues of Chinese prisoners to be cut off, lost him the Democratic support of California. He has, instead, the approval of his own judgment, and of all intelligent, thoughtful men throughout the country.

There are other traits of his intellectual character and of his work, in themselves worthy of mention, such as his diligence, his capacity for continued labor, his rapidity of execution, and particularly his clear and accurate style of literary composition, which renders some of his more carefully prepared opinions models of judicial argumentation; but I pass them by without further notice as not being distinctive, since they are shared with him in an equal and sometimes in a superior degree, by others judges both of the State and the national courts.

I pass to a consideration of the work which he did while a member of the Supreme Court of California. This must be merely a brief reference. Any full account would necessarily be a reproduction of the matters contained in pages 16 to 38 of the printed volume. I shall, therefore, simply enumerate the leading decisions, arranged in groups according to their subject-matter, which best exhibit his distinctive qualities as a judge, and embody his most important judicial work. They naturally fall into two main divisions: (1) Those which deal with common law and equitable doctrines of general interest to the profession of all the States; and (2) Those which deal with mere local matters, of which the interest is chiefly confined to the profession and people of California and the other Pacific States.

1. *Matters of a general interest.*—Among the most important of these topics were the following. *The powers and
liabilities of Municipal Corporations.* Certain transactions
entered into and acts done by the governing body of San-
Francisco gave rise to a bitter judicial controversy extending through several litigations, in which the Supreme
Court was called upon to examine, from their very foundations, the doctrines of the American common law concerning the powers and liabilities of Municipal Corporations, in the absence of express charter or other statutory
provisions defining and limiting the same.* The opinions
of Judge Field in these cases are universally regarded as of
the highest authority. They are able, thorough, and exhaustive decisions of the law, and reach conclusions based
both upon principle and precedent which have been accepted by the ablest text-writers, and especially by Judge
Dillon, as final.

Mortgages.—The Supreme Court, while he was a member of it, freed the jurisprudence of California from the
last vestige of the old common-law notions concerning the
nature and effect of the mortgage, and adopted the rational
and consistent equitable theory as the single system which
should determine all private relations and should prevail
in all tribunals, both of law and of equity. His opinions
explaining, advocating, and enforcing this single equitable conception of the mortgage as purely a hypothecation,
as creating no estate in the land, as a mere lien, and not a
jus ad rem nor a *jus in re*, have not been excelled in their
clearness of statement and cogency of argument by those
of any other Court which has maintained the same view,
and they have undoubtedly done much to promote its acceptance in other States.† No opinions upon the subject

---

* McCraken vs. San Francisco, 16 Cal., 591; Grogan vs. The Same, 18
Cal., 608; Pimental vs. The Same, 21 Cal., 359; Argenti vs. The Same,
16 Cal., 282; Zottman vs. The Same, 20 Cal., 96.—See the printed volume,
pp. 30–32.

† McMillan vs. Richards, 9 Cal., 365; Nagle vs. Macy, 9 Cal., 426;
Johnson vs. Sherman, 15 Cal., 287; Goodenow vs. Ewer, 16 Cal., 461.—See
printed vol., pp. 32, 33.

are more instructive for the student in all parts of the country.

Sunday Laws.—Under a constitutional provision substantially the same as that in most other States, a majority of the Supreme Court pronounced unconstitutional and void a statute which simply prohibited the keeping open of business places (with certain specified exceptions) and the selling of goods, or exposing them for sale, on Sunday. It will be noticed that this statute was far less stringent than the type of similar legislation prevailing in most of the States. A majority of the Court saw fit to repudiate the authority of the numerous decided cases unanimously sustaining the validity of such a law. The prevailing opinion professed to uphold religious freedom, and delared all statutes for the preservation of quiet and good order on Sunday to be *sectarian*.* Judge Field firmly and most emphatically dissented. His dissenting opinion is an exhaustive examination and triumphant settlement of all the questions involved, and most effectually exposes the weak positions of the majority. It vindicates both the validity and the wisdom of such statutes, shows their universal approval, and demonstrates their secure foundation, not as intended for the purpose of directly supporting religion, but for the purpose of promoting and preserving good order among the entire community. This opinion was received with the utmost satisfaction by all intelligent and thoughtful persons, not only in California, but throughout the country. At a later day its reasonings and its conclusions were adopted by the Court in a subsequent case, and the former decision was overruled.†

Legal-tender act and taxes.—Soon after the passage of the Legal-tender act by Congress the question arose, of vital importance not only to California, but to every other State, whether it applied to the payment of State taxes. It was held, in an opinion delivered by Judge Field, that the

---

* *Ex-parte* Newman, 9 Cal., 502.—See printed vol., pp. 34–37.

† *Ex-parte* Andrews, 18 Cal., 680.

clause making treasury notes " a legal tender in payment
of all debts, private and public," is confined in its operations to obligations for the payment of money founded
upon contract, and does not extend to taxes imposed under State authority; that a debt is a sum of money due by
contract, express or implied, while a tax is a charge upon
persons or property to raise money for public purposes,
and operates *in invitum*.* The doctrine of this case was
approved and followed by the Supreme Court of the
United States.† Besides, the power of taxation is one of
the highest functions of government, given to the individual States as well as to the nation, and so far as it is
conferred upon, and may be exercised by the States, it is
beyond the scope of congressional interference. State
taxes are, therefore, payable in such kind of money as
State laws shall prescribe, entirely unaffected by the so-
called " Legal-tender act."

2. *Matters of a local interest.*—The long series of decisions pronounced by Judge Field, dealing with matters of
local interest to the Pacific Slope, discuss legal questions
of the greatest magnitude and difficulty, affecting property
of enormous value, and determine, in fact, the whole
course of private industries in the Mining States. The vast
amount of research, labor, learning, and intellectual force
which these cases required, cannot be appreciated by those
whose only knowledge of them has been obtained from
the volumes of Reports. Nothing at all analogous to them
can be found in the modern judicial records of the English
Bench. The judges of a new, half-settled American State
were called upon to decide controversies far surpassing in
the number and difficulty of the legal questions presented,
and in the pecuniary interests at stake, anything which
the present generation has brought before the House of

---

* Perry vs. Washburn, 20 Cal., 318.

† Lane County vs. Oregon, 7 Wall., 71, per C. J. Chase, a most able exposition of the fundamental theory of our national government, and of
the relations between the nation and the States.—See printed vol., p. 38.

Lords, or the Privy Council, or other highest tribunal of the British Empire; and many of these decisions themselves would reflect credit upon the ablest of the English judiciary. A detailed account of these controversies might, in the hands of a graphic writer, be made a narrative of intense and highly dramatic interest to the general as well as to the professional reader. Such a narrative, however, I cannot attempt. I can only enumerate the most important questions which were finally settled by these successive judicial contests, and must refer to the pages of the printed volume for all the particulars. It is enough to say that these questions, in their universality, their variety, and their far-reaching consequences, lay at the very bottom of the social organization in California; upon them depended the titles to a large portions of the lands; they determined the success or the destruction of the great mining and agricultural industries of the whole southern coast west of the Rocky Mountains. The following is a bare statement of the most important which were settled in greater part, even if not entirely, through Judge Field's influence, and the adoption of his views by the Court.

1. *The Mexican governmental land-grants*, embracing as collateral or subordinate incidents, the validity of their titles, and the system of legal rules by which they were to be established and governed; the extent, location, and boundaries of the tracts included in the grants; the rights of the original grantees or of their assigns; and the conflicting rights and claims of the actual occupants and of adjacent settlers.*

2. *The occupation of the United States public lands by settlers*, before any measures had been adopted by the government regulating their sale or use, that is, before the lands were surveyed and brought under the general public

---

* Ferris vs. Coover, 10 Cal., 589; Cornwall vs. Culver, 16 Cal , 429; Mahoney vs. Van Winkle, 21 Cal., 576–580.

See the printed volume, pp. 20–24; and also Judge Field's "Personal Reminiscences of Early Days in California," pp. 138–143.

D

land system. This embraced, as incidental and auxiliary questions, the mode of treating such settlers, whether they were to be regarded and dealt with as unlawful intruders and trespassers ; the nature and extent of the usufructuary interest which each individual settler obtained in the parcel of land appropriated by him from his actual occupation, and his rights thereto as against all the world except the United States; in considering which questions the Court boldly disregarded the settled common-law rules concerning the necessity of a legal title in order to maintain ejectment. It also embraced a consideration of the rights of such settlers to mines on the lands occupied by them, and to appropriate water for irrigation and other purposes, and a great number of similar ancillary questions growing out of the altogether anomalous condition of the country, and the absence of legislation by Congress.*

3. *The ownership of the gold and silver in the soil,* and the claim of the State to such ownership. In one or two early cases the Supreme Court had, without fully examining the reasons originally given for the doctrine or their applicability to our own country, adopted the ancient common-law dogma that the ownership of gold and silver contained in all lands within the State was vested in the State itself by virtue of its sovereignty.† The miners soon took advantage of this doctrine. Claiming to act under an authority derived from a State statute, and even without any such legislative permission, they asserted the right to carry on their mining, not only in the public lands of the United States, but also in all land which had been granted, either by Mexico, or by the United States, or by the State, to private owners. They even asserted this right with respect to private lands which were actually occupied by their owners, and were used by them for other pur-

---

* Coryell vs. Cain, 16 Cal., 572.

† Hicks vs. Bell, 3 Cal., 227 ; Stoakes vs. Barrett, 5 Cal., 37.—See the printed volume, pp. 26, 27 ; and " Early Days in California," pp. 145-149.

poses than mining, for agriculture, for grazing, or for
residence. This claim was not an empty theory; it was
carried into actual operation. The miners entered upon
private lands at will, used and occupied for farms, cattle
ranches, vineyards, or any other similar purpose, in search
for gold and silver, heaving up the soil, and sometimes
destroying improvements and doing great damage.* In
this condition of things the Supreme Court nobly performed its duty. With the certainty of encountering the
hostility of large masses of prejudiced and lawless men,
Judge Field, as the organ of the Court, swept away the
old common-law dogma; demonstrated the absurdity of
the reasoning upon which it had originally been rested,
and showed its inapplicability to the institutions and social
condition of this country. His opinions, which are most
able specimens of judicial reasoning, established the doctrine that the gold and silver in the soil belong to the
owner of it, and that the precious metals are entirely
unconnected with whatever of sovereignty inheres in the
State. As the United States originally owned the soil,
so it owned all the gold and silver contained within the
same ; and this ownership passed to and vested in the
grantees of the United States and their assigns. No more
important decisions were made by the Court while Judge
Field was a member of it, and although they aroused
temporary opposition, they have long been acknowledged
as wise and just as well as legally correct.†

4. *United States patents for lands,* involving their peculiar
force and effect, the rights which they confer, the legal
estate of the patentees; the equitable estates which may

---

* This was specially so on the Mariposa and Fernandez grants. Henshaw vs. Clark, 14 Cal., 463 ; Biddle-Boggs vs. Merced Mining Co., Id.,
379.

† Biddle-Boggs vs. Merced Mining Co., 14 Cal., 373–380; Fremont vs.
Fowler, and Moore vs. Smaw, 17 Cal., 200.

See the printed vol., pp. 26–29; " Early Days in California," pp. 145–
153.

exist either under or in opposition to them, and a number of other incidents.*

5. *The Pueblo of San Francisco,* and the proprietary rights derived therefrom. The decision of the Supreme Court that a " pueblo " existed at the site of San Francisco, and that the city had succeeded to its proprietary rights under the Mexican laws, settled a dispute which had existed since the very beginning of the American settlement. The opinion in the first and leading case was written by Judge Baldwin and concurred in by Judge Field.† The latter's most important work in connection with this matter was done by him as United States judge, presiding in the U. S. Circuit Court. He there rendered a final decree establishing the proprietary rights of San Francisco, which was afterwards confirmed by Congress, and now constitutes the foundation of all the titles within a large part of the city limits.‡

6. *The community property* of husband and wife, its nature, and the rules regulating its management, disposition, and dissolution, and determining the rights in it of the two spouses.‖

7. *Other subjects.*—A number of other subjects of great importance, which were considered by the State Court, are mentioned in the printed volume; such as the claim of the State to five hundred thousand acres of land granted by the 8th section of the act of Congress of September 4th, 1841, for purposes of internal improvement, and its right to dispose of the lands in advance of the public surveys;

---

* Moore vs. Wilkinson, 13 Cal., 478 ; Biddle-Boggs vs. Merced Mining Co., 14 Cal., 361–366 ; Stark vs. Barrett, 15 Cal., 362 ; Mott vs. Smith, 16 Cal., 534 ; Teschemacker vs. Thompson, 18 Cal., 20 ; Leese vs. Clark, 18 Cal., 565 ; 20 Cal., 411 ; Estrada vs. Murphy, 18 Cal., 268 ; Beard vs. Federy, 3 Wall., 478.—See printed vol., p. 30.

† Hart vs. Burnett, 15 Cal., 530.

‡ The Pueblo Case, 4 Sawyer, 553. See " Early Days in California," pp. 153–163 ; pp. 241–243.

‖ Myer vs. Kinzer, 12 Cal., 247 ; Smith vs. Smith, 12 Cal., 216–225 ; Pixley vs. Huggins, 15 Cal., 128 ; Van Maren vs. Johnson, Id., 308 ; Scott vs. Ward, 13 Id., 458.

contracts of the State for the support and labor of its convicts; the power of the Courts to compel by mandamus
officers of the State to do their duty; conflicting rights of
miners to the use of the water of streams in the mountains for the purpose of mining; the construction of wills;
the distinction between mortgages and deeds of trust, and
many other matters.*

III.—*His work as a Member of the United States Supreme
Court.*

It is upon his character as a constitutional lawyer, as an
authoritative interpreter of the National Constitution, that
Judge Field's reputation as a judge of the United States
Supreme Court must ultimately and mainly rest. Legal
questions of a countless number and variety, affecting
private rights, and involving every department of jurisprudence—common law and equity, admiralty, maritime
and prize law, patent law and copyright, the civil law as
embodied in Louisiana and Mexican codes, statutes of
Congress and of State Legislatures, everything except
pure matters of probate—may come before that Court for
adjudication. Probably no other single tribunal in the
world is called upon to exercise a jurisdiction extending
over so many different subjects, and demanding from its
judges such a variety of legal knowledge. But the highest power of the Court, that incident of transcendent importance which elevates it far above any other judicial
tribunal, is its authority as a final arbiter in all controversies depending upon a construction of the United States
Constitution, in the exercise of which exalted function,
as the final interpreter of the organic law, it determines

* Butte Canal and Ditch Co. vs. Vaughan, 11 Cal., 153; Baker vs. Baker,
13 Id., 87; Pierce vs. Robinson, 13 Id., 116; Blanding vs. Burr, 13 Id.,
343; Koch vs. Briggs, 14 Id., 256; Noe vs. Card, 14 Id., 577; Norris vs.
Harris, 15 Id., 226; State of California vs. McCauley, 15 Id., 429; Holliday vs. Frisbie, 15 Id., 630; McCauley vs. Brooks, 16 Id., 12; Koppikus
vs. State Capital Commissioners, 16 Id., 249; Brumagim vs. Tillinghast,
16 Id., 266; Doll vs. Meador, 16 Id., 295; Halleck vs. Mixer, 16 Id., 575.

the bounds beyond which neither the national nor the State governments may rightfully pass. It is the unique feature of our civil polity, the element which distinguishes our political institutions from all others, the crowning conception of our system, the very keystone of the vast arch, upon which depend the safety and permanence of the whole fabric, that the extent and limits of the legislative and executive powers, under the Constitution, both of the nation and of the individual States, are judicially determined by a body completely independent of all other departments, conservative in its essential nature and tendencies, and inferior to no authority except the deliberate organic will of the people expressed through the elective franchise. This special function of the Supreme Court was from the outset denied by a small school of impracticable theorists, and during the whole period of our history it has been the object of bitter hostility from those by whom the very conception of one united people is rejected. It has, however, been uniformly exercised from the beginning of Washington's administration down to the present day; it has grown in the public favor, and it has finally been accepted by the overwhelming weight of popular approval as one of the fundamental axioms of our governmental system. With the vast majority of intelligent men in all parties, the well-considered decisions of the Supreme Court are regarded as authoritatively settling disputed questions of power and right, for the government as well as for individuals, and alike for the government of the nation and of the separate States. As a student of political science, and especially of our own public law, I am profoundly convinced that this peculiar function of the National Judiciary, as the final interpreter of the organic law, is the very corner-stone upon which rest all our institutions, and the permanence of our present organization into nation and States, each with its own powers, and as a consequence the perpetuation of our civil and political liberties.

No more need be said to show that the character of a
United States judge as a constitutional lawyer, is a matter
of the highest importance. It is chiefly in this character that
I shall examine the work of Judge Field. In such examination I shall follow the method already adopted in the
preceding subdivision. There will be no unnecessary rep-
etition of matter contained in the accompanying selection
from his decisions and opinions. As a prelude or introduction to that selection, I shall portray his general character as a constitutional lawyer; state the fundamental
principles of constitutional interpretation which he adopted
and promulgated, describe the most important of his judicial work by which those principles have been carried into
operation, and mention some of the leading cases in which
the results of that work have been embodied. For fuller
details and particulars, reference must be had to the books
of reports and to the volume of selections annexed.

Within the past year or two, and especially since certain
recent decisions from which he dissented, the charge has
been repeatedly made by some political newspapers, whose
extreme partisanship is only equalled by their absolute
ignorance of constitutional law, that Judge Field is an
advocate of the so-called " State-sovereignty " theory,
and that he denies the validity of, and is endeavoring to
judicially break down, the XIVth Amendment of the
Constitution. Nothing can be more absurdly false. The
"State-sovereignty" theory, as I understand it, denies *in toto*
that the National Judiciary can authoritatively pass upon
the validity of State legislation; and asserts in the most
positive manner that the power to determine finally the
validity of State laws and of State governmental acts, belongs exclusively to each State—*i. e.*, to the judiciary
thereof—by itself; and insists that the construction of all
provisions of the United States Constitution imposing restrictions upon the State governments, is a judicial function irrevocably possessed by each State, with which the
United States or its judiciary cannot interfere. In at least

one-half the cases involving questions of constitutional law decided by Judge Field, he bas reviewed State legislation, inquired into its validity, and pronounced it void, asserting in the strongest manner the revisory power thus exercised by the Supreme Court. Even as a single judge, sitting in the Circuit Court, he has annulled the statutes of a State. In the face of these facts he is foolishly charged with being a judicial supporter of the " State-sovereignty " dogma, as above defined, by editors who are ignorant of the very meaning of the term.

While in the Supreme Court of California he had occasion, in a very important and carefully-considered opinion, to explain the true meaning of the word " sovereignty," as it is applied to individual States under our political system, and to show that it is only in a partial and qualified sense that the word can with propriety be used to designate any attribute belonging to a State. In the great case of Fremont vs. Fowler,* he thus describes the sovereignty of a State:

" Sovereignty is a term used to express the supreme political authority of an independent State or nation. Whatever rights are essential to the existence of this authority are rights of sovereignty. Thus the right to declare war, to make treaties of peace, to levy taxes, to take private property for public uses—termed the right of eminent domain—are all rights of sovereignty, for they are rights essential to the existence of supreme political authority. In this country, *this authority is rested in the people*, and is exercised through the joint action of their federal and State governments. To the federal government is delegated the exercise of certain rights and powers of sovereignty, and with respect to sovereignty, rights and powers are synonymous terms; and the exercise of all other rights of sovereignty, except as expressly prohibited, is reserved to the people of the respective States, or vested by them in their local governments. When we say, therefore, that a State of the Union is sovereign, we only mean that she possesses supreme political authority, except as to those matters over

---

* 17 Cal., 200.

which such authority is delegated to the federal government, or prohibited to the States; in other words, that she possesses all the rights and powers essential to the existence of an individual political organization, except as they are withdrawn by the provisions of the Constitution of the United States. To the existence of this political authority of the State—*this qualified sovereignty,* or any part of it—tl e ownership of the minerals of gold and silver found within her limits is in no way essential."

This extract shows in the clearest possible light that Judge Field repudiates the notion of an absolute sovereignty, such as is the essential attribute of a completely independent political society, being vested in each individual State; which is the very fundamental conception of the " State-sovereignty " theory; on the contrary, he asserts the true principle,—the very central thought of all correct interpretation,—that the absolute sovereignty *is vested in the people;* that a part of its sovereign powers is exercised by the federal government and a part by each State government; and that the sovereignty thus exercised by a State is partial and qualified. To this conception of the relations between the divided sovereignty, wielded in part by the central government and in part by the States, he has adhered during his whole judicial career.

Passing now to an affirmative view of his work as a constitutional interpreter, I think that in no other department of the law has the element of consistency, described in a preceding paragraph, been displayed in a more remarkable manner than in this. He has adopted clear and definite principles of constitutional law, applicable both to the nation and to the State, to the powers conferred upon the government of each, and to the limitation imposed upon those powers, and to this system, whether it be correct or not, he has unquestionably adhered with absolute consistency through the entire course of his numerous decisions. No external influence has been able to sway him from those settled convictions. When the Court has conformed to and announced those principles, he has agreed with it, and has often been its mouth-piece in making the decision. Whenever the majority of the Court, as has sometimes been the case, has temporarily departed from those principles on either side, whether in the direction of sustaining State legislation or of sustaining legislation of Congress, he has dissented. It should be especially remarked, for the benefit of those who charge him with being a supporter of the " State-sovereignty theory," so called, that some of his ablest, best considered, and most forcible dissents have been from decisions of the Court which upheld State statutes transgressing, in his opinion, the restrictions either of the original Constitution or of the XIVth Amendment.

The fundamental principles which Judge Field has thus adopted,—the system of constitutional interpretation which as a whole he has consistently maintained,—are, in my opinion, correct. They are substantially the same broad, comprehensive, liberal doctrines which were promulgated, and enforced with a cogency of reasoning absolutely crushing, by the great Chief Justice Marshall, and supported by such judges as Washington, Story, Wayne, and Catron. Whether he has correctly applied them in every individual case coming before him as a member of the Court, or whether he may not sometimes have erred in such application, are questions concerning which there may, perhaps, be a difference of opinion even among those who entirely agree with him in his general system.

These principles which thus underlie all his work in interpreting the Constitution, and to which he has so consistently adhered, whether acting with the Court or dissenting from it, are, I think, the following: (1) The political sovereignty and absolute supremacy of the United States and of its government, with respect to all matters within the scope of its legitimate functions, embracing all the legislative, executive, and judicial powers conferred upon it by the Constitution, and especially the power conferred upon its judiciary, of authoritatively and finally interpreting the organic law, and determining the nature and extent of all its grants and limitations of power. (2) Corresponding qualified political sovereignty exercised by the individual States, and *their exclusive powers*, free from federal interference with respect to all matters coming within the scope of their legitimate functions, which include all powers not conferred upon the general government, or not reserved by the people themselves, incapable, therefore, of being exercised by either government, or not expressly prohibited to the States. (3) The recognition, preservation, and maintenance, firm and inviolate, of all the limitations and restrictions, whether expressed or necessarily implied, imposed upon the governments, both of the United States and of the individual States, by the original Constitution or by the amendments thereto. (4) The upholding and enforcement, as a matter of special moment, of all those particular restrictions upon the governmental action, both of the United States and of the several States, contained in the original Constitution and in the amendments, which are intended directly to protect the private rights of life, liberty, and property, and, in fact, that entire body of private rights which constitute "civil liberty."

These principles may be still further generalized, and are summed up in two ideas: *First*, the preservation from every interference or invasion by each other, of all the powers and functions allotted to the national government and the State governments; and *second*, the perfect security and protection of private rights from all encroachments, either by the United States or by the individual States. These two ideas he has steadily kept in view and has made the basis of his decisions. He has demonstrated that a constant and firm maintenance of the powers justly belonging to the federal government, is not incompatible with an equally firm upholding of the powers entrusted to the States, with an undeviating adherence to the sacred doctrine of local self-government, and with zealous protection of private rights, because all, in fact, rest upon the same foundation.

My purpose, in the remaining portion of this sketch, is to show that Judge Field has uniformly and consistently asserted and applied these fundamental principles through his whole course of decisions upon the United States Bench. If I shall refer with more detail to decisions in which he has asserted the power and supremacy of the United States Government, it is because the other side of his system, and the cases in which he sustains the State authority and the civil rights of persons, are fully set forth in the accompanying volume.

Judge Field's opinions concerning the essential and historical nationality of the United States; the nature of the Union; its relations with the States; the indestructible character, both of the Union and the States, as an organization which not only exists under the Constitution, but existed prior to it, may be learned from the cases of Lane Co. vs. Oregon and Texas vs. White, in 7 Wallace. In these cases the Court was called upon to examine more profoundly and to declare more correctly, than had ever before been done by Marshall, Story, Taney, and the whole line of former judges, the true nature of the relations of the United States and of the States with each other, and of the peculiar organization resulting from their union. The Court for the first time found a solid basis, historical as well as logical, on which to rest the inherent existence and supremacy of the United States. Placing the Union upon a sure foundation, it also defined the status of the States, and asserted their necessary existence and peculiar rights in a manner no less clear and certain. The Court by these judgments established the United States and the States upon exactly the same footing; whatever weakens the one weakens the other; whoever denies the historic origin of the one, denies the same of the other. As we have in this theory the greatest security for the nation, we have also the greatest security for the several States. The opinions in these two cases were delivered by Mr. Justice Chase, and were concurred in by Judge Field and others who composed the majority rendering the decision. It is undoubtedly true, as a general rule, that concurring judges are not necessarily required to agree with all of the views expressed in the prevailing opinion of the Court. While they must agree with its conclusions, there may be modes of reasoning, forms of argument, personal notions of the one writing the opinion, to which the concurring judges do not wholly assent. There are, however, special reasons why this ordinary rule cannot be applied to these two cases. They were test cases, most carefully considered by the Court, and intended by the majority to put the questions involved, forever at rest. This was especially true of Texas vs. White. Again, the conclusions reached, and concurred in by the majority, are such as necessarily required an assent to the whole course of reasoning contained in the opinions. It would be impossible to reject any substantial position taken by the Chief Justice, or any particular argument in his chain of reasoning, without at the same time rejecting the conclusions which he finally reaches, and which form the basis of the judgment. To this I may add the testimony of Chief Justice Chase himself. In a letter written to me shortly after the decision of Texas vs. White was announced, he says, concerning the opinion in that case :

" That opinion was very much discussed, especially by the judges who concurred in it, and may, I think, be regarded as a tolerably correct expression of the views of the Court as to the nature of the National Union, of its relations to the States, and of the principles of re-organization of States disorganized by rebellion, and of the restoration of national relations interrupted by civil war."

It may, therefore, be considered as certain that these two cases express the deliberate convictions and opinions held by Judge Field; and in no subsequent case has he expressed any sentiment, or adopted any course of reasoning, or announced any doctrine, in opposition to these most important and profound judgments.

The same high view concerning the supremacy of the United States Government, within the field of its delegated powers, and concerning the limitations placed upon State action, is exhibited in his interpretation of the XIVth Amendment—that crowning and consummate provision of the organic law. So far from the absurd charge that he is hostile to this amendment being true, it was Judge Field himself who first, in a dissenting opinion, gave to the amendment that broad, liberal, and universal construction which renders it, as was intended, the most perfect safeguard against the encroachments of State governmental action upon the private civil rights of all persons. The first cases involving the amendment which came before the Court were the Slaughter-House Cases.—(16 Wall., 36.) The majority of the Court, in an opinion by Mr. Justice Miller,* put upon the amendment a most narrow interpretation, which would utterly destroy its value as a protection of private civil rights. They adopted as their fundamental proposition the strange notion that the amendment was confined in its operations to negroes. They held that the XIIIth, XIVth, and XVth Amendments were steps in the accomplishment of one final object—the abolition of slavery and the perfect freedom and protection of the negro race. They declared that, although expressed in general terms, the primary design and main purport of the XIVth Amendment was to confirm the status of negroes as citizens, and to prevent the encroachments of State laws which would discriminate against them. This was all the meaning which the majority could find in provisions designed to protect all persons against

---

* This opinion is the more strange and inconsistent since Judge Miller has always advocated views which tend to break down almost all limitations upon the general government, and to make the legislative powers of Congress almost universal. While maintaining a general theory concerning the nationality of the U. S., which I believe to be on the whole correct, he is inclined to ignore or weaken the restrictions which the Constitution has everywhere placed upon the exercise of full national powers by Congress.

unjust action of the local government. Mr. Justice Miller went so far, while commenting upon the last and most sweeping provision—"nor shall any State deny to any person within its jurisdiction the equal protection of the laws "—as to say of it: " We doubt very much whether any action of a State, not directed by way of discrimination against the negroes as a class, or on account of their race, will ever be held to come within the province of this provision." Four judges dissented from this narrow construction, in a most powerful opinion written by Judge Field. He asserted in the strongest terms the universality of the amendment, its application to all classes of persons. He denied that its operation was confined to the negroes. It afforded the same protection to *all* persons against local oppressive laws; it secured to all persons the equal protection of the laws. In a word, the XIVth Amendment was enacted to supply a great want, which had existed since the foundation of the government. While the States were from the outset forbidden to pass *ex post facto* laws, or bills of attainder, or laws impairing the obligation of contracts, they might in many other ways invade the rights of citizens, and the national courts could grant no relief.

This beneficial amendment throws the protection of the national courts around the lives, liberty, and property of all persons, and enables the supreme tribunal to annul all oppressive laws which the partisanship of local courts might perhaps sustain. To limit the meaning of the amendment, to confine its effect to one portion of the inhabitants, and that a comparatively small part, was to defeat its most important design, and to destroy its highest usefulness. The construction then put upon it by the majority simply emasculated the amendment. The broad, liberal, and national interpretation of Judge Field and the minority, is clearly correct; and to it he has steadily adhered in every subsequent case coming before the Supreme Court, or before himself in the Circuit Court, down to and including the somewhat famous " Chinese

Queue Case," in which he directly held that certain local legislation was annulled by the amendment. Judge Field's position in this matter should not be misunderstood. In the recent cases which have attracted so much attention, involving the validity of certain legislation of Congress purporting to be based upon the XIVth Amendment, he does not deny the validity nor the efficacy of that amendment; on the contrary, he reiterates all the views which he had before expressed. He dissents from the Court solely with respect to the legislation which Congress may properly enact for the purpose of carrying it into effect. He declares that no affirmative legislation is either necessary or appropriate. Like the clauses forbidding States to pass *ex post facto* laws, or bills of attainder, or laws impairing the obligation of contracts, the prohibitions of the amendment execute themselves. They are addressed to the States in their corporate capacity, and not to individuals, and they annul all State legislation which conflicts with their provisions. He regards the sacred principles of local self-government as lying at the very foundation of our institutions. The theory of the Constitution is, that all affirmative control over and legislation concerning private rights and relations, are confided exclusively to the individual States, and are not delegated to Congress. The XIVth Amendment has enabled the national courts to exercise a judicial scrutiny over this State legislation, to determine its validity, and to pronounce it null and void when discriminating or oppressive or violative of private civil rights; but the amendment cannot be regarded as revolutionizing the entire theory of our political organization, and as transferring to Congress the power of legislating with respect to private and personal rights. This is, in outline, the position maintained by Judge Field. It is entirely consistent with his doctrines concerning the supremacy of the General Government; it is, in fact, a part of one rounded, complete, and consistent system.

The supremacy of the General Government within the scope of those powers delegated to it by the Constitution, is also maintained in the most positive manner by a long series of decisions, in many of which he delivered the opinion of the Court, and in the others concurred, dealing with foreign commerce, inter-state commerce, the objects of State taxation, and other analogous subjects of congressional legislation. In numerous decisions covering every aspect of the question, and in language as pointed and emphatic as any that was ever used by Marshall or Story, he has affirmed the supreme and exclusive power of Congress over all branches and kinds of foreign or inter-state commerce which are national in their character, or requiring a uniform rule, the invalidity of State statutes which either directly or indirectly interfere with the freedom of inter-state traffic, or with the equality of civil rights belonging to citizens of other States. Did my time and space permit, it would be both interesting and instructive to quote some passages from the opinions of this class; but I must be content with collecting and arranging the most important cases in the foot-note.* Here, also, it should be noticed that Judge Field has been uniformly consistent, even when the Court has departed from its established principles, as it did in some of the so-called Granger Cases involving the validity of State statutes which interfered with and prescribed regulations affecting the inter-state transportation of goods and persons, and the inter-state traffic in goods.†

---

*See the following cases in which he delivered the opinion of the Court : Welton vs. Missouri, 1 Otto, 275 ; Sherlock vs. Alling, 3 Otto, 99 ; The Daniel Ball, 10 Wall., 357, 365 ; State Tax on Foreign Bondholders, 15 Wall., 300 ; County of Mobile vs. Kimball, 12 Otto. 691 ; Tiernan vs. Rinker, Ibid., 123 ; *In re* Ah Fong, 3 Sawyer, 144, 151 ; and also the following, among numerous others, in which he concurred : Case of State Freight Tax, 15 Wall., 232 ; Chy Lung vs. Freeman, 2 Otto, 275 ; Railroad vs. Husen, 5 Otto, 465 ; Henderson vs. Mayor of N. Y., 2 Otto, 259.

† Munn vs. Illinois, 4 Otto, 113, 135 ; Chicago, &c., R. R. vs. Iowa, 4 Otto, 155, 163 ; Peik vs. Chicago, &c., R. R., 4 Otto, 164, 177. Judge Field's dissent in this group of cases is a noble protest against State legislation invading the rights of private property, and as a course of reasoning is, as it seems to me, unanswerable.

E

One of the most distinguishing features of Judge Field's character as an interpreter of the Constitution, and of his work as a member of the National Judiciary, appears in the steady, uniform, and energetic manner in which he has enforced all the safeguards which the Constitution and its amendments have thrown around the personal rights of life, liberty, and property, by inhibiting all legislative or executive action, either of the federal or of the State governments, which would encroach upon those rights. He has clearly perceived that the primary object of all constitutional government is the protection of those sacred rights and immunities which constitute " civil liberty," and that a government which can only be maintained by ignoring or violating those rights is not worth preserving and maintaining. On the other hand, he has perceived, with an equally clear vision, that our own national organization, our political institutions, the integrity of our Union, and the autonomy of the States, could be upheld, preserved, and maintained by means of a strict and faithful adherence to the restrictions and limitations embodied in the Bill of Rights; that the preservation of the Union, the suppression of insurrection, and the ultimate triumph of the principles of freedom and equality, did not require any abandonment of, or interference with, local self-government, or the civil liberties of the private citizen. This element of his character and work is fully displayed in the accompanying volume and needs no further description.

At the outbreak of the civil war a species of political insanity seems to have seized upon large numbers of otherwise thoughtful and intelligent men. The power of the President to disregard all the legal securities of life, liberty, and property, to enforce martial law against civilians, to establish military courts in States removed from the scene of war, and subject persons there to military trials and punishments, was asserted in the most positive manner ; any denial or even doubt of the authority was treated as disloyalty. It is simply amazing to look back to that period and to recall the opinions which were then publicly maintained.* The whole subject, in fact, presented two aspects, namely: the effect of suspending the writ of habeas corpus, and the power to enforce martial law. It was asserted that the authority given to suspend the writ of habeas corpus during insurrection or invasion included the authority to disregard all the safeguards which the Bill of Rights has thrown around life, liberty, and property, and drew after it, as a necessary consequence, the power to make military arrests of citizens, and subject them to military trials and punishments. Even at the very outset a warning voice was raised against these monstrous conclusions. The venerable Horace Binney, the acknowledged leader of the American Bar, the associate and friend of all the greatest statesmen and judges of our earlier period, who, as a scholar in the Philadelphia High School, walked in public procession at the adoption of the United States Constitution, and then first felt, as he wrote to me, that he belonged to a nation, to something he could call his country,—Horace Binney wrote and published three essays in which he examined the subject of suspending the writ of habeas corpus in a most exhaustive manner, and showed, by a course of reasoning which amounts to absolute demonstration, that suspending the writ does not in the least affect the authority over arrests; that it does not enable Congress to allow, nor the Executive to make, arrests without legal cause or in an arbitrary manner; that it does not legalize seizures otherwise arbitrary, nor give any greater authority than that of detaining suspected persons in custody whom the government would else be obliged to bring to a speedy trial or to release on bail.

---

* A large volume was written and published called "The War Powers under the Constitution," a book maintaining sentiments suited, perhaps, to the autocratic despotism of Russia in its struggle with the Nihilists, but which are simply the negation of every fundamental principle of civil liberty and of private rights contained in our own political institutions.

These conclusions thus reached by Horace Binney were adopted by the Supreme Court in the Milligan Case (4 Wall., 2, 115), in the decision of which Judge Field concurred. The claim to exercise martial law against civilians was still more terrible. A most elaborate and exhaustive examination of the power to enforce martial law under or by virtue of the common law was made a few years ago by Lord Chief Justice Cockburn, one of the ablest chiefs who ever sat on the English Bench, and whose recent death is a great loss to the English administration of justice.* After a review of the precedents, ancient and modern, set forth in the wonderfully clear manner for which he was so pre-eminently distinguished, the Chief Justice reached the conclusion that under the common law there is no authority to enforce the martial law in any part of the British Empire where the common law prevails; in other words, the common law knows no such attribute of executive power. This conclusion the Supreme Court also adopted in the Milligan case. There can be no martial law in the United States except as an instrument and means of carrying on actual warfare, of conducting actual hostilities in regions occupied by the opposing armies. This doctrine received the hearty approval of Judge Field, and has been on every occasion maintained by him. See especially his dissenting opinion in ·Beckwith vs. Bean, (8 Otto, 285-306.)

I must not pursue this analysis into any further detail. I have shown that his system of constitutional construction is consistent and complete; that it recognizes and maintains alike the lawful supremacy and exclusive authority of the General Government within the scope of powers delegated to it, and the just rights of individual

---

* Charge of the Lord Chief Justice of England in the case of the Queen vs. Nelson and Brand, London, 1867, a case growing out of the negro insurrection, or rather tumult, in Jamaica, and the conduct of the Governor.

States; that it preserves unimpaired all the restrictions and limitations imposed upon the governmental action both of the States and of the nation; that it jealously guards the private and civil rights and immunities of persons; and that it respects and keeps in force the sacred principles of local self-government, and of civil and constitutional liberty, which underlie all our political institutions. From his opinions alone, a complete and consistent system of constitutional law might be composed, in which the American citizen would find a perfect text-book of political science, an exhaustive treatise upon the institutions of his country.

In conclusion, the proposition is, in my opinion, established by the foregoing sketch, that by his creative force as a state legislator, as a state judge, and, above all, as a member of the Supreme National Tribunal, Judge Field has, as much as any jurist of the present generation, impressed himself upon the jurisprudence of his country.

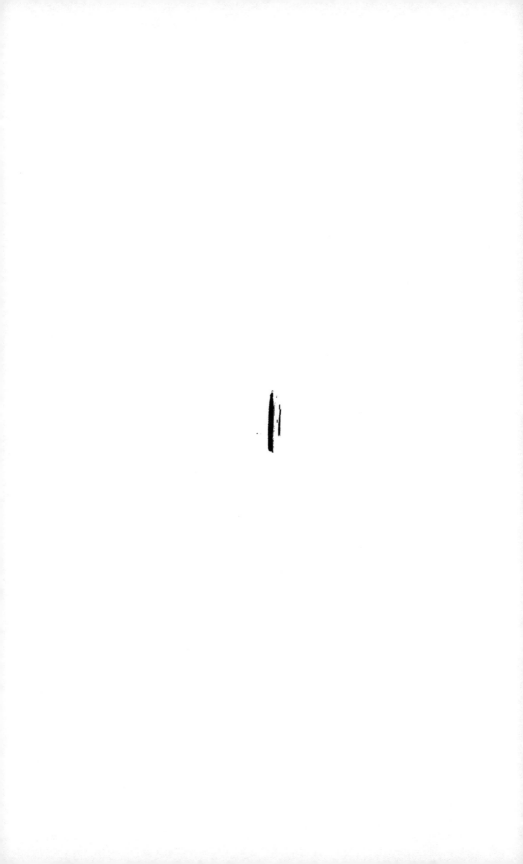

Note.

The articles in this volume are a compilation made by political and personal friends of Judge Field. The greater part of them were prepared in 1880. Those added since have been furnished principally by members of the Bar of California. The whole are now published at the request of gentlemen of that State, where it is believed they will be favorably received from the number of important public questions considered in them, and the ability with which the questions are treated.

No reference is made to the action of the associates of Judge Field on the Bench or in the Electoral Commission further than is necessary to illustrate and explain his conduct and positions. It is only with his career that the volume is concerned, and its limits would not allow any extended statement of their views and acts.

CHAUNCEY F. BLACK.
SAMUEL B. SMITH.

NEW YORK, *July*, 1881.

STEPHEN J. FIELD

AS A

LEGISLATOR, STATE JUDGE, AND JUDGE OF THE SUPREME COURT OF THE UNITED STATES.

JUDGE FIELD AS A LEGISLATOR.

The Legislation secured by him for the Protection of Miners in their Mining Claims.

From the San José DAILY HERALD *(California) of November* 18, 1879.

" The long judicial service of our distinguished fellow-citizen, embracing nearly six years in the Supreme Court of the State, and more than sixteen in the Supreme Court of the United States, has been marked by most able opinions on many great leading questions. This fact has very naturally connected his name in the public mind mainly with those questions, and few are aware of other, and even more important services, rendered our State by him, as a legislator, in the early days of the State's history. He was a member of the second legislature which was chosen in the Fall of 1850, and represented the then county of Yuba, which at that time included also what are now Sierra and Nevada counties.

" The first legislature had enacted a general system of laws, such as are indispensable to the government of any community. It had done nothing, however, toward the protection or regulation of that great interest which had gathered together from every State in the Union, and from every nation of the world, the restless and sometimes turbulent population of the California of thirty years ago. The gold seekers were left to jostle each other, and to settle their disputes as best they might. The ownership of the mines was held by some to be in the United States, and by others to be in the State, while all were alike extremely jealous of any assertion of power over them by the government of either. It was evident that the miners could not long be left to fight among themselves over questions of priority or extent of claims, while it was equally evident that legislation on the subject must be in accord with generally accepted opinion or it would be a dead letter. The situation was a grave one, and it demanded statesmanlike treatment. To do nothing was to leave the peace of the State at the mercy of those whose fierce thirst for gold might outrun their respect for fair dealing. Honest misunderstandings as to facts were oftenest settled by immediate appeal to brute force. The world has probably never seen a similar spectacle—that of extensive gold-fields suddenly peopled by masses of men from all States and countries, restrained by no law, and not agreed as to whence the laws ought to emanate by which they would consent to be bound. As in all other emergencies, the one man was there to bring forward the saving measure. Stephen J. Field solved the difficult problem. He saw that the rude society around him would shatter to fragments any system in which its own strong will and native common sense were not taken into account. The miners had, in each camp, held meetings, and enacted rules and regulations by which they agreed to be governed in that place. These had reference to the extent of each claim in the given locality, the acts necessary to constitute location or appropriation of the same, and the amount of work which should entitle the claimant to continued possession. The State could not safely attempt to substitute for these various rules any of a more general and uniform character. This fact was the basis of the measure brought forward by Judge Field in the Legislature of 1851, and by him urged to final success. He did not leave the miners to be a law unto themselves, but held them to the laws they had made for themselves. His plan was simple and at the same time thorough and sound. It was that the rules made by the miners should be enforced by the State. What they had declared to be fair play should be the law of the land, and should govern the courts in their decisions in mining disputes. Here is the language :

" In actions respecting ' Mining Claims ' proof shall be admitted of the customs, usages, or regulations established and in force at the bar, or diggings, embracing such claims, and such customs, usages, or regulations, when not in conflict with the constitution and laws of this State, shall govern the decision of the action."

" The principle contained in the fifty-two words above quoted was adopted in other mining regions of the country, and finally by the Congress of the United States. The author of it has seen its wisdom vindicated by more than twenty-eight years of experience, and for it the people of the State and of Nevada should ever hold him in grateful remembrance. When they think of him only as a judge deciding upon the administration of laws framed by others, let them be reminded that in a single sentence he laid the foundation of our mining system so firmly that it has not been, and cannot be, disturbed."

At the time the above legislation was had actions for mining claims, the mines being in the lands of the United States, were usually brought upon an alleged forcible or unlawful detainer. The rule adopted by the enactment in question, originally applicable only in actions before local magistrates, was soon extended to actions for mining claims in all courts, and, as stated above, now prevails in all the mining regions of the country.

Many years afterwards Mr. Field, in giving the opinion of the Supreme Court of the United States in an important case before it, spoke of the usages and regulations of miners, to which this legislation gave the force of law, as follows :

"The discovery of gold in California was followed, as is well known, by an immense immigration into the State, which increased its population within three or four years from a few thousand to several hundred thousand. The lands in which the precious metals were found belonged to the United States, and were unsurveyed, and not open, by law, to occupation and settlement. Little was known of them further than that they were situated in the Sierra Nevada Mountains. Into these mountains the emigrants in vast numbers penetrated, occupying the ravines, gulches, and cañons, and probing the earth in all directions for the precious metals. Wherever they went they carried with them that love of order and system and of fair dealing which are the prominent characteristics of our people. In every district which they occupied they framed certain rules for their government, by which the extent of ground they could severally hold for mining was designated, their possessory right to such ground secured and enforced, and contests between them either avoided or determined. These rules bore a marked similarity, varying in the several districts only according to the extent and character of the mines, distinct provisions being made for different kinds of mining, such as placer mining, quartz mining, and mining in drifts or tunnels. They all recognized discovery followed by appropriation as the foundation of the possessor's title, and development by working as the condition of its retention. And they were so framed as to secure to all comers, within practicable limits, absolute equality of right and privilege in working the mines. Nothing but such equality would have been tolerated by the miners, who were emphatically the law-makers, as respects mining, upon the public lands in the State. The first appropriator was everywhere held to have, within certain well-defined limits, a better right than others to the claims taken up; and in all controversies, except as against the government, he was regarded as the original owner, from whom title was to be traced. But the mines could not be worked without water. Without water the gold would remain forever buried in the earth or rock. To carry water to mining localities, when they were not on the banks of a stream or lake, became, therefore, an important and necessary business in carrying on mining. Here, also, the first appropriator of water to be conveyed to such localities for mining or other beneficial purposes, was recognized as having, to the extent of actual use, the better right. The doctrines of the common law respecting the rights of riparian owners were not considered as applicable, or only in a very limited degree, to the condition of miners in the mountains. The waters of rivers and lakes were consequently carried great distances in ditches and flumes, constructed with vast labor and enormous expenditures of money, along the sides of mountains and through cañons and

ravines to supply communities engaged in mining, as well as for agricul-
turists and ordinary consumption. Numerous regulations were adopted,
or assumed to exist from their obvious justness, for the security of these
ditches and flumes, and the protection of rights to water, not only between different appropriators, but between them and the holders of
mining claims. These regulations and customs were appealed to in controversies in the State courts, and received their sanction; and properties
to the value of many millions rested upon them. For eighteen years,
from 1848 to 1866, the regulations and customs of miners, as enforced
and moulded by the courts, and sanctioned by the legislation of the
State, constituted the law governing property in mines and in water on
the public mineral lands. Until 1866 no legislation was had looking to
a sale of the mineral lands. The policy of the country had previously
been, as shown by the legislation of Congress, to exempt such lands from
sale. In that year the act, the ninth section of which we have quoted,
was passed.* In the first section it declared that the mineral lands of
the United States were free and open to exploration and occupation by
citizens of the United States, and those who had declared their intention
to become citizens, subject to such regulations as might be prescribed by
law and the local customs or rules of miners in the several mining districts, so far as the same were not in conflict with the laws of the United
States. In other sections it provided for acquiring the title of the United
States to claims in veins or lodes of quartz bearing gold, silver, cinnabar,
or copper, the possessory right to which had been previously acquired
under the customs and rules of miners. In no provision of the act was
any intention manifested to interfere with the possessory rights previously acquired, or which might be afterwards acquired; the intention
expressed was to secure them by a patent from the government. The
Senator of Nevada,† the author of the act, in advocating its passage in
the Senate, spoke in high praise of the regulations and customs of miners,
and portrayed in glowing language the wonderful results that had followed the system of free mining which had prevailed with the tacit
consent of the government. The Legislature of California, he said, had
wisely declared that the rules and regulations of miners should be received in evidence in all controversies respecting mining claims, and
when not in conflict with the constitution or laws of the State or of the
United States, should govern their determination; and a series of wise
judicial decisions had moulded these regulations and customs into 'a
comprehensive system of common law, embracing not only mining law,
properly speaking, but also regulating the use of water for mining purposes.' The miner's law, he added, was a part of the miner's nature. He
had made it, and he trusted it and obeyed it. He had given the honest

---

* The act of July 26, 1866, "granting the right of way to ditch and
canal owners over the public lands, and for other purposes."—(14 U. S.
Statutes, 251.)

† Hon. Wm. M. Stewart.

toil of his life to discover wealth, which, when found, was protected by no higher law than that enacted by himself under the implied sanction of a just and generous government. And the act proposed continued the system of free mining, holding the mineral lands open to exploration and occupation subject to legislation by Congress and to local rules. It merely recognized the obligation of the government to respect private rights which had grown up under its tacit consent and approval. It proposed no new system, but sanctioned, regulated, and confirmed a system already established, to which the people were attached."—(Jennison vs. Kirk, 98 U. S. Rep., 457.)

JUDGE FIELD AS A LEGISLATOR.

The Legislation secured by him for the Exemption from Forced Sale for Debts of the Tools and other Personal Property of the Debtor.

From the San José DAILY HERALD *of November* 21, 1879.

"Last Wednesday we gave a portion of Judge Field's record as a legislator in this State, showing that his services have been of great value and that he is one of the most thorough statesmen claimed by this coast. We referred particularly to the mining law, and we now call attention to another most beneficial law of which Judge Field was the author. We refer to the law exempting from sale for debt (other than the purchase money, or to satisfy a mortgage thereon) certain property. The law reads as follows :

"The following property shall be exempt from execution, except as herein otherwise specially provided :

"1. Chairs, tables, desks, and books, to the value of one hundred dollars, belonging to the judgment debtor ;

"2. Necessary household, table, and kitchen furniture, belonging to the judgment debtor, including stove, stovepipe, and stove furniture, wearing apparel, beds, bedding, and bedsteads, and provisions actually provided for individual or family use sufficient for one month ;

" 3. The farming utensils, or implements of husbandry, of the judgment debtor ; also two oxen, or two horses, or two mules, and their harness, and one cart or wagon, and food for such oxen, horses, or mules for one month ;

" 4. The tools and implements of a mechanic necessary to carry on his trade, the instruments and chests of a surgeon, physician, surveyor, and dentist necessary to the exercise of their professions, with their professional library, and the law libraries of an attorney or counsellor ;

" 5. The tent and furniture, including a table, camp stools, bed and bedding, of a miner ; also his rocker, shovels, spades, wheelbarrows, pumps, and other instruments used in mining, with provisions necessary for his support for one month ;

" 6. Two oxen, or two horses, or two mules, and their harness, and one cart or wagon, by the use of which a cartman, teamster, or other laborer habitually earns his living ; and food for such oxen, horses, or mules for one month ; and a horse, harness, and vehicle used by a physician or surgeon in making his professional visits ;

" 7. All arms and accoutrements required by law to be kept by any person. But no article mentioned in this section shall be exempt from an execution issued on a judgment recovered for its price, or upon a mortgage thereon." *

" This was far in advance of any similar provision in other States, and was a bold and novel proposition. Thousands have enjoyed its benefits without being aware that its author was Stephen J. Field. The wisdom of it is manifest when we consider that it merely preserves to the unfortunate debtor the instrumentalities for future effort. A rapacious creditor might feel entitled to " the uttermost farthing " in the possession of the man indebted to him.

---

* These provisions are contained in section 219 of the act of 1851, regulating proceedings in civil cases, which is one of the many original sections in that act drawn by Judge Field. Until this legislation there was no exemption at all of personal property in California; and no exemption equally extensive is found in the previous legislation of any State of the Union.

But this law interposes and says to the debtor : " You shall have the right to reserve a hundred dollars' worth of property, your necessary household furniture, wearing apparel, and a month's provisions ; and then besides this, if you are a farmer, you shall be allowed to retain all your farming implements, and also a wagon and a pair of animals, with one month's food for them. This will enable you to go to work and repair your fortunes. The law will not see you disabled." To the mechanic and miner this humane law says : " Be of good cheer. You shall keep the tools with which you ply your calling. These shall be regarded as a part of your own physical system ; as well might your hands be cut off as your tools taken from them." To the workingman using a cart and horse, as so many laborers do, this law, which has stood for twenty-eight years on our statute book, says : " You must pay your debts, but need not sell the good horse and cart by which you are aided to feed your children. Nay, you may keep a wagon and two horses, if you are so fortunate as to have them. These make you independent, and the sheriff shall not take them." Others were also protected. The instruments of the surgeon and surveyor, the library of the physician and the lawyer, and the horse and buggy of the physician, were all declared exempt from forced sale. This law has never been complained of or tampered with, and remains a monument to the wisdom, humanity, and thoughtfulness of its author, Judge Field, who, in framing it, made application, for the benefit of the debtor, of the truth uttered by that harshest of creditors—Shylock—when he said :

———— You take my life
When you do take the means
Whereby I live.

These measures—the mining law, and the law exempting certain property from forced sale under execution—are but a small portion of the valuable legislative work of Judge Field, but we bring them to public attention at this time as furnishing high evidence of the practical wisdom of one whose name we read oftenest of late years in connection with judicial decisions, but whose friends could, if they chose, claim for him a place among statesmen as high as that he occupies among jurists. His conservatism has never made him the enemy of wholesome changes, and his progressiveness has never made him the supporter of any of the isms of the times. He has been as great a student of men and of affairs as of books."

---•◦•---

JUDGE FIELD AS A LEGISLATOR.

General Legislation secured by him.

From the San José DAILY HERALD *of December* 26, 1879.

"We have already referred to legislation concerning mining customs and regulations, and exemptions of certain personal property from forced sale, of which Judge Field was the author. We desire to make some further reference to his brief but most honorable, and we might truly say brilliant legislative career.

"His service was only for a single session—that of 1851 —and yet whilst there he left his mark permanently upon the laws of the State. He was appointed on the Judiciary Committee ; and as a member of that Committee he prepared and reported a bill concerning the Courts of Justice and Judicial Officers of the State, which was passed. The immense labor, difficulty, and responsibility attending the preparation of this bill will be seen, when it is stated that by it the whole Judiciary System of the State was reorganized, and the jurisdiction, powers, and duties of the several courts, and of all judicial officers, were designated and defined. And it may be here added that the act of 1853 with the same title—which was the original act carefully revised, and introduced into the Legislature by Mr. Samuel B. Smith of Sutter County—was also prepared by him.

" He also prepared and introduced bills to regulate proceedings in civil and criminal cases. These bills were taken from the proposed codes of New York as reported by the Commissioners of that State ; but the great labor involved nevertheless in their preparation may be estimated from the fact, that in order to adapt them to the peculiar condition of the new State and the requirements of its constitution, as well as to his own views of what would constitute the best practice, he redrafted over three hundred sections, and added over one hundred new ones. Among the new sections are those to which we have already referred relating to actions respecting mining claims and the admission in evidence of the customs and regulations of miners, and respecting exemptions from forced sale of personal property. These bills became laws and with some amendments—found necessary during a period of nearly twenty-two years, and particularly from the constitutional amendments of 1862—remained on the statute book until the adoption of the recent codes, in which they are substantially embodied.

" He also drew bills creating the counties of Nevada and Klamath and gave those counties their names. Many counties also sought legislation correcting or changing their boundary lines, and several bills on the subject being referred to him he reported a general bill, dividing the State into counties and establishing the Seats of Justice therein, which was passed. Judge Field drew the charters of the cities of Marysville, Nevada, and Monterey— the latter being reported as a substitute for the bill introduced by the member of Monterey County. The principal provisions of these charters have been adopted in subsequent acts creating municipal incorporations.

" He also drafted the act concerning divorces which was reported from the Judiciary Committee as a substitute for a bill on the same subject introduced by Mr. Jesse D. Carr.

" It has always been a source of great satisfaction to him that he gave most earnest support to the Homestead Exemption Bill. That bill was introduced by Mr. Gavin D. Hall, then of El Dorado, now of San Francisco, and was assailed violently as tending to obstruct the collection of debts. An effort to reduce the amount of the Homestead Exemption from $5,000 to $3,000 was stoutly and successfully resisted by Judge Field, Judge McCorkle, and the author of the bill.

" The session of 1851 was the most important in the history of the State. It was the first one held after the admission of California into the Union ; and some of the best timbers of the new governmental structure are of the handiwork of Judge Field. His labors there, as in every other station to which he has been called, exhibit great devotion to the public service, untiring industry, and a high sense of the responsibility of a public officer. Many bad bills were defeated through his influence and many defective ones amended by his suggestions. He was seldom absent from his seat ; he carefully watched all measures ; and there were few debates in which he did not participate. Such is the universal testimony of all the survivors of the legislative body of 1851, and its truth is established by the Journals of the Assembly and the papers of the time.

" We are specially indebted for the materials of this article to information derived from Judge McCorkle, Hon. Samuel A. Merritt, and Hon. Jesse D. Carr, who were members of the Legislature with Judge Field."

In addition to the above, Judge Field was the author of the act concerning attorneys and counsellors-at-law, in

which he incorporated provisions rendering it impossible
for any judge to disbar an attorney in an arbitrary manner without notice of the charges against him, and giving
him an opportunity to be heard upon them ; of the act
concerning county recorders, in which the present system
of keeping the records of conveyances was adopted ; and of
the act concerning county sheriffs, in which their duties
in the execution of process and in keeping prisoners were
declared and defined.

STEPHEN J. FIELD

AS A

JUDGE OF THE SUPREME COURT OF CALIFORNIA.

In 1857 Mr. Field was elected Judge of the Supreme Court of California for six years, commencing January 1st, 1858. There were two candidates besides himself before the people for the position, and 93,000 votes were polled. He received a majority of 36,000 over each of his opponents, and 17,000 over them both together.*

In September, 1857, the Chief Justice of the Court, Hugh L. Murray, died, and one of the associate judges was appointed to fill the vacancy. This left the balance of the associate judge's term of service, which extended to the following January, unoccupied, and Mr. Field was appointed by the governor of the State—a political opponent—to fill it. He accepted the appointment, and took his seat on the bench October 13th, 1857. He held the office of associate judge until the resignation of Chief Justice Terry in September, 1859, when he became Chief Justice.

---

* The exact vote was as follows :

For S. J. Field	55,216
For Nathaniel Bennett	18,944
For J. P. Ralston	19,068
Total vote	93,228
Majority of Field over Bennett	36,272
Majority of Field over Ralston	36,148
Majority of Field over both	17,204

In 1863 Mr. Field was appointed by President Lincoln an Associate Justice of the Supreme Court of the United States. The appointment was made upon the unanimous recommendation of the congressional delegation of the Pacific Coast, then consisting of four Senators and four Members of the House, of whom five were Democrats and three Republicans ; all of them were Union men. His commission was dated March 10th, 1863, but as he desired, prior to leaving the State bench, to dispose of the cases which had been argued before him, he did not take the oath of office until the 20th of May following. He sent in his resignation to the governor to take effect on that day.

Judge Joseph G. Baldwin, who had been his associate on the bench for three years, hearing of the resignation, gave expression to his estimate of Mr. Field's judicial career in the following communication to the Sacramento Union, which appeared in that paper May 6th, 1863. Judge Baldwin was himself distinguished alike for his legal and literary attainments, and was warmly attached to his friend.

JUDGE FIELD.

" The resignation by Judge Field of the office of Chief Justice of the Supreme Court of California, to take effect on the 20th instant, has been announced. By this event the State has been deprived of the ablest jurist who ever presided over her courts. Judge Field came to California from New York in 1849, and settled in Marysville. He immediately commenced the practice of law, and rose at once to a high position at the local bar, and upon the organization of the Supreme Court soon commanded a place in the first class of the counsel practicing in that forum. For many years, and until his promotion to the bench, his practice was as extensive, and probably as remunerative, as that of any lawyer in the State. He served one or two sessions in the Legislature, and the State is indebted to him for very many of the laws which constitute the body of her legislation.* In 1857 he was nominated for Judge of the Supreme Court for a full term, and in October of the same year was appointed by Govenor Johnson to fill the unexpired term of Justice Heydenfeldt, resigned. He immediately entered upon the office, and has continued ever since to discharge its duties. Recently, as the reader knows, he was appointed by the unanimous request of our delegation in Congress, to a seat upon the Bench of the Supreme Court of the United States, and was confirmed, without opposition, by the Senate.

"Like most men who have risen to distinction in the United States, Judge Field commenced his career without the advantages of wealth, and he prosecuted it without the factitious aids of family influence or patronage. He had the advantage, however—which served him better than wealth or family influence—of an accomplished education, and careful study and mental discipline. He brought to the practice of his profession a mind stored with professional learning, and embellished with rare scholarly attainments. He was distinguished at the bar for his fidelity to his clients, for untiring industry, great care and accuracy in the preparation of his cases, uncommon legal acumen, and extraordinary solidity of judgment. As an adviser, no man had more the confidence of his clients, for he trusted nothing to chance or accident when certainty could be attained, and felt his way cautiously to his conclusions, which, once reached, rested upon sure foundations, and to which he clung with remarkable pertinacity. Judges soon learned to repose confidence in his opinions, and he always gave them the strongest proofs of the weight justly due to his conclusions.

"When he came to the bench, from various unavoidable causes the calendar was crowded with cases involving immense interests, the most important questions, and various and pecular litigation. California was then, as now, in the

---

* He was in the Legislature only one session.

2

development of her multiform physical resources. The judges were as much pioneers of law as the people of settlement. To be sure something had been done, but much had yet to be accomplished ; and something, too, had to be undone of that which had been done in the feverish and anomalous period that had preceded. It is safe to say that, even in the experience of new countries hastily settled by heterogeneous crowds of strangers from all countries, no such example of legal or judicial difficulties was ever before presented as has been illustrated in the history of California. There was no general or common source of jurisprudence. Law was to be administered almost without a standard. There was the civil law, as adulterated or modified by Mexican provincialisms, usages, and habitudes, for a great part of the litigation; and there was the common law for another part, but *what that was* was to be decided from the conflicting decisions of any number of courts in America and England, and the various and diverse considerations of policy arising from local and other facts. And then, contracts made elsewhere, and some of them in semi-civilized countries, had to be interpreted here. Besides all which may be added that large and important interests peculiar to this State existed—mines, ditches, etc.—for which the courts were compelled to frame the law, and make a system out of what was little better than chaos.

" When, in addition, it is considered that an unprecedented number of contracts, and an amount of business without parallel, had been made and done in hot haste, with the utmost carelessness ; that legislation was accomplished in the same way, and presented the crudest and most incongruous materials for construction ; that the whole scheme and organization of the government, and the relation of the departments to each other, had to be adjusted by judicial construction—it may well be conceived what task even the ablest jurist would take upon himself when he assumed this office. It is no small compliment to say that Judge Field entered upon the duties of this great trust with his usual zeal and energy, and that he leaves the office not only with greatly increased reputation, but that he has raised the character of the jurisprudence of the State. He has more than any other man given tone, consistency, and system to our judicature, and laid broad and deep the foundation of our civil and criminal law. The land titles of the State—the most important and permanent of the interests of a great commonwealth—have received from his hand their permanent protection, and this alone should entitle him to the lasting gratitude of the bar and the people.

" His opinions, whether, for their learning, logic, or diction, will compare favorably, in the judgment of some of our best lawyers, with those of any judge upon the Supreme Bench of the Union. It is true what he has accomplished has been done with labor ; but this is so much more to his praise, for such work was not to be hastily done, and it was proper that the time spent in perfecting the work should bear some little proportion to the time it should last. We know it has been said of Judge Field that he is too much of a ' case lawyer,' and not sufficiently broad and comprehensive in his views. This criticism is not just. It is true he is reverent of authority, and likes to be sustained by precedent ; but an examination of his opinions will show that, so far from being a timid copyist, or the passive slave of authority, his rulings rest upon clearly defined principles and strong common sense.

" He retires from office without a stain opon his ermine. Millions might have been amassed by venality. He retires as poor as when he entered—owing nothing and owning little, except the title to the respect of good men, which malignant mendacity can not wrest from a public officer who has deserved, by a long and useful career, the grateful appreciation of his fellow-citizens. We think that we may safely predict that, in his new place, Justice Field will fulfill the sanguine expectations of his friends."

SAN FRANCISCO, *May* 1, 1863.   J. G. B.

It will be observed that in his communication Judge Baldwin places great stress upon the action of Judge Field in the settlement of land titles. Their unsettled condition when he went on the bench was the occasion of much litigation as well as animosity between persons who otherwise would have been on amicable terms. This condition arose principally from three causes: 1st, the immense extent and indefinite boundaries of grants from the former Mexican government ; 2d, the occupation by settlers of lands of the United States in advance of measures by the government for their sale; and 3d, the claim of California to own the gold and silver found in all lands in the State.

The following is a brief statement as to these causes of disturbance and their disposition :

1st. *As to the Mexican grants :*

" When California was acquired, the population was small and widely scattered. To encourage colonization, grants of land in large quantities, varying from one to eleven leagues, had been made to settlers by the Mexican government. Only small tracts were subjected to cultivation. The greater part of the land was used for grazing cattle, which were kept in immense herds. The grants were sometimes of tracts with defined boundaries, and sometimes of places by name, but more frequently of specified quantities lying within boundaries embracing a greater amount. By the Mexican law, it was incumbent upon the magistrates of the vicinage to put the grantees in possession of the land granted to them ; and for that purpose to measure off and segregate the quantity designated. Owing to the sparseness of the population there was little danger of disputes as to boundaries, and this segregation in the majority of cases had been neglected before our acquisition of the country. From the size of the grants and the want of definite boundaries, arose nearly all the difficulties and complaints of the early settlers. Upon the discovery of gold, immigrants from all parts of the world rushed into the country, increasing the population in one or two years from a few thousand to several hundred thousand. A large number crossed the plains from the Western States, and many of them sought for farming lands upon which to settle. To them a grant of land leagues in extent seemed a monstrous wrong to which they could not be reconciled. The vagueness, also, in many instances, of the boundaries of the land claimed gave force and apparent reason to their objections. They accordingly settled upon what they found unenclosed or uncultivated, without much regard to the claims of the Mexican grantees. If the land upon which they thus settled was within the tracts formerly occupied by the grantees with their herds, they denied the validity of grants so large in extent. If the boundaries designated enclosed a greater amount than that specified in the grants, they undertook to locate the supposed surplus. Thus, if a grant were of three leagues within boundaries embracing four, the immigrant would undertake to appropriate to himself a portion of what he deemed the surplus ; forgetting that other immigrants might do the same thing, each claiming that what he had taken was a portion of such surplus, until the grantee was deprived of his entire property.

"When the Supreme Court of California was brought to consider the questions to which this condition of things gave rise, it assumed at the outset that the obligations of the treaty with Mexico were to be respected and enforced. This treaty had stipulated for the protection of all rights of property of the citizens of the ceded country; and that stipulation embraced inchoate and equitable rights, as well as those which were perfect. It was not for that Court to question the wisdom or policy of Mexico in making grants of such large portions of her domain, or of the United States in stipulating for their protection. As Judge Grier said in his opinion in the case of The United States vs. Sutherland, in the 19th of Howard, the rhetoric which denounced the grants as enormous monopolies and princedoms might have a just influence when urged to those who had a right to give or refuse; but as the United States had bound themselves by a treaty to acknowledge and protect all *bona-fide* titles granted by the previous government, the court had no discretion to enlarge or contract such grants to suit its own sense of propriety or to defeat just claims, however extensive, by stringent technical rules of construction to which they were not originally subjected." *

* In the Fossatt case this obligation of our government to protect the rights of Mexican grantees in California is stated in brilliant and powerful language by Judge Black. Referring to the land claimed by one Justo Larios, a Mexican grantee, he said: "The land we are claiming never belonged to this government. It was private property under a grant made long before our war with Mexico. When the treaty of Guadalupe Hidalgo came to be ratified—at the very moment when Mexico was feeling the sorest pressure that could be applied to her by the force of our armies and the diplomacy of our statesmen—she utterly refused to cede her public property in California unless upon the express condition that all private titles should be faithfully protected. We made the promise. The gentleman sits on this bench (Judge Clifford) who was then our Minister there. With his own right hand he pledged the sacred honor of this nation that the United States would stand over the grantees of Mexico and keep them safe in the enjoyment of their property. The pledge was not only that the government itself would abstain from all disturbance of them, but that every blow aimed at their rights, come from what quarter it might, should be caught upon the broad shield of our blessed Constitution and our equal laws. It was by this assurance thus solemnly given that we won the reluctant consent of Mexico to part with California. It gave us a domain of more than imperial grandeur. Besides the vast extent of that country, it has natural advantages such as no other can boast. Its valleys teem with unbounded fertility, and its mountains are filled with inexhaustible treasures of mineral wealth. The navigable rivers run hundreds of miles into the interior, and the coast is indented with the most capacious harbors in the world. The climate is more healthful than any other on the globe: men can labor longer with less fatigue. The vegetation is more vigorous and the products more abundant; the face of the earth is more varied, and the sky bends over it with a lovelier blue. ——— That was what we gained by the promise to protect men in the situation of Justo Larios, their children, their alienees, and others claiming through them. It is impossible that in this nation they will ever be plundered in the face of such a pledge."— (2 Wallace, 703.)

"Acting on the principle — that fidelity to a nation's pledge is a sacred duty, and that justice is the highest interest of the country, Judge Field endeavored, whenever the occasion presented itself, and his associates co-operated with him, to protect the Mexican grantees. Their grants contained a stipulation for the possession of the lands granted, inasmuch as they were subject to the conditions of cultivation and occupancy, and a failure to comply with the conditions was considered by the tribunals of the United States as a most material circumstance in the determination of the right of the grantees to a confirmation of their claims. He held, therefore, with the concurrence of his associates, that the grantees, whether they were to be considered as having a legal or an equitable right to the lands, were entitled to their possession until the action of the government upon their claims, and, therefore, that they could recover in ejectment." If the grant was a mere float, or of a quantity to be selected within vague undefinable boundaries like mountains, as in the case of the Mariposa grant, no line on such mountains, from their base to their summit, being designated, he held that the grantee was to be confined in his recovery to the tract actually used and occupied by him, until the government intervened and determined that the quantity granted to him should be elsewhere located. But if the grant was not a mere float, but was of land within clearly defined boundaries, which embraced a greater quantity than that specified in it, with a provision that the surplus should be measured of by the government, he held that until such measurement the grantee was a tenant in common with the government and could hold the whole as against mere intruders and trespassers. As he said in one of his opinions, speaking for the court, until such measurement no individual could complain, much less could he be permitted to determine in advance, that any particular locality would fall within the supposed surplus, and thereby justify its forcible seizure and detention by himself. " If one person could in this way appropriate a particular parcel to himself, all persons could do so ; and thus the grantee, who is the donee of the government, would be stripped of its bounty for the benefit of those who were not in its contemplation and were never intended to be the recipients of its favors." *

These views have since met with general assent in California and have been approved by the Supreme Court of the United States.† But at that time they gave offence to a large class, and the judges were accused of acting in the interest of monopolists and land-grabbers, when in fact they were only extending to the grantees the protection which our treaty with Mexico stipulated.

2d. As to the occupation by settlers of lands of the United States in advance of measures by the government for their sale.

" The position of a large portion of the people of California, previous to 1860, with respect to the public lands, was unprecedented. The discovery of gold had brought, as stated, an immense immigration to the country. The slopes of the Sierra Nevada were traversed by many of the immigrants in search of the precious metals, and by others the tillable land was occupied for agricultural purposes. The title was in the United States, and until 1853 there had been no legislation authorizing a settlement upon any of the public lands, and for some years afterwards the public surveys were extended over only a portion of them. Conflicting possessory claims naturally arose, and the question was presented as to the law applicable to them. The Legislature in 1851 had provided that in suits before magistrates for mining claims, evidence of the customs, usages, and regulations of miners in their vicinage should be admissible, and, when not in conflict

---

* Cornwall vs. Culver, 16 Cal., 429, and Mahoney vs. Van Winkle, 21 Id., 576–580.

† Van Reynegan vs. Bolton, 95 U. S., 33.

with the constitution and laws of the state, should govern their decision, and the principle thus approved was
soon applied in actions for mining claims in all courts.
In those cases it was considered that the first possessor or
appropriator of the claim had the better right as against
all parties except the government, and that he, and persons claiming under him, were entitled to protection. This
principle received the entire concurrence of the court, and
was applied, in its fullest extent, for the protection of all
possessory rights on the public lands. Thus, in Coryell vs.
Cain, Judge Field said, speaking for the court:

"It is undoubtedly true, as a general rule, that the claimant in ejectment must recover upon the strength of his own title, and not upon the
weakness of his adversary's, and that it is a sufficient answer to his action
to show title out of him and in a third party. But this general rule has,
in this State, from the anomalous condition of things arising from the
peculiar character of the mining and landed interests of the country,
been to a certain extent qualified and limited. The larger portion of the
mining lands within the State belong to the United States, and yet that
fact has never been considered as a sufficient answer to the prosecution of
actions for the recovery of portions of such lands. Actions for the possession of mining claims, water privileges, and the like, situated upon the
public lands, are matters of daily occurrence, and if the proof of the paramount title of the government would operate to defeat them, confusion
and ruin would be the result. In determining controversies between
parties thus situated, this court proceeds upon the presumption of a
grant from the government to the first appropriator of mines, water
privileges, and the like. This presumption, which would have no place
for consideration as against the assertion of the rights of the superior proprietor, is held absolute in all those controversies. And with the public
lands which are not mineral lands, the title, as between citizens of the
State, where neither connects himself with the government, is considered
as vested in the first possessor, and to proceed from him."—(16 Cal., p.
572.)

The doctrine thus laid down was of incalculable benefit
to all occupants of the public lands of the United States
in advance of measures by the government for their sale.
It preserved peace among them, and gave them assurance
that they would be protected in their possessions until
the general government should interfere and assert its
superior title.

3d. As to the claim of California to own the gold and silver found in all lands in the State.

"The difficulties attendant upon any attempt to give security to landed possessions in the State, arising from the circumstances narrated, were increased by an opinion, which for some time prevailed, -that the precious metals, gold and silver, found in various parts of the country, whether in public or private lands, belonged to the State by virtue of her sovereignty. To this opinion a decision of the Supreme Court of the State, made in 1853, gave great potency. In Hicks vs. Bell, decided that year, the court came to that conclusion, relying upon certain decisions of the courts of England recognizing the right of the Crown to those metals. The principal case on the subject was that of The Queen vs. The Earl of Northumberland, reported in Plowden. The counsel of the Queen in that case gave, according to our present notions, some very fanciful reasons for the conclusion reached, though none were stated in the judgment of the court. The Supreme Court of the State, without considering the force of the reasons assigned in that case adopted its conclusion ; and as the gold and silver in the British realm are there held to belong to the Crown, it was concluded, on the hypothesis that the United States have no municipal sovereignty within the limits of the State, that they must belong in this country to the State. The State, therefore, said the court, "has solely the right to authorize them" (the mines of gold and silver) "to be worked ; to pass laws for their regulation ; to license miners ; and to affix such terms and conditions as she may deem proper to the freedom of their use. In her legislation upon this subject she has established the policy of permitting all who desire it to work her mines of gold and silver, with or without conditions; and she has wisely provided that their conflicting claims shall be adjudicated by the rules and customs which may be established by bodies of them working in the same vicinity."—(3 Cal., 227.)

" The miners soon grasped the full scope of the decision thus rendered, and the lands of private proprietors were invaded for the purpose of mining as freely as the public lands. It was the policy of the State to encourage the development of the mines, and no greater latitude in exploration could be desired than was thus sanctioned by the highest tribunal of the State.

" It was not long before a cry came up from private proprietors against this invasion of their possessions. There was gold in limited quantities scattered through large and valuable districts, where the land was held in private proprietorship, and under the doctrine announced the whole might be invaded, and, for all useful purposes, destroyed, no matter how little remunerative the product of the mining. The entry might be made at all seasons, whether the land was under cultivation or not, and without reference to its condition, whether covered with orchards, vineyards, gardens, or otherwise. It was evident that under such a state of things the owner of mineral land would never be secure in his possessions. His title would be of little value if there was a right of invasion in the whole world. In fact, the land would be to him poor and valueless just in proportion to the actual richness and abundance of its products.

" The Court was, therefore, compelled to put some limitation upon the enjoyment by the citizen of this asserted right of the State. Accordingly, within two years afterwards, it held that although the State was the owner of the gold and silver found in the lands of private individuals as well as in the public lands, " yet to authorize an invasion of private property in order to enjoy a public franchise would require more specific legislation than any yet resorted to."—(Stoakes vs. Barrett, 5 Cal., 39.)

" The spirit to invade other people's lands, to which the original decision gave increased force, could not, however, be as easily repressed as it was raised in the crowd of adventurers who filled the mining regions. And when Judge

Field went on the bench, in 1857, the right to dig for the precious metals on the lands of private individuals, under an assumed license of the State, was still asserted." But afterwards, in the case of Biddle Boggs vs. The Merced Mining Company* the whole subject was elaborately examined, and the doctrine repudiated. Judge Field wrote the opinion of the Court, which attracted much attention. The fallaciousness of the reasoning upon which the doctrine rested was so clearly shown, that the doctrine has never been reasserted since.

" At a later day the court took up the doctrine, that the precious metals belonged to the State by virtue of her sovereignty, and exploded it. The question arose in Moore vs. Smaw, and Fremont vs. Flower, which were heard together.† In disposing of it, Judge Field, speaking for the court, used the following language respecting the sovereignty of the State :

" It is undoubtedly true that the United States held certain rights of sovereignty over the territory which is now embraced within the limits of California, only in trust for the future State, and that such rights at once vested in the new State upon her admission into the Union. But the ownership of the precious metals found in public or private lands was not one of those rights. Such ownership stands in no different relation to the sovereignty of a State than that of any other property which is the subject of barter and sale. Sovereignty is a term used to express the supreme political authority of an independent State or Nation. Whatever rights are essential to the existence of this authority are rights of sovereignty. Thus the right to declare war, to make treaties of peace, to levy taxes, to take private property for public uses, termed the right of eminent domain, are all rights of sovereignty, for they are rights essential to the existence of supreme political authority. In this country, this authority is vested in the people, and is exercised through the joint action of their federal and State governments. To the federal government is delegated the exercise of certain rights or powers of sovereignty; and with respect to sovereignty, rights and powers are synonymous terms; and the exercise of all other rights of sovereignty, except as expressly prohibited, is reserved to the people of the respective States, or vested by them in their local governments. When we say, therefore, that a State of the Union is sovereign, we only mean that she possesses supreme political authority, except as to those matters over which such au-

---

* 14 Cal. Rep., 373–380. .   † 17 Cal. Rep., 200.

thority is delegated to the federal government, or prohibited to the States; in other words, that she possesses all the rights and powers essential to the existence of an independent political organization, except as they are withdrawn by the provisions of the Constitution of the United States. To the existence of this political authority of the State—this qualified sovereignty, or any part of it—the ownership of the minerals of gold and silver found within her limits is in no way essential./ The minerals do not differ from the great mass of property, the ownership of which may be in the United States, or in individuals, without affecting in any respect the political jurisdiction of the State. They may be acquired by the State, as any other property may be, but when thus acquired she will hold them in the same manner that individual proprietors hold their property, and by the same right; by the right of ownership, and not by any right of sovereignty."

"The court also held that, although under the Mexican law the gold and silver found in land did not pass with a grant of the land, a different result followed, under the common law, when a conveyance of land was made by an individual or by the government. By such a conveyance, without a special reservation, everything passed in any way connected with the land, forming a portion of its soil or fixed to its surface.

"The doctrine of the right of the State by virtue of her sovereignty to the mines of gold and silver within her limits perished with this decision. It was never afterwards seriously asserted." *

---

* The opinions of the court in the cases cited above—that of Biddle-Boggs vs. Merced Mining Company, and that of Fremont vs. Flower—were the subject of an article in the American Law Register of June, 1862, by Mr. Emory Washburn, Professor of Law in Harvard University. As the two cases grew out of the Mariposa grant, the Professor treated them as substantially one case, and concluded his article in the following language:

"It would be pleasant, if this article had not become so extended, to dwell for a moment upon the reflections that are at once awakened, as one contemplates the various phases of this celebrated case, upon the silent yet resistless majesty of the law, so long as its robes of office are worn by men of learning, uprightness, and unsuspected moral courage, acting within their sphere. Here has been a controversy involving, it is said, millions in value, as well as many considerations of great hardship, exciting not a little local as well as personal feeling and animosity. It has been passed upon by three men, personally without power, the organs and officers of the law, and there the contest ends, for the law has spoken, and we are, after all, a law-abiding people."

Patents for Land by the United States.

Patents for land by the United States, particularly those issued upon a confirmation of grants in California of the former Mexican government, were the subject of repeated consideration by the Supreme Court of the State while Judge Field was on its bench. In many opinions written by him, the operation of such patents was elaborately and exhaustively treated, and the law by which they were to be construed, their effect in giving quiet and security to the patentees in the possession of their lands, the extent to which they are conclusive against attacks at law, and the circumstances under which they can be assailed in equity, were stated with a clearness and precision, which left nothing in doubt and closed the door to much vexatious and harassing litigation touching the ownership of the lands covered by them. The doctrines advanced by him have never been successfully controverted, and they have been approved by the Supreme Court of the United States.*

Municipal Corporations.

Municipal corporations, their powers, rights, and obligations, were also the subject of consideration in numerous opinions of the Supreme Court of California written by Judge Field. Judge Dillon, in his recent work on Municipal Corporations, speaks of these opinions in terms of the highest praise, makes frequent citations from them, and recognizes the fact that the views contained in them have been concurred in very generally by the courts of other States.

In a series of adjudications in what are known in California as the " City Slip Cases," where property of the city of

---

* Moore vs. Wilkinson, 13 Cal., 478; Biddle Boggs vs. Merced Mining Co., 14 Id., 361–366; Stark vs. Barrett, 15 Id., 362; Mott vs. Smith, 16 Id., 534; Teschemacker vs. Thompson, 18 Id., 20; Leese vs. Clark, Id., 565; Same case a second time before the court in 20 Cal., 411; Estrada vs. Murphy, 19 Id., 268. See also Beard vs. Federy, 3d Wallace, 478.

San Francisco was sold under a void ordinance and the proceeds appropriated for municipal purposes, it was held, that no title passed, and that under the charter of the city (which required sales of its property to be made, by an ordinance adopted for that purpose, after advertisement of the time and place and terms of sale) the appropriation of the proceeds did not operate to ratify the sales, while at the same time it imposed upon the city the liability to pay back the money to the purchasers. It would seem plain that if the mere appropriation of the proceeds obtained under a void ordinance could give validity to a sale of the city's property, the restraints imposed by the legislature upon the action of the city would be easily defeated. Referring to the principles stated in these decisions, Judge Dillon says that they " are vindicated with characteristic clearness and striking logical force, in able and interesting opinions of Mr. Chief Justice Field." *

Among other objections against a recovery of the money paid by the purchasers upon the void sale, it was urged, that the common council of the city was forbidden by its charter to create or permit to be created any debt or liabilities, which in the aggregate, with all former debts or liabilities, should exceed $50,000 over and above its annual revenue, unless specially authorized by an ordinance providing the ways and means for the payment of the annual interest and of the principal, and such ordinance were approved by a vote of the people. To this objection Judge Field, in speaking for the court, thus replied:

"We are clear that the provision refers only to the acts or contracts of the city, and not to liabilities which the law may cast upon her. It was intended to restrain extravagant expenditures of the public moneys; not to justify the detention of the property of her citizens which she may have unlawfully obtained. The plaintiff claims that the city has got his money without any consideration—by mistake—and has appro-

---

* McCracken vs. The City of San Francisco, 16 Cal., 591; Grogan vs. San Francisco, 18 Id., 607; Pimental vs. San Francisco, 21 Id., 359. See also Argenti vs. City of San Francisco, 16 Cal., 282, and Zottman vs. San Francisco, 20 Cal., 96.

priated it to municipal purposes, and he insists that she is responsible to him for it, because the law—not her contract or permission—renders her liable. Her liability, in this respect, is independent of the restraining clauses of the charter; it arises from the obligation to do justice—to restore what belongs to others—which rests upon all persons, whether natural or artificial. And it may well be doubted whether it would be competent for the legislature to exempt the city, any more than private individuals, from liability under circumstances of this character. Suppose, for example, that the city should recover judgment against an individual for $100,000, and collect the money upon execution, and upon appeal the judgment should be reversed; would it be pretended that the money could not afterwards be recovered? Could the city defend against the claim for restitution upon the pretense that she was already indebted over $50,000? Could she, to use the language of counsel, *owe herself out of liability?* Suppose, again, an individual should pay the taxes upon his property, in ignorance that they had already been paid by his agent, could the city retain the amount thus paid by mistake? Could she plead her previous indebtedness as an excuse for the detention of the money to which she had no legal or equitable right? Suppose, again, the city should neglect to keep the streets in repair, and an individual should be injured in consequence—should break his leg or be otherwise crippled— could she allege her insolvency against his claim for damages? Would her pecuniary condition be an answer for the neglect of every duty, legal and moral? If this were so, she would be the most irresponsible corporation on earth, and her treasury would be, in many instances, but a receptacle for others' property without possibility of restitution. The truth is, there is no such exemption from liability on her part. The same obligations to do justice rest upon her as rest upon individuals. She cannot appropriate to her own use the property of others, and screen herself from responsibility upon any pretense of excessive indebtedness. The law casts upon her the legal liability from the moral duty to make restitution. Admitting that the charter restricts her power to incur liabilities by her own acts, ———— it still leaves her liable according to the general law. The restriction can, in any event, only apply to liabilities dependent for their creation upon the volition of the common council, and hence does not include liabilities arising from torts, or trespasses, or mistakes."—(McCracken vs. The City of San Francisco, 16 Cal., 631–2.)

MORTGAGES.

While Judge Field was on the bench the law of mortgages in California was settled in conformity with the common understanding of men. Opinions of the court, written by him, made that the rule of law which was before the rule of equity, namely : that a mortgage is not a

conveyance, but a pledge only, redeemable by compliance
with the condition on which it was given. Herman, the
author of a recent and most learned work on mortgages,
expresses the opinion that "No man in this country has
done as much in developing sound principles in regard to
mortgages—that they are mere hypothecations—as Judge
Field. To his labors on the Supreme Bench of California,
and in the United States Supreme Court, have been indebted the courts of every State where the doctrine is
maintained; and his California opinions are cited as leading and decisive of the true principle."*

OTHER CASES.

Numerous other cases besides those to which reference
has been made, presenting a great variety of questions,
some of general and public interest, and others of local
concern, were before the court whilst Judge Field was
on the bench, in which he gave the opinion of the court.
It would extend this sketch beyond the design of the writer
to give even a syllabus of the cases. They related to
the claim of the State to five hundred thousand acres of
land donated by the 8th section of the Act of Congress of
Sept. 4th, 1841, for purposes of internal improvement,
and to its right to dispose of the lands in advance of the
public surveys;—to contracts of the State for the support
and labor of its convicts;—to the power of the courts to
compel by mandamus officers of the State to do their
duty;—to the conflicting rights of miners to the use of
the water of streams in the mountains for the purpose of
mining;—to the right of the wife to a share of the community property under the law of Mexico and the law of
California;—to the title of the City of San Francisco to
lands within her limits as successor of a former Mexican
Pueblo and under the grant of beach and water lots by the

* McMillan vs. Richards, 9 Cal., 365; Nagle vs. Macy, 9 Id., 426; Johnson vs. Sherman, 15 Id., 287; Goodenow vs. Ewer, 16 Id., 461.

3

State in 1851 ;—to the construction of wills ;—to the distinction between mortgages and deeds of trust ; and to a great number of other subjects. A citation is given in the note of several of these cases.*

Two cases not included among these deserve special notice;—in one of which—*Ex-parte Newman*, (9 Cal., 502,) relating to a law making Sunday a day of rest—Judge Field wrote a dissenting opinion; and in the other—*Perry vs. Washburn*, (20 Cal., 318,) asserting the non-receivability of legal-tender notes for State taxes—he wrote the opinion of the court.

A Sunday Law, or a Law for a Day of Rest.

In Ex-parte Newman the question arose as to the validity of a law of California, which provided that no person should keep open on Sunday " any store, warehouse, mechanic shop, workshop, banking-house, manufacturing establishment, or other business house, for business purposes ;" or " sell or expose for sale any goods, wares, or merchandise" on that day ; and that a violation of these provisions should be deemed a misdemeanor for which a penalty was prescribed. The law excepted from its operation the keepers of hotels, inns, taverns, restaurants, boarding houses, and livery stables, and the retailers of drugs and medicines, and certain articles of fresh food and articles required in cases of necessity or charity. Nor did the law apply to such manufacturing or other business establishments as were necessarily required to be kept in continual operation to accomplish their business.

---

*Butte Canal and Ditch Co. vs. Vaughan, 11 Cal., 153; Baker vs. Baker, 13 Id., 87; Pierce vs. Robinson, 13 Id., 116; Blanding vs. Burr, 13 Id., 343; Scott vs. Ward, 13 Id., 458; Koch vs. Briggs, 14 Id., 256; Noe vs. Card, 14 Id., 577; Pixley vs. Huggins, 15 Id., 128; Norris vs. Harris, 15 Id., 226; State of California vs. McCauley, 15 Id., 429; Holliday vs. Frisbie, 15 Id., 630; McCauley vs. Brooks, 16 Id., 12; Koppikus vs. State Capital Commissioners, 16 Id., 249; Brumagim vs. Tillinghast, 16 Id., 267; Doll vs. Meador, 16 Id., 295; Halleck vs. Mixer, 16 Id., 575.

This law the majority of the court decided to be in conflict with the clause of the constitution which declared
that "the free exercise and enjoyment of religious profession and worship, without discrimination or preference,"
should forever be allowed in the State, holding that in
enforcing cessation from labor on a day held sacred by a
religious sect was a discrimination in favor of that sect.
The court also decided that the Legislature had no right
to forbid the pursuit of a lawful occupation on one day of
a week, any more than it had a right to forbid it altogether,
under the clause of the constitution declaring that all
men have the inalienable right of "acquiring, possessing,
and protecting property."

From this decision Judge Field dissented, holding that
the law only prescribed a day of rest from certain occupations as a rule of civil conduct, and had nothing to do
with religious profession or worship, to which it did not
allude in any of its provisions. And he thus vindicated
its wisdom :

"In its enactment the Legislature has given the sanction of law to a
rule of conduct which the entire civilized world recognizes as essential
to the physical and moral well-being of society. Upon no subject is
there such a concurrence of opinion among philosophers, moralists, and
statesmen of all nations, as on the necessity of periodical cessations from
labor. One day in seven is the rule, founded in experience and sustained by science. There is no nation, possessing any degree of civilization, where the rule is not observed, either from the sanctions of the law
or the sanctions of religion. This fact has not escaped the observation
of men of science, and distinguished philosophers have not hesitated to
pronounce the rule founded upon a law of our race.

"The Legislature possesses the undoubted right to pass laws for the
preservation of health and the promotion of good morals, and if it is of
opinion that periodical cessation from labor will tend to both, and thinks
proper to carry its opinion into a statutory enactment on the subject,
there is no power, outside of its constituents, which can sit in judgment
upon its action. It is not for the judiciary to assume a wisdom which it
denies to the Legislature, and exercise a supervision over the discretion
of the latter. It is not the province of the judiciary to pass upon the
wisdom and policy of legislation ; and when it does so, it usurps a power
never conferred by the constitution.

"It is no answer to the requirements of the statute to say that mankind
will seek cessation from labor by the natural influences of self-preserva-

tion. The position assumes that all men are independent, and at liberty to work whenever they choose. Whether this be true or not in theory, it is false in fact; it is contradicted by every day's experience. The relations of superior and subordinate, master and servant, principal and clerk, always have and always will exist. Labor is in a great degree dependent upon capital, and unless the exercise of the power which capital affords is restrained, those who are obliged to labor will not possess the freedom for rest which they would otherwise exercise.——The law steps in to restrain the power of capital. Its object is not to protect those who can rest at their pleasure, but to afford rest to those who need it, and who, from the conditions of society, could not otherwise obtain it. Its aim is to prevent the physical and moral debility which springs from uninterrupted labor; and in this aspect it is a beneficent and merciful law. It gives one day to the poor and dependent; from the enjoyment of which no capital or power is permitted to deprive them. It is theirs for repose, for social intercourse, for moral culture, and, if they choose, for divine worship. Authority for the enactment I find in the great object of all government, which is protection. Labor is a necessity imposed by the condition of our race, and to protect labor is the highest office of our laws."

Indeed, every one can see that the only chance for rest to the over-worked laboring classes in our factories and workshops, and in the heated rooms of our cities, is in a law compelling cessation from secular pursuits at regular intervals. Without it there would be for them only ceaseless toil. To them, therefore, such a law is a great blessing. It enables them, one day in a week, to be with their families ; to seek with them the pure air of the country; to visit gardens, and places for quiet enjoyment ; to exchange courtesies with friends and relatives, and to be free from the perpetual din of the shop, and the ever-pressing thought that only by the sweat of their brow they can earn their daily bread. To the objection that Sunday is a day of religious observance by certain sects; Judge Field answered as follows :

" The power of selection being in the Legislature, there is no valid reason why Sunday should not be designated as well as any other day. Probably no day in the week could be taken which would not be subject to some objection. That the law operates with inconvenience to some is no argument against its constitutionality. Such inconvenience is an incident to all general laws. A civil regulation cannot be converted into a religious institution because it is enforced on a day that a particular religious sect regards as sacred.——The fact that the civil regulation finds support in the religious opinion of a vast majority of the people of California is no argument against its establishment. It would be fortunate for society if all wise civil rules obtained a ready obedience from the citizen, not merely from the requirements of the law, but from conscientious or religious convictions of their obligation. The law against homicide is not the less wise and necessary because the divine command is 'thou shalt do no murder.' The legislation against perjury is not the less useful and essential for the due administration of justice because the injunction comes from the Most High, 'thou shalt not bear false witness against thy neighbor.' The establishment by law of Sunday as a day of rest from labor, is none the less a beneficent and humane regulation because it accords with the divine precept that upon that day 'thou shalt do no manner of work; thou, and thy son, and thy daughter, thy man-servant and thy maid-servant, thy cattle, and the stranger that is within thy gates.' "

To the objection that the law was in conflict with the clause declaring the inalienable rights of all men to acquire, possess, and protect property, he answered that the clause was never intended to inhibit legislation upon them, and that the mode and manner of acquiring, possessing, and protecting property were matters upon which laws were passed at every every session of the Legislature.

"All sorts of restrictions and regulations," he added, "are placed upon the acquisition and disposition of property. What contracts are valid, and what are invalid, when they must be in writing, and when they can be made by parol, what is essential to transfer chattels, and what to convey realty, are matters of constant legislation. Some modes of acquisition are subject to licenses, and some are prohibited. The right to acquire property, with the use of it, must be considered in relation to other rights. It may be regulated for the public good, though thereby the facility of acquisition is lessened, as in the sale of gunpowder and drugs, and in the practice of different professions. —— To say that a prohibition of work on Sunday prevents the acquisition of property, is to beg the question. With more truth it may be said, that rest upon one day in seven better enables men to acquire on the other six."—(9 Cal., 527.)

The decision of the court was rendered at the April term in 1858. In 1861 the Legislature passed another Sunday law similar in its provisions to the one declared to be unconstitutional, and at the July term of that year the court held it to be constitutional, thus overruling the decision in *Ex-parte Newman*, and adopting the views expressed by Judge Field in his dissenting opinion in that case.

THE NON-RECEIVABILITY OF LEGAL-TENDER NOTES FOR STATE TAXES.

In Perry vs. Washburn the question arose whether Treasury notes of the United States were receivable for state and county taxes. The act of Congress made such notes " a legal tender in payment of all debts, private and public." The court held that Congress only intended by debts such obligations for the payment of money as are founded upon contract. Judge Field gave the opinion of the court, and in speaking on this point he said :

" The act does not, in our judgment, have any reference to taxes levied under the laws of the State. It only speaks of taxes due to the United States, and distinguishes between them and debts. Its language is, 'for all *taxes*, internal duties, excises, *debts*, and demands of every kind due to the United States, the notes shall be receivable." When it refers to obligations other than those to the United States it only uses the term 'debts'; the notes it declares shall be 'a legal tender in payment of all *debts* public and private.' Taxes are not debts within the meaning of this provision. A debt is a sum of money due by contract, express or implied. A tax is a charge upon persons or property to raise money for public purposes. It is not founded upon contract; it does not establish the relation of debtor and creditor between the taxpayer and State; it does not draw interest; it is not the subject of attachment; and it is not liable to set-off. It owes its existence to the action of the legislative power, and does not depend for its validity or enforcement upon the individual assent of the taxpayer. It operates *in invitum.*"

Independent of the consideration mentioned, it is evident that the States can collect their taxes in such way as they may see fit—in goods as well as money, as was formerly done in some of the States; and that this right has never been surrendered to the general government. This case is important as being the first one in which the receivability of legal-tender notes for State taxes was brought before the courts for adjudication.

The Supreme Court of the United States cited the decision with approval and followed it in Lane County vs. Oregon (7 Wall., 71).

STEPHEN J. FIELD

AS A

JUDGE OF THE SUPREME COURT OF THE UNITED STATES.

Mr. Field was commissioned as a Justice of the Supreme Court of the United States on the 10th of March, 1863, but he did not take the oath of office until the 20th of May afterwards. In June following he was assigned by the President to the Tenth Circuit, then consisting of the States of California and Oregon.* When Nevada became a State she was included in the circuit. As a member of the Supreme Court he was required to attend the sessions of the court at Washington in the winter, and hold the Circuit Court in his circuit in the summer. He was thus compelled, until the overland railroad was completed, to travel, going by the way of the Isthmus, over twelve thousand miles a year, and now since the completion of the road he is obliged to travel over eight thousand miles a year. When his office was created he was allowed one thousand dollars a year for his travelling expenses, but in 1871 Congress repealed the law allowing this sum; and now, notwithstanding the immense distance he has to travel, and the

---

* Under the 5th section of the "Act to amend the judicial system of the United States" of April 29th, 1802, (2 Stats. at Large, p. 156,) the President is authorized to allot the Justices of the Supreme Court to the circuits when a new justice is appointed in the recess of the court; such allotment to remain until a new allotment is made by the justices among themselves.—(See 2d Black's Rep., p. 7.)

great expenses to which he is thus subjected beyond those imposed upon his associates, he is forced to meet them out of his regular salary. He has never failed to visit his circuit any year since his appointment, although since the passage of the act of 1869, providing for the appointment of circuit judges, he has not been required to attend a term in his circuit but once in two years. Of the many important cases tried and disposed of by him there, mention will be made hereafter.

When he went on the Supreme Bench, Taney was Chief Justice, and Wayne, Catron, Nelson, Grier, Clifford, Swayne, Miller, and Davis were associate justices. Chief Justice Taney died in the following year, and Mr. Chase was appointed his successor. The business of the court is always greater than can be disposed of by the judges, and at every session cases involving important principles are decided. But those which have attracted the greatest attention, and excited the deepest interest since 1863, have grown out of the civil war and the legislation to which it gave rise.

The Milligan Case.

" One of the earliest and most important cases of this kind was the Milligan case. In October, 1864, Milligan, a citizen of the United States and a resident of Indiana, was arrested by order of the military commander of the district and confined in a military prison near the capital of the State. He was subsequently, on the 21st of the same month, put on trial, before a military commission convened at Indianapolis, in that State, upon charges of: 1st, Conspiring against the Government of the United States ; 2d, Affording aid and comfort to the rebels against the authority of the United States ; 3d, Inciting insurrection ; 4th, Disloyal practices ; and 5th, Violation of the laws of war ; and was found guilty and sentenced to death by hanging. He was never in the military service ; there was no rebellion in Indiana ; and the civil courts were open in that State and in the undisturbed exercise of their jurisdiction. The sentence of the military commission was affirmed by the President, who directed that it should be carried into immediate execution. The condemned thereupon presented a petition to the Circuit Court of the United States in Indiana for a writ of *habeas corpus,* praying to be discharged from custody, alleging the illegality of his arrest and of the proceedings of the military commission. The judges of the Circuit Court were divided in opinion upon the question whether the writ should be issued and the petitioner discharged, which, of course, involved the jurisdiction of the military commission to try him. Upon a certificate of division the case was brought to the Supreme Court at the December term of 1865.

The case was elaborately argued by able and distinguished counsel, consisting of Mr. Joseph E. McDonald, now U. S. Senator from Indiana, Mr. James A. Garfield, a distinguished member of Congress, Mr. Jeremiah S. Black, the eminent jurist of Pennsylvania, and Mr. David Dudley Field, of New York, for the petitioner ; and by Mr. Henry Stanbery, the Attorney-General, and Gen. B. F. Butler, for the government. Their arguments were remarkable for learning, research, ability, and eloquence, and will repay the careful perusal not only of the student of law, but of all lovers of constitutional liberty. The judgment of the court was for the liberty of the citizen. All the judges agreed to his discharge, but the opinion, which has given so much celebrity to the case, and placed the protection of the citizen, in States where the civil courts are open, on solid grounds, obtained the approval of only five of the judges against four of them. *Judge Field was one of the five; his vote was essential to make that opinion the judgment of the court.* " The opinion was written by Mr. Justice Davis, and it will be a perpetual monument to his honor. It laid down in clear and unmistakable terms the doctrine that military commissions organized during the war, in a State not invaded nor engaged in rebellion, in which the federal courts were open and in the undisturbed exercise of their judicial functions, had no jurisdiction to try a citizen, who was not a resident of a State in rebellion, nor a prisoner of war, nor a person in the military or naval service ; and that Congress could not invest them with any such power ; and that in States where the courts were thus open and undisturbed, the guaranty of trial by jury contained in the Constitution was intended for a state of war as well as a state of peace, and is equally binding upon rulers and people at all times and under all circumstances."

THE CUMMINGS CASE.

" At the same term with the Milligan case the test-oath case from Missouri was brought before the court and argued. In January, 1865, a convention had assembled in that State to amend its constitution. Its members had been elected in November previous. In April, 1865, the constitution, as revised and amended, was adopted by the convention, and in June following by the people. Elected, as the members were, in the midst of the war, it exhibited throughout traces of the animosities which the war had engendered. By its provisions the most stringent and searching oath as to past conduct known in history was required, not only of officers under it, but of parties holding trusts and pursuing avocations in no way connected with the administration of the government. The oath, divided into its separate parts, contained more than thirty distinct affirmations touching past conduct, and even embraced the expression of sympathies and desires. Every person unable to take it was declared incapable of holding in the State "any office of honor, trust, or profit under its authority, or of being an officer, councilman, director or trustee, or other manager of any corporation, public or private, now existing or hereafter established by its authority, or of acting as a professor or teacher in any educational institution, or in any common or other school, or of holding any real estate or other property in trust for the use of any church, religious society, or congregation. "

And every person holding, at the time the amended constitution took effect, any of the offices, trusts, or positions mentioned, was required, within sixty days thereafter, to take the oath ; and, if he failed to comply with this requirement, it was declared that his office, trust, or position should *ipso facto* become vacant.

No person, after the expiration of the sixty days, was permitted, without taking the oath, "to practice as an attorney or counsellor-at-law," nor, after that period could "any person be competent as a bishop, priest, deacon, minister, elder, or other clergyman, of any religious persuasion, sect, or denomination, to teach, or preach, or solemnize marriages."

Fine and imprisonment were prescribed as a punishment for holding or exercising any of "the offices, positions, trusts, professions, or functions" specified, without having taken the oath ; and false swearing or affirmation in taking it was declared to be perjury, punishable by imprisonment in the penitentiary.

Mr. Cummings of Missouri, a priest of the Roman Catholic Church, was indicted and convicted, in one of the circuit courts of that State, of the crime of teaching and preaching as a priest and minister of that religious denomination without having first taken the oath thus prescribed, and was sentenced to pay a fine of five hundred dollars and to be committed to jail until the same was paid. On appeal to the Supreme Court of the State the judgment was affirmed, and the case was brought on a writ of error to the Supreme Court of the United States. It was there argued with great learning and ability by distinguished counsel, consisting of Mr. Montgomery Blair, of Washington, Mr. David Dudley Field, of New York, and Mr. Reverdy Johnson, of Maryland, for Mr. Cummings ; and by Mr. G. P. Strong and Mr. John B. Henderson, of Missouri, the latter then United States Senator, for the State.

" It was evident that the power asserted by the State of Missouri to exact this oath for past conduct from parties, as a condition of their continuing to pursue certain professions, or to hold certain trusts, might, if sustained, be often exercised in times of excitement to the oppression, if not ruin, of the citizen. For, if the State could require the oath for the acts mentioned, it might require it for any acts of one's past life, the number and character of which would depend upon the mere will of its legislature. It might compel one to affirm, under oath, that he had never violated the Ten Commandments, nor exercised his political rights except in conformity with the views of the existing majority. Indeed, under this kind of legislation, the most flagrant wrongs might be committed and whole classes of people deprived, not only of their political, but of their civil rights.

" It is difficult to speak of the whole system of expurgatory oaths for past conduct without a shudder at the suffering and oppression they were not only capable of effecting but often did effect. Such oaths have never been exacted in England, nor on the Continent of Europe. Test-oaths there have always been limited to an affirmation on matters of present belief, or as to present disposition towards those in power. It was reserved for the ingenuity of legislators in our country during the civil war to make test-oaths reach to past conduct.

" The court held that enactments of this character, operating, as they did, to deprive parties, by legislative decree, of existing rights for past conduct, without the formality and the safeguard of a judicial trial, fell within the inhibition of the Constitution against the passage of bills of attainder. In depriving parties of existing rights for past conduct, the provisions of the constitution of Missouri imposed, in effect, a punishment for such conduct. Some of the acts for which such deprivation was imposed were not punishable at the time ; and for some this deprivation was added to the punishments previously prescribed, and thus they fell under the further prohibition of the Constitution against the passage of an *ex post facto* law. The decision of the court, therefore, was for the discharge of the Cath-olic priest. The judgment against him was reversed, and the Supreme Court of Missouri was directed to order the inferior court by which he was tried to set him at liberty."

This judgment obtained the concurrence of only five judges against four of them. *Judge Field was one of the five; his vote was essential to that judgment; and he wrote the opinion of the court.*

THE GARLAND CASE.

Immediately following the case of Cummings that of *Ex-parte* Garland was argued, involving the validity of the iron-clad oath, as it was termed, prescribed for attorneys and counsellors-at-law by the act of Congress of January 24th, 1865. Mr. A. H. Garland, now United States Sena-tor from Arkansas, had been a member of the bar of the Supreme Court of the United States before the civil war. When Arkansas passed her ordinance of secession and joined the Confederate States, he went with her, and was one of her representatives in the Congress of the Confed-eracy. In July, 1865, he received from the President a full pardon for all offences committed by his participation, direct or implied, in the rebellion. At the following term of the court he produced his pardon, and asked permission to continue to practice as an attorney and counsellor with-out taking the oath required by the act of Congress, and the rule of the court made in conformity with it, which he was unable to take by reason of the offices he had held under the Confederate Government.

The application was argued by eminent counsel, con-sisting of Mr. Matthew H. Carpenter, of Wisconsin, and Mr. Reverdy Johnson, of Maryland, for the petitioner, Mr. Garland, and Mr. Marr, another applicant for admis-sion, who had participated in the rebellion, filing written arguments; and by Mr. Speed, of Kentucky, and Mr.

Henry Stanbery, the Attorney-General, on the other side. The whole subject of expurgatory oaths was discussed, and all that could be said on either side was fully and elaborately presented.

"The court in its decision followed the reasoning of the Cummings case and held that the law was invalid, as applied to the exercise of the petitioner's right to practice his profession; that such right was not a mere indulgence, a matter of grace and favor, revocable at the pleasure of the court, or at the command of the legislature ; but was a right of which the petitioner could be deprived only by the judgment of the court for moral or professional delinquency. The court also held that the pardon of the petitioner released him from all penalties and disabilities attached to the offence of treason committed by his participation in the rebellion, and that, so far as that offence was concerned, he was placed beyond the reach of punishment of any kind. But to exclude him by reason of that offence—that is, by requiring him to take an oath that he had never committed it—was to enforce a punishment for it notwithstanding the pardon ; and that it was not within the constitutional power of Congress thus to inflict punishment beyond the reach of executive clemency."

The judgment in this case also was pronounced by five of the judges against four of them. *Judge Field here again was one of the five. His vote was essential to the judgment; and he wrote the opinion of the court.**

THE McARDLE CASE.

"The Reconstruction Acts, so-called—that is, 'An act to provide for the more efficient government of the rebel

---

* In the decision of the two test-oath cases—the Cummings case and the Garland case—Justices Wayne, Nelson, Grier, Clifford, and Field concurred. Chief Justice Chase and Justices Swayne, Miller, and Davis dissented. Afterwards Chief Justice Chase expressed his concurrence in the opinion of the majority; and the decision was followed by the whole court, with the exception of Mr. Justice Bradley, in the case of Pierce vs. Carskadon, decided at the December term, 1872.—(16 Wallace, 234.)

States,' of March 2d, 1867, and an act of the 23d of the same month, supplementary to the former—were violently attacked in Congress when before it for consideration, as invalid, unconstitutional, and arbitrary measures of the government; and as soon as they were passed various steps were taken to bring them to the test of judicial examination and arrest their enforcement. Those acts divided the late insurgent States, except Tennessee, into five military districts, and placed them under military control to be exercised until constitutions, containing various provisions stated, were adopted and approved by Congress, and the States declared to be entitled to representation in that body. The State of Georgia, in April following their passage filed a bill in the Supreme Court invoking the exercise of its original jurisdiction, against Stanton, Secretary of War, Grant, General of the Army, and Pope, Major-General, assigned to the command of the Third Military District, consisting of the States of Georgia, Florida, and Alabama; to restrain those officers from carrying into effect the provisions of the acts. The bill set forth the existence of the State of Georgia as one of the States of the Union; the civil war in which she, with other States forming the Confederate States, had been engaged with the government of the United States; the surrender of the Confederate armies in 1865, and her submission afterwards to the Constitution and laws of the Union ; the withdrawal of the military government from Georgia by the President as Commander-in-Chief of the army of the United States; the re-organization of the civil government of the State under his direction and with his sanction; and that the government thus re-organized was in full possession and enjoyment of all the rights and privileges, executive, legislative, and judicial, belonging to a State in the Union under the Constitution, with the exception of a representation in the Senate and House of Representatives. The bill alleged that the acts were designed to overthrow and annul the existing government of the State, and to erect another and a different government in its place, unauthorized by the Constitution and in defiance of its guaranties ; and that the defendants, acting under orders of the President, were about to set in motion a portion of the army to take military possession of the State, subvert her government, and subject her people to military rule."

The court, however, dismissed the bill, holding that it called for judgment upon a political question.—(6 Wallace, 50.) Other attempts were made to obtain the judgment of the court upon the legislation in question, but until the McArdle case, they failed from the assumed want of jurisdiction in the court to pass upon its validity as the question was presented. But in the McArdle case the validity of that legislation came up in such a form that its consideration could not be avoided. In November, 1867, McArdle had been arrested and held in custody by a military commission organized in Mississippi under the Reconstruction Acts, for trial upon charges of (1) disturbing the public peace ; (2) inciting to insurrection, disorder, and violence ; (3) libel ; and (4) impeding reconstruction. He thereupon applied to the Circuit Court of the United States for the District of Mississippi for a writ of *habeas corpus*, in order that he might be discharged from his alleged illegal imprisonment. The writ was accordingly issued, but on the return of the officer showing the authority under which the petitioner was held, he was ordered to be remanded. From that judgment he appealed to the Supreme Court. Of course, if the Reconstruction Acts were invalid the petitioner could not be held, and he was entitled to his discharge. The case excited great interest throughout the country. Judge Sharkey and Robert J. Walker, of Mississippi, David Dudley Field and Charles O'Connor, of New York, and Jeremiah S. Black, of Pennsylvania, appeared for the appellant ; and Matthew H. Carpenter, of Wisconsin, Lyman Trumbull, of Illinois, and Henry Stanbery, the Attorney-General, appeared for the other side. The case was thoroughly argued, as any one must know from the character of the counsel.

" Seldom has the court listened to arguments equal in learning, ability, and eloquence. The whole subject was exhausted. As the arguments were widely published in the public journals, and read throughout the country, they produced a profound effect. The impression was general that the Reconstruction Acts could not be sustained ; that they were revolutionary and destructive of a republican form of government in the States, which the Constitution required the federal government to guarantee. Of course what the judgment of the court would have been cannot be known, as it never expressed its opinion. The argument was had on the 2d, 3d, 4th, and 9th of March, 1868, and it was expected that the case would be decided in regular course of proceedings when it was reached on the second subsequent consultation day, the 21st. In the meantime an act was quietly introduced into the House, and passed, repealing so much of the law of February 5th, 1867, as authorized an appeal to the Supreme Court from the judgment of the Circuit Court on writs of *habeas corpus*, or the exercise of jurisdiction on appeals already taken. The President vetoed the bill, but Congress passed it over his veto, and it became a law on the 27th of the month.* Whilst it was pending in Congress the attention of the Judges was called to it, and in consultation on the 21st they postponed the decision of the case until it should be disposed of. It was then that Mr. Justice Grier wrote the following protest, which he afterwards read in court : "

IN RE }
MCARDLE. }   PROTEST OF MR. JUSTICE GRIER.

This case was fully argued in the beginning of this month. It is a case that involves the liberty and rights not only of the appellant, but of millions of our fellow-citizens. The country and the parties had a right to expect that it would receive the immediate and solemn attention of this court. By the postponement of the case we shall subject ourselves,

---

* 15 Stats. at Large, 44.

whether justly or unjustly, to the imputation that we have evaded the performance of a duty imposed on us by the Constitution, and waited for legislation to interpose to supersede our action and relieve us from our responsibility. I am not willing to be a partaker either of the eulogy or opprobrium that may follow; and can only say:

"Pudet hæc opprobria nobis,
Et dici potuisse; et non potuisse repelli."*

R. C. GRIER.

I am of the same opinion with my brother Grier, and unite in his protest.
FIELD, J.

After the passage of the repealing act, the case was continued; and at the ensuing term the appeal was dismissed for want of jurisdiction.—(7 Wall., 506.) No further direct attempt was ever afterwards made to obtain the judgment of the court upon the constitutionality of the Reconstruction Acts.

CONFISCATION CASES.

On the 17th of July, 1862, the President approved of the act of Congress commonly known as the Confiscation Act. It is entitled "An act to suppress insurrection, to punish treason and rebellion, to seize and confiscate the property of rebels, and for other purposes." Its first section prescribed the punishment for treason thereafter committed. It punished it with death, or, in the discretion of the court, with imprisonment for not less than five years and a fine of not less than ten thousand dollars; and it provided that the slaves of the party adjudged guilty, if any he had, should be declared free. The second section provided for the punishment of the offence of inciting, setting on foot, or engaging in any rebellion or insurrection against the authority of the United States or the laws thereof, or engaging in or giving aid and comfort to the rebellion or insurrection then existing. The third section declared that parties guilty of either of the offences thus described

---

* "It fills us with shame that these reproaches can be uttered, and cannot be repelled." The words are found in Ovid's Metamorphoses, Book I., lines 758-9. In some editions the last word is printed *refelli*.

should be forever incapable and disqualified to hold any office under the United States. The fourth section provided that the act should not affect the prosecution, conviction, or punishment of persons guilty of treason before the passage of the act, unless such persons were convicted under the act itself. The fifth section declared " that to insure the speedy termination " of the rebellion, it should be the duty of the President to cause the " seizure of all the estate and property, money, stocks, credits, and effects " of certain persons named therein, and to apply and use the same and their proceeds for the support of the army of the United States. Among the classes named were included persons who might thereafter act as officers, military or civil, under the Confederate States, or hold any agency under them, or any of the States composing the Confederacy, and persons owning property in any loyal State or Territory of the United States, or in the District of Columbia, who should thereafter assist and give aid and comfort to the rebellion. The sixth section declared that if any person within any State or Territory of the United States, other than those above named, after the passage of the act, being engaged in armed rebellion against the United States, or in aiding or abetting such rebellion, should not, within sixty days after public warning and proclamation of the President, cease to aid and abet it, and return to his allegiance to the United States, all his " estate and property, moneys, stocks and credits " should be liable to seizure ; and that " all sales, transfers, or conveyances of any such property after the expiration of the said sixty days " should be " null and void," and that it should be " a sufficient bar to any suit brought by such person for the possession or the use of such property, or any of it, to allege and prove " that he was one of the persons described in the section.

The other sections of the act prescribed the proceedings to be taken for the condemnation of the property after it had been seized and for its disposition The " other purposes" mentioned in the title of the act related principally to slaves, their employment or colonization, and the power of the President to proclaim annesty and pardon.—(12 Stats., 590.)

The proclamation of the President, reference to which was made in the sixth section, was issued and published on the 25th of July 1862.—(12 Stats., 1266.)

Before the constitutionality of this act was passed upon by the Supreme Court, the question arose as to the import and meaning of the last clause of the sixth section, declaring "all sales, transfers, and conveyances" of property by persons not heeding the warning of the President and ceasing to aid the rebellion, to be null and void. In Corbett vs. Nutt (10 Wall., 479) it was contended that *a devise* to one Mrs. Hunter, a resident in Virginia, within the Confederate lines, was a transfer within the meaning of the act, and by its provisions was invalid. But the court answered, that assuming that a devise was included within "the sales, transfers, and conveyances" invalidated by the act, such invalidity could only be asserted by the United States. The act contemplated the seizure and confiscation of the property of certain persons engaged in the rebellion, and authorized the institution of proceedings for that purpose; and Judge Field, speaking for the court, said :

"It was to prevent these provisions from being evaded by the parties whose property was liable to seizure that 'sales, transfers, and conveyances' of the property were declared invalid. They were null and void as against the belligerent or sovereign right of the United States to appropriate and use the property for the purpose designated, but in no other respect, and not as against any other party. Neither the object sought, nor the language of the act, requires any greater extension of the terms used. The United States were the only party who could institute the proceedings for condemnation; the offence for which such condemnation was decreed was against the United States, and the property condemned, or its proceeds, went to their sole use. They alone could, therefore, be affected by the sales.

"Any other construction would impute to the United States a severity in their legislation entirely foreign to their history. No people can exist without exchanging commodities. There must be buying and selling and exchanging in every community, or the greater part of its inhabitants would have neither food nor raiment. And yet the argument of the defendant, if good for anything, goes to this extent, that by the act of Congress 'all sales, transfers, and conveyances' of property of the vast numbers engaged in the late rebellion against the United States, constituting the great majority of many towns and cities, and even of several States, were utterly null and void ; that even the commonest transactions of exchange in the daily life of these people were tainted with invalidity. It is difficult to conceive the misery which would follow from a legislative decree of this wide-sweeping character in any community, where its execution was conceived to be possible, or confidence was reposed in its validity."—(10 Wall., 479-480.)

In the case of Miller vs. United States (11 Wall., 268) the question of the constitutionality of the act came directly before the court. In that case 200 shares of stock in the Michigan Southern and Northern Indiana Railroad Company, and 343 shares in the Detroit, Monroe and Toledo Railroad Co., the property of one Samuel Miller, a resident of Virginia, was seized by the marshal of the District of Michigan under the act, and, by proceedings in the District Court of that district, were condemned as forfeited to the United States. The U. S. Circuit Court affirmed the decision, and the case was taken to the Supreme Court. Besides various objections urged to the decree, for irregularities in the alleged seizure and proceedings, the unconstitutionality of the act under which it was rendered was asserted. The court met this question directly, and affirmed the validity of the act, holding that, while so much of it as imposed penalties for treason was passed in the exercise of the municipal power of Congress to legislate for the punishment of offences against the sovereignty of the United States, all that portion which provided for the confiscation of property of rebels was passed in the exercise of the war powers of the government. The opinion of the court was delivered by Judge Strong, and received the concurrence, on this point, of all the judges present at the argument, except Judges Clifford and Field. Chief Justice Chase was absent from the court the whole term on account of ill-health. Judge Nelson was engaged on the

Joint High Commission for the settlement, by treaty, of questions in dispute between the United States and Great Britain. Judges Clifford and Field dissented, Judge Field giving a dissenting opinion. They did not deny the strict legal right of the government to confiscate the private property of enemies, that is, of permanent inhabitants of the enemies' country, although by the humane policy of modern times such property, unless taken in the field or besieged towns, or as a military contribution, is usually exempt from confiscation; but they contended that the act in question was not directed against enemies as such, but against persons who were guilty of certain alleged offences.

After stating the several provisions of the act, Judge Field said as follows :

"It would seem clear, therefore, that the provisions of the act were not passed in the exercise of the war powers of the government, but in the exercise of the municipal power of the government to legislate for the punishment of offences against the United States. It is the property of persons guilty of certain acts, wherever they may reside, in loyal or disloyal States, which the statute directs to be seized and confiscated. It is also for acts committed after the passage of the statute, except in one particular, corrected by the joint resolution of the two houses, that the forfeiture is to be declared. If it had been the intention of the statute to confiscate the property of enemies, its prospective character would have been entirely unnecessary, for whenever public war exists the right to order the confiscation of enemies' property, according to Mr. Chief Justice Marshall, exists with Congress.

"That the legislation in question was directed, not against 'enemies, but against persons who might be guilty of certain designated public offences, and that the forfeiture ordered was intended as a punishment for the offences, is made further evident by what followed the passage of the act of Congress. After the bill was sent to the President it was ascertained that he was of opinion that it was unconstitutional in some of its features, and that he intended to veto it. His objections were that the restriction of the Constitution concerning forfeitures not extending beyond the life of the offender had been disregarded. To meet this objection, which had been communicated to members of the House of Representatives, where the bill originated, a joint resolution explanatory of the act was passed by the House and sent to the Senate. That body, being informed of the objections of the President, concurred in the joint resolution. It was then sent to the President and was received by him before the expiration of the ten days allowed him for the consideration of the original bill. He returned the bill and resolution together to the House, where they originated, with a message, in which he stated that, considering the act and the resolution explanatory of the act as being substantially one, he had approved and signed both. That joint resolution declares that the provisions of the third clause of the fifth section of the act shall be so construed as not to apply to any act or acts done prior to its passage, 'nor shall any punishment or proceedings under said act be so construed as to work a forfeiture of the real estate of the offender beyond his natural life.'

"The terms here used, 'forfeiture' of the estate of the 'offender,' have no application to the confiscation of enemies' property under the law of nations. They are, as justly observed by counsel, strictly and exclusively applicable to punishment for crime. It was to meet the constitutional requirement that the punishment by forfeiture should not extend beyond the life of the offender that the joint resolution was passed. The President said to Congress, the act is penal, and does not conform to the requirement of the Constitution in the extent of punishment which it authorizes, and I cannot, therefore, sign it. Congress accepts his interpretation, and by its joint resolution directs a construction of the act in accordance with his views. And this construction, thus directed, is decisive, as it appears to me, of the character of the act. Indeed it is difficult to conceive of any reason for the limitation of the forfeiture of an estate to the life of the owner, if such forfeiture was intended to apply only to the property of public enemies.*

"The inquiry, then, arises whether proceedings in rem for the confiscation of the property of parties charged to be guilty of certain overt acts of treason, can be maintained without their previous conviction for the alleged offences. Such proceedings, according to Mr. Chief Justice Marshall, may be had for the condemnation of enemies' property when authorized by Congress. The proceedings in such cases are merely to authenticate the fact, upon which, under the law of nations, the confiscation follows. But here the inquiry is, whether, upon the assumption that a party is guilty of a particular public offence, his property may be seized, and upon proof of his guilt, or its assumption upon his failure to appear upon publication of citation, condemnation may be decreed. The inquiry is prompted from the supposed analogy of these cases to proceedings in rem for the confiscation of property for offences against the revenue laws, or the laws for the suppression of the slave-trade. But in these cases, and in all cases where proceedings in rem are authorized for a disregard of some municipal or public law, the offence constituting the ground of condemnation inheres, as it were, in the thing itself. The thing is the instrument of wrong, and is forfeited by reason of the unlawful use made

---

* See Bigelow vs. Forrest, 9 Wall., 350, and McVeigh vs. United States, 11 Wallace, 259.

of it, or the unlawful condition in which it is placed. And generally the thing, thus subject to seizure, itself furnishes the evidence for its own condemnation. Thus, goods found smuggled, not having been subjected to the inspection of the officers of the customs, or paid the duties levied by law, prove of themselves nearly all that is desired to establish the right of the government to demand their confiscation. A ship entering the mouth of a blockaded port furnishes by its position evidence of its intention to break the blockade, and the decree of condemnation follows. A ship captured whilst engaged in the slave-trade furnishes, in the use to which it was subjected, the material fact to be established for its forfeiture. In all these cases the proceeding is against the offending thing. And it is true that in these cases criminal proceedings will also lie against the smuggler or slave-trader, if arrested, and that the procedings in rem are wholly independent of, and unaffected by, the criminal proceedings against the person. But in the two cases the proof is entirely different. In the one case there must be proof that the thing proceeded against was subjected to some unlawful use or was fouud in some unlawful condition. In the other case the personal guilt of the party must be established, and when condemnation is founded upon such guilt, it must be preceded by due conviction of the offender, according to the forms prescribed by the Constitution. 'Confiscations of property,' says Mr. Justice Sprague in the Amy Warwick,* ' not for any use that has been made of it, which go not against an offending thing, but are inflicted for the personal delinquency of the owner are punitive, and punishment should be inflicted only upon due conviction of personal guilt.'

"If we examine the cases found in the reports, where proceedings in rem have been sustained, we shall find the distinction here stated constantly observed. Indeed, were this not so, and proceedings in rem for the confiscation of property could be sustained, without any reference to the uses to which the property is applied, or the condition in which it is found, but whilst, so to speak, it is innocent and passive, and removed at a distance from the owner and the sphere of his action, on the ground of the personal guilt of the owner, all the safeguards provided by the Constitution for the protection of the citizen against punishment, without previous trial and conviction, and after being confronted by the witnesses against him, would be broken down and swept away."—(11 Wall., 319–323.)

The court having adjudged that the statute, in authorizing suits *in rem* for the confiscation of the property of persons alleged to have been guilty of certain overt acts of treason, was valid, proceedings under it were sustained, which, though taken ostensibly in the interest of the United States, were in many instances prosecuted for the

---

* Sprague's Decisions, 2ud vol., 150.

benefit of parties connected with the court in which they were had, or their immediate relatives or friends. A deplorable instance of the kind is stated in the opinion of the Court of Appeals in Virginia, in the case of Underwood vs. McVeigh.—(23 Grattan, 409.) There the district judge ordered the appearance of the owner of the property seized, and his answer and claim to be stricken from the files of the court, because he was in the position of an alien enemy; and thereupon adjudged that the property be confiscated and forfeited to the United States. At the sale under the decree thus rendered, the wife of the judge became the purchaser of the property at a price greatly below its value. Some evidence of the abuses practiced under the statute will also be found in the opinion of the Supreme Court in McVeigh vs. Windsor (11 Wall., 259); Osborn vs. United States (91 U. S., 475); and Windsor vs. McVeigh (93 U. S., 274).

The owners of the property seized did not often appear in the suits, usually not having information of the proceedings until after a decree of condemnation had passed, and the property had been sold. Persons immediately connected with the court, where these suits were prosecuted, were in a position to take great advantage of the government, and that they availed themselves of the opportunity, the records of the courts abundantly show. A distinguished member of the profession at the South, formerly on the Supreme Bench (Judge Campbell), who had occasion to look a good deal into these proceedings, has stated that the statute as a financial expedient was abortive, only about $150,000 having been realized from the confiscation decrees of the courts, and most of that sum after the war had nearly or quite ended. And he thinks that President Lincoln, in insisting upon the explanatory resolution before signing the act, must have agreed with one of the greatest of statesmen, " that speculative plunder, contingent spoil, future, long-adjourned, uncertain booty, pillage to supply troops and sustain armies, would not serve to maintain even a mercenary war ; " and have regarded the act—comprehending as it did in its scope nine-tenths of the property and white persons within the limits of the Confederate States—as a mere *brutum fulmen*, which, if not available as such, it was not worthy an enlightened and civilized people to enforce in spirit or detail.

In Conrad vs. Wafles (96 U. S., 279) the court held that the act, in its provisions for the confiscation of property, applied only to the property of persons who thereafter might be guilty of acts of disloyalty and treason ; that sales and conveyances between enemies of real property in the enemies' country passed the title, subject only to be defeated if the government should afterwards proceed for its condemnation ; and that the provision of the act declaring all transfers of property by enemies null and void only invalidated the transactions as against the right of the United States to claim the forfeiture of the property, affirming in this respect the decision in Corbett vs. Nutt, cited above. In giving its opinion Judge Field said :

"A different doctrine would unsettle a multitude of titles passed during the war between residents of the insurrectionary territory, temporarily absent therefrom whilst it was dominated by the federal forces. Such residents were deemed enemies by the mere fact of being inhabitants of that territory, without reference to any hostile disposition manifested or hostile acts committed by them. In numerous instances, also, transfers of property were made in loyal States, bordering on the line of actual hostilities, by parties who had left those States and joined the insurgents. This was particularly the case in Missouri and Kentucky. No principle of public policy would be advanced, or principle of public law sustained, by holding such transfers absolutely void, instead of being merely inoperative as against the right of the United States to appropriate the property *jure belli :* on the contrary, such a holding would create unnecessary hardship, and therefore add a new cruelty to the war."

In Burbank vs. Conrad (96 U. S., 291) the court held that by the decree of condemnation under the act, the United States acquired only the life-estate of the alleged offender, actually possessed by him at the time of its seizure, not the estate which the records in the register's office may have shown to be in him. Accordingly a previous sale was not affected, although not recorded. On this point Judge Field, in speaking for the court, said :

"The object of requiring a public record of instruments affecting the title to real property is to protect third parties dealing with the vendor, by imparting notice to them of any previous sale or hypothecation of the property, and to protect the purchaser against any subsequent attempted disposition of it. In Louisiana the conveyance is valid between the parties without registration and passes the title. The only consequence of a failure of the purchaser to place his conveyance on the records of the parish where the property is situated, is that he is thereby subjected to the risk of losing the property if it be again sold or hypothecated by his vendor to an innocent third party ; or if it be seized and sold by a creditor of his vendor for the latter's debts. The second purchaser from the vendor and the bidder at the judicial sale would in that case hold the property. The United States never stood in the position of a second purchaser of the property sold by the elder Conrad. They were not purchasers at any sale of his property. They had caused his estate in the land, whatever that was, to be seized and condemned. By the decree of condemnation that estate vested in them for the period of his life. His estate for that period was then their property. The statute declares that the property condemned ' shall become the property of the United States, and may be disposed of as the court shall decree.' It was the property of the United States, therefore, which was sold and conveyed at the marshal's sale. The United States acquired by the decree, for the life of the offender, only the estate which at the time of the seizure he actually possessed ; not what he may have appeared from the public records to possess, by reason of the omission of his vendees to record the act of sale to them ; and that estate, whatever it was, for that period passed by the marshal's sale and deed ; nothing more and nothing less. The registry act was not intended to protect the United States in the exercise of their power of confiscation from the consequences of previous unrecorded sales of the alleged offender. It was in the power of Congress to provide for the confiscation of the entire property, as being within the enemy's country, without limiting it to the estate remaining in the offender ; but not having done so, the court cannot enlarge the operation of the stringent provisions of the statute. The plaintiff had notice of the character and legal effect of the decree of condemnation when he purchased, and is therefore presumed to have known that if the alleged offender possessed no estate in the premises at the time of their seizure, nothing passed to the United States by the decree, or to him by his purchase."

CASES ON PARDON AND AMNESTY.

In his great speech on conciliation with America, Burke observed, what all must admit to be true, " that there is a wide difference in reason and policy between the mode of proceeding on the irregular conduct of scattered individuals, or even of bands of men who disturb order within the State, and the civil dissensions which may, from time to time, on great questions, agitate the several communities which compose a great empire;" and said that it looked to him to be narrow and pedantic to apply the ordinary ideas of criminal justice to the great public contest then going on in America ; and that he did not know the method of drawing up an indictment against a whole people.

This language must have occurred to the belligerents in the late civil war. And yet the Constitution declares that " treason against the United States shall consist only in levying war against them, or in adhering to their enemies, giving them aid and comfort." The people of the Confederate States, in making war against the United States, came within the terms of this definition, however unwise and monstrous the proposition, that under it they were all exposed to criminal prosecution. The attempt to pass sentence upon them as a people would, as Burke said, be a proceeding " for wise men, not judicious; for sober men, not decent; for minds tinctured with humanity, not mild and merciful." But under the legislation of Congress and of several of the States, it was of the highest moment to many of these people, that they should be relieved from the disabilities to which their participation in the rebellion subjected them ; and that could only be accomplished, whilst that legislation remained in force, by pardon or amnesty. The term amnesty is not found in the Constitution, but is generally used to denote the clemency extended to a whole community or to a class of persons. Pardon is the generic term and includes every species of executive clemency, individual or general, conditional or absolute.

The first case after the war, in which the Supreme Court had occasion to speak of the effect and operation of a pardon, was that of Garland, who was precluded, as stated above, from continuing the practice of his profession as an attorney and counsellor-at-law in the Supreme Court, by his inability to take the oath required by the act of Congress, that he had never participated in the rebellion or given it aid and comfort. Judge Field, speaking in that case for the court, said :

"The Constitution provides that the President 'shall have power to grant reprieves and pardons for offences against the United States, except in cases of impeachment.'

"The power thus conferred is unlimited, with the exception stated. It extends to every offence known to the law, and may be exercised at any time after its commission, either before legal proceedings are taken or during their pendency, or after conviction and judgment. This power of the President is not subject to legislative control. Congress can neither limit the effect of his pardon nor exclude from its exercise any class of offenders. The benign prerogative of mercy reposed in him cannot be fettered by any legislative restrictions.

"Such being the case, the inquiry arises as to the effect and operation of a pardon, and on this point all the authorities concur. A pardon reaches both the punishment prescribed for the offence and the guilt of the offender; and when the pardon is full, it releases the punishment and blots out of existence the guilt, so that in the eye of the law the offender is as innocent as if he had never committed the offence. If granted before conviction, it prevents any of the penalties and disabilities consequent upon conviction from attaching; if granted after conviction, it removes the penalties and disabilities, and restores him to all his civil rights; it makes him, as it were, a new man, and gives him a new credit and capacity.

"There is only this limitation to its operation: it does not restore offices forfeited, or property or interests vested in others in consequence of the conviction and judgment.

"The pardon produced by the petitioner is a full pardon 'for all offences by him committed, arising from participation, direct or implied, in the rebellion,' and is subject to certain conditions which have been complied with. The effect of this pardon is to relieve the petitioner from all penalties and disabilities attached to the offence of treason, committed by his participation in the rebellion. So far as that offence is concerned, he is thus placed beyond the reach of punishment of any kind."
—(4 Wall., 380–381.)

In several cases subsequently before the court, on appeal from the Court of Claims, which were brought for the recovery of the proceeds of cotton seized by officers of the United States under the captured and abandoned property act of March 12th, 1863, the doctrine of the Garland case was followed and applied, so as to relieve the petitioners from the necessity of showing that they had never given any aid or comfort to the rebellion, which otherwise would have been required under the act.

In Paddleford's case, (9 Wall., 531,) the petitioner having taken the oath of allegiance prescribed by the proclamation of President Lincoln, of December 8th, 1863, and kept it inviolate, it was held, that he was entitled to claim the proceeds of cotton subsequently seized and sold under that act. The court cited the language in the Garland case as to the effect of a pardon, that by it " in the eye of the law the offender is as innocent as if he had never committed the offence." The pardon had purged him of the offence when the seizure was made. In the words of the Chief Justice, who gave the opinion of the court, "the law made the grant of pardon a complete substitute for proof that he gave no aid or comfort to the rebellion."

In Klein's case, (13 Wall., 129,) subsequently before the court, an act of Congress, which undertook to do away with this effect and operation of a pardon, was brought to its notice. That act declared that a pardon should not supersede the necessity of proof of loyalty by its recipient, but that its acceptance, without an express disclaimer and protestation, should be conclusive evidence of his guilt of the acts pardoned, and be inoperative as evidence of the rights which the court had adjudged were conferred by it. The court, to its great honor, held the act to be unconstitutional—an attempt to prescribe to the judiciary the effect to be given to the previous pardon of the President. The Chief Justice, in giving its opinion, said: " It is clear that the legislature cannot change the effect of such a pardon any more than the executive can change a law. Yet this is attempted by the provision under consideration. The court is required to receive special pardons as evidence of guilt and to treat them as null and void. It is required to disregard pardons granted by proclamation on condition, though the condition has been fulfilled, and to deny them their legal effect. This certainly impairs the executive authority, and directs the court to be instrumental to that end."

In Mrs. Armstrong's case, (13 Wall., 154,) which was heard after the decision in Klein's case, the court declined to consider whether the evidence was sufficient to prove that the claimant had given aid and comfort to the rebellion, and held that the proclamation of pardon and amnesty issued by the President entitled her to the proceeds of her captured and abandoned property in the Treasury, without proof that she never gave such aid and comfort. The Chief Justice, in delivering the opinion of the court, observed that the proclamation granting pardon, unconditionally and without reservation, " was a public act of which all courts of the United States are bound to take notice, and to which all courts are bound to give effect."

Subsequently, at the December term, 1872, in Carlisle vs. The United States, the question again arose as to the effect of the proclamation of pardon and amnesty made by the President, December 25th, 1868, upon the rights of parties who had given aid and comfort to the rebellion, and were claiming the proceeds of cotton seized by the officers of the United States and turned over to the agents of the Treasury Department; and the court said, speaking through Judge Field :

"Assuming that they [the claimants] are within the terms of the proclamation, the pardon and amnesty granted relieve them from the legal consequences of their participation in the rebellion, and from the necessity of proving that they had not thus participated, which otherwise would have been indispensable to a recovery. It is true, the pardon and amnesty do not and cannot alter the fact that aid and comfort were given by the claimants, *but they forever close the eyes of the court to the perception of that fact as an element in its judgment, no rights of third parties having intervened.*"

In Osborn vs. The United States, decided at the October term, 1875, (91 U. S., 474,) the question was as to the effect of the President's pardon upon the rights of the petitioner to the proceeds of his property confiscated by the decree of the District Court. The Circuit Court — Judge Miller presiding — was of opinion that, subject to the exceptions specified therein, the pardon restored all rights of property lost by the offence pardoned, unless the property had by judicial process become vested in other persons; and that the proceeds of property confiscated, paid into court, were under its control until an order for their distribution was made, or they were paid into the hands of the informer entitled to receive them, or into the Treasury of the United States; and that until then no vested right to the proceeds had accrued so as to prevent the pardon from restoring them to the petitioner. This ruling was assailed by officers of the District Court, who were called upon to make restitution of a portion of the proceeds they had obtained. But the Supreme Court, in affirming it, speaking through Judge Field, replied as follows :

" It is not a matter for these officers to complain that proceeds of property adjudged forfeited to the United States are held subject to the further disposition of the court, and possible restitution to the original owner. That is a matter which concerns only the United States, and they have not seen fit to object to the decision. But independently of this consideration we are clear that the decision was correct. The pardon, as is seen, embraces all offences arising from participation of the petitioner, direct or indirect, in the rebellion. It covers, therefore, the offences for which the forfeiture of his property was decreed. The confiscation law of 1862, though construed to apply only to public enemies, is limited to such of them as were engaged in and gave aid and comfort to the rebellion. The pardon of that offence necessarily carried with it the release of the penalty attached to its commission, so far as such release was in the power of the government, unless specially restrained by exceptions embraced in the instrument itself. It is of the very essence of a pardon that it releases the offender from the consequences of his offence. If in the proceedings to establish his culpability and enforce the penalty, and before the grant of the pardon, the rights of others than the government have vested, those rights cannot be impaired by the pardon. The government having parted with its power over such rights, they necessarily remain as they existed previously to the grant of the pardon. The government can only release what it holds. But unless rights of others in the property condemned have accrued, the penalty of forfeiture annexed to the commission of the offence must fall with the pardon of the offence itself, provided the full operation of the pardon be not restrained by the conditions upon which it is granted."

In Knote vs. United States, (95 U. S., 154,) heard at the October term, 1877, the question was whether the pardon and amnesty granted by the President's proclamation entitled one, who had received its benefits, to the proceeds of his property previously condemned and sold under the confiscation act, after such proceeds had been paid into the Treasury. And upon this subject, Judge Field, speaking for the court, said :

" Moneys once in the Treasury can only be withdrawn by an appropriation by law. However large, therefore, may be the power of pardon possessed by the President, and however extended may be its application, there is this limit to it, as there is to all his powers : it cannot touch moneys in the Treasury of the United States, except expressly authorized by act of Congress. The Constitution places this restriction upon the pardoning power.

" Where, however, property condemned, or its proceeds, have not thus vested, but remain under control of the executive or of officers subject to his orders, or are in the custody of the judicial tribunals, the property will be restored or its proceeds delivered to the original owner upon his full pardon. The property and the proceeds are not considered as so absolutely vesting in third parties or in the United States as to be unaffected by the pardon until they have passed out of the jurisdiction of the officer or tribunal. The proceeds have thus passed when paid over to the individual entitled to them, in the one case, or are covered into the Treasury, in the other."

LEGAL-TENDER CASES AND CONFEDERATE NOTES.

Next to the questions relating to reconstruction, test-oaths, pardon, and amnesty, those relating to the notes issued by the government to be used as a circulating medium, excited, after the war, the greatest interest. On the 25th of February, 1862, the President approved of an act of Congress entitled " An act to authorize the issue of United States notes, and for the redemption or funding thereof, and for funding the floating debt of the United States," commonly known as the legal-tender act.—(12 Stats., 345.)

5

It authorized the Secretary of the Treasury to issue notes on the credit of the United States to the amount of one hundred and fifty millions, not drawing interest, payable to bearer, of such denominations as he might deem expedient, not less than five dollars each. And it declared that such notes should be "receivable in payment of all taxes, internal duties, excises, debts, and demands of every kind due to the United States, except duties on imports, and of all claims and demands against the United States of every kind whatsoever, except for interest upon bonds and notes," which was to be paid in coin, and be "lawful money and a legal tender in payment of all debts, public and private, within the United States, except duties on imports and interest as aforesaid."

No serious question was ever raised as to the power of the government to issue the notes as a means of borrowing money, or to make them payable to bearer, and of such denominations as would suit the convenience of the lender, or to make them receivable for dues to the United States. The only objection to the act was the provision making them "a legal tender in payment of all debts public and private," so far as it applied to private debts and debts owing by the United States.

As Congress could only exercise such powers as were expressly delegated to it, or were necessary and proper to the execution of those powers, and as it was not expressly invested with control over the subject of legal tender, and the States were prohibited in terms from making anything but gold and silver such tender, the validity of the provision, so far as it applied to private debts, was at once raised. The question was one of immediate and pressing importance, not only from the fact that the amount authorized by the act mentioned was issued, but by subsequent acts, containing a similar provision, the issue of a much larger amount was authorized, and in denominations as low as one dollar. These notes, not being convertible on demand into coin, soon depreciated in value in the market, so at times during the war they were fifty cents below par, and long after the war their purchasable power was greatly less than their nominal amount. Unscrupulous debtors at once seized the occasion to discharge their previous obligations by these notes, thus paying their creditors nominally the whole, but in fact only a portion, of their dues. The great corporations of the country, which had contracted a large indebtedness prior to the war, did not hesitate to offer to their creditors these notes, both for the interest and principal of their bonds. They measured their sense of justice, not by the rules of common honesty, but by what the law permitted.

In the case of Lane County vs. Oregon (7 Wall., 72) an attempt was made to compel the officials of that State to receive these notes for taxes in the face of legislation requiring such taxes to be paid in gold and silver. But the Supreme Court held that taxes were not debts within the meaning of the legal-tender act, and that by the term *debts* were meant only such obligations for the payment of money as were founded upon contract, citing and following in this respect the opinion of Judge Field, given by him when on the bench of the Supreme Court of California, in Perry vs Washburn (20 Cal., 318).

The Chief Justice, who spoke for the court in the case, referred to the power of taxation in the general government conferred by the Constitution, and to its limitations. He also mentioned the restrictions upon the States to tax exports or imports except for a single purpose, or to lay any duty on tonnage, and then added :

"In respect, however, to property, business, and persons, within their respective limits, their power of taxation remained and remains entire. It is, indeed, a concurrent power, and in the case of a tax on the same subject by both governments, the claim of the United States, as the supreme authority, must be preferred; but, with this qualification, it is absolute. The extent to which it shall be exercised, the subjects upon which it shall be exercised, and the mode in which it shall be exercised, are all equally within the discretion of the Legislatures, to which the States commit the exercise of the power. That discretion is restrained only by the will of the people expressed in the State constitutions or through elections, and by the condition that it must not be so used as to burden or embarrass the operations of the national government.* There is nothing in the Constitution which contemplates or authorizes any direct abridgment of this power by national legislation. To the extent just indicated, it is as complete in the States as the like power, within the limits of the Constitution, is complete in Congress. If, therefore, the condition of any State, in the judgment of its Legislature, requires the collection of taxes in kind—that is to say, by the delivery to the proper officers of a certain proportion of products, or in gold and silver bullion, or in gold and silver coin—it is not easy to see upon what principle the National Legislature can interfere with the exercise, to that end, of this power, original in the States, and never as yet surrendered."

In Bronson vs. Rodes (7 Wall., 229) the question was raised whether a previous contract for the payment of a certain sum in gold and silver coin could be specifically enforced, or whether it could be discharged, under the legal-tender act, by a tender of treasury notes. The court held that the contract could be specifically enforced. It is difficult, at this day, to appreciate fully the earnestness of the opposition to this position. The fact that the law recognized two different kinds of currency, and that one only could be used for a certain class of payments—that is, for duties on imports—would seem to be a conclusive answer to the objections urged. As two kinds of currency were made lawful, a contract for either must be lawful also. A person might wish coin to remit abroad or to pay duties, or because it could be more safely kept at his residence, not being liable to be destroyed by fire or injured by water or other casualties. As the Chief Justice, who gave the opinion of the court, said :

"The currency acts themselves provide for payments in coin. Duties on imports must be paid in coin, and interest on the public debt, in the absence of other express provisions, must also be paid in coin. And it hardly requires argument to prove that these positive requirements cannot be fulfilled if contracts between individuals to pay coin dollars can be satisfied by offers to pay their nominal equivalent in note dollars.

---

* Or, it may be added, to impose greater burdens upon the business or property in the State of non-resident, than upon the business or property of resident citizens.—(Ward vs. Maryland, 12 Wall., 418.)

The merchant who is to pay duties in coin must contract for the coin which he requires; the bank which receives the coin on deposit contracts to repay coin on demand; the messenger who is sent to the bank or the custom-house contracts to pay or deliver the coin according to his instructions. These are all contracts, either express or implied, to pay coin. Is it not plain that duties cannot be paid in coin if these contracts cannot be enforced?

"An instructive illustration may be derived from another provision of the same acts. It is expressly provided that all dues to the government, except for duties on imports, may be paid in United States notes. If, then, the government, needing more coin than can be collected from duties, contracts with some bank or individual for the needed amount, to be paid at a certain day, can this contract for coin be performed by the tender of an equal amount in note dollars? Assuredly it may if the note dollars are a legal tender to the government for all dues except duties on imports. And yet a construction which will support such a tender will defeat a very important intent of the act.

"Another illustration, not less instructive, may be found in the contracts of the government with depositors of bullion at the mint to pay them the ascertained value of their deposits in coin. These are demands against the government other than for interest on the public debt; and the letter of the acts certainly makes United States notes payable for all demands against the government except such interest. But can any such construction of the act be maintained? Can judicial sanction be given to the proposition that the government may discharge its obligation to the depositors of bullion by tendering them a number of note dollars equal to the number of gold or silver dollars which it has contracted by law to pay?

"But we need not pursue the subject further. It seems to us clear beyond controversy that the act must receive the reasonable construction, not only warranted, but required, by the comparison of its provisions with the provisions of other acts, and with each other, and that upon such reasonable construction it must be held to sustain the proposition that express contracts to pay coined dollars can only be satisfied by the payment of coined dollars."

The Confederate States also issued their notes, to be used as currency, but, unlike our government, they did not make them a legal tender. Contracts at the South during the war had reference generally to these notes when dollars were mentioned. After the war, suits being brought upon many of these contracts, the question was raised as to the meaning to be attached to the term "dollars" used in them. On the one hand, it was said, and correctly, that by " dollars," as defined in the statutes, were meant pieces of gold and silver coin of a prescribed fineness and weight, each bearing the stamp of the United States, expressive of its value. On the other hand, it was manifest that there would be great injustice in giving this meaning to the term, when by it only Confederate notes were intended. As well might it be claimed that to contracts made in Germany, where the term " dollars " is used, a similar construction should be given when the contracts are sought to be enforced in this country, although the German dollar is worth only sixty-nine cents of our dollar.

In Thorington vs. Smith, (8 Wall., 1,) which was before the court at the December term of 1868, this question was presented. In that case a tract of land in Alabama had been sold in 1864 by the plaintiff, Thorington, to the defendants for $45,000, of which $35,000 were paid; and for the residue a promissory note of the purchasers was given. Upon the suppression of the rebellion, Confederate notes became, of course, valueless, and, in 1867, Thorington filed a bill against the purchasers for the enforcement of his lien as vendor, claiming $10,000 in the only money then current, that of the United States. The defendants answered that at the time of the purchase Alabama was one of the Confederate States, and from that portion where the parties resided, and the contract was made, the authority of the United States was excluded ; that there was no gold or silver coin nor were any notes of the United States in circulation there ; that the only currency in use for the ordinary transactions of business consisted of Confederate notes ; that the land purchased was worth only $3,000 in lawful money of the United States ; that the contract was to be paid, by agreement of parties, in Confederate notes, of which $35,000 were thus paid, and that the balance was to be discharged in the same way. It was, therefore, insisted, upon this state of facts, that the plaintiff was not entitled to any relief. The court below, being of opinion that the contract was illegal because payable in these notes, dismissed the bill, but the Supreme Court reversed the decision, holding that the Confederate States had established a government of paramount force over the States of the Confederacy, and that by its authority their notes were placed in circulation and became almost exclusively the currency of those States ; that contracts payable in them could not for that reason be regarded as made in aid of the insurrection ; that they had no necessary relations to the insurgent government, but were transactions in the ordinary course of civil society, and were without blame, except when proved to have been entered into with actual intent to further the rebellion. The court also held that evidence of the character and value of this currency was competent and admissible. Upon this latter point the court, speaking through the Chief Justice, said :

" It is quite clear that a contract to pay dollars, made between citizens of any State of the Union, while maintaining its constitutional relations with the national government, is a contract to pay lawful money of the United States, and cannot be modified or explained by parol evidence. But it is equally clear, if in any other country, coins or notes denominated dollars should be authorized of different value from the coins or notes which are current here under that name, that in a suit upon a contract to pay dollars, made in that country, evidence would be admitted to prove what kind of dollars were intended, and if it should turn out that foreign dollars were meant, to prove their equivalent value in lawful money of the United States. Such evidence does not modify or alter the contract. It simply explains an ambiguity, which, under the general rules of evidence, may be removed by parol evidence."

It was accordingly adjudged that the vendor could recover only the actual value of the Confederate notes at the time and place of the contract, in lawful money of the United States.

At the December term of 1872, in Hanauer vs. Woodruff, this case was cited, and in reference to the alleged illegality of the contract, because made in Confederate currency, Judge Field, speaking for the court, said :

" The transaction was in a currency imposed by irresistible force upon the community, in which currency the commonest transactions in the daily life of millions of people, even in the minutest particulars, were carried on, and without the use of which there would have been no medium of exchange among them. The simplest purchase in the market of daily food would, without its use, have been attended with inconveniences which it is difficult to estimate. It would have been a cruel and oppressive judgment, if all the transactions of the many millions of people, composing the inhabitants of the insurrectionary States, for the several years of the war, had been held tainted with illegality because of the use of this forced currency, when those transactions were not made with any reference to the insurrectionary government."—(15 Wall., 448. See, also, the Confederate note case, 19 Wall., 555.)

The constitutionality of the legal-tender clause of the act of Congress was discussed in Lane County vs. Oregon, Bronson vs. Rodes, and in other cases before the court, but they either went off on some other point, or their decision was reserved until judgment should be rendered in Hepburn vs. Griswold, where the question was directly presented and could not be avoided. That case, which was before the court both at the December term of 1868, and the December term of 1869, was elaborately argued, first on briefs and then orally, by counsel of eminent ability, and it was long held under advisement. Indeed it was afterwards said by some of the judges that no case before the court since its organization had been more fully presented or more deliberately considered. The question was whether the holder of a note payable in dollars, made before the legal-tender act was passed, was obliged in law to accept in payment United States notes, equal in nominal amount to the sum due, when tendered by the maker ; or in other words, whether debts contracted previous to the legal-tender act could be discharged, against the consent of the holder, by legal-tender notes. The presentation of the question placed the Chief Justice in a very embarrassing position. The provision assailed had been recommended by him when Secretary of the Treasury, though with much doubt and hesitation. It did not, however meet the approval of all the lawyers of the Senate.

Some of the ablest of them, like Collamer and Fessenden, opposed it as both unnecessary and unconstitutional. But as the war continued, and immense drafts were made upon the Treasury, the validity of the provision was generally acquiesced in as a matter of necessity. So when the question came before the court for adjudication a large portion of the people had come to believe in its constitutionality, and several supreme courts in the loyal States had pronounced in its favor. In addition to all this, three of the judges expressed themselves strongly on the subject as having no doubt whatever of the validity of the provision. A regard for consistency urged him to concur with their views. His mind was sorely perplexed, and the question was examined and re-examined by him with painful anxiety. But his sense of duty prevailed. He could not be false to his convictions as a judge in order to preserve his consistency as a statesman. He pronounced against the validity of the provision and read the opinion of the court. That opinion is well known to the country. It presents the unconstitutionality of the provision in the clearest light. In it he alludes to his own change of views on the question, as follows :

"It is not surprising that amid the tumult of the late civil war, and under the influence of apprehensions for the safety of the Republic, almost universal, different views, never before entertained by American statesmen or jurists, were adopted by many. The time was not favorable to considerate reflection upon the constitutional limits of legislative or executive authority. If power was assumed from patriotic motives, the assumption found ready justification in patriotic hearts. Many who doubted yielded their doubts; many who did not doubt were silent. Some who were strongly averse to making government notes a legal tender felt themselves constrained to acquiesce in the views of the advocates of the measure. Not a few who then insisted upon its necessity, or acquiesced in that view, have, since the return of peace, and under the influence of the calmer time, reconsidered their conclusions, and now concur in those which we have just announced."—(8 Wall., 625.)

The views of the Chief Justice, as well as the action of the court, in the several cases under the legal-tender act,

have been fully stated, because they had the entire concurrence and earnest support of Judge Field, and because
of what subsequently occurred to bring about a reconsid-
eration of the question decided and a reversal of the judgment of the court. The Judge had frequent consultations
upon the questions raised with the Chief Justice, who
never hesitated to express in strong terms his appreciation
of the Judge's counsel.

The decision was received by the country, excepting
the debtor class, with favor. Many who did not object
to the application of the act to future contracts were rejoiced that the injustice, likely to attend its application to
past contracts, was prevented. As to future contracts,
they said, parties acted with the law before them. But
from the debtor class, and especially the large corporations
of the country, the greater part of whose liabilities had
been created before the war, the decision met with decided
hostility. A movement was at once set on foot to obtain
its reversal. The legislation of Congress, suggested by
the court in the hope that it might to some degree be relieved of the great pressure of labor upon it, favored this
movement. In the winter of 1869 members of the Judiciary Committee of the Senate informed the court that
they would be glad to receive from it suggestions for
changes in the judicial system with a view to facilitate
the discharge of its business. The members of the court
thereupon met and appointed Judges Miller and Field a
committee to consider the subject and report what changes
should be recommended. They suggested a bill for the
appointment of independent circuit judges. The suggestion was favorably received, and a bill for that purpose was
prepared by them, and, after some verbal changes, was
approved by the judges and sent to the Judiciary Committee of the Senate. It was then reported by Senator
Trumbull from that committee, with some slight changes,
and was soon after passed by both Houses. President
Johnson refused to sign it, but after Gen. Grant became

President it was again introduced into the Senate and was soon passed, to take effect on the 1st of December, 1869. It increased the number of judges of the Supreme Court to nine, thus necessitating the appointment of a new member, and created nine independent circuit judges. As the court then consisted of only eight judges, it was necessary, to obtain a majority in favor of the legal-tender provision, that two new judges should be appointed who would agree with the three who had opposed the late decision. It was, therefore, suggested that the physical infirmities of Judge Grier were such that he should retire. At that time he was unable to walk without assistance from others, and he was accompanied by his servant into the court-room whenever he took his seat on the bench. Owing to the frequent comments in the public journals upon his infirmities, and the suggestions of some friends, he was induced to send in his resignation. His mind was then as clear as ever, but his physical system was greatly impaired. The letter of the Judges to him on his resignation testifies to their high appreciation of the purity of his character, the great powers of his intellect, and his profound knowledge of the law. His resignation took effect the 1st of February, 1870. Mr. Stanton was appointed his successor, but he died a few days afterwards, before even Judge Grier's resignation took effect. So it was said by the present Secretary of State, Mr. Evarts, that Judge Grier had the singular experience of attending the funeral of his successor whilst he himself was still on the bench. Judge Strong was then nominated and confirmed. For the new judgeship created Mr. E. R. Hoar, of Massachusetts, the Attorney-General, was nominated, but he was rejected by the Senate. Judge Bradley was then nominated and confirmed.

There have been many things of an unpleasant character said in regard to the appointment of Judges Strong and Bradley, but the writer of this narrative cannot give any approval of them. Undoubtedly Mr. Hoar, the Attorney-General, was very active and earnest to secure the appointment of judges who would favor a reversal of the decision against the legal-tender provision. He openly said as much. It is also true that Judge Strong was known to be in favor of the constitutionality of that provision. Whilst a judge of the Supreme Court of Pennsylvania he had written an opinion to that effect. It was also well known that Judge Bradley, as counsel of the Camden and Amboy Railroad Company, had given a similar opinion. - Their appointment was undoubtedly advocated partly in view of these facts, and this can be said without any injurious reflection upon them. It is probable that nearly all appointments of judges are made with some reference to their opinions as to the construction to be given to the Constitution. It is not at all likely that during the war any one would have been nominated, or, if nominated, have been confirmed, who believed that under it secession was a constitutional remedy of the States for their grievances, or who did not approve of the forcible suppression of the rebellion by the General Government. There could be, therefore, no just ground of reproach against those gentlemen because they were appointed in view of their previously expressed opinions. The complaint against them arose from the reversal, through their aid, of the previously well-considered judgment of the majority of the Court, without any reasons being advanced different from those presented when the case was originally heard. Thoughtful men, without questioning the learning and ability of Judges Strong and Bradley, felt that it was wrong that a solemn judgment of the Court, affecting great public interests, reached only after long and careful consideration, should be reversed by a mere change in its personnel.

Soon after the new judges had taken their seats, Attorney-General Hoar moved that two cases then pending undecided—the Latham case and the Deming case, appealed from the Court of Claims—should be set down for argument, and suggested that the legal-tender provision should be considered in them. This application created a good deal of feeling, and led to an unpleasant controversy among members of the court. The majority—consisting of the three judges who had previously dissented from the opinion in Hepburn vs. Griswold, and the two newly appointed judges—ordered the argument, and it would have taken place but from the fact that the appeals were dismissed by the appellants and the rehearing of the question thus prevented. Those who take any interest in this unfortunate controversy will find the particulars stated in the life of Chief Justice Chase and in the journals of the day. It is not the intention of the writer of this narrative to recall them. Judges Nelson, Clifford, and Field were on pleasant terms with all their associates, and however great the difference of opinion between them and the other judges, their personal relations were not disturbed.

At the following term of December, 1870, two other cases came before the court involving the constitutionality of the legal-tender cases—Knox vs. Lee and Parker vs. Davis. They are reported in 12th Wallace, under the title of "Legal-Tender Cases." In them the whole question of the constitutionality of the legal-tender clause was reargued and reconsidered. The previous judgment in Hepburn vs. Griswold was reversed by the judgment of five against four, and the constitutionality of the tender clause asserted. Judge Strong gave the opinion of the court. The Chief Justice and Judges Clifford and Field each gave a dissenting opinion. Of these dissenting opinions this can be said: that they exhaust the whole subject, and it is difficult to understand how any one, after reading them, can doubt that the Constitution intended that gold and silver alone should be a legal tender in the United States. As said by Judge Field in his opinion :

"If we consider the history of the times when the Constitution was adopted; the intentions of the framers of that instrument, as shown in their debates; the contemporaneous exposition of the coinage power in the State conventions assembled to consider the Constitution, and in the public discussions before the people; the natural meaning of the terms used; the nature of the Constitution itself as creating a government of enumerated powers; the legislative exposition of nearly three-quarters of a century; the opinions of judicial tribunals, and the recorded utterances of statesmen, jurists, and commentators, it would seem impossible to doubt that the only standard of value authorized by the Constitution was to consist of metallic coins struck or regulated by the direction of Congress, and that the power to establish any other standard was denied by that instrument."

No adequate account of these dissenting opinions can be given without a much fuller citation than this narrative permits. A few extracts will be made from the one by Judge Field, as it is only with his judicial career that this narrative is concerned.

Referring to the position urged on the argument of the case, that as the issue of the notes was authorized under the power to borrow money, the annexing to them the quality of legal tender was an appropriate means to the execution of that power, as it enhanced their value, and thus increasing their circulation, induced parties the more readily to advance upon them, the Judge said as follows:

The power of Congress to borrow money "is not different in its nature or essential incidents from the power to borrow possessed by individuals, and is not to receive a larger definition. Nor is it different from the power often granted to public and private corporations. The grant, it is true, is usually accompanied in these latter cases with limitations as to the amount to be borrowed, and a designation of the objects to which the money shall be applied,—limitations which in no respect affect the nature of the power. The terms 'power to borrow money' have the same meaning in all these cases, and not one meaning when used by individuals, another when granted to corporations, and still a different one when possessed by Congress. They mean only a power to contract for a loan of money upon considerations to be agreed between the parties. The amount of the loan, the time of repayment, the interest it shall bear, and the form in which the obligation shall be expressed are simply matters of arrangement between the parties. They concern no one else. It is no part or incident of a contract of this character that the rights or interests of third parties, strangers to the matter, shall be in any respect affected. The transaction is completed when the lender has parted with his money, and the borrower has given his promise of repayment at the time, and in the manner, and with the securities stipulated between them.

" As an inducement to the loan, and security for its repayment, the borrower may of course pledge such property or revenues, and annex to his promises such rights and privileges as he may possess. His stipulations in this respect are necessarily limited to his own property, rights, and privileges, and cannot extend to those of other persons.

" Now, whether a borrower—be the borrower an individual, a corporation, or the government—can annex to the bonds, notes, or other evidences of debt given for the money borrowed, any quality by which they will serve as a means of satisfying the contracts of other parties, must necessarily depend upon the question whether the borrower possesses any right to interfere with such contracts, and determine how they shall be satisfied. The right of the borrower in this respect rests upon no different foundation than the right to interfere with any other property of third parties. And if it will not be contended, as I think I may assume it will not be, that the borrower possesses any right, in order to make a loan, to interfere with the tangible and visible property of third parties, I do not perceive how it can be contended that he has any right to interfere with their property when it exists in the form of contracts. A large part of the property of every commercial people exists in that form, and the principle which excludes a stranger from meddling with another's property which is visible and tangible, equally excludes him from meddling with it when existing in the form of contracts.

" That an individual or a corporation borrowing possesses no power to annex to his evidences of indebtedness any quality by which the holder will be enabled to change his contracts with third parties, strangers to the loan, is admitted ; but it is contended that Congress possesses such power because, in addition to the express power to borrow money, there is a clause in the Constitution which authorizes Congress to make all laws ' necessary and proper' for the execution of the powers enumerated. This clause neither augments nor diminishes the expressly designated powers. It only states in terms what Congress would equally have had the right to do without its insertion in the Constitution. It is a general principle that a power to do a particular act includes the power to adopt all the ordinary and appropriate means for its execution."

——— " That is only appropriate which has some relation of fitness to an end. Borrowing, as already stated, is a transaction by which, on one side, the lender parts with his money, and on the other the borrower agrees to repay it in such form and at such time as may be stipulated. Though not a necessary part of the contract of borrowing, it is usual for the borrower to offer securities for the repayment of the loan. The fitness which would render a means appropriate to this transaction thus considered must have respect to the terms which are essential to the con-

tract, or to the securities which the borrower may furnish as an inducement to the loan. The quality of legal tender does not touch the terms
of the contract of borrowing, nor does it stand as a security for the loan.
A security supposes some right or interest in the thing pledged, which
is subject to the disposition of the borrower.

"There has been much confusion on this subject from a failure to distinguish between the adaptation of particular means to an end and the
effect, or supposed effect. of those means in producing results desired by
the government. The argument is stated thus: the object of borrowing is to raise funds; the annexing of the quality of legal tender to
the notes of the government induces parties the more readily to loan upon
them; the result desired by the government—the acquisition of funds—
is thus accomplished; therefore, the annexing of the quality of legal
tender is an appropriate means to the execution of the power to borrow.
But it is evident that the same reasoning would justify, as appropriate
means to the execution of this power, any measures which would result
in obtaining the required funds. The annexing of a provision by which
the notes of the government should serve as a free ticket in the public
conveyances of the country, or for ingress into places of public amuse-
ment, or which would entitle the holder to a percentage out of the revenues of private corporations, or exempt his entire property, as well as
the notes themselves, from State and municipal taxation, would produce
a ready acceptance of the notes. But the advocate of the most liberal
construction would hardly pretend that these measures, or similar measures touching the property of third parties, would be appropriate as a
means to the execution of the power to borrow. Indeed, there is no invasion by government of the rights of third parties which might not
thus be sanctioned upon the pretence that its allowance to the holder of
the notes would lead to their ready acceptance, and produce the desired
loan.

"The actual effect of the quality of legal tender in inducing parties to
receive them was necessarily limited to the amount required by existing
debtors, who did not scruple to discharge with them their pre-existing
liabilities. For moneys desired from other parties, or supplies required
for the use of the army or navy, the provision added nothing to the
value of the notes. Their borrowing power or purchasing power depended, by a general and an universal law of currency, not upon the
legal-tender clause, but upon the confidence which the parties receiving
the notes had in their ultimate payment. Their exchangeable value was
determined by this confidence, and every person dealing in them advanced his money and regulated his charges accordingly."

———— "Without the legal-tender provision the notes would have circulated equally well and answered all the purposes of government—the
only direct benefit resulting from that provision arising, as already stated,
from the ability it conferred upon unscrupulous debtors to discharge with
them previous obligations. The notes of State banks circulated without

possessing that quality and supplied a currency for the people just so long as confidence in the ability of the banks to redeem the notes continued. The notes issued by the national bank associations during the war, under the authority of Congress, amounting to three hundred millions, which were never made a legal tender, circulated equally well with the notes of the United States. Neither their utility nor their circulation was diminished in any degree by the absence of a legal-tender quality. They rose and fell in the market under the same influences and precisely to the same extent as the notes of the United States, which possessed this quality."

Referring to the position that the annexing of the quality of legal tender was a necessary means to the exercise of other powers of Congress, particularly to declare war, to suppress insurrection, to raise and support armies, and to provide and maintain a navy, all of which were called into exercise and severely taxed at the time, the Judge said as follows :

"It is evident that the notes have no relation to these powers, or to any other powers of Congress, except as they furnish a convenient means for raising money for their execution. The existence of the war only increased the urgency of the government for funds. It did not add to its powers to raise such funds, or change, in any respect, the nature of those powers or the transactions which they authorized. If the power to engraft the quality of legal tender upon the notes existed at all with Congress, the occasion, the extent, and the purpose of its exercise were mere matters of legislative discretion ; and the power may be equally exerted when a loan is made to meet the ordinary expenses of government in time of peace, as when vast sums are needed to raise armies and provide navies in time of war. The wants of the government can never be the measure of its powers.

"The Constitution has specifically designated the means by which funds can be raised for the uses of the government, either in war or peace. These are taxation, borrowing, coining, and the sale of its public property. Congress is empowered to levy and collect taxes, duties, imposts, and excises to any extent to which the public necessity may require. Its power to borrow is equally unlimited. It can convert any bullion it may possess into coin, and it can dispose of the public lands and other property of the United States or any part of such property. The designation of these means exhausts the powers of Congress on the subject of raising money. The designation of the means is a negation of all others, for the designation would be unnecessary and absurd if the use of any and all means were permissible without it. These means exclude a resort to forced loans, and to any compulsory interference with the property of third persons, except by regular taxation in one of the forms mentioned."

6

After showing that the act of Congress impaired the obligation of past contracts, and referring to the statement of Judge Miller, in his dissenting opinion in Hepburn vs. Griswold, that the Constitution does not forbid legislation having that effect, the Judge said as follows :

"It is true there is no provision in the Constitution forbidding in express terms such legislation. And it is also true that there are express powers delegated to Congress, the execution of which necessarily operates to impair the obligation of contracts. It was the object of the framers of that instrument to create a national government competent to represent the entire country in its relations with foreign nations, and to accomplish by its legislation measures of common interest to all the people, which the several States in their independent capacities were incapable of effecting, or if capable, the execution of which would be attended with great difficulty and embarrassment. They, therefore, clothed Congress with all the powers essential to the successful accomplishment of these ends, and carefully withheld the grant of all other powers. Some of the powers granted, from their very nature, interfere in their execution with contracts of parties. Thus war suspends intercourse and commerce between citizens or subjects of belligerent nations; it renders during its continuance the performance of contracts, previously made, unlawful. These incidental consequences were contemplated in the grant of the war power. So the regulation of commerce and the imposition of duties may so affect the prices of articles imported or manufactured as to essentially alter the value of previous contracts respecting them; but this incidental consequence was seen in the grant of the power over commerce and duties. There can be no valid objection to laws passed in execution of express powers that consequences like these follow incidentally from their execution. But it is otherwise when such consequences do not follow incidentally, but are directly enacted.

" The only express authority for any legislation affecting the obligation of contracts is found in the power to establish a uniform system of bankruptcy, the direct object of which is to release insolvent debtors from their contracts upon the surrender of their property. From this express grant in the Constitution I draw a very different conclusion from that drawn in the dissenting opinion in Hepburn vs. Griswold, and in the opinion of the majority of the court just delivered. To my mind it is a strong argument that there is no general power in Congress to interfere with contracts, that a special grant was regarded as essential to authorize an uniform system of bankruptcy. If such general power existed the delegation of an express power in the case of bankrupts was unnecessary. As very justly observed by counsel, if this sovereign power could be taken in any case without express grant, it could be taken in connection with bankruptcies, which might be regarded in some respects as a regulation of commerce made in the interest of traders.

· "The grant of a limited power over the subject of contracts necessarily implies that the framers of the Constitution did not intend that Congress should exercise unlimited power, or any power less restricted. The limitation designated is the measure of congressional power over the subject. This follows from the nature of the instrument, as one of enumerated powers.

"The doctrine that where a power is not expressly forbidden it may be exercised would change the whole character of our government. As I read the writings of the great commentators and the decisions of this court, the true doctrine is the exact reverse, that if a power is not in terms granted, and is not necessary and proper for the exercise of a power thus granted, it does not exist."

And, after referring to the interference with contracts by the legislation of the several States, previous to the adoption of the Constitution, in the form of tender laws, appraisement laws, installment laws, and suspension laws, which was the cause of great oppression and injustice, and which Judge Story declared prostrated all private credit and all private morals, the Judge continued as follows :

"It would require very clear evidence, one would suppose, to induce a belief that with the evils, resulting from what Marshall terms the system of lax legislation following the Revolution, deeply impressed on their minds, the framers of the Constitution intended to vest in the new government created by them this dangerous and despotic power which they were unwilling should remain with the States, and thus widen the possible sphere of its exercise.

"When the possession of this power has been asserted in argument, (for until now it has never been asserted in any decision of this court) it has been in cases where a supposed public benefit resulted from the legislation, or where the interference with the obligation of the contract was very slight. Whenever a clear case of injustice, in the absence of such supposed public good, is stated, the exercise of the power by the government is not only denounced, but the existence of the power is denied. No one, indeed, is found bold enough to contend that if A has a contract for one hundred acres of land, or one hundred pounds of fruit, or one hundred yards of cloth, Congress can pass a law compelling him to accept one-half of the quantity in satisfaction of the contract. But Congress has the same power to establish a standard of weights and measures as it has to establish a standard of value, and can, from time to time, alter such standard. It can declare that the acre shall consist of · eighty square rods instead of one hundred and sixty, the pound of eight ounces instead of sixteen, and the foot of six inches instead of twelve, and if it could compel the acceptance of the same *number* of acres, pounds, or yards after such alteration, instead of the actual *quantity* stipulated, then the acceptance of one-half of the quantity originally designated could be directly required without going through the form of altering the standard. No just man could be imposed upon by this use of words in a double sense, where the same names were applied to denote different quantities of the same thing, nor would his condemnation of the wrong committed in such case be withheld because the attempt was made to conceal it by the jugglery of words.

" The power of Congress to interfere with contracts for the payment of money is not greater or in any particular different from its power with respect to contracts for lands or goods. The contract is not fulfilled any more in one case than in the other by the delivery of a thing which is not stipulated, because by legislative action it is called by the same name. Words in contracts are to be construed in both cases in the sense in which they were understood by the parties at the time of the contract.

" Let us for a moment see where the doctrine of the power asserted will lead. Congress has the undoubted right to give such denominations as it chooses to the coin struck by its authority, and to change them. It can declare that the dime shall hereafter be called a dollar, or, what is the same thing, it may declare that the dollar shall hereafter be composed of the grains of silver which now compose the dime. But would anybody pretend that a contract for dollars, composed as at present, could be satisfied by the delivery of an equal number of dollars of the new issue? I have never met any one who would go to that extent. The answer always has been that would be too flagrantly unjust to be tolerated. Yet enforcing the acceptance of paper promises or paper dollars, if the promises can be so called, in place of gold or silver dollars, is equally enforcing a departure from the terms of the contract, the injustice of the measure depending entirely upon the actual value at the time of the promises in the market. Now reverse the case. Suppose Congress should declare that hereafter the eagle should be called a dollar or that the dollar should be composed of as many grains of gold as the eagle, would any body for a moment contend that a contract for dollars, composed as now of silver, should be satisfied by dollars composed of gold? I am confident that no judge sitting on this bench, and, indeed, that no judge in christendom could be found, who would sanction the monstrous wrong by decreeing that the debtor could only satisfy his contract in such case by paying ten times the value originally stipulated. The natural sense of right which is implanted in every mind would revolt from such supreme injustice. Yet there cannot be one law for debtors and another law for creditors. If the contract can at one time be changed by congressional legislation for the benefit of the debtor, it may at another time be changed for the benefit of the creditor.

" For acts of flagrant injustice such as those mentioned there is no authority in any legislative body, even though not restrained by any express constitutional prohibition. For as there are unchangeable principles of right and morality, without which society would be impossible, and men would be but wild beasts preying upon each other, so there are fundamental principles of eternal justice, upon the existence of which all constitutional government is founded, and without which government would be an intolerable and hateful tyranny."

Referring to the asserted power of Congress to require its own promises to be received in discharge of its previous obligations, the Judge said :

" It follows, then, logically, from the doctrine advanced by the majority of the court as to the power of Congress over the subject of legal tender, that Congress may borrow gold coin upon a pledge of the public faith to repay gold at the maturity of its obligations, and yet, in direct disregard of its pledge, in open violation of faith, may compel the lender to take, in place of the gold stipulated, its own promises ; and that legislation of this character would not be in violation of the Constitution, but in harmony with its letter and spirit.

" What is this but declaring that repudiation by the government of the United States of its solemn obligations would be constitutional? Whenever the fulfillment of the obligation in the manner stipulated is refused, and the acceptance of something different from that stipulated is enforced against the will of the creditor, a breach of faith is committed ; and to the extent of the difference of value between the thing stipulated and the thing which the creditor is compelled to receive, there is repudiation of the original obligation. I am not willing to admit that the Constitution, the boast and glory of our country, would sanction or permit any such legislation. Repudiation in any form, or to any extent, would be dishonor, and for the commission of this public crime no warrant, in my judgment, can ever be found in that instrument."

And, referring to the argument that Congress can regulate the alloy of the coins issued under its authority, and has exercised its power in that respect without question, by diminishing in some instances the actual quantity of gold or silver they contain, the Judge said :

" Undoubtedly Congress can alter the value of the coins issued by its authority by increasing or diminishing, from time to time, the alloy they contain, just as it may alter, at its pleasure, the denominations of the several coins issued, but there its power stops. It cannot make these altered coins the equivalent of the coins in their previous condition ; and, if the new coins should retain the same names as the original, they would only be current at their true value. Any declaration that they should have any other value would be inoperative in fact, and a monstrous disregard by Congress of its constitutional duty. The power to coin money, as already declared by this court, is a great trust devolved upon Congress, carrying with it the duty of creating and maintaining an uniform standard of value throughout the Union, and it would be a manifest abuse of this trust to give to the coins issued by its authority any other than their real value. By debasing the coins, when once the standard is fixed, is meant giving to the coins, by their form and impress, a certificate of their having a relation to that standard different from that which, in truth, they possess; in other words, giving to the coins a false certificate of their value. Arbitrary and profligate governments have often resorted to this miserable scheme of robbery, which Mills designates as a shallow and impudent artifice, the 'least covert of all modes of knavery, which consists in calling a shilling a pound, that a debt of one hundred pounds may be cancelled by the payment of one hundred shillings.' "

The Judge concluded his opinion as follows :

" I know that the measure, the validity of which I have called in question, was passed in the midst of a gigantic rebellion, when even the bravest hearts sometimes doubted the safety of the Republic, and that the patriotic men who adopted it did so under the conviction that it would increase the ability of the government to obtain funds and supplies, and thus advance the national cause. Were I to be governed by my appreciation of the character of those men, instead of my views of the requirements of the Constitution, I should readily assent to the views of the majority of the court. But, sitting as a judicial officer, and bound to compare every law enacted by Congress with the greater law enacted by the people, and being unable to reconcile the measure in question with that fundamental law, I cannot hesitate to pronounce it as being, in my judgment, unconstitutional and void.

"In the discussions which have attended this subject of legal tender there has been at times what seemed to me to be a covert intimation, that opposition to the measure in question was the expression of a spirit not altogether favorable to the cause, in the interest of which that measure was adopted. All such intimations I repel with all the energy I can express. I do not yield to any one in honoring and reverencing the noble and patriotic men who were in the councils of the nation during the terrible struggle with the rebellion. To them belong the greatest of all glories in our history,—that of having saved the Union, and that of having emancipated a race. For these results they will be remembered and honored so long as the English language is spoken or read among men. But I do not admit that a blind approval of every measure which they may have thought essential to put down the rebellion is any evidence of loyalty to the country. The only loyalty which I can admit consists in obedience to the Constitution and laws made in pursuance of it. It is only by obedience that affection and reverence can be shown to a superior having a right to command. So thought our great Master when he said to his disciples : 'If ye love me, keep my commandments.' "

THE LEGISLATIVE POWER OF THE INSURGENT STATES DURING THE CIVIL WAR, AND THE EXTENT TO WHICH THE CONFEDERATE GOVERNMENT COULD BE REGARDED AS A DE FACTO GOVERNMENT.

The States do not derive their powers from the general government. Thirteen of them existed before that government was formed ; and the others have come under it with similar powers and rights. If there were no States there would of course be no such political organization as the United States. If the Union were destroyed the States as independent political communities would remain, though a government like that of the Union would be necessary to their prosperity. That government preserves peace among them, thus ensuring domestic tranquillity, regulates commercial intercourse between them, secures to citizens of the several States equality of privileges and immunities in all of them, and exercises control over foreign affairs and matters of general concern, which could not be managed by the States acting separately, except in a few particulars, without great embarrassment and difficulty. It is essential, therefore, as all must see, to the whole country. But as the original States existed before the Constitution, and the States subsequently formed have been admitted into the Union upon terms of equality with them—all possess the attributes and powers of distinct political communities, except as limited and restrained by that instrument. When the civil war broke out the character of the insurgent States as such communities was not changed. They retained and exercised the powers previously possessed, which were essential to the security of persons and property, the preservation of order, and the due administration of justice. Their attempt to sever their relations to the government of the Union and to form a confederation with a part only of the States, and a new central government for themselves, could have, under the Constitution, no validity. To those who regard that instrument as creating a perpetual Union, to be dissolved only by the consent of the people of the several States, this new confederation could be nothing more than a rebellious organization—treasonable in its designs and actions—to be suppressed, if necessary, by armed force. That instrument prohibits any treaty, alliance, or confederation between one State and another, and the new confederation was in open defiance and contempt of this prohibition. It also declares that the Constitution, and the laws of the United States made in pursuance thereof, shall be the supreme law of the land. The new confederation denied this supremacy, repudiated the authority of the Constitution and of the laws passed in pursuance thereof, and endeavored to maintain its position by force of arms. The United States could, therefore, only treat it, and the government created by it, as the military representative of the insurrection against their authority. The concession of belligerent rights gave to its armed forces in the conduct of the war the position and rights of parties engaged in lawful warfare. But no further recognition was ever extended to it. Its legislation was never treated as valid, and when its forces were overthrown, its whole organization disappeared.

The insurgent States, however, were in a different position. They remained as previously to the war, with similar legislative powers, their acts being invalid only so far as they impaired or tended to impair the supremacy of the government of the Union or the rights of loyal citizens.

The Constitution, after delegating to the Congress of the United States certain enumerated powers, declares that it may make any laws necessary or proper to carry its powers into execution. Judge Field was always a "Union man," and when the rebellion broke out, he never hesitated a moment to give his earnest support to the government for its suppression. He had no patience with the doctrine of non-coercion, and denounced it as the suggestion of treason, or the utterance of stupidity. And to this day he never refers to it except with an expression of contempt. In a charge to a grand jury at San Francisco in 1872, in alluding to the results of the war, he thus spoke of it :

"That war has done away forever with the miserable notion, which extensively prevailed at the time of the outbreak of the rebellion, that the general government, because it was formed by the people of the several States, sovereign in some of their powers, should not exert any coercion to enforce its laws. No one is now willing to run a tilt against common sense by adducing any argument in support of this absurd position; and the war has demonstrated that the general government possesses all the power necessary to enforce obedience to its laws throughout the limits of the Republic."

The views stated as to the legislative powers of the insurgent States, and the character given to the Confederate government as the representative of the military insurrection, have been sanctioned by the Supreme Court in many decisions, notwithstanding some hesitation and some doubtful expressions in the early cases. These decisions deny all validity to any legislative action of the States favoring the insurrection, or against the rights of loyal citizens, but they sustain all other acts of ordinary legislation; and they treat the government of the Confederate States as a wholly illegal and traitorous combination.

In Texas vs. White, at the December term, 1868, Chief Justice Chase, after observing that the Legislature of Texas, during the war, constituted one of the departments of a state government established in hostility to the Constitution, and could not therefore be regarded in the courts of the United States as a lawful legislature, said that, as a department of the government having actual control of the State, he was of opinion that its acts, when not hostile to the United States, should be regarded as valid. Speaking for the court, he said :

" It is not necessary to attempt any exact definitions within which the acts of such a state government must be treated as valid or invalid. It may be said, perhaps with sufficient accuracy, that acts necessary to peace and good order among citizens—such, for example, as acts sanctioning and protecting marriage and the domestic relations, governing the course of descents, regulating the conveyance and transfer of property, real and personal, and providing remedies for injuries to person and estate, and other similar acts, which would be valid if emanating from a lawful government—must be regarded, in general, as valid when proceeding from an actual though unlawful government; and that acts in furtherance or support of rebellion against the United States, or intended to defeat the just rights of citizens, and other acts of like nature, must, in general, be regarded as invalid and void."—(7 Wall., 733.)

In Horn vs. Lockhart, before the court at the October term of 1873, these views are reasserted with still greater emphasis. There a bill had been filed by the legatees in a will to compel an executor in Alabama to account for funds received by him belonging to the estate of his testator, and to pay to them their distributive shares. He had, under a law of that State, invested the funds in bonds of the Confederate States, and the investment was approved by the decree of the probate court; and the question was whether this disposition of the moneys received, and the decree of the court, were a sufficient answer to the suit of the legatees to compel an accounting. In reply to it, Judge Field, speaking for the court, said :

"The bonds of the Confederate States were issued for the avowed purpose of raising funds to prosecute the war then waged by them against the government of the United States. The investment was, therefore, a direct contribution to the resources of the Confederate government; it was an act giving aid and comfort to the enemies of the United States; and the invalidity of any transaction of that kind, from whatever source originating, ought not to be a debatable matter in the courts of the United States. No legislation of Alabama, no act of its convention, no judgment of its tribunals, and no decree of the Confederate government could make such a transaction lawful.

"We admit that the acts of the several States in their individual capacities—executive, judicial, and legislative—during the war, so far as they did not impair or tend to impair the supremacy of the national authority, or the just rights of citizens under the Constitution, are, in general, to be treated as valid and binding. The existence of a state of insurrection and war did not loosen the bonds of society, or do away with civil government or the regular administration of the law. Order was to be preserved, police regulations maintained, crime prosecuted, property protected, contracts enforced, marriages celebrated, estates settled, and the transfer and descent of property regulated precisely as in time of peace. No one, that we are aware of, seriously questions the validity of judicial or legislative acts in the insurrectionary States touching these and kindred subjects, where they were not hostile in their purpose or mode of enforcement to the authority of the national government, and did not impair the rights of citizens under the Constitution."—(17 Wall., 580.)

In United States vs. Insurance Companies, at the October term of 1874, these views were reiterated and affirmed, the court citing with approbation the passages from the opinions in Texas vs. White and Lockhart vs. Horn, given above. These corporations, created by the Legislature of Georgia during the war, were held to be lawful institutions, capable of suing in the federal courts, not being in their purposes or operation hostile to the Union, or in conflict with the Constitution, but creatures of ordinary legislation, such as might have been created if there had been no war or attempted secession. In giving the opinion of the court, Judge Strong, after making the above and other similar citations, said :

" After these emphatic utterances controversy upon this subject should cease. All the enactments of the *de facto* legislatures in the insurrectionary States during the war, which were not hostile to the Union or to the authority of the general government, and which were not in conflict with the Constitution of the United States, or of the States, have the same validity as if they had been enactments of legitimate legislatures. Any other doctrine than this would work great and unnecessary hardship upon the people of those States, without any corresponding benefit to the citizens of other States, and without any advantage to the national government."—(22 Wall., 103. See also Sprott vs. United States, 20 Wall., 464.)

The character in which the government of the Confederate States was to be regarded, in view of the concession of belligerent rights to its armed forces, was the subject of frequent consideration by the Supreme Court. In Thorington vs. Smith, at the December term of 1868, the Chief Justice, in delivering the opinion of the court, spoke of the different kinds of *de facto* governments, and compared the government of the Confederate States with the government imposed upon Castine, in Maine, by the British forces in 1814, and that imposed upon Tampico, in Mexico, by the

Americans in 1846, and designated it as a government of paramount force, to which obedience, being a matter of necessity, became a duty for the preservation of civil order; but said that by the government of the United States it had been regarded, from an early period of the civil war to its close, as simply the military representative of the insurrection against their authority—(7 Wall., 9.) But by far the most thorough and exhaustive consideration of the character of the government of the Confederate States, and its relation to the government of the Union, is contained in the opinion in Bruffy vs. Williams, decided at the October term of 1877. In that case the question arose as to the validity of an act of the Confederate States, during the war, confiscating a debt due from a citizen of Virginia to a citizen of Pennsylvania. The former having died, an action was brought after the war against his administrator to recover the debt. The defendant took the ground that the enactment of the Confederate States was that of an independent nation, and must be so treated. His contention was substantially this : that the Confederate government, from April, 1861, until it was overthrown in 1865, was a government *de facto*, complete in all its parts, exercising jurisdiction over a well-defined territory, which included that portion of Virginia where the deceased resided, and as such *de facto* government it had engaged in war with the United States ; and possessed and was justified in exercising within its territorial limits all the rights of war which belonged to an independent nation, and among them, that of confiscating debts due by its citizens to its enemies.

In support of this position reference was made to numerous instances of *de facto* governments which had existed in England and in other parts of Europe and in America, to the doctrines of jurists and writers on public law respecting the powers of such governments, and the validity accorded to their acts, to the opinion of the Supreme Court of the United States, in Thorington vs. Smith and in the Prize Cases, to the concession of belligerent rights to the

Confederate government, and to the action of the States during the revolutionary war and the period immediately following it.

In reply to this position, Judge Field, in delivering the opinion of the court said as follows :

" We do not question the doctrines of public law which have been invoked, nor their application in proper cases, but it will be found upon examination that there is an essential difference between the government of the Confederate States and those *de facto* governments. The latter are of two kinds. One of them is such as exists after it has expelled the regularly constituted authorities from the seats of power and the public offices, and established its own functionaries in their places, so as to represent in fact the sovereignty of the nation. Such was the government of England under the commonwealth established upon the execution of the King and the overthrow of the loyalists. As far as other nations are concerned such a government is treated as in most respects possessing rightful authority; its contracts and treaties are usually enforced; its acquisitions are retained; its legislation is in general recognized; and the rights acquired under it are, with few exceptions, respected after the restoration of the authorities which were expelled. All that counsel say of *de facto* governments is justly said of a government of this kind. But the Confederate government was not of this kind. It never represented the nation; it never expelled the public authorities from the country; it never entered into any treaties; nor was it ever recognized as that of an independent power. It collected an immense military force and temporarily expelled the authorities of the United States from the territory over which it exercised an usurped dominion; but in that expulsion the United States never acquiesced; on the contrary, they immediately resorted to similar force to regain possession of that territory and re-establish their authority, and they continued to use such force until they succeeded. It would be useless to comment upon the striking contrast between a government of this nature, which with all its military strength never had undisputed possession of power for a single day, and a government like that of the Commonwealth of England under Parliament or Cromwell.

" The other kind of *de facto* governments, to which the doctrines cited relate, is such as exists where a portion of the inhabitants of a country have separated themselves from the parent state and established an independent government. The validity of its acts, both against the parent state and its citizens or subjects, depends entirely upon its ultimate success. If it fail to establish itself permanently, all such acts perish with it. If it succeed and become recognized, its acts from the commencement of its existence are upheld as those of an independent nation. Such was the case of the state governments under the old confederation on their separation from the British Crown. Having made good their declaration of independence, everything they did from that date was as valid as if their independence had been at once acknowledged. Confiscations, therefore, of enemy's property made by them were sustained as if made by an independent nation. But if they had failed in securing their independence, and the authority of the King had been re-established in this country, no one would contend that their acts against him, or his loyal subjects, could have been upheld as resting upon any legal foundation. ———

" When a rebellion becomes organized and attains such proportions as to be able to put a formidable military force in the field, it is usual for the established government to concede to it some belligerent rights. This concession is made in the interests of humanity, to prevent the cruelties which would inevitably follow mutual reprisals and retaliations. But belligerent rights, as the terms import, are rights which exist only during war; and to what extent they shall be accorded to insurgents depends upon the considerations of justice, humanity, and policy controlling the government. The rule stated by Vattel, that the justice of the cause between two enemies being by the law of nations reputed to be equal, whatsoever is permitted to the one in virtue of war is also permitted to the other, applies only to cases of regular war between independent nations. It has no application to the case of a war between an established government and insurgents seeking to withdraw themselves from its jurisdiction, or to overthrow its authority.* The concession made to the Confederate government in its military character was shown in the treatment of captives as prisoners of war, the exchange of prisoners, the recognition of flags of truce, the release of officers on parole, and other arrangements having a tendency to mitigate the evils of the contest. The concession placed its soldiers and military officers in its service on the footing of those engaged in lawful war, and exempted them from liability for acts of legitimate warfare. But it conferred no further immunity or any other rights. It in no respect condoned acts against the government not committed by armed force in the military service of the rebellious organization. It sanctioned no hostile legislation ; it gave validity to no contracts for military stores; and it impaired in no respect the rights of loyal citizens as they had existed at the commencement of the hostilities. Parties residing in the insurrectionary territory, having property in their possession as trustees or bailees of loyal citizens, may in some instances have had such property taken from them by force, and in that event they may perhaps be released from liability. Their release will depend upon the same principles which control in ordinary cases of violence by an unlawful combination too powerful to be successfully resisted.

" But debts not being tangible things subject to physical seizure and removal, the debtors cannot claim release from liability to their creditors by reason of the coerced payment of equivalent sums to an unlawful combination. The debts can only be satisfied when paid to the creditors to whom they are due, or to others by direction of lawful authority. Any

---

* Halleck's Inter. Law, ch. xiv., sec. 9.

sum which the unlawful combination may have compelled the debtors to pay to its agents on account of debts to loyal citizens cannot have any effect upon their obligations ; they remain subsisting and unimpaired. The concession of belligerent rights to the rebellious organization yielded nothing to its pretensions of legality. If it had succeeded in its contest it would have protected the debtor from further claim for the debt, but as it failed the creditor may have recourse to the courts of the country as prior to the rebellion. It would be a strange thing, if the nation, after succeeding in suppressing the rebellion and re-establishing its authority over the insurrectionary district, should by any of its tribunals recognize as valid the attempt of the rebellious organization to confiscate a debt due to a loyal citizen as a penalty for his loyalty. Such a thing would be unprecedented in the history of unsuccessful rebellions, and would rest upon no just principle.

" The immense power exercised by the government of the Confederate States for nearly four years, the territory over which it extended, the vast resources it wielded, and the millions who acknowledged its authority, present an imposing spectacle, well fitted to mislead the mind in considering the legal character of that organization. It claimed to represent an independent nation and to possess sovereign powers ; and as such to displace the jurisdiction and authority of the United States from nearly half of their territory, and instead of their laws to substitute and enforce those of its own enactment. Its pretensions being resisted, they were submitted to the arbitrament of war. In that contest the Confederacy failed, and in its failure its pretensions were dissipated, its armies scattered, and the whole fabric of its government broken in pieces. The very property it had amassed passed to the nation. The United States during the whole contest never for one moment renounced their claim to supreme jurisdiction over the whole country, and to the allegiance of every citizen of the Republic. They never acknowledged in any form, or through any of their departments, the lawfulness of the rebellious organization, or the validity of any of its acts, except so far as such acknowledgment may have arisen from conceding to its armed forces in the conduct of the war the standing and rights of those engaged in lawful warfare. They never recognized its asserted power of rightful legislation."

The Judge then proceeded to show that there was nothing in conflict with these views in Thorington vs. Smith, or in the Prize Cases, or in Wheaton or Vattel, and then added, that it was unnecessary to pursue the subject further; that—

" Whatever *de facto* character may be ascribed to the Confederate government consists solely in the fact, that it maintained a contest with the United States for nearly four years, and dominated for that period over a large extent of territory. When its military forces were overthrown it utterly perished, and with it all its enactments."

He concluded as follows :

" Whilst thus holding that there was no validity in any legislation of the Confederate States which this court can recognize, it is proper to observe that the legislation of the States stands on very different grounds. The same general form of government, the same general laws for the administration of justice and the protection of private rights, which had existed in the States prior to the rebellion, remained during its continuance and afterwards. As far as the acts of the States did not impair or tend to impair the supremacy of the national authority or the just rights of citizens under the Constitution, they are, in general, to be treated as valid and binding."—(Citing from Horn vs. Lockhart, 76 U. S.)

PROTECTION FROM MILITARY ARREST AND IMPRISONMENT DURING THE WAR OF CITIZENS NOT IN THE MILITARY SERVICE, IN STATES WHERE THE CIVIL COURTS WERE OPEN AND IN THE UNDISTURBED EXERCISE OF THEIR JURISDICTION.

After the decision of the Supreme Court in the Milligan case, at the December term of 1865, declaring military commissions in the loyal States, for the trial of citizens not in the military service or prisoners of war, to be illegal, no attempt was made to bring the decrees of such irregular and unauthorized tribunals before the court. Their illegality was accepted without further contest. But during the war there were in some instances arbitrary and oppressive acts committed in the loyal States by military officers, particularly those filling the positions of provost-marshals, for which redress was sought by civil action. An instance of this kind was before the Supreme Court in Beckwith vs. Bean, at the October term of 1878. That action was brought against the provost-marshal and assistant provost-marshal of a military district embracing the State of Vermont, and was for an assault and battery upon the plaintiff, and his imprisonment in the state prison for several months—from November, 1864, to April, 1865—

without process of law and under circumstances of great cruelty and oppression. It appeared from the evidence in the case that on the 11th of November, 1864, the plaintiff, whilst returning from a trip to Boston to his home in Canada, where he temporarily resided, though a citizen of the United States, was arrested by one of the defendants, the assistant provost-marshal, without any warrant or process of law, and detained until the following day ; that he was then forcibly taken by order of the other defendant, the provost-marshal, and placed in the state prison at Windsor, where he remained until the 26th of April, 1865, a period of nearly five months, when he was admitted to bail and released from imprisonment; that during this period he was locked up at night, and for the first few days in the daytime also, in a narrow and scantily furnished cell, being one in which convicts were confined at night ; that after the first few days he was allowed, upon his complaint of the coldness of the cell, to spend the day in the shops where the convicts worked, but he was required to go out and to return when they did, and at no time to be out of sight of a keeper, and not to go on the corridor or in the yard for exercise ; that the food offered to him was the fare served to the convicts, which he could not eat, and that afterwards he obtained his meals from the keeper's table by paying a small sum each week ; and that during this period no complaint against him was filed with any magistrate ; and that he was simply held upon the order of the defendants.

The excuse offered by them for this imprisonment and treatment of the plaintiff was, that they suspected that he had aided or been privy to the desertion from the army of two substitutes, who had been furnished upon a contract with a substitute broker, and for whom the latter had paid $1,200, of which sum $800 had been received by the plaintiff and two others. Suspecting the plaintiff, the defendants determined to hold him in the state prison until they should coerce him to pay not merely what he had received, but what his supposed confederates had received also. After he had been in the state prison for a few days, the provost-marshal called upon him, and verbally informed him that he was charged with aiding or being privy to the desertion of the substitutes, but that he would be discharged on payment of the $800, and $25 additional for expenses. The plaintiff protested that he was innocent of the charge, and demanded a trial. He was told in reply that " he could not have a trial, and could not get one," but that his case would be reported to the officer's superiors.

During his imprisonment he made constant efforts to obtain a trial, or release on bail which he was able and willing to furnish. But no trial was allowed him, and not until intercession was made on his behalf at Washington by a member of Congress was he permitted to give bail and be discharged. When the grand jury of the United States court subsequently met in Vermont they found no cause for prosecution against him, although the provost-marshal made a statement of the case to them.

At the time of his arrest and during his imprisonment there was no rebellion in the State of Vermont against the laws and government of the United States, nor were there any military operations carried on within its limits. The courts of justice, both federal and state, were open and in the full exercise of their jurisdiction; and the plaintiff was not in the military service or in any way connected with such service; and for the offence of which he was sus-pected, or for any other offence, could have been brought before them on any day of the year. By his imprison-ment, and the report that he was in the state prison, his business was ruined, his personal property and furniture were seized by creditors and sacrificed at sheriff's sale, and his wife was compelled to leave his home and return to her friends in Vermont.

On the trial of the action, the defendants relied for their defence upon the fourth section of the act of Congress of March 3d, 1863, " relating to habeas corpus, and regulating judicial proceedings in certain cases;" and upon the act of March 2d, 1867, to declare valid and conclusive certain proclamations of the President, and acts done in pursuance thereof, or of his orders in the suppression of the late rebellion; contending that under them the defendants were to be presumed to have acted by the orders of the President, and that they were thereby justified for the matters complained of. And if they were not thus justified, then they sought to give in evidence in mitigation of damages the testimony of certain parties, which was discovered after the arrest and imprisonment of the plaintiff, tending to establish facts, which, if known at that time, would have justified, to some extent, their suspicions as to his complicity in the escape of the substitutes. The court below, in refusing to give certain instructions asked, held that the defendants were not justified under the acts of Congress and the proclamations of the President mentioned. It also held that evidence of the possible guilt of the plaintiff, discovered after the commission of the grievances complained of, was inadmissible in mitigation of damages.

The plaintiff accordingly obtained a verdict and judgment for $15,000 damages, and the case was carried to the Supreme Court. There the Attorney-General appeared for the military officers, and contended, substantially, as follows :

1st. That the defendants were to be presumed to have acted, in the arrest and imprisonment of the plaintiff, by the orders of the President; and that by the acts of Congress they were justified for the matters complained of.

2d. That the evidence of the possible guilt of the plaintiff, discovered after the commission of the grievances, was admissible in mitigation of damages.

The first proposition was not passed upon, the court observing that the instruction requested ignored the evidence introduced, that the defendants had, under circumstances of oppression and wantonness, and by improper and fraudulent representations, procured their superior officers

" to continue the imprisonment longer than necessary, and prevented them from having a speedy trial" for the offence charged; and on that ground, and not on the ground that the acts of Congress justifying the conduct of the defendants were invalid, or that the orders of the President, if issued, would have afforded no justification to them, the court overruled the objection to the ruling of the court below. But the second proposition the court sustained, and, for the refusal of the court below to admit the subsequently discovered evidence, reversed the judgment and ordered a new trial.

From this decision Judges Clifford and Field dissented, Judge Field giving an elaborate dissenting opinion, in which the invalidity of the acts of Congress, and of any orders of the President, if issued, to justify the conduct of the defendants, is conclusively shown. The subject is so important, and is so fully considered, that no apology is necessary for extended citations from the opinion. Both propositions of the Attorney-General were discussed at length.

Upon the first proposition the Judge, after citing the acts of Congress, said as follows :

" These statutes, as is apparent on their face, extend only to acts done in compliance with express orders or proclamations of the President. They do not cover acts done by persons upon their own will and discretion, who may have been at the time in the service of the government, simply because they were under the general direction of the President as commander-in-chief. They were not intended to protect against judicial inquiry and redress every act of a surbordinate in the military service in suppressing or punishing what he may have regarded as a disloyal practice, no matter how flagrant the outrage he may have thus committed against life, liberty, or property.———

" It is not pretended that any proof was produced that the arrest and imprisonment of the plaintiff were made under any express order or proclamation of the President ; but it is contended by the Attorney-General, that under the last clause of the act of 1867 it is to be presumed that their action [the defendants'] was authorized by the President, and that they are thus relieved from accountability for it.

" The court below held, that assuming the construction placed by the Attorney-General upon the statute to be correct, and that from the commission of the act the presumption arose that it was authorized by the President—the act thus presumptively establishing its own validity—the presumption in this case was repelled, inasmuch as it appeared in evidence by whose direction the orders were issued under which the plaintiff was arrested and imprisoned. It appeared that they never originated with or had the sanction of the President.

"If, however, the court below erred in this respect, there is another and a conclusive answer to the defence—one which renders futile and abortive all attempts to justify the action of the defendants under any presumed orders of the President—and that is, that it was not within the competency of the President or of Congress to authorize or approve the acts here complained of, so as to shield the perpetrators from responsibility.

"Persons engaged in the military service of the United States are, of course, subject to what is termed military law; that is, to those rules and regulations which Congress has provided for the government of the army and the punishment of offences in it. Congress possesses authority under the Constitution to prescribe the tribunals, as well as the manner in which offenders against the discipline of the army and the laws for the protection of its men and officers shall be summarly tried and punished; and to the jurisdiction thus created, all persons in the military service are amenable. But that jurisdiction does not extend to persons not in the military service, who are citizens of States where the civil courts are open.

"It may be true, also, that on the actual theatre of military operations, what is termed martial law, but which would be better called martial rule, for it is little else than the will of the commanding general, applies to all persons, whether in the military service or civilians. It may be true that no one, whatever his station or occupation, can there interfere with or obstruct any of the measures deemed essential for the success of the army, without subjecting himself to immediate arrest and summary punishment. The ordinary laws of the land are there superseded by the laws of war. The jurisdiction of the civil magistrate is there suspended, and military authority and force are substituted. The success of the army is the controlling consideration, and to that everything else is required to bend. To secure that success, persons may be arrested and confined, and property taken and used or destroyed at the command of the general, he being responsible only to his superiors for an abuse of his authority. His orders, from the very necessity of the case, there constitute legal justification for any action of his officers and men. This martial rule—in other words, this will of the commanding general, except in the country of the enemy occupied and dominated by the army—is limited to the field of military operations. In a country not hostile, at a distance from the movements of the army, where they cannot be immediately and directly interfered with, and the courts are open, it has no existence.

"The doctrine sometimes advanced by men, with more zeal than wisdom, that whenever war exists in one part of the country, the constitutional guaranties of personal liberty, and of the rights of property, are suspended everywhere, has no foundation in the principles of the common law, the teachings of our ancestors, or the language of the Constitution, and is at variance with every just notion of a free government. Our system of civil polity is not such a rickety and ill-jointed structure, that when one part is disturbed the whole is thrown into confusion and jostled to its foundation. The fact that rebellion existed in one portion of the country could not have the effect of superseding or suspending the laws and Constitution in a loyal portion widely separated from it. The war in the Southern States did not disturb Vermont from her constitutional propriety. She did not assent to the theory that war and disturbance elsewhere could destroy the security given by her laws and government. The same juridical institutions, and the same constitutional guaranties for the protection of the personal liberty of the citizen, with all the means for their enforcement, remained there as completely as before ; and the Constitution and laws of the United States were as capable of enforcement in all their vigor in that State during the war as at any time before or since. The arrest and imprisonment of the plaintiff, even if made by direct order of the President, were, therefor, in plain violation of the fifth constitutional amendment, which declares that no person shall be deprived of his liberty without due process of law. No mere order or proclamation of the President for the arrest and imprisonment of a person not in the military service, in a State removed from the scene of actual hostilities, where the courts are open and in the unobstructed exercise of their jurisdiction, can constitute due process of law ; nor can it be made such by any act of Congress. Those terms, as is known to every one, were originally used to express what was meant by the terms 'the law of the land ' in Magna Charta, and had become synonymous with them. They were intended, as said by this court, ' to secure the individual from the arbitrary exercise of the powers of government, unrestrained by the established principles of private right and distributive justice.'* They were designed to prevent the government from depriving any individual of his rights except by due course of legal proceedings, according to those rules and principles established in our systems of jurisprudence for the protection and enforcement of the rights of all persons.———

"To me, therefore, it is a marvel, that in this country, under a Constitution ordained by men who were conversant with the principles of Magna Charta, and claimed them as their birthright—a Constitution which declares in its preamble that it is established ' to secure the blessings of liberty to ourselves and our posterity '—it could ever be contended that an order of the Executive, issued at his will, for the arrest and imprisonment of a citizen, where the courts are open and in the full exercise of their jurisdiction, is due process of law, or could ever be made such by an act of

---

* Bank of Columbia vs. Okely, 4 Wheat., 235.

Congress. I certainly never supposed that such a proposition could be seriously asserted before the highest tribunal of the Republic by its chief legal officer. I had supposed that we could justly claim that in America, under our republican government, the personal liberty of the citizen was greater and better guarded than that of the subject in England. It is only the extraordinary claim made by the counsel of the government in this case which justifies any argument in support of principles so fundamental and heretofore so universally recognized. It may be necessary at times with respect to them, as it is necessary at times with respect to admitted principles of morality, to re-state them in order to rescue them from the forgetfulness caused by their universal admission.

" The assertion that the power of the government to carry on the war and suppress the rebellion, would have been crippled and its efficiency impaired, if it could not have authorized the arrest of persons and their detention without examination or trial, on suspicion of their complicity with the enemy, or of disloyal practices, rests upon no foundation whatever, so far as Vermont was concerned. There was no invasion or insurrection there, nor any disturbance which obstructed the regular administration of justice. A claim to exemption from the restraints of law is always made in support of arbitrary power, whenever unforeseen exigencies arise in the affairs of government. It is inconvenient; it causes delay; it takes time to furnish to committing magistrates evidence which, in a country where personal liberty is valued and guarded by constitutional guaranties, would justify the detention of the suspected ; and, therefore, in such exigencies, say the advocates of the exercise of arbitrary power, the evidence should not be required. A doctrine more dangerous than this to free institutions could not be suggested by the wit of man. The proceedings required by the general law for the arrest and detention of a party for a public offence—the charge under oath, the examination of witnesses in the presence of the accused, with the privilege of cross-examination, and of producing testimony in his favor, creating the objectionable delays—constitute the shield and safeguard of the honest and loyal citizen. They were designed not merely to insure punishment to the guilty, but to insure protection to the innocent, and without them every one would hold his liberty at the mercy of the government. ' All the ancient, honest, juridical principles and institutions of England,' says Burke—and it is our glory that we inherit them—' are so many clogs to check and retard the headlong course of violence and oppression. They were invented for this one good purpose, that what was not just should not be convenient.' *
Whoever, therefore, favors their subversion or suspension, except when in the presence of actual invasion or insurrection the laws are silent, is consciously or unconsciously an enemy to the Republic.

" If neither the order of the President nor the act of Congress could suspend, in a State where war was not actually waged, any of the guar-

---

* Letter to the Sheriffs of Bristol.

anties of the Constitution intended for the protection of the plaintiff from unlawful arrest and imprisonment, neither could they shield the defendants from responsibility in disregarding them. Protection against the deprivation of liberty and property would be defeated if remedies for redress, where such deprivation was made, could be denied."

In answer to the second proposition of the Attorney-General, that evidence of the possible guilt of the plaintiff discovered after the commission of the grievances complained of, was admissible in mitigation of damages, the Judge said as follows :

"As facts not known at that time [when the grievances were committed] could not have influenced the conduct of the defendants, it is difficult to comprehend how proof of those facts could be received to show the motives—of malice or good faith—with which they then acted.

"Independently of this consideration, it seems to me, that the evidence of the guilt or innocence of the plaintiff was entirely immaterial. Assuming that he was guilty of the complicity alleged—that he had admitted his guilt to the defendants—that circumstance would not have justified their conduct in the slightest degree. They would have been equally bound upon that assumption, as they were in fact bound—no more and no less—to take the plaintiff before the proper magistrate to be proceeded against according to law. To keep him for nearly six months in the state prison among convicts, without taking him before the proper officer to be held to bail or brought to trial, was a gross outrage upon his rights, whether he were guilty or innocent. There were magistrates in every county of the State competent to act upon the charge, and the district attorney was ready to take control of all cases against the laws of the United States and prosecute them. The defendants not only omitted this plain, imperative duty, but detained the plaintiff in prison, not with a view to punish him for the offence of which they suspected him to be guilty, but to coerce from him payment of money alleged to be due by him and others to a substitute broker. Where is the law or reason for allowing one, who by force holds another in confinement in order to extort the payment of money, to show in extenuation of his conduct that the man had been guilty of some offence against the law? The answer in all such cases should be, that the law attaches the proper penalties to its violation, and appoints the ministers by whom those penalties are to be enforced ; and whenever they can act, whoever usurps their authority and attempts to punish supposed offenders, in any other mode than that provided by law, is himself a criminal. For, as it was said by a distinguished statesman and jurist of England, when the laws can act, 'every other mode of punishing supposed crimes is itself an enormous crime.'

"The doctrine announced by the decision of the court in this case is nothing less than this: that a gross outrage upon the rights of a person may be extenuated or excused by proof that the outraged party had himself been guilty of some crime, or, at least, that the perpetrators of the outrage had reason to suspect that he had. This doctrine is pregnant with evil. I know not why, under it, the violence of mobs, excited against guilty or suspected parties, may not find extenuation. Let such a doctrine be once admitted, and a greater blow will be dealt to personal security than any given to it for a century.———

"It will appear from an examination of the adjudged cases, as it must on principle, that when illegal measures have been taken to redress private wrongs, or to punish for offences against the public, it is inadmissible to prove, in mitigation of actual or exemplary damages, that the party injured was guilty of the offence or misconduct constituting the provocation to the illegal measures, except where the provocation is of a personal character calculated to excite passion, and so recent as to create the presumption that the acts complained of were committed under the influence of the passion thus excited.———They are founded upon the plain principle, that no one can be allowed to undertake the punishment of wrongdoers according to his own notions ; that the administration of punitive justice for all offences is confided by the law to certain public officers, and whoever assumes their functions without being authorized, usurps the prerogative of sovereign power and becomes himself amenable to punishment. He shall not be permitted to set up the real or supposed offences of others to justify his own wrong."

PROTECTION TO OFFICERS AND SOLDIERS OF THE ARMY OF THE UNITED STATES IN THE ENEMY'S COUNTRY DURING THE WAR.

In the prosecution of the late war the armies of the United States were, as a matter of course, sent into the States in insurrection. The destruction which necessarily attended their march, together with acts of violence of individual soldiers, which no discipline could wholly prevent, produced the natural result—great bitterness and hostility on the part of the inhabitants of the invaded country. With the close of the war this feeling did not entirely cease, and where a crime had been committed the whole community would naturally desire to have its perpetrator punished. Where a personal wrong had been suffered, or a wanton injury to private property committed, the sufferer would naturally consider the possibility of redress in the courts. Hence criminal prosecutions were in many instances begun against parties who had been in the federal armies for alleged offences during the war, and numerous private suits were brought for injuries to persons and property. Some of these found their way to the Supreme Court, where decisions were rendered extending protection to the officers and soldiers of the army against prosecution in the tribunals of the enemy's country for offences or injuries committed there by them during the war.

The first of these cases was that of Coleman from Tennessee, which was before the court at the October term of 1878. Coleman was indicted in October, 1874, in one of the district courts of Tennessee for the murder of a young woman in March, 1865. To the indictment he pleaded not guilty, and a former conviction for the same offence by a general court-martial regularly convened for his trial at Knoxville, Tennessee, on the 27th of March, 1865, the United States at that time, and when the offence was committed, occupying with their armies East Tennessee as a military district, and the defendant being a regular soldier in their military service, subject to the articles of war, military orders, and such military laws as were there in force by their authority, alleging that he was arraigned by that tribunal upon a charge of murder, in having killed the same person mentioned in the indictment, and was afterwards, on the 9th of May, 1865, tried and convicted of the offence and sentenced to death by hanging, and that said sentence was still standing as the judgment of the court-martial, approved as required by law in such cases, without any other or further action thereon. He, therefore, prayed that the indictment might be quashed.

The local court held this plea bad on the ground, among others, that the defendant's conviction of the offence charged by a court-martial, under the laws of the United States, on the 9th of May, 1865, was not a bar to the indictment for the same offence; because by the murder

alleged he was also guilty of an offence against the laws
of Tennessee. He was thereupon put upon his trial in
that court, convicted of murder, and sentenced to death.
On appeal to the Supreme Court of the State the judgment
was affirmed, and the case was taken to the Supreme
Court of the United States. It was there argued as though
its determination depended upon the construction given
to the 30th section of the act of Congress of March 3d
1863, to enroll and call out the national forces, the defendant's counsel contending that the section vested in general
courts-martial and military commissions the right to punish for the offences designated therein, when committed
in time of war, by persons in the military service of the
United States and subject to the articles of war, to the
exclusion of jurisdiction over them by the state courts.
That section enacted: " That in time of war, insurrection,
or rebellion, murder, assault and battery with an intent to
kill, manslaughter, mayhem, wounding by shooting or
stabbing with an intent to commit murder, robbery, arson,
burglary, rape, assault and battery with an intent to commit rape, and larceny, shall be punishable by the sentence
of a general court-martial or military commission, when
committed by persons who are in the military service of
the United States, and subject to the articles of war; and
the punishment for such offences shall never be less than
those inflicted by the laws of the State, territory, or district
in which they may have been committed."* But in delivering the opinion of the court, Judge Field replied as
follows :

" The section is part of an act containing numerous provisions for the
enrollment of the national forces, designating who shall constitute such
forces; who shall be exempt from military service; when they shall be
drafted for service; when substitutes may be allowed; how deserters and
spies and persons resisting the draft shall be punished; and many other
particulars, having for their object to secure a large force to carry on the
then existing war, and to give efficiency to it when called into service.
It was enacted not merely to insure order and discipline among the men

* 12 U. S. Stats., p. 736.

composing those forces, but to protect citizens not in the military service from the violence of soldiers. It is a matter well known that the march even of an army not hostile is often accompanied with acts of violence and pillage by straggling parties of soldiers, which the most rigid discipline is hardly able to prevent. The offences mentioned are those of most common occurrence, and the swift and summary justice of a military court was deemed necessary to restrain their commission.

"But the section does not make the jurisdiction of the military tribunals exclusive of that of the state courts. It does not declare that soldiers committing the offences named shall not be amenable to punishment by the state courts. It simply declares that the offences shall be 'punishable,' not that they shall be punished by the military courts; and this is merely saying that they may be thus punished.

"Previous to its enactment the offences designated were punishable by the state courts, and persons in the military service who committed them were delivered over to those courts for trial; and it contains no words indicating an intention on the part of Congress to take from them the jurisdiction in this respect which they had always exercised. With the known hostility of the American people to any interference by the military with the regular administration of justice in the civil courts, no such intention should be ascribed to Congress in the absence of clear and direct language to that effect.

"We do not mean to intimate that it was not within the competency of Congress to confer exclusive jurisdiction upon military courts over offences committed by persons in the military service of the United States. As Congress is expressly authorized by the Constitution 'to raise and support armies,' and 'to make rules for the government and regulation of the land and naval forces,' its control over the whole subject of the formation, organization, and government of the national armies, including therein the punishment of offences committed by persons in the military service, would seem to be plenary. All we now affirm is that by the law to which we are referred, the 30th section of the enrollment act, no such exclusive jurisdiction is vested in the military tribunals mentioned. No public policy would have been subserved by investing them with such jurisdiction, and many reasons may be suggested against it. Persons in the military service could not have been taken from the army by process of the state courts without the consent of the military authorities; and, therefore, no impairment of its efficiency could arise from the retention of jurisdiction by the state courts to try the offences. The answer of the military authorities to any such process would have been : 'We are empowered to try and punish the persons who have committed the offences alleged, and we will see that justice is done in the premises.' Interference with the army would thus have been impossible; and offences committed by soldiers, discovered after the army had marched to a distance, when the production of evidence before a court-martial would have been difficult, if not impossible, or discovered after the war was over and the army disbanded, would not go unpunished. Surely Congress could not have intended that in such cases the guilty should go free.

" In denying to the military tribunals exclusive jurisdiction, under the section in question, over the offences mentioned, when committed by persons in the military service of the United States and subject to the articles of war, we have reference to them when they were held in States occupying, as members of the Union, their normal and constitutional relations to the federal government, in which the supremacy of that government was recognized and the civil courts were open and in the undisturbed exercise of their jurisdiction. When the armies of the United States were in the territory of the insurgent States, banded together in hostility to the national government and making war against it; in other words, when the armies of the United States were in the enemy's country the military tribunals mentioned had, under the laws of war, and the authority conferred by the section named, exclusive jurisdiction to try and punish offences of every grade committed by persons in the military service. Officers and soldiers of the armies of the Union were not subject during the war to the laws of the enemy or amenable to his tribunals for offences committed by them. They were answerable only to their own government, and only by its laws, as enforced by its armies, could they be punished.

" It is well settled that a foreign army permitted to march through a friendly country, or to be stationed in it, by authority of its government or sovereign, is exempt from the civil and criminal jurisdiction of the place. The sovereign is understood, said this court in the celebrated case of The Exchange, to cede a portion of his territorial jurisdiction when he allows the troops of a foreign prince to pass through his dominions :—' In such case, without any express declaration waiving jurisdiction over the army to which this right of passage has been granted, the sovereign who should attempt to exercise it would certainly be considered as violating his faith. By exercising it, the purpose for which the free passage was granted would be defeated, and a portion of the military force of a foreign independent nation would be diverted from those national objects and duties to which it was applicable, and would be withdrawn from the control of the sovereign whose power and whose safety might greatly depend on retaining the exclusive command and disposition of this force. The grant of a free passage, therefore, implies a waiver of all jurisdiction over the troops during their passage, and permits the foreign general to use that discipline and to inflict those punishments which the government of his army may require.'

" If an army marching through a friendly country would thus be exempt from its civil and criminal jurisdiction, *a fortiori* would an army invading an enemy's country be exempt. The fact that war is waged between two countries negatives the possibility of jurisdiction being exercised by the tribunals of the one country over persons engaged in the military service of the other for offences committed while in such ser-vice. Aside from this want of jurisdiction there would be something incongruous and absurd in permitting an officer or soldier of an invading army to be tried by his enemy, whose country he had invaded.

"The fact that when the offence was committed, for which the defendant was indicted, the State of Tennessee was in the military occupation of the United States, with a military governor at its head, appointed by the President, cannot alter this conclusion. Tennessee was one of the insurgent States forming the organization known as the Confederate States, against which the war was waged. Her territory was enemy's country, and its character in this respect was not changed until long afterwards.

"The doctrine of international law on the effect of military occupation of enemy's territory upon its former laws is well established. Though the late war was not between independent nations, but between different portions of the same nation, yet having taken the proportions of a territorial war, the insurgents having become formidable enough to be recognized as belligerents, the same doctrine must be held to apply. The right to govern the territory of the enemy during its military occupation is one of the incidents of war, being a consequence of its acquisition; and the character and form of the government to be established depend entirely upon the laws of the conquering State or the order of its military commander. By such occupation the political relations between the people of the hostile country and their former government or sovereign are for the time severed; but the municipal laws, that is, the laws which regulate private rights, enforce contracts, punish crime, and regulate the transfer of property, remain in full force, so far as they affect the inhabitants of the country among themselves, unless suspended or superseded by the conqueror. And the tribunals by which the laws are enforced continue as before unless thus changed. In other words, the municipal laws of the State and their administration remain in full force so far as the inhabitants of the country are concerned unless changed by the occupying belligerent. *

"This doctrine does not affect in any respect the exclusive character of the jurisdiction of the military tribunals over the officers and soldiers of the army of the United States in Tennessee during the war; for, as already said, they were not subject to the laws, nor amenable to the tribunals of the hostile country. The laws of the State for the punishment of crime were continued in force only for the protection and benefit of its own people. As respects them, the same acts which constituted offences before the military occupation constituted offences afterwards; and the same tribunals, unless superseded by order of the military commanders, continued to exercise their ordinary jurisdiction.

"If these views be correct, the plea of the defendant of a former conviction for the same offence by a court-martial under the laws of the United States was not a proper plea in the case. Such a plea admits the

* Halleck's Int. Law, chap. xxxiii.

jurisdiction of the criminal court to try the offence if it were not for the former conviction. Its inapplicability, however, will not prevent our giving effect to the objection which the defendant in this irregular way attempted to raise, that the state court had no jurisdiction to try and punish him for the offence alleged. The judgment and conviction in the criminal court should have been set aside and the indictment quashed for want of jurisdiction. Their effect was to defeat an act done under the authority of the United States by a tribunal of officers appointed under the law enacted for the government and regulation of the army in time of war, and whilst that army was in a hostile and conquered State. The judgment of that tribunal at the time it was rendered, as well as the person of the defendant, were beyond the control of the State of Tennessee. The authority of the United States was then sovereign and their jurisdiction exclusive. Nothing which has since occurred has diminished that authority or impaired the efficacy of that judgment.

"In thus holding, we do not call in question the correctness of the general doctrine asserted by the Supreme Court of Tennessee, that the same act may, in some instances, be an offence against two governments, and that the transgressor may be held liable to punishment by both when the punishment is of such a character that it can be twice inflicted, or by either of the two governments if the punishment, from its nature, can be only once suffered. It may well be that the satisfaction which the transgressor makes for the violated law of the United States is no atonement for the violated law of Tennessee. But here there is no case presented for the application of the doctrine. The laws of Tennessee with regard to offences and their punishment, which were allowed to remain in force during its military occupation, did not apply to the defendant, as he was at the time a soldier in the army of the United States and subject to the articles of war. He was responsible for his conduct to the laws of his own government only as enforced by the commander of its army in that State, without whose consent he could not even go beyond its lines. Had he been caught by the forces of the enemy, after committing the offence, he might have been subjected to a summary trial and punishment by order of their commander, and there would have been no just ground of complaint, for the marauder and assassin are not protected by any usages of civilized warfare. But the courts of the State, whose regular government was superseded, and whose laws were tolerated from motives of convenience, were without jurisdiction to deal with him."

The Supreme Court of the United States accordingly reversed the judgment of the Supreme Court of Tennessee; but it did not allow the criminal to escape. It added to its reversal the following direction :

"But as the defendant was guilty of murder, as clearly appears not only by the evidence in the record in this case, but in the record of the proceedings of the court-martial, a murder committed, too, under circum-

stances of great atrocity, and as he was convicted of the crime by that
court and sentenced to death, and it appears by his plea that said judgment was duly approved and still remains without any action having
been taken upon it, he may be delivered up to the military authorities
of the United States, to be dealt with as required by law."

The prisoner was soon afterwards turned over to the
military authorities of the United States, when his punishment was commuted to imprisonment for life at hard labor,
and he is now thus imprisoned.

In the case of Dow vs. Johnson, at the October term of
1879, the question came before the court whether an officer
of the army of the United States, whilst in service during
the late war in the enemy's country, was liable to a civil
action in the courts of that country for injuries resulting
from acts of war ordered by him in his military character;
and it was held that he was not thus liable, and that he
could not be called upon to justify or explain his military
conduct in a civil tribunal upon any allegation of the injured party that the acts complained of were not justified
by the necessities of war. He was responsible only to his
own government, and only by its laws, administered by its
authority, could he be called to account.

The case was one which excited a good deal of interest,
and the question presented was elaborately discussed. The
defendant, Neal Dow, was a brigadier-general in the army
of the United States, and in 1862 and 1863 was stationed
in Louisiana in command of Forts Jackson and St. Philip,
on the Mississippi River, below New Orleans. These
forts surrendered to the forces of the United States in
April, 1862. The fleet under Admiral Farragut had passed
them and reached New Orleans on the 25th of the month,
and soon afterwards the city was occupied by the forces of
the United States under General Butler. On taking possession of the city, the General issued a proclamation,
bearing date on the 1st of May, 1862, in which, among
other things, he declared that until the restoration of the

authority of the United States the city would be governed
by martial law; that all disorders, disturbances of the peace,
and crimes of an aggravated nature, interfering with the
forces or laws of the United States, would " be referred to
a military court for trial and punishment ;" that other
misdemeanors would be subject to the municipal authority
if it desired to act ; and that civil causes between parties
would " be referred to the ordinary tribunals." Under
this proclamation, the Sixth District Court of the City and
Parish of New Orleans was allowed to continue in existence, the judge having taken the oath of allegiance to the
United States.

In January, 1863, General Dow was sued in that court
by one Johnson, who set forth in his petition that he was
a citizen of New York, and for several years had been the
owner of a plantation and slaves in Louisiana, on the Mississippi River, about forty-three miles from New Orleans;
that on the sixth of September, 1862, during his temporary absence, the steamer Avery, in charge of Captain
Snell, of Company B, of the Thirteenth Maine Regiment,
with a force under his command, had stopped at the plantation, and taken from it twenty-five hogsheads of sugar;
and that said force had plundered the dwelling-house of
the plantation and carried off a silver pitcher, half a dozen
silver knives, and other table ware, the private property
of the plaintiff, the whole property taken amounting in
value to $1,611.29; that these acts of Captain Snell and
of the officers and soldiers under his command, which the
petition characterized as " illegal, wanton, oppressive, and
unjustifiable," were perpetrated under a verbal and secret
order of Brigadier-General Neal Dow, then in the service
of the United States, and in command of Forts Jackson
and St. Philip, who, by his secret orders, which the petition declared were " unauthorized by his superiors, or by
any provision of martial law, or by any requirements of
necessity growing out of a state of war," wantonly abused
his power and inflicted upon the plaintiff the wrongs of

8

which he complained; and, therefore, he prayed judgment against the General for the value of the property.

To this suit General Dow, though personally served with citation, made no appearance. He may have thought, as the Supreme Court in its opinion suggests, that during the existence of the war, in a district where insurrection had recently been suppressed, and was only kept from breaking out again by the presence of the armed forces of the United States, he was not called upon by any rule of law to answer to a civil tribunal for his military orders, and satisfy it that they were authorized by his superiors, or by the necessities growing out of a state of war. He may have supposed that for his military conduct he was responsible only to his military superiors and the government whose officer he was.

Be that as it may, or what ever other reason he may have had, he made no response to the petition ; he was therefore defaulted. The Sixth District Court of the Parish of New Orleans did not seem, as the Supreme Court observes, to consider that it was at all inconsistent with his duty, as an officer in the army of the United States, to leave his post at the forts, which guarded the passage of the Mississippi, nearly a hundred miles distant, and attend upon its summons to justify his military orders, or seek counsel and procure evidence for his defence. Nor did it appear to have occurred to the court that if jurisdiction over him was recognized there might spring up such a multitude of suits as to keep the officers of the army stationed in its district so busy that they would have little time to look after the enemy and guard against his attacks. The default of the General being entered, testimony was received showing that the articles mentioned were seized by a military detachment sent by him and removed from the plantation, and that their value amounted to $1,454.81. Judgment was thereupon entered in favor of the plaintiff for that sum with interest and costs. It bore date April 9th, 1863.

Upon this judgment an action was brought in the Circuit Court of the United States for the District of Maine. The declaration stated the recovery of the judgment mentioned and made profert of an authenticated copy. To it the defendant pleaded the general issue, *nul tiel* record, and certain special pleas, the object of which was to show that the district court had no jurisdiction to render the judgment in question, for the reason that at the time its district was a part of the country in insurrection against the government of the United States, and making war against it, and was held in subjection by its armed forces ; that the defendant was then a brigadier-general in the military service of the United States, commissioned by the President, and acting in that State under his orders and the articles of war; and was authorized by the general order of the President of July 22d, 1862, to seize and use any property, real or personal, which might be necessary or convenient for his command as supplies, or for other military purposes; that by his order the troops under his command seized from the plaintiff then a citizen of that State, certain chattels necessary and convenient for supplies for the army of the United States, and other military purposes ; and that for that seizure the action was brought in the Sixth District Court of New Orleans against him, in which the judgment in question was rendered ; that the general government had deprived that court of all jurisdiction, except such as was conferred by the commanding general, and that no jurisdiction over persons in the military service of the United States for acts performed in the line of their duty was ever thus conferred upon it.

Upon these pleas the main question stated above was discussed. In deciding it, Judge Field, who gave the opinion of the court, after disposing of a preliminary objection, said as follows :

"This brings us to the consideration of the main question involved, which we do not regard as at all difficult of solution, when reference is had to the character of the late war. The war, though not between independent nations, but between different portions of the same nation, was accompanied by the general incidents of an international war. It was waged between people occupying different territories, separated from each other by well-defined lines. It attained proportions seldom reached in the wars of modern nations. Armies of greater magnitude and more formidable in their equipments than any known in the present century were put into the field by the contending parties. The insurgent States united in an organization known as the Confederate States, by which they acted through a central authority guiding their military movements; and to them belligerent rights were accorded by the federal government. This was shown in the treatment of captives as prisoners of war, the exchange of prisoners, the release of officers on parole, and in numerous arrangements to mitigate as far as possible the inevitable sufferings and miseries attending the conflict. The people of the loyal States on the one hand, and the people of the Confederate States on the other, thus became enemies to each other, and were liable to be dealt with as such without reference to their individual opinions and dispositions. Commercial intercourse and correspondence between them were prohibited, as well by express enactments of Congress as by the accepted doctrines of public law. The enforcement of contracts previously made between them was suspended, partnerships were dissolved, and the courts of each belligerent were closed to the citizens of the other, and its territory was to the other enemies' country. When, therefore, our armies marched into the country which acknowledged the authority of the Confederate government, that is, into the enemy's country, their officers and soldiers were not subject to its laws, nor amenable to its tribunals for their acts. They were subject only to their own government, and only by its laws, administered by its authority, could they be called to account. As was observed in the recent case of Coleman vs. Tennessee, it is well settled that a foreign army, permitted to march through a friendly country, or to be stationed in it by authority of its sovereign or government, is exempt from its civil and criminal jurisdiction. The law was so stated in the celebrated case of The Exchange, reported in the seventh of Cranch. Much more must this exemption prevail where a hostile army invades an enemy's country. There would be something singularly absurd in permitting an officer or soldier of an invading army to be tried by his enemy, whose country it had invaded. The same reasons for his exemption from criminal prosecution apply to civil proceedings. There would be as much incongruity, and as little likelihood of freedom from the irritations of the war, in civil as in criminal proceedings prosecuted during its continuance. In both instances, from the very nature of war, the tribunals of the enemy must be without jurisdiction to sit in judgment upon the military conduct of the officers and soldiers of the invading army. It is difficult to reason upon a proposition so manifest; its correctness is evident upon its bare announcement, and no additional force can be given to it by any amount of statement as to the proper conduct of war. It is manifest that if officers or soldiers of the army could be required to leave their posts and troops, upon the summons of every local tribunal, on pain of a judgment by default against them, which at the termination of hostilities could be enforced by suit in their own States, the efficiency of the army as a hostile force would be utterly destroyed. Nor can it make any difference with what denunciatory epithets the complaining party may characterize their conduct. If such epithets could confer jurisdiction they would always be supplied in every variety of form. An inhabitant of a bombarded city would have little hesitation in declaring the bombardment unnecessary and cruel. Would it be pretended that he could call the commanding general, who ordered it, before a local tribunal to show its necessity or be mulcted in damages? The owner of supplies seized, or property destroyed, would have no difficulty, as human nature is constituted, in believing and affirming that the seizure and destruction were wanton and needless. All this is too plain for discussion and will be readily admitted.

"Nor is the position of the invading belligerent affected, or his relation to the local tribunals changed, by his temporary occupation and domination of any portion of the enemy's country. As a necessary consequence of such occupation and domination, the political relations of its people to their former government are, for the time, severed. But for their protection and benefit, and the protection and benefit of others not in the military service; or, in other words, in order that the ordinary pursuits and business of society may not be unnecessarily deranged, the municipal laws, that is, such as affect private rights of persons and property, and provide for the punishment of crime, are generally allowed to continue in force, and to be administered by the ordinary tribunals as they were administered before the occupation. They are considered as continuing unless suspended or superseded by the occupying belligerent. But their continued enforcement is not for the protection or control of the army or its officers or soldiers. These remain subject to the laws of war, and are responsible for their conduct only to their own government, and the tribunals by which those laws are administered. If guilty of wanton cruelty to persons, or of unnecessary spoliation of property, or of other acts not authorized by the laws of war, they may be tried and punished by the military tribunals. They are amenable to no other tribunal, except that of public opinion, which, it is to be hoped, will always brand with infamy all who authorize or sanction acts of cruelty and oppression.

"If, now, we apply the views thus expressed to the case at bar, there will be no difficulty in disposing of it. The condition of New Orleans and of the district connected with it, at the time of the seizure of the property of the plaintiff and the entry of the judgment against Dow, was not that of a country restored to its normal relations to the Union, by the fact that they had been captured by our forces, and were held in subjection. A feeling of intense hostility against the government of the Union prevailed as before with the people, which was ready to break out into insurrection upon the appearance of the enemy in force, or upon the withdrawal of our troops. The country was under martial law; and its armed occupation gave no jurisdiction to the civil tribunals over the officers and soldiers of the occupying army. They were not to be harassed and mulcted at the complaint of any person aggrieved by their action. The jurisdiction which the district court was authorized to exercise over civil cases between parties, by the proclamation of General Butler, did not extend to cases against them. The third special plea alleges that the court was deprived by the general government of all jurisdiction except such as was conferred by the commanding general, and that no jurisdiction over persons in the military service for acts performed in the line of their duty was ever thus conferred upon it. It was not for their control in any way, or the settlement of complaints against them, that the court was allowed to continue in existence. It was, as already stated, for the protection and benefit of the inhabitants of the conquered country and others there not engaged in the military service.

"If private property there was taken by an officer or a soldier of the occupying army, acting in his military character, when, by the laws of war, or the proclamation of the commanding general, it should have been exempt from seizure, the owner could have complained to that commander, who might have ordered restitution, or sent the offending party before a military tribunal, as circumstances might have required, or he could have had recourse to the government for redress. But there could be no doubt of the right of the army to appropriate any property there, although belonging to private individuals, which was necessary for its support or convenient for its use. This was a belligerent right, which was not extinguished by the occupation of the country, although the necessity for its exercise was thereby lessened. However exempt from seizure on other grounds private property there may have been, it was always subject to be appropriated when required by the necessities or convenience of the army, though the owner of property taken in such case may have had a just claim against the government for indemnity.———

"This doctrine of non-liability to the tribunals of the invaded country for acts of warfare is as applicable to members of the Confederate army when in Pennsylvania, as to members of the National army when in the insurgent States. The officers or soldiers of neither army could be called to account civilly or criminally in those tribunals for such acts, whether those acts resulted in the destruction of property or the destruction of life; nor could they be required by those tribunals to explain or justify their conduct upon any averment of the injured party that the acts complained of were unauthorized by the necessities of war. It follows that, in our judgment, the District Court of New Orleans was without jurisdiction to render the judgment in question, and the special pleas in this case constituted a perfect answer to the declaration.—(See People vs. Coleman, 97 U. S., 509; Ford vs. Surget, Id., 605; also LeCaux vs. Eden, 2 Doug., 594; Lamar vs. Browne, 92 U. S., 197, and Coolidge vs. Guthrie, 2 Amer. Law. Reg., N. S., 22.)

"We fully agree with the presiding justice of the circuit court in the doctrine that the military should always be kept in subjection to the laws of the country to which it belongs, and that he is no friend to the Republic who advocates the contrary. The established principle of every free people is, that the law shall alone govern; and to it the military must always yield. We do not controvert the doctrine of Mitchell vs. Harmony; on the contrary, we approve it. But it has no application to the case at bar. The trading for which the seizure was there made had been permitted by the Executive Department of our government. The question here is, what is the law which governs an army invading an enemy's country? It is not the civil law of the invaded country; it is not the civil law of the conquering country; it is military law—the law of war—and its supremacy for the protection of the officers and soldiers of the army, when in service in the field in the enemy's country, is as essential to the efficiency of the army as the supremacy of the civil law at home, and in time of peace, is essential to the preservation of liberty."

PROTECTION OF SEALED MATTER IN THE MAIL FROM INSPECTION BY OFFICIALS OF THE POST-OFFICE.

How far matter in the mail can be protected from inspection by officials of the post-office, and at the same time the mail prevented from being the vehicle of circulating publications having a tendency to corrupt the public morals, has been for many years the subject of frequent discussion and of much conflict of opinion. It was the occasion of an earnest debate in the Senate of the United States in 1836. President Jackson, in his annual message of the previous year, had referred to the attempted circulation through the mail of inflammatory appeals, addressed to the passions of the slaves, in prints, and in various publications, tending to stimulate them to insurrection, and suggested to Congress the propriety of passing a law prohibiting, under severe penalties, such circulation of "incendiary publications" in the Southern States. In the Senate, that portion of the message was referred to a select committee, of which Mr. Calhoun was chairman; and he made an elaborate report on the subject, in which he contended that it belonged to the States, and not to Congress, to determine what is and what is not calculated to disturb their security, and that to hold otherwise would be fatal to the States; for if Congress might determine what papers were incendiary, and as such prohibit their circulation through the mail, it might also determine what were not incendiary and enforce their circulation. Whilst, therefore, condemning in the strongest terms the circulation of the publications, he insisted that Congress had not the power to pass a law prohibiting their transmission through the mail, on the ground that it would abridge the liberty of the press. " To understand," he said, " more fully the extent of the control which the right of prohibiting circulation through the mail would give to the government over the press, it must be borne in mind that the power of Congress over the post-office and the mail is an exclusive power. It must also be remembered that Congress, in the exercise of this power, may declare any road or navigable water to be a post-road; and that, by the act of 1825, it is provided ' that no stage, or other vehicle which regularly performs trips on a post-road, or on a road parallel to it, shall carry letters.' The same provision extends to packets, boats, or other vessels on navigable waters. Like provision may be extended to newspapers and pamphlets, which, if it be admitted that Congress has the right to discriminate in reference to their character, what paper shall or what shall not be transmitted by the mail, would subject the freedom of the press, on all subjects, political, moral, and religious, completely to its will and pleasure. It would, in fact, in some respects, more effectually control the freedom of the press than any sedition law, however severe its penalties." Mr. Calhoun, at the same time, contended that when a State had pronounced certain publications to be dangerous to its peace and prohibited their circulation, it was the duty of Congress to respect its laws and co-operate in their enforcement; and whilst, therefore, Congress could not prohibit the transmission of the incendiary documents through the mails, it could prevent their delivery by the postmasters in the States where their circulation was forbidden. In the discussion upon the bill reported by him, similar views against the power of Congress were expressed by other Senators, who did not concur in the opinion that the delivery of papers could be prevented when their transmission was permitted.

The question thus presented came before the Supreme Court of the United States at the October term of 1877, in Ex-parte Jackson. A section of the Revised Statutes provided that " no letter or circular concerning lotteries, so-called gift concerts, or other similar enterprises offering prizes," should be carried in the mail, and declared that any person knowingly depositing anything in the mail to be conveyed in violation of this section should be punished by a fine of from one to five hundred dollars, with costs of prosecution. Under this section one Jackson was indicted in the Circuit Court of the United States for the Southern District of New York, for depositing in the mail at New York, to be conveyed to another person, a circular concerning a lottery offering prizes. Upon being arraigned he stood mute, refusing to plead, and thereupon a plea of not guilty was entered in his behalf by order of the court. He was subsequently tried, convicted, and sentenced to pay a fine of one hundred dollars, with the costs of the prosecution, and to be committed to the county jail until the fine and costs were paid. Upon his commitment he presented to the Supreme Court a petition, alleging, among other things, that he was illegally restrained of his liberty, as the court had no jurisdiction to punish for the matters charged, because the act of Congress was unconstitutional and void. He therefore prayed for a writ of habeas corpus to be directed to the marshal to bring him before the court, and a writ of certiorari to be directed to the clerk of the circuit court to send up the record of his conviction, that the court might inquire into the cause and legality of his imprisonment. Accompanying the petition, as exhibits, were copies of the indictment and of the record of conviction. The court, instead of ordering that the writs issue at once, entered a rule, the counsel of the petitioner consenting thereto, that cause be shown, on a day designated, why the writs should not issue as prayed, and that a copy of the rule be served on the Attorney-General of the United States, the marshal of the Southern District of New York, and the clerk of the Circuit Court. On the return day the validity of the act was argued. The court decided the act to be valid and refused the writs, drawing a distinction, in the right of inspection by officials of the post-office, between sealed matter and unsealed matter, and holding that sealed matter in the mail is equally protected from unreasonable search as papers in one's household. In giving the opinion of the court, Judge Field said as follows :

"The power vested in Congress 'to establish post-roads and post-offices' has been practically construed, since the foundation of the government, to authorize not merely the designation of the routes over which the mail shall be carried, and the offices where letters and other documents shall be received to be distributed or forwarded, but the carriage of the mail, and all measures necessary to secure its safe and speedy transit, and the prompt delivery of its contents. The validity of legislation prescribing what should be carried, and its weight and form, and the charges to which it should be subjected, has never been questioned. What should be mailable has varied at different times, changing with the facility of transportation over the post-roads. At one time only letters, newspapers, magazines, pamphlets, and other printed matter, not exceeding eight ounces in weight, were carried ; afterwards books were added to the list ; and now small packages of merchandise, not exceeding a prescribed weight, as well as books and printed matter of all kinds, are transported in the mail. The power possessed by Congress embraces the regulation of the entire postal system of the country. The right to designate what shall be carried necessarily involves the right to determine what shall be excluded. The difficulty attending the subject arises, not from the want of power in Congress to prescribe regulations as to what shall constitute mail matter, but from the necessity of enforcing them consistently with rights reserved to the people, of far greater importance than the transportation of the mail. In their enforcement a distinction is to be made between different kinds of mail matter ; between what is intended to be kept free from inspection, such as letters and sealed packages subject to letter postage ; and what is open to inspection, such as newspapers, magazines, pamphlets, and other printed matter, purposely left in a condition to be examined. Letters and sealed packages of this kind in the mail are as fully guarded from examination and inspection, except as to their outward form and weight, as if they were retained by the parties forwarding them in their own domiciles. The constitutional guaranty of the right of the people to be secure in their papers against unreasonable searches and seizures extends to their papers, thus closed against inspection, wherever they may be. Whilst in the mail they can only be opened and examined under like warrant, issued upon similar oath or affirmation, particularly describing the thing to be seized, as is required when papers are subjected to search in one's own household. No law of Congress can place in the hands of officials connected with the postal service any authority to invade the secrecy of letters and such sealed packages in the mail; and all regulations adopted as to mail matter of this kind must be in subordination to the great principle embodied in the fourth amendment of the Constitution.

"Nor can any regulation be enforced against the transportation of printed matter in the mail, which is open to examination, so as to interfere in any manner with the freedom of the press. Liberty of circulating is as essential to that freedom as liberty of publishing; indeed, without the circulation the publication would be of little value. If, therefore, printed matter be excluded from the mails, its transportation in any other way cannot be forbidden by Congress."

Referring to the views expressed by Mr. Calhoun and other Senators in the Senate in 1836, stated above, the Judge said as follows :

" It is evident that they were founded upon the assumption that it was competent for Congress to prohibit the transportation of newspapers and pamphlets over postal routes in any other way than by mail; and of course it would follow that if, with such a prohibition, the transportation in the mail could also be forbidden, the circulation of the documents would be destroyed and a fatal blow given to the freedom of the press. But we do not think that Congress possesses the power to prevent the transportation in other ways, as merchandise, of matter which it excludes from the mails. To give efficiency to its regulations and prevent rival postal systems, it may perhaps prohibit the carriage by others for hire over postal routes of articles which legitimately constitute mail matter, in the sense in which those terms were used when the Constitution was adopted—consisting of letters, and of newspapers and pamphlets when not sent as merchandise—but further than this its power of prohibition cannot extend.

" Whilst regulations excluding matter from the mail cannot be enforced in a way which would require or permit an examination into letters or sealed packages subject to letter postage, without warrant issued upon oath or affirmation, in the search for prohibited matter, they may be enforced upon competent evidence of their violation obtained in other ways, as from the parties receiving the letters or packages, or from agents de-

positing them in the post-office, or others cognizant of the facts. And as
to objectionable printed matter, which is open to examination, the regulations may be enforced in a similar way, by the imposition of penalties
for their violation through the courts; and in some cases, by the direct
action of the officers of the postal service. In many instances those officers can act upon their own inspection, and from the nature of the case
must act without other proof, as where the postage is not prepaid, or
where there is an excess of weight over the amount prescribed, or where
the object is exposed and shows unmistakably that it is prohibited, as in
the case of an obscene picture or print. In such cases, no difficulty
arises, and no principle is violated, in excluding the prohibited articles
or refusing to forward them. The evidence respecting them is seen by
every one and is in its nature conclusive."

THE FOURTEENTH AMENDMENT AND THE SLAUGHTER-HOUSE
CASES.—EQUALITY OF RIGHT IN THE PURSUIT OF ANY LAW-
FUL TRADE OR AVOCATION MAINTAINED.

The institution of slavery, with the irritations and reproaches to which it gave rise between the States, where
it existed, and the free States, was the cause of the civil
war. Its extinction was the natural consequence of the
success of the forces of the Union. The Constitutional
amendment, which destroyed it, declared that "neither
slavery nor involuntary servitude, except as a punishment
for crime, whereof the party shall have been duly convicted, shall exist within the United States or any place
subject to their jurisdiction." It thus not only abolished
the existing institution, but forever prohibits its future establishment. And by its comprehensive language it embraces not merely slavery of the African race, as it previously existed, but involuntary servitude in any form—
peonage, villanage, serfage, and all other modes by which
man can be subjected to compulsory labor for the pleasure,
profit, or caprice of others. It was intended to make every
one within the jurisdiction of the United States a free
man, and as such to allow him to pursue his happiness by
the ordinary avocations of life upon the same terms and
conditions as others.

To give effect to this purpose of the amendment, Congress, soon after its adoption, passed the civil rights act. The amendment was ratified on the 18th of December 1865, that is, the official proclamation of its ratification was made on that day. In April of the following year the civil rights act was passed. Its first section is as follows: "*Be it enacted, &c.*, That all persons born in the United States and not subject to any foreign power, excluding Indians not taxed, are hereby declared to be citizens of the United States, and such citizens, of every race and color, without regard to any previous condition of slavery or involuntary servitude, except as a punishment for crime, whereof the party shall have been duly convicted, shall have the same right, in every State and Territory in the United States, to make and enforce contracts, to sue, be parties, and give evidence, to inherit, purchase, lease, sell, hold, and convey real and personal property, and to full and equal benefit of all laws and proceedings for the security of person and property, as is enjoyed by white citizens, and shall be subject to like punishment, pains, and penalties, and to none other, any law, statute, ordinance, regulation, or custom to the contrary notwithstanding."

The other sections of the act are designed to secure the rights thus declared.[*]

The bill for this act was earnestly discussed in Congress and its validity was violently assailed. On the one hand it was contended that the amendment was only designed to do way with slavery of the colored race, and, except as it affected that institution, it left all the powers of the State untouched, with a right in its legislation to discriminate against persons of that race and others. On the other hand it was insisted that the amendment was intended to secure to all persons equality of civil rights. Senator Trumbull drew the bill and introduced it into the Senate, and in opening the discussion upon it in that body stated

---

[*] 14 Statutes-at-Large, 27.

that the object of the measure was to give effect to the declaration of the amendment, observing that there was very little importance in the general declaration of abstract truths and principles unless they could be carried into effect;—unless the persons who were to be affected by them had some means of availing themselves of their benefits; that the first section of the bill proposed declared what were the rights of all persons; that the other sections contained the necessary machinery to give effect to them; and that if Congress had not authority to give practical effect to the great declaration that slavery shall not exist in the United States, by a bill of that kind, nothing would be accomplished by the adoption of the constitutional amendment.

The Senator then referred to the clause of the Constitution which declares that " the citizens of each State shall be entitled to all privileges and immunities of citizens in the several States," and asked, " What rights are secured to the citizens of each State under that provision ? " And he answered, " Such fundamental rights as belong to every free person; " citing from Story the statement that the intention of this clause was to confer on citizens, if one may so say, a general citizenship, and to communicate all the privileges and immunities which the citizens of the same State would be entitled to under the like circumstances. He also quoted with special approval the language of Judge Washington, in Corfield vs. Coryell, that by the expression privileges and immunities of citizens, as here used, were meant those privileges and immunities which are in their nature fundamental, and belong of right to the citizens of all free governments. He added that the people of the insurgent States had not regarded the colored race as citizens, and on that principle many of their laws making discriminations between the whites and the colored people were based, and said : " But it is competent for Congress to declare, under the Constitution of the United States, who are citizens. If there were any question about it, it would be settled by the passage of a law declaring all persons born in the United States to be citizens thereof. That this bill proposes to do. Then they will be entitled to the rights of citizens. And what are they ? The great fundamental rights set forth in this bill: the right to acquire property, the right to go and come at pleasure, the right to enforce rights in the courts, to make contracts, and to inherit and dispose of property. These are the very rights that are set forth in this bill as appertaining to every freeman."

Other Senators expressed similar views in advocating the measure. The bill was passed in both Houses of Congress by a large majority, but it was vetoed by the President; it was then passed over the veto by the required two-thirds vote. But notwithstanding its passage by a large majority of both Houses, and over the veto of the President, grave doubts of its constitutionality were entertained by men of distinguished ability, many of whom were not hostile to its object. In some of the State courts also its validity was denied; and in others, able judges dissented from judgments recognizing its obligation. Complaints also were made that, notwithstanding the amendment abolishing slavery and involuntary servitude, except for crime, the freedmen in some of the insurrectionary States were subjected to burdens and disabilities in the acquisition and enjoyment of property and in the pursuit of happiness, which to a great extent destroyed the value of their freedom. Hostile sentiments were also alleged to exist towards citizens of the North seeking business or residence among them, and towards their own citizens who adhered to the government of the Union during the war. No doubt there was much exaggeration in the complaints of these things, but they were nevertheless believed to be well founded. To remove the cause of them, and to obviate at the same time the grounds of objection to the validity of the civil rights act, or to similar legislation, and prevent hostile and discriminating legislation by any State against citizens of the United States, and thus secure to all persons within the jurisdiction of every State the equal protection of its laws, the fourteenth amendment was brought forward and adopted. This purpose was avowed in all the discussions of the measure in both Houses of Congress. A very instructive and able article upon this subject, by William L. Royall, Esq., of Richmond, Va., is found in the number of the Southern Law Review for October and November of 1878, in which he shows by citations from the remarks of every one who participated in the debate, that it was the purpose of its framers and advocates to obviate objections to legislation similar to that contained in the civil rights act.

At the session of Congress following the adoption of the amendment abolishing slavery and involuntary servitude, propositions for further amendments were numerous. All of them were sent to a committee of the two Houses on Reconstruction, consisting of fifteen, of whom Mr. Fessenden was chairman on the part of the Senate, and Mr. Thaddeus Stevens on the part of the House. That committee reported on the 30th of April, 1866, as the result of their deliberations, in the form of a joint resolution, an amendment to the Constitution. As it came from the committee the first section of the proposed amendment was as follows :

" No State shall make or enforce any law which shall abridge the privileges or immunities of citizens of the United States; nor shall any State deprive any person of life, liberty, or property without due process of law, nor deny to any person within its jurisdiction the equal protection of the laws."

The second section provided the basis of representation; the third declared that no person who had voluntarily aided the late insurrection should have the right to vote for representatives in Congress, or for electors for P.esident and Vice-President, until July 4, 1870 ; the fourth prohibited the payment of the Confederate debt; and the fifth provided that Congress should have power to enforce the provisions of the article by appropriate legislation.

The resolution was first brought forward in the House, the Senate awaiting its action. The principal debate was on the third section, which was not thought to be sufficiently punitive. It, however, was adopted without alteration. Mr. Stevens opened the discussion and said :

"The first section prohibits the States from abridging the privileges and immunities of citizens of the United States, or unlawfully depriving them of life, liberty, or property, or of denying to any person within their jurisdiction the 'equal' protection of the laws. I can hardly believe that any person can be found who will not admit that every one of these provisions is just. They are all asserted, in some form or other, in our Declaration or organic law. But the Constitution limits only the action of Congress, and is not a limitation on the States. This amendment supplies that defect, and allows Congress to correct the unjust legislation of the States, so far that the law which operates upon one man shall operate equally upon all."

Mr. Fink, a Democrat, followed Mr. Stevens, and made the point that the first section was, in substance, the civil rights bill which Congress had just passed over the President's veto; and that by voting to so amend the Constitution of the United States as to put the civil rights bill into it was the same thing as to admit that the civil rights bill was unconstitutional.

To this Mr. Garfield replied :

"I am glad to see this first section here, which purposes to hold over every American citizen, without regard to color, the protecting shield of law. The gentleman who has just taken his seat undertakes to show that because we propose to vote for this section we therefore acknowledge that the civil rights bill was unconstitutional. He was anticipated in that objection by the gentleman from Pennsylvania (Mr. Stevens). The civil rights bill is now a part of the law of the land. But every gentleman knows it will cease to be a part of the law whenever the sad moment arrives when that gentleman's party comes into power. It is precisely for that reason that we propose to lift that great and good law above the reach of political strife, beyond the reach of plots and machinations of any party, and fix it in the serene sky, in the eternal firmament of the Constitution, where no storm of passion can shake it, and no cloud can obscure it. For this reason, and not because I believe the civil rights bill unconstitutional, I am glad to see that first section here."

9

Mr. Thayer, a Republican, in the course of his remarks said :

"With regard to the first section of the proposed amendment to the Constitution, it simply brings into the Constitution what is found in the bill of rights of every State of the Union; as I understand it, it is but incorporating in the Constitution of the United States the principle of the civil rights bill which has lately become a law, and that not, as the gentleman from Ohio (Mr. Fink) suggested, because, in the estimation of this House, that law cannot be sustained as constitutional, but in order, as was justly said by the gentleman from Ohio who last addressed the House (Mr. Garfield), that that provision, so necessary for the equal administration of the law, so just in its operation, so necessary for the protection of the fundamental rights of citizenship, shall be forever incorporated in the Constitution of the United States." .

The language of all the other speakers in the House was to the same purport. The first section of the proposed amendment passed the House as it came from the committee, and it thus went to the Senate. The health of Mr. Fessenden, the chairman of the committee of the Senate, disabled him from taking charge of the resolution, and it was entrusted to the custody of Mr. Howard, Senator from Michigan. In his opening speech, explaining the various sections and defining as far as he was able the privileges and immunities of a citizen of the United States, comprising as well those which he had as a citizen of the State as those which he had as a citizen of the United States, he said :

"The great object of the first section of this amendment is, therefore, to restrain the power of the States and compel them at all times to respect their fundamental guarantees."

It is to be observed that the resolution, as reported from the committee and discussed in the House and in the Senate, did not have the clause defining citizenship of the United States. It opened with the provision " No State shall make or enforce any law which shall abridge the privileges and immunities of citizens of the United States," and it is plain that no one who either favored or opposed the amendment understood that in that form it was designed to protect only the rights of citizens of the United

States, and not the rights of citizens of the State. The provision defining citizenship of the United States was offered by the Senator from Michigan, after the resolution had passed the House and been under discussion in the Senate for several days. In the House, Mr. Bingham, of Ohio, had contended that the civil rights bill was unconstitutional, arguing that the rights of citizens which it undertook to protect were left by the Constitution to the protection of the States, and that Congress had no right to legislate on the subject. Attention was also called to the fact that the act made negroes citizens of the United States, whereas the Supreme Court had decided in the Dred Scott case that no person of African descent could become such a citizen. The clause as to citizenship was added to the proposed amendment in order to obviate these objections. No one intimated during the whole debate that its purpose was to qualify in any respect the subsequent general language of the amendment.

There was a perfect unanimity of opinion between Senators and Representatives, Democrats and Republicans, that the purpose of the first section was to incorporate the civil rights bill into the Constitution, or rather to authorize legislation of a similar character and thus obviate the objections that had been made to that bill on account of the supposed limitation of the amendment abolishing slavery and the Dred Scott decision. The Republicans contended for the adoption of the amendment because such was its purpose and would be its effect; the Democrats opposed it for the same reason. All agreed in declaring its purpose; and there was no difference in their understanding of it after the declaration of citizenship was added to the amendment from what it was previously. No one supposed that this addition limited or changed the character of rights which were to be protected.

The amendment, in its present form, passed both Houses of Congress by large majorities, and was ratified by the States on the 28th of July, 1868; that is to say, on that day the proclamation of its ratification was made.

The first cases under this amendment which came before the Supreme Court grew out of an act of the Legislature of the State of Louisiana, entitled "An act to protect the health of the city of New Orleans, to locate the stock-landings and slaughter-houses, and to incorporate 'The Crescent City Live-Stock Landing and Slaughter-House Company,'" which was approved on the 8th of March, 1869, and went into operation the 1st of June following. The act created the corporation mentioned in its title, which was composed of seventeen persons designated by name, and invested them and their successors with the powers usually conferred upon corporations, and certain special and exclusive privileges.

It first declared that it should not be lawful, after the 1st day of June, 1869, to land, keep, or slaughter any animals, or to have, keep, or establish any stock-landing, yards, slaughter-houses, or abattoirs within the city of New Orleans, or the parishes of Orleans, Jefferson, and St. Bernard, except as provided in the act, and imposed a penalty of $250 for each violation of its provisions.

The act then authorized the corporation to establish and erect, within the parish of St. Bernard and the corporate limits of New Orleans, at a designated place, (which was on the river below the occupied portions of the city,) wharves, stables, sheds, yards, and buildings necessary to land, stable, shelter, protect, and preserve all kinds of horses, mules, cattle, and other animals, and provided that animals destined for sale or slaughter in the city of New Orleans or its environs, should be landed at the wharves and yards of this company and be there yarded, sheltered, and protected, if necessary; and that the company should be entitled to certain prescribed fees for the use of its wharves and for each animal landed, and be authorized to detain the animals until the fees were paid, and if not paid within fifteen days to take proceedings for their sale. Every person violating any of these provisions, or landing, yarding, or keeping animals elsewhere was subjected to a fine of $250.

The act then required the corporation to erect a grand slaughter-house of sufficient dimensions to accommodate all butchers, in which five hundred animals might be slaughtered a day, with a sufficient number of sheds and stables for the stock received at the port of New Orleans, and provided that when these buildings were completed and thrown open for use, public notice should be given for thirty days, and within that time all other stock-landings and slaughter-houses within the parishes of Orleans, Jefferson, and St. Bernard were to be closed, and it should no longer be lawful to slaughter animals in them, the meat of which was destined for sale within those parishes.

The act then provided that the company should receive for every animal slaughtered in its buildings certain prescribed fees, besides the head, feet, gore, and entrails of all animals, except of swine.

Other provisions of the act required the inspection of the animals before they were slaughtered. The exclusive privileges mentioned were granted for the period of twenty-five years. The language of the act was that the corporation should " have the *sole and exclusive privilege* of conducting and carrying on the live-stock landing and slaughter-house business, within the limits and privileges granted by the provisions of the act ; " and, after the 1st of June, 1869, should have " *the exclusive privilege* of having landed at their landing places all animals intended for sale or slaughter " in the parishes of Orleans and Jefferson, and " the *exclusive privilege* of having slaughtered" in its slaughter-houses all animals the meat of which was intended for sale in these parishes.

The character of these special privileges will be better understood when the extent of country and of population which they affected are stated. The parish of Orleans contains an area of country of 150 square miles ; the parish of Jefferson, 384 square miles; and the parish of St. Bernard, 620 square miles. The three parishes together contain an area of 1,154 square miles, and they had a population of between two and three hundred thousand people.

Previous to the passage of the act there were more than a thousand persons in the territory mentioned who supported themselves and their families by the business of procuring, preparing, and selling animal food, but by the act in question they were all deprived of the business in which they were thus engaged, or subjected to onerous conditions in its prosecution.

Three cases were brought involving the validity of this legislation. The first was brought by an association of butchers to prevent the assertion and enforcement of the privileges. One was brought by the attorney-general of the State to protect the corporation in the enjoyment of those privileges, and to prevent an association of stock-dealers and butchers from acquiring a tract of land in the same district with the corporation, upon which to erect suitable buildings for receiving, keeping, and slaughtering cattle and preparing animal food for market. The third case was brought by the corporation itself to restrain the defendants from carrying on a business similar to its own, in violation of its alleged exclusive privileges.

The substance of the averments of the parties complaining of this legislation was, that prior to its adoption they were engaged in the lawful and necessary business of procuring and bringing to the parishes mentioned animals suitable for human food, and in preparing such food for market; that in the prosecution of their business they had provided in those parishes suitable establishments for landing, sheltering, keeping, and slaughtering cattle, and the sale of meat; that with their association about four hundred persons were connected, and that in the parishes named about a thousand persons were engaged in procuring, preparing, and selling animal food. And they complained that the business of landing, yarding, and keeping, within the parishes named, cattle intended for sale or slaughter, which was lawful for them to pursue before the 1st day of June, 1869, was made by that act unlawful for any one except the corporation named; and that the business of slaughtering cattle and preparing animal food for market, which it was lawful for them to pursue in those parishes before that day, was made by that act unlawful for them to pursue afterwards, except in the buildings of the company, and upon payment of certain prescribed fees, and a surrender of a valuable portion of each animal slaughtered. And they contended that the lawful business of landing, yarding, sheltering, and keeping cattle intended for sale or slaughter, which they, in common with every individual in the community of the three parishes, had a right to follow, could not be thus taken from them and given over for a period of twenty-five years for the sole and exclusive enjoyment of a corporation of seventeen persons, or of anybody else. And they also contended that the lawful and necessary business of slaughtering cattle and preparing animal food for market, which they and all other individuals had a right to follow, could not be thus restricted, within this territory of 1,154 square miles, to the buildings of this corporation, or be subjected to tribute for the emolument of that body.

The Supreme Court of the State of Louisiana held the act constitutional and gave judgment in all the cases for the protection of the exclusive privileges of the corporation. The cases were then brought to the Supreme Court of the United States and were there twice argued with great ability; Judge Campbell, formerly a member of the court, and Mr. Fellowes appearing against the act; and Senator Carpenter and Mr. Durant for the corporation. The exclusive privileges were assailed as being in conflict with the 13th amendment, and also with the inhibition of the 14th amendment, declaring that " No State shall make or enforce any law which shall abridge the privileges or immunities of citizens of the United States."

The Supreme Court, by a vote of five of its members against four, affirmed the judgment of the Louisiana court, holding that the legislation of Louisiana gave no special privileges which the State could not grant, and that the fourteenth amendment only inhibited an invasion by the States of the rights of citizens of the United States as distinguished from those of citizens of the State. Judges Clifford, Davis, Strong, Miller, and Hunt composed the majority. Chief Justice Chase and Judges Swayne, Field, and Bradley dissented from this view. Judge Miller wrote the opinion of the majority. Judges Field, Bradley, and Swayne each wrote a dissenting opinion. The Chief Justice concurred with Judge Field, as did also Judges Swayne and Bradley, although they each wrote a separate opinion.

Both the majority and minority not only considered the claim made that the legislation of Louisiana was to be regarded as the exercise of the police power of the State; but they gave an extended examination to the inhibition mentioned contained in the fourteenth amendment.

As to the police power, the majority were of opinion that the legislation of Louisiana was passed in its legitimate exercise, and made reference to the necessity of having the landing of live-stock in large droves from steamboats on the bank of the river and from railroad trains limited to particular places, so as to secure the safety and comfort of the people of the city; and observed that it could not be "injurious to the general community that while the duty of making ample preparation for this is imposed upon a few men, or a corporation, they should, to enable them to do it successfully, have the exclusive right of providing such landing places, and receiving a fair compensation for the service."

And as to the slaughter-house privilege, they said, speaking through Judge Miller:

"It is not, and cannot be successfully controverted, that it is both the right and the duty of the legislative body—the supreme power of the State or municipality—to prescribe and determine the localities where the business of slaughtering for a great city may be conducted. To do this effectively it is indispensable that all persons who slaughter animals for food shall do it in those places *and no where else.* The statute under consideration defines these localities and forbids slaughtering in any other. It does not, as has been asserted, prevent the butcher from doing his own slaughtering. On the contrary, the Slaughter-House Company is required, under a heavy penalty, to permit any person who wishes to do so, to slaughter in their houses, and they are bound to make ample provision for the convenience of all the slaughtering for the entire city. The butcher, then, is still permitted to slaughter, to prepare, and to sell his own meats; but he is required to slaughter at a specified place and to pay a reasonable compensation for the use of the accommodations furnished him at that place.

"The wisdom of the monopoly granted by the legislature may be open to question, but it is difficult to see a justification for the assertion that the butchers are deprived of the right to labor in their occupation, or the people of their daily service in preparing food, or how this statute, with the duties and guards imposed upon the company, can be said to destroy the business of the butcher, or seriously interfere with its pursuit. The power here exercised by the Legislature of Louisiana is, in its essential nature, one which has been, up to the present period in the constitutional history of this country, always conceded to belong to the States, however it may *now* be questioned in some of its details."

He then cites from Kent and Shaw as to the extent of that power, and continues :

"This power is, and must be, from its very nature, incapable of any very exact definition or limitation. Upon it depends the security of social order, the life and health of the citizen, the comfort of an existence in a thickly populated community, the enjoyment of private and social life, and the beneficial use of property. 'It extends,' says another eminent judge, 'to the protection of the lives, limbs, health, comfort, and quiet of all persons, and the protection of all property within the State; . . . and persons and property are subjected to all kinds of restraints and burdens in order to secure the general comfort, health, and prosperity of the State. Of the perfect right of the legislature to do this no question ever was, or, upon acknowledged general principles, ever can be made, so far as natural persons are concerned.'"

To this proposition the minority of the court replied, speaking through Judge Field :

"That power [the police power of the State] undoubtedly extends to all regulations affecting the health, good order, morals, peace, and safety of society, and is exercised on a great variety of subjects, and in almost numberless ways. All sorts of restrictions and burdens are imposed under it, and when these are not in conflict with any constitutional prohibitions or fundamental principles, they cannot be successfully assailed in a judicial tribunal. With this power of the State and its legitimate exercise I shall not differ from the majority of the court. But under the pretence of prescribing a police regulation the State cannot be permitted to encroach upon any of the just rights of the citizen, which the Constitution intended to secure against abridgment.

"In the law in question there are only two provisions which can properly be called police regulations—the one which requires the landing and slaughtering of animals below the city of New Orleans, and the other which requires the inspection of the animals before they are slaughtered. When these requirements are complied with the sanitary purposes of the act are accomplished. In all other particulars the act is a mere grant to a corporation created by it of special and exclusive privileges by which the health of the city is in no way promoted. It is plain that if the corporation can, without endangering the health of the public, carry on the business of landing, keeping, and slaughtering cattle within a district below the city embracing an area of over a thousand square miles, it would not endanger the public health if other persons were also permitted to carry on the same business within the same district under similar conditions as to the inspection of the animals. The health of the city might require the removal from its limits and suburbs of all buildings for keeping and slaughtering cattle, but no such object could possibly justify legislation removing such buildings from a large part of the State for the benefit of a single corporation. The pretence of sanitary regulations for the grant of the exclusive privileges is a shallow one, which merits only this passing notice. ———

"The act of Louisiana presents the naked case, unaccompanied by any public considerations, where a right to pursue a lawful and necessary calling, previously enjoyed by every citizen, and in connection with which a thousand persons were daily employed, is taken away and vested exclusively for twenty-five years, for an extensive district and a large population, in a single corporation, or its exercise is for that period restricted to the establishments of the corporation, and there allowed only upon onerous conditions.

"If exclusive privileges of this character can be granted to a corporation of seventeen persons, they may, in the discretion of the legislature, be equally granted to a single individual. If they may be granted for twenty-five years they may be equally granted for a century, and in perpetuity. If they may be granted for the landing and keeping of animals intended for sale or slaughter they may be equally granted for the landing and storing of grain and other products of the earth, or for any article of commerce. If they may be granted for structures in which animal food is prepared for market they may be equally granted for structures in which farinaceous or vegetable food is prepared. They may be granted for any of the pursuits of human industry, even in its most simple and common forms. Indeed, upon the theory on which the exclusive privileges granted by the act in question are sustained, there is no monopoly, in the most odious form, which may not be upheld."

The great interest, however, manifested in the opinions of the court, both in that of the majority and in those of the minority, arose from the discussion they contained as to the import and meaning of the inhibition of the fourteenth amendment.

The majority held that the State was authorized to confer the special privileges unless restrained by that amendment. Its first section, the only one which had any bearing upon the question presented, is as follows: "All persons born or naturalized in the United States, and subject to the jurisdiction thereof, are citizens of the United States and of the State wherein they reside. No State shall make or enforce any law which shall abridge the privileges or immunities of citizens of the United States, nor shall any State deprive any person of life, liberty, or property without due process of law, nor deny to any person within its jurisdiction the equal protection of the laws."

The majority of the court in their opinion first give a history of the three amendments adopted since the war, the thirteenth, fourteenth and fifteenth, and state that their pervading purpose was the freedom of the slave race, the security and firm establishment of their freedom, and the protection of the newly-made freeman and citizen from the oppressions of those who had formerly exercised unlimited dominion over them, and that in any fair and just construction of any section or phrase of the amendments it is necessary to keep this pervading purpose in view. They then take up the fourteenth amendment and observe that it opens with a definition of citizenship, not only of the United States, but of the States, and that it recognizes and establishes a distinction between the two. Their language is as follows:

"Not only may a man be a citizen of the United States without being a citizen of a State, but an important element is necessary to convert the former into the latter. He must reside within the State to make him a citizen of it, but it is only necessary that he should be born or naturalized in the United States to be a citizen of the Union.

" It is quite clear, then, that there is a citizenship of the United States and a citizenship of a State, which are distinct from each other, and which depend upon different characteristics or circumstances in the individual.

" We think this distinction and its explicit recognition in this amendment of great weight in this argument, because the next paragraph of this same section, which is the one mainly relied on by the plaintiffs in error, speaks only of privileges and immunities of citizens of the United States, and does not speak of those of citizens of the several States. The argument, however, in favor of the plaintiffs rests wholly on the assumption that the citizenship is the same, and the privileges and immunities guaranteed by the clause are the same.

"The language is, 'No State shall make or enforce any law which shall abridge the privileges or immunities of citizens of *the United States*.' It is a little remarkable, if this clause was intended as a protection to the citizen of a State against the legislative power of his own State, that the word citizen of the State should be left out when it is so carefully used, and used in contradistinction to citizens of the United States, in the very sentence which precedes it. It is too clear for argument that the change in phraseology was adopted understandingly and with a purpose.

"Of the privileges and immunities of the citizen of the United States, and of the privileges and immunities of the citizen of the State, and what they respectively are we will presently consider; but we wish to state here that it is only the former which are placed by this clause under the protection of the federal Constitution, and that the latter, whatever they may be, are not intended to have any additional protection by this paragraph of the amendment.

"If, then, there is a difference between the privileges and immunities belonging to a citizen of the United States as such, the latter must rest for their security and protection where they have heretofore rested; for they are not embraced by this paragraph of the amendment."

The doctrine advanced in this passage is the special feature of the opinion and has been the occasion of discussion and disagreement among judges and members of the profession throughout the country.

The majority then consider the meaning attached to the terms "privileges and immunities" contained in the amendment and adopt substantially as correct the view expressed by Judge Washington in Corfield vs. Coryell, that they embrace those rights of citizens which are fundamental in their nature, such as belong to citizens of all free governments; and hold that their protection rests with the States and not with the United States. Their language is as follows:

"It would be the vainest show of learning to attempt to prove by citations of authority, that up to the adoption of the recent amendments no claim or pretence was set up that those rights depended on the federal government for their existence or protection, beyond the very few express

limitations which the federal Constitution imposed upon the States—
such, for instance, as the prohibition against *ex post facto* laws, bills of attainder, and laws impairing the obligation of contracts. But with the
exception of these and a few other restrictions, the entire domain of the
privileges and immunities of citizens of the States, as above defined, lay
within the constitutional and legislative power of the States, and without that of the federal government. Was it the purpose of the fourteenth amendment, by the simple declaration that no State should make
or enforce any law which shall abridge the privileges and immunities of
citizens of the United States, to transfer the security and protection of all
the civil rights which we have mentioned, from the States to the federal
government? And where it is declared that Congress shall have the
power to enforce that article, was it intended to bring within the power
of Congress the entire domain of civil rights heretofore belonging exclusively to the States?

" All this and more must follow, if the proposition of the plaintiffs in
error be sound, for not only are these rights subject to the control of Congress, whenever in its discretion any of them are supposed to be abridged
by State legislation, but that body may also pass laws in advance, limiting and restricting the exercise of legislative power by the States, in their
most ordinary and most useful functions, as in its judgment it may think
proper on all such subjects. And still further, such a construction followed by the reversal of the judgments of the Supreme Court of Louisiana
in these cases, would constitute this court a perpetual censor upon all
legislation of the States, on the civil rights of their own citizens, with
authority to nullify such as it did not approve as consistent with those
rights as they existed at the time of the adoption of this amendment."

The passage here given is generally cited as showing
the evil consequences of any other construction than the
one adopted. The majority then refer to such privileges
and immunities of citizens of the United States as they
suppose are intended, when the States are inhibited from
making or enforcing any law abridging them. These are
the right of the citizen to come to the seat of government,
to assert any claim he may have upon that government,
to transact any business he may have with it, to seek its
protection, to share its offices, to engage in administering
its functions, to have free access to its seaports, to demand
the care and protection of that government over his life,
liberty, and property on the high seas, or within the jurisdiction of a foreign government; the right to peaceably
assemble and petition for redress of grievances; the right

to use the navigable waters of the United States, and other similar rights.

To these positions of the majority of the court several objections naturally arise.

In the first place, if the inhibition upon the States does not refer to the fundamental rights of citizens, such as belong to the citizens of all free governments, such as are expressed in the Declaration of Independence as the inalienable rights of men, it is difficult to see what was accomplished by its insertion in the amendment. The privileges and immunities which citizens previously enjoyed under the Constitution and laws of the United States, no State could lawfully interfere with. Any attempted interference with them could have been successfully resisted through the courts. The parties who drafted and advocated the fourteenth amendment thought that they would obtain thereby additional security for the rights of a citizen of the United States, not that they were merely contending for words which could have no efficacy beyond provisions already in force.

In the second place, the construction asserted entirely ignores the avowed purpose of the framers of the amendment, as stated in the discussion of the measure in both Houses of Congress. There was an entire concurrence of views on the part of all persons—Democrats and Republicans, Senators and Representatives—that the object of the amendment was to obviate the objections which had been urged to the validity of the civil rights act, or rather to legislation of a similar character. That act had stated in express terms that citizens of the United States had the right "to make and enforce contracts, to sue, be parties and give evidence, to inherit, purchase, lease, sell, hold, and convey real and personal property, and to full and equal benefit of all the laws and proceedings for the security of person and property." These were rights which, according to the interpretation of the majority, are now dependent for their protection upon the States alone.

Though the debates in Congress cannot be used to qualify the meaning of language, which is not susceptible of misconstruction, they can be resorted to in order to show the general purpose of the framers of legislation, and it is certainly a matter of no slight significance that the purpose of the amendment, as thus shown, is consistent with the obvious meaning of its language. "All persons born or naturalized in the United States, and subject to the jurisdiction thereof, are citizens of the United States and of the State wherein they reside." The citizenship of the United States is the general and primary citizenship which accompanies the individual everywhere. The State citizenship is local and movable at the option of the party by a mere change of his residence. The command upon the States is not to abridge the privileges and immunities of the citizen of the United States, and thus all the privileges and immunities of the citizen, be he of the United States or be he of the State, are secured.

In the third place, the alleged evil consequences of the opposite construction are purely imaginary. The inhibition of the amendment is upon the States, and if only appropriate legislation be adopted for its enforcement, no such interference with their legislation, no such censorship over it as indicated in the opinion, can exist. Legislation to annul the act of a State can only be appropriate so far as it authorizes application to the courts to meet the exigency, and by their action the act which is forbidden will be declared null or its enforcement restrained.

Every inhibition in the amendment every patriot ought to desire to see enforced. Can any one object to the clause forbidding a State to abridge the privileges and immunities of citizens of the United States ; that is, to take away or impair any of their fundamental rights? Can any one find fault with the clause which declares that no State shall deprive any person of life, liberty, or property without due process of law ? Can any one object to the provision which declares that no State shall deny to any person

within its jurisdiction the equal protection of its laws?
Surely not. The amendment does not limit the subjects
upon which the States can legislate ; it only inhibits discriminating and partial enactments favoring some to the
impairment of the rights of others; it simply requires that
every one shall be allowed to pursue his happiness unrestrained except by just, equal, and impartial laws.

The amendment has been the subject of complaint from
the manner in which legislation has attempted to enforce
its prohibitions, not from the prohibitions themselves.
That manner has in most cases been clearly wrong. The
only appropriate manner is that which has been applied
with reference to other prohibitions previously existing in
the Constitution, such as the prohibition against a State
passing a law impairing the obligation of contracts, or a
bill of attainder, or an *ex post facto* law. No machinery is
necessary to annul any legislation in disregard of these
prohibitions, except such as may facilitate proceedings for
that purpose in the courts; and no other legislation can be
appropriate as against the action of a State.

The answers of the dissenting judges to the opinion of
the majority were full, and are generally regarded by the
profession as satisfactory. An extended citation is made
from the one delivered by Judge Field. He considered
the law of Louisiana in the light of the thirteenth and
fourteenth amendments, although he only rested his judgment on the fourteenth.

" That amendment [the thirteenth] prohibits slavery and involuntary
servitude, except as a punishment for crime, but I have not supposed it
was susceptible of a construction which would cover the enactment in
question. I have been so accustomed to regard it as intended to meet
that form of slavery which had previously prevailed in this country, and
to which the recent civil war owed its existence, that I was not prepared,
nor am I yet, to give it the extent and force ascribed by counsel. Still it
is evident that the language of the amendment is not used in a restrictive
sense. It is not confined to African slavery alone. It is general and universal in its application. Slavery of white men as well as of black men
is prohibited, and not merely slavery in the strict sense of the term, but
involuntary servitude in every form.

. " The words 'involuntary servitude' have not been the subject of any judicial or legislative exposition, that I am aware of, in this country, except that which is found in the civil rights act, which will be hereafter noticed. It is, however, clear that they include something more than slavery in the strict sense of the term; they include also serfage, vassalage, villanage, peonage, and all other forms of compulsory service for the mere benefit or pleasure of others. Nor is this the full import of the terms. The abolition of slavery and involuntary servitude was intended to make every one born in this country a freeman, and as such, to give to him the right to pursue the ordinary avocations of life without other restraint than such as affects all others, and to enjoy equally with them the fruits of his labor. A prohibition to him to pursue certain callings, open to others of the same age, condition, and sex, or to reside in places where others are permitted to live, would so far deprive him of the rights of a freeman, and would place him, as respects others, in a condition of servitude. A person allowed to pursue only one trade or calling, and only in one locality of the country, would not be, in the strict sense of the term, in a condition of slavery, but probably none would deny that he would be in a condition of servitude. He certainly would not possess the liberties nor enjoy the privileges of a freeman. The compulsion which would force him to labor even for his own benefit only in one direction, or in one place, would be almost as oppressive, and nearly as great an invasion of his liberty as the compulsion which would force him to labor for the benefit or pleasure of another, and would equally constitute an element of servitude. The counsel of the plaintiffs in error, therefore, contend that 'wherever a law of a State or a law of the United States makes a discrimination between classes of persons, which deprives the one class of their freedom or their property, or which makes a caste of them, to subserve the power, pride, avarice, vanity, or vengeance of others,' there involuntary servitude exists within the meaning of the thirteenth amendment.

" It is not necessary, in my judgment, for the disposition of the present case in favor of the plaintiffs in error, to accept as entirely correct this conclusion of counsel. It, however, finds support in the act of Congress known as the civil rights act, which was framed and adopted upon a construction of the thirteenth amendment, giving to its language a similar breadth. That amendment was ratified on the eighteenth of December, 1865,* and in April of the following year the civil rights act was passed.† Its first section declares that all persons born in the United States, and not subject to any foreign power, excluding Indians not taxed, are 'citizens of the United States,' and that 'such citizens, of every race and color, without regard to any previous condition of slavery, or involuntary servitude, except as a punishment for crime, whereof the party shall have been duly convicted, shall have the same right in every State and terri-

---

* 13 Stat. at Large, 774.   † 14 Ib., 27.

10

tory in the United States, to make and enforce contracts, to sue, be parties, and give evidence, to inherit, purchase, lease, sell, hold, and convey real and personal property, and to full and equal benefit of all laws and proceedings for the security of person and property, as enjoyed by white citizens.'

" This legislation was supported upon the theory that citizens of the United States as such were entitled to the rights and privileges enumerated, and that to deny to any such citizen equality in these rights and privileges with others, was, to the extent of the denial, subjecting him to an involuntary servitude. Senator Trumbull, who drew the act and who was its earnest advocate in the Senate, stated, on opening the discussion upon it in that body, that the measure was intended to give effect to the declaration of the amendment, and to secure to all persons in the United States practical freedom. After referring to several statutes passed in some of the Southern States, discriminating between the freedmen and white citizens, and after citing the definition of civil liberty given by Blackstone, the Senator said: ' I take it that any statute which is not equal to all, and which deprives any citizen of civil rights, which are secured to other citizens, is an unjust encroachment upon his liberty ; and it is in fact a badge of servitude which by the Constitution is prohibited.' *

" By the act of Louisiana, within the three parishes named, a territory exceeding one thousand one hundred square miles, and embracing over two hundred thousand people, every man who pursues the business of preparing animal food for market must take his animals to the buildings of the favored company, and must perform his work in them, and for the use of the buildings must pay a prescribed tribute to the company, and leave with it a valuable portion of each animal slaughtered. Every man in these parishes who has a horse or other animal for sale, must carry him to the yards and stables of this company, and for their use pay a like tribute. He is not allowed to do his work in his own buildings, or to take his animals to his own stables or keep them in his own yards, even though they should be erected in the same district as the buildings, stables, and yards of the company, and that district embraces over eleven hundred square miles. The prohibition imposed by this act upon butchers and dealers in cattle in these parishes, and the special privileges conferred upon the favored corporation, are similar in principle and as odious in character as the restrictions imposed in the last century upon the peasantry in some parts of France, where, as says a French writer, the peasant was prohibited ' to hunt on his own lands, to fish in his own waters, to grind at his own mill, to cook at his own oven, to dry his clothes on his own machines, to whet his instruments at his own grindstone, to make his own wine, his oil, and his cider at his own press, ... or to sell his commodities at the public market.' The exclusive right to all

---

* Cong. Globe, 1st Sess., 39th Cong., Part I., p. 474.

these privileges was vested in the lords of the vicinage. ' The history of the most execrable tyranny of ancient times,' says the same writer, ' offers nothing like this. This category of oppressions cannot be applied to a free man, or to the peasant, except in violation of his rights.'

"But if the exclusive privileges conferred upon the Louisiana corporation can be sustained, it is not perceived why exclusive privileges for the construction and keeping of ovens, machines, grindstones, winepresses, and for all the numerous trades and pursuits for the prosecution of which buildings are required, may not be equally bestowed on other corporations or private individuals, and for periods of indefinite duration.

"It is not necessary, however, as I have said, to rest my objections to the act in question upon the terms and meaning of the thirteenth amendment. The provisions of the fourteenth amendment, which is properly a supplement to the thirteenth, cover, in my judgment, the case before us, and inhibit any legislation which confers special and exclusive privileges like these under consideration. The amendment was adopted to obviate objections which had been raised and pressed with great force to the validity of the civil rights act, and to place the common rights of American citizens under the protection of the national government. It first declares that ' all persons born or naturalized in the United States, and subject to the jurisdiction thereof, are citizens of the United States and of the State wherein they reside.' It then declares that 'no State shall make or enforce any law which shall abridge the privileges or immunities of citizens of the United States, nor shall any State deprive any person of life, liberty, or property without due process of law, nor deny to any person within its jurisdiction the equal protection of the laws.'

"The first clause of this amendment determines who are citizens of the United States, and how their citizenship is created. Before its enactment there was much diversity of opinion among jurists and statesmen whether there was any such citizenship independent of that of the State, and, if any existed, as to the manner in which it originated. With a great number the opinion prevailed that there was no such citizenship independent of the citizenship of the State. Such was the opinion of Mr. Calhoun and the class represented by him. In his celebrated speech in the Senate upon the force bill, in 1833, referring to the reliance expressed by a Senator upon the fact that we are citizens of the United States, he said : 'If by citizen of the United States he means a citizen at large, one whose citizenship extends to the entire geographical limits of the country without having a local citizenship in some State or territory, a sort of citizen of the world, all I have to say is that such a citizen would be a perfect nondescript ; that not a single individual of this description can be found in the entire mass of our population. Notwithstanding all the pomp and display of eloquence on the occasion, every citizen is a citizen of some State or territory, and as such, under an express provision of the Constitution, is entitled to all the privileges and immunities of citizens of the several States; and it is in this and no other sense that we are citizens of the United States.'*

"In the Dred Scott case this subject of citizenship of the United States was fully and elaborately discussed. The exposition in the opinion of Mr. Justice Curtis has been generally accepted by the profession of the country as the one containing the soundest views of constitutional law. And he held that, under the Constitution, citizenship of the United States in reference to natives was dependent upon citizenship in the several States, under their constitutions and laws.

"The Chief Justice in that case, and the majority of the court with him, held that the words 'people of the United States' and 'citizens' were synonymous terms; that the people of the respective States were the parties to the Constitution; that these people consisted of the free inhabitants of those States; that they had provided in their Constitution for the adoption of an uniform rule of naturalization; that they and their descendants and persons naturalized were the only persons who could be citizens of the United States, and that it was not in the power of any State to invest any other person with citizenship so that he could enjoy the privileges of a citizen under the Constitution, and that, therefore, the descendants of persons brought to this country and sold as slaves were not, and could not be, citizens within the meaning of the Constitution.

"The first clause of the fourteenth amendment changes this whole subject, and removes it from the region of discussion and doubt. It recognizes in express terms, if it does not create, citizens of the United States, and it makes their citizenship dependent upon the place of their birth, or the fact of their adoption, and not upon the constitution or laws of any State or the condition of their ancestry. A citizen of a State is now only a citizen of the United States residing in that State. The fundamental rights, privileges, and immunities which belong to him as a free man and a free citizen, now belong to him as a citizen of the United States, and are not dependent upon his citizenship of any State. The exercise of these rights and privileges, and the degree of enjoyment received from such exercise, are always more or less affected by the condition and the local institutions of the State, or city, or town where he resides. They are thus affected in a State by the wisdom of its laws, the ability of its officers, the efficiency of its magistrates, the education and morals of its people, and by many other considerations. This is a result which follows from the constitution of society, and can never be avoided, but in no other way can they be affected by the action of the State, or by the residence of the citizen therein. They do not derive their existence from its legislation, and cannot be destroyed by its power.

"The amendment does not attempt to confer any new privileges or immunities upon citizens, or to enumerate or define those already exist-

---

* Calhoun's Works, vol. 2, p. 242.

ing. It assumes that there are such privileges and immunities which belong of right to citizens as such, and ordains that they shall not be abridged by state legislation. If this inhibition has no reference to privileges and immunities of this character, but only refers, as held by the majority of the court in their opinion, to such privileges and immunities as were before its adoption specially designated in the Constitution or necessarily implied as belonging to citizens of the United States, it was a vain and idle enactment, which accomplished nothing, and most unnecessarily excited Congress and the people on its passage. With privileges and immunities thus designated or implied, no State could ever have interfered by its laws, and no new constitutional provision was required to inhibit such interference. The supremacy of the Constitution and the laws of the United States always controlled any State legislation of that character. But if the amendment refers to the natural and inalienable rights which belong to all citizens, the inhibition has a profound significance and consequence.

"What, then, are the privileges and immunities which are secured against abridgment by State legislation?

"In the first section of the civil rights act Congress has given its interpretation to these terms, or, at least, has stated some of the rights which, in its judgment, these terms include; it has there declared that they include the right 'to make and enforce contracts, to sue, be parties and give evidence, to inherit, purchase, lease, sell, hold, and convey real and personal property, and to full and equal benefit of all laws and proceedings for the security of person and property.' That act, it is true, was passed before the fourteenth amendment, but the amendment was adopted, as I have already said, to obviate objections to the act, or, speaking more accurately, I should say, to obviate objections to legislation of a similar character, extending the protection of the national government over the common rights of all citizens of the United States. Accordingly, after its ratification, Congress re-enacted the act, under the belief that whatever doubts may have previously existed of its validity, they were removed by the amendment.*

"The terms, privileges and immunities are not new in the amendment; they were in the Constitution before the amendment was adopted. They are found in the second section of the fourth article, which declares that 'the citizens of each State shall be entitled to all privileges and immunities of citizens in the several States,' and they have been the subject of frequent consideration in judicial decisions. In Corfield vs. Coryell,† Mr. Justice Washington said he had 'no hesitation in confining these expressions to those privileges and immunities which were, in their nature, fundamental; which belong of right to citizens of all free governments, and which have at all times been enjoyed by the citizens of the several

---

* May 31st, 1870; 16 Stat. at Large, 144.
† 4 Washington, Cir. Ct., 380.

States which compose the Union, from the time of their becoming free, independent, and sovereign ;' and, in considering what these fundamental privileges were, he said that perhaps it would be more tedious than difficult to enumerate them, but that they might be 'all comprehended under the following general heads : protection by the government; the enjoyment of life and liberty, with the right to acquire and possess property of every kind, and to pursue and obtain happiness and safety, subject, nevertheless, to such restraints as the government may justly prescribe for the general good of the whole.' This appears to me to be a sound construction of the clause in question. The privileges and immunities designated are those *which of right belong to the citizens of all free governments.* Clearly among these must be placed the right to pursue a lawful employment in a lawful manner, without other restraint than such as equally affects all persons. In the discussions in Congress upon the passage of the civil rights act repeated reference was made to this language of Mr. Justice Washington. It was cited by Senator Trumbull with the observation that it enumerated the very rights belonging to a citizen of the United States set forth in the first section of the act, and with the statement that all persons born in the United States, being declared by the act citizens of the United States, would thenceforth be entitled to the rights of citizens, and that these were the great fundamental rights set forth in the act; and that they were set forth 'as appertaining to every freeman.'

" The privileges and immunities designated in the second section of the fourth article of the Constitution are, then, according to the decision cited, those which of right belong to the citizens of all free governments, and they can be enjoyed under that clause by the citizens of each State in the several States upon the same terms and conditions as they are enjoyed by the citizens of the latter States. No discrimination can be made by one State against the citizens of other States in their enjoyment, nor can any greater imposition be levied than such as is laid upon its own citizens. It is a clause which insures equality in the enjoyment of these rights between citizens of the several States whilst in the same State.

" Nor is there anything in the opinion in the case of *Paul* vs. *Virginia*⁕ which at all militates against these views, as is supposed by the majority of the court.————

" The whole purport of the decision [in that case] was, that citizens of one State do not carry with them into other States any special privileges or immunities conferred by the laws of their own States, of a corporate or other character. That decision has no pertinency to the questions involved in this case. The common privileges and immunities which of right belong to all citizens, stand on a very different footing. These the citizens of each State do carry with them into other States and are secured by the clause in question, in their enjoyment upon terms of equality with

---

⁕ 8 Wallace, 168.

citizens of the latter States. This equality in one particular was enforced by this court in the recent case of Ward vs. The State of Maryland, reported in the 12th of Wallace. A statute of that State required the payment of a larger sum from a non-resident trader for a license to enable him to sell his merchandise in the State, than it did of a resident trader, and the court held that the statute in thus discriminating against the non-resident trader contravened the clause securing to the citizens of each State the privileges and immunities of citizens of the several States. The privilege of disposing of his property, which was an essential incident to his ownership, possessed by the non-resident, was subjected by the statute of Maryland to a greater burden than was imposed upon a like privilege of her own citizens. The privileges of the non-resident were in this particular abridged by that legislation.

"What the clause in question did for the protection of the citizens of one State against hostile and discriminating legislation of other States, the fourteenth amendment does for the protection of every citizen of the United States against hostile and discriminating legislation against him in favor of others, whether they reside in the same or in different States. If, under the fourth article of the Constitution, equality of privileges and immunities is secured between citizens of different States, under the fourteenth amendment the same equality is secured between citizens of the United States.

"It will not be pretended that under the fourth article of the Constitution any State could create a monopoly in any known trade or manufacture in favor of her own citizens, or any portion of them, which would exclude an equal participation in the trade or manufacture monopolized by citizens of other States. She could not confer, for example, upon any of her citizens the sole right to manufacture shoes or boots or silk, or the sole right to sell those articles in the State, so as to exclude non-resident citizens from engaging in a similar manufacture or sale. The non-resident citizens could claim equality of privilege under the provisions of the fourth article with the citizens of the State exercising the monopoly as well as with others, and thus, as respects them, the monopoly would cease. If this were not so, it would be in the power of the State to exclude at any time the citizens of other States from participation in particular branches of commerce or trade, and extend the exclusion from time to time so as effectually to prevent any traffic with them.

"Now, what the clause in question does for the protection of citizens of one State against the creation of monopolies in favor of citizens of other States, the fourteenth amendment does for the protection of every citizen of the United States against the creation of any monopoly whatever. The privileges and immunities of citizens of the United States, of every one of them, is secured against abridgment in any form by any State. The fourteenth amendment places them under the guardianship of the national authority. All monopolies in any known trade or manufacture are an invasion of these privileges, for they encroach upon the liberty of citizens to acquire property and pursue happiness, and were held void at common law in the great case of Monopolies, decided during the reign of Queen Elizabeth.

"A monopoly is defined 'to be an institution or allowance from the sovereign power of the State, by grant, commission, or otherwise, to any person or corporation, for the sole buying, selling, making, working, or using of anything whereby any person or persons, bodies politic or corporate, are sought to be restrained of any freedom or liberty they had before, or hindered in their lawful trade.' All such grants relating to any known trade or manufacture have been held by all the judges of England, whenever they have come up for consideration, to be void at common law, as destroying the freedom of trade, discouraging labor and industry, restraining persons from getting an honest livelihood, and putting it in the power of the grantees to enhance the price of commodities. The definition embraces, it will be observed, not merely the sole privilege of buying and selling particular articles, or of engaging in their manufacture, but also the sole privilege of using anything by which others may be restrained of the freedom or liberty they previously had in any lawful trade, or hindered in such trade. It thus covers in every particular the possession and use of suitable yards, stables, and buildings for keeping and protecting cattle and other animals, and for their slaughter. Such establishments are essential to the free and successful prosecution by any butcher of the lawful trade of preparing animal food for market. The exclusive privilege of supplying such yards, buildings, and other conveniences for the prosecution of this business in a large district of country, granted by the act of Louisiana to seventeen persons, is as much a monopoly as though it had granted to the company the exclusive privilege of buying and selling the animals themselves. It equally restrains the butchers in the freedom and liberty they previously had and hinders them in their lawful trade.

"The reasons given for the judgment in the case of Monopolies apply with equal force to the case at bar. In that case a patent had been granted to the plaintiff giving him the sole right to import playing-cards, and the entire traffic in them, and the sole right to make such cards within the realm. The defendant, in disregard of this patent, made and sold some gross of such cards and imported others, and was accordingly sued for infringing upon the exclusive privileges of the plaintiff. As to a portion of the cards made and sold within the realm, he pleaded that he was a haberdasher in London and a free citizen of that city, and as such had a right to make and sell them. The court held the plea good and the grant void, as against the common law and divers acts of Parliament. 'All trades,' said the court, 'as well mechanical as others, which prevent idleness (the bane of the commonwealth) and exercise men and youth in labor for the maintenance of themselves and their families, and for the increase of their substance, to serve the Queen when occasion shall require, are profitable for the commonwealth, and therefore the grant to the plaintiff to have the sole making of them is *against the com-mon law and the benefit and liberty of the subject.'* * The case of Davenant and Hurdis was cited in support of this position. In that case a com-pany of merchant tailors in London, having power by charter to make ordinances for the better rule and government of the company, so that they were consonant to law and reason, made an ordinance that any brother of the society who should have any cloth dressed by a cloth-worker, not being a brother of the society, should put one-half of his cloth to some brother of the same society who exercised the art of a cloth-worker, upon pain of forfeiting ten shillings, 'and it was adjudged that the ordinance, although it had the countenance of a charter, was against the common law, *because it was against the liberty of the subject; for every subject, by the law, has freedom and liberty to put his cloth to be dressed by what cloth-worker he pleases, and cannot be restrained to certain persons, for that in effect would be a monopoly,* and, therefore, such ordinance, by color of a charter or any grant by charter to such effect, would be void.'

"Although the court, in its opinion, refers to the increase in prices and deterioration in quality of commodities which necessarily result from the grant of monopolies, the main ground of the decision was their interfer-ence with the liberty of the subject to pursue for his maintenance and that of his family any lawful trade or employment. This liberty is as-sumed to be the natural right of every Englishman.

" The struggle of the English people against monopolies forms one of the most interesting and instructive chapters in their history. It finally ended in the passage of the statute of 21st James I., by which it was declared 'that all monopolies and all commissions, grants, licenses, charters, and letters-patent, to any person or persons, bodies politic or corporate, what-soever, of or for the sole buying, selling, making, working, or using of anything' within the realm or the dominion of Wales, were altogether contrary to the laws of the realm and utterly void, with the exception of patents for new inventions for a limited period, and for printing, then supposed to belong to the prerogative of the King, and for the prepara-tion and manufacture of certain articles and ordnance intended for the prosecution of war.

"The common law of England, as is thus seen, condemned all monopolies in any known trade or manufacture, and declared void all grants of special privileges whereby others could be deprived of any liberty which they previously had, or be hindered in their lawful trade. The statute of James I., to which I have referred, only embodied the law as it had been previously declared by the courts of England, although frequently disre-garded by the sovereigns of that country.

" The common law of England is the basis of the jurisprudence of the United States. It was brought to this country by the Colonists, together with the English statutes, and was established here so far as it was ap-

* 1 Coke Rept., part XI., p. 86.

plicable to their condition. That law and the benefit of such of the English statutes as existed at the time of their colonization, and which they had by experience found to be applicable to their circumstances, were claimed by the Congress of the United Colonies in 1774 as a part of their 'indubitable rights and liberties.'* Of the statutes, the benefit of which was thus claimed, the statute of James I. against monopolies was one of the most important. And when the colonies separated from the mother country, no privilege was more fully recognized or more completely incorporated into the fundamental law of the country, than that every free subject in the British Empire was entitled to pursue his happiness by following any of the known established trades and occupations of the country, subject only to such restraints as equally affected all others. The immortal document which proclaimed the independence of the country declared as self-evident truths that the Creator had endowed all men 'with certain inalienable rights, and that among these are life, liberty, and the pursuit of happiness; and that to secure these rights governments are instituted among men.'

"If it be said that the civil law and not the common law is the basis of the jurisprudence of Louisiana, I answer that the decree of Louis XVIth, in 1776, abolished all monopolies of trades and all special privileges of corporations, guilds, and trading companies, and authorized every person to exercise, without restraint, his art, trade, or profession, and such has been the law of France and her colonies ever since, and that law prevailed in Louisiana at the time of her cession to the United States. Since then, notwithstanding the existence in that State of the civil law as the basis of her jurisprudence, freedom of pursuit has been always recognized as the common right of her citizens. But were this otherwise, the fourteenth amendment secures the like protection to all citizens in that State against any abridgment of their common rights, as in other States. That amendment was intended to give practical effect to the declaration of 1776 of inalienable rights, rights which are the gift of the Creator, which the law does not confer, but only recognizes. If the trader in London could plead that he was a free citizen of that city against the enforcement to his injury of monopolies, surely under the fourteenth amendment every citizen of the United States should be able to plead his citizenship of the Republic as a protection against any similar invasion of his privileges and immunities.

"So fundamental has this privilege of every citizen to be free from disparaging and unequal enactments in the pursuit of the ordinary avocations of life been regarded, that few instances have arisen where the principle has been so far violated as to call for the interposition of the courts. But whenever this has occurred, with the exception of the present cases from Louisiana, which are the most barefaced and flagrant of all, the enactment interfering with the privilege of the citizen has been pro-

---

*Journals of Congress, Vol. 1, pp. 28–30.

nounced illegal and void. When a case under the same law under which the present cases have arisen came before the Circuit Court of the United States in the District of Louisiana, there was no hesitation on the part of the court in declaring the law, in its exclusive features, to be an invasion of one of the fundamental privileges of the citizen.* The presiding justice, in delivering the opinion of the court, observed that it might be difficult to enumerate or define what were the essential privileges of a citizen of the United States, which a State could not by its laws invade, but that so far as the question under consideration was concerned, it might be safely said that ' it is one of the privileges of every American citizen to adopt and follow such lawful industrial pursuit, not injurious to the community, as he may see fit, without unreasonable regulation or molestation, and without being restricted by any of those unjust, oppressive, and odious monopolies or exclusive privileges which have been 'condemned by all free governments.' And again, ' there is no more sacred right of citizenship than the right to pursue unmolested a lawful employment in a lawful manner. It is nothing more nor less than the sacred right of labor.' "

Other cases were cited in support of the position of the opinion. The Judge concluded as follows :

"In all these cases there is a recognition of the equality of right among citizens in the pursuit of the ordinary avocations of life, and a declaration that all grants of exclusive privileges, in contravention of this equality, are against common right and void.

"This equality of right, with exemption from all disparaging and partial enactments, in the lawful pursuits of life, throughout the whole country, is the distinguishing privilege of citizens of the United States. To them, everywhere, all pursuits, all professions, all avocations are open without other restrictions than such as are imposed equally upon all others of the same age, sex, and condition. The State may prescribe such regulations for every pursuit and calling of life as will promote the public health, secure the good order and advance the general prosperity of society, but when once prescribed, the pursuit or calling must be free to be followed by every citizen who is within the conditions designated, and will conform to the regulations. This is the fundamental idea upon which our institutions rest, and unless adhered to in the legislation of the country our government will be a republic only in name. The fourteenth amendment, in my judgment, makes it essential to the validity of the legislation of every State that this equality of right should be respected. How widely this equality has been departed from ; how entirely rejected and trampled upon by the act of Louisiana, I have already shown. And it is to me a matter of profound regret that its validity is

---

* Live Stock, &c., Association vs. The Crescent City, &c., Company, 1 Abbott's U. S. Rep., p. 398.

recognized by a majority of this court, for by it the right of free labor, one of the most sacred and imprescriptible rights of man, is violated.* As stated by the Supreme Court of Connecticut in the case cited, grants of exclusive privileges, such as is made by the act in question, are opposed to the whole theory of free government, and it requires no aid from any bill of rights to render them void. That only is a free government, in the American sense of the term, under which the inalienable right of every citizen to pursue his happiness is unrestrained, except by just, equal, and impartial laws."†

The Power of the State to Control the Compensation Receivable for the Use of Private Property, and for Services in connection with it.—The Chicago Warehouse Case.

It is a recognized principle under all governments that every one must hold, use, and enjoy his property subject to such restrictions as the legislative authority of the State

---

* "The property which every man has in his own labor," says Adam Smith, "as it is the original foundation of all other property, so it is the most sacred and inviolable. The patrimony of the poor man lies in the strength and dexterity of his own hands; and to hinder him from employing this strength and dexterity in what manner he thinks proper, without injury to his neighbor, is a plain violation of this most sacred property. It is a manifest encroachment upon the just liberty both of the workman and of those who might be disposed to employ him. As it hinders the one from working at what he thinks proper, so it hinders the others from employing whom they think proper."—(Smith's Wealth of Nations, b. 1, ch. 10, part 2.)

In the edict of Louis 16th, in 1776, giving freedom to trades and professions, prepared by his minister, Turgot, he recites the contributions that had been made by the guilds and trade companies, and says: "It was the allurement of these fiscal advantages undoubtedly that prolonged the illusion and concealed the immense injury they did to industry and their infraction of natural right. This illusion had extended so far that some persons asserted that the right to work was a royal privilege which the king might sell, and that his subjects were bound to purchase from him. We hasten to correct this error and to repel the conclusion. God in giving to man wants and desires rendering labor necessary for their satisfaction, conferred the right to labor upon all men, and this property is the first, most sacred and imprescriptible of all." . . . He, therefore, regards it " as the first duty of his justice, and the worthiest act of benevolence, to free his subjects from any restriction upon this inalienable right of humanity."

† "Civil liberty, the great end of all human society and government, is that state in which each individual has the power to pursue his own happiness according to his own views of his interest, and the dictates of his conscience, unrestrained, except by equal, just, and impartial laws."—(1 Sharswood's Blackstone, 127, note 8.)

may prescribe for the good order, peace, health, and morals of the community, and so as not to interfere with the equal use and enjoyment by others of their property. And every one must, also, hold his property subject to taxation for the support of government, or to be appropriated for public purposes, upon a regular appraisement and payment of its value. But unless there is some special privilege conferred by the government in connection with one's property or with its use, interference with his control over it for any other purpose has not generally been considered in this country, of late years, a legitimate subject of legislation. Formerly, in European governments, where, theoretically, all power was in the sovereign, or in legislative assemblies or councils sitting under his sanction, the case was different. Numerous regulations, as to the use of property and the compensation receivable for its use, were there prescribed by law. In England, also, this was a common thing; and many acts of legislation have been adopted in this country from the fact that precedents for like legislation have existed there, without considering their propriety or validity under our different system.

In the recent case of Munn & Scott against the State of Illinois, this subject was brought to the consideration and judgment of the Supreme Court of the United States, and the decision rendered has attracted unusual attention as indicating a departure from what was previously considered to be the settled rule in this country. Munn & Scott were warehousemen in Chicago, Illinois, engaged in the storage of grain. They had constructed their warehouse and elevator in 1862 with their own means, upon ground leased by them for that purpose; and from that time until the filing of an information against them by the State, they had transacted the business of receiving and storing grain for hire. The rates of storage charged by them were annually established by arrangement with the owners of different elevators in Chicago, and were published in the month of January. In 1870 the State of Illinois adopted a new constitution, and by it "all elevators or storehouses where grain, or other property, is stored for a compensation, whether the property stored be kept separate or not, are declared to be public warehouses."

In April, 1871, the legislature of the State passed an act to regulate these warehouses, thus declared to be public, and the warehousing and inspection of grain, and to give effect to this article of the constitution. By that act, public warehouses, as defined in the constitution, were divided into three classes, the first of which embraced all warehouses, elevators, or granaries located in cities having not less than one hundred thousand inhabitants, in which grain was stored in bulk, and the grain of different owners was mixed together, or stored in such manner that the identity of different lots or parcels could not be accurately preserved. To this class the warehouse of Munn & Scott belonged. The act prescribed the maximum of charges which the proprietor, lessee, or manager of the warehouse was allowed to make for storage and handling of grain, including the cost of receiving and delivering it, for the first thirty days or any part thereof, and for each succeeding fifteen days or any part thereof; and it required him to procure from the circuit court of the county a license to transact business as a public warehouseman, and to give a bond to the people of the State in the penal sum of ten thousand dollars for the faithful performance of his duty as such warehouseman of the first class, and for his full and unreserved compliance with all laws of the State in relation thereto. The license was made revocable by the circuit court upon a summary proceeding for any violation of such laws. And a penalty was imposed upon every person transacting business as a public warehouseman of the first class without first procuring a license, or continuing in such business after his license had been revoked, of not less than one hundred or more than five hundred dollars for each day on which the business was thus carried on. The court was also authorized to refuse for one year to renew the license, or to grant a new one to any person whose license had been revoked. The maximum of charges prescribed by the act for the receipt and storage of grain was different from that which Munn & Scott had previously charged, and which had been agreed to by the owners of the grain. More extended periods of storage were required of them than they formerly gave for the same charges. What they formerly charged for the first twenty days of storage, the act allowed them to charge only for the first thirty days of storage; and what they formerly charged for each succeeding ten days after the first twenty, the act allowed them to charge only for each succeeding fifteen days after the first thirty. Munn & Scott, deeming that they had a right to use their own property in such manner as they desired, not inconsistent with the equal right of others to a like use, and denying the power of the legislature to fix prices for the use of their property and their services in connection with it, refused to comply with the act by taking out the license and giving the bond required; but continued to carry on the business and to charge for receiving and storing grain such prices as they had been accustomed to charge, and as had been agreed upon between them and the owners of the grain. For thus transacting their business without procuring a license as required by the act, they were prosecuted and fined, and the judgment against them was affirmed by the Supreme Court of the State. The case was then carried to the Supreme Court of the United States.

The question thus presented for adjudication was whether it is within the competency of a State to fix the compensation which an individual may receive for the use of his own property in his private business and for his services in connection with it? It was argued with great ability by distinguished counsel, Messrs. Goudy and Jewett, for Munn & Scott, and the Attorney-General of Illinois, for

. the State. The Supreme Court affirmed the judgment, two judges only, Field and Strong, disagreeing with it. Chief Justice Waite gave the opinion of the court; Judge Field filed a dissenting opinion.

The Chief Justice, after stating generally that when one becomes a member of society he necessarily parts with some rights or privileges which as an individual, not affected by his relations to others, he might retain; that government acting for all, under what are termed its police powers, regulates the conduct of its citizens toward each other, and the manner in which each shall use his property when such regulation becomes necessary for the public good, and that in their exercise it has been customary in England from time immemorial, and in this country from its first colonization, to regulate ferries, common carriers, hackmen, bakers, millers, wharfingers, and innkeepers, said as follows:

"From this it is apparent that, down to the time of the adoption of the fourteenth amendment, it was not supposed that statutes regulating the use, or even the price of the use, of private property necessarily deprived an owner of his property without due process of law. Under some circumstances they may, but not under all. The amendment does not change the law in this particular; it simply prevents the States from doing that which will operate as such a deprivation.

"This brings us to inquire as to the principles upon which this power of regulation rests, in order that we may determine what is within and what is without its operative effect. Looking, then, to the common law, from whence came the right, which the Constitution protects, we find that when private property is 'affected with a public interest, it ceases to be *juris privati* only.' This was said by Lord Chief Justice Hale more than two hundred years ago, in his treatise *De Portibus Maris*, (1 Harg. Law Tracts, 78,) and has been accepted without objection as an essential element in the law of property ever since. Property does become clothed with a public interest when used in a manner to make it of public consequence, and affect the community at large. When, therefore, one devotes his property to a use in which the public has an interest, he, in effect, grants to the public an interest in that use, and must submit to be controlled by the public for the common good, to the extent of the interest he has thus created. He may withdraw his grant by discontinuing the use; but so long as he maintains the use he must submit to the control."—(94 U. S., 125-6.)

The doctrine here announced as to property being affected with a public interest, and the statement of the circumstances under which property is thus affected, constitute the principle of the decision, the reason of the judgment rendered.

Several cases were also cited by the Chief Justice in supposed support of his position. Judge Field, as stated above, filed a dissenting opinion. In that he answered the position of the Chief Justice, and examined the authorities referred to by him, and in the view of many very able judges and lawyers overthrew the position and showed that the authorities sustain the very contrary of the doctrine to uphold which they were invoked. Speaking for himself and his associate the Judge said as follows:

"The declaration of the constitution [of Illinois] of 1870, that private buildings used for private purposes shall be deemed public institutions, does not make them so. The receipt and storage of grain in a building erected by private means for that purpose does not constitute the building a public warehouse. There is no magic in the language, though used by a constitutional convention, which can change a private business into a public one, or alter the character of the building in which the business is transacted. A tailor's or a shoemaker's shop would still retain its private character even though the assembled wisdom of the State should declare by organic act or legislative ordinance that such a place was a public workshop, and that the workmen were public tailors or public shoemakers. One might as well attempt to change the nature of colors by giving them a new designation. The defendants were no more public warehousemen, as justly observed by counsel, than the merchant who sells his merchandise to the public is a public merchant, or the blacksmith who shoes horses for the public is a public blacksmith; and it was a strange notion that by calling them so they would be brought under legislative control.

"The Supreme Court of the State—divided, it is true, by three to two of its members—has held that this legislation was a legitimate exercise of State authority over private business; and the Supreme Court of the United States, two only of its members dissenting, has decided that there is nothing in the Constitution of the United States, or its recent amendments, which impugns its validity. It is, therefore, with diffidence I presume to question the soundness of the decision.

"The validity of the legislation was, among other grounds, assailed in the State court as being in conflict with that provision of the State constitution which declares that no person shall be deprived of life, liberty,

11

or property without due process of law, and with that provision of the 14th amendment of the federal Constitution which imposes a similar restriction upon the action of the State. The State court held in substance that the constitutional provision was not violated so long as the owner was not deprived of the title and possession of his property ; and that it did not deny to the legislature the power to make all needful rules and regulations respecting the use and enjoyment of the property, referring, in support of the position, to instances of its action in prescribing the interest on money, in establishing and regulating public ferries and public mills, and fixing the compensation in the shape of tolls, and in delegating power to municipal bodies to regulate the charges of hackmen and draymen and the weight and price of bread. In this court the legislation was also assailed on the same ground, our jurisdiction arising upon the clause of the 14th amendment ordaining that no State shall deprive any person of life, liberty, or property without due process of law. But it would seem from its opinion that the court holds that property loses something of its private character when employed in such a way as to be generally useful. The doctrine declared is that property 'becomes clothed with a public interest when used in a manner to make it of public consequence and affect the community at large ;' and from such clothing the right of the legislature is deduced to control the use of the property and to determine the compensation which the owner may receive for it. When Sir Matthew Hale, and the sages of the law in his day, spoke of property as affected by a public interest, and ceasing from that cause to be *juris privati* solely, that is, ceasing to be held merely in private right, they referred to property dedicated by the owner to public uses, or to property the use of which was granted by the government, or in connection with which special privileges were conferred. Unless the property was thus dedicated, or some right bestowed by the government was held with the property, either by specific grant or by prescription of so long a time as to imply a grant originally, the property was not affected by any public interest so as to be taken out of the category of property held in private right. But it is not in any such sense that the terms 'clothing property with a public interest' are used in this case. From the nature of the business under consideration—the storage of grain—which, in any sense in which the word can be used, is a private business, in which the public are interested only as they are interested in the storage of other products of the soil, or in articles of manufacture, it is clear that the court intended to declare that whenever one devotes his property to a business which is useful to the public—'affects the community at large '—the legislature can regulate the compensation which the owner may receive for its use and for his own services in connection with it. ' When, therefore,' says the court, 'one devotes his property to a use in which the public has an interest, he, in effect, grants to the public an interest in that use, and must submit to be controlled by the public for the common good to the extent of the interest he has thus created. He may withdraw his grant by discontinuing the use, but so long as he maintains the use he must submit to the control.' The building used by the defendants was for the storage of grain; in such storage, says the court, the public has an interest; therefore the defendants, by devoting the building to that storage, have granted to the public an interest in that use, and must submit to have their compensation regulated by the legislature.

"If this be sound law, if there be no protection either in the principles upon which our republican government is founded, or in the prohibitions of the Constitution against such invasion of private rights, all property and all business in the State are held at the mercy of a majority of its legislature. The public has no greater interest in the use of buildings for the storage of grain than it has in the use of buildings for the residences of families, nor, indeed, anything like so great an interest; and, according to the doctrine announced, the legislature may fix the rent of all tenements used for residences, without reference to the' cost of their erection. If the owner does not like the rates prescribed, he may cease renting his houses. He has granted to the public, says the court, an interest in the use of the buildings, and ' he may withdraw his grant by discontinuing the use; but so long as he maintains the use he must submit to the control.' The public is interested in the manufacture of cotton, woolen, and silken fabrics, in the construction of machinery, in the printing and publication of books and periodicals, and in the making of utensils of every variety, useful and ornamental; indeed, there is hardly an enterprise or business engaging the attention and labor of any considerable portion of the community in which the public has not an interest in the sense in which that term is used by the court in its opinion; and the doctrine which allows the legislature to interfere with and regulate the charges which the owners of property thus employed shall make for its use, that is, the rates at which all these different kinds of business shall be carried on, has never before been asserted, so far as I am aware, by any judicial tribunal in the United States.

" The doctrine of the State court, that no one is deprived of his property, within the meaning of the constitutional inhibition, so long as he retains its title and possession, and the doctrine of this court, that whenever one's property is used in such a manner as to affect the community at large, it becomes by that fact clothed with a public interest and ceases to be *juris privati* only, appear to me to destroy for all useful purposes the efficacy of the constitutional guaranty. All that is beneficial in property arises from its use and the fruits of that use; and whatever deprives a person of them deprives him of all that is desirable or valuable in the title and possession. If the constitutional guaranty extends no further than to prevent a deprivation of title and possession, and allows a deprivation of use and the fruits of that use, it does not merit the encomiums it has received. Unless I have misread the history of the provision now incorporated into all our State constitutions, and by' the fifth and fourteenth amendments into our federal Constitution, and have misunderstood the interpretation it has received, it is not thus limited in its scope and thus impotent for good. It has a much more extended operation than either court, State or federal, has given to it. The provision, it is to be observed, places property under the same protection as life and liberty. Except by due process of law no State can deprive any person of either. The provision has been supposed to secure to every individual the essential conditions for the pursuit of happiness, and for that reason has not been heretofore, and should never be, construed in any narrow or restricted sense.

"No State 'shall deprive any person of life, liberty, or property without due process of law,' says the 14th amendment to the Constitution. By the term 'life,' as here used, something more is meant than mere animal existence. The inhibition against its deprivation extends to all those limbs and faculties by which life is enjoyed. The provision equally prohibits the mutilation of the body by the amputation of an arm or leg, or the putting out of an eye, or the destruction of any other organ of the body through which the soul communicates with the outer world. The deprivation, not only of life, but of whatever God has given to every one with life, for its growth and enjoyment, is prohibited by the provision in question, if its efficacy be not frittered away by judicial decision.

"By the term 'liberty,' as used in the provision, something more is meant than mere freedom from physical restraint or the bounds of a prison. It means freedom to go where one may choose, and to act in such manner, not inconsistent with the equal rights of others, as his judgment may dictate for the promotion of his happiness—that is, to pursue such callings and avocations as may be most suitable to develop his capacities and give to them their highest enjoyment.

"The same liberal construction which is required for the protection of life and liberty, in all particulars in which life and liberty are of any value, should be applied to the protection of private property. If the legislature of a State, under pretence of providing for the public good, or for any other reason, can determine, against the consent of the owner, the uses to which private property shall be devoted, or the prices which the owner shall receive for its uses, it can deprive him of the property as completely as by a special act for its confiscation or destruction. If, for instance, the owner is prohibited from using his building for the purposes for which it was designed, it is of little consequence that he is permitted to retain the title and possession. Or if he is compelled to take as compensation for its use less than the expenses to which he is subjected by its ownership, he is for all practical purposes deprived of the property, as effectually as if the legislature had ordered his forcible dispossession. If it be admitted that the legislature has any control over the compensation, the extent of that compensation becomes a mere matter of legislative discretion. The amount fixed will operate as a partial destruction of the value of the property, if it fall below the amount which the owner would obtain by contract, and, practically, as a complete destruction, if it be less than the cost of retaining its possession. There is, indeed, no protection of any value under the constitutional provision which does not extend to the use and income of the property as well as to its title and possession.

"This court has heretofore held in many instances that a constitutional provision intended for the protection of rights of private property should be liberally construed. It has so held in the numerous cases where it has been called upon to give effect to the provision prohibiting the States from legislation impairing the obligation of contracts; the provision being construed not only to secure the contract itself from direct attack, but all the essential incidents which give it value and enable its owner to enforce it. Thus, in Bronson vs. Kinzie, reported in the 1st of Howard, it was held that an act of the Legislature of Illinois giving to a mortgagor twelve months within which to redeem his mortgaged property from a judicial sale, and prohibiting its sale for less than two-thirds of its appraised value, was void as applied to mortgages executed prior to its passage. It was contended, in support of the act, that it affected only the remedy of the mortgagee and did not impair the contract; but the court replied that there was no substantial difference between a retrospective law declaring a particular contract to be abrogated and void and one which took away all remedy to enforce it, or encumbered the remedy with conditions that rendered it useless or impracticable to pursue it. And, referring to the constitutional provision, the court said, speaking through Mr. Chief Justice Taney, that 'it would be unjust to the memory of the distinguished men who framed it to suppose that it was designed to protect a mere barren and abstract right, without any practical operation upon the business of life. It was undoubtedly adopted as a part of the Constitution for a great and useful purpose. It was to maintain the integrity of contracts and to secure their faithful execution throughout this Union by placing them under the protection of the Constitution of the United States. And it would but ill become this court, under any circumstances, to depart from the plain meaning of the words used and to sanction a distinction between the right and the remedy which would render this provision illusive and nugatory, mere words of form, affording no protection and producing no practical result.'

"And in Pumpelly vs. Green Bay Company, reported in the 13th of Wallace, the language of the court is equally emphatic. That case arose in Wisconsin, the constitution of which declares, like the constitutions of nearly all the States, that private property shall not be taken for public use without just compensation; and this court held that the flooding of one's land by a dam constructed across a river under a law of the State was a taking within the prohibition, and required compensation to be made to the owner of the land thus flooded. The court, speaking through Mr. Justice Miller, said: 'It would be a very curious and unsatisfactory result, if, in construing a provision of constitutional law, always understood to have been adopted for protection and security to the rights of the individual as against the government, and which has received the commendation of jurists, statesmen, and commentators, as placing the just principles of the common law on that subject beyond the power of ordinary legislation to change or control them, it shall be held that if the government refrains from the absolute conversion of real property to the uses of the public it can destroy its value entirely, can inflict irreparable and permanent injury to any extent, can, in effect, subject it to total destruction, without making any compensation, because, in the narrowest sense of the word, it is not *taken* for the public use. Such a construction would pervert the constitutional provision into a restriction on the rights of the citizen, as those rights stood at the common law, instead of the government, and make it an authority for invasion of private right under the pretext of the public good, which had no warrant in the laws or practices of our ancestors.' The views expressed in these citations, applied to this case, would render the constitutional provision invoked by the defendants effectual to protect them in the uses, income, and revenues of their property as well as in its title and possession. The construction actually given by the State court and by this court makes the provision, in the language of Taney, a protection to ' a mere barren and abstract right, without any practical operation upon the business of life,' and renders it ' illusive and nugatory, mere words of form, affording no protection and producing no practical result.'

" The power of the State over the property of the citizen under the constitutional guaranty is well defined. The State may take his property for public uses upon just compensation being made therefor. It may take a portion of his property by way of taxation for the support of the government. It may control the use and possession of his property so far as may be necessary for the protection of the rights of others, and to secure to them the equal use and enjoyment of their property. The doctrine that each one must so use his own as not to injure his neighbor—*sic utere tuo ut alienum non lædas*—is the rule by which every member of society must possess and enjoy his property ; and all legislation essential to secure this common and equal enjoyment is a legitimate exercise of State authority. Except in cases where property may be destroyed to arrest a conflagration or the ravages of pestilence, or be taken under the pressure of an immediate and overwhelming necessity to prevent a public calamity, the power of the State over the property of the citizen does not extend beyond such limits.

" It is true that the legislation which secures to all protection in their rights and the equal use and enjoyment of their property embraces an almost infinite variety of subjects. Whatever affects the peace, good order, morals, and health of the community comes within its scope, and every one must use and enjoy his property subject to the restrictions which such legislation imposes. What is termed the police power of the State, which from the language often used respecting it one would suppose to be an undefined and irresponsible element in government, can only interfere with the conduct of individuals in their intercourse with each other, and in the use of their property, so far as may be required to secure these objects. The compensation which the owners of property, not having any special rights or privileges from the government in connection with it, may demand for its use, or for their own services in union with it, forms no element of consideration in prescribing regulations for that purpose. If one construct a building in a city, the State, or the municipality exercising a delegated power from the State, may require its walls to be of sufficient thickness for the uses intended; it may forbid the employment of inflammable materials in its construction, so as not to endanger the safety of his neighbors; if designed as a theatre, church, or public hall, it may prescribe ample means of egress so as to afford facility for escape in case of accident; it may forbid the storage in it of powder, nitro-glycerine, or other explosive material; it may require its occupants daily to remove decayed vegetable and animal matter which would otherwise accumulate and engender disease; it may exclude from it all occupations and business calculated to disturb the neighborhood or infect the air. Indeed, there is no end of regulations with respect to the use of property which may not be legitimately prescribed, having for their object the peace, good order, safety, and health of the community, thus securing to all the equal enjoyment of their property; but in establishing these regulations it is evident that compensation to the owner for the use of his property, or for his services in union with it, is not a matter of any importance; whether it be one sum or another does not affect the regulation, either in respect to its utility or mode of enforcement. One may go in like manner through the whole round of regulations authorized by legislation, State or municipal, under what is termed the police power, and in no instance will he find that the compensation of the owner for the use of his property has any influence in establishing them. It is only where some right or privilege is conferred by the government or municipality upon the owner which he can use in connection with his property, or by means of which the use of his property is rendered more valuable to him, or he thereby enjoys an advantage over others, that the compensation to be received by him becomes a legitimate matter of regulation. Submission to the regulation of compensation in such cases is an implied condition of the grant, and the State in exercising its power of prescribing the compensation only determines the conditions upon which its concession shall be enjoyed. When the privilege ends the power of regulation ceases.

"Jurists and writers on public law find authority for the exercise of this police power of the State and the numerous regulations which it prescribes in the doctrine already stated, that every one must use and enjoy his property consistently with the rights of others and the equal use and enjoyment by them of their property. 'The police power of the State,' says the Supreme Court of Vermont, 'extends to the protection of the lives, limbs, health, comfort, and quiet of all persons, and the protection of all property in the State. According to the maxim, *sic utere tuo ut alienum non lædas,* which being of universal application, it must, of course, be within the range of legislative action *to define the mode and manner in which every one may so use his own as not to injure others.*'* 'We think it a settled principle growing out of the nature of well-ordered civil society,' says the Supreme Court of Massachusetts, 'that every holder of property, however absolute and unqualified may be his title, holds it under the implied liability that his use of it *shall not be injurious to the equal enjoyment of others having an equal right to the enjoyment of their property, nor injurious to the rights of the community.*'† In his commentaries, after speaking of the protection afforded by the Constitution to private property, Chancellor Kent says: ' But though property be thus protected, it is still to be understood that the lawgiver has the right to prescribe the mode and manner of using it, *so far as may be necessary to prevent the abuse of the right, to the injury or annoyance of others, or of the public.* The government may, by general regulations, interdict such uses of property as would create nuisances and become dangerous to the lives, or health, or peace, or comfort of the citizens. Unwholesome trades, slaughter-houses, operations offensive to the senses, the deposit of powder, the application of steam-power to propel cars, the building with combustible materials, and the burial of the dead may all be interdicted by law, in the midst of dense masses of population, *on the general and rational principle that every person ought so to use his property as not to injure his neighbors, and that private interest must be subservient to the general interests of the community.*'‡

"The italics in these citations are mine. The citations show what I have already stated to be the case, that the regulations which the State, in the exercise of its police power, authorizes with respect to the use of property are entirely independent of any question of compensation for such use or for the services of the owner in connection with it.

"There is nothing in the character of the business of the defendants as warehousemen which called for the interference complained of in this case. Their buildings are not nuisances; their occupation of receiving and storing grain infringes upon no rights of others, disturbs no neighborhood, infects not the air, and in no respect prevents others from using and enjoying their property as to them may seem best. The legislation in question is nothing less than a bold assertion of absolute power by the State to control at its discretion the property and business of the citizen, and fix the compensation he shall receive. The will of the legislature is made the condition upon which the owner shall receive the fruits of his property and the just reward of his labor, industry, and enterprise. ' That government,' says Story, ' can scarcely be deemed to be free where the rights of property are left solely dependent upon the will of a legisla-

---

* Thorpe vs. Rutland & Burlington R. R. Co., 27 Vt., 149.
† Commonwealth vs. Alger, 7 Cushing, 84.
‡ 2 Kent, 340.

tive body without any restraint. The fundamental maxims of a free government seem to require that the rights of personal liberty and private property should be held sacred.'* The decision of the court in this case gives unrestrained license to legislative will.

"The several instances mentioned by counsel in the argument and by the court in its opinion, in which legislation has fixed the compensation which parties may receive for the use of their property and services, do not militate against the views I have expressed of the power of the State over the property of the citizen. They were mostly cases of public ferries, bridges, and turnpikes, of wharfingers, hackmen, and draymen, and of interest on money. In all these cases, except that of interest on money, which I shall presently notice, there was some special privilege granted by the State or municipality; and no one, I suppose, has ever contended that the State had not a right to prescribe the conditions upon which such privilege should be enjoyed. The State in such cases exercises no greater right than an individual may exercise over the use of his own property when leased or loaned to others. The conditions upon which the privilege shall be enjoyed being stated or implied in the legislation authorizing its grant, no right is, of course, impaired by their enforcement. The recipient of the privilege in effect stipulates to comply with the conditions. It matters not how limited the privilege conferred, its acceptance implies an assent to the regulation of its use and the compensation for it. The privilege which the hackman and drayman have to the use of stands on the public streets, not allowed to the ordinary coachman or laborer with teams, constitutes a sufficient warrant for the regulation of their fares. In the case of the warehousemen of Chicago, no right or privilege is conferred by the government upon them, and hence no assent of theirs can be alleged to justify any interference with their charges for the use of their property.

"The quotations from the writings of Sir Matthew Hale, so far from supporting the positions of the court, do not recognize the interference of the government even to the extent which I have admitted to be legitimate. They state merely that the franchise of a public ferry belongs to the King, and cannot be used by the subject except by license from him, or prescription time out of mind; and that when the subject has a public wharf by license from the King, or from having dedicated his private wharf to the public, as in the case of a street opened by him through his own land, he must allow the use of the wharf for reasonable and moderate charges. Thus, in the first quotation, which is taken from his treatise 'De Jure Maris,' Hale says that the King has a 'right of franchise or privilege, that no man may set up a common ferry for all passengers without a prescription time out of mind or a charter from the King. He may make a ferry for his own use or the use of his family, but not for the common use of all the King's subjects passing that way;

---

* Wilkeson vs. Leland, 2 Peters, 657.

because it doth in consequent tend to a common charge, and is become a thing of public interest and use, and every man for his passage pays a toll, which is a common charge, and every ferry ought to be under a public regulation, viz., that it give attendance at due times, keep a boat in due order, and take but reasonable toll; for if he fail in these he is fineable.' Of course one who obtains a license from the King to establish a public ferry at which 'every man for his passage pays a toll,' must take it on condition that he charge only reasonable toll, and indeed subject to such regulations as the King may prescribe.

" In the second quotation, which is taken from his treatise ' De Portibus Maris,' Hale says: ' A man, for his own private advantage, may, in a port or town, set up a wharf or crane, and may take what rates he and his customers can agree for cranage, wharfage, housellage, pesage; for he doth no more than is lawful for any man to do, viz., makes the most of his own. . . . If the King or subject have a public wharf, unto which all persons that come to that port must come and unlade or lade their goods as for the purpose, because they are the wharves only licensed by the King, . . . or because there is no other wharf in that port, as it may fall out where a port is newly erected, in that case there cannot be taken arbitrary and excessive duties for cranage, wharfage, pesage, &c., neither can they be enhanced to an immoderate rate, but the duties must be reasonable and moderate, though settled by the King's license or charter. For now the wharf and crane and other conveniences are affected with a public interest, and they cease to be *juris privati* only; as if a man set out a street in new building on his own land, it is now no longer bare private interest, but is affected by the public interest.' The purport of which is that if one have a public wharf, by license from the government or his own dedication, he must exact only reasonable compensation for its use. By its dedication to public use a wharf is as much brought under the common law rule of subjection to reasonable charges as it would be if originally established or licensed by the Crown. All property dedicated to public use by an individual owner, as in the case of land for a park or street, falls at once, by force of the dedication, under the law governing property appropriated by the government for similar purposes.

" I do not doubt the justice of the encomiums passed upon Sir Matthew Hale as a learned jurist of his day, but I am unable to perceive the pertinency of his observations upon *public* ferries and *public* wharves, found in his treatises on 'The Rights of the Sea ' and on ' The Ports of the Sea,' to the questions presented by the warehousing law of Illinois undertaking to regulate the compensation receivable by the owners of *private* property, when that property is used for *private* purposes.

" The principal authority cited in support of the ruling of the court is that of Alnutt vs. Inglis, decided by the King's Bench, and reported in the 12th of East. But that case, so far from sustaining the ruling, establishes, in my judgment, the doctrine that every one has a right to charge for his property, or for its use, whatever he pleases, unless he enjoys in connection with it some right or privilege from the government not accorded to others; and even then it only decides what is above stated in the quotations from Sir Matthew Hale, that he must submit, so long as he retains the right or privilege, to reasonable rates. In that case the London Dock Company, under certain acts of Parliament, possessed the exclusive right of receiving imported goods into their warehouses before the duties were paid; and the question was whether the company was bound to receive them for a reasonable reward, or whether it could arbitrarily fix its compensation. In deciding the case, the Chief Justice, Lord Ellenborough, said: 'There is no doubt that the general principle is favored both in law and justice, that every man may fix what price he pleases upon his own property, or the use of it; but if, for a particular purpose, the public have a right to resort to his premises and make use of them, and he have a monopoly in them for that purpose, if he will take the benefit of that monopoly, he must, as an equivalent, perform the duty attached to it on reasonable terms.' And coming to the conclusion that the company's warehouses were invested with 'the monopoly of a public privilege,' he held that by law the company must confine itself to take reasonable rates; and added that if the Crown should thereafter think it advisable to extend the privilege more generally to other persons and places, so that the public would not be restrained from exercising a choice of warehouses for the purpose, the company might be enfranchised from the restriction which attached to a monopoly; but so long as its warehouses were the only places which could be resorted to for that purpose, the company was bound to let the trade have the use of them for a reasonable hire and reward. The other judges of the court placed their concurrence in the decision upon the ground that the company possessed a legal monopoly of the business, having the only warehouses where goods imported could be lawfully received without previous payment of the duties. From this case it appears that it is only where some privilege in the bestowal of the government is enjoyed in connection with the property, that it is affected with a public interest in any proper sense of the term. It is the public privilege conferred with the use of the property which creates the public interest in it.

"In the case decided by the Supreme Court of Alabama, where a power granted by the city of Mobile to license bakers and to regulate the weight and price of bread, was sustained so far as regulating the weight of bread was concerned, no question was made as to the right to regulate the price.* There is no doubt of the competency of the State to prescribe the weight of a loaf of bread, as it may declare what weight shall constitute a pound or a ton. But I deny the power of any legislature under our government to fix the price which one shall receive for his property of any kind. If the power can be exercised as to one article it may as to all articles, and

---

* 3 Ala., 137.

the prices of everything from a calico gown to a city mansion may be the subject of legislative direction.

"Other instances of a similar character may no doubt be cited of attempted legislative interference with the rights of property. The act of Congress of 1820, mentioned by the court, is one of them. There Congress undertook to confer upon the city of Washington power to regulate the rates of wharfage at private wharves, and the fees for sweeping chimneys. Until some authoritative adjudication is had upon these and similar provisions, I must adhere, notwithstanding the legislation, to my opinion that those who own property have the right to fix the compensation at which they will allow its use, and that those who control services have a right to fix the compensation at which they will be rendered. The chimney-sweeps may, I think, safely claim all the compensation which they can obtain by bargain for their work. In the absence of any contract for property or services the law allows only a reasonable price or compensation, but what is a reasonable price in any case will depend upon a variety of considerations, and is not a matter for legislative determination.

"The practice of regulating by legislation the interest receivable for the use of money, when considered with reference to its origin, is only the assertion of a right of the government to control the extent to which a privilege granted by it may be exercised and enjoyed. By the ancient common law it was unlawful to take any money for the use of money; all who did so were called usurers, a term of great reproach, and were exposed to the censure of the Church. And if, after the death of a person, it was discovered that he had been a usurer whilst living, his chattels were forfeited to the King, and his lands escheated to the lord of the fee. No action could be maintained on any promise to pay for the use of money, because of the unlawfulness of the contract. Whilst the common law thus condemned all usury, Parliament interfered and made it lawful to take a limited amount of interest. It was not upon the theory that the legislature could arbitrarily fix the compensation which one could receive for the use of property, which by the general law was the subject of hire for compensation, that Parliament acted, but in order to confer a privilege which the common law denied. The reasons which led to this legislation originally have long since ceased to exist, and if the legislation is still persisted in, it is because a long acquiescence in the exercise of a power, especially when it was rightfully assumed in the first instance, is generally received as sufficient evidence of its continued lawfulness.*

---

* 10 Bacon's Abridgment, 264. The statute of 13 Elizabeth, C. 8, which allows ten per cent. interest, recites "that all usury being forbidden by the law of God is sin and detestable;" and the statute of 21 James the First, reducing the rate to eight per cent., provided that nothing in the law should be "construed to allow the practice of usury in point of religion or conscience," a clause introduced, it is said, to satisfy the bishops, who would not vote for the bill without it.

"There was also recognized in England by the ancient common law certain privileges as belonging to the lord of the manor, which grew out of the state of the country, the condition of the people, and the relation existing between him and his tenants under the feudal system. Among these was the right of the lord to compel all the tenants within his manor to grind their corn at his mill. No one, therefore, could set up a mill except by his license or by the license of the Crown, unless he claimed the right by prescription, which presupposed a grant from the lord or Crown, and, of course, with such license went the right to regulate the tolls to be received. Hence originated the doctrine which at one time obtained generally in this country, that there could be no mill to grind corn for the public without a grant or license from the public authorities. It is still, I believe, asserted in some States. This doctrine being recognized, all the rest followed. The right to control the toll accompanied the right to control the establishment of the mill.

"It requires no comment to point out the radical differences between the cases of public mills and interest on money and that of the warehouses in Chicago. No prerogative or privilege of the Crown to establish warehouses was ever asserted at the common law. The business of a warehouseman was at common law a private business, and is so in its nature. It has no special privileges connected with it, nor did the law ever extend to it any greater protection than it extended to all other private business. No reason can be assigned to justify legislation interfering with the legitimate profits of that business that would not equally justify an intermeddling with the business of every man in the community, so soon at least as his business became generally useful."*

THE RELATIONS BETWEEN THE FEDERAL GOVERNMENT AND THE STATE GOVERNMENTS.—THE RIGHTS OF THE STATES. —THE VIRGINIA JURY CASES AND THE ELECTION CASES FROM OHIO AND MARYLAND.

The government of the Union is a government of delegated powers. It can exercise only those powers and such as may be necessary and proper to give them full execution. All other powers which are not thus delegated, and which are not prohibited by the Constitution, are reserved to the States or to the people. This is not a matter of argu-

---

* See a learned note by Prof. Denslow upon the opinion of the court in the 16th vol., new series, of the American Law Register, p. 539-545.

ment and inference. It is the express language of the tenth amendment, which is as follows :

"The powers not delegated to the United States by the Constitution, nor prohibited by it to the States, are reserved to the States respectively, or to the people."

All that there is of " State rights," properly understood, is contained in this amendment. When reference is made to the authority and jurisdiction of States, and not merely to their proprietary interests, " rights " and " powers " are synonymous terms. The rights of the States, or " State rights," as the phrase is, are nothing more than the powers of the States reserved to them under the Constitution.

The government of the Union is invested with great powers, such as are essential to present the whole country as one nation in its intercourse with other countries, whether in peace or war, and such as are essential to the preservation of peace at home, and to facilitate intercourse and commerce among its people. In all its powers that government is supreme, and to their enforcement no impediment can be lawfully interposed. No true advocate for the maintenance of the rights of the States can ever claim otherwise. The Constitution itself on its face declares that it, and laws made in pursuance thereof, " shall be the supreme law of the land."

But the same supreme authority over matters delegated to it, which the government of the Union possesses, the States retain over matters not thus delegated. Over such matters the powers of the States are those of their original sovereignty. It was not for local matters, such as the management of the police of towns and cities, the opening of highways, the care of the sick, the education of children, the establishment of universities, the regulation, transfer, and descent of property, and the direction of the local interests of a community, that the government of the Union was created. It was created for the control of matters of common interest to all the States, which they could not in their separate capacities adequately manage.

The dual government of our fathers—that of the general government and that of the States—acting together solved the problem of a free government over a vast country, embracing different climates, furnishing different products, and having, in different sections, people of different habits and pursuits. Each State can have its local policy to suit its people, without interfering with a different policy pursued by another State. Take, for example, the three States of Maine, Georgia, and California. Maine, with its cool climate, its mountains of timber, its water-power for manufacturing establishments, and its neighboring fishing-grounds, may desire special legislation to develop its industries and promote its prosperity. Georgia, with its cotton fields, its balmly air, and its productive soil, may require a very different system of measures for which the legislation of Maine would be unsuitable. California, with its gold and silver mines, its seasons of rain and drought, the latter requiring provision for irrigation ; its vast production of cereals and fruits, its position on the Pacific Ocean encouraging commerce with Asia, may well call for other and different legislation. Under our federal system each of these States can pursue its own policy without any jarring between them. The government of the Union is over all, preserving peace among them, and protecting them all from foreign aggression or violence.

In the argument of the Cruikshank case before the Supreme Court, one of the counsel* used the following language, which well presents this subject :

" This complex government was curiously contrived to give liberty and safety to the people of all the States. It was fashioned by the people, in the name of the people. and for the people. Its aim was to keep the peace among the States and to manage affairs of common concern, while it left to the States the entire management of their own affairs. Its founders were wise and practical men. They knew what history had taught from the beginning of Greek civilization. that a number of small republics would perish without federation, and that federation would destroy the small republics without such a barrier as it was impossible to pass.

---

* David Dudley Field.

Liberty and safety were the ends to be won by the double and complex organization; liberty from the States, and safety from the Union, and the founders thought that they had contrived a scheme which would make the States and the Union essential parts of a great whole; that they had set bounds to each which they could not pass; in short, that they had founded 'liberty and union, one and inseparable.'

"No man in his senses could have supposed, at the formation of the Constitution, or can now suppose, that a consolidated government, extending over so much territory and so many people, can last a generation without the destruction of the States and of republican government with them. History is a fable, and political philosophy a delusion, if any government other than monarchical can stretch itself over fifty degrees of longitude and half as many of latitude, with fifty millions of people, where there are no local governments capable of standing by themselves and resisting all attempts to imperil their self-existence or impair their authority. The moment it is conceded that Washington may, at its discretion, regulate all the concerns of New York and California, of Louisiana and Maine; that the autonomy of the States has no defence stronger than the self-denial of fluctuating congressional majorities; at that moment the republic of our fathers will have disappeared, and a republic in name, but a despotism in fact, will have taken its place, to give way in another generation to a government with another name, and other attributes."

In his dissenting opinion in the Pensacola Telegraph case Judge Field gave expression to similar views, as follows:

"The late war was carried on at an enormous cost of life and property that the Union might be preserved ; but unless the independence of the States within their proper spheres be also preserved the Union is valueless. In our form of government the one is as essential as the other ; and a blow at one strikes both. The general government was formed for national purposes, principally that we might have within ourselves uniformity of commercial regulations, a common currency, one postal system and that the citizens of the several States might have in each equality of right and privilege ; and that in our foreign relations we might present ourselves as one nation. But the protection and enforcement of private rights of both persons and property, and the regulation of domestic affairs, were left chiefly with the States, and unless they are allowed to remain there it will be impossible for a country of such vast dimensions as ours, with every variety of soil and climate, creating different pursuits and conflicting interests in different sections, to be kept together in peace. As long as the general government confines itself to its great but limited sphere, and the States are left to control their domestic affairs and business, there can be no ground for public unrest and disturbance. Disquiet can only arise from the exercise of ungranted powers."—(96 U. S., 23.)

The fourteenth amendment has not changed this control of the States over matters of local concern. It only prohibits partial and discriminating legislation by them, requiring that all persons within their jurisdiction shall receive the equal protection of the laws. It interferes with the previous powers of the States in no other respect.

But by far the most exhaustive and elaborate consideration of the relations between the general government and that of the States, which has ever been had in the Supreme Court, is found in the dissenting opinions of Judge Field in the recent jury cases from Virginia, and in the election cases from Ohio and Maryland.

There were two jury cases; one arising upon the indictment of a county judge for not selecting as jurors persons of the colored race; and the other upon the removal of prisoners from a State court to a federal court after their conviction because persons of that race were not selected as jurors in the State court.

The first case arose as follows:

In Virginia all male citizens between the ages of twenty-one and sixty, who are entitled to vote and hold office under the constitution and laws of the State, are liable, with certain exceptions, not material to be here mentioned, to serve as jurors. The judge of each county or corporation court is required to prepare annually a list of such inhabitants of the county or corporation, not less than one hundred, nor exceeding three hundred in number, " as he shall think well qualified to serve as jurors, being persons of sound judgment and free from legal exception." The name of each person on the list thus prepared is to be written on a separate ballot and placed in a box to be kept by the clerk of the court. From this box the names of persons to be summoned as grand and petit jurors of the county are to be drawn.

The law, in thus providing for the preparation of the list of persons from whom the jurors are to be taken, makes no discrimination against persons of the colored

12

race. The judge of the county or corporation court is restricted in his action only by the condition that the persons selected shall, in his opinion, be "well qualified to serve as jurors," be "of sound judgment," and "free from legal exception." Whether they possess these qualifications, is left to his determination.

In 1878 J. D. Coles was the judge of the County Court of the County of Pittsylvania, in Virginia, and had held that office for some years. It was not pretended that, in the discharge of his judicial duties, he had ever selected as jurors persons who were not qualified to serve in that character, or who were not of sound judgment, or who were not free from legal exception. It was not even suggested in argument that he had not at all times faithfully obeyed the law of the State ; yet he was indicted in the District Court of the United States for the Western District of Virginia for having, on some undesignated day in the year 1878, excluded and failed to select as grand and petit jurors, citizens of the county, on account of race, color, and previous condition of servitude. The indictment did not state who those citizens were, or set forth any particulars of the offence, but charged it in the general words of a definition. The district court, nevertheless, issued a bench warrant, upon which the judge was arrested and, refusing to give bail, he was held in custody to answer the indictment. He thereupon presented to the Supreme Court of the United States a petition for a certiorari to that court to send up the record of its proceedings for examination, and for a writ of habeas corpus, alleging that its action was without jurisdiction, and that his imprisonment thereunder was unlawful, and praying to be released therefrom.

The Commonwealth of Virginia also presented a similar petition, declaring that she was injured by being deprived of the services of her judicial officer, by his unlawful arrest and imprisonment.

The indictment was founded upon the fourth section of

the act of Congress of March 1st, 1875, "to protect all citizens in their civil and legal rights," which declares: "That no citizen possessing all other qualifications, which are or may be prescribed by law, shall be disqualified for service as grand or petit juror, in any court of the United States, or of any State, on account of race; color, or previous condition of servitude ; and any officer or other person charged with any duty in the selection or summoning of jurors, who shall exclude or fail to summon any citizen for the cause aforesaid, shall, on conviction thereof, be deemed guilty of a misdemeanor, and be fined not more than five thousand dollars."

The case was elaborately and ably argued by Judge Robertson and the Attorney-General of Virginia for the petitioner, Coles, and the Commonwealth ; and by the Attorney-General of the United States and Judge Willoughby in opposition.

The court held the act of Congress constitutional, the indictment valid, and denied the petitions of Judge Coles and the Commonwealth of Virginia. A very elaborate opinion on sustaining their action was given by Judge Strong for the majority of the court. Judges Clifford and Field dissented, Judge Field delivering a dissenting opinion. In that opinion he contended that the district court exceeded its jurisdiction in issuing its process for the arrest of Judge Coles, on two grounds: 1st, because, assuming that the act of Congress of 1875 was constitutional and valid legislation, the indictment described no offence under it, but was void on its face; and 2ud, because that act, in the section upon which the indictment was founded, so far as it related to jurors in State courts, was unconstitutional and void. On the second ground Judge Field said as follows :

"Previous to the late amendments it would not have been contended, by any one familiar with the Constitution, that Congress was vested with any power to exercise supervision over the conduct of State officers in the discharge of their duties under the laws of the State, and prescribe a punishment for disregarding its directions. It would have been conceded that the selection of jurors was a subject exclusively for regulation by the States; that it was for them to determine who should act as jurors in their courts, from what class they should be taken, and what qualifications they should possess; and that their officers in carrying out the laws in this respect were responsible only to them. The States could have abolished jury trials altogether, and required all controversies to be submitted to the courts without their intervention. The sixth and seventh amendments, in which jury trials are mentioned, apply only to the federal courts, as has been repeatedly adjudged.

" The government created by the Constitution was not designed for the regulation of matters of purely local concern. The States required no aid from any external authority to manage their domestic affairs. They were fully competent to provide for the due administration of justice between their own citizens in their own courts, and they needed no directions in that matter from any other government, any more than they needed directions as to their highways and schools, their hospitals and charitable institutions, their public libraries, or the magistrates they should appoint for their towns and counties. It was only for matters which concerned all the States, and which could not be managed by them in their independent capacity, or managed only with great difficulty and embarrassment, that a general and common government was desired. Whilst they retained control of local matters, it was felt necessary that matters of general and common interest, which they could not wisely and efficiently manage, should be entrusted to a central authority. And so to the common government, which grew out of this prevailing necessity, was granted exclusive jurisdiction over external affairs, including the great powers of declaring war, making peace, and concluding treaties; but only such powers of internal regulation were conferred as were essential to the successful and efficient working of the government established; to facilitate intercourse and commerce between the people of the different States, and secure to them equality of protection in the several States.

" That the central government was created chiefly for matters of a general character, which concerned all the States and their people, and not for matters of interior regulation, is shown as much by the history of its formation, as by the express language of the Constitution. The Union preceded the Constitution. As happily expressed by the late Chief Justice, ' it began among the Colonies and grew out of common origin, mutual sympathies, kindred principles, similar interests, and geographical relations. It was confirmed and strengthened by the necessities of war, and received definite form and character and sanction from the Articles of Confederation.'—(Texas vs. White, 725.) Those articles were prepared by the Continental Congress, which was called to provide measures for the common defence of the colonies against the encroachments of the British Crown, and which, failing to secure redress, declared their independence. Its members foresaw that when the independence of the Colonies was established and acknowledged, their condition as separate and independent States would be beset with dangers threatening their peace and safety ; that disputes arising from conflicting interests and rivalries, always incident to neighboring nations, would lead to armed collisions and expose them to re-conquest by the mother country. To provide against the possibility of evils of this kind, the Articles of Confederation were prepared and submitted to the legislatures of the several States, and finally in 1781 were adopted. They declared that the States entered into a firm league of friendship with each other for their common defence ; the security of their liberties and their mutual and general welfare ; and they bound themselves to assist each other against attacks on account of religion, sovereignty, trade, or any other pretence. They clothed the new government created by them with powers supposed to be ample to secure these ends, and declared that there should be freedom of intercourse and commerce between the inhabitants of the several States. They provided for a general Congress, and, among other things, invested it with the exclusive power of determining on peace and war, except in case of invasion of a State by enemies or imminent danger of such invasion by Indians; of sending and receiving ambassadors, entering into treaties and alliances; of regulating the alloy and value of coin struck by the authority of the States or of the United States; of fixing the standard of weights and measures ; of regulating the trade and managing all affairs with the Indians; and of establishing and regulating post-offices from one State to another ; and they placed numerous restraints upon the States. But by none of the articles was any interference authorized with the purely internal affairs of the States, or with any of the instrumentalities by which the States administered their governments and dispensed justice among their people ; and they declared in terms that each State retained its sovereignty, freedom, and independence, and every power, jurisdiction, and right which was not by the articles expressly delegated to the United States in Congress assembled.

"When the government of the Confederation failed, chiefly through the want of all coercive authority, to carry into effect its measures, its power being only that of recommendation to the States, and the present Constitution was adopted, the same general ends were sought to be attained, namely, the creation of a central government, which would take exclusive charge of all our foreign relations, representing the people of all the States in that respect as one nation, and would at the same time secure at home freedom of intercourse between the States, equality of protection to citizens of each State in the several States, uniformity of commercial regulations, a common currency, a standard of weights and measures, one postal system, and such other matters as concerned all the States and their people.

" Accordingly, the new government was invested with powers adequate to the accomplishment of these purposes, with which it could act directly upon the people, and not by recommendation to the States, and enforce its measures through tribunals and officers of its own creation. There were also restraints placed upon the action of the States to prevent interference with the authority of the new government, and to secure to all persons protection against punishment by legislative decree, and ensure the fulfillment of contract obligations. But the control of matters of purely local concern, not coming within the scope of the powers granted or the restraints mentioned, was left, where it had always existed, with the States. The new government being one of granted powers, its authority was limited by them and such as were necessarily implied for their execution. But lest from a misconception of their extent these powers might be abused, the tenth amendment was at an early day adopted, declaring that 'the powers not delegated to the United States by the Constitution, nor prohibited by it to the States, are reserved to the States respectively, or to the people.'

"Now, if we look into the Constitution we shall not find a single word from its opening to its concluding line. nor in any of the amendments in force before the close of the civil war, nor, as I shall hereafter endeavor to show, in those subsequently adopted, which authorizes any interference by Congress with the States in the administration of their governments, and the enforcement of their laws with respect to any matter over which jurisdiction was not surrendered to the United States. The design of its framers was not to destroy the States. but to form a more perfect union between them, and whilst creating a central government for certain great purposes, to leave to the States in all matters, the jurisdiction of which was not surrendered, the functions essential to separate and independent existence. And so the late Chief Justice. speaking for the court in 1869, said: 'Not only, therefore. can there be no loss of separate and independent autonomy to the States, through their union under the Constitution, but it may be not unreasonably said that the preservation of the States, and the maintenance of their governments, are as much within the design and care of the Constitution as the preservation of the Union and the maintenance of the national government.' and then he adds, in that striking language which gives to an old truth new force and significance, that 'the Constitution. in all its provisions, looks to an indestructible Union composed of indestructible States.'—(Texas vs. White, 7 Wall., 725.)

"And Mr. Justice Nelson, also speaking for the court, in 1871, used this language: 'The general government, and the States, although both exist within the same territorial limits, are separate and distinct sovereignties. acting separately and independently of each other, within their respective spheres. The former in its appropriate sphere is supreme; but the States within the limits of their powers not granted, or, in the language of the tenth amendment. 'reserved,' are as independent of the general government as that government within its sphere is independent of the States.' And again : ' We have said that one of the reserved powers was that to establish a judicial department; it would have been more accurate, and in accordance with the existing state of things at the time, to have said the power to maintain a judicial department. All of the thirteen States were in the possession of this power and had exercised it at the adoption of the Constitution; and it is not pretended that any grant of it to the general government is found in that instrument. It is, therefore, one of the sovereign powers vested in the States by their constitutions, which remained unaltered and unimpaired, and in respect to which the State is as independent of the general government as that government is independent of the States.'—(The Collector vs. Day, 11 Wall., 124-6.)

"The cases of Texas vs. White, and Collector vs. Day, were decided after the thirteenth and fourteenth amendments, upon which it is sought to maintain the legislation in question, were adopted; and with their provisions the Chief Justice and Mr. Justice Nelson, and the court for which they spoke, were familiar. Yet neither they, nor any other judge of the court, suggested that the doctrines announced in the opinions, from which I have quoted, were in any respect modified or affected by the amendments.

"Nothing, in my judgment, could have a greater tendency to destroy the independence and autonomy of the States; reduce them to a humiliating and degrading dependence upon the central government; engender constant irritation; and destroy that domestic tranquillity which it was one of the objects of the Constitution to insure, than the doctrine asserted in this case, that Congress can exercise coercive authority over judicial officers of the States in the discharge of their duties under State laws. It will be only another step in the the same direction towards consolidation, when it assumes to exercise similar coercive authority over governors and legislators of the States.

"The Constitution declares that a 'person charged in any State with treason, felony, or other crime, who shall flee from justice and be found in another State, shall, on demand of the executive authority of the State from which he fled, be delivered up, to be removed to the State having jurisdiction of the crime.' And yet in the case of The Commonwealth of Kentucky vs. Dennison, where a fugitive from justice from Kentucky was demanded from the governor of Ohio, and on his refusal application was made to this court for a mandamus to compel him to perform his duty in this respect, it was held that there was no clause or provision in the Constitution which armed the government of the United States with authority to compel the executive of a State to perform his duty, nor to inflict any punishment for his neglect or refusal. 'Indeed, such a power,' said Mr. Chief Justice Taney, speaking for the whole court, ' would place every State under the control and dominion of the general government even in the administration of its internal concerns and reserved rights.'—(24 How., 107.) And Mr. Justice Nelson, in the case of Collector vs. Day, where it was held that it was not competent for Congress to impose a tax upon the salary of a judicial officer of a State, said, that 'any government whose means employed in conducting its operations are made subject to the control of another and distinct government, can exist only at the mercy of that government.' I could add to these authorities, if anything more were required, that all the recorded utterances of the statesmen who participated in framing the Constitution and urging its adoption, and of the publicists and jurists who have since studied its language and aided in the enforcement of its provisions, are inconsistent with the pretension advanced in this case by the counsel of the government.

" The duties of the county judge in the selection of jurors were judicial in their nature. They involved the exercise of discretion and judgment. He was to determine who were qualified to serve in that character, and for that purpose whether they possessed sound judgment and were free from legal exceptions. The law under which he acted had been in force for many years, and had been always considered by the judicial authorities of Virginia to be in conformity with its constitution, which inhibits the legislature from requiring of its judges any other than judicial duties. A test as to the character of an act is found in the power of a writ of mandamus to enforce its performance in a particular way. If the act be a judicial one, the writ can only require the judge to proceed in the discharge of his duty with reference to it; the manner of performance cannot be dictated. Here the writ could not command the county judge to select as jurors any particular persons, black or white, but only to proceed and select such as are qualified, its command in that respect being subject to the limitation incident to all commands of such writs upon judicial officers touching judicial acts.

" The thirteenth and fourteenth amendments are relied upon, as already stated, to support the legislation in question. The thirteenth amendment declares 'That neither slavery nor involuntary servitude, except as a punishment for crime, whereof the party shall have been duly convicted, shall exist within the United States, or any place subject to their jurisdiction.' The fourteenth amendment, in its first section, which is the only one having any bearing upon the questions involved in this case, declares that 'All persons born or naturalized in the United States, and subject to the jurisdiction thereof, are citizens of the United States and of the State wherein they reside. No State shall make or enforce any law which shall abridge the privileges or immunities of citizens of the United States; nor shall any State deprive any person of life, liberty, or property without due process of law; nor deny to any person within its jurisdiction the equal protection of the laws.' The fifteenth amendment, which declares that 'the right of citizens of the United States to vote shall not be denied or abridged by the United States, or by any State, on account of race, color, or previous condition of servitude,' is not material to the question before us, except as showing that it was only with respect to the suffrage that an interdict was in terms placed against legislation on account of race, color, or previous condition of servitude. Equality in their civil rights was in other ways secured to persons of the colored race ; and the ballot being assured to them, an effectual means against unjust legislation was placed in their hands. To each of these amendments a clause is added authorizing Congress to enforce its provisions by 'appropriate legislation.'

"The history of the amendments is fresh in the recollection of all of us. They grew out of the late civil war and the events which followed it. They were primarily designed to give freedom to persons of the African race, prevent their future enslavement, make them citizens, prevent discriminating State legislation against their rights as freemen, and secure to them the ballot. The generality of the language used necessarily extends some of their provisions to all persons of every race and color; but in construing the amendments and giving effect to them, the occasion of their adoption and the purposes they were designed to attain should be always borne in mind. Nor should it be forgotten that they are additions to the previous amendments, and are to be construed in connection with them and the original Constitution as one instrument. They do not, in terms, contravene or repeal anything which previously existed in the Constitution and those amendments. Aside from the extinction of slavery, and the declaration of citizenship, their provisions are merely prohibitory upon the States; and there is nothing in their language or purpose which indicates that they are to be construed or enforced in any way different from that adopted with reference to previous restraints upon the States. The provision authorizing Congress to enforce them by appropriate legislation does not enlarge their scope, nor confer any authority which would not have existed independently of it. No legislation would be appropriate which should contravene the express prohibitions upon Congress previously existing, as, for instance, that it should not pass a bill of attainder or an ex post facto law. Nor would legislation be appropriate which should conflict with the implied prohibitions upon Congress. They are as obligatory as the express prohibitions. The Constitution, as already stated, contemplates the existence and independence of the States in all their reserved powers. If the States were destroyed there could of course be no United States. In the language of this court, in Collector vs. Day, ' without them the general government itself would disappear from the family of nations.' Legislation could not, therefore, be appropriate which, under pretence of prohibiting a State from doing certain things, should tend to destroy it, or any of its essential attributes. To every State, as understood in the American sense, there must be, with reference to the subjects over which it has jurisdiction, absolute freedom from all external interference in the exercise of its legislative, judicial, and executive authority. Congress could not undertake to prescribe the duties of a State legislature and the rules it should follow, and the motives by which it should be governed, and authorize criminal prosecutions against the members if its directions were disregarded ; for the independence of the legislature is essential to the independence and autonomy of the State. Congress could not lay down rules for the guidance of the State judiciary, and prescribe to it the law and the motives by which it should be controlled, and if these were disregarded, direct criminal proceedings against its members; because a judiciary independent of external authority is essential to the independence of the State, and, also, I may add, to a just and efficient administration of justice in her courts. Congress could not dictate to the executive of a State the bills he might approve, the pardons and reprieves he might grant, or the manner in which he might discharge the functions of his office, and assume to punish him if its dictates were disregarded, because his independence, within the reserved powers, is essential to that of the State. Indeed, the independence of a State consists in the independence of its legislative, executive, and judicial officers, through whom alone it acts. If this were not so, a State would cease to be a self-existing and an indestructible member of the Union, and would be brought to the level of a dependent municipal corporation, existing only with such powers as Congress might prescribe.

"I cannot think I am mistaken in saying that a change so radical in the relation between the federal and State authorities, as would justify legislation interfering with the independent action of the different departments of the state governments, in all matters over which the States retain jurisdiction, was never contemplated by the recent amendments. The people in adopting them did not suppose they were altering the fundamental theory of their dual system of governments. The discussions attending their consideration in Congress, and before the people, when presented to the legislatures of the States for adoption, can be successfully appealed to in support of this assertion. The Union was preserved at a fearful cost of life and property. The institution of slavery in a portion of the country was the cause of constant irritation and crimination between the people of the States where it existed and those of the free States, which finally led to a rupture between them and to the civil war. As the war progressed its sacrifices and burdens filled the people of the loyal States with a determination, that not only should the Union be preserved, but that the institution, which, in their judgment, had threatened its dissolution, should be abolished. The emancipation proclamation of President Lincoln expressed this determination, though placed on the ground of military necessity. The thirteenth amendment carried it into the organic law. That amendment prohibits slavery and involuntary servitude, except for crime, within the United States, or any place subject to their jurisdiction. Its language is not restricted to the slavery of any particular class. It applies to all men; and embraces in its comprehensive language not merely that form of slavery which consists in the denial of personal rights to the slave, and subjects him to the condition of a chattel, but also serfage, vassalage, peonage, villanage, and every other form of compulsory service for the benefit, pleasure, or caprice of others. It was intended to render every one within the domain of the Republic a freeman, with the right to follow the ordinary pursuits of life without other restraints than such as are applied to all others, and to enjoy equally with them the earnings of his labor. But it confers no political rights; it leaves the States free, as before its adoption, to determine who shall hold their offices and participate in the administration of their laws. A similar prohibition of slavery and involuntary servitude was in the constitution of several States previous to its adoption by the United States; and it was never held to confer any political rights.

"On the eighteenth of December, 1865, this amendment was ratified, that is, the official proclamation of its ratification was then made; and in April of the following year the civil rights act was passed. Its first section declares that all persons born in the United States, and not subject to any foreign power, excluding Indians not taxed, are 'citizens of the United States,' and that 'such citizens, of every race and color, without regard to any previous condition of slavery or involuntary servitude, except as a punishment for crime, of which the party shall have been duly convicted, shall have the same right in every State and territory in the United States, to make and enforce contracts, to sue, be parties and give evidence, to inherit, purchase, lease, sell, hold, and convey real and personal property, and to full and equal benefit of all laws and proceedings for the security of person and property as is enjoyed by white persons.' This legislation was intended to secure to all persons in the United States practical freedom. But its validity was questioned in many quarters entitled to consideration, and some of its provisions not long afterwards were declared by State courts to be beyond the constitutional authority of Congress.—(Bowlin vs. Commonwealth, 2 Bush, 5.) There were also complaints made that notwithstanding the amendment abolishing slavery and involuntary servitude, except for crime, the freedmen were, by legislation in some of the Southern States, subjected to such burdensome disabilities in the acquisition and enjoyment of property, and the pursuit of happiness, as to render their freedom of little value.—(Slaughter-House Cases, 16 Wall., 70.) There were, besides, complaints of the existence, in those sections, of a feeling of dislike towards citizens of the North seeking residence there, and towards such of their own citizens as had adhered to the national government during the war, which could not fail to find expression in hostile and discriminating legislation. It is immaterial whether these complaints were justified or not; they were believed by many persons to be well-founded. To remove the cause of them; to obviate objections to the validity of legislation similar to that contained in the first section of the civil rights act; to prevent the possibility of hostile and discriminating legislation in future by a State against any citizen of the United States, and the enforcement of any such legislation already had; and to secure to all persons within the jurisdiction of the States the equal protection of the laws, the first section of the fourteenth amendment was adopted. Its first clause declared who are citizens of the United States and of the States. It thus removed from discussion the question, which had previously been debated, and though decided, not settled, by the judgment in the Dred Scott case, whether descendants of persons brought to this country and sold as slaves were citizens within the meaning of the Constitution. It also recognized, if it did not create, a national citizenship, as contradistinguished from that of the States. But the privilege or the duty, whichever it may be called, of acting as a juror in the courts of the country, is not an incident of citizenship. Women are citizens; so are the aged above sixty, and children in their minority ; yet they are not allowed in Virginia to act as jurors. Though some of these are in all respects qualified for such service, no one will pretend that their exclusion by law from the jury list impairs their rights as citizens.

" The second clause of the first section of the amendment declares that 'no State shall make or enforce any law which shall abridge the privileges or immunities of citizens of the United States.' In the Slaughter-House cases, it was held by a majority of the court that this clause had reference only to privileges and immunities of citizens of the United States, as distinguished from those of citizens of the States, and, therefore, did not apply to those fundamental civil rights which belong to citizens of all free governments, such as the right to acquire and enjoy property and pursue happiness, subject only to such just restraints as might be prescribed for the general good. If this construction be correct there can be no pretence that the privilege or duty of acting as a juror in a State court is within the inhibition of the clause. Nor could it be within that inhibition if a broader construction were given to the clause, and it should be held, as contended by the minority of the court in the Slaughter-House cases, that it prohibits the denial or abridgment by any State of those fundamental privileges and immunities which of right belong to citizens of all free governments; and with which the Declaration of Independence proclaimed that all men were endowed by their Creator, and to secure which governments were instituted among men. These fundamental rights were secured, previous to the amendment, to citizens of each State in the other States, by the second section of the fourth article of the Constitution, which declares that ' the citizens of each State shall be entitled to all privileges and immunities of citizens in the several States.' Among those privileges and immunities, it was never contended that jury duty or jury service was included.

" The third clause in the first section of the amendment declares that no State ' shall deprive any person of life, liberty, or property without due process of law.' It will not be contended that this clause confers upon the citizen any right to serve as a juror in the State courts. It exists in the constitutions of nearly all the States, and is only an additional security against arbitrary deprivation of life and liberty, and arbitrary spoliation of property. It means that neither can be taken, or the enjoyment thereof impaired, except in the course of the regular administration of the law in the established tribunals. The existence of this clause in the amendment is to me a persuasive argument that those who framed it, and the legislatures of the States which adopted it, never contemplated that the prohibition was to be enforced in any other way than through the judicial tribunals, as previous prohibitions upon the States had always been enforced. If Congress could, as an appropriate means to enforce the prohibition, prescribe criminal prosecutions for its infraction against legislators, judges, and other officers of the States, it would be authorized to frame a vast portion of their laws, for there are few subjects upon which legislation can be had besides life, liberty, and property. In determining what constitutes a deprivation of property, it might prescribe the conditions upon which property shall be acquired and held; and declare as to what subjects property rights shall exist. In determining what constitutes deprivation of liberty, it might prescribe in what way and by what means the liberty of the citizen shall be deemed protected. In prescribing punishment for deprivation of life, it might prescribe a code of criminal procedure. All this and more might be done if it once be admitted, as the court asserts in this case, that Congress can authorize a criminal prosecution for the infraction of the prohibitions. It cannot prescribe punishment without defining crime, and, therefore, must give expression to its own views as to what constitutes protection to life, liberty, and property.

" The fourth clause in the first section of the amendment declares that no State shall 'deny to any person within its jurisdiction the equal protection of the laws.' Upon this clause the counsel of the district judge chiefly rely to sustain the validity of the legislation in question. But the universality of the protection secured necessarily renders their position untenable. All persons within the jurisdiction of the State, whether permanent residents or temporary sojourners, whether old or young, male or female, are to be equally protected. Yet no one will contend that equal protection to women, to children, to the aged, to aliens, can only be secured by allowing persons of the class to which they belong to act as jurors in cases affecting their interests. The equality of protection intended does not require that all persons shall be permitted to participate in the government of the State and the administration of its laws, to hold its offices, or be clothed with any public trusts. As already said, the universality of the protection assured repels any such conclusion.

" The equality of the protection secured extends only to civil rights as distinguished from those which are political, or arise from the form of the government and its mode of administration. And yet the reach and influence of the amendment are immense. It opens the courts of the country to every one, on the same terms, for the security of his person and property, the prevention and redress of wrongs, and the enforcement of contracts; it assures to every one the same rules of evidence and modes of procedure; it allows no impediments to the acquisition of property and the pursuit of happiness, to which all are not subjected; it suffers no other or greater burdens or charges to be laid upon one than such as are equally borne by others; and in the administration of criminal justice it permits no different or greater punishment to be imposed upon one than such as is prescribed to all for like offences. It secures to all persons their civil rights upon the same terms; but it leaves political rights, or such as arise from the form of goverpment and its administration, as they stood previous to its adoption. It has no more reference to them than it has to social rights and duties, which do not rest upon any positive law, though they are more potential in controlling the intercourse of individuals. In the consideration of questions growing out of these amendments much confusion has arisen from a failure to distinguish between the civil and the political rights of citizens. Civil rights are absolute and personal. Political rights on the other hand are conditioned and dependent upon the discretion of the elective or appointing power, whether that be the people acting through the ballot, or one of the departments of their government. The civil rights of the individual are never to be withheld, and may be always judicially enforced. The political rights which he may enjoy, such as holding office and discharging a public trust, are qualified because their possession depends on his fitness, to be adjudged by those whom society has clothed with the elective authority. The thirteenth and fourteenth amendments were designed to secure the civil rights of all persons of every race, color, and condition, but they left to the States to determine to whom the possession of political power should be entrusted. This is manifest from the fact that when it was desired to confer political power upon the newly-made citizens of the States, as was done by inhibiting the denial to them of the suffrage on account of race, color, or previous condition of servitude, a new amendment was required.

"The doctrine of the district judge, for which the counsel contend, would lead to some singular results. If, when a colored person is accused of a criminal offence, the presence of persons of his race on the jury by which he is to be tried is essential to secure to him the equal protection of the laws, it would seem that the presence of such persons on the bench would be equally essential, if the court should consist of more than one judge, as in many cases it may; and if it should consist of a single judge, that such protection would be impossible. A similar objection might be raised to the composition of any appellate court to which the case, after verdict, might be carried.

"The position that in cases where the rights of colored persons are concerned, justice will not be done to them unless they have a mixed jury, is founded upon the notion that in such cases white persons will not be fair and honest jurors. If this position be correct there ought not to be any white persons on the jury where the interests of colored porsons only are involved. That jury would not be an honest or fair one, of which any of its members should be governed in his judgment by other considerations than the law and the evidence; and that decision would hardly be considered just which should be reached by a sort of compromise, in which the prejudices of one race were set off against the prejudices of the other. To be consistent, those who hold this notion should contend that in cases affecting members of the colored race only the juries should be composed entirely of colored persons, and that the presiding judge should be of the same race. To this result the doctrine asserted by the District Court logically leads. The jury *de medietate linguæ*, anciently allowed in England for the trial of an alien, was expressly authorized by statute probably as much because of the difference of language and customs between him and Englishmen, and the greater probability of his defence being more fully understood, as because it would be heard in a more friendly spirit by jurors of his own country and language.

"If these views as to the purport and meaning of the thirteenth and fourteenth amendments of the Constitution be correct, there is no warrant for the act of Congress under which the indictment in this case was found, and the arrest and imprisonment of the petitioner were unlawful, and his release should be ordered.

"The case is one which should not be delayed for the slow process of a trial in the court below, and a subsequent appeal, in case of conviction, to this court to be heard years hence. The Commonwealth of Virginia has represented to us that the services of her judicial officer are needed in her courts for the administration of justice between her citizens, and she asks that the highest tribunal of the Union will release him from his unlawful arrest, in order that he may perform the duties of his office. Those who regard the independence of the States in all their reserved powers—and this includes the independence of their legislative, judicial, and executive departments—as essential to the successful maintenance of our form of government, cannot fail to view with the gravest apprehension for the future, the indictment, in a court of the United States, of a judicial officer of a State for the manner in which he has discharged his duties under her laws, and of which she makes no complaint. The proceeding is a gross offence to the State; it is an attack upon her sovereignty in matters over which she has never surrendered her jurisdiction. The doctrine which sustains it, carried to its logical results, would degrade and sink her to the level of a mere local municipal corporation; for if Congress can render an officer of a State criminally liable for the manner in which he discharges his duties under her laws, it can prescribe the nature and extent of the penalty to which he shall be subjected on conviction; it may imprison him for life or punish him by removal from office. And if it can make the exclusion of persons from jury service on account of race or color a criminal offence, it can make their exclusion from office on that account also criminal; and, adopting the doctrine of the district judge in this case, the failure to appoint them to office will be presumptive evidence of their exclusion on that ground. To such a result are we logically led. The legislation of Congress is founded, and is sustained by this court, as it seems to me, upon a theory as to what constitutes the equal protection of the laws, which is purely speculative, not warranted by any experience of the country, and not in accordance with the understanding of the people as to the meaning of those terms since the organization of the government."

The decision of the court in this case attracted great attention throughout the country, for the views expressed seemed to indicate a wide departure from previous doctrines, and to recognize in the general government a power over the States never before supposed to exist. All the principal journals contained comments upon it. The following extracts from a leading Republican paper of California express with much force the sentiments of thoughtful men of all parties :

"THE LAST STEP TOWARDS CENTRALIZATION.

From the RECORD-UNION *of March 20th*, 1880.

" In the interpretation of the last judicial advance towards governmental centralization, the public judgment is warped by partisan prejudice, and Republicans are led to believe that they have witnessed a fresh triumph for the principles of their party, when in reality they are unwittingly consenting to the removal of all those checks to centralization which afford the strongest guarantees of popular liberty. The decision of the United States Supreme Court, in the matter of J. D. Coles and the Commonwealth of Virginia, petioners for the writ of habeas corpus, marks a decided forward step in that modern policy of governmental metamorphosis which is gradually withdrawing from and denying to the States those elements of independent sovereignty and local self-government never surrendered by them to the federal government. So insidiously is this transformation proceeding, that it promises to have extended beyond the possibility of check or retracement before the nation has clearly realized what it is that is being done. Twenty years ago the perception of the reserved rights of the States was so much keener than now that such a decision as this would certainly have created a profound sensation, and as certainly have provoked the most energetic and earnest censure, whereas to-day it passes with no more notice than consists in the customary indorsement held indispensable by every party serf when a doctrine supposed to be partisan in its character is promulgated. In fact the concernment here is not partisan, but national. Because the Commonwealth of Virginia is a party to the proceeding, and the political rights of negroes are in question, it has been hastily concluded that the whole matter was one of reconstruction, and that inasmuch as the court had ruled against the State, another defeat for the ' Secessionists ' was to be scored. It is necessary to point out that, though in truth reconstruction is here dealt with, it is not alone the technical reconstruction of the Southern States, but the absolute reconstruction of the Union between the States that is now in course of being arranged.———

" It is neither necessary nor desirable to import any political bias into the consideration of this subject. It transcends all party issues, for it involves the question of the future of the whole Republic. It is here deliberately set forth by the highest judicial authority that the constitutional amendments give the federal government powers over the States which are incompatible with the maintenance of any independence whatever, and which not only facilitate but hasten the transformation of the government from a federation of sovereign States to a centralized democratic absolutism. The doctrine now asserted goes the length of subordinating *all* State authority to federal authority; for it involves the right of the latter to traverse all State legislation, to set aside the rules made by State legislatures for the government of the State judiciary, to punish State officials for obeying State laws, and in a word, to reduce all the States to the level of mere municipalities, existing only at the will and caprice of Congress. The tendency in this direction has, as we have often pointed out, increased continually since the close of the war.———All history shows that the diffusion of institutional self-government to the greatest possible extent is necessary to the securing of the largest measure of freedom and the most just and least burdensome government. This diffusion the American States enjoyed originally, and it is this which is threatened.———The danger lies not alone in the strongly marked centralizing policy of the Supreme Court, but in the formidable support which the corrupt condition of politics gives to this movement.———The greater a country becomes, the denser its population, the more complex its interests, the more necessary is it that the people everywhere should keep the levers of self-government in their own hands. For the removal of authority to a distance always involves the weakening of responsibility and the encouragement of corruption."

The second jury case from Virginia arose in this wise: Two colored persons in Virginia were indicted in a county court in that State for the crime of murder. The person alleged to have been murdered was a white man. On being arraigned they pleaded not guilty, and on their demand their trial was removed to the circuit court of the county. They there moved that the panel of jurors summoned, which was composed entirely of white persons, should be so modified as to allow one-third of the number to be persons of the colored race.

This motion was denied, as it satisfactorily appeared that the jurors had been drawn from the jury-box according to law. The prisoners then presented a petition for the removal of the case to the United States Circuit Court, alleging, in substance, that the rights secured by the law providing for the equal civil rights of all citizens of the

United States were denied to them, inasmuch as their application for a mixed jury had been refused. It also alleged that a strong prejudice existed in the community against them on the ground of their color, the person alleged to have been murdered being a white man. Their petition was denied and the prisoners were separately tried and convicted of murder. Both obtained new trials, one by motion to the court, and one on appeal to the Court of Appeals. When they were brought up for a second trial they again moved to have the prosecution removed to the Circuit Court of the United States. This was also denied. They were then tried separately. In one case the jury disagreed and the prisoner was removed to jail to await another trial. In the other case the prisoner was convicted and he was sentenced to imprisonment in penitentiary.

Whilst the prisoners were in jail, one waiting for a new trial and the other until he could be removed under his sentence to the penitentiary, they procured a copy of the record of proceedings against them and presented it to the Circuit Court of the United States for the Western District of Virginia, then held by Alexander Rives, the district judge, with the petition for removal presented to the State court, and prayed that the prosecution might be there docketed and proceeded with. The circuit court granted the petition, directed the cases to be placed on the docket and authorized the clerk to issue a writ of *habeas corpus* to the marshal of the district to take the prisoners into his custody, and to summon for their trial twenty-five jurors to attend at the next term. A writ of *habeas corpus* was accordingly issued, and pursuant to its command the prisoners were taken into the custody of the marshal. Thereupon the Commonwealth of Virginia presented a petition to the Supreme Court of the United States praying for a mandamus to be directed to the district judge, commanding him to order the marshal to re-deliver the prisoners to her authorities, upon the ground that the judge in his proceedings had transcended the jurisdiction of his court, and exercised powers not vested in him. An order was accordingly issued to the judge to show cause why the writ should not issue. In his return he admitted the facts stated, and justified his action on the ground that the refusal of the State court to set aside the panel of jurors, and to give the prisoners a jury composed in part of their own race, was a denial to them of the equal protection of the laws, and brought their cases within the provision of the act of Congress authorizing a removal of criminal prosecutions to the federal courts. The attorney-general of Virginia, contending that the return was insufficient, moved that the writ might be issued as prayed.

The application was argued by the same counsel who argued the first jury case. The court granted the writ and ordered that the prisoners should be returned to the State court, but it placed its decision on the ground that the act of Congress, providing for the removal of criminal prosecutions from State to federal courts, was only intended for cases where the application was made before a trial or final hearing had commenced, and that the denial of rights for which a removal was authorized was such as resulted from the constitution or laws of the State and not such as might be manifested at the trial or hearing ; but it left open the question whether Congress could not authorize a transfer of a case to the federal courts at any stage of its proceedings whenever a ruling is made denying to the defendant the equal protection of the laws. Judges Field and Clifford concurred in the judgment of the court that the prisoners should be returned to the officers of Virginia from whose custody they were taken ; that the prosecution against them should be remanded to the State court from which it was removed, and that a mandamus to the district judge was an appropriate remedy to effect those ends, but as they did not agree with all the views expressed in the opinion of the court, and there were other reasons equally cogent with those given for the decision rendered, Judge Field thought proper to

state, in a separate opinion, the grounds of their concurrence. After discussing at length the right of the court
to issue a mandamus in the case, and referring to the act
of Congress, he said as follows :

"By this enactment it appears that in order to obtain a removal of a
prosecution from a State to a federal court—except where it is against a
public officer or other person for certain trespasses or conduct not material to consider in this connection—the petition of the accused must
show a denial of, or an inability to enforce in the tribunals of the State,
or of that part of the State where the prosecution is pending, some right
secured to him by the law providing for the equal rights of citizens or
persons within the jurisdiction of the United States. But how must the
denial of a right under such a law, or the accused's inability to enforce
it in the judicial tribunals of the State, be made to appear? So far as
the accused is concerned, the law requires him to state and verify the
facts, and from them the court will determine whether such denial or
inability exists. His naked averment of such denial or inability can
hardly be deemed sufficient; if it were so, few prosecutions would be
retained in a State court for insufficient allegations when the accused
imagined he would gain by the removal.—(Texas vs. Gaines, 2 Woods,
344.) There must be such a presentation of facts as to lead the court to
the conclusion that the averments of the accused are well founded.
There are many ways in which a person may be denied his rights, or be
unable to enforce them in the tribunals of a State. The denial or inability may arise from direct legislation, depriving him of their enjoyment or the means of their enforcement, or discriminating against him or
the class, sect, or race to which he belongs. And it may arise from popular
prejudices, passions, or excitement, biasing the minds of jurors and
judges. Religious animosities, political controversies, antagonisms of
race, and a multitude of other causes will always operate, in a greater or
less degree, as impediments to the full enjoyment and enforcement of civil
rights. We cannot think that the act of Congress contemplated a denial
of, or an inability to enforce one's rights from these latter and similar
causes, and intended to authorize a removal of a prosecution by reason
of them from a State to a federal court. Some of these causes have always existed in some localities in every State, and the remedy for them
has been found in a change of the place of trial to other localities where
like impediments to impartial action of the tribunals did not exist. The
civil rights act, to which reference is made in the section in question,
was only intended to secure to the colored race the same rights and privileges as are enjoyed by white persons ; it was not designed to relieve them
from those obstacles in the enjoyment of their rights to which all other persons are subject, and which grow out of popular prejudices and passions.
"The denial of rights or the inability to enforce them, to which the
section refers, is, in my opinion, such as arises from legislative action of

the State, as, for example, an act excluding colored persons from being witnesses, making contracts, acquiring property, and the like. With respect to obstacles to the enjoyment of rights arising from other causes, persons of the colored race must take their chances of removing or providing against them with the rest of the community.

" This conclusion is strengthened by the provisions of the 14th amendment to the Constitution. The original civil rights act was passed, it is true, before the adoption of that amendment, but great doubt was expressed as to its validity, and to obtain authority for similar legislation, and thus obviate the objections which had been raised to its first section, was one of the objects of the amendment. After its adoption the civil rights act was re-enacted, and upon the first section of that amendment it rests. That section is directed against the State. Its language is that ' no State shall make or enforce any law which shall abridge the privileges or immunities of citizens of the United States ; nor shall any State deprive any person of life, liberty, or property without due process of law, nor deny to any person within its jurisdiction the equal protection of the laws.' As the State, in the administration of its government, acts through its executive, legislative, and judicial departments, the inhibition applies to them. But the executive and judicial departments only construe and enforce the laws of the State ; the inhibition, therefore, is in effect against passing and enforcing any laws which are designed to accomplish the ends forbidden. If an executive or judicial officer exercises power with which he is not invested by law, and does unauthorized acts, the State is not responsible for them. The action of the judicial officer in such a case, where the rights of a citizen under the laws of the United States are disregarded, may be reviewed and corrected or reversed by this court; it cannot be imputed to the State, so as to make it evidence that she in her sovereign or legislative capacity denies the rights invaded or refuses to allow their enforcement. It is merely the ordinary case of an erroneous ruling of an inferior tribunal. Nor can the unauthorized action of an executive officer, impinging upon the rights of the citizen, be taken as evidence of her intention or policy so as to charge upon her a denial of such rights.

" If these views are correct, no cause is shown in the petition of the prisoners that justified a removal of the prosecutions against them to the federal court. No law of Virginia makes any discrimination against persons of the colored race, or excludes them from the jury. The law respecting jurors provides that ' all male citizens, twenty-one years of age and not over sixty, who are entitled to vote and hold office under the constitution and laws of the State,' with certain exemptions not material to the question presented, may be jurors; and it authorizes an annual selection in each county, by the county judge, from the citizens at large, of from one to three hundred persons, whose names are to be placed in a box, and from them the jurors, grand and petit, of the county are to be drawn. There is no restriction placed upon the county judge in selecting them, except that they shall be such as he shall think ' well qualified to serve as jurors, being persons of sound judgment and free from legal exception.' The mode thus provided, properly carried out, cannot fail to secure competent jurors. Certain it is that no rights of the prisoners are denied by this legislation. The application to the State court, upon the refusal of which the peti.ion was presented, was for a venire composed of one-third of their race, a proceeding wholly inadmissible in any jury system which obtains in the several States.

" From the return of the district judge it would seem that in his judgment the presence of persons of the colored race on the jury is essential to secure to them ' the equal protection of the laws ;' but how this conclusion is reached is not apparent, except upon the general theory that such protection can only be afforded to parties when persons of the class to which they belong are allowed to sit on their juries. The correctness of this theory is contradicted by every day's experience. Women are not allowed to sit on juries ; are they thereby denied the equal protection of the laws ? Foreigners resident in the country are not permitted to act as jurors, yet they are protected in their rights equally with citizens. Persons over sixty years of age in Virginia are disqualified as jurors, yet no one will pretend that they do not enjoy the equal protection of the laws. If when a colored person is indicted for a criminal offence it is essential, to secure to him the equal protection of the laws, that persons of his race should be on the jury by which he is tried, it would seem that the presence of such persons on the bench should be equally essential, where the court consists of more than one judge ; and that if it should consist of only a single judge, such protection would be impossible. To such an absurd result does the doctrine lead, which the circuit court announced as controlling its action.

" The equality of protection assured by the fourteenth amendment to all persons in the State does not imply that they shall be allowed to participate in the administration of its laws, or to hold any of its offices, or to discharge any duties of a public trust. The universality of the protection intended excludes any such inference. Were this not so, aliens resident in the country, or temporarily here, of whom there are many thousands in each State, would be without that equal protection which the amendment declares that no State shall deny to any person within its jurisdiction.

" It follows from these views as to the meaning and purpose of the act of Congress that the removal of the prosecution in this case from the State to the federal court is unauthorized by it ; and that the order of the circuit court to the marshal to take the prisoners from the custody of the State authorities is illegal and void.

" The second objection of the Commonwealth to the legality of the removal is equally conclusive. The prosecution is for the crime of murder, committed within her limits by persons and at a place subject to her jurisdiction. The offence charged is against her authority and laws, and she alone has the right to inquire into its commission, and to punish the offender. Murder is not an offence against the United States, except when committed on an American vessel on the high seas, or in some port or haven without the jurisdiction of the State, or in the District of Columbia, or in the Territories, or at other places where the national government has exclusive jurisdiction. The offence within the limits of a State, except where jurisdiction has been ceded to the United States, is as much beyond the jurisdiction of their courts as though it had been committed on another continent. The prosecution of the offence in such a case does not, therefore, arise under the Constitution and laws of the United States; and the act of Congress which attempts to give the federal courts jurisdiction of it is, to my mind, a clear infraction of the Constitution. That instrument defines and limits the judicial power of the United States.

" It declares, among other things, that the judicial power shall extend to cases in law and equity arising under the Constitution, laws, and treaties of the United States, and to various controversies to which a State is a party ; but it does not include in its enumeration controversies between a State and its own citizens. There can be no ground, therefore, for the assumption by a federal court of jurisdiction of offences against the laws of a State. The judicial power granted by the Constitution does not cover any such case or controversy. And whilst it is well settled that the exercise of the power granted may be extended to new cases as they arise under the Constitution and laws, the power itself cannot be enlarged by Congress. The Constitution creating a government of limited powers puts a bound upon those which are judicial as well as those which are legislative, which cannot be lawfully passed.

" This view would seem to be conclusive against the validity of the attempted removal of the prosecution in this case from the State court. The federal court could not in the first instance have taken jurisdiction of the offence charged, and summoned a grand jury to present an indictment against the accused ; and if it could not have taken jurisdiction at first, it cannot do so upon a removal of the prosecution to it. The jurisdiction exercised upon the removal is original and not appellate, as is sometimes erroneously asserted, for, as stated by Chief Justice Marshall in Marbury vs. Madison, already, cited, it is of the essence of appellate jurisdiction that it revises and corrects proceedings already had. The removal is only an indirect mode by which the federal court acquires original jurisdiction.—(Railroad Co. vs. Whitton, 13 Wall., 287.)

" The Constitution, it is to be observed, in the distribution of the judicial power, declares that in the cases enumerated in which a State is a party, the Supreme Court shall have original jurisdiction. Its framers seemed to have entertained great respect for the dignity of a State, which was to remain sovereign at least in its reserved powers, notwithstanding the new government, and therefore provided that when a State should have occasion to seek the aid of the judicial power of the new government, or should be brought under its subjection, that power should be invoked only in its highest tribunal. It is difficult to believe that the wise men who sat in the convention which framed the Constitution and advocated its adoption, ever contemplated the possibility of a State being required to assert its authority over offenders against its laws in other tribunals than those of its own creation, and least of all in an inferior tribunal of the new government. I do not think I am going too far in asserting that had it been supposed a power so dangerous to the independence of the States, and so calculated to humiliate and degrade them, lurked in any of the provisions of the Constitution, that instrument would never have been adopted.

"There are many other difficulties in maintaining the position of the circuit court, which the counsel of the accused and the Attorney-General have earnestly defended. If a criminal prosecution of an offender against the laws of a State can be transferred to a federal court, what officer is to prosecute the case? Is the attorney of the Commonwealth to follow the case from his county, or will the United States district attorney take charge of it? Who is to summon the witnesses and provide for their fees? In whose name is judgment to be pronounced? If the accused is convicted and ordered to be imprisoned, who is to enforce the sentence? If he is deemed worthy of executive clemency, who is to exercise it—the governor of the State, or the President of the United States? Can the President pardon for an offence against the State? Can the governor release from the judgment of a federal court? These and other questions which might be asked show, as justly observed by the counsel of Virginia, the incongruity and absurdity of the attempted proceeding.

"Undoubtedly, if in the progress of a criminal prosecution as well as in the progress of a civil action, a question arise as to any matter under the Constitution and laws of the United States, upon which the defendant may claim protection, or any benefit in the case, the decision thereon may be reviewed by the federal judiciary, which can examine the case so far and so far only as to determine the correctness of the ruling. If the decision be erroneous in that respect it may be reversed and a new trial had. Provision for such revision was made in the 25th section of the judiciary act of 1789 and is retained in the Revised Statutes. That great act was penned by Oliver Ellsworth, a member of the convention which framed the Constitution, and one of the early chief justices of this court. It may be said to reflect the views of the founders of the Republic as to the proper relations between the federal and State courts. It gives to the federal courts the ultimate decision of federal questions without infringing upon the dignity and independence of the State courts. By it harmony between them is secured, the rights of both federal and State governments maintained, and every privilege and immunity which the accused could assert under either can be enforced."

*The Election Cases from Ohio and Maryland: Ex-parte
Clarke and Ex-parte Siebold.*

The Constitution declares that " the times, places, and manner of holding elections for senators and representatives shall be prescribed in each State by the legislature thereof ; but the Congress may, at any time, by law, make or alter such regulations, except as to the places of choosing senators." Congress is thus authorized to make such regulations itself or to alter those prescribed by the States, the making or alteration embracing every particular of time, place, and manner except the place of choosing senators. The regulations, however, can only extend to the designation of the mode in which the will of the voter shall be expressed and ascertained. The power is not lodged in Congress to prescribe the qualifications of voters; that matter is left to the States, subject to the provision that the electors of representatives in Congress must have the qualifications required of electors of the most numerous branch of the State legislature, and the provision of the fifteenth amendment relating to the suffrage of the colored race. Whatever is involved in the *manner of holding* Congress can prescribe, and it is possible that so far as the election of representatives is concerned this may embrace all necessary provisions for ascertaining the names of the voters—thus sanctioning a registry law—and the appointment of officers of election to collect the votes and announce the result. So far as the election of senators is concerned, whatever regulations are prescribed, they must be such as a legislative body can conform to without impairment of its independent functions.

The constitutional provision was adopted in order that the general government might have the means of its own preservation against a possible dissolution from the refusal or neglect of the States to provide for the election of representatives. To obtain this end in case of hostile action of the States, Congress must be able to authorize all necessary measures to ensure the holding of an election.

No one disputes this doctrine. The dispute between the two great parties of the country upon the election laws of Congress has not arisen from any exercise of the powers conferred by the clause of the Constitution in question, for no regulations have been adopted by Congress as to the holding of the elections, except as to the times of electing representatives and senators, and in case of senators by requiring the separate and joint action of the two houses of of the State legislatures. These regulations require no interference in their execution with the officers of the State. The dispute has arisen from the attempt of Congress to enforce the regulations prescribed by the State and to exercise a supervision over its officers, interfering with their action, and endeavoring to arrest and punish them for alleged violations of State laws.

Previous to the election laws of Congress it was supposed to be a well-established doctrine that State officers were responsible only to the State for the manner in which they discharged their duties under State laws ; that whenever the federal government desired to enforce by coercive measures and punitive sanctions the performance of a duty which it could prescribe, it was bound to appoint its own officers, upon whom its power could be exerted; and that if it entrusted the performance of such duty to officers of a State, it was obliged to take their agency on the terms which the State permitted. In other words, although Congress could by law prescribe regulations for the election of representatives, and appoint its own officers for their execution, if it entrusted their execution to State officers it must take their agency upon the conditions which the State might exact. If on the other hand regulations were prescribed by the State, it was for the officers of the State to enforce them, and not the officers of the United States.

Again, regulations for the election of State officers can only be prescribed by the State, and any regulations by Congress for the election at the same time of representatives in Congress must be so framed as not to interfere with the free election of State officers under the State laws. Complaint has been made that by the laws of Congress that freedom of election was invaded.

This subject came up for consideration before the Supreme Court of the United States at the October term, 1879. At an election held in the First Congressional District of Ohio, in October, 1878, at which a representative in Congress was voted for, one Clarke was appointed under the laws of the State, and acted as a judge of election at a precinct in one of the wards of Cincinnati. At an election held in the Fourth and Fifth Congressional Districts of Maryland, in November, 1878, at which a like representative was voted for, one Siebold and four others were appointed under the laws of the State and acted as judges of election at different precincts in the city of Baltimore. For alleged misconduct as such officers of election these parties were indicted in the Circuit Court of the United States for their respective districts, tried, convicted, and sentenced to imprisonment for twelve months, and in some of the cases also to pay a fine. Clarke was charged in the indictment with having violated a law of the State of Ohio. The parties from Maryland were charged with having prevented federal officers from interfering with them and supervising their action in the execution of the laws of that State. All of them petitioned the Supreme Court for writs of *habeas corpus*, praying that they might be released, on the alleged ground that their imprisonment was unlawful, in that the acts of Congress under which they were prosecuted were unconstitutional and void.

The cases were elaborately argued by George Hoadly, of Cincinnati, for the petitioner from Ohio ; by Bradley Johnson, of Baltimore, for the petitioners from Maryland, and by the Attorney-General of the United States on the other side.

The Supreme Court held that the acts of Congress were valid, and that the parties were rightly indicted and convicted. They, therefore, refused the writs. Judges Clifford and Field dissented from the judgment, Judge Field reading a dissenting opinion. In it he confined himself principally to the case of the petitioner from Ohio, as the principle which governed that case disposed of all of them; for, as he said, if Congress could not punish an officer of a State for the manner in which he discharged his duties under her laws, it could not subject him to the supervision and control of others in the performance of such duties, and punish him for resisting their interference. In the cases from Maryland, it appeared that the laws of the State under which the petitioners were appointed judges of election, and the registration of voters for the election of 1878 was made, were not in existence when the act of Congress was passed providing for the appointment of supervisors to examine the registration and scrutinize the lists, and of special deputy marshals to aid and protect them. The act of Congress was passed in 1871, and re-published in the Revised Statutes, which are declaratory of the law in force, December 1st, 1873. The law of Maryland, under which the registration of voters was had, was enacted in 1874, and the law under which the judges of election were appointed was enacted in 1876, and these judges were required to possess different qualifications from those required of judges of election in 1871 and 1873.

The act of Congress upon which the indictment of the petitioner of Ohio was founded is contained in section 5,515 of the Revised Statutes, which declares that " every officer of an election, at which any representative or delegate in Congress is voted for, whether such officer of election be appointed or created by or under any law or authority of the United States, or by or under any State, territorial, district, or municipal law or authority, who neglects or refuses to perform any duty in regard to such election required of him by any law of the United States, or of any State or Territory thereof ; or who violates any duty so imposed; or who knowingly does any acts thereby unauthorized, with intent to affect any such election or the result thereof, . . . shall be punished as prescribed" in a previous section, that is, by a fine not exceeding one thousand dollars, or imprisonment not more than one year, or by both.

The provisions of the act of Congress relating to the appointment of supervisors of election, for resisting and interfering with whom the petitioners from Maryland were convicted, authorized the supervisors to supervise the action of the State officers from the registration of voters down to the close of the polls on the day of election; required the marshals to aid and protect them; provided for the appointment of special deputy marshals in towns and cities of over twenty thousand inhabitants; and invested them with a power to arrest and take into custody persons without process, more extended than has ever before been entrusted to any one in this country in time of peace.

In his dissenting opinion Judge Field, speaking for himself and associate, said as follows:

" In what I have to say I shall endeavor to show; 1st, that it is not competent for Congress to punish a State officer for the manner in which he discharges duties imposed upon him by the laws of the State, or to subject him in the performance of such duties to the supervision and control of others, and punish him for resisting their interference; and, 2d, that it is not competent for Congress to make the exercise of its punitive power dependent upon the legislation of the States.

" There is no doubt that Congress may adopt a law of a State, but in that case the adopted law must be enforced as a law of the United States. Here there is no pretence of such adoption. In the case from Ohio it is for the violation of a State law, not a law of the United States, that the indictment was found, The judicial power of the United States does not extend to a case of that kind. The Constitution defines and limits that power. It declares that it shall extend to cases in law and equity arising under the Constitution, the laws of the United States, and treaties made under their authority ; to cases affecting ambassadors, other public ministers and consuls; to cases of admiralty and maritime jurisdiction, and to various controversies to which the United States or a State is a party, or between citizens of different States, or citizens of the same State claiming lands under grants of different States, or between citizens of a State and any foreign State, citizens, or subjects. The term controversies as here used refers to such only as are of a civil as distinguished from those of a criminal nature. The judicial power thus defined may be applied to new cases as they arise under the Constitution and laws of the United States, but it cannot be enlarged by Congress so as to embrace cases not enumerated in the Constitution. It has been so held by this court from the earliest period. It was so adjudged in 1803 in Marbury vs. Madison, and the adjudication has been affirmed in numerous instances since. This limitation upon Congress would seem to be conclusive of the case from Ohio. To authorize a criminal prosecution in the federal courts for an offence against a law of a State, is to extend the judicial power of the United States to a case not arising under the Constitution or laws of the United States.

"But there is another view of this subject which is equally conclusive against the jurisdiction of the federal court. The act of Congress asserts a power inconsistent with, and destructive of, the independence of the States. The right to control their own officers, to prescribe the duties they shall perform, without the supervision or interference of any other authority, and the penalties to which they shall be subjected for a violation of duty is essential to that independence. If the federal government can punish a violation of the laws of the State, it may punish obedience to them, and graduate the punishment according to its own judgment of their propriety and wisdom. It may thus exercise a control over the legislation of the States subversive of all their reserved rights. However large the powers conferred upon the government formed by the Constitution, and however numerous its restraints, the right to enforce their own laws by such sanctions as they may deem appropriate is left, where it was originally, with the States. It is a right which has never been surrendered. Indeed a State could not be considered as independent in any matter, with respect to which its officers, in the discharge of their duties, could be subjected to punishment by any external authority; nor in which its officers, in the execution of its laws, could be subject to the supervision and interference of others.

"The invalidity of coercive measures by the United States, to compel an officer of a State to perform a duty imposed upon him by a law of Congress, is asserted in explicit terms in the case of The Commonwealth of Kentucky vs. Dennison.—(24 How., 66.) The Constitution declares that 'a person charged in any State with treason, felony, or other crime, who shall flee from justice, and be found in another State, shall, on demand of the executive authority of the State from which he fled, be delivered up to be removed to the State having jurisdiction of the crime.' And the act of Congress of 1793, to give effect to this clause, made it the duty of the executive authority of the State, upon the demand mentioned, and the production of a properly authenticated copy of the indictment or affidavit charging the person demanded with the commission of treason, felony, or other crime, to surrender the fugitive. The governor of Ohio having refused upon a proper demand to surrender a fugitive from justice from Kentucky, the governor of the latter State applied to this court for a mandamus to compel the performance of that duty. But the court, after observing that, though the words 'it shall be the duty,' in ordinary legislation implied the assertion of the power to command and to cause obedience, said, that looking to the subject-matter of the law and 'the relations which the United States and the several States bear to each other,' it was of opinion that the words were not used as mandatory and compulsory, but as declaratory of the moral duty created, when Congress had provided the mode of carrying the provision into execution. 'The act does not provide,' the court added, 'any means to compel the execution of this duty, nor inflict any punishment for neglect or refusal on the part of the executive of the State; nor is there any clause or provision in the Constitution which arms the government of the United States with this power. Indeed, such a power would place every State under the control and dominion of the general government, even in the administration of its internal concerns and reserved rights. And we think it clear that the federal government, under the Constitution, has no power to impose on a State officer, as such, any duty whatever, and compel him to perform it; for if it possessed this power it might overload the officer with duties which would fill up all his time, and disable him from performing his obligations to the State, and might impose on him duties of a character incompatible with the rank and dignity to which he was elevated by the State. It is true that Congress may authorize a particular State officer to perform a particular duty; but if he declines to do so, it does not follow that he may be coerced or punished for his refusal. And we are very far from supposing that in using this word 'duty,' the statesmen who framed and passed the law, or the President who approved and signed it, intended to exercise a coercive power over State officers not warranted by the Constitution.' And again: 'If the governor of Ohio refuses to discharge this duty, there is no power delegated to the general government, either through the judicial department or any other department, to use any coercive means to compel him.'

"If it be incompetent for the federal government to enforce, by coercive measures, the performance of a plain duty imposed by a law of Congress upon the executive officer of a State, it would seem to be equally incompetent for it to enforce, by similar measures, the performance of a duty imposed upon him by a law of a State. If Congress cannot impose upon a State officer, as such, the performance of any duty, it would seem logically to follow that it cannot subject him to punishment for the neglect of such duties as the State may impose. It cannot punish for the non-performance of a duty which it cannot prescribe. It is a contradiction in terms to say that it can inflict punishment for disobedience to an act, the performance of which it has no constitutional power to command.

"I am not aware that the doctrine of this case, which is so essential to the harmonious working of the State and federal governments, has ever been qualified or departed from by this court until the recent decisions in the Virginia cases, of which I shall presently speak. It is true that, at an early period in the history of the government, laws were passed by Congress authorizing State courts to entertain jurisdiction of proceedings by the United States, to enforce penalties and forfeitures under the revenue laws, and to hear allegations, and take proofs if applications were made for their remission. To these laws reference is made in the Kentucky case, and the court observes, that the powers, which they conferred, were for some years exercised by the State tribunals without objection, until in some of the States their exercise was declined because it interfered with and retarded the performance of duties which properly belonged to them as State courts; and in other States because doubts arose as to the power of the State courts to inflict penalties and forfeitures for offences against the general government, unless specially authorized to do so by the States; and that the co-operation of the States in those cases was a matter of comity which the several sovereignties extended to one another for their mutual benefit, and was not regarded by either party as an obligation imposed by the Constitution.

" It is to be observed that by the Constitution the demand for the surrender of a fugitive is to be made by the executive authority of the State from which he has fled, but it is not declared upon whom the demand shall be made. That was left to be determined by Congress, and it provided that the demand should be made upon the executive of the State where the fugitive was found. It might have employed its own agents, as in the enforcement of the fugitive slave law, and compel them to act. But in both cases, if it employed the officers of the State it could not restrain nor coerce them.

" Whenever, therefore, the federal government, instead of acting through its own officers, seeks to accomplish its purposes through the agency of officers of the States, it must accept the agency with the conditions upon which the officers are permitted to act. For example, the Constitution invests Congress with the ' power to establish a uniform rule of naturalization;' and this power, from its nature, is exclusive. A concurrent power in the States would prevent the uniformity of regulations required on the subject.—(Chirac vs. Chirac, 2 Wheaton, 259; The Federalist, No. 42.) Yet Congress, in legislating under this power, has authorized courts of record of the States to receive declarations under oath by aliens of their intention to become citizens, and to admit them to citizenship after a limited period of residence, upon satisfactory proof as to character and attachment to the Constitution. But when Congress prescribed the conditions and proof upon which aliens might, by the action of the State courts, become citizens, its power ended. It could not coerce the State courts to hold sessions for such applications, nor fix the time when they should hear the applicants, nor the manner in which they should administer the required oaths, nor regulate in any way their procedure. It could not compel them to act by mandamus from its own tribunals; nor subject their judges to criminal prosecution for their non-action. It could accept the agency of those courts only upon such terms as the States should prescribe. The same thing is true in all cases where the agency of State officers is used; and this doctrine applies with special force to judges of elections at which numerous State officers are chosen at the same time with representatives to Congress. So far as the election of State officers and the registration of voters for their election are concerned, the federal government has confessedly no authority to interfere. And yet the supervision of and interference with the State regulations, sanctioned by the act of Congress, when representatives to Congress are voted for, amount practically to a supervision of and an interference with the election of State officers, and constitute a plain encroachment upon the rights of the States, which is well calculated to create irritation towards the federal government, and disturb the harmony that all good and patriotic men should desire to exist between it and the State governments.

"It was the purpose of the framers of the Constitution to create a government which could enforce its own laws, through its own officers and tribunals without reliance upon those of the States, and thus avoid the principal defect of the government of the Confederation; and they fully accomplished their purpose, for, as said by Chief Justice Marshall in the McCullough case, ' No trace is to be found in the Constitution of an intention to create a dependence of the federal government on the governments of the States for the execution of the great powers assigned to it. Its means are adequate to its ends, and on those means alone was it expected to rely for the accomplishment of its ends.' When, therefore, the federal government desires to compel by coercive measures and punitive sanctions the performance of any duties devolved upon it by the Constitution, it must appoint its own officers and agents, upon whom its power can be exerted. If it sees fit to entrust the performance of such duties to officers of a State, it must take their agency, as already stated, upon the conditions which the State may impose. The co-operative scheme to which the majority of the court give their sanction, by which the general government may create one condition and the States another, and each make up for and supplement the omissions or defects in the legislation of the other, touching the same subject, with its separate penalties for the same offence, and thus produce a harmonious mosaic of statutory regulation, does not appear to have struck the great jurist as a feature in our system of government or one that had been sanctioned by its founders.

"It is true that since the recent amendments of the Constitution there has been legislation by Congress asserting, as in the instance before us, a direct control over State officers, which previously was never supposed to be compatible with the independent existence of the States in their reserved powers. Much of that legislation has yet to be brought to the test of judicial examination; and until the recent decisions in the Virginia cases, I could not have believed that the former carefully considered and repeated judgments of this court upon provisions of the Constitution, and upon the general character and purposes of that instrument, would

14

have been disregarded and overruled. These decisions do indeed, in my judgment, constitute a new departure. They give to the federal government the power to strip the States of the right to vindicate their authority in their own courts against a violator of their laws, when the transgressor happens to be an officer of the United States, or alleges that he is denied or cannot enforce some right under their laws. And they assert for the federal government a power to subject a judicial officer of a State to punishment for the manner in which he discharges his duties under her laws. The power to punish at all existing, the nature and extent of the punishment must depend upon the will of Congress, and may be carried to a removal from office. In my judgment, and I say it without intending any disrespect to my associates, no such advance has ever before been made toward the conversion of our federal system into a consolidated and centralized government. I cannot think that those who framed and advocated, and the States which adopted the amendments, contemplated any such fundamental change in our theory of government as those decisions indicate. Prohibitions against legislation on particular subjects previously existed, as, for instance, against passing a bill of attainder and an *ex post facto* law, or a law impairing the obligation of contracts; and in enforcing those prohibitions it was never supposed that criminal prosecutions could be authorized against members of the State legislature for passing the prohibited laws, or against members of the State judiciary for sustaining them, or against executive officers for enforcing the judicial determinations. Enactments prescribing such prosecutions would have given a fatal blow to the independence and autonomy of the States. So of all or nearly all the prohibitions of the recent amendments the same doctrine may be asserted. In few instances could legislation by Congress be deemed appropriate for their enforcement, which should provide for the annulment of prohibited laws in any other way than through the instrumentality of an appeal to the judiciary, when they impinged upon the rights of parties. If in any instance there could be such legislation authorizing a criminal prosecution for disregarding a prohibition, that legislation should define the offence and declare the punishment, and not invade the independent action of the different departments of the State governments within their appropriate spheres. Legislation by Congress can neither be necessary nor appropriate which would subject to criminal prosecution State officers for the performance of duties prescribed by State laws, not having for their object the forcible subversion of the government.

"The clause of the Constitution, upon which reliance was placed by counsel, on the argument, for the legislation in question, does not, as it seems to me, give the slightest support to it. That clause declares that 'the times, places, and manner of holding elections for senators and representatives shall be prescribed in each State by the legislature thereof; but the Congress may, at any time, by law, make or alter such regulations, except as to the places of choosing senators.' The power of Congress thus conferred is either to alter the regulations prescribed by the State or to make new ones; the alteration or new creation embracing every particular of time, place, and manner, except the place of choosing senators. But in neither mode nor in any respect has Congress interfered with the regulations prescribed by the legislature of Ohio, or with those prescribed by the legislature of Maryland. It has not altered them or made new ones. It has simply provided for the appointment of officers to supervise the execution of the State laws, and of marshals to aid and protect them in such supervision, and has added a new penalty for disobeying those laws. This is not enforcing an altered or a new regulation. Whatever Congress may properly do touching the regulations, one of two things must follow; either the altered or the new regulation remains a State law, or it becomes a law of Congress. If it remain a State law, it must, like other laws of the State, be enforced through its instrumentalities and agencies, and with the penalties which it may see fit to prescribe, and without the supervision or interference of federal officials. If, on the other hand, it become a law of Congress, it must be carried into execution by such officers and with such sanctions as Congress may designate. But as Congress has not altered the regulations for the election of representatives prescribed by the Legislature of Ohio or of Maryland, either as to time, place, or manner, nor adopted any regulations of its own, there is nothing for the federal government to enforce on the subject. The general authority of Congress to pass all laws necessary to carry into execution its granted powers, supposes some attempt to exercise those powers. There must, therefore, be some regulations made by Congress, either by altering those prescribed by the State, or by adopting entirely new ones, as to the times, places, and manner of holding elections for representatives, before any incidental powers can be invoked to compel obedience to them. In other words, the implied power cannot be invoked until some exercise of the express power is attempted, and then only to aid its execution. There is no express power in Congress to enforce State laws by imposing penalties for disobedience to them; its punitive power is only implied as a necessary or proper means of enforcing its own laws; nor is there any power delegated to it to supervise the execution by State officers of State laws.

"If this view be correct, there is no power in Congress, independently of all other considerations, to authorize the appointment of supervisors and other officers to superintend and interfere with the election of representatives under the laws of Ohio and Maryland, or to annex a penalty to the violation of those laws, and the action of the circuit courts was without jurisdiction and void. The act of Congress in question was passed, as it seems to me, in disregard of the object of the constitutional provision. That was designed simply to give to the general government the means of its own preservation against a possible dissolution from the hostility of the States to the election of representatives, or from their neglect to provide suitable means for holding such elections. This is evident from the language of its advocates, some of them members of the convention, when the Constitution was presented to the country for adoption. In commenting upon it in his report of the debates, Mr. Madison said, that it was meant ' to give the national legislature a power not only to alter the provisions of the States, but to make regulations, *in case the States should fail or refuse altogether.*'—(Elliott's Debates, 402.) And in the Virginia convention called to consider the Constitution, he observed that ' it was found impossible to fix the time, place, and manner of the election of representatives in the Constitution. It was found necessary to leave the regulation of these, in the first place, to the State governments, as being best acquainted with the situation of the people, subject to the control of the general government, in order to enable it to *produce uniformity, and prevent its own dissolution.*'—(3 Elliott's Debates, 367.) And in the Federalist, Hamilton said, that the propriety of the clause in question rested ' upon the evidence of the plain proposition that every government should contain in itself the means of its own preservation.'

"Similar language is found in the debates in conventions of the other States and in the writings of jurists and statesmen of the period. The conduct of Rhode Island was referred to as illustrative of the evils to be avoided. That State was not represented by delegates in Congress for years, owing to the character and views of the prevailing party; and Congress was often embarrassed by their absence. The same evil, it was urged, might result from a similar cause, and Congress should, therefore, possess the power to give the people an opportunity of electing representatives if the States should neglect or refuse to make the necessary regulations.

" In the conventions of several States which ratified the Constitution, an amendment was proposed to limit in express terms the action of Congress to cases of neglect or refusal of a State to make proper provisions for congressional elections, and was supported by a majority of the thirteen States; but it was finally abandoned upon the ground of the great improbability of congressional interference so long as the States performed their duty. When Congress does interfere and provide regulations, the duty of rendering them effectual, so far as they may require affirmative action, will devolve solely upon the federal government. It will then be federal power which is to be exercised, and its enforcement, if promoted by punitive sanctions, must be through federal officers and agents; for, as said by Mr. Justice Story in Prigg vs. Pennsylvania. ' The national government, in the absence of all positive provisions to the contrary, is bound, through its own proper department, legislative, judicial, or executive, as the case may require, to carry into effect all the rights and duties imposed upon it by the Constitution.' If State officers and State agents are employed, they must be taken, as already said, with the conditions upon which the States may permit them to act, and without responsibility to the federal authorities. The power vested in Congress is to alter the regulations prescribed by the legislatures of the States, or to make new ones, as to the times, places, and manner of *holding* the elections. Those which relate to the times and places will seldom require any affirmative action beyond their designation. And regulations as to the *manner of holding* them cannot extend beyond the designation of the mode in which the will of the voters shall be expressed and ascertained. The power does not authorize Congress to determine who shall participate in the election, or what shall be the qualifications of voters. These are matters not pertaining to or involved in the *manner of holding* the election, and their regulation rests exclusively with the States. The only restriction upon them with respect to these matters is found in the provision that the electors of representatives in Congress shall have the qualifications required for electors of the most numerous branch of the State legislature, and the provision relating to the suffrage of the colored race. And whatever regulations Congress may prescribe as to the manner of holding the election for representatives must be so framed as to leave the election of State officers free, otherwise they cannot be maintained. In one of the numbers of the Federalist, Mr. Hamilton, in defending the adoption of the clause in the Constitution, uses this language: ' Suppose an article had been introduced into the Constitution empowering the United States to regulate the elections for the particular States, would any man have hesitated to condemn it, both as an unwarrantable transposition of power, and as a premeditated engine for the destruction of the State governments? The violation of principle in this case would have required no comment.' By the act of Congress sustained by the court an interference with State elections is authorized almost as destructive of their control by the States as the direct regulation which he thought no man would hesitate to condemn.

"The views expressed derive further support from the fact that the constitutional provision applies equally to the election of senators, except as to the place of choosing them, as it does to the election of representatives. It will not be pretended that Congress could authorize the appointment of supervisors to examine the roll of members of State legislatures and pass upon the validity of their titles, or to scrutinize the balloting for senators; or could delegate to special deputy marshals the power to arrest any member resisting and repelling the interference of the supervisors. But if Congress can [authorize such officers to interfere with the judges of election appointed under State laws in the discharge of their duties when representatives are voted for, it can authorize such officers to interfere with members of the State legislatures when senators are voted for. The language of the Constitution conferring power upon Congress to alter the regulations of the States, or to make new regulations on the subject, is as applicable in the one case as in the other. The objection to such legislation in both cases is that State officers are not responsible to the federal government for the manner in which they perform their duties, nor subject to its control. Penal sanctions and coercive measures by federal law cannot be enforced against them. Whenever, as in some instances is the case, a State officer is required by the Constitution to perform a duty, the manner of which may be prescribed by Congress, as in the election of senators by members of State legislatures, those officers are responsible only to their States for their official conduct. The federal government cannot touch them. There are remedies for their disregard of its regulations, which can be applied without interfering with their official character as State officers. Thus if its regulations for the election of senators should not be followed, the election had in disregard of them might be invalidated ; but no one, however extreme in his views, would contend that in such a case the members of the legislature could be subjected to criminal prosecution for their action. With respect to the election of representatives, so long as Congress does not adopt regulations of its own and enforce them through federal officers, but permits the regulations of the States to remain, it must depend for a compliance with them upon the fidelity of the State officers and their responsibility to their own government. All the provisions of the law, therefore, authorizing supervisors and marshals to interfere with those officers in the discharge of their duties, and providing for criminal prosecutions against them in the federal courts, are, in my judgment, clearly in conflict with the Constitution. The law was adopted, no doubt, with the object of preventing frauds at elections for members of Congress, but it does not seem to have occurred to its authors that the States are as much interested as the general government in guarding against frauds at those elections and in maintaining their purity, and, if possible, more so, as their principal officers are elected at the same time. If fraud be successfully perpetrated in any case, they will be the first and the greatest sufferers. They are invested with the sole power to regulate domestic affairs of the highest moment to the prosperity and happiness of their people, affecting the acquisition, enjoyment, transfer, and descent of property ; the marriage relation, and the education of children ; and if such momentous and vital concerns may be wisely and safely entrusted to them, I do not think that any apprehension need be felt if the supervision of all elections in their respective States should also be left to them.

" Much has been said in argument of the power of the general government to enforce its own laws, and in so doing to preserve the peace, though it is not very apparent what pertinency the observations have to the questions involved in the cases before us. No one will deny that in the powers granted to it the general government is supreme, and that, upon all subjects within their scope, it can make its authority respected and obeyed throughout the limits of the Republic ; and that it can repress all disorders and disturbance which interfere with the enforcement of its laws. But I am unable to perceive in this fact, which all sensible men acknowledge, any cause for the exercise of ungranted power. The greater its lawful power, the greater the reason for not usurping more. Unrest, disquiet, and disturbance will always arise among a people, jealous of their rights, from the exercise by the general government of powers which they have reserved to themselves or to the States.

" My second proposition is that it is not competent for Congress to make the exercise of its punitive power dependent upon the legislation of the States. The act, upon which the indictment of the petitioner from Ohio is founded, makes the neglect or violation of a duty prescribed by a law of the State in regard to an election at which a representative in Congress is voted for, a criminal offence. It does not say that the neglect or disregard of a duty prescribed by any *existing* law shall constitute such an offence. It is the neglect or disregard of *any duty* prescribed by *any law* of the State, *present or future*. The act of Congress is not changed in terms with the changing laws of the State ; but its penalty is to be shifted with the shifting humors of the State legislatures. I cannot think that such punitive legislation is valid which varies, not by direction of the federal legislators, upon new knowledge or larger experience, but by the direction of some external authority which makes the same act lawful in one State and criminal in another, not according to the views of Congress as to its propriety, but to those of another body. The Constitution vests all the legislative power of the federal government in Congress ; and from its nature this power cannot be delegated to others, except as its delegation may be involved by the creation of an inferior local government or department. Congress can endow territorial governments and municipal corporations with legislative powers, as the possession of such powers for certain purposes of local administration is indispensable to their existence. So, also, it can invest the heads of departments and of the army and navy with power to prescribe regulations to enforce discipline, order, and efficiency. Its possession is implied in their creation ; but legislative power over subjects which come under the immediate control of Congress, such as defining offences against the United States, and prescribing punishment for them cannot be delegated to any other government or authority. Congress cannot, for example, leave to the States the enactment of laws and restrict the United States to their enforcement. There are many citizens of the United States in foreign countries, in Japan, China, India, and Africa. Could Congress enact that a crime against one of those States should be punished as a crime against the United States? Can Congress abdicate its functions and depute foreign countries to act for it? If Congress cannot do this with respect to offences against those States, how can it enforce penalties for offences against any other States, though they be of our own Union ? If Congress could depute its authority in this way ; if it could say that it will punish as an offence what another power enacts as such, it might do the same thing with respect to the commands of any other authority, as, for example, of the President or the head of a department. It could enact that what the President proclaims shall be law ; that what he declares to be offences shall be punished as such. Surely no one will go so far as this, and yet I am unable to see the distinction in principle between the existing law and the one I suppose, which seems so extravagant and absurd.

" I will not pursue the subject further, but those who deem this question at all doubtful or difficult, may find something worthy of thought in the opinions of the Court of Appeals of New York and of the supreme courts of several other States, where this subject is treated with a fullness and learning, which leaves nothing to be improved and nothing to be added."

CORPORATIONS. — CASES RELATING TO THEIR POWERS AND LIABILITIES, AND THEIR SUBJECTION TO THE CONTROL OF THE STATE.

Corporations of all kinds, public and private, foreign and domestic, commercial, benevolent, and religious, have been the frequent subject of consideration by the Supreme Court. Their powers and liabilities, their creation, amendment, and dissolution; how far they are to be regarded as contracts within the prohibition of the Constitution against State impairment, and how far they are subject to the control of the State, have been treated in numerous cases with exhaustive fullness. Every judge on the bench has given opinions in some of the cases. Judge Field has given opinions in several of them; and, among others, in the following: Paul vs. Virginia (8 Wallace, 168); Marsh vs. Fulton County (10 Wallace, 676); Tomlinson vs. Jessup (15 Wallace, 454); Minot vs. The Philadelphia, Wilmington and Baltimore Railroad Company (18 Wallace, 206); Board of Commissioners of Tippecanoe County vs. Lucas, Treasurer (93 U. S., 108); Broughton vs. Pensacola (Ibid., 266); and United States vs. New Orleans (98 U. S., 381). In the case of The Pensacola Telegraph Company vs. The Western Union Telegraph Company he wrote a dissenting opinion (96 U. S., 14).

In Paul vs. Virginia the court held that corporations were not citizens within the meaning of the clause of the Constitution which declares that " the citizens of each State shall be entitled to all the privileges and immunities of citizens in the several States ;" that the terms " citizens " as there used applied only to natural persons, members of the body-politic, owing allegiance to the State, and not to artificial persons created by the legislature and possessing only the attributes which the legislature had prescribed. It was true, the court observed, that it had been held that where contracts or rights of property were to be enforced by or against a corporation, the courts of the United States will, for the purpose of maintaining jurisdiction, consider the corporation as representing citizens of the State under the laws of which it was created, and to that extent would treat a corporation as a citizen within the clause of the Constitution extending the judicicial power of the United States to controversies between citizens of different States; but the court added that in no case had a corporation been considered a citizen within the meaning of the provision, which declares that " the citizens of each State shall be entitled to all the privileges and immunities of citizens in the several States." With respect to that provision Judge Field, speaking for the court, said as follows :

" It was undoubtedly the object of the clause in question to place the citizens of each State upon the same footing with citizens of other States, so far as the advantages resulting from citizenship in those States are concerned. It relieves them from the disabilities of alienage in other States ; it inhibits discriminating legislation against them by other States ; it gives them the right of free ingress into other States, and egress from them ; it insures to them in other States the same freedom possessed by the citizens of those States in the acquisition and enjoyment of property and in the pursuit of happiness ; and it secures to them in other States the equal protection of their laws. It has been justly said that no provision in the Constitution has tended so strongly to constitute the citizens of the United States one people as this.* Indeed, without some provision of the kind removing from the citizens of each State the disabilities of alienage in the other States, and giving them equality of privilege with citizens of those States, the Republic would have constituted little more than a league of States; it would not have constituted the Union which now exists.

" But the privileges and immunities secured to citizens of each State in the several States, by the provision in question, are those privileges and immunities which are common to the citizens in the latter States under

* Lemmon vs. The People, 20 New York, 607.

their constitution and laws by virtue of their being citizens. Special
privileges enjoyed by citizens in their own States are not secured in other
States by this provision. It was not intended by the provision to give to
the laws of one State any operation in other States. They can have no
such operation, except by the permission, express or implied, of those
States. The special privileges which they confer must, therefore, be enjoyed at home, unless the assent of other States to their enjoyment therein
be given.

"Now a grant of corporate existence is a grant of special privileges to
the corporators, enabling them to act for certain designated purposes as a
single individual, and exempting them (unless otherwise specially provided) from individual liability. The corporation being the mere creation
of local law, can have no legal existence beyond the limits of the sovereignty where created. As said by this court in *Bank of Augusta vs.
Earle*, ' it must dwell in the place of its creation, and cannot migrate to
another sovereignty.' The recognition of its existence even by other
States, and the enforcement of its contracts made therein, depend purely
upon the comity of those States—a comity which is never extended where
the existence of the corporation or the exercise of its powers are prejudicial to their interests or repugnant to their policy. Having no absolute
right of recognition in other States, but depending for such recognition
and the enforcement of its contracts upon their assent, it follows, as a
matter of course, that such assent may be granted upon such terms and
conditions as those States may think proper to impose. They may exclude the foreign corporation entirely ; they may restrict its business to
particular localities, or they may exact such security for the performance
of its contracts with their citizens as in their judgment will best promote
the public interest. The whole matter rests in their discretion.

" If, on the other hand, the provision of the Constitution could be construed to secure to citizens of each State in other States the peculiar
privileges conferred by their laws, an extra-territorial operation would be
given to local legislation utterly destructive of the independence and the
harmony of the States. At the present day corporations are multiplied
to an almost indefinite extent. There is scarcely a business pursued requiring the expenditure of large capital, or the union of large numbers,
that is not carried on by corporations. It is not too much to say that the
wealth and business of the country are to a great extent controlled by
them. And if, when composed of citizens of one State, their corporate
powers and franchises could be exercised in other States without restriction, it is easy to see that, with the advantages thus possessed, the most
important business of those States would soon pass into their hands.
The principal business of every State would, in fact, be controlled by corporations created by other States.

" If the right asserted of the foreign corporation, when composed of
citizens of one State, to transact business in other States were even restricted to such business as corporations of those States were authorized

to transact, it would still follow that those States would be unable to limit the number of corporations doing business therein. They could not charter a company for any purpose, however restricted, without at once opening the door to a flood of corporations from other States to engage in the same pursuits. They could not repel an intruding corporation, except on the condition of refusing incorporation for a similar purpose to their own citizens, and yet it might be of the highest public interest that the number of corporations in the State should be limited; that they should be required to give publicity to their transactions; to submit their affairs to proper examination; to be subject to forfeiture of their corporate rights in case of mismanagement, and that their officers should be held to a strict accountability for the manner in which the business of the corporation is managed, and be liable to summary removal.

" ' It is impossible,' to repeat the language of this court in *Bank of Augusta vs. Earle*, 'upon any sound principle, to give such a construction to the article in question,'—a construction which would lead to results like these."

In Marsh vs. Fulton County the court held that where bonds of a county were issued without authority by its supervisors to a railroad company, they were invalid in the hands of an innocent purchaser; that the authority to contract must exist before any protection as such purchaser can be claimed by the holder. And further, that where the supervisors possessed no authority to make a subscription or issue bonds to a railroad company in the first instance, without the previous sanction of the qualified voters of the county, they could not ratify a subscription to the company already made without such authority. Said the court, speaking through Judge Field, as follows :

" A ratification is, in its effect upon the act of an agent, equivalent to the possession by him of a previous authority. It operates upon the act ratified in the same manner as though the authority of the agent to do the act existed originally. It follows that a ratification can only be made when the party ratifying possesses the power to perform the act ratified. The supervisors possessed no authority to make the subscription or issue the bonds in the first instance without the previous sanction of the qualified voters of the county. The supervisors, in that particular, were the mere agents of the county. They could not, therefore, ratify a subscription without a vote of the county, because they could not make a subscription in the first instance without such authorization. It would be absurd to say that they could, without such vote, by simple expressions of approval, or in some other indirect way, give validity to acts, when they were directly in terms prohibited by statute from doing those acts until after such vote was had. That would be equivalent to saying that an agent, not having the power to do a particular act for his principal, could give validity to such act by its indirect recognition.*

"We do not mean to intimate that liabilities may not be incurred by counties independent of the statute. Undoubtedly they may. The obligation to do justice rests upon all persons, natural and artificial, and if a county obtains the money or property of others without authority, the law, independent of any statute, will compel restitution or compensation. But this is a very different thing from enforcing an obligation attempted to be created in one way, when the statute declares that it shall only be created in another and different way."

In Tomlinson vs. Jessup the court held that, where a general law of South Carolina passed in 1841 provided that the charter of every corporation subsequently granted, and any renewal, amendment, or modification thereof, should be subject to amendment, alteration, or repeal by legislative authority, unless the act granting the charter or the renewal, amendment, or modification, in express terms excepted it from the general law, it was competent for the legislature of the State to alter an amendment to a corporation subsequently created, which exempted its property from taxation without such exception, and to subject the property to taxation; that the power reserved to the State by the general law authorized any change in the contract of the corporation, created by the charter between the corporators and the State, as it originally existed, or as subsequently modified, or its entire revocation. On this point, Judge Field, speaking for the court, said as follows:

"The object of the reservation, and of similar reservations in other charters, is to prevent a grant of corporate rights and privileges in a form which will preclude legislative interference with their exercise if the public interest should at any time require such interference. It is a provision intended to preserve to the State control over its contract with the corporators, which without that provision would be irrepealable and protected from any measures affecting its obligation.———Immunity from taxation, constituting in these cases a part of the contract with the government, is, by the reservation of power such as is contained in the law

---

* McCracken vs. City of San Francisco, 16 Cal., 624.

of 1841, subject to be revoked equally with any other provision of the charter whenever the legislature may deem it expedient for the public interests that the revocation shall be made. The reservation affects the entire relation between the State and the corporation, and places under legislative control all rights, privileges, and immunities derived by its charter directly from the State. Rights acquired by third parties, and which have become vested under the charter, in the legitimate exercise of its powers, stand upon a different footing; but of such rights it is unnecessary to speak here. The State only asserts in the present case the power under the reservation to modify its own contract with the corporators; it does not contend for a power to revoke the contracts of the corporation with other parties, or to impair any vested rights thereby acquired."

In Minot vs. The Philadelphia, Wilmington and Baltimore Railroad Company—designated in the reports as "The Delaware Railroad Tax"—the court gave strong expression to the rule that exemption from taxation by the State must be strictly pursued. On this point, speaking through Judge Field, it said as follows :

"It has also been repeatedly held by this court that the legislature of a State may exempt particular parcels of property or the property of particular persons or corporations from taxation either for a specified period or perpetually, or may limit the amount or rate of taxation to which such property shall be subjected. And when such immunity is conferred, or such limitation is prescribed by the charter of a corporation, it becomes a part of the contract, and is equally inviolate with its other stipulations. But before any such exemption or limitation can be admitted, the intent of the legislature to confer the immunity or prescribe the limitation, must be clear beyond a reasonable doubt. All public grants are strictly construed. Nothing can be taken against the State by presumption or inference. The established rule of construction in such cases is that rights, privileges, and immunities, not expressly granted, are reserved. There is no safety to the public interests in any other rule. And with special force does the principle, upon which the rule rests, apply when the right, privilege, or immunity claimed calls for any abridgment of the powers of the government, or any restraint upon their exercise. The power of taxation is an attribute of sovereignty, and is essential to every independent government. As this court has said, the whole community is interested in retaining it undiminished, and has ' a right to insist that its abandonment ought not to be presumed in a case in which the deliberate purpose of the State to abandon it does not appear.'* If the point were not already adjudged, it would admit of grave consideration, whether

* Providence Bank vs. Billings, 4 Peters, 561.

the legislature of a State can surrender this power, and make its action in this respect binding upon its successors, any more than it can surrender its police power or its right of eminent domain. But the point being adjudged, the surrender, when claimed, must be shown by clear, unambiguous language, which will admit of no reasonable construction consistent with the reservation of the power. If a doubt arise as to the intent of the legislature, that doubt must be solved in favor of the State."

The same doctrine is reiterated in equally emphatic terms in the case of Hoge vs. The Railroad Company (99 U. S., 354–5).

In the case of Board of Commissioners of Tippecanoe County vs. Lucas, Treasurer, the court held that municipal corporations are mere instrumentalities of the State for the convenient administration of government, and that their powers may be qualified, enlarged, or withdrawn at the pleasure of the legislature; that the tenure of property, derived from the State for specific public purposes, or obtained for such purposes through means which the State alone can authorize,—that is, taxation—is so far subject to the control of the legislature, that the property may be applied to other public uses of the municipality than those originally designated, and, therefore, that it was competent for the legislature to direct a restitution to taxpayers of a county, or other municipal corporation, of property exacted from them by taxation, into whatever form the property may have been changed, so long as it remained in the possession of the municipality.

In Broughton vs. Pensacola the court held that a change in the charter of a municipal corporation, in whole or in part, by an amendment of its provisions, or the substitution of a new charter in place of the old one, embracing substantially the same coporators and the same territory, would not be deemed, in the absence of express legislative declaration otherwise, to affect the identity of the corporation, or to relieve it from its previous liabilities, although different powers were possessed under the amended or new charter, and different officers administered its affairs. The court said, speaking through Judge Field, as follows :

"Although a municipal corporation, so far as it is invested with subordinate legislative powers for local purposes, is a mere instrumentality of the State for the convenient administration of government, yet, when authorized to take stock in a railroad company, and issue its obligations in payment of the stock, it is to that extent to be deemed a private corporation, and its obligations are secured by all the guaranties which protect the engagements of private individuals. The inhibition of the Constitution, which preserves against the interference of a State the sacredness of contracts, applies to the liabilities of municipal corporations created by its permission, and although the repeal or modification of the charter of a corporation of that kind is not within the inhibition, yet it will not be admitted, where its legislation is susceptible of another construction, that the State has in this way sanctioned an evasion of or escape from liabilities, the creation of which it authorized. When, therefore, a new form is given to an old municipal corporation, or such a corporation is reorganized under a new charter, taking, in its new organization, the place of the old one, embracing substantially the same corporators and the same territory, it will be presumed that the legislature intended a continued existence of the same corporation, although different powers are possessed under the new charter, and different officers administer its affairs; and in the absence of express provision for their payment otherwise, it will also be presumed in such case that the legislature intended that the liabilities, as well as the rights of property of the corporation in its old form, should accompany the corporation in its reorganization. That such was the intention of the State of Florida in the present case, we have no doubt; to suppose otherwise would be to impute to her an insensibility to the claims of morality and justice, which nothing in her history warrants.

"The principle which applies to the State would seem to be applicable to cases of this kind. Obligations contracted by its agents continue against the State whatever changes may take place in its constitution of government. 'The new government,' says Wheaton, 'succeeds to the fiscal rights, and is bound to fulfill the fiscal obligations of the former government. It becomes entitled to the public domain and other property of the State, and is bound to pay its debts previously contracted.'—(Inter. Law, 30.) So a change in the charter of a municipal corporation, in whole or part, by an amendment of its provisions, or the substitution of a new charter in place of the old one, should not be deemed, in the absence of express legislative declaration otherwise, to affect the identity of the corporation, or to relieve it from its previous liabilities."

In the case of the United States vs. New Orleans, the court held that where municipal corporations are created, the power of taxation is vested in them as an essential attribute for all the purposes of their existence, unless its exercise be in express terms prohibited; and that when,

in order to execute a public work, they have been vested
with authority to borrow money or incur an obligation,
they have the power to levy a tax to raise revenue to pay
the money or discharge the obligation without any special
mention that such power is granted, and that in case of a
refusal to provide for the payment of the indebtedness
contracted, a mandamus should be issued to compel the
levying of such tax.   On this point the court said, speaking through Judge Field :

"The position that the power of taxation belongs exclusively to the
legislative branch of the government, no one will controvert. Under our
system it is lodged nowhere else. But it is a power that may be delegated by the legislature to municipal corporations, which are merely the
instrumentalities of the State for the better administration of the government in matters of local concern. When such a corporation is created
the power of taxation is vested in it as an essential attribute for all the
purposes of its existence, unless its exercise be in express terms prohibited. For the accomplishment of those purposes, its authorities, however
limited the corporation, must have the power to raise money and control
its expenditure. In a city, even of small extent, they have to provide
for the preservation of peace, good order, and health, and the execution
of such measures as conduce to the general good of its citizens; such as
the opening and repairing of streets, the construction of sidewalks, sew-
ers, and drains, the introduction of water, and the establishment of a fire
and police department. In a city like New Orleans, situated on a navigable stream, or on a harbor of a lake or sea, their powers are usually enlarged so as to embrace the building of wharves and docks or levees for
the benefit of commerce, and they may extend also to the construction of
roads leading to it, or the contributing of aid towards their construction.
The number and variety of works which may be authorized, having a
general regard to the welfare of the city or of its people, are mere matters of legislative discretion. All of them require for their execution
considerable expenditures of money. Their authorization without providing the means for such expenditures would be an idle and futile proceeding. Their authorization, therefore, implies and carries with it the
power to adopt the ordinary means employed by such bodies to raise
funds for their execution, unless such funds are otherwise provided.
And the ordinary means in such cases is taxation. A municipality without the power of taxation would be a body without life, incapable of acting, and serving no useful purpose.

"For the same reason, when authority to borrow money or incur an
obligation in order to execute a public work is conferred upon a municipal corporation, the power to levy a tax for its payment or the discharge
of the obligation accompanies it; and this, too, without any special men-

tion that such power is granted. This arises from the fact that such corporations seldom possess—so seldom, indeed, as to be exceptional—any means to discharge their pecuniary obligations except by taxation. 'It is, therefore, to be inferred,' as observed by this court in *Loan Association vs. Topeka*, (20 Wall., 660,) ' that when the legislature of a State authorizes a county or city to contract a debt by bond, it intends to authorize it to levy such taxes as are necessary to pay the debt, unless there is in the act itself, or in some general statute, a limitation upon the power of taxation which repels such an inference.' "

In the case of The Pensacola Telegraph Company vs. The Western Union Telegraph Company a bill was filed to obtain an injunction restraining the defendant, the Western Union Co., from erecting, using, or maintaining a telegraph line in the county of Escambia, Florida, on the ground that by a statute of the State, passed in December, 1866, the complainant, the Pensacola Co., had acquired the exclusive right to erect and use lines of telegraph in that county for the period of twenty years. The court below denied the injunction and dismissed the bill, upon the ground that the statute was in conflict with the act of Congress of July 24th, 1866, entitled " An act to aid in the construction of telegraph lines, and to secure to the government the use of the same for postal, military, and other purposes," the first section of which provides " that any telegraph company now organized, or which may hereafter be organized, under the laws of any State in this Union, shall have the right to construct, maintain, and operate lines of telegraph through and over any portion of the public domain of the United States, over and along any of the military or post roads of the United States, which have been or may hereafter be declared such by act of Congress, and over, under, or across the navigable streams or waters of the United States: *Provided*, That such lines of telegraph shall be so constructed and maintained as not to obstruct the navigation of such streams and waters, or interfere with the ordinary travel on such military or post roads. And any of said companies shall have the right to take and use from such public lands the necessary stone, timber, and other materials for its posts,

15

piers, stations, and other needful uses in the construction, maintenance, and operation of said lines of telegraph, and may pre-empt and use such portion of the unoccupied public lands subject to pre-emption, through which its said lines of telegraph may be located, as may be necessary for its stations, not exceeding forty acres for each station, but such stations shall not be within fifteen miles of each other." *

The statute of Florida incorporated the Pensacola Telegraph Company, which had been organized in December of the previous year, and in terms declared that it should enjoy "the sole and exclusive privilege and right of establishing and maintaining lines of electric telegraph in the counties of Escambia and Santa Rosa, either from different points within said counties, or connecting with lines coming into said counties, or either of them, from other points in this or any other State."

Soon after its organization and in 1866 the company erected a line of telegraph from the city of Pensacola, through the county of Escambia, to the southern boundary of Alabama, a distance of forty-seven miles, which has since been open and in continuous operation. It was located, by permission of the Alabama and Florida Railroad Company, along its line of railway. After the charter was obtained, the line was substantially rebuilt, and two other lines in the county were erected by the company.

In February, 1873, the Legislature of Florida passed an act granting to the Pensacola and Louisville Railroad Company, which had become the assignee of the Alabama and Florida Railroad Company, the right to construct and operate telegraph lines upon its right-of-way from the bay of Pensacola to the junction of its road with the Mobile and Montgomery railroad, and to connect the same with the lines of other companies. By an amendatory act passed in the following year (February, 1874), the railroad company was authorized to construct and operate the

---

* 14 Statutes at Large, 221.

lines, not only along its road as then located, but as it might be thereafter located, and along connecting roads in the county, to the boundary of Alabama, and to connect and consolidate them with other telegraph companies, and to sell and assign the property appertaining to them, and the rights, privileges, and franchises conferred by the act; and it empowered the assignee, in such case, to construct and operate the lines and to enjoy these rights, privileges, and franchises.

Under this amendatory act, and soon after its passage, the railroad company assigned the rights, privileges, and franchises thus acquired to the Western Union Telegraph Company, a corporation created under the laws of the State of New York, which at once proceeded to erect a line from the city of Pensacola to the southern boundary of Alabama, along the identical railway on which the complainant's line was erected in 1866, and ever afterwards located, with the avowed intention of using it to transmit for compensation messages for the public in the county and State. By the erection and operation of this line, the complainant alleged that its property would become valueless, and that it would lose the benefits of the franchises conferred by its charter.

The Supreme Court affirmed the decision of the circuit court, dismissing the bill, holding that the act of Congress of July 24, 1866, so far as it declared that the erection of telegraph lines should, as against State interference, be free to all who accepted its terms and conditions, and that a telegraph company of one State should not, after accepting them, be excluded by another State from prosecuting its business within her jurisdiction, was a legitimate regulation of commercial intercourse among the States, and appropriate legislation to execute the powers of Congress over the postal service. And further, that the right-of-way which the act granted was not limited to such military and post roads as were upon the public domain. The Chief Justice, who delivered the opinion of the court, said as follows :

" It [the act of Congress of 1866] substantially declares, in the interest of commerce and the convenient transmission of intelligence from place to place by the government of the United States and its citizens, that the erection of telegraph lines shall, so far as State interference is concerned, be free to all who will submit to the conditions imposed by Congress, and that corporations organized under the laws of one State for constructing and operating telegraph lines shall not be excluded by another from prosecuting their business within its jurisdiction, if they accept the terms proposed by the national government for this national privilege. To this extent, certainly, the statute is a legitimate regulation of commercial intercourse among the States, and is appropriate legislation to carry into execution the powers of Congress over the postal service. It gives no foreign corporation the right to enter upon private property without the consent of the owner and erect the necessary structures for its business, but it does provide that, whenever the consent of the owner is obtained, no State legislation shall prevent the occupation of post roads for telegraph purposes by such corporations as are willing to avail themselves of its privileges.

" It is insisted, however, that the statute extends only to such military and post roads as are upon the public domain ; but this, we, think, is not so. The language is, ' Through and over any portion of the public domain of the United States, over and along any of the military or post roads of the United States which have been or may hereafter be declared such by act of Congress, and over, under, or across the navigable streams or waters of the United States.' There is nothing to indicate an intention of limiting the effect of the words employed, and they are, therefore, to be given their natural and ordinary signification. Read in this way, the grant evidently extends to the public domain, the military and post roads, and the navigable waters of the United States. These are all within the dominion of the national government to the extent of the national powers, and are, therefore, subject to legitimate congressional regulation. No question arises as to the authority of Congress to provide for the appropriation of private property to the uses of the telegraph, for no such attempt has been made. The use of public property alone is granted. If private property is required, it must, so far as the present legislation is concerned, be obtained by private arrangement with its owner. No compulsory proceedings are authorized. State sovereignty under the Constitution is not interfered with. Only national privileges are granted."

From this decision Judges Field and Hunt dissented, Judge Field delivering a dissenting opinion. In that opinion he said as follows :

" There can be no serious question that the State of Florida possessed the absolute right to confer upon a corporation created by it the exclusive privilege for a limited period to construct and operate a telegraph line within its borders. Its constitution, in existence at the time, empowered the legislature to grant exclusive privileges and franchises to private corporations for a period not exceeding twenty years. The exclusiveness of a privilege often constitutes the only inducement for undertakings holding out little prospect of immediate returns. The uncertainty of the results of an enterprise will often deter capitalists, naturally cautious and distrustful, from making an investment without some assurance that in case the business become profitable they shall not encounter the danger of its destruction or diminution by competition. It has, therefore, been a common practice in all the States to encourage enterprises having for their object the promotion of the public good, such as the construction of bridges, turnpikes, railroads, and canals, by granting for limited periods exclusive privileges in connection with them. Such grants, so far from being deemed encroachments upon any rights or powers of the United States, are held to constitute contracts, and to be within the protecting clause of the Constitution prohibiting any impairing of their obligation.

. "The grant to the complainant was invaded by the subsequent grant to the Pensacola and Louisville Railroad Company. If the first grant was valid, the second was void, according to all the decisions of this court upon the power of a State to impair its grant since the Dartmouth College case. The court below did not hold otherwise, and I do not understand that a different view is taken here; but it decided, and this court sustains the decision, that the statute making the first grant was void by reason of its conflict with the act of Congress of July 24th, 1866.

. " With all deference to my associates, I cannot see that the act of Congress has anything to do with the case before us. In my judgment, it has reference only to telegraph lines over and along military and post roads on the public domain of the United States. The title of the act expresses its purpose, namely, 'to aid in the construction of telegraph lines and to secure to the government the use of the same for postal, military, and other purposes.' The aid conferred was the grant of a right of way over the public domain; the act does not propose to give aid in any other way. Its language is that any telegraph company organized under the laws of a State 'shall have the right to construct, maintain, and operate lines of telegraph through and over any portion of the public domain, over and along any of the military and post roads which have been, or may hereafter be, declared such by act of Congress, and over and across the navigable streams or waters of the United States.' The portion of the public domain which may be thus used is designated by reference to the military and post roads upon it. Were there any doubt that this is the correct construction of the act, the provision which follows in the same section would seem to remove it, namely, that any of the said companies shall ' have the right to take and use from *such public lands* the necessary stone, timber, and other materials for its posts, piers, stations, and other needful uses in the construction, maintenance, and operation of said lines of telegraph, and may pre-empt and use such portion of the *unoccupied public lands*, subject to pre-emption, through which its said lines of telegraph may be located, as may be necessary for its stations, not exceeding forty acres for each station, but such sections shall not be within fifteen miles of each other.' In the face of this language, the italics of which are mine, there ought not to be a difference of opinion as to the object of the act, or as to its construction. The conclusion reached by the majority of the court not only overlooks this language, but implies that Congress intended to give aid to the telegraph companies of the country—those existing or thereafter to be created—not merely by allowing them to construct their lines over and along post roads upon the public lands, but also over and along such roads within the States which are not on the public lands, where heretofore it has not been supposed that it could rightfully exercise any power.

" The only military roads belonging to the United States within the States are in the military reservations ; and to them the act obviously does not apply. And there are no post roads belonging to the United States within the States. The roads upon which the mails are carried by parties, under contract with the government, belong either to the States or to individuals or to corporations, and are declared post roads only to protect the carriers from being interfered with, and the mails from being delayed in their transportation, and the postal service from frauds. The government has no other control over them. It has no proprietary interest in them or along them to bestow upon any one. It cannot use them without paying the tolls chargeable to individuals for similar uses. It cannot prevent the State from changing or discontinuing them at its pleasure ; and it can acquire no ownership or property interest in them, except in the way in which it may acquire any other property in the States, namely, by purchase or by appropriation upon making just compensation,*

" The public streets in some of our cities are post roads under the declaration of Congress ;† and it would be a strange thing if telegraph lines could be erected by a foreign corporation along such streets without the consent of the municipal and State authorities, and, of course, without power on their part to regulate its charges or control its management. Yet the doctrine asserted by the majority of the court goes to this length : that if the owners of the property along the streets consent to the erection of such lines by a foreign corporation, the municipality and the State are powerless to prevent it, although the exclusive right to erect them may have been granted by the State to a corporation of its own creation.

" If by making a contract with a party to carry the mails over a particular road in a State, which thus becomes by act of Congress for that purpose a post road, Congress acquires such rights with respect to the road that it can authorize corporations of other States to construct along

---

* Dickey vs. Turnpike Road Co., 7 Dana (Ky.), 113.

† Rev. Stats., sec. 3,964.

and over it a line of telegraph, why may it not authorize them to construct along the road a railway, or a turnpike, or a canal, or any other work which may be used for the promotion of commerce? If the authority exists in the one case, I cannot see why it does not equally exist in the other. And if Congress can authorize the corporations of one State to construct telegraph lines and railways in another State, it must have the right to authorize them to condemn private property for that purpose. The act under consideration does not, it is true, provide for such condemnation, but if the right exist to authorize the construction of the lines, it cannot be defeated from the inability of the corporations to acquire the necessary property by purchase. The power to grant implies a power to confer all the authority necessary to make the grant effectual. It was for a long time a debated question whether the United States, in order to obtain property required for their own purposes, could exercise the right of eminent domain within a State. It has been decided, only within the past two years, that the government, if such property cannot be obtained by purchase, may appropriate it upon making just compensation to the owner,* but never has it been suggested that the United States could enable a corporation of one State to condemn property in another State, in order that it might transact its private business there.

" We are not called upon to say that Congress may not construct a railroad as a post road, or erect for postal purposes a telegraph line. It may be that the power to establish post roads is not limited to designating the roads which shall be used as postal routes ; a limitation which has been asserted by eminent jurists and statesmen.† If it be admitted that the power embraces also the construction of such roads, it does not follow that Congress can authorize the corporation of one State to construct and operate a railroad or telegraph line in another State for the transaction of private business, or even to exist there, without the permission of the latter State. By reason of its previous grant to the complainant Florida was incompetent to give such permission to the assignor of the defendant, or to any other company, to construct a telegraph line in the county of Escambia. The act of the State of February 3d, 1874, in the face of this grant, can only be held to authorize the construction of telegraph lines by different companies in other counties. If, therefore. the defendant has any rights in that county they are derived solely from the act of Congress.

"A corporation can have no legal existence beyond the limits of the sovereignty which created it. In The Bank of Augusta vs. Earle, it was said by this court that ' it must dwell in the place of its creation and

---

* Kohl vs. U. S., 1 Otto, 367.

† Elliott's Debates, edition of 1836, 433, 487 ; Views of President Monroe accompanying his veto message of May 4th, 1822; Views of Judge McLean in his dissenting opinion in the Wheeling Bridge Case, 18 How., p. 441-2.

cannot migrate to another sovereignty.'* And in Paul vs. Virginia we added that 'the recognition of its existence even by other States, and the enforcement of its contracts made therein, depend purely upon the comity of those States, a comity which is never extended where the existence of the corporation or the exercise of its powers is prejudicial to their interests or repugnant to their policy. Having no absolute right of recognition in other States, but depending for such recognition and the enforcement of its contracts upon their assent, it follows, as a matter of course, that such assent may be granted upon such terms and conditions as those States may think proper to impose. They may exclude the foreign corporation entirely; they may restrict its business to particular localities, or they may exact such security for the performance of its contracts with their citizens as in their judgment will best promote the public interest. The whole matter rests in their discretion.'† If, therefore, foreign corporations can exist in the State of Florida, and do business there by the authority of Congress, it must be because Congress can create such corporations for local business,—a doctrine to which I cannot assent, and which to my mind is pregnant with evil consequences.

"In all that has been said of the importance of the telegraph as a means of intercourse, and of its constant use in commercial transactions, I fully concur. Similar language may be used with regard to railways; indeed, of the two the railway is much the more important instrument of commerce. But it is difficult to see how from this fact can be deduced the right of Congress to authorize the corporations of one State to enter within the borders of another State and construct railways and telegraph lines in its different counties for the transaction of local business. The grant to the complainant in no way interferes with the power of Congress, if it possess such power, to construct telegraph lines or railways for postal service or for military purposes, or with its power to regulate commerce between the States. The imputation that Florida designed by the grant to obstruct the powers of Congress in these respects, is not warranted by anything in her statute. A like imputation, and with equal justice, might be made against every State in the Union which has authorized the construction of a railway or telegraph line in any of its counties, with a grant of an exclusive right to operate the road or line for a limited period. It is true the United States, equally with their citizens, may be obliged in such cases to use the road or line, but it has not heretofore been supposed that this fact impaired the right of the State to make the grant. When the general government desires to transact business within a State it necessarily makes use of the highways and modes of transit provided under the laws of the State, in the absence of those of its own creation.

"The position advanced, that if a corporation be in any way engaged in commerce it can enter and do business in another State without the latter's consent, is novel and startling.———Let this doctrine be once established, and the greater part of the trade and commerce of every State will soon be carried on by corporations created without it. The business of the country is to a large extent conducted or controlled by corporations, and it may be, as was said by this court in the case referred to (Paul vs. Virginia),' of the highest public interest that the number of corporations in the State should be limited, that they should be required to give publicity to their transactions, to submit their affairs to proper examination, to be subject to forfeiture of their corporate rights in case of mismanagement, and that their officers should be held to a strict accountability for the manner in which the business of the corporations is managed, and be liable to summary removal.' All these guards against corporate abuses the State would be incapable of taking against a corporation of another State operating a railway or a telegraph line within its borders under the permission of Congress, however extortionate its charges or corrupt its management. The corporation might have a tariff of rates and charges prescribed by its charter, which would be beyond the control of the State; and thus, by the authority of Congress, a State might be reduced to the condition of having the rates of charges for transportation of persons and freight and messages within its borders regulated by another State. Indeed, it is easy to see that there will remain little of value in the reserved rights of the States if the doctrine announced in this case be accepted as the law of the land.

" The power vested in Congress to regulate commerce ' among the several States' does not authorize any interference with the commerce which is carried on entirely within a State. 'Comprehensive as the word 'among' is,' says Chief Justice Marshall, 'it may very properly be restricted to that commerce which concerns more States than one,' and 'the completely internal commerce of a State, then, may be considered as reserved for the State itself.' That commerce embraces the greater part of the business of every State. Every one engaged in the transportation of property or persons, or in sending messages, between different points within the State, not destined to points beyond it, or in the purchase or sale of merchandise within its borders, is engaged in its commerce; and the doctrine that Congress can authorize foreign corporations to enter within its limits and participate in this commerce without the State's consent is utterly subversive of our system of local State government. State control in local matters would thus be imposible."

The case of The Union Pacific Railroad Company vs. The United States, and that of Gallatin vs. The Central Pacific Railroad Company, before the Supreme Court at the October term, 1878, were brought to test the validity of the funding act of Congress of May 7th, 1878, commonly called the Thurman act.

By the first section of the act of Congress of July, 1862, certain persons therein designated were created a corporation by the name of the Union Pacific Railroad Company, and authorized to construct and operate a continuous railroad and telegraph line from a designated point on the 100th meridian of longitude west from Greenwich to the western boundary of Nevada Territory, and were invested with the powers, privileges, and immunities necessary for that purpose, and with such as are usually conferred upon corporations.

By subsequent provisions of the act and the amendatory act of 1864, three grants were made to the company thus created: a grant of a right-of-way over the public lands of the United States for the road and telegraph line; a grant of ten alternate sections of land on each side of the road, to aid in its construction and that of the telegraph line; and a grant of a certain number of subsidy bonds of the United States, each in the sum one thousand dollars, payable in thirty years, with semi-annual interest—patents for the lands and the bonds to be issued as each twenty consecutive miles of the road and telegraph should be completed.

These grants were made upon certain conditions as to the completion of the road and telegraph line, their construction and use by the government. These conditions are expressed in the sixth section, which is as follows:

"SEC. 6. *And be it further enacted,* That the grants aforesaid are made upon condition that said company shall pay said bonds at maturity, and shall keep said railroad and telegraph line in repair and use, and shall at all times transmit dispatches over said telegraph line, and transport mails, troops, and munitions of war, supplies, and public stores upon said railroad for the government whenever required to do so by any department thereof, and that the government shall at all times have the preference in the use of the same for all the purposes aforesaid (at fair and reasonable rates of compensation, not to exceed the amounts paid by private parties for the same kind of service); and all compensation [by the act of 1864 reduced to one-half] for services rendered for the government shall be applied to the payment of said bonds and interest until the whole amount is fully paid. Said company may also pay the United

States, wholly or in part, in the same or other bonds, treasury notes, or other evidences of debt against the United States, to be allowed at par; and after said road is completed, until said bonds and interest are paid, at least five per centum of the net earnings of said road shall also be annually applied to the payment thereof."

By the same act which incorporated the Union Pacific Company, the Central Pacific Company, a corporation existing under the laws of the State of California, was authorized to construct a railroad and telegraph line from the Pacific Coast, at or near San Francisco, or the navigable waters of the Sacramento River, to the eastern boundary of California, upon the same terms and conditions in all respects as those contained in the act for the construction of the road and telegraph line of the Union Pacific, and to meet and connect with that road and telegraph line on the eastern boundary of California. Each of the companies was required to file its acceptance of the conditions of the act in the Department of the Interior within six months after its passage. The Central Pacific was also authorized, after completing its road across the State of California, to continue the construction of the road and telegraph through the territories of the United States. The number of bonds that were to be issued to the company were sixteen for each mile, excepting for 450 miles between the western base of the Sierra Nevada Mountains and the eastern base of the Rocky Mountains. For 150 miles of that distance double the usual amount, namely, thirty-two bonds a mile, were to be issued, and for 300 miles of the most mountainous and difficult portion treble the amount a mile, namely, forty-eight, were to be issued. These bonds were to constitute a first mortgage on the whole line of railroad and telegraph, together with its rolling-stock and property of every kind.

By the act of 1864 the United States waived its priority of lien and allowed the companies to issue their first mortgage bonds on their respective roads to an amount not exceeding the amount of the bonds of the United States. The act of 1862 provided that in case the companies failed to comply with the terms and conditions prescribed by not completing the road and telegraph line within a reasonable time, or not keeping the same in repair and use, Congress might pass an act to ensure their speedy completion, or to put them in repair and use, and if the road were not completed by the first of July, 1876, the whole road and property were to be forfeited to the United States.

Its eighteenth section was as follows :

"SEC. 18. *And be it further enacted,* That whenever it appears that the net earnings of the entire road and telegraph, including the amount allowed for services rendered for the United States, after deducting all expenditures—including repairs and the furnishing, running, and managing of said road—shall exceed ten per centum upon its cost, (exclusive of the five per centum to be paid to the United States,) Congress may reduce the rates of fare thereon, if unreasonable in amount, and may fix and establish the same by law. And the better to accomplish the object of this act, namely, to promote the public interest and welfare by the construction of said railroad and telegraph line, and keeping the same in working order, and to secure to the government at all times (but particularly in time of war) the use and benefits of the same for postal, military, and other purposes, Congress may at any time—having due regard for the rights of said companies named herein—add to, alter, amend, or repeal this act."

The amendatory act closes with a section providing that Congress "may at any time alter, amend, or repeal this act."

The two companies—the Union Pacific and the Central Pacific—both filed their acceptance of the conditions of the act with the Department of the Interior, and proceeded to the construction of their respective roads. These were completed several years before the time limited by the act, and they have been kept at all times since in repair and use. They have also been at the service of the government whenever required, and no complaint of their inefficiency has been made.

Soon after the completion of the roads a question arose between the companies and the government, whether the companies were bound to pay the interest on the bonds of the United States as it became due from year to year, or only at the maturity of the bonds at the end of the thirty years, and was carried before the Court of Claims for adjudication, and came, on appeal from its decision, before the Supreme Court of the United States at the October term of 1875. It was there held by the court unanimously that the interest was not payable by the company until the maturity of the bonds. Judge Davis gave the opinion of the court.—(See United States vs. The Union Pacific Railroad, 91 U. S., 72.)

The same conclusion was reached by the Judiciary Committee of both Houses of Congress. The Committee on the Judiciary of the Senate consisted at the time of Senators Trumbull, Stewart, Edmunds, Carpenter, Conkling, Thurman, and Rice.

Notwithstanding there was no complaint against the companies that they had not complied in all respects with the acts of Congress, or that there was any impairment of the value of their property, on the 7th of May, 1878, Congress passed the funding act, commonly known as the "Thurman act." It is entitled "An act to alter and amend the railroad acts of 1862 and 1864," giving their titles.

This act requires that the whole amount of compensation which may from time to time be due to the companies for services rendered for the government, shall be retained by the United States, one half to be applied to the liquidation of the interest paid by the United States on its bonds, and the other half to be turned into a sinking fund, which the act establishes, in the treasury of the United States. The act requires the Secretary of the Treasury to invest moneys of that fund in bonds of the United States. It also provides that on the 1st of February of each year, one half of the compensation for services mentioned shall be credited to that fund, and requires the Central Pacific Company to pay into that fund on that day in each year $1,200,000, or so much thereof as may be necessary to make the five per centum of the net earnings payable to the United States under the act of

1862, and the whole sum earned as compensation for services, and the sum thus paid to amount in the aggregate to twenty-five per centum of the whole net earnings of the company. The act requires the Union Pacific Company to pay $850,000 into the sinking fund on the 1st day of February of each year, or so much thereof as, with the five per centum and compensation for services, and the amount paid, shall equal twenty-five per cent. of its net earnings. And the act declares that no dividend shall be voted or paid to any stockholder or stockholders in either of the companies, when the company is in default in respect of the payment of the sums required into the sinking fund, or in respect of the five per centum of the net earnings, or in respect of any interest upon any debt the lien of which is paramount to that of the United States; and any officer or person who shall vote, declare, or pay any stockholder of said companies any dividend contrary to the provisions of the act, and any stockholder who shall receive any, shall be liable to the United States for the amount, and shall be deemed guilty of a misdemeanor, and, on conviction, shall be punished by a fine not exceeding $10,000, and by imprisonment not exceeding one year.

It is the validity of this act, thus changing the conditions and obligations of the companies under the acts of 1862 and 1864, which was considered in the cases mentioned. In both cases judgments were given in the courts below as a matter of form against the companies, and by them appeals were taken to the Supreme Court. The questions involved were there elaborately and ably argued by distinguished counsel. Messrs. Samuel Shellabarger and Jeremiah M. Wilson appearing for the Union Pacific; Mr. B. H. Hill, of the United States Senate, and Mr. S. W. Sanderson, of California, appearing for the Central Pacific; the Attorney-General, and Mr. George H. Williams, and Mr. Edwin B. Smith, the Assistant Attorney-General, appearing for the United States. The Supreme Court affirmed the judgment in both cases, holding that the act of May

7th, 1878, was constitutional, and that the establishment of the sinking fund was a reasonable regulation for the administration of the affairs of the companies and was warranted under the clauses reserving to Congress the right to alter and amend the acts of 1862 and 1864.

Judges Strong, Bradley, and Field dissented from the judgment, and each of them read a dissenting opinion, Judge Field confining himself principally to the case of the Central Pacific. His opinion is as follows :

" The decision [rendered] will, in my opinion, tend to create insecurity in the title to corporate property in the country. It, in effect, determines that the general government, in its dealings with the Pacific Railroad Companies, is under no legal obligation to fulfill its contracts, and that whether it shall do so is a question of policy and not of duty. It also seems to me to recognize the right of the government to appropriate by legislative decree the earnings of those companies without judicial inquiry and determination as to its claim to such earnings, thus sanctioning the exercise of judicial functions in its own cases. And in respect to the Central Pacific Company it asserts a supremacy of the federal over the State government in the control of the corporation which, in my judgment, is subversive of the rights of the State. I, therefore, am constrained to add some suggestions to those presented by my associates, Justices Strong and Bradley. In what I have to say I shall confine myself chiefly to the case of the Central Pacific Company. That company is a State corporation, and is the successor of a corporation of the same name, created before the railroad acts of Congress were passed, and of four other corporations organized under the laws of the State. No sovereign attributes possessed by the general government were exercised in calling into existence the original company, or any of the companies with which it is now consolidated. They all derived their powers and capacities from the State, and held them at its will.

" The relation of the general government to the Pacific companies is two-fold : that of sovereign in its own territory, and that of contractor. As sovereign, its power extends to the enforcement of such acts and regulations by the companies as will insure, in the management of their roads, and conduct of their officers in its territory, the safety, convenience, and comfort of the public. It can exercise such control in its territory over all common carriers of passengers and property. As a contractor, it is bound by its engagements equally with a private individual ; it cannot be relieved from them by any assertion of its sovereign authority.

" Its relation to the original Central Pacific Company, and to the present company as its successor, in the construction and equipment of its road, and its use for public purposes, was and is that of a contractor, and the rights and obligations of both are to be measured, as in the case of sim-ilar relations between other parties, by the terms and conditions of the contract.

" By the first section of the original railroad act of Congress, passed in July, 1862, certain persons therein designated were created a corporation by the name of the Union Pacific Railroad Company, and authorized to construct and operate a continuous railroad and telegraph line from a designated point on the 100th meridian of longitude west from Green-wich to the eastern boundary of Nevada Territory, and were invested with the powers, privileges, and immunities necessary for that purpose, and with such as are usually conferred upon corporations.

" By subsequent provisions of the act and the amendatory act of 1864, three grants were made to the company thus created : a grant of a right-of-way over the public lands of the United States for the road and tele-graph line ; a grant of ten alternate sections of land on each side of the road, to aid in its construction and that of the telegraph line ; and a grant of a certain number of subsidy bonds of the United States, each in the sum of one thousand dollars, payable in thirty years, with semi-annual interest—patents for the lands and the bonds to be issued as each twenty consecutive miles of the road and telegraph should be completed. These grants were made upon certain conditions as to the completion of the road and telegraph line, their construction and use by the government, and their pledge as security for the ultimate payment of the bonds. They were the considerations offered by the government to the company for the work which it undertook.

" By the act which thus incorporated the Union Pacific Company, and made the grants mentioned, the United States proposed to the Central Pacific that it should construct in like manner a railroad and a telegraph line through the State of California from a point near the Pacific Coast to its eastern boundary, upon the same terms and conditions, and after com-pleting them across the State, to continue their construction through the territories of the United States until they should meet and connect with the road and telegraph line of the Union Pacific.

" They, in effect, said to the company, that if it would construct a rail-road and a telegraph line from the Pacific Ocean eastward to a connection with the Union Pacific—the road to be in all respects one of first class—and keep them in repair, so that they could be used at all times by any department of the government for the transmission of despatches and the transportation of mails, troops, munitions of war, supplies, and public stores, at reasonable rates of compensation, not exceeding such as were charged private persons for similar services, and allow the government at all times the preference in the use of the road and telegraph,—they would grant the company a right-of-way over the public lands for the construc-tion of the road and telegraph line, and grant to it ten alternate sections of land on each side of the road, and give it their bonds, each for the sum of $1,000, payable thirty years after date, with semi-annual interest, such bonds to be issued at the rate of sixteen, thirty-two, or forty-eight the mile, according to the character of the country over which the road should be constructed; and would issue patents for the lands, and the subsidy bonds as each twenty consecutive miles of the road and telegraph should be completed in the manner prescribed; it being agreed that the company should pay the bonds as they should mature, and that for the security of their payment they should constitute a second mortgage upon the whole line of the road and telegraph, and that one-half of the compensation earned for services to the government, and, after the completion of the road, five per cent. of its net earnings should be retained and applied to the payment of the bonds; and also, that the company should complete the road by the first of July, 1876, and keep it in repair and use thereafter, or upon failure to do so, that the government might take possession of the road and complete it, or keep it in repair and use as the case might be. And they further, in effect, said that if these terms and conditions were satisfactory, the company should file its written acceptance thereof with the Secretary of the Interior, within six months thereafter; and that thereupon there should be a contract between them.

" This proposition of the government the Central Pacific accepted, and filed its acceptance as required, and thereupon the provisions of the act became a contract between it and the United States, as complete and perfect as could be made by the most formal instrument. The United States thus came under obligation to the company to make the grants and issue the bonds stipulated, upon the construction of the road and telegraph line in the manner prescribed. The corporate capacity of the company in no respect affected the nature of the contract, or made it in any particular different from what it would have been had a natural person been one of the parties. The company was not a creature of the United States, and Congress could neither add to nor subtract from its corporate powers. The exercise of the right of eminent domain allowed in the Territories was not the exercise of a corporate power. That right belongs to the sovereign authority, and whoever exercises it does so as the agent of that sovereignty. Nor was its character as a State institution changed by the fact that it was permitted by Congress to extend its road through the territory of the United States. This permission was no more than the license which is usually extended by positive agreement, or by comity in the absence of such agreement, by one State to the corporations of another State, to do business and own property in its jurisdiction. Such license is not the source of the corporate powers exercised. Insurance companies, express companies, and, indeed, companies organized for almost every kind of business, are, by comity, permitted throughout the United States, and generally throughout the civilized world, to do business, make contracts, and exercise their corporate powers in a jurisdiction where, in a strict legal sense, they have no corporate existence. The Pacific Mail Steamship Company, for example, to take an illustration mentioned by counsel, is a corporation created under the laws of the State of New York,

16

and, like the Central Pacific, has been subsidized by the United States. Its ships visit Central America, California, Japan, and China, and in all these places it leases or owns wharves and makes and enforces contracts necessary to the transaction of its business, yet no one has ever pretended or suggested that it derived any of its corporate powers from the United States, or from the authorities of any of the places named.* By consent of those authorities, expressed in terms, or implied in what is understood as their comity, it exercises powers derived solely from the State of New York.

"When, therefore, Congress assented to the extension into the territory of the United States of the road which the Central Pacific was authorized by its charter to construct in California, it was deemed important for the company to obtain also the consent and authority of the State to act without its limits and assume responsibilities not originally contemplated. Accordingly, in 1864, the legislature of the State at its second session after the adoption of the original railroad act of Congress, in order to enable the company to comply with its provisions and conditions, authorized the company to construct, maintain, and operate the road in the territory lying east of the State, and invested it with rights, privileges, and powers granted by the act of Congress, with the reservation, however, that the company should *be subject to all the laws of the State concerning railroad and telegraph lines*, except that messages and property of the United States, of the State, and of the company should have priority of transmission and transportation. The extent of the power which was thus reserved we shall hereafter consider. It is sufficient at present to observe that it was as ample and complete as it is possible for one sovereignty to exert over institutions of its own creation, and that its exercise is incompatible with the control asserted by the law of Congress of 1878, which has given rise to the present suit.

"The Central Pacific Company having accepted, as already stated, the conditions proffered by Congress, proceeded at once to the execution of its contract. In the face of great obstacles, doubts, and uncertainties its directors commenced and prosecuted the work, and within a period several years less than that prescribed, its telegraph line and road were completed, the latter with all the appurtenances of a first-class road, and were accepted by the government. Patents for the land granted, and the subsidy bonds mentioned, were accordingly issued to the company. Since then the road and telegraph line have been kept in repair and use and the government has enjoyed all the privileges in the transmission of despatches over the telegraph, and in the transportation of mails, troops, munitions of war, supplies, and public stores over the road, which were stipulated. There has been no failure on the part of the company to comply with its engagements, nor is any complaint of delinquency or neglect in its action made by the government. The road is more valuable now than on the day of its completion; it has been improved in its rails, bridges, cars, depots, turn-outs, machine-shops, and all other appurtenances. Its earnings have been constantly increasing, and it constitutes to-day a far better security to the United States for the ultimate payment of the subsidy bonds than at any period since its completion, and to the government it has caused, with the connecting road of the Union Pacific, an immense saving of expense. The records of the different departments show an annual saving, as compared with previous expenditures, in the item of transportation alone of the mails, troops, and public stores, of five millions, aggregating at this day over fifty millions of dollars.

"Whilst the company was thus complying in all respects with its engagements, the act of May 7, 1878, was passed, altering in essential particulars the contract of the company and greatly increasing its obligations. By the contract only one-half of the compensation for transportation for the government is to be retained and applied towards the payment of the bonds. By the act of 1878 the whole of such compensation is to be retained and thus applied. By the contract five per cent. only of the net earnings of the road are to be paid to the United States to be applied upon the subsidy bonds. By the act of 1878 twenty-five per cent. of the net earnings are to be thus paid and applied. By the contract the only security which the government had for its subsidy bonds was a second mortgage on the road and its appurtenances and telegraph line; and the company was allowed to give a first mortgage as security for its own bonds, issued for an equal amount. By the act of 1878 additional security is required for the ultimate payment of its own bonds, and the subsidy bonds of the United States, by the creation of what is termed a sinking fund, that is, by compelling the company to deposit twelve hundred thousand dollars a year in the treasury of the United States, to be held for such payment, or so much thereof as may be necessary to make the five per cent. net earnings, the whole sum earned as compensation for services, and sufficient in addition to make the whole reach twenty-five per cent. of the net earnings.

"It is not material, in the view I take of the subject, whether the deposit of this large sum in the treasury of the creditor be termed a payment, or something else. It is the exaction from the company of money for which the original contract did not stipulate, which constitutes the objectionable feature of the act of 1878. The act thus makes a great change in the liabilities of the company. Its purpose, however disguised, is to coerce the payment of money years in advance of the time prescribed by the contract. That such legislation is beyond the power of Congress I cannot entertain a doubt. The clauses of the original acts reserving a right to Congress to alter or amend them do not, in my judgment, justify the legislation. The power reserved under these clauses is declared to be for a specific purpose. The language in the act of 1862 is as follows: 'And the better to accomplish the object of this act, to promote the public interest and welfare by the construction of said railroad and telegraph line, and keeping the same in working order, and to secure the government at all times (but particularly in time of war) the use and benefits of the same for postal, military, and other purposes, Congress may at any time—having due regard for the rights of said companies named herein—add to, alter, amend, or repeal this act.'—(Sec. 18.) The language of the amendatory act of 1864 is more general: ' That Congress may at any time alter, amend, or repeal this act.' The two acts are to be read together; they deal with the same subject; and are to be treated as if passed at the same time.—(Prescott vs. Railroad Co., 16 Wall., 603.) The limitations, therefore, imposed upon the exercise of the power of alteration and amendment in the act of 1862 must be held to apply to the power reserved in the act of 1864. They are not repealed, either expressly or impliedly, by anything in the latter act. If this be so, the legislation of 1878 can find no support in the clauses. The conditions upon which the reserved power could be exercised under them did not then exist. The road and telegraph had years before been constructed, and always kept in working order; and the government has at all times been secured in their use and benefits for postal, military, and other purposes.

"But if the reserved power of alteration and amendment be considered as freed from the limitations designated, it cannot be exerted to affect the contract so far as it has been executed, or the rights vested under it. When the road was completed in the manner prescribed and accepted, the company became entitled as of right to the land and subsidy bonds stipulated. The title to the land was perfect on the issue of the patents; the title to the bonds vested on their delivery. Any alteration of the acts under the reservation clauses, or their repeal, could not revoke the title to the land or recall the bonds or change the right of the company to either. So far as these are concerned the contract was, long before the act of 1878, an executed and closed transaction, and they were as much beyond the reach of the government as any other property vested in private proprietorship. The right to hold the subsidy bonds for the period at which they are to run without paying or advancing money on them before their maturity, except as originally provided, or furnishing other security than that originally stipulated, was, on their delivery, as perfect as the right to hold the title to the land patented unencumbered by future liens of the government. Any alteration or amendment could only operate for the future and affect subsequent acts of the company; it could have no operation upon that which had already been done and vested.

"There have been much discussion and great difference of opinion on many points as to the meaning and effect of a similar reservation in statutes of the States, but on the point that it does not authorize any interference with vested rights all the authorities concur. Such was the language of Chief Justice Shaw in the case cited from the Supreme Court of Massachusetts; and such is the language of Mr. Justice Clifford in the cases cited from this court. And such must be the case or there would be no safety in dealing with the government where such a clause is inserted in its legislation. It could undo at pleasure everything done under its authority, and despoil of their property those who had trusted to its faith.—(Essex Co. vs. The Commonwealth, 13 Gray, 253; Miller vs. The State, 15 Wall., 498; Holyoke Co. vs. Lyman, Ibid., 522; see also Shields vs. Ohio, 95 U. S., 324, and Sage vs. Dillard, 15 B. Monroe, 35.)

" The object of a reservation of this kind in acts of incorporation is to insure to the government control over corporate franchises, rights, and privileges which, in its sovereign or legislative capacity, it may call into existence, not to interfere with contracts which the corporation created by it may make. Such is the purport of our language in Tomlinson vs. Jessup, where we state the object of the reservation to be ' to prevent a grant of *corporate* rights and privileges in a form which will preclude legislative interference with their exercise, if the public interest should at any time require such interference,' and that ' the reservation affects the entire relation between the State and corporation, and places under legislative control all rights, privileges, and immunities *derived by its charter directly from the State.'*—(15 Wall., 454.) The same thing we repeated, with greater distinctness, in the case of The Railroad Company vs. Maine, where we said that by the reservation the State retained the power to alter the act incorporating the company, in all particulars *constituting the grant to it of corporate rights, privileges, and immunities;* and that 'the existence of the corporation, and its franchises and immunities, derived directly from the State, were thus kept under its control.' But, we added, that ' rights and interests acquired by the company, *not constituting a part of the contract of incorporation,* stand upon a different footing.'—(96 U. S., 499.)

" Now, there was no grant by the United States to the Central Pacific Company, of corporate rights, privileges, and immunities. No attribute of sovereignty was exercised by them in its creation. It took its life, and all its attributes and capacities, from the State. Whatever powers, rights, and privileges it acquired from the United States it took under its contract with them and not otherwise. The relation between the parties being that of contractors, the rights and obligations of both, as already stated, are to be measured by the terms and conditions of the contract. And when the government of the United States entered into that contract, it laid aside its sovereignty and put itself on terms of equality with its contractor. It was then but a civil corporation, as incapable as the Central Pacific of releasing itself from its obligations, or of finally determining their extent and character. It could not, as justly observed by one of the counsel who argued this case, ' *release itself and hold the other party* to the contract. It could not change its *obligations* and hold its *rights* unchanged. It cannot bind itself as a *civil corporation,* and loose itself by its sovereign legislative power.' This principle is aptly expressed by the great conservative statesman, Alexander Hamilton, in his report to Congress on the public credit, in 1795: ' When a government,' he observes, ' enters into a contract with an individual, it deposes, as to the matter of the contract, its constitutional authority, and exchanges the character of legislator for that of a moral agent, with the same rights and obligations as an individual. Its promises may be justly considered out of its *power to legislate,* unless in aid of them. It is, in theory, impossible to reconcile the two ideas of a *promise which obliges* with a power *to make a law which can vary the effect of it.*'—(Hamilton's Works, vol. 3, p. 518, 519.)

"When, therefore, the government of the United States entered into the contract with the Central Pacific, it could no more than a private corporation or a private individual finally construe and determine the extent of the company's rights and liabilities. If it had cause of complaint against the company, it could not undertake itself, by legislative decree, to redress the grievance, but was compelled to seek redress as all other civil corporations are compelled, through the judicial tribunals. If the company was wasting its property, of which no allegation is made, or impairing the security of the government, the remedy by suit was ample. To declare that one of two contracting parties is entitled, under the contract between them, to the payment of a greater sum than is admitted to be payable, or to other or greater security than that given, is not a legislative function. It is a judicial action; it is the exercise of judicial power—and all such power, with respect to any transaction arising under the laws of the United States, is vested by the Constitution in the courts of the country.

"In the case of The Commonwealth vs. The Proprietors of New Bedford Bridge, a corporation of Massachusetts, the supreme court of that State, speaking with reference to a contract between the parties, uses this language: 'Each has equal rights and privileges under it, and neither can interpret its terms authoritatively so as to control and bind the rights of the other. The Commonwealth has no more authority to construe the charter than the corporation. By becoming a party to a contract with its citizens, the government divests itself of its sovereignty in respect to the terms and conditions of the contract and its construction and interpretation, and stands in the same position as a private individual. If it were otherwise, the rights of parties contracting with the government would be held at the caprice of the sovereign, and exposed to all the risks arising from the corrupt or ill-judged use of misguided power. The interpretation and construction of contracts when drawn in question belong exclusively to the *judicial* department of the government. The legislature has no more power to construe their own contracts with their citizens than those which individuals make with each other. They can do neither without exercising judicial powers which would be contrary to the elementary principles of our government, as set forth in the Declaration of Rights.'—(2 Gray, 350.)

"In that case the charter of the corporation authorized the building of a toll-bridge across a navigable river, with two suitable draws at least thirty feet wide. A subsequent act required draws to be made of a greater width; but the court held that the question whether the draws already made were suitable, and constructed so as not unreasonable or uunceessarily to obstruct or impede public navigation, was not a question to be determined by the legislature, or by the corporation, but by the courts. It was a question which could not be authoritatively determined by either party so as to control and bind the other, 'Like all other matters involving a controversy concerning public duty and private rights,' said the court, 'it is to be adjusted and settled in the regular tribunals, where questions of law and fact are adjudicated on fixed and established principles, and according to the forms and usages best adapted to secure the impartial administration of justice.' In the case at bar, the government, by the act of 1878, undertakes to decide authoritatively what the obligations of the Central Pacific are, and in effect declares that if the directors of the company do not respect its construction, and obey its mandates, founded upon such construction, they shall be subject to fine and imprisonment.

"The distinction between a judicial and a legislative act is well defined. The one determines what the law is, and what the rights of parties are, with reference to transactions already had; the other prescribes what the law shall be in future cases arising under it. Wherever an act undertakes to determine a question of right or obligation, or of property, as the foundation upon which it proceeds, such act is to that extent a judicial one, and not the proper exercise of legislative functions. Thus an act of the Legislature of Illinois authorizing the sale of the lands of an intestate, to raise a specific sum, to pay certain parties their claims against the estate of the deceased for moneys advanced and liabilities incurred, was held unconstitutional on the ground that it involved a judicial determination that the estate was indebted to those parties for the moneys advanced and liabilities incurred. The ascertainment of indebtedness from one party to another, and a direction for its payment, the court considered to be judicial acts which could not be performed by the legislature.—(3 Scam., 238.) So also an act of the Legislature of Tennessee authorizing a guardian of infant heirs to sell certain lands of which their ancestors died seized, and directing the proceeds to be applied to the payment of the ancestor's debts, was, on similar grounds, held to be unconstitutional.—(Jones vs. Perry, 10 Yerger, 59.) Tested by the principles thus illustrated the act of 1878 must be held in many ways to transcend the legislative power of Congress.

"I cannot assent to the doctrine which would ascribe to the federal government a sovereign right to treat as it may choose corporations with which it deals, and would exempt it from that great law of morality which should bind all governments, as it binds all individuals, to do justice and keep faith. Because it was deemed important, on the adoption of the Constitution, in the light of what was known as tender laws, appraisement laws, stay laws, and installment laws of the States, which Story says had prostrated all private credit and all private morals, to insert a clause prohibiting the States from passing any law impairing the obligation of contracts, and no clause prohibiting the federal government from like legislation is found, it is argued that no such prohibition upon it exists.

"'It is true,' as I had occasion to observe in another case, 'there is no provision in the Constitution forbidding in express terms such legislation. And it is also true that there are express powers delegated to Congress, the execution of which necessarily operates to impair the obligation of contracts. It was the object of the framers of that instrument to create a national government, competent to represent the entire country in its relations with foreign nations and to accomplish by its legislation measures of common interest to all the people, which the several States in their independent capacities were incapable of effecting, or if capable, the execution of which would be attended with great difficulty and embarrassment. They, therefore, clothed Congress with all the powers essential to the successful accomplishment of these ends, and carefully withheld the grant of all other powers. Some of the powers granted, from their very nature, interfere in their execution with contracts of parties. Thus war suspends intercourse and commerce between citizens or subjects of belligerent nations; it renders during its continuance the performance of contracts previously made, unlawful. These incidental consequences were contemplated in the grant of the war power. So the regulation of commerce and the imposition of duties may so affect the prices of articles imported or manufactured as to essentially alter the value of previous contracts respecting them; but this incidental consequence was seen in the grant of the power over commerce and duties. There can be no valid objection to laws passed in execution of express powers, that consequences like these follow incidentally from their execution. But it is otherwise when such consequences do not follow incidentally, but are directly enacted.'

"'The only express authority for any legislation affecting the obligation of contracts is found in the power to establish a uniform system of bankruptcy, the direct object of which is to release insolvent debtors from their contracts upon the surrender of their property.'—(12 Wallace, 663.) From this express grant in the case of bankrupts the inference is deducible that there was no general power to interfere with contracts. If such general power existed there could have been no occasion for the delegation of an express power in the case of bankrupts. The argument for the general power from the absence of a special prohibition proceeds upon a misconception of the nature of the federal government as one of limited powers. It can exercise only such powers as are specifically granted or are necessarily implied. All other powers, not prohibited to the States, are reserved to them or to the people. As I said in the case referred to, the doctrine that where a power is not expressly forbidden it may be exercised, would change the whole character of our government. According to the great commentators on the Constitution, and the opinions of the great jurists, who have studied and interpreted its meaning, the true doctrine is, that where a power is not in terms granted, and is not necessary or proper for the exercise of a power thus granted, it does not exist. It would not be pretended, for example, had there been no amendments to the Constitution as originally adopted, that Congress could have passed a law respecting an establishment of religion or prohibiting the free exercise thereof, or abridging the freedom of speech, or the right of the people to assemble and petition for a redress of grievances. The amendments prohibiting the exercise of any such power were adopted in the language of the preamble accompanying them, when presented to the States, ' in order to prevent misconception or abuse' of the powers of the Constitution.

" Independent of these views, there are many considerations which lead to the conclusion that the power to impair contracts, by direct action to that end, does not exist with the general government. In the first place, one of the objects of the Constitution, expressed in its preamble, was the establishment of justice, and what that meant in its relations to contracts is not left, as was justly said by the late Chief Justice, in Hepburn vs. Griswold, to inference or conjecture. As he observes, at the time the Constitution was undergoing discussion in the Convention, the Congress of the Confederation was engaged in framing the ordinance for the government of the Northwestern Territory, in which certain articles of compact were established between the people of the original States and the people of the territory, for the purpose, as expressed in the instrument, of extending the fundamental principles of civil and religious liberty, upon which the States, their laws and constitutions, were erected. By that ordinance it was declared, that in the just preservation of rights and property, 'no law ought ever to be made, or have force in the said territory, that shall, in any manner, interfere with or affect private contracts or engagements *bona fide* and without fraud previously formed.' The same provision, adds the Chief Justice, found more condensed expression in the prohibition upon the States against impairing the obligation of contracts, which has ever been recognized as an efficient safeguard against injustice, and. though the prohibition is not applied in terms to the government of the United States, he expressed the opinion, speaking for himself and the majority of the court at the time, that it was clear ' that those who framed and those who adopted the Constitution, intended that the spirit of this prohibition should pervade the entire body of legislation, and that the justice which the Constitution was ordained to establish was not thought by them to be compatible with legislation of an opposite tendency.'—(8 Wallace, 623.)

" Similar views are found expressed in the opinions of other judges of this court. In Calder vs. Bull, which was here in 1798, Mr. Justice Chase said, that there were acts which the federal and State legislatures could not do without exceeding their authority, and among them he mentioned a law which punished a citizen for an innocent act ; a law that destroyed or impaired the lawful private contracts of citizens ; a law that made a man judge in his own case ; and a law that took the property from A and gave it to B. 'It is against all reason and justice,' he added, ' for a people to entrust a legislature with such powers, and, therefore, it cannot be presumed that they have done it. They may command what is right and prohibit what is wrong; but they cannot change innocence into guilt or punish innocence as a crime, or violate the right of an antecedent lawful private contract, or the right of private property. To maintain that a federal or State legislature possesses such powers if they had not been expressly restrained, would, in my opinion, be a political heresy altogether inadmissible in all free republican governments.'—(3 Dallas, 388.)

" In Ogden vs. Saunders, which was before this court in 1827, Mr. Justice Thompson, referring to the clauses of the Constitution prohibiting the State from passing a bill of attainder, an *ex post facto law*, or a law impairing the obligation of contracts, said : ' Neither provision can strictly be considered as introducing any new principle, but only for greater security and safety to incorporate into this charter provisions admitted by all to be among the first principles of our government. No State court would, I presume, sanction and enforce an *ex post facto* law, if no such prohibition was contained in the Constitution of the United States; so, neither would retrospective laws, taking away vested rights, be enforced. Such laws are repugnant to those fundamental principles upon which every just system of laws is founded.'

" In the Federalist, Mr. Madison declared that laws impairing the obligation of contracts were contrary to the first principles of the social compact and to every principle of sound legislation ; and in the Dartmouth College case Mr. Webster contended that acts, which were there held to impair the obligation of contracts, were not the exercise of a power properly legislative, as their object and effect was to take away vested rights. ' To justify the taking away of vested rights,' he said, ' there must be a forfeiture, to adjudge upon and declare which is the proper province of the judiciary.' Surely the Constitution would have failed to establish justice had it allowed the exercise of such a dangerous power to the Congress of the United States.

" In the second place, legislation impairing the obligation of contracts impinges upon the provision of the Constitution which declares that no one shall be deprived of his property without due process of law ; and that means by law in its regular course of administration through the courts of justice. Contracts are property, and a large portion of the wealth of the country exists in that form. Whatever impairs their value diminishes, therefore, the property of the owner, and if that be effected by direct legislative action operating upon the contract, forbidding its enforcement or transfer, or otherwise restricting its use, the owner is as much deprived of his property without due process of law as if the contract were impounded, or the value it represents were in terms wholly or partially confiscated.

" In the case at bar the contract with the Central Pacific is, as I have said, changed in essential particulars. The company is compelled to accept it in its changed form, and by legislative decree, without the intervention of the courts, that is, without due process of law, to pay out of its earnings each year to its contractors, the United States, or deposit with them, a sum that may amount to twelve hundred thousand dollars, and this, twenty years before the debt to which it is to be applied becomes due and payable by the company. If this taking of the earnings of the company and keeping them from its use during these twenty years to come is not depriving the company of its property, it would be difficult to give any meaning to the provision of the Constitution. It will only be necessary hereafter to give to the seizure of another's property or earnings a new name—to call it the creation of a sinking fund, or the providing against the possible wastefulness or improvidence of the owner—to get rid of the constitutional restraint. To my mind the evasion of that clause, the frittering away of all sense and meaning to it, are insuperable objections to the legislation of Congress. Where contracts are impaired, or when operating against the government are sought to be evaded and avoided by legislation, a blow is given to the security of all property. If the government will not keep its faith, little better can be expected from the citizen. If contracts are not observed, no property will in the end be respected; and all history shows that rights of person are unsafe where property is insecure. Protection to one goes with protection to the other; and there can be neither prosperity nor progress where this foundation of all just government is unsettled. ' The moment,' said the elderAdams, ' the idea is admitted into society that property is not as sacred as the laws of God, and that there is not a force of law and public justice to protect it, anarchy and tyranny commence.'

" I am aware of the opinion which prevails generally that the Pacific railroad corporations have, by their accumulation wealth, and the numbers in their employ, become so powerful as to be disturbing and dangerous influences in the legislation of the country ; and that they should, therefore, be brought by stringent measures into subjection to the State. This may be true; I do not say that it is not; but if it is, it furnishes no justification for the repudiation or evasion of the contracts made with them by the government. The law that protects the wealth of the most powerful, protects also the earnings of the most humble ; and the law which would confiscate the property of the one would in the end take the earnings of the other.

" There are many other objections to the act of Congress besides those I have mentioned—each to my mind convincing—but why add to what has already been said. If the reasons given will not convince, neither would any others which could be presented. I will, therefore, refer only to the interference of the law with the rights of the State of California.

" The Central Pacific being a State corporation, the law creating it is, by the constitution of California, subject to alteration, amendment, and repeal by its legislature at any time—a power which the legislature can neither abdicate nor transfer. In its assent given to the company to extend its road into the territory of the United States—the general government having authorized the extension—the legislature reserved the same control which it possesses over other railroad and telegraph companies created by it. That control under the new constitution, goes, as is claimed, to the extent of regulating the fares and freights of the company, thus limiting its income or earnings; and of supervising all its business, even to the keeping of its accounts, making disobedience of its directors to the regulations established for its management punishable by fine and imprisonment; and the legislature may impose the additional penalty of a forfeiture of the franchises and privileges of the company. The law in existence when the corporation was created, and still in force, requires the creation of a sinking fund by the company to meet its bonds, and under it large sums have been accumulated for that purpose, and still further sums must be raised. In a word, the law of the State undertakes to control and manage the corporation, in all particulars required for the service, convenience, and protection of the public; and can there be a doubt in the mind of any one that over its own creations the State has, within its own territory, as against the United States, the superior authority? Yet the power asserted by the general government in the passage of the act of 1878 would justify legislation affecting all the affairs of the company, both in the State and in the Territories of the United States. It could treble the amount of the sum to be annually deposited in the sinking fund; it could command the immediate deposit of the entire amount of the ultimate indebtedness; it could change the order of the liens held by the government and the first mortgage bondholders; it could extend the lien of the government beyond the property to the entire income of the company, and, in fact, does so by the act in question (sec. 9); it could require the transportation for the government to be made without compensation, and it could subject the company to burdens which, if anticipated at the time, would have prevented the construction of the road. A power thus vast, once admitted to exist, might be exerted to control the entire affairs of the company, in direct conflict with the legislation of the State; its exercise would be a mere matter of legislative discretion in Congress. Yet it is clear that both governments cannot control and manage the company in the same territory, subjecting its directors to fine and imprisonment for disobeying their regulations. Under the Constitution the management of local affairs is left chiefly to the States, and it never entered into the conception of its framers that under it the creations of the States could be taken from their control. Certain it is that over no subject is it more important for their interests that they should retain the management and direction than over corporations brought into existence by them. The decision of the majority goes a great way—further, it appears to me, than any heretofore made by the court—to weaken the authority of the States, in this respect, as against the will of Congress. According to my understanding of its scope and reach, the United States have only to make a contract with a State corporation, and a loan to it, to oust the jurisdiction of the State, and place the corporation under their direction. It would seem plain that if legislation, taking institutions of the State from its control, can be sustained by this court, the government will drift from the limited and well-guarded system established by our fathers into a centralized and consolidated government."

A leading journal of California thus speaks of the invasion made by the decision of the court upon the rights of the State of California, to which the dissenting opinion refers :

"The position taken by him [Judge Field] upon the question of congressional invasion of State sovereignty is one which would beyond doubt have ranged the framers of the United States Constitution upon his side, and it includes a revelation of dangers and perplexities which sober men will do well to heed, and which it behooves every earnest politician to study seriously, because of the certainty of the approaching importance of this and similar questions, in both State and national affairs. The argument of Judge Field in regard to the peculiar relations existing between the Central Pacific, the State, and Congress, ought indeed to be mastered thoroughly by all who desire to keep themselves informed concerning the nature of the movements by which the original character of the union between the States is being changed, and a centralized government is being gradually erected upon the wrecks of State sovereignty, already little more than an empty name.

"In the first place, Judge Field points out that the Central Pacific was a creature of the State, and not of the United States. It draws its powers and its life from California, not from Congress. 'There was no grant by the United States to the Central Pacific Company of corporate rights, privileges, and immunities. No attribute of sovereignty was exercised by them in its creation. It took its life and all its attributes and capacities from the State. Whatever power, rights, and privileges it acquired from the United States it took under its contract with them, and not otherwise.' This is the key to the argument. Here is a distinct exercise of State sovereignty, not lapsed, or dormant, or inchoate, but in active, present operation. At every step this State sovereignty is affirmed and acted upon. It is made the basis of legislation. It is made the basis for radical changes in the organic law. The right of the State to deal with the corporations it has created, and whose charters it can 'alter, amend, or repeal' at will, does not seem a question concerning which there can be two opinions. And yet this very question has been raised in the decision of the Supreme Court on the Thurman act, and not only raised, but settled adversely to the right of the State to control its own creatures. As the State has nevertheless undertaken to exercise such control very vigorously, and as during the coming session of the legislature that right must be still further exerted, it is evident that the importance of this whole question is very considerable. And now let us hear Judge Field upon this topic somewhat further: ' The Central Pacific being a State corporation, the law creating it is, by the constitution of California, subject to alteration, amendment, and repeal by its legislature at any time—a power which the legislature can neither abdicate nor transfer. In its assent given to the company to extend its road into the territory of the United States—the general government authorizing the extension—the legislature reserved the same control which it possesses over other railroad and telegraph companies created by it. That control, under the new Constitution, goes, as is claimed, to the extent of regulating the fares and freights of the company, thus limiting its incomes or earnings ; and of supervising all its business, even to the keeping of its accounts, making disobedience of its directors to the regulations established for its management punishable by fine and imprisonment ; and the legislature may impose the additional penalty of a forfeiture of the franchises and privileges of the company.' ———

" Here are two distinct and necessarily antagonistic authorities set up, both claiming control of the same corporation. And it is perfectly evident that the assumption by Congress of the right to interfere with a creation of the State involves the assumption of a right to carry the same interference to such lengths as may destroy the last pretence of State sovereignty. In this case Congress interferes to compel the payment of a debt before it is due, in open violation of a solemn contract. Having undertaken to perpetrate an act of such marked injustice toward the corporation, it is at least possible that so reckless and irresponsible a body may err as widely on the other side at some future time. For if Congress can supersede the rights of the State, it certainly can ignore the interests of the State ; and the disposition to do the first implies no serious disinclination to proceed to the second. Congress in short can, under the ruling of the court, so alter the conditions of the Central Pacific Company by imposts and burdens, that it shall be disabled either from meeting its obligations or operating its roads ; and it will be in vain for the State to protest against this legislation. Indeed, it becomes a highly important question whether, under this decision, the ensuing legislature can venture to handle the railroad question at all, for Congress has in practice formally assumed control of the subject. As Judge Field says : ' Under the Constitution the management of local affairs is left chiefly to the States, and it never entered into the conception of its framers that under it the creations of the States could be taken from under their control. Certain it is that over no subject is it more important for their interests that they should retain the management and direction than over corporations brought into existence by them. The decision of the majority goes a great way— further, it appears to me, than any heretofore made by the court—to weaken the authority of the States, in this respect, as against the will of Congress. According to my understanding of its scope and reach, the United States has only to make a contract with a State corporation and a loan to it, to oust the jurisdiction of the State and place the corporation under their their direction.' It is scarcely possible to escape from this conclusion, or to perceive where the right of congressional interference can be checked, after going so far. Nor is this the only serious view of the matter imposed on the State. For what Congress has done is practically to undertake the management of the railroads of California, and the conflict of authority here decided in favor of Congress has implications which will not improbably cause great embarrassment in the near future. The Supreme Court says that Congress has the right to alter, amend, or repeal State charters. It does not make this claim in terms, but this is the actual outcome of its definition of State authority. The State, therefore, is thrust aside, and can no longer control the corporations it has endowed with life and functions. It cannot hope to exercise sovereignty over agencies which are already claimed by a higher jurisdiction. It is clearly impossible that the corporations concerned can pay allegiance equally to the State and to Congress. The mere suggestion of such a divided or duplicated sovereignty must be fatal to the financial standing of the enterprise so fixed between the upper and the nether millstone. Since either power may ruin the corporation, and since both powers claim the right to confiscate its property for disobedience of orders, the situation is sufficiently difficult. —— The powers of the State are certainly circumscribed and diminished very seriously by this decision, and, in the words of Judge Field, ' It would seem plain that if legislation, taking institutions of the State from its control, can be sustained by this court, the government will drift from the limited and well-guarded system established by our fathers, into a centralized and consolidated government.' If this is States rights doctrine, it is a kind of States rights doctrine which the best friends of republican government ought to subscribe to, for it is founded upon principles the neglect or abandonment of which must destroy the firmest supports of popular liberty, and prepare the way for the advent of a centralized despotism."

The Thurman act, besides being open to the objections thus stated, operates with special hardship upon the people of the Pacific Coast, as the increased charges for transportation which the Central Pacific will be required to make to meet the annual payment into the treasury of the United States of the sum of $1,200,000 many years before it is due, will fall principally upon them. This is a circumstance which seems to have escaped the attention of the advocates of the measure.

OTHER CASES.

The opinions from which the quotations above are made have attracted more general attention than any others written by Judge Field, yet they constitute a very small portion of his labors in the Supreme Court. His career on the bench covers many years, and in a large number of cases, of great importance, he has been called upon either to speak for the court or to express his dissent from its views. The questions involved in these cases have been of infinite variety, as one may suppose from the multitude of subjects upon which litigation can arise in the federal courts. It would occupy many pages to give an intelligent statement of them. They relate to many matters of a public character, as well as those of mere private concern; to treaties and international disputes; to foreign commerce and commerce between the States; to the power of taxation of the States and of the general government, and the limits upon both, as affected by contract and residence; to the public lands of the United States and the cessions made by Congress to the different States, and to public institutions; to the law governing the right to the use of water by miners and settlers on the public lands; to the jurisdiction of the admiralty; to the debts of cities, counties, and States; to corporations of every kind, but especially to railroad corporations and grants to them; to subjects of prize and of revenue; to acts of the military and naval forces; and to a great number of other matters arising in a highly civilized community having commercial and diplomatic relations with the rest of the world.

The following are some of the cases :

The Moses Taylor, 4 Wallace, 411.
The Siren, 7 Wallace, 152.
The Iron-clad Atlanta, 3 Wallace, 425.
The Daniel Ball, 10 Wallace, 557.
Welton vs. State of Missouri, 1 Otto, 275.
Sherlock vs. Alling, 3 Otto, 99.

State Tax on Foreign-held Bonds, 15 Wallace, 300.

Low vs. Austin, 13 Wallace, 29.

Tarble's Case, 13 Wallace, 397.

Trebilcock vs. Wilson, 12 Wallace, 687.

Carlisle vs. United States, 16 Wallace, 147.

Horn vs. Lockhart, 17 Wallace, 570.

Boyd vs. Alabama, 4 Otto, 645.

New Orleans vs. Clark, 5 Otto, 644.

United States vs. Fox, 5 Otto, 670.

Railroad Co. vs. Whitton, 13 Wallace, 270.

Morgan vs. Louisiana, 3 Otto, 217.

Chamberlain vs. St. Paul & Sioux City R. R. Co., 2 Otto, 299.

Farnsworth vs. Minnesota & Pacific R. R. Co., 2 Otto, 49.

Clark vs. Iowa City, 20 Wallace, 583.

Weber vs. The board of Harbor Commissioners, 18 Wallace, 57.

Telegraph Co. vs. Davenport, 7 Otto, 369.

The Nitro-Glycerine Case, 15 Wallace, 524.

The Confederate Note Case, 19 Wallace, 548.

Boom vs. Patterson, 8 Otto, 403.

Cromwell vs. County of Sac, 4 Otto, 351.

Cromwell vs. County of Sac, 6 Otto, 51.

Russell vs. Place, 4 Otto, 606.

Bradley vs. Fisher, 13 Wallace, 335.

Ex-parte Robinson, 19 Wallace, 505.

Atchison vs. Peterson, 20 Wallace, 507.

Basey vs. Gallagher, Ib., 670.

Jennison vs. Kirk, 8 Otto, 453.

Beard vs. Federy, 3 Wallace, 478.

Hornsby vs. United States, 10 Wallace, 224.

Gibson vs. Chouteau, 13 Wallace, 92.

Henshaw vs. Bissell, 18 Wallace, 255.

Shulenberg vs. Harriman, 21 Wallace, 44.

Langdeau vs. Hanes, 21 Wallace, 521.

The Yosemite Valley Case, 15 Wallace, 77.

Shepley vs. Cowan, 1 Otto, 330.

17

Beecher vs. Wetherby, 5 Otto, 517.
Grisar vs. McDowell, 6 Wallace, 363.
Stark vs. Starrs, 6 Wallace, 402.
Galpin vs. Page, 18 Wallace, 350.
Pennoyer vs. Neff, 5 Otto, 714.
Windsor vs. McVeigh, 3 Otto, 274.

The writing of opinions is but a small part of the labors of a judge of the Supreme Court. He is obliged to study and master every case which comes before the court and give his judgment upon it. About three hundred cases are thus considered by him every session, which usually lasts seven months. Some of the cases are decided without written opinions being given, some by a divided court, and those in which opinions are written are distributed among nine judges. The great labor of each judge consists in mastering the cases before the court so as to be able to give an intelligent judgment.

Note.

The preceding pages were printed a year ago, but their publication was afterwards abandoned. Since then many friends of Judge Field in California have expressed a desire that some account of other decisions of his should be added, and the whole published in a pamphlet form. The other decisions particularly mentioned are those relating to inter-state commerce, taxation by the general and State governments, the trust character of directors of corporations, the use of running waters on the public lands, and various subjects of interest arising in the Circuit Court of the United States for California, such as the Pueblo of San Francisco and legislation of the State against the Chinese. In compliance with this desire the following pages have been prepared. To them is added a notice of his action in the Electoral Commission of 1876, of which he was a member.

June, 1881.

Inter-State Commerce. — Cases relating to this subject.

The Constitution of the United States vests in Congress the power " to regulate commerce with foreign nations and among the several States, and with the Indian tribes ;" and no provision of that instrument is of more importance, or has been the subject of greater discussion. The meaning of the term commerce, and how far the grant of power to regulate it is exclusive of State interference, how far, if at all, it is concurrent with the authority of the State, and what is the effect of non-action by the general government with respect to any particular subject of commerce, have all been the occasion of earnest discussion and of wide

18

differences of opinion. The earlier judges of the Supreme Court disagreed in their views. It is only of late years that there has been any concurrence on the subject among the members of that Court. Important opinions leading to this uniformity have been rendered by nearly all of the judges. It is the object of this compilation to refer only to those delivered by Judge Field.

In Welton vs. The State of Missouri, (1 Otto, 275,) the Court, at its October term of 1875, was called upon to consider the validity of a statute of Missouri discriminating in favor of goods, wares, and merchandise which were the growth, product, or manufacture of the State, and against those which were the growth, product, or manufacture of other States or countries, in the conditions upon which their sale could be made by traveling dealers. One Welton was a dealer in sewing machines which were manufactured without the State of Missouri, and went from place to place in the State selling them without a license for that purpose. For this offence he was indicted and convicted in one of the Circuit Courts of the State, and was sentenced to pay a fine of fifty dollars, and to be committed until the same was paid. On appeal to the Supreme Court of the State the judgment was affirmed.

The statute under which the conviction was had declared that whoever dealt in the sale of goods, wares, or merchandise, except books, charts, maps, and stationery, which were not the growth, produce, or manufacture of the State, by going from place to place to sell the same, should be deemed a pedlar; and then enacted that no person should deal as a pedlar without a license, and prescribed the rates of charge for the licenses, these varying according to the manner in which the business was conducted, whether by the party carrying the goods himself on foot, or by the use of beasts of burden, or by carts or other land carriage, or by boats or other river vessels. Penalties were imposed for dealing without the license prescribed. No license was required for selling in a similar way—by going from place to place in the State—goods which were the growth, product, or manufacture of the State.

The license charge exacted was sought to be maintained as a tax upon a calling. It was held to be such a tax by the Supreme Court of the State; a calling, said the Court, which was limited to the sale of merchandise not the growth or product of the State. To this view the Supreme Court of the United States, speaking through Judge Field, said :

"The general power of the State to impose taxes in the way of licenses upon all pursuits and occupations within its limits is admitted, but like all other powers must be exercised in subordination to the requirements of the federal Constitution. Where the business or occupation consists in the sale of goods, the license tax required for its pursuit is in effect a tax upon the goods themselves. If such a tax be within the power of the State to levy, it matters not whether it be raised directly from the goods, or indirectly from them through the license to the dealer. But if such tax conflict with any power vested in Congress by the Constitution of the United States, it will not be any the less invalid because enforced through the form of a personal license.

"In the case of Brown vs. Maryland * the question arose whether an act of the Legislature of Maryland requiring importers of foreign goods to pay the State a license tax before selling them in the form and condition in which they were imported, was valid and constitutional. It was contended that the tax was not imposed on the importation of foreign goods, but upon the trade and occupation of selling such goods by whole-sale after they were imported. It was a tax. said the counsel, upon the profession or trade of the party when that trade was carried on within the State, and was laid upon the same principle as the usual taxes upon retailers, or inn-keepers. or hawkers and pedlars, or upon any other trade exercised within the State. But the Court in its decision replied that it was impossible to conceal the fact that this mode of taxation was only varying the form without varying the substance, that a tax on the occupation of an importer was a tax on importation, and must add to the price of the article and be paid by the consumer or by the importer himself in like manner as a direct duty on the article itself. Treating the exaction of the license tax from the importer as a tax on the goods imported, the Court held that the act of Maryland was in conflict with the Constitution ; with the clause prohibiting a State, without the consent of Congress, from laying any impost or duty on imports or exports, and with the clause investing Congress with the power to regulate commerce with foreign nations.

* 12 Wheaton, 425, 444.

" So, in like manner, the license tax exacted by the State of Missouri from dealers in goods which are not the product or manufacture of the State, before they can be sold from place to place within the State, must be regarded as a tax upon such goods themselves. And the question presented is, whether legislation thus discriminating against the products of other States in the conditions of their sale by a certain class of dealers is valid under the Constitution of the United States. It was contended in the State Courts, and it is urged here, that this legislation violates that clause of the Constitution which declares that Congress shall have the power to regulate commerce with foreign nations and among the several States. The power to regulate conferred by that clause upon Congress, is one without limitation; and to regulate commerce is to prescribe rules by which it shall be governed, that is, the conditions upon which it shall be conducted; to determine how far it shall be free and untrammeled; how far it shall be burdened by duties and imposts, and how far it shall be prohibited.

" Commerce is a term of the largest import; it comprehends intercourse for the purposes of trade in any and all its forms, including the transportation, purchase, sale, and exchange of commodities between the citizens of our country and the citizens or subjects of other countries, and between the citizens of different States. The power to regulate it embraces all the instruments by which such commerce may be conducted. So far as some of these instruments are concerned, and some subjects which are local in their operation, it has been held that the States may provide regulations until Congress acts with reference to them. But where the subject to which the power applies is national in its character, or of such a nature as to admit of uniformity of regulation, the power is exclusive of all State authority.

" It will not be denied that that portion of commerce with foreign countries and between the States, which consists in the transportation and exchange of commodities, is of national importance, and admits and requires uniformity of regulation. The very object of investing this power in the general government was to insure this uniformity against discriminating State legislation. The depressed condition of commerce and the obstacles to its growth previous to the adoption of the Constitution, from the want of some single controlling authority, has been frequently referred to by this Court in commenting upon the power in question. 'It was regulated,' says Chief Justice Marshall, in delivering the opinion in Brown vs. Maryland, 'by foreign nations with a single view to their own interests, and our disunited efforts to counteract their restrictions were rendered impotent by want of combination. Congress, indeed, possessed the power of making treaties, but the inability of the Federal Government to enforce them became so apparent as to render that power in a great degree useless. Those who felt the injury arising from this state of things, and those who were capable of estimating the influence of commerce on the prosperity of nations, perceived the necessity of giving the control over this important subject to a single government. It may be doubtful whether any of the evils proceeding from the feebleness of the Federal Government contributed more to that great revolution which introduced the present system, than the deep and general conviction that commerce ought to be regulated by Congress.'

" The power which insures uniformity of commercial regulation must cover the property which is transported as an article of commerce from hostile or interfering legislation until it has mingled with and become a part of the general property of the country and subjected like it to similar protection, and to no greater burdens. If at any time before it has thus become incorporated into the mass of property of the State or nation, it can be subjected to any restrictions by State legislation, the object of investing the control in Congress may be entirely defeated. If Missouri can require a license tax for the sale by traveling dealers of goods which are the growth, product, or manufacture of other States or countries, it may require such license tax as a condition of their sale from ordinary merchants, and the amount of the tax will be a matter resting exclusively in its discretion.

" The power of the State to exact a license tax of any amount being admitted, no authority would remain in the United States or in this Court to control its action, however unreasonable or oppressive. Imposts operating as an absolute exclusion of the goods would be possible, and all the evils of discriminating State legislation, favorable to the interests of one State and injurious to the interests of other States and countries, which existed previous to the adoption of the Constitution, might follow, and the experience of the last fifteen years shows would follow from the action of some of the States.

" There is a difficulty, it is true, in all cases of this character, in drawing the line precisely where the commercial power of Congress ends and the power of the State begins. A similar difficulty was felt by this Court in Brown vs. Maryland, in drawing the line of distinction between the restriction upon the power of the States to lay a duty on imports, and their acknowledged power to tax persons and property, but the Court observed that the two, though quite distinguishable when they do not approach each other, may yet, like the intervening colors between white and black, approach so nearly as to perplex the understanding, as colors perplex the vision in marking the distinction between them, but that, as the distinction exists, it must be marked as the cases arise. And the Court, after observing that it might be premature to state any rule as being universal in its application, held that when the importer had so acted upon the thing imported that it had become incorporated and mixed up with the mass of property in the country, it had lost its distinctive character as an import, and become subject to the taxing power of the State, but that while remaining the property of the importer, in his warehouse in the original form and' package in which it was imported, the tax upon it was plainly a duty on imports, prohibited by the Constitution.

" Following the guarded language of the Court in that case we observe here, as was observed there, that it would be premature to state any rule which would be universal in its application to determine when the commercial power of the Federal Government over a commodity has ceased and the power of the State has commenced. It is sufficient to hold now that the commercial power continues until the commodity has ceased to be the subject of discriminating legislation by reason of its foreign character. That power protects it, even after it has entered the State, from any burden imposed by reason of its foreign origin. The act of Missouri encroaches upon this power in this respect, and is, therefore, in our judgment, unconstitutional and void.

" The fact that Congress has not seen fit to prescribe any specific rules to govern inter-state commerce does not affect the question. Its inaction on this subject, when considered with reference to its legislation with respect to foreign commerce, is equivalent to a declaration that inter-state commerce shall be free and untrammeled. As the main object of that commerce is the sale and exchange of commodities, the policy thus established would be defeated by discriminating legislation like that of Missouri."

The doctrine of this case has been approved in Tiernan vs. Rinker (12 Otto, 123); and in Webber vs. State of Virginia (13 Id.), in both of which cases Judge Field delivered -the opinion of the Court. In the first of these the Court said, that the doctrine had never been questioned but had been uniformly recognized and followed, and expresses now its " settled judgment." In the second one, which involved the consideration of the validity of a license tax imposed under a statute of Virginia, discriminating in favor of resident manufacturers and against manufacturers of other States, the Court, in holding the law invalid said, that " commerce among the States in any commodity can only be free when the commodity is exempted from all discriminating regulations and burdens imposed by local atuhority by reason of its foreign growth or manufacture."

In the subsequent case of Sherlock vs. Alling, (3 Otto, 99,) the Court was called upon to consider the validity of State legislation not directed against foreign or inter-state commerce or any of its regulations, but indirectly and remotely affecting persons engaged in it. In December, 1858, two steamboats collided on the Ohio River at a point opposite the main land of the State of Indiana. By the collision the hull of one of them was broken in, and a fire started, which burned the boat to the water's edge, destroying it and causing the death of one of its passengers, a citizen of Indiana. The administrator of the deceased brought an action for his death in one of the Courts of Common Pleas of Indiana, under a statute of that State, which provides " that when the death of one is caused by the wrongful act or omission of another, the personal representatives of the former may maintain an action therefor against the latter, if the former might have maintained an action, had he lived, against the latter for an injury for the same act or omission."

· The complaint in the action alleged that the collision occurred within the territorial jurisdiction of Indiana, above the line of low-water mark of the river, and charged it generally to the careless and negligent navigation of the steamboat of the defendants by their servants and officers of the vessel. To defeat this action the defendants relied upon substantially the following grounds of defence: 1st, that the injuries complained of occurred on the river Ohio beyond low-water mark on the Indiana side, and within the limits of the State of Kentucky; and that by a law of that State an action for the death of a party from the carelessness of another could only be brought within one year from such death, which period had elapsed when the present action was brought; and, 2d, that at the time of the alleged injuries the colliding boats were engaged in carrying on inter-state commerce under the laws of the United States, and the defendants as their owners were not liable for injuries occurring in their navigation through the carelessness of their officers, except as prescribed by those laws; and that these did not cover the liability asserted by the plaintiff under the statute of Indiana.

The plaintiff recovered judgment in the Court of Common Pleas, which the Supreme Court of the State affirmed, and the case was taken to the Supreme Court of the United States. There the first ground of defence was not considered as open to consideration under the admission of the parties, but upon the second ground, the Court, speaking through Judge Field, said as follows:

" Under this head it is contended that the statute of Indiana creates a new liability, and could not, therefore, be applied to cases where the injuries complained of were caused by marine torts, without interfering with the exclusive regulation of commerce vested in Congress. The position of the defendants, as we understand it, is that as by both the common and maritime law the right of action for personal torts dies with the person injured, the statute which allows actions for such torts, when resulting in the death of the person injured, to be brought by the personal representatives of the deceased, enlarges the liability of parties for such torts, and that such enlarged liability, if applied to cases of marine torts, would constitute a new burden upon commerce.

" In supposed support of this position numerous decisions of this Court are cited by counsel, to the effect that the States cannot by legislation place burdens upon commerce with foreign nations or among the several States. The decisions go to that extent, and their soundness is not questioned. But upon an examination of the cases in which they were rendered it will be found that the legislation adjudged invalid imposed a tax upon some instrument or subject of commerce, or exacted a license fee from parties engaged in commercial pursuits, or created an impediment to the free navigation of some public waters, or prescribed conditions in accordance with which commerce in particular articles or between particular places was required to be conducted. In all the cases the legislation condemned operated directly upon commerce, either by way of tax upon its business, license upon its pursuit in particular channels, or conditions for carrying it on. Thus, in the Passenger Cases,* the laws of New York and Massachusetts exacted a tax from the captains of vessels bringing passengers from foreign ports for every passenger landed. In the Wheeling-Bridge Case † the statute of Virginia authorized the erection of a bridge, which was held to obstruct the free navigation of the river Ohio. In the case of Sinnot vs. Davenport‡ the statute of Alabama required the owner of a steamer navigating the waters of the State to file, before the boat left the port of Mobile, in the office of the probate judge of Mobile County, a statement in writing, setting forth the name of the vessel and of the owner or owners, and his or their place of residence and interest in the vessel, and prescribed penalties for neglecting the requirement. It thus imposed conditions for carrying on the coasting trade in the waters of the State in addition to those prescribed by Congress. And in all the other cases where legislation of a State

---

* 7 How., 445.   † 13 Id., 518.   ‡ 22 Id., 227.

has been held to be null for interfering with the commercial power of Congress, as in Brown vs. Maryland,* the Tonnage Tax Cases,† and Welton vs. Missouri,‡ the legislation created, in the way of tax, license, or condition, a direct burden upon commerce, or in some way directly interfered with its freedom. In the present case no such operation can be ascribed to the statute of Indiana. That statute imposes no tax, prescribes no duty, and in no respect interferes with any regulations for the navigation and use of vessels. It only declares a general principle respecting the liability of all persons within the jurisdiction of the State for torts resulting in the death of parties injured. And in the application of the principle it makes no difference where the injury complained of occurred in the State, whether on land or on water. General legislation of this kind prescribing the liabilities or duties of citizens of a State, without distinction as to pursuit or calling, is not open to any valid objection because it may affect persons engaged in foreign or inter-state commerce. Objection might with equal propriety be urged against legislation prescribing the form in which contracts shall be authenticated, or property descend or be distributed on the death of its owner, because applicable to the contracts or estates of persons engaged in such commerce. In conferring upon Congress the regulation of commerce, it was never intended to cut the States off from legislating on all subjects relating to the health, life, and safety of their citizens, though the legislation might indirectly affect the commerce of the country. Legislation in a great variety of ways may affect commerce and persons engaged in it without constituting a regulation of it, within the meaning of the Constitution.

" It is true that the commercial power conferred by the Constitution is one without limitation. It authorizes legislation with respect to all the subjects of foreign and inter-state commerce, the persons engaged in it, and the instruments by which it is carried on. And legislation has largely dealt, so far as commerce by water is concerned, with the instruments of that commerce. It has embraced the whole subject of navigation, prescribed what shall constitute American vessels, and by whom they shall be navigated ; how they shall be registered or enrolled and licensed ; to what tonnage, hospital, and other dues they shall be subjected ; what rules they shall obey in passing each other ; and what provision their owners shall make for the health, safety, and comfort of their crews. Since steam has been applied to the propulsion of vessels, legislation has embraced an infinite variety of further details to guard against accident and consequent loss of life.

" The power to prescribe these and similar regulations necessarily involves the right to declare the liability which shall follow their infraction. Whatever, therefore, Congress determines, either as to a regulation or the liability for its infringement, is exclusive of State authority. But with reference to a great variety of matters touching the rights and lia-

---

* 12 Wheat., 425.   † 12 Wallace, 204.   ‡ 1st Otto, 275.

bilities of persons engaged in commerce, either as owners or navigators of vessels, the laws of Congress are silent, and the laws of the State govern. The rules for the acquisition of property by persons engaged in navigation, and for its transfer and descent, are, with some exceptions, those prescribed by the State to which the vessels belong. And it may be said generally that the legislation of a State, not directed against commerce or any of its regulations, but relating to the rights, duties, and liabilities of citizens, and only indirectly and remotely affecting the operations of commerce, is of obligatory force upon citizens within its territorial jurisdiction, whether on land or water, or engaged in commerce, foreign or inter-state, or in any other pursuit. In our judgment the statute of Indiana falls under this class. Until Congress, therefore, makes some regulation touching the liability of parties for marine torts resulting in the death of the persons injured, we are of opinion that the statute of Indiana applies, giving a right of action in such cases to the personal representatives of the deceased, and that, as thus applied, it constitutes no encroachment upon the commercial power of Congress."*

But the most elaborate consideration of the commercial clause of the Constitution, and the extent to which the power of Congress is exclusive of State authority, found among the recent decisions of the Court, is contained in an opinion rendered at the last term, in the case of County of Mobile vs. Kimball.—(12 Otto., 691.) In February, 1867, the Legislature of Alabama passed an act to "provide for the improvement of the river, bay, and harbor of Mobile." It created a board of commissioners for the improvement of the river, harbor, and bay of Mobile, and required the president of the Commissioners of Revenue of Mobile County to issue bonds to the amount of one million dollars, and deliver them, when called for, to the board, to meet the expenses of the work directed. The board was authorized to apply the bonds or their proceeds to the cleaning out, deepening, and widening of the river, harbor, and bay, or any part thereof, or to the construction of an artificial harbor in addition to such improvements.

In June, 1872, the board of commissioners entered into a contract with Messrs. Kimball & Slaughter to dredge

---

* United States vs. Bevans, 3 Wheat., 337.

and cut a channel through a designated bar in the bay, of a specified width, depth, and distance, at a named price per cubic yard of material excavated and removed, and to receive in payment the bonds of the county issued under the act mentioned. In pursuance of this contract, the work agreed upon was at once undertaken by Kimball & Slaughter, and was completed in March, 1873, and accepted by the board through its authorized engineer. The amount due to them was paid, with the exception of six bonds, and to obtain the delivery of those six, or payment of their value, suit was brought against the county. Among other defences to the suit, it was contended that the act of the State, under which the work was done, conflicted with the commercial power vested in Congress, and was, therefore, void. To this objection the Court, speaking through Judge Field, said as follows:

"The objection that the law of the State, in authorizing the improvement of the harbor of Mobile, trenches upon the commercial power of Congress, assumes an exclusion of State authority from all subjects in relation to which that power may be exercised not warranted by the adjudications of this Court, notwithstanding the strong expressions used by some of its judges. That power is indeed without limitation. It authorizes Congress to prescribe the conditions upon which commerce in all its forms shall be conducted between our citizens and the citizens or subjects of other countries, and between the citizens of the several States, and to adopt measures to promote its growth and insure its safety. And as commerce embraces navigation, the improvement of harbors and bays along our coast, and of navigable rivers within the States connecting with them, falls within the power. The subjects, indeed, upon which Congress can act under this power are of infinite variety, requiring for their successful management different plans or modes of treatment. Some of them are national in their character, and admit and require uniformity of regulation, affecting alike all the States; others are local, or are mere aids to commerce, and can only be properly regulated by provisions adapted to their special circumstances and localities. Of the former class may be mentioned all that portion of commerce with foreign countries or between the States which consists in the transportation, purchase, sale, and exchange of commodities. Here there can, of necessity, be only one system or plan of regulations, and that Congress alone can prescribe. Its non-action in such cases, with respect to any particular commodity or mode of transportation, is a declaration of its purpose that the commerce in that commodity or by that means of transportation shall be free. There would otherwise be no security against conflicting regulations of different States, each discriminating in favor of its own products and citizens and against the products and citizens of other States. And it is a matter of public history that the object of vesting in Congress the power to regulate commerce with foreign nations and among the States was to insure uniformity of regulation against conflicting and discriminating State legislation.

" Of the class of subjects local in their nature, or intended as mere aids to commerce, which are best provided for by special regulations, may be mentioned harbor pilotage, buoys, and beacons to guide mariners to the proper channel in which to direct their vessels.

" The rules to govern harbor pilotage must depend in a great degree upon the peculiarities of the ports where they are to be enforced. It has been found by experience that skill and efficiency on the part of local pilots is best secured by leaving this subject principally to the control of the States. Their authority to act upon the matter and regulate the whole subject, in the absence of legislation by Congress, has been recognized by this Court in repeated instances. In Cooley vs. The Board of Wardens of the Port of Philadelphia, the Court refers to the act of Congress of 1789, declaring that pilots should continue to be regulated by such laws as the States might respectively thereafter enact for that purpose; and observes that 'it manifests the understanding of Congress, at the outset of the government, that the nature of this subject is not such as to require its exclusive legislation. The practice of the States and of the national government has been in conformity with this declaration, from the origin of the national government to this time ; and the nature of the subject, when examined, is such as to leave no doubt of the superior fitness and propriety, not to say the absolute necessity, of different systems of regulation, drawn from local knowledge and experience, and conformed to local wants.'—(12 How., p. 320.)

" Buoys and beacons are important aids, and sometimes are essential to the safe navigation of vessels, in indicating the channel to be followed at the entrance of harbors and in rivers; and their establishment by Congress is undoubtedly within its commercial power. But it would be extending that power, to the exclusion of State authority, to an unreasonable degree, to hold that, whilst it remained unexercised upon this subject, it would be unlawful for the State to provide the buoys and beacons required for the safe navigation of its harbors and rivers, and in case of their destruction, by storms or otherwise, it could not temporarily supply their places until Congress could act in the matter and provide for their re-establishment. That power which every State possesses, sometimes termed its police power, by which it legislates for the protection of the lives, health, and property of its people, would justify measures of this kind.

" The uniformity of commercial regulations, which the grant to Congress was designed to secure against conflicting State provisions, was necessarily intended only for cases where such uniformity is practicable. Where, from its nature or the sphere of its operation, the subject is local and limited, special regulations adapted to the immediate locality could only have been contemplated. State action upon such subjects can constitute no interference with the commercial power of Congress; for when that acts, the State authority is superseded. Inaction of Congress upon these subjects of a local nature or operation, unlike its inaction upon matters affecting all the States and requiring uniformity of regulation, is not to be taken as a declaration that nothing shall be done with respect to them, but is rather to be deemed a declaration that, for the time being, and until it sees fit to act, they may be regulated by State authority.

"The improvement of harbors, bays, and navigable rivers within the States falls within this last category of cases. The control of Congress over them is to insure freedom in their navigation, so far as that is essential to the exercise of its commercial power. Such freedom is not encroached upon by the removal of obstructions to their navigability, or by other legitimate improvement. The States have as full control over their purely internal commerce as Congress has over commerce among the several States and with foreign nations; and to promote the growth of that internal commerce and insure its safety, they have an undoubted right to remove obstructions from their harbors and rivers, deepen their channels, and improve them generally, if they do not impair their free navigation as permitted under the laws of the United States, or defeat any system for the improvement of their navigation provided by the general government. Legislation of the States for the purposes and within the limits mentioned do not infringe upon the commercial power of Congress; and so we hold that the act of the State of Alabama, of February 16, 1867, to provide for the 'improvement of the river, bay, and harbor of Mobile' is not invalid.

"There have been, it is true, expressions by individual judges of this Court going to the length that the mere grant of the commercial power, anterior to any action of Congress under it, is exclusive of all State authority; but there has been no adjudication of the Court to that effect. In the opinion of the Court in Gibbons vs. Ogden, the first and leading case upon the construction of the Constitution, and which opinion is recognized as one of the ablest of the great Chief Justice then presiding, there are several expressions which would indicate, and his general reasoning would tend to the same conclusion, that in his judgment the grant of the commercial power was of itself sufficient to exclude all action of the States; and it is upon them that the advocates of the exclusive theory chiefly rely; and yet he takes care to observe that the question was not involved in the decision required by that case. 'In discussing the question whether this power is still in the States,' he observes that 'in the case under consideration we may dismiss from it the inquiry, whether it is surrendered by the mere grant to Congress, or is retained until Congress shall exercise the power. We may dismiss that inquiry because, it has been exercised, and the regulations which Congress deemed it proper to make are now in full operation. The sole question is, can a State regulate commerce with foreign nations and among the several States while Congress is regulating it?' And the decision was necessarily restricted by the limitations of the question presented. It determined that the grant of power by the Constitution, accompanied by legislation under it, operated as an inhibition upon the States from interfering with the subject of that legislation. The acts of New York giving to Livingston and Fulton an exclusive right to navigate all the waters within its jurisdiction, with vessels propelled by steam, for a certain period, being in collision with the laws of Congress regulating the coasting trade, were, therefore, adjudged to be unconstitutional. This judgment was rendered in 1824.—(9 Wheat., 1.) Some years later (1829) the case of Wilson vs. Blackbird Creek Marsh Company came before the Court. There, a law of Delaware authorizing the construction of a bridge over one of its small navigable streams, which obstructed the navigation of the stream, was held to be repugnant to the commercial power of Congress. The Court, Chief Justice Marshall delivering its opinion, placed its decision entirely upon the absence of any congressional legislation on the subject. Its language was: ' If Congress had passed any act which bore upon the case —any act in execution of the power to regulate commerce, the object of which was to control State legislation over these small navigable creeks into which the tide flows, and which abound throughout the lower country of the Middle and Southern States, we should not feel much difficulty in saying that a State law coming in conflict with such act would be void. But Congress has passed no such act. The repugnancy of the law of Delaware to the Constitution is placed entirely on its repugnancy to the power to regulate commerce with foreign nations and among the several States—a power which has not been so exercised as to affect the question.'—(2 Peters, 282.)

" In the License Cases, which were before the Court in 1847, there was great diversity of views in the opinions of the different judges upon the operation of the grant of the commercial power of Congress in the absence of congressional legislation. Extreme doctrines upon both sides of the question were asserted by some of the judges, but the decision reached, so far as it can be viewed as determining any question of construction, was confirmatory of the doctrine that legislation of Congress is essential to prohibit the action of the States upon the subjects there considered.

" But in 1851, in the case of Cooley vs. The Wardens of the Port of Philadelphia, to which we have already referred, the attention of the Court appears to have been for the first time drawn to the varying and different regulations required by the different subjects upon which Congress may legislate under the commercial power; and from this consideration the conclusion was reached that, as some of these subjects are national in their nature, admitting of one uniform plan or system of regulation, whilst others, being local in their nature or operation, can be best regulated by the States, the exclusiveness of the power in any case is to be determined more by the nature of the subject upon which it is to operate than by the terms of the grant, which, though general, are not accompanied by any express prohibition to the exercise of the power by the States. The decision was confined to the validity of regulations by the States of harbor pilotage ; but the reasoning of the Court suggested as satisfactory a solution as perhaps could be obtained of the question which had so long divided the judges. The views expressed in the opinion delivered are followed in Gilman vs. Philadelphia (3 Wall.,727), and are mentioned with approval in Crandall vs. State of Nevada (6 Wall., 42). In the first of these cases the Court, after stating that some subjects of commerce call for uniform rules and national legislation, and that others can 'be best regulated by rules and provisions suggested by the varying circumstances of different localities, and limited in their operation to such localities respectively,' says, 'whether the power in any given case is vested exclusively in the general government, depends upon the nature of the subject regulated.' The doctrine was subsequently recognized in the case of Welton vs. Missouri (91 U. S., 282), in Henderson vs. Mayor of New York (95 U. S., 259), and in numerous other cases ; and it may be considered as expressing the final judgment of the Court.

Perhaps some of the divergence of views upon this question among former judges may have arisen from not always bearing in mind the distinction between commerce, as strictly defined, and its local aids or instruments or measures taken for its improvement. Commerce with foreign countries and among the States, strictly considered, consists in intercourse and traffic, including in these terms navigation and the transportation and transit of persons and property as well as the purchase, sale, and exchange of commodities. For the regulation of commerce as thus defined there can be only one system of rules applicable alike to the whole country ; and the authority which can act for the whole country can alone adopt such a system. Action upon it by separate States is not, therefore, permissible. Language affirming the exclusiveness of the grant of power over commerce as thus defined may not be inaccurate, when it would be so if applied to legislation upon subjects which are merely auxiliary to commerce."

THE POWER OF TAXATION BY THE GENERAL AND STATE GOVERNMENTS, AND SOME OF ITS LIMITATIONS.

It has been settled by numerous decisions of the Supreme Court of the United States that the obligations and instrumentalities of the general government, that is, the means by which its functions are executed, are not subject to taxation by the States.

In McCullough vs. Maryland, (4 Wheaton, 432,) decided in 1819,—which is the leading case on this subject,—a statute of Maryland imposing a tax upon a branch of the Bank of the United States established at Baltimore, in that State, was considered. The Court held that the bank, being one of the instrumentalities of the government in the execution of its powers, was not subject to taxation by the State; that the power to create the bank implied the power to preserve it, and that the right of the State to tax, if conceded, might be so exercised as to destroy the institution, and thus wholly defeat the operations of the Federal Government. " If the States," said Chief Justice Marshall, " may tax one instrument employed by the government in the execution of its powers, they may tax any and every other instrument. They may tax the mail; they may tax the mint; they may tax patent rights; they may tax the papers of the custom-house, they may tax judicial process; they may tax all the means employed by the government to an excess which would defeat all the ends of government. This was not intended by the American people. They did not design to make their government dependent on the States."

In Weston vs. Charleston, (2d Peters, 449,) decided in 1829, an ordinance of the city of Charleston imposing a tax upon all personal estate owned in the said city, including, among other things, six and seven per cent. stock of the United States, was considered. The Court held that the tax in question was a tax upon the contract subsisting between the government and individuals, and, therefore, operated directly upon the power to borrow money on the credit of the United States; that if the right to impose it existed with the States, it was a right which in its nature acknowledged no limits, and might be exercised to the serious embarrassment of the Federal Government; that such a right was, therefore, inconsistent with the supremacy of that government in the powers granted to it.

In Dobbins vs. The Commissioners of Erie County, (16 Peters, 435,) decided in 1842, a law of Pennsylvania, authorizing an assessment upon all " offices and positions of profit," was held invalid so far as it applied to offices of the United States, the Court re-affirming the doctrine that the States cannot impose a tax upon the means and instrumentalities of the general government in the execution of its powers. The compensation, said the Court, of an officer of the United States is fixed by a law of Congress passed in the exercise of its discretion; such law confers upon him the right to the compensation in its entireness, and any act of a State imposing a tax upon the office in diminishing its recompense conflicts with that law.

The principle involved in these decisions, that the means and instrumentalities by which the general government executes its powers cannot be embarrassed and burdened by the action of the States, is equally applicable to prevent the means and instrumentalities of the governments of the States, essential to the execution of their reserved powers, from being in like manner embarrassed and burdened by the general government, and was so applied in the case of Collector vs. Day.—(11 Wall., 113.) Under an act of Congress a tax had been levied upon the salary of a judge of probate in Massachusetts. The judge paid the tax under protest, and brought suit to recover it back. The Supreme Court held that it was not competent for Congress to impose a tax upon the salary of a judicial officer of a State. Referring to the case of Dobbins vs. The Commissioners of Erie County, the Court, speaking through Judge Nelson, said:

" If the means and instrumentalities employed by that government [the general government] to carry into operation the powers granted to it are, necessarily, and, for the sake of self-preservation, exempt from taxation by the States, why are not those of the States depending upon their reserved powers, for like reasons, equally exempt from federal taxation? Their unimpaired existence in the one case is as essential as in the other. It is admitted that there is no express provision in the Constitution that prohibits the general government from taxing the means and instrumentalities of the States, nor is there any prohibiting the States from taxing the means and instrumentalities of that government. In both cases the exemption rests upon necessary implication, and is upheld by the great law of self-preservation ; as any government, whose means employed in conducting its operations, if subject to the control of another and distinct government, can exist only at the mercy of that government."

In addition to this restriction upon both governments in the power of taxation,—that it cannot be exercised so as to impair the existence and efficiency of the other—there is a further restriction necessarily arising from the limits of their territorial jurisdiction. Neither can exercise the taxing power upon property or persons beyond that jurisdiction. The attempt to exercise it in that way would be regarded elsewhere as a mere abuse of authority. Says Chief Justice Marshall: " All subjects over which the sovereign power of a State extends are objects of taxation, but those over which it does not extend are upon the soundest principles exempt from taxation. This proposition may almost be pronounced self-evident."—(4 Wheaton, 429.)

This subject came before the Supreme Court for special consideration in the case of Railroad Company vs. Pennsylvania, which is reported under the title of State Tax on Foreign-Held Bonds.—(15 Wall., 300.) In May, 1868, the Legislature of that State passed an act requiring the president, treasurer, or cashier of every corporation, except savings banks created under its laws and doing business there, which paid interest to bondholders or other creditors, to retain from them before such payment a tax of five per cent. upon every dollar of interest, and to pay over the same semi-annually to the State treasurer for the use of the Commonwealth.

In 1848 the Legislature of Ohio incorporated the Cleveland, Painesville and Ashtabula Railroad Company, and authorized it to construct a railroad from the city of Cleveland, in that State, to the line of the State of Pennsylvania. Under this act and its supplement, passed in 1850, the road was constructed. In 1854 the Legislature of Pennsylvania authorized the company to construct a road from Erie, in that State, to the State line of Ohio, so as to connect with the road from Cleveland, and to purchase a road already constructed between those places. This road was constructed, or the one constructed was purchased, so that the two roads effected a continuous line between the cities of Cleveland and Erie—a distance of ninety-five and one-half miles, twenty-five of which were in Pennsylvania. The company, so far as it acted in Pennsylvania under the authority of an act of its Legislature, was held to be a corporation in that State and subject to its laws for the taxation of incorporated companies, though there was only one board of directors for both companies. In 1868 the funded debt of the company amounted to two and one-half millions of dollars, and was in bonds secured by three mortgages,—one for five hundred thousand dollars, made in 1854; one for a million of dollars, made in 1859, and one for a million dollars, made in 1867. Each of these was upon the entire road from Erie, in Pennsylvania, to Cleveland, in Ohio, including the right-of-way and all the buildings and other property of every kind connected with the road. The principal and interest of the bonds first issued were payable in Philadelphia. The principal and interest of the other bonds were payable in New York. All of them were executed and delivered in Cleveland, Ohio, and nearly all of them were issued, and were afterwards held by non-residents of Pennsylvania and citizens of other States. The officers of the State of Pennsylvania endeavored to enforce the tax imposed by the act of 1868 upon the interest on these bonds, having first apportioned it according to the length of the road, assigning to the part in the State of Pennsylvania an amount in proportion to the whole indebtedness which that part bore to the whole road. The validity of the tax, so far as it applied to the interest on the bonds made payable out of the State, issued to and held by non-residents of the State and citizens of other States, was contested in the courts of the State, first in the Common Pleas and then in the Supreme Court, and being by them sustained, was brought to the consideration of the Supreme Court of the United States. In denying the validity of the tax, that Court, speaking through Judge Field, said as follows:

"The power of taxation, however vast in its character and searching in its extent, is necessarily limited to subjects within the jurisdiction of the State. These subjects are persons, property, and business. Whatever form taxation may assume, whether as duties, imposts, excises, or licenses, it must relate to one of these subjects. It is not possible to conceive of any other, though, as applied to them, the taxation may be exercised in a great variety of ways. It may touch property in every shape, in its natural condition, in its manufactured form, and in its various transmutations; and the amount of the taxation may be determined by the value of the property, or its use, or its capacity, or its productiveness. It may touch business in the almost infinite forms in which it is conducted, in professions, in commerce, in manufactures, and in transportation. Unless restrained by provisions of the Federal Constitution, the power of the State as to the mode, form, and extent of taxation is unlimited, where the subjects to which it applies are within her jurisdiction. Corporations may be taxed like natural persons upon their property and business; but debts owing by corporations, like debts owing by individuals, are not property of the debtors in any sense. They are obligations of the debtors and only possess value in the hands of the creditors. With them they are property, and in their hands they may be taxed. To call debts property of the debtors, is simply to misuse terms. All the property there can be in the nature of things in debts of corporations, belongs to the creditors to whom they are payable, and follows their domicile wherever that may be. Their debts can have no locality separate from the parties to whom they are due. This principle might be stated in many different ways, and supported by citations from numerous adjudications; but no number of authorities and no forms of expression could add anything to its obvious truth, which is recognized upon its simple statement.

"The bonds issued by the railroad company in this case are undoubtedly property, but property in the hands of the holders, not property of the obligors. So far as they are held by non-residents of the State, they are property beyond the jurisdiction of the State. The law which requires the treasurer of the company to retain five per cent. of the interest due to the non-resident bondholder is not, therefore, a legitimate exercise of the taxing power. It is a law which interferes between the company and the bondholder, and under the pretence of levying a tax commands the company to withhold a portion of the stipulated interest and pay it over to the State. It is a law which thus impairs the obligation of a contract between the parties. The obligation of a contract depends upon its terms and the means which the law in existence at the time affords for its enforcement. A law which alters the terms of a contract by imposing new conditions, or dispensing with those expressed, is a law which impairs its obligations, for, as stated on another occasion, such a law relieves the parties from the moral duty of performing the original stipulations of the contract, and it prevents their legal enforcement. The Act of Pennsylvania of May 1st, 1868, falls within this description. It directs the treasurer of every incorporated company to retain from the interest stipulated to its bondholders five per cent. upon every dollar and pay it into the treasury of the Commonwealth. It thus sanctions and commands a disregard of the express provisions of the contracts between the company and its creditors. It is only one of many cases where, under the name of taxation, an oppressive exaction is made without constitutional warrant, amounting to little less than an arbitrary seizure of private property. It is, in fact, a forced contribution levied upon property held in other States, where it is subjected, or may be subjected, to taxation upon an estimate of its full value."

"The case of *Maltby vs. The Reading and Columbia Railroad Company*, decided by the Supreme Court of Pennsylvania in 1866, was referred to by the Common Pleas in support of its ruling, and is relied upon by counsel in support of the tax in question. The decision in that case does go to the full extent claimed, and holds that bonds of corporations held by non-residents are taxable in that State. But it is evident, from a perusal of the opinion of the Court, that the decision proceeded upon the idea that the bond of the non-resident was itself property in the State, because secured by mortgage on property there. 'It is undoubtedly true,' said the Court, 'that the Legislature of Pennsylvania cannot impose a personal tax upon the citizen of another State, but the constant practice is to tax property within our jurisdiction which belongs to non-residents.' And again: 'There must be jurisdiction over either the property or the person of the owner, else the power cannot be exercised; but when the property is within our jurisdiction, and enjoys the protection of our State government, it is justly taxable, and it is of no moment that the owner, who is required to pay the tax, resides elsewhere.' There is no doubt of the correctness of these views. But the Court then proceeds to state that the principle of taxation as the correlative of protection is as applicable to a non-resident as to a resident; that the loan to the non-resident is made valuable by the franchises which the company derived from the Commonwealth, and as an investment rests upon State authority, and therefore ought to contribute to the support of the State government. It also adds that though the loan is for some purposes subject to the law of the domicile of the holder, 'yet, in a very high sense,' it is also property in Pennsylvania, observing in support of this position that the holder of a bond of the company could not enforce it except in that State, and that the mortgage given for its security was upon property and franchises within her jurisdiction. The amount of all which is this : that the State which creates and protects a corporation ought to have the right to tax the loans negotiated by it, though taken and held by non-residents, a proposition which it is unnecessary to controvert. The legality of a tax of that kind would not be questioned if, in the charter of the company, the imposition of the tax were authorized, and in the bonds of the company, or its certificates of loan, the liability of the loan to taxation were stated. The tax in that case would be in the nature of a license tax for negotiating the loan, for, in whatever manner made payable, it would ultimately fall on the company as a condition of effecting the loan, and parties contracting with the company would provide for it by proper stipulations. But there is nothing in the observations of the Court, nor is there anything in the opinion, which shows that the bond of the non-resident was property in the State, or that the non-resident had any property in the State which was subject to taxation, within the principles laid down by the Court itself, which we have cited. The property mortgaged belonged entirely to the company, and so far as it was situated in Pennsylvania was taxable there. If taxation is the correlative of protection, the taxes which it there paid were the correlative for the protection which it there received. And neither the taxation of the property nor its protection was augmented or diminished by the fact that the corporation was in debt or free from debt. The property in no sense belonged to the non-resident bondholder or to the mortgagee of the company. The mortgage transferred no title; it created only a lien upon the property. Though in form a conveyance, it was both at law and in equity a mere security for the debt. That such is the nature of a mortgage in Pennsylvania has been frequently ruled by her highest Court. In Witmer's Appeal the Court said : ' The mortgagee has no estate in the land, any more than the judgment creditor. Both have liens upon it, and no more than liens.' And in that State all possible interests in lands, whether vested or contingent, are subject to levy and sale on execution ; yet it has been held, on the ground that a mortgagee has no estate in the lands, that the mortgaged premises cannot be taken in execution for his debt. . . . . . . Such being the character of a mortgage in Pennsylvania, it cannot be said, as was justly observed by counsel, that the non-resident holder and owner of a bond, secured by a mortgage in that State, owns any real estate there. A mortgage being there a mere chose in action, it only confers upon the holder, or the party for whose benefit the mortgage is given, a right to proceed against the property mortgaged, upon a given contingency, to enforce, by its sale, the payment of his demand. This right has no locality independent of the party in whom it resides. It may undoubtedly be taxed by the State when held by a resident therein, but when held by a non-resident, it is as much beyond the jurisdiction of the State as the person of the owner.

"It is undoubtedly true that the actual *situs* of personal property, which has a visible and tangible existence, and not the domicile of its owner, will, in many cases, determine the State in which it may be taxed. The same thing is true of public securities, consisting of State bonds and bonds of municipal bodies, and circulating notes of banking institutions; the former, by general usage, have acquired the character of and are treated as property in the place where they are found, though removed from the domicile of the owner; the latter are treated and pass as money wherever they are. But other personal property, consisting of bonds, mortgages, and debts generally, has no *situs* independent of the domicile of the owner, and certainly can have none where the instruments, as in the present case, constituting the evidences of debt, are not separated from the possession of the owners.

"Cases were cited by counsel on the argument from the decisions of the highest Courts of several States, which accord with the views we have expressed. In *Davenport vs. The Mississippi and Missouri Railroad Company* (12 *Iowa*, 539), the question arose before the Supreme Court of Iowa, whether mortgages on property in that State held by non-residents could be taxed under a law which provided that all property, real and personal, within the State, with certain exceptions not material to the present case, should be subject to taxation, and the Court said: 'Both in law and equity the mortgagee has only a chattel interest. It is true that the *situs* of the property mortgaged is within the jurisdiction of the State, but the mortgage itself, being personal property, a chose in action, attaches to the person of the owner. It is agreed by the parties that the owners and holders of the mortgages are non-residents of the State. If so, and the property of the mortgage attaches to the person of the owner, it follows that these mortgages are not property within the State, and if not, they are not the subject of taxation.' . . . . .

"Some adjudications in the Supreme Court of Pennsylvania were also cited on the argument, which appear to recognize doctrines inconsistent with that announced in *Maltby vs. Reading and Columbia Railroad Company*, particularly the case of *McKeen vs. The County of Northampton*, and the case of *Short's Estate*, but we do not deem it necessary to pursue the matter further. We are clear that the tax cannot be sustained; that the bonds, being held by non-residents of the State, are only property in their hands, and that they are thus beyond the jurisdiction of the taxing power of the State. Even where the bonds are held by residents of the State, the retention by the company of a portion of the stipulated interest can only be sustained as a mode of collecting a tax upon that species of property in the State. When the property is out of the State, there can then be no tax upon it for which the interest can be retained. The tax laws of Pennsylvania can have no extra-territorial operation, nor can any law of that State, inconsistent with the terms of a contract made with or payable to parties out of the State, have any effect upon the contract whilst it is in the hands of such parties or other non-residents. The extra-territorial invalidity of State laws discharging a debtor from his contracts with citizens of other States, even though made and payable in the State after the passage of such laws, has been judicially determined by this Court. A like invalidity must, on similar grounds, attend State legislation which seeks to change the obligation of such contracts in any particular, and on stronger grounds where the contracts are made and payable out of the State."

There are other limitations upon the power of taxation by the States imposed by their respective constitutions, designed to secure, as far as practicable, an equal distribution of the burdens of government, by requiring a uniform rate of taxation upon property of the same kind, and a uniform mode of assessment or appraisement of value. Of these it is not the purpose of this narrative to speak. There is, however, in the Fourteenth Amendment a clause which, according to the force attributed to it by Judge Field, may yet be invoked to prevent the imposition of unequal taxation by the States, of which there are so many daily complaints throughout the country—the clause which declares that no State shall " deny to any person, within its jurisdiction, the equal protection of the laws." In his opinion in the Virginia Jury Cases, he contended that the prohibitions of the Fourteenth Amendment being against the State, can only be properly enforced through the action of the judiciary, in like manner as the prohibition against the passage of a bill of attainder or an *ex post facto* law, or a law impairing the obligation of contracts ;—in other words, that a law of a State can be annulled only through the judiciary, and not by criminal proceedings against its legislators, judges, and other officers. He also contended that the clause mentioned applies only to civil rights and not to political or social rights; and yet he gave to it an immense force for the protection of private rights against arbitrary and unequal legislation of the States. His language is as follows :

" It opens the Courts of the country to every one, on the same terms, for the security of his person and property, the prevention and redress of wrongs, and the enforcement of contracts; it assures to every one the same rules of evidence and modes of procedure ; it allows no impediments to the acquisition of property and the pursuit of happiness, to which all are not subjected; *it suffers no other or greater burdens or charges to be laid upon one than such as are equally borne by others;* and in the administration of criminal justice it permits no different or greater punishment to be imposed upon one than such as is prescribed to all for like offences."

The clause was intended to secure equality of right to every person within the States, and this necessarily implies that he shall not be subjected to any greater burdens than his fellows. If one, therefore, is arbitrarily taxed by a law of a State at five per cent. on the value of his property, while others are taxed on the value of the same kind of property only one per cent., or if he be thus taxed because he pursues one calling or trade, or because he is black or brown or yellow in his color, whilst those of another pursuit or of a different color are taxed at a lower rate, he is subjected to an unequal share of the public burdens and may justly invoke the protection of the amendment against the action of the State.

In People vs. Weaver, where equality in taxation was disregarded by a law of the State of New York in the face of a law of Congress, the Supreme Court declared the State law invalid.—(10 Otto, 539.) Upon the same principle a State law sanctioning the imposition of unequal burdens must fall before the constitutional amendment.

THE TRUST CHARACTER OF DIRECTORS OF CORPORATIONS.

In the preceding pages, from 216 to 255 inclusive, a statement is made of several opinions of Judge Field respecting the powers and liabilities of corporations. During the past term, in the case of Wardell vs. The Union Pacific Railroad Company, he delivered another opinion touching the obligations of the directors of such bodies and the fiduciary character of their office. The case arose in this way. The road of the Union Pacific Company passes for its entire length, from Omaha, on the Missouri

River, to Ogden, in Utah, a distance of over one thousand miles, through a country almost destitute of timber fit for fuel. During its construction, however, large deposits of coal, of excellent quality and easily worked, were discovered in land along its line from which abundant supplies could be obtained for the use of the company. The engineers, appointed to survey the route for the road, reported the existence of such deposits. In June, 1868, one Thomas Wardell made explorations for coal in the lands of the company, and reported to its managers the information which he had thus acquired, which was confirmatory of that previously obtained from the engineers. A contract was then entered into between the company and himself and one Godfrey, with whom he had become associated in business, to furnish the company with coal required for its use. This contract, which is dated July 16th, 1868, stipulated for exorbitant prices; and by it all the coal lands of the company were leased to Wardell and Godfrey for fifteen years. They immediately entered upon the execution of the contract and began work on several mines along the line of the road. Soon afterwards Godfrey transferred his interest in the contract to Wardell. A new company was then formed called the Wyoming Coal and Mining Company, of which the directors of the Union Pacific Railroad Company became the chief shareholders. To this company Wardell assigned his contract without any consideration. The company continued the execution of the contract, Wardell acting as its superintendent, secretary, and general manager, and delivered coal as needed to the railroad company up to March, 1874, when the officers and agents of that company, by order of its directors, took forcible possession of the mines and of the books, papers, tools, and other personal property of the coal company, which they continued to hold and use. Some months after this the two companies, through their directors, made a settlement of their matters of difference, by which the contract of July 16th, 1868, was rescinded

and one million dollars was allowed to the coal company. Of this million the railroad company set apart
and tendered to Wardell one hundred thousand dollars
for his share. He, not being satisfied with the settlement, brought a suit, in his own name, against the railroad company, alleging as a reason that a majority of the
directors and stockholders of the coal company were also
directors and stockholders of the railroad company, and
that therefore he could obtain no relief by a suit in
the name of the coal company. He prayed that an
account might be taken of the amount due for the
coal delivered to the railroad company, for drawback on
freight from the date of the contract, for coal extracted
from the mines since their seizure and for the property of
the coal company taken, and for the damages arising from
the attempted abrogation of the contract. To this suit the
railroad company set up, among other things, that the contract of July 16th, 1868, was a fraud upon the company,
that it was made on the part of the executive committee
of its board of directors, a majority of whom were, by previous agreement, to be equally interested with the contractors, and for that reason its terms were made so favorable to them and unfavorable to the company, as to enable
the former to make large gains at the expense of the latter; and that the organization of the coal company was a
mere device to enable those directors to participate in the
profits; and also that a settlement had been made between
the two companies of all their transactions,

The court below held that the contract of July 16, 1868,
was a fraud upon the company, but that the complainant
was, apart from it, entitled to some compensation for his
time, skill, and services while engaged in taking out the
coal, with the return of the money actually invested and
compensation for its use, the amount to be credited with
what he had actually received out of the business; and
that at his election he could have an accounting upon that
basis or take the one hundred thousand dollars tendered

by the company. Of the alternatives thus offered he elected to take the one hundred thousand dollars instead of having the accounting mentioned, but appealed to the Supreme Court from the decree, contending that the contract itself was valid, and that he was entitled to an accounting upon that hypothesis, but the judgment was there affirmed. Of the contract and of the obligations of the directors of the railroad company, that Court, speaking through Judge Field, said as follows :

"The evidence in the case justifies the conclusion of the court below as to the nature of the contract of July 16th, 1868. It was evidently drawn more for the benefit of the contractors than for the interest of the company. The extent, value, and accessibility of the coal deposits along the line of the road of the company were, as stated above, well known at the time to its directors, having the immediate control and management of its business. Wardell, the principal contractor, informed those with whom he chiefly dealt in negotiating the contract, that coal could be delivered to the company at a cost of two dollars per ton, yet the contract, which was to remain in force fifteen years, stipulated that the company should pay treble this amount per ton for the coal the first two years, two and a half times the amount for the next three years, twice the amount for the following four years, and one-half more for the balance of the time. And lest these rates might prove too little, the contract further provided that the sum paid should not be less than ten per cent. added to the cost of the coal to the contractors. These terms and the leasing of all the coal lands of the company for fifteen years to those parties upon a royalty of twenty-five cents a ton for the first nine years, and without any royalty afterwards if the price of the coal should be reduced to three dollars, with the stipulation to provide side-tracks to the mines, and also to furnish cars for transportation of coal for general consumption, and after charging them only what was charged to others, to allow them a drawback of twenty-five per cent. on the sums paid, gave to them a contract of the value of millions of dollars. These provisions would of themselves justly excite a suspicion that the directors of the railroad company, who authorized the contract on its behalf, had been greatly deceived and imposed upon, or that they were ignorant of the cost at which the coal could be taken from the mines and delivered to the company. But the evidence shows that those directors were neither deceived nor imposed upon, nor were they without information as to the probable cost of taking out and delivering the coal. And what is of more importance, it shows, as alleged, their previous agreement with the contractors for a joint interest in the contract, and, in order that they might not appear as co-contractors, that a corporation should be formed in which they should become stockholders, and to which the contract should be assigned ; and that this agreement was carried out by the subsequent formation of the Wyoming Mining and Coal Company and their taking stock in it. This matter was so well understood that when the contractors commenced their work in developing the mines and taking out the coal, they kept their accounts in the name of the proposed company, though no such company was organized until months afterwards.

" It hardly requires argument to show that the scheme thus designed to enable the directors, who authorized the contract, to divide with the contractors large sums which should have been saved to the company, was utterly indefensible and illegal. Those directors, constituting the executive committee of the board, were clothed with power to manage the affairs of the company for the benefit of its stockholders and creditors. Their character as agents forbade the exercise of their powers for their own personal ends against the interest of the company. They were thereby precluded from deriving any advantage from contracts made by their authority as directors, except through the company for which they acted. Their position was one of great trust, and to engage in any matter for their personal advantage inconsistent with it was to violate their duty and to commit a fraud upon the company.

" It is among the rudiments of the law that the same person cannot act for himself and at the same time, with respect to the same matter, as the agent for another whose interests are conflicting. Thus a person cannot be a purchaser of property and at the same time the agent of the vendor. The two positions impose different obligations, and their union would at once raise a conflict between interest and duty ; and 'constituted as humanity is, in the majority of cases duty would be overcome in the struggle.'—(Marsh vs. Whitmore, 21 Wallace, 183.) The law, therefore, will always condemn the transactions of a party on his own behalf when, in respect to the matter concerned, he is the agent of others, and will relieve against them whenever their enforcement is seasonably resisted. Directors of corporations, and all persons who stand in a fiduciary relation to other parties, and are clothed with power to act for them, are subject to this rule ; they are not permitted to occupy a position which will conflict with the interest of parties they represent and are bound to protect. They cannot, as agents or trustees, enter into or authorize contracts on behalf of those for whom they are appointed to act, and then personally participate in the benefits. Hence all arrangements by directors of a railroad company, to secure an undue advantage to themselves at its expense, by the formation of a new company as an auxiliary to the original one, with an understanding that they, or some of them, shall take stock in it, and then that valuable contracts shall be given to it, in the profits of which they, as stockholders in the new company, are to share, are so many unlawful devices to enrich themselves to the detriment of the stockholders and creditors of the original company, and will be condemned whenever properly brought before the Courts for consideration.—(Great Luxembourg Co. vs. Magnay, 25 Beavan, 586; Benson vs. Heathorn, 1 Young & Coll., 326; Flint & Pere Marquette R. R. Co. vs. Dewey, 14 Michigan, 477; European & N. American R. R. Co. vs. Poor, 59 Maine, 277; and Drury vs. Cross, 7 Wall., 299.)

"The scheme disclosed here has no feature which relieves it of its fraudulent character, and the contract of July 16, 1868, which was an essential part of it, must go down with it. It was a fraudulent proceeding on the part of the directors and contractors who devised and carried it into execution, not only against the company, but also against the government, which had largely contributed to its aid by the loan of bonds and by the grant of lands. By the very terms of the charter of the company five per cent. of its net earnings were to be paid to the government. Those earnings were necessarily reduced by every transaction which took from the company its legitimate profits. It is true that some of the directors, who approved of or did not dissent from the contract, early stated that they held their stock in the coal company for the benefit of the railroad company, and transferred it, or were ready to transfer it, to the latter; but the majority expressed such a purpose only when the character and terms of the contract became known and they were desirous to screen themselves from censure for their conduct.

"The complainant, therefore, can derive no benefit from the contract thus tainted, or sustain any claim against the railroad company for its repudiation."—(13 Otto.)

The Use of Running Waters on the Public Lands.

When it was known that gold had been discovered in California, and existed in such form and quantity as to reward individual exploration and labor, an immense immigration set in for the country. Gold-seekers came from all parts of the world, and in such numbers as to swell the population in three or four years from a few thousands to over half a million. A great number of these— perhaps one-third—remained in the cities and engaged in commerce, or settled upon the fertile lands in the valleys and cultivated the soil, or raised cattle from the rich pasturage afforded. The greater portion spread over the mineral region, which was chiefly in the Sierra Nevada Mountains. The title to the whole of the lands composing this region was in the United States, and no law had

been passed which provided for their occupation and purchase. The rights which the miners asserted were merely
possessory, and to protect each other in their psssession
and in extracting gold from the lands, they were compelled to adopt certain rules for their government. The
character, justice, and wisdom of the rules established by
them in different localities, are fully stated in an opinion
delivered by Judge Field in the Supreme Court, in the
case of Jennison vs. Kirk, (8 Otto, 457,) an extract of
which is given on pages 6, 7, and 8 of this volume.

In working the mines water was a necessity; without it
gold could not be separated from the earth or rock in
which it was buried. The doctrines of the common law
relating to the rights of riparian proprietors were not applicable to the conditions and wants of the miners. They
accordingly adopted rules for the regulation of the possession and use of water, as they had done for the possession and working of their mining claims. These regulations controlled the disposition of properties of the value
of many millions.

The same general system of regulations, so intrinsically
just were they deemed, was established by miners in the
territory east of the Sierra Nevada Mountains—in Nevada, Montana, and Idaho; indeed, wherever the precious
metals were found. Questions arising under them were
constantly before the local Courts, and in some instances
found their way to the Supreme Court of the United States.

In Atchison vs. Peterson,* which was before that Court
in 1874, the question was presented as to the right, from
prior appropriation, to the use for mining purposes of the
water of a stream without deterioration in quality and
value. The suit was brought to restrain the defendants
from carrying on certain mining work on a creek in the
Territory of Montana, on the alleged ground that the
water, diverted by the complainants from the stream for
mining purposes, was, by such work, thus deteriorated.

---

* 20 Wall., 507.

The complainants were the owners of two ditches or canals, constructed at a cost of $117,000, by which the creek was tapped and the water diverted and conveyed a distance of eighteen miles to certain mining districts, and there sold to miners. At a point about fifteen miles above the place where the creek was thus tapped the defendants were working mining ground, which they had acquired subsequently to the time when the complainants commenced the construction of the ditches. In some places in their work the defendants washed down the earth from the side of the hills bordering on the stream; in other places they excavated the earth, and threw such portions as were supposed to contain gold into sluices, upon which the water was turned. The earth from the washings on the hillsides, and from the sluices, was carried into the creek and affected its whole current, filling the water to some extent with mud, sand, and sediment. The evidence as to the extent of the deterioration was conflicting, but the great preponderance of it was to the effect that the injury in quality from this cause, at the point where the complainants tapped the stream, was so slight as not, in any material extent, to impair the value of the water for mining, or to render it less salable to the miners at the places where it was carried.

The District Court denied the injunction, and the Supreme Court of the Territory affirmed the decree, and the case was taken to the Supreme Court. In affirming the decree that Court, speaking through Judge Field, said as follows:

"By the custom which has obtained among miners in the Pacific States and Territories, where mining for the precious metals is had on the public lands of the United States, the first appropriator of mines, whether in placers, veins, or lodes, or of waters in the streams on such lands for mining purposes, is held to have a better right than others to work the mines or use the waters. The first appropriator who subjects the property to use, or takes the necessary steps for that purpose, is regarded, except as against the government, as the source of title in all controversies relating to the property. As respects the use of water for mining purposes, the doctrines of the common law declaratory of the rights of riparian owners were, at an early day, after the discovery of gold, found to be inapplicable or applicable only in a very limited extent to the necessities of the miners, and inadequate to their protection. By the common law the riparian owner on a stream not navigable, takes the land to the centre of the stream, and such owner has the right to the use of the water flowing over the land as an incident to his estate. And as all such owners on the same stream have an equality of right to the use of the water, as it naturally flows, in quality, and without diminution in quantity, except so far as such diminution may be created by a reasonable use of the water for certain domestic, agricultural, or manufacturing purposes, there could not be, according to that law, any such diversion or use of the water by one owner as would work material detriment to any other owner below him. Nor could the water by one owner be so retarded in its flow as to be thrown back to the injury of another owner above him. 'It is wholly immaterial,' says Mr. Justice Story, in Tyler vs. Wilkinson, 'whether the party be a proprietor above or below in the course of the river; the right being common to all the proprietors on the river, no one has a right to diminish the quantity which will, according to the natural current, flow to the proprietor below, or to throw it back upon a proprietor above. This is the necessary result of the perfect equality of right among all the proprietors of that which is common to all.'* 'Every proprietor of lands on the banks of a river,' says Kent, 'has naturally an equal right to the use of the water which flows in the stream adjacent to his lands, as it was wont to run (currere solebat) without diminution or alteration. No proprietor has a right to use the water to the prejudice of other proprietors above or below him, unless he has a prior right to divert it, or a title to some exclusive enjoyment. He has no property in the water itself, but a simple usufruct while it passes along. Aqua currit et debet currere ut currere solebat. Though he may use the water while it runs over his land as an incident to the land, he cannot unreasonably detain it or give it another direction, and he must return it to its ordinary channel when it leaves his estate. Without the consent of the adjoining proprietors he cannot divert or diminish the quantity of the water which would otherwise descend to the proprietors below, nor throw the water back upon the proprietors above without a grant or an uninterrupted enjoyment of twenty years, which is evidence of it. This is the clear and settled doctrine on the subject, and all the difficulty which arises consists in the application.'†

"This equality of right among all the proprietors on the same stream would have been incompatible with any extended diversion of the water by one proprietor, and its conveyance for mining purposes to points from which it could not be restored to the stream. But the government being the sole proprietor of all the public lands, whether bordering on streams or otherwise, there was no occasion for the application of the com-

---

* 4 Mason, 379.   † 3 Kent's Comm., 439,

20

mon-law doctrine of riparian proprietorship with respect to the waters of those streams. The government, by its silent acquiescence, assented to the general occupation of the public lands for mining, and, to encourage their free and unlimited use for that purpose, reserved such lands as were mineral from sale and the acquisition of title by settlement. And he who first connects his own labor with property thus situated and open to general exploration, does, in natural justice, acquire a better right to its use and enjoyment than others who have not given such labor. So the miners on the public lands throughout the Pacific States and Territories by their customs, usages, and regulations everywhere recognized the inherent justice of this principle, and the principle itself was at an early period recognized by legislation and enforced by the courts in those States and Territories. In Irwin vs. Phillips,* a case decided by the Supreme Court of California in January, 1855, this subject was considered. After stating that a system of rules had been permitted to grow up with repect to mining on the public lands by the voluntary action and assent of the population, whose free and unrestrained occupation of the mineral region had been tacitly assented to by the federal government, and heartily encouraged by the expressed legislative policy of the State, the Court said : ' If there are, as must be admitted, many things connected with this system which are crude and undigested, and subject to fluctuation and dispute, there are still some which a universal sense of necessity and propriety have so firmly fixed as that they have come to be looked upon as having the force and effect of *res adjudicata*. Among these the most important are the rights of miners to be protected in their selected localities, and the rights of those who, by prior appropriation, have taken the waters from their natural beds, and by costly artificial works have conducted them for miles over mountains and ravines to supply the necessities of gold diggers, and without which the most important interests of the mineral region would remain without development. So fully recognized have become these rights, that without any specific legislation conferring or confirming them, they are alluded to and spoken of in various acts of the Legislature in the same manner as if they were rights which had been vested by the most distinct expression of the will of the lawmakers.'

" This doctrine of right by prior appropriation, was recognized by the legislation of Congress in 1866.† The act granting the right of way to ditch and canal owners over the public lands, and for other purposes, passed on the 26th of July of that year, in its ninth section declares ' that whenever, by priority of possession, rights to the use of water for mining, agricultural, manufacturing, or other purposes, have vested and accrued, and the same are recognized and acknowledged by the local customs, laws, and decisions of courts, the possessors and owners of such vested rights shall be maintained and protected in the same.'

---

* 5 Cal., 140.   † 14 Stats. at Large, 253.

" The right to water by prior appropriation, thus recognized and established as the law of miners on the mineral lands of the public domain, is limited in every case, in quantity and quality, by the uses for which the appropriation is made. A different use of the water subsequently does not affect the right; that is subject to the same limitations, whatever the use. The appropriation does not confer such an absolute right to the body of the water diverted that the owner can allow it, after its diversion, to run to waste, and prevent others from using it for mining or other legitimate purposes; nor does it confer such a right that he can insist upon the flow of the water without deterioration in quality, where such deterioration does not defeat nor impair the uses to which the water is applied.

" Such was the purport of the ruling of the Supreme Court of California in Butte Canal and Ditch Company vs. Vaughn,* where it was held that the first appropriator had only the right to insist that the water should be subject to his use and enjoyment to the extent of his original appropriation, and that its quality should not be impaired so as to defeat the purpose of that appropriation. To this extent, said the Court, his rights go, and no farther; and that, in subordination to them, subsequent appropriators may use the channel and waters of the stream, and mingle with its waters other waters, and divert them as often as they choose; that whilst enjoying his original rights, the first appropriator had no cause of complaint. In the subsequent case of Ortman vs. Dixon † the same Court held to the same purport, that the measure of the right of the first appropriator of the water, as to extent, follows the nature of the appropriation, or the uses for which it is taken.

" What diminution of quantity, or deterioration in quality, will constitute an invasion of the rights of the first appropriator, will depend upon the special circumstances of each case, considered with reference to the uses to which the water is applied. A slight deterioration in quality might render the water unfit for drink or domestic purposes, whilst it would not sensibly impair its value for mining or irrigation. In all controversies, therefore, between him and parties subsequently claiming the water, the question for determination is necessarily whether his use and enjoyment of the water, to the extent of his original appropriation, have been impaired by the acts of the defendant. But whether, upon a petition or bill asserting that his prior rights have been thus invaded, a Court of Equity will interfere to restrain the acts of the party complained of, will depend upon the character and extent of the injury alleged, whether it be irremediable in its nature, whether an action at law would afford adequate remedy, whether the parties are liable to respond for the damages resulting from the injury, and other considerations which ordinarily govern a Court of Equity in the exercise of its preventive process of injunction."

---

* 11 Cal., 143.   See, also, Lobdell vs. Simpson, 2 Nev., 274,
† 13 Cal., 33.

The Court then proceeded to apply the principles thus stated to the solution of the questions presented, and affirmed the decree.

In Basey vs. Gallagher * the question arose whether a right to running waters on the public lands of the United States for purposes of irrigation could be acquired by prior appropriation as against parties not having the title of the government. The District and Supreme Courts of Montana having sustained the affirmative of this question, the case in which it arose was brought before the Supreme Court of the United States. In giving its judgment the Court referred to Atchison vs. Peterson, above mentioned, which was decided at the same term, stated what had been held in that case, and then, speaking through Judge Field, said as follows:

"The views there expressed and the rulings made are equally applicable to the use of water on the public lands for purposes of irrigation. No distinction is made in those States and Territories [of the Pacific Coast] by the custom of miners or settlers, or by the Courts, in the rights of the first appropriator from the use made of the water, if the use be a beneficial one.

"In the case of Tartar vs. The Spring Creek Water and Mining Company, decided in 1855, the Supreme Court of California said: 'The current of decisions of this Court go to establish that the policy of this State, as derived from her legislation, is to permit settlers in all capacities to occupy the public lands, and by such occupation to acquire the right of undisturbed enjoyment against all the world but the true owner. In evidence of this, acts have been passed to protect the possession of agricultural lands acquired by mere occupancy; to license miners; to provide for the recovery of mining claims; recognizing canals and ditches which were known to divert the water of streams from their natural channel for mining purposes; and others of like character. This policy has been extended equally to all pursuits, and no partiality for one over another has been evinced, except in the single case where the rights of the agriculturalist are made to yield to those of the miner where gold is discovered in his land. . . . . The policy of the exception is obvious. Without it the entire gold region might have been inclosed in large tracts, under the pretence of agriculture and grazing, and eventually what would have sufficed as a rich bounty to many thousands would be reduced to the proprietorship of a few. Aside from this the legislation and decisions have been uniform in awarding the right of

* 20 Cal., 671.

peaceable enjoyment to the first occupant, either of the land or of anything incident to the land.'*

"Ever since that decision it has been held generally throughout the Pacific States and Territories that the right to water by prior appropriation for any beneficial purpose is entitled to protection. Water is diverted to propel machinery in flour-mills and saw-mills, and to irrigate land for cultivation, as well as to enable miners to work their mining claims; and in all such cases the right of the first appropriator, exercised within reasonable limits, is respected and enforced. We say within reasonable limits, for this right to water, like the right by prior occupancy to mining ground or agricultural land, is not unrestricted. It must be exercised with reference to the general condition of the country and the necessities of the people, and not so as to deprive a whole neighborhood or community of its use, and vest an absolute monopoly in a single individual. The act of Congress of 1866 recognizes the right to water by prior appropriation for agricultural and manufacturing purposes, as well as for mining. Its language is: 'That whenever by priority of possession rights to the use of water for mining, agricultural, manufacturing, or other purposes have vested and accrued, and the same are recognized and acknowledged by the local customs, laws, and decisions of courts, the possessors and owners of such vested rights shall be maintained and protected in the same.'

"It is evident that Congress intended, although the language used is not happy, to recognize as valid the customary law with respect to the use of water, which had grown up among the occupants of the public land under the peculiar necessities of their condition; and that law may be shown by evidence of the local customs, or by the legislation of the State or Territory, or the decisions of the courts. The union of the three conditions, in any particular case, is not essential to the perfection of the right by priority; and in case of conflict between a local custom and a statutory regulation, the latter, as of superior authority, must necessarily control."

---

* Per Heydenfeldt, J., 5 California, 397.

CASES IN THE CIRCUIT COURT OF THE UNITED
STATES FOR THE DISTRICT OF CALIFORNIA.

_____

As mentioned in the preceding pages, Judge Field, upon
his appointment, was assigned to the circuit composed of
the Pacific States, California and Oregon, to which Nevada,
on her becoming a State, was added. It was his duty to
attend the sessions of the Supreme Court at Washington
in the winter, and to hold the Circuit Court in his circuit
in summer. Until the passage of the act of 1869, providing for the appointment of Circuit Judges, the Circuit
Court, in his absence, was held by the District Judge of
the district. Since then he has only been required to attend a term in each district of his circuit once in two
years. He has, however, visited the circuit every year,
until the present one (1881), since his appointment, and
has generally held court in all its districts.

The cases brought before the Circuit Court have not
only been of the variety and importance, which have generally characterized the litigation in the Federal Courts
of other circuits, but many of them have had special interest, arising either from accidental circumstances or circumstances peculiar to the coast.

UNITED STATES VS. GREATHOUSE.

At the first term of the circuit at which Judge Field
presided, after his appointment, the case of the United
States vs. Greathouse and others, was tried. Growing out
of the civil war, then pending, it excited unusual interest

throughout the country. Its history is briefly this. In March, 1863, the schooner *J. M. Chapman* was seized in the harbor of San Francisco by the United States revenue officers, while sailing, or about to sail, on a cruise, in the service of the Confederate States, against the commerce of the United States, and the leaders of the expedition, named Greathouse, Harpending, Rubery, Law, and Libby, were indicted under the act of Congress of July 17th, 1862, for engaging in and giving aid and comfort to the then existing rebellion against the government of the United States. The case was called for trial at the October term of 1863. A *nolle prosequi* was entered as to Law and Libby, and they became witnesses for the prosecution.

Their testimony and that of others showed that Harpending, a native of Kentucky, and Rubery, a native of England, had for some time contemplated the fitting out of a privateer at San Francisco, for the purpose of taking several of the mail steamships plying between that port and Panama, and other vessels. With this object in view, Harpending had gone across the country to Richmond, Virginia, and procured from Jefferson Davis, the President of the Confederate States, a letter of marque, authorizing him to prey upon the commerce of the United States, and to burn, board, or take any vessel of their citizens; and also a letter of instructions directing him how to act, and containing the form of a bond, in case any prize taken should be bonded. Upon his return to San Francisco he and Rubery made arrangements for the purchase of a vessel which would suit their purpose; but these arrangements afterwards failed, on account of the dishonor of the drafts drawn for the purchase-money by Rubery, and the consequent want of funds. They also made a voyage to Cerros Island for the purpose of examining into its fitness as a depot and as a rendezvous whence to attack the steamers going to Panama.

In January or February, 1863, Harpending made the acquaintance, at San Francisco, of Law, a ship captain;

broached to him the project of fitting out a privateer; stated what had been done; exhibited his letter of marque and instructions; solicited him to enter into the enterprise and assist in procuring a vessel; and said, among other things, that if he had succeeded in carrying out his previous arrangements, he could easily have taken three of the mail steamers. Law agreed to take part in the scheme, and soon afterwards pointed out the schooner *J. M. Chapman,* a vessel of about ninety tons burden and a fast sailer, as well adapted for the intended cruise. Several meetings in reference to the subject took place between Harpending, Rubery, Law, and Greathouse, (who had been introduced by Harpending to Law as a capitalist,) and the result was that Greathouse purchased the schooner, and furnished money to procure arms, ammunition, and stores, and to engage a mate and a crew. The next morning Law took charge of the schooner, moved it to a wharf at the city front, informed Libby of the project, and induced him to go as mate, and engaged four seamen and a cook.

All this time Greathouse gave out that he was acting in the interest of the " Liberal Party " in Mexico, and under this pretext, arms and ammunition were purchased, consisting of two brass rifled twelve-pounders, shells, fuse, powder, muskets, pistols, lead, caps, and knives. These were packed in cases marked " oil mill " and " machinery," and shipped as quietly as possible, and there was also shipped a number of uniforms, such as are usually worn by men on vessels of war. A large amount of lumber was also purchased and shipped, with which to construct berths, a prison room, and a lower deck. The intention of the parties was to sail from San Francisco on Sunday the 15th of March, 1863, to the island of Guadalupe, which lies some three hundred miles off the coast of California; there land Harpending and the fighting men, who were to be shipped on the night of Saturday the 14th; thence proceed to Manzanillo, and discharge such freight as might be taken; then return to Guadalupe, and fit the schooner for privateering purposes; then proceed again to Manzanillo, where the men were to be enrolled and their names inserted in the letter of marque, a copy of which was thereupon to be forwarded to the government of the Confederate States. It was their plan first to capture a steamer bound from San Francisco to Panama, on its arrival at Manzanillo, land its passengers, and with the steamer thus taken capture a second steamer; next to seize a vessel from San Francisco, then engaged in recovering treasure from the wreck of the steamer Golden Gate; thence to go to the Chincha Islands, and burn vessels there belonging to citizens of the United States, and thence to proceed to the China Sea, and finally into the Indian Ocean. There they expected to join Admiral Semmes of the Confederate Navy. In pursuance of this plan, and to prevent suspicion, the schooner was " put up " for Manzanillo. A partial cargo was shipped on board, and Law cleared at the custom-house for that port, signing and swearing to a false manifest. On the night of March 14th, in accordance with the scheme arranged, all the participants went on board. Fifteen persons, who had been employed by Harpending as privateersmen, were placed in the hold in an open space left for them among the cargo, directly under the main hatch. The only person absent was Law, who remained on shore with the understanding that he should be on hand before morning. It afterwards appeared that he had became intoxicated, and did not get down to keep his appointment until after the schooner had been seized.

During the evening, Rubery had heard rumors that the vessel was to be overhauled, and as the morning approached and Law did not appear, he proposed sailing without him. At daylight, Law being still absent, Libby cast off the lines, and began working the schooner out from the wharf into the stream. The main-sail was partially hoisted; but no sooner had the wharf been left, than two boats were observed putting off from the United States sloop-of-war

Cyane, then lying at anchor in the bay. As they headed for the schooner, Libby, pointing at them, said to Greathouse that they were after them. Rubery then insisted on running up the sails, but Libby replied that there was no wind, and it would be useless. In a few minutes afterwards the schooner was boarded and seized by the officers of the United States, and the enterprise nipped in the bud. Scarcely had the seizure been effected when Law made his appearance on board and was arrested with the others.

The revenue officers of the United States had been aware of the intended enterprise from an early period, and maintained a constant watch on the vessel night and day.

They knew the character of the cargo, which had been carefully noted by the watchmen; were aware of the shipment of arms, and saw the cases with their false marks. On the Saturday afternoon when the schooner was cleared for Manzanillo, they increased the watch, chartered a steam-tug, and put policemen on board. They also made arrangements for the reception and confinement of prisoners at the United States fortifications on Alcatraz Island, and procured the two boats with their crews from the war-ship Cyane, to act in conjunction with them on a given signal. In the evening, the revenue officers themselves went on board the tug, proceeded to a wharf next that at which the *J. M. Chapman* lay, and watched the men going on board. When the schooner cast off its lines at daylight and headed out into the stream, the boats from the Cyane put off and boarded it according to previous arrangement; and at the same time the tug steamed up. Greathouse and Libby were on deck; the others were below. Fifteen men were found in the hold under the hatch, besides two sailors, who had been placed there over night to prevent them from leaving the vessel. A search being instituted for papers, a number of scraps, some torn, some chewed, and some partially burned, were found strewn about the hold. The two sailors confined testified that some of the party had employed the time intervening between the boarding of the vessel and the opening of the hatchway in destroying papers. Loaded pistols and bowie-knives were found stowed away in the interstices between the packages of the cargo. In the baggage of Harpending and Rubery were found, among other papers, a proclamation to the people of California to throw off the authority of the United States; a plan for the capture of the United States forts at San Francisco, and particularly Alcatraz; also, the form of an oath of fidelity to their cause, with an imprecation of vengeance on all who should prove false. It was shown that some of these papers were in the handwriting of Harpending; and Rubery admitted that he and one of the defendants had spent some time in preparing the oaths.

After the seizure and arrest, the prisoners were taken to Alcatraz and confined. The schooner was unloaded, and the arms and munitions examined. An army officer testified that, in his opinion, the schooner might have destroyed a Panama steamer; but naval officers expressed a doubt whether this could have been done.

The defence offered no testimony, but claimed, among other things, that a state of war existed between the United States and the Confederate States; that the latter were entitled to, and had in fact received from the former, belligerent rights; and that privateering on the part of either side was a legitimate mode of warfare, and made those engaged amenable only to the laws of war. They also claimed that the schooner had not started on her voyage, but had left the wharf with the intention of anchoring in the stream and waiting there for the captain and papers; that whatever the ultimate intention might have been, there had, in fact, been no commencement of the cruise, and that, at any rate, no offence could have been committed until the schooner had reached Manzanillo, and been ready to commence hostilities. They finally insisted that there could be no treason and no conviction under the indictment, for the reason that "aid and comfort" had not been actually given.

The trial lasted three weeks. Judge Hoffman of the District Court sat with Judge Field, and each of the judges gave their views to the jury, following in that respect the practice which was adopted in some of the early State cases in the Circuit Courts, at the close of the last century.—(See Wharton's State Trials, Fries' Case, pages 584 and 587.)

In his charge Judge Field defined what constituted treason under the Constitution of the United States, following in that respect the definition of Chief Justice Marshall in *Ex-parte* Bollman and *Ex-parte* Swartwout, (4 Cranch, 127,) and commented upon and explained the act of July, 1862, under which the indictment was found, and then proceeded as follows :

" The existence of the rebellion is a matter of public notoriety, and like matters of general and public concern to the whole country, may be taken notice of by judges and juries without that particular proof which is required of the other matters charged. The public notoriety, the proclamation of the President, and the acts of Congress are sufficient proof of the allegation of the indictment in this respect. The same notoriety and public documents are also sufficient proof that the rebellion is organized and carried on under a pretended government called the Confederate States of America.

"As to the treasonable purposes of the defendants there is no conflict in the evidence. It is true the principal witnesses of the government are, according to their own statements, co-conspirators with the defendants, and equally involved in guilt with them, if guilt there be in any of them. But their testimony, as you have seen, has been corroborated in many of its essential details. You are, however, the exclusive judges of its credibility. The Court will only say to you that there is no rule of law which excludes the testimony of an accomplice, or prevents you from giving credence to it, when it has been corroborated in material particulars. Indeed, gentlemen, I have not been able to perceive from the argument of counsel that the truth of the material portions of their testimony has been seriously controverted.

" It is not necessary that I should state in detail the evidence produced. I do not propose to do so. It is sufficient to refer to its general purport. It is not denied, and will not be denied, that the evidence tends to establish that Harpending obtained from the president of the so-called Confederate States a letter of marque—a commission to cruise in their service on the high seas, in a private armed vessel, and commit hostilities against the citizens, vessels, and property of the United States ;

that his co-defendants and others entered into a conspiracy with him to purchase and fit out, and arm a vessel, and cruise under the said letter of marque, in the service of the rebellion; that in pursuance of the conspiracy they purchased the schooner J. M. Chapman; that they purchased cannon, shells, and ammunition, and the means usually required in enterprises of that kind, and placed them on board the vessel; that they employed men for the management of the vessel; and that, when everything was in readiness, they started with the vessel from the wharf, with the intention to sail from the port of San Francisco on the arrival on board of the captain, who was momentarily expected. Gentlemen I do not propose to say anything to you upon the much disputed questions whether or not the vessel ever did, in fact, sail from the port of San Francisco, or whether, if she did sail, she started on the hostile expedition. In the judgment of the Court they are immaterial, if you find the facts to be what I have said the evidence tends to establish.

"'When Harpending received the letter of marque, with the intention of using it, if such be the case (and it is stated by one of the witnesses that he represented that he went on horseback over the plains expressly to obtain it), he became leagued with the insurgents—the conspiracy between him and the chiefs of the rebellion was complete; it was a conspiracy to commit hostilities on the high seas against the United States, their authority and laws. If the other defendants united with him to carry out the hostile expedition, they, too, became leagued with him and the insurgent chiefs in Virginia in the general conspiracy. The subsequent purchasing of the vessel, and the guns, and the ammunition, and the employment of the men to manage the vessel, if these acts were done in futherance of the common design, were overt acts of treason. Together, these acts complete the essential charge of the indictment. In doing them the defendants were performing a part in aid of the great rebellion. They were giving it aid and comfort.'

"It is not essential to constitute the giving of aid and comfort that the enterprise commenced should be successful and actually render assistance. If, for example, a vessel fully equipped and armed in the service of the rebellion should fail in its attack upon one of our vessels, and be itself captured, no assistance would in truth be rendered to the rebellion; but yet in judgment of law, in legal intent, the aid and comfort would be given. So if a letter containing important intelligence for the insurgents be forwarded, the aid and comfort are given, though the letter be intercepted on its way. Thus Foster, in his Treatise on Crown Law, says: 'And the bare sending money or provisions, or sending intelligence to rebels or enemies, which in most cases is the most effectual aid that can be given them, will make a man a traitor, though the money or intelligence should happen to be intercepted; for the party in sending it did all he could; the treason was complete on his part, though it had not the effect he intended.'

"Whenever overt acts have been committed which, in their natural consequence if successful, would encourage and advance the interests of the rebellion, in judgment of law aid and comfort are given. Whether aid and comfort are given—the overt acts of treason being established—is not left to the balancing of probabilities; it is a conclusion of law.

" If the defendants obtained a letter of marque from the president of the so-called Confederate States, the fact does not exempt them from prosecution in the tribunals of the country for the acts charged in the indictment. The existence of civil war, and the application of the rules of war to particular cases, under special circumstances, do not imply the renunciation or waiver by the Federal Government of any of its municipal rights as sovereign toward the citizens of the seceded States.

"As matter of policy and humanity, the government of the United States has treated the citizens of the so-called Confederate States, taken in open hostilities, as prisoners of war, and has thus exempted them from trial for violation of its municipal laws. But the Courts have no such dispensing power; they can only enforce the laws as they find them upon the statute-book. They cannot treat any new government as having authority to issue commissions or letters of marque which will afford protection to its citizens until the legislative and executive departments have recognized its existence. The judiciary follows the political department of the government in these particulars. By that department the rules of war have been applied only in special cases; and, notwithstanding the application, Congress has legislated in numerous instances for the punishment of all parties engaged in or rendering assistance in any way to the existing rebellion. The law under which the defendants are indicted was passed after captives in war had been treated and exchanged as prisoners of war in numerous instances.

" But even if full belligerent rights had been conceded to the Confederate States, such rights could not be invoked for the protection of persons entering within the limits of States which have never seceded, and secretly getting up hostile expeditions against our government and its authority and laws. The local and temporary allegiance which every one—citizen or alien—owes to the government under which he at the time lives, is sufficient to subject him to the penalties of treason."—(4 Sawyer, 470-4.)

The last part of this charge is undoubtedly correct, for whatever protection the concession of belligerent rights may have given to persons engaged in actual warfare on the Confederate side, none could be allowed to persons in league with them, engaged in getting up hostile expeditions within the limits of the States which had never seceded. Under no aspect of the law of belligerency could they be exempted from prosecution. The extent of protection which the concession of belligerent rights gives to insurgents against an established government is stated by the Supreme Court in Williams vs. Bruffy (6 Otto, 187).— See above, page 94.

Happily the great Act of Amnesty promulgated by President Johnson on the 25th of December, 1868, has removed all ground for legal accusation against parties engaged in the great insurrection against the government of the United States.—See language of Burke cited above at page 60, and comments upon it.

The jury found the defendants guilty, and sentence imposing both fine and imprisonment was pronounced upon them. Rubery was subsequently pardoned by President Lincoln at the request of John Bright of England. The other defendants were subsequently released from imprisonment upon taking the oath prescribed in the proclamation of President Lincoln of December 8, 1863, and giving a bond for their future good behavior.

UNITED STATES VS. KNOWLES.

This case was also one of special interest. It was tried in the Circuit Court in 1864. Knowles was the captain of the American ship " Charger," and in April of that year one of its sailors, by the name of Swainson, whilst on the royal yard engaged in furling sail, accidentally fell overboard. The captain refused to stop the vessel and lower either of its boats—it had three—or to make any attempt to rescue the man, and he was drowned. An indictment was accordingly found against him, alleging that the sailor might have been saved had the captain stopped his ship and lowered either of its boats and made any attempt to rescue him, and that for his negligence and omission in this respect the sailor was drowned, and hence charging the captain with murder. At the outset of the trial the public prosecutor only asked a verdict for manslaughter.

Judge Field, after stating the nature of the indictment, charged the jury as follows:

"As you will thus perceive, gentleman, the charge is that the death of Swainson was occasioned by the willful omission of the defendant to stop the ship, lower the boats, and rescue him, or to make any attempt for his rescue. In the majority of cases where manslaughter is charged, the death alleged has resulted from direct violence on the part of the accused. Here the death is charged to have been occasioned by the willful omission of the defendant to perform a plain duty.

" There may be, in the omission to do a particular act under some circumstances, as well as in the commission of an act, such a degree of criminality as to render the offender liable to indictment for manslaughter. The law on the subject is this : that where death is the direct and immediate result of the omission of a party to perform a plain duty imposed upon him by law or contract, he is guilty of a felonious homicide. There are several particulars in this statement of the law to which your attention is directed.

" In the first place, the duty omitted must be a plain duty, by which I mean that it must be one that does not admit of any discussion as to its obligatory force; one upon which different minds must agree, or will generally agree. Where doubt exists as to what conduct should be pursued in a particular case, and intelligent men differ as to the proper action to be had, the law does not impute guilt to any one, if, from omission to adopt one course instead of another, fatal consequences follow to others. The law does not enter into any consideration of the reasons governing the conduct of men in such cases, to determine whether they are culpable or not.

" In the second place, the duty omitted must be one which the party is bound to perform by law or contract, and not one the performance of which depends simply upon his humanity, or his sense of justice or propriety. In the absence of such obligations it is undoubtedly the moral duty of every person to extend to others assistance when in danger; to throw, for instance, a plank or rope to a drowning man, or make other efforts for his rescue, and if such efforts should be omitted by any one when they could be made without imperiling his own life, he would, by his conduct, draw upon himself the just censure and reproach of good men; but this is the only punishment to which he would be subjected by society.

" In the third place, the death which follows the duty omitted must be the immediate and direct consequence of the omission. There are many cases in the reports in which this doctrine of liability for negligence resulting in death is asserted. In one case a defendant had been employed to give signals to railway trains of obstructions on the road. Having, on one occasion, neglected to give the proper signal of an obstruction, a collision followed, causing the death of a passenger. The negligence was held to be criminal and the defendant was convicted of manslaughter.— (Regina vs. Pargeter, 3 Cox C. C., 191.) In another case the defendant was employed as the ground bailiff of a mine, and as such it was his duty to cause the mine to be ventilated, by directing air-headings to be placed where necessary. By his omission to do this in a particular place the damp in the mine exploded and several persons were killed. The defendant was indicted for manslaughter, and the Court instructed the jury that if they were satisfied that it was the ordinary and plain duty of the prisoner to cause the air-heading to be made in the mine, and that a person using reasonable diligence would have had it done, and that by the omission the death of the deceased occurred, they should find the prisoner guilty.—(Regina vs. Karmes, 2 Carrington & Kirwin, 368.) In these cases you will perceive that the omission which resulted fatally was of a plain personal duty, and that the accident was the immediate and direct consequence of the omission.

"Now, in the case of a person falling overboard from a ship at sea, whether passenger or seaman, when he is not killed by the fall, there is no question as to the duty of the commander. He is bound, both by law and by contract, to do everything, consistent with the safety of the ship and of the passengers and crew, necessary to rescue the person overboard, and for that purpose to stop the vessel, lower the boats, and throw to him such buoys or other articles which can be readily obtained, that may serve to support him in the water until he is reached by the boats and saved. No matter what delay in the voyage may be occasioned, or what expense to the owners may be incurred, nothing will excuse the commander for any omission to take these steps to save the person overboard, provided they can be taken with a due regard to the safety of the ship and others remaining on board. Subject to this condition, every person at sea, whether passenger or seaman, has a right to all reasonable efforts of the commander of the vessel for his rescue in case he should by accident fall or be thrown overboard. Any neglect to make such efforts would be criminal, and if followed by the loss of the person overboard, when by them he might have been saved, the commander would be guilty of manslaughter, and might be indicted and punished for that offence.

"In the present case it is not pretended that any efforts were made by the defendant to save Swainson, nor is the law as to the duty of the commander, and his liability for omitting to perform it under the conditions stated, controverted by counsel. The positions taken in the defence of the accused are: 1. That Swainson was killed by his fall from the yard; 2. That if not killed it would have been impossible to save him in the existing condition of the sea and weather; 3. That to have attempted to save him would have endangered the safety of the ship and the lives of the crew. If, in your judgment, either of these positions is sustained by the evidence, the defendant is entitled to an acquittal.

"The killing of Swainson from his fall is alleged from the distance he must have fallen, and the absence of any appearance of subsequent motion on his part in the water. The distance was one hundred and ten feet, as stated by one of the witnesses from actual measurement. Another witness says that Swainson struck the water on his back or front:

21

a third witness states that the feet of Swainson struck the water first, but the position of the body was somewhat inclined. From the noise made in falling the mate was of the opinion that Swainson struck the channels on the side of the vessel in his fall. You can judge of the probabilities of the man being alive after a fall of this kind. If you believe from the evidence that he was killed by the fall, that is an end of this case, and you need not pursue your inquiries further. But more, if you have any reasonable doubt, by which I mean a doubt founded upon a consideration of all the circumstances and evidence, and not a doubt resting upon mere conjecture or speculation, whether he was killed by the fall, you need not go further. The prosecution proceeds upon the ground that he was not thus killed, the district attorney relying upon the general presumption of the law that a man known to be alive at a particular time continues alive until his death is proved, or some event is shown to have happened to him which usually, in the experience of men, proves fatal. The fall of a person into the sea from a height of one hundred and ten feet is not an event which is necessarily fatal. Nor can it be said that in the experience of men it is usually so. Its effect depends very much, if not entirely, upon the manner in which the party falling strikes the water, and the existence of obstacles breaking the force of the fall. The fact, therefore, that the fall of Swainson appears in the evidence presented by the prosecution, does not change the presumption of the law which I have mentioned. The burden still remains upon the defendant of showing that the fall was fatal, or of showing such attending circumstances as to create a reasonable doubt whether such was not the fact. You will not take the fall itself as conclusive on this point, but will consider it in connection with the evidence of the manner in which the party fell, and particularly of the manner in which he struck the water in falling.

"If you are satisfied that the fall was not immediately fatal, the next inquiry will be whether Swainson could have been saved by any reasonable efforts of the captain, in the then condition of the sea and weather. That the wind was high there can be no doubt. The vessel was going, at the time, at the rate of twelve knots an hour; it had averaged for several hours ten knots an hour. A wind capable of propelling a vessel at that speed would in a few hours create a strong sea. To stop the ship, change its course, go back to the position where the seaman fell overboard, and lower the boats, would have required a good deal of time, according to the testimony of several witnesses. In the meanwhile, the man overboard must have drifted a good way from the spot where he fell. To these considerations you will add the probable shock and consequent exhaustion which Swainson must have experienced from the fall, even supposing that he was not immediately killed.

"It is not sufficient for you to believe that possibly he might have been saved. To find the defendant guilty you must come to the conclusion that he would, beyond a reasonable doubt, have been saved if proper efforts to save him had been seasonably made, and that his death was the consequence of the defendant's negligence in this respect. Besides the condition of the weather and sea, you must also take into consideration the character of the boats attached to the ship. According to the testimony of the mate they were small and unfit for a rough sea.

"During the trial much evidence was offered as to the character of the defendant as a skillful and able officer and as a humane man. The act charged is one of gross inhumanity; it is that of allowing a sailor falling overboard whilst at work upon the ship, to perish, without an effort to save him, when by proper efforts, promptly made, he could have been saved. If there be any doubt as to the conduct of the defendant, his past life and character should have some consideration with you.

"With these views I leave the case with you. It is one of much interest, but I do not think that, under the instructions given, you will have any difficulty in arriving at a just conclusion."—(4 Sawyer, 518–23.)

The jury returned a verdict of acquittal.

UNITED STATES vs. SMILEY.

This was another case which excited much interest at the time. It arose as follows: The steamer Golden Gate left San Francisco for Panama on the 21st July, 1862, with two hundred and forty-two passengers and a crew of ninety-six persons. At about five o'clock on the afternoon of Sunday, July 27th, while running within three and a half miles of the Mexican coast, she was discovered to be on fire. An examination disclosed that the fire had originated between one of the galleys and the smoke-stack, and it soon became apparent that it was impossible to save her. She was then immediately headed for the shore, and half an hour later struck on a shelving beach of sand about two hundred and fifty feet from the shore, at a point fifteen miles north of the port of Manzanillo. The surf, which was breaking heavily, soon swung her stern around so that she lay nearly parallel with the beach when she went to pieces. At eight o'clock of that evening all that remained visible were her engines, boilers, and wheel frames. Of the three hundred and thirty-eight souls on board only one hundred and forty were saved. The treasure which she carried, amounting to one million four hundred and fifty thousand dollars was sunk about forty feet inside of the wreck, where in a space of sixty feet square upwards of one million two hundred thousand dollars were subsequently recovered.

Soon after the loss of the steamer was known, a vessel was fitted out by the underwriters to proceed to the scene of disaster and recover whatever was possible of the treasure. The parties employed soon returned and abandoned the idea of finding it. Immediately another vessel, the "Active," was sent by a party of capitalists, on the same errand, but she returned likewise unsuccessful. In December, 1862, another party of capitalists started another vessel, the schooner "William Ireland," fitted with pumps and wrecking appliances and accompanied by sub-marine divers, under the command of Ireland, one of the projectors of the enterprise. The men in this expedition succeeded in recovering $800,000. In August, 1863, they again returned to the wreck and were successful in recovering seventy-six thousand dollars more, when it was believed that any further efforts to secure any additional amount would be unsuccessful. Afterwards, in September, 1863, Thomas Smiley and others fitted out another expedition with a party of divers and a more complete equipment of diving and wrecking apparatus, and returned in January following, having succeeded in recovering $303,000. On a second trip they found thirty-three thousand more ; and with this voyage all efforts in that direction were closed. The treasure recovered by Smiley and others, was carried in wooden boxes, each containing from $500 to $44,000, and was stowed in a room near the stern of the ship. The locality where the greater part was found was about one hundred and fifty feet from the shore of Mexico and in from six to nine feet of water. Beneath the water was an equal depth of sand under which was a hard clay stratum. On this hard pan beneath the water and the sand the treasure boxes lay.

Before commencing his operations, Smiley had obtained from the Mexican government a license to explore for

the treasure lost. On his return to San Francisco, claim
was made by shippers for the specie recovered, but it was
not given up, as the parties could not agree as to the
amount which the recovering company should retain as
compensation for the recovery. The result was that a
complaint was made against Smiley and others of his company, and in March, 1864, they were indicted in the Circuit Court of the United States for plundering and
stealing the treasure from the Golden Gate, under the
ninth section of the act of Congress of March 3d, 1825,
which provides: "That, if any person or persons shall
plunder, steal, or destroy any money, goods, merchandise,
or other effects, from. or belonging to any ship, or vessel,
or boat, or raft, which shall be in distress, or which shall
be wrecked, lost, stranded, or cast away upon the sea, or
upon any reef, shoal, bank, or rocks of the sea, or in any
other place within the admiralty and maritime jurisdiction
of the United States," —- [he] "shall be deemed guilty
of felony, and shall, on conviction thereof, be punished by
fine, not exceeding five thousand dollars, and imprisonment and confinement to hard labor not exceeding ten
years, according to the aggravation of the offence."*

To the indictment a demurrer was interposed on various
technical grounds. As the expedition conducted by Smiley
was an open one, after all other efforts for the recovery of the treasure had been abandoned, and Smiley was
a man of previously good character and standing in the
community, the indictment was generally regarded as per-
secution—as an attempt to coerce the treasure from him
without allowing proper compensation to him and his associates for its recovery. The counsel engaged in the case
appeared to recognize this. It was, therefore, agreed that
the facts stated above should be deemed admitted, and that
upon them the following questions should be presented
to the Court for determination: 1st, Whether the act of
Congress applied to a case where the taking of the prop-

---

* 4 Stat. at Large, p. 116.

erty, of which larceny was alleged, was after the vessel had gone to pieces and disappeared; and, 2d, Whether, if the act covered such a case, the Circuit Court had jurisdiction to try the offence charged, it having been committed within a marine league of the shore of Mexico; with a stipulation that if the Court should be of opinion that the act did not apply to the case, or that it had not jurisdiction to try the offence charged, the demurrer should be sustained. Upon this stipulation the questions were argued. In disposing of them the Court said, speaking through Judge Field:

"We are not prepared to decide that the statute does not apply to a case where the vessel has gone to pieces, to which the goods belonged of which larceny is alleged. It would fail of one of its objects if it did not extend to goods, which the officers and men of a stranded or wrecked vessel had succeeded in getting ashore, so long as a claim is made by them to the property, though before its removal the vessel may have been broken up. We are inclined to the conclusion that, until the goods are removed from the place where landed, or thrown ashore, from the stranded or wrecked vessel, or cease to be under the charge of the officers or other parties interested, the act would apply if a larceny of them were committed, even though the vessel may in the meantime have gone entirely to pieces and disappeared from the sea. But in this case the treasure taken had ceased to be under the charge of the officers of the ' Golden Gate,' or of its underwriters, when the expedition of Smiley was fitted out, and all efforts to recover the property had been given up by them. The treasure was then in the situation of derelict or abandoned property, which could be acquired by any one who might have the energy and enterprise to seek its recovery. In our judgment the act was no more intended to reach cases where property thus abandoned is recovered, than it does to reach property voluntarily thrown into the sea, and afterwards fished from its depths.

"But if the act covered a case where the property was recovered after its abandonment by the officers of the vessel and others interested in it, we are clear that the Circuit Court has not jurisdiction of the offence here charged. The treasure recovered was buried in the sand several feet under the water, and was within one hundred and fifty feet from the shore of Mexico. The jurisdiction of that country over all offences committed within a marine league of its shore, not on a vessel of another nation, was complete and exclusive.

"Wheaton, in his treatise on International Law, after observing that ' the maritime territory of every State extends to the ports, harbors, bays, and mouths of rivers and adjacent parts of the sea inclosed by headlands.

belonging to the same State,' says: 'The general usage of nations superadds to this extent of territorial jurisdiction a distance of a marine league, or as far as a cannon-shot will reach from the shore, along all the coasts of the State. Within these limits its rights of property and territorial jurisdiction are absolute, and exclude those of every other nation.' —(Part 2, Chap. 4, Section 6.)

" The criminal jurisdiction of the government of the United States—that is, its jurisdiction to try parties for offences committed against its laws—may in some instances extend to its citizens everywhere. Thus, it may punish for violation of treaty stipulations by its citizens abroad—for offences committed in foreign countries where, by treaty, jurisdiction is conceded for that purpose, as in some cases in China and in the Barbary States; it may provide for offences committed on deserted islands, and on an uninhabited coast, by the officers and seamen of vessels sailing under its flag. It may also punish derelictions of duty by its ministers, consuls, and other representatives abroad. But in all such cases it will be found that the law of Congress indicates clearly the ex-territorial character of the act at which punishment is aimed. Except in cases like these, the criminal jurisdiction of the United States is necessarily limited to their own territory, actual or constructive. Their actual territory is co-extensive with their possessions, including a marine league from their shores into the sea.

" This limitation of a marine league was adopted because it was formerly supposed that a cannon-shot would only reach to that extent. It is essential that the absolute domain of a country should extend into the sea so far as necessary for the protection of its inhabitants against injury from combating belligerents while the country itself is neutral. Since the great improvement of modern times in ordnance, the distance of a marine league, which is a little short of three English miles, may, perhaps, have to be extended so as to equal the reach of the projecting power of modern artillery. The constructive territory of the United States embraces vessels sailing under their flag; wherever they go they carry the laws of their country, and for a violation of them their officers and men may be subjected to punishment. But when a vessel is destroyed and goes to the bottom, the jurisdiction of the country over it necessarily ends, as much so as it would over an island which should sink into the sea.

" In this case it appears that the ' Golden Gate ' was broken up; not a vestige of the vessel remained. Whatever was afterwards done with reference to property once on board of her, which had disappeared under the sea, was done out of the jurisdiction of the United States as completely as though the steamer had never existed.

" We are of opinion, therefore, that the Circuit Court has no jurisdiction to try the offence charged, even if, under the facts admitted by the parties, any offence was committed. According to the stipulation, judgment sustaining the demurrer will be, therefore, entered and the defendants discharged."

Ex-parte Cavanaugh on Habeas Corpus.

In this case the petitioner, James C. Cavanaugh, was brought before the Circuit Court, in the summer of 1864, on a writ of *habeas corpus*, alleging in his petition the un-lawful restraint of his liberty by an officer claiming to be a deputy marshal of the Consular Court at Nagasaki, in Japan, and praying for his discharge. It appeared that the petitioner had been convicted in that Court, in September of the previous year,—the consul sitting with four assessors,—of the crime of manslaughter in an aggravated degree, and sentenced to five years' imprisonment, at hard labor, in the jail at that port, and that the sentence had been approved by the resident minister in Japan. Upon the request of the petitioner, his sentence was changed to confinement in the State prison of California, there being no provision made by Congress for a jail at the port of Nagasaki. He was accordingly brought to San Francisco, and there he applied for his discharge.

Two points were made before the Court: 1st. That the legislation of Congress carrying out the provisions of the treaty with Japan, by which the Consular Court was authorized to try citizens of the United States charged with the commission of crimes in that empire, was unconstitutional; and, 2d, if constitutional, that there was no provision of law authorizing the confinement of prisoners, sentenced by that Court, in the penitentiary of California, or their detention by the marshal of the United States for that district.

The Court held that the legislation of Congress was constitutional, but discharged the prisoner on the second ground. Its opinion has not been reported. It placed the validity of the legislation upon the treaty clause of the Constitution, holding that that clause authorized treaties upon all subjects of foreign commerce and for the protection of persons engaged in it, and, if necessary, to prevent citizens of the United States, charged with offences, from being

fendants took the legal title with notice of the invalidity of the means by which it was obtained, and should, therefore, upon obvious principles of justice, be required to give it up to the true owners. The bill is filed for the purpose of having a trust declared and enforced, the complainants relying upon the established doctrine that whenever property is acquired by fraud, or under such circumstances as to render it inequitable for the holder of the legal title to retain it, a Court of Equity will convert him into a trustee of the party actually entitled to its beneficial enjoyment. And the bill presents a clear case for the application of this doctrine. The Prefect of Sonoma had no jurisdiction over the estate of the deceased, nor any authority to appoint an administrator. Prefects were executive officers of the government. It was their duty to maintain public order and tranquillity, to publish and enforce the laws, and to exercise a general supervision over the subordinate officers and the public interests of their districts. They were empowered to impose small fines in the enforcement of their authority, and to hear complaints against inferior officers of the district, but beyond this extent they were not clothed with any judicial functions.

" Nor did the Probate Court of Solano County acquire any jurisdiction over the estate of the deceased after the transfer of the papers from the Prefect. The statute of California for the settlement of the estates of deceased persons has no application to the estates of parties who died previous to the organization of the State government. This was expressly held by the Supreme Court of California in Grimes' Estate vs. Norris, with reference to the probate of a will executed in 1848 (6 Cal., 621) ; and the ruling in this respect was affirmed by the same Court in the subsequent case of Tevis vs. Pitcher.—(10 Cal., 465.) The act which provides for the probate of wills also regulates the manner in which the estates of parties dying intestate shall be closed, and is equally limited in its application to cases arising subsequent to the adoption of the constitution. It was obviously the intention of the Legislature to leave all estates of decedents who died previously to be settled under the law as it then existed; and such is the ruling in a recent case of the Supreme Court of the State.—(Downer vs. Smith, 24 Cal., 114.)

" It was, therefore, under color of legal proceedings, every step of which was a nullity, that the conveyance of the alleged administrator was executed. That conveyance enabled the purchasers, and parties holding under them, to present the grant made to Hardy by the Mexican government to the Board of Land Commissioners, and to obtain a confirmation of the claim asserted by them to the land it embraces, and ultimately the patent of the United States. Thus, by means of an instrument purporting to transfer the interest of which Hardy died possessed, but in fact transferring nothing, they obtained a standing before the federal tribunals, and have secured to themselves the legal title from the government of the United States. It is the possession of this legal title, as shown by the confirmation and patent, which precludes the complainants, who are the sole surviving heirs of the deceased, from instituting or maintaining ejectment for the premises, and forces them to seek relief from a Court of Equity. And it is upon the confirmation and patent that the defendants rely to resist the claim of the complainants. Their position is that the confirmation enured to the benefit of the confirmees, and that the patent is conclusive evidence of the validity of their title; that it is the record of the government upon it, which cannot be questioned except in direct proceedings instituted in the name of the government or by its authority.

" It is undoubtedly true that the confirmation enured to the benefit of the confirmees, so far as the legal title to the premises was concerned. It established the legal title in them, but it determined nothing as to the equitable relations between them and third parties. The object of the government in the passage of the act of March 3d, 1851, was to separate the public lands from those which were private property, and to discharge its treaty obligations by protecting private claims. The only question in which the government was concerned, and which demanded its consideration, was what interests in land had the former sovereignty parted with, not what had transpired between private parties subsequent to the action of that sovereignty. And in conformity with this view is the language of the Supreme Court of the United States in Castro vs. Hendricks. —(23 How., 412.) After stating that to accomplish the purposes of the act of March 3, 1851, every person claiming lands in California by virtue of any title or right derived from the Spanish or Mexican governments, was required to present the same to a Board of Commissioners, the Court said : 'The mesne conveyances were also required, but not for any aim of submitting their operation and validity to the Board, but simply to enable the Board to determine if there was a *bona fide* claimant before it under a Mexican grant; and so this Court have repeatedly determined that the government had no interest in the contests between persons claiming *ex post facto* the grant.' And the Supreme Court of California, whilst declaring that the confirmation enured to the benefit of the confirmee, has in frequent instances qualified the declaration by stating that equities between the confirmees and third parties remained unaffected. Thus, in Estrada vs. Murphy (19 Cal., 272), the Court said : ' If the confirmee, in presenting his claim, acted as agent, or trustee, or guardian, or in any other fiduciary capacity, a Court of Equity, upon a proper proceeding, will compel a transfer of the legal title to the principal, *cestui que trust*, ward, or other party equitably entitled to the same, or subject it to the proper trusts in the confirmee's hands. It matters not whether the presentation was made by the confirmee in his own name in good faith, or with intent to defraud the actual owner of the claim, a Court of Equity will control the legal title in his hands so as to protect the just rights of others.'

" The patent is undoubtedly a record of the government upon the title of the claimant. Before it is issued numerous proceedings are required to be taken before the tribunals and officers of the United States, having for their object the ascertainment of the validity of the grant, preferred under Mexican law and authorities, and the identification of the land to which it is or should be restricted. As the last act in the series of proceedings, and as a result of those previously taken, it is issued. It is, therefore, record evidence on the part of the government that the previous grant was genuine, and entitled to recognition and confirmation by the law of nations, or the stipulations of the treaty between Mexico and the United States, and is correctly located so as to embrace the premises described. Until vacated and set aside by proceedings instituted in the name, or by the authority of the government, it is evidence that the title had passed by the grant from the former government, or that such equities had existed under that government in favor of the alleged grantee, as to require or justify the cession of the title, and also that by conveyances, regular on their face, the legal title had apparently passed from the grantee to the claimant; but it is not evidence of any equitable relations of the holders of subsequent conveyances from the grantees to each other or to third parties, for such relations were not submitted to the tribunals of the United States for adjudication in the settlement of private land claims under Spanish and Mexican grants.

" There is nothing in the numerous decisions of the Supreme Court of the State upon patents of the United States which militates against this view. Those decisions, with one or two exceptions, were rendered in actions of ejectment, and only affirmed the conclusiveness of the patents in determining the title of the patentees in such actions, as against attempts to resist their operation by parties holding either under unconfirmed grants, or by alleged pre-emption and settlement under the laws of the United States. It is true, it is said in Stark vs. Barret (15 Cal., 316), that the patent, in recognizing the validity of the grant, upon the confirmation of which it is issued, necessarily establishes the validity of all properly executed intermediate transfers of the grantee's interest, but this is no more than saying that if the grant was valid, a valid title was transferred by properly executed conveyances of the grantee—a proposition which requires no explanation. And the decision in Clark vs. Lockwood (20 Cal., 220), to which counsel refer, only goes to the extent of declaring that in an action of ejectment by the vendee of the confirmee, it is unnecessary to introduce the intermediate conveyances from the Mexican grantee to the confirmee, the confirmation being an adjudication that the legal title was in him at the date of the presentation of his petition to the Land Commissioners. The opinion of the Court expressly limits the conclusiveness of the adjudication to the legal title in that action, and cites from the case of Estrada vs. Murphy to show that equities against such titles may be enforced by proper proceedings in a Court of Equity.

"The action of ejectment deals with legal titles; the patent determines the position of such title, and when the patentee is other than the Mexican grantee, it is evidence that he had made such a *prima facie* showing before the proper authorities of having a transfer of the grantee's interest, as to justify its having been issued to him. In the opinions filed on rendering the decisions in the State Courts cited by counsel, though relating to the legal title, reference is made in several instances to possible equities of third parties, for the purpose of qualifying the general language used as to the conclusive effect of the patents, and to direct parties asserting such equities to the proper tribunal for relief."

The Judge then referred to the cases of Brush vs. Ware (15 Peters, 93), Reeder vs. Barr (4 Ohio, 458), and proceeded as follows :

" The principle upon which these decisions proceed is the familiar one, that where a purchaser cannot make out his title except through an instrument which leads to a particular fact, he is chargeable with notice of such fact.

" In the case at bar the principle applies and is a full answer to those of the defendants who took their title from the patentees. The patent, we must presume, was issued in the ordinary form of such instruments upon the confirmation of a Mexican grant, with a recital of the existence of the grant, the conveyance of the grantee's interest by the administrator, the confirmation of the claim under the grant, its survey upon the confirmation, and the approval of the survey by the proper officers of the government. Such are the usual recitals, and, of course, in the present case they directed the attention of all subsequent purchasers to the examination of the conveyance of the administrator, and the proceedings upon which it was made.

" The position that the complainants are not entitled to relief because by the act of March 3, 1851, all lands, the claim to which was not presented within two years thereafter, were to be deemed part of the public domain, hardly merits serious consideration. It cannot be affirmed that if the sale by the administrator had not taken place, friends of the deceased would not have made efforts to ascertain whether there were any heirs to the estate, and have not succeeded in finding them ; nor that the property would not have been taken in charge by officers of the State as a vacant inheritance, and the grant presented for adjudication to the proper tribunals of the United States ; nor that relief might not have been afforded the heirs when the property was discovered by appropriate legislation. The finder of personal property might with equal propriety justify its retention on the ground that the true owner would never have found it.

" The claim presented by the claimants, resting upon solid principles of justice and right, must be sustained, upon the showing of the bill, unless barred by the statute of limitations.

" The statute of limitations of this State is peculiar. It differs essentially from the English statute, and from the statute of limitations in force in most of the other States of the Union. Those statutes, in terms, apply only to particular legal remedies, and Courts of Equity are said to be bound by them only in cases of concurrent jurisdiction, and in other cases to act only by analogy to the statutes, and not in obedience to them. But in this State the statute applies both to equitable and to legal remedies. It is directed to the subject-matter, and not to the form of the action or the tribunal before which it is prosecuted. Such is the language of the Supreme Court, the only authoritative interpreter of the laws of the State.—(Lord vs. Morris, 18 Cal., 486.)

" The question then is, whether the statute barred the relief prayed, and not whether, as insisted by counsel, the claim on general principles adopted in the administration of equity is a stale claim, although we may add on this latter head that the claim has upon such principles no feature that should bar its enforcement on that ground. The statute provides that certain actions shall be brought within three years after the cause of action shall have accrued, but declares that in action for relief on the ground of fraud, the cause of action ' shall not be deemed to have accrued until the discovery by the aggrieved party of the facts constituting the fraud.' This exception covers the case at bar. The patentees secured to themselves the legal title by the presentation to the Board of Land Commissioners of a worthless document as a transfer of the grantee's interest, and they prosecuted a claim under this document for years. By these proceedings a fraud was committed upon the heirs of Hardy, and not until its discovery did the statute commence running against their rights. The bill avers such discovery within the years prescribed. And the defendants who took title under the patentees are chargeable with notice of the character of the claim under which the patentees secured the title, and, consequently, are precluded from protection as innocent purchasers. They are, therefore, chargeable with constructive fraud in taking title from the patentees, however ignorant in fact of the rights of the heirs, and however honest in their intentions they may have been. 'Another class of constructive frauds,' says Mr. Justice Story, after enumerating several classes, ' consists of those where a person purchases with full notice of the legal or equitable title of other persons to the same property. In such cases he will not be permitted to protect himself against such claims ; but his own title will be postponed and made subservient to theirs.' "

This case is reported in 4th Sawyer, 536. Its doctrine was affirmed in Norton vs. Meader, Ibid., 604.

HALL vs. UNGER.

California passed under the jurisdiction of the United States on the 7th of July, 1846; at least at that date the forces of the United States took possession of Monterey, the Capital of the Department, and from it the authority of Mexican officials over the country is regarded by the political department of the government, as having ceased. In that respect the judiciary follows the action of the political department.—(United States vs. Yorba, 1 Wall., 423.) At that time there was a Mexican pueblo at the site of the present city of San Francisco. This term, " pueblo," has all the vagueness of signification of the English word " town," and is applied indiscriminately to a mere collection of individuals residing at a particular place, a settlement, a village, and also to a regularly organized municipality. The pueblo at San Francisco, was a small settlement, though it was of sufficient importance, as early as 1835, to have a Council [Ayuntamiento], composed of alcaldes and other officers, for its government. When our forces took possession of the town, citizens of the United States were appointed, by the military and naval commanders, to act as alcaldes in place of the Mexican officers.

Under the laws of Mexico, a pueblo—or town—when once recognized as such by public authority, became entitled to the use of four square leagues of land, embracing its site and adjoining country. San Francisco, as a pueblo, asserted a claim to such lands. The Mexican alcaldes were authorized to distribute these lands in small tracts to the inhabitants of the town for building, cultivation, or other uses, the remainder being reserved for commons or other public purposes. The American alcaldes, appointed by our military or naval commanders, at once asserted a right to exercise this power of distribution, and as a consequence they had numerous applications for grants, some of which were from officers of the army and navy.

In December, 1848, John Hall, a lieutenant in the navy, received from Alcalde Leavenworth a grant of a hundred-vara lot, that is, a lot two hundred and seventy-five feet square. Whatever title the city, or the State, or the United States may have possessed to the land, was afterwards relinquished by city, state, and congressional legislation.

His title, therefore, if not so at the time, subsequently became perfect.

In 1849 Hall became unwell, and his health was so much affected that he was sent from California to the Eastern States in the charge of a physician. He arrived in New York and joined his family in June, 1849, and remained with them until June, 1851. During this period there were such indications of insanity that, by the advice of his physician and consent of his family, he was sent to the asylum at Frankford. There he remained under treatment for insanity until January, 1854, when he was removed to the State insane asylum, where he died in September, 1860.

On the 27th of December, 1852, whilst he was in the asylum at Frankford, he signed a power of attorney to one James W. Harris, empowering him to sell and convey the lot in San Francisco, and also to appoint a substitute to act for him. This power bore a certificate of due acknowledgment before a commissioner of California, resident in Pennsylvania. The attorney mentioned appointed one David B. Rising as his substitute, and he, as such substituted attorney, executed a conveyance to parties who entered into possession of the premises. Against them the widow and heirs of the deceased Hall brought ejectment for the property, contending that, at the time the power of attorney purported to have been executed, Hall was insane, and incapable, by reason of his insanity, of attending to any business.

The case was tried at the October term of 1867, with a jury, whom Judge Field charged, as follows:

"Gentlemen, I do not propose to attempt any nice or philosophical exposition of the subject of insanity. I should certainly fail if I made the attempt; and if I could succeed, the result would not be of any service to you in determining this case. Any elaborate and extended dissertation, if it were possible for me to present such a one, would only tend to perplex and confuse your minds. I shall make a few plain observations on this subject, and refer to the rules laid down by the authorities to guide you in considering it, and then call your attention briefly to the evidence in the case.

22

"The physicians who have been examined, and the text-writers, declare that it is impossible to give any consistent definition of insanity; that no words can comprise the different forms and characters which this malady may assume. The most common forms, in which it presents itself, are those of mania, monomania, and dementia. All these imply a derangement of the faculties of the mind from their normal or natural condition. Idiocy, which is usually classed under the general designation of insanity, is more properly the absence of mind than the derangement of its faculties; it is congenital, that is, existing at birth, and consists not in the loss or derangement of the mental powers, but in the destitution of powers never possessed.

"Mania is that form of insanity where the mental derangement is accompanied with more or less of excitement. Sometimes the excitement amounts to a fury. The individual in such cases is subject to hallucinations and illusions. He is impressed with the reality of events which have never occurred, and of things which do not exist, and acts more or less in conformity with his belief in these particulars. The mania may be general and affect all or most of the operations of the mind; or it may be partial, and be confined to particular subjects. In the latter case it is generally termed monomania.

"Dementia is that form of insanity where the mental derangement is accompanied with a general enfeeblement of the faculties. It is characterized by forgetfulness, inability to follow any train of thought, and indifference to passing events. 'In dementia,' says Ray, a celebrated writer on medical jurisprudence, 'the mind is susceptible of only feeble and transitory impressions, and manifests but little reflection even upon these. They come and go without leaving any trace of their presence behind them. The attention is incapable of more than a momentary effort, one idea succeeding another with but little connection or coherence. The mind has lost the power of comparison, and abstract ideas are utterly beyond its grasp. The memory is peculiarly weak; events the most recent and most nearly connected with the individual being rapidly forgotten. The language of the demented is not only incoherent, but they are much inclined to repeat isolated words and phrases without the slightest meaning.'

"These common forms of insanity—mania, monomania, and dementia— present themselves in an infinite variety of ways, seldom exhibiting themselves in any two cases exactly in the same manner. Mania sometimes affects, as already observed, all the operations of the mind; and sometimes the mental derangement appears to be limited to particular subjects. An absence of reason on one matter, indeed on many matters, may exist, and at the same time the patient may exhibit a high degree of intelligence and wisdom on other matters. The books are full of such cases. Many of them have been cited to you by counsel on the argument. They show, indeed, a want of entire soundness of mind; they show partial insanity, but this does not necessarily unfit the individuals affected for the transaction of business on all subjects. In a case which arose in the Prerogative Court of England (Dew vs. Clark, 3 Addams Eccl. R., 79), it was said by counsel that partial insanity was something unknown to the law of England. To this suggestion the Court replied: ' If he meant by this that the law of England never deems a person both sane and insane at the same time upon one and the same subject, the assertion is a mere truism. But if by that position he meant and intended that the law of England never deems a party both sane and insane at different times on the same subject, and both sane and insane at the same time on different subjects, there can scarcely be a position more destitute of legal foundation, or rather there can scarcely be one more adverse to the current of legal authority.' In that case the Court cited the language of Locke, that 'a man who is very sober and of a right understanding in all other things, may, in one particular, be as frantic as any man in Bedlam ;' and of Lord Hale, who says, ' There is a partial insanity of mind and a total insanity ; in the first, as it respects particular things or persons, or in respect of degrees, which is the condition with very many, especially melancholy persons, who for the most part discover their defect in excessive fears and grief, and yet are not wholly destitute of the use of reason.'

"So, too, in dementia, where there is a general enfeeblement of the mental powers, there is not usually equal weakness exhibited on all subjects, nor in all the faculties. Those matters which, previous to the existence of the malady, the patient frequently thought of and turned over in his mind, are generally retained with greater clearness than less familiar objects. One faculty may be greatly impaired—the memory, for example—while other faculties retain some portion of their original vigor. The disease is of all degrees from slight weakness to absolute loss of reason. The enfeeblement usually progresses gradually—through a twilight, as it were, of reason, before the darkness of night settles upon the mind.

" It is important to bear these observations in mind, for it does not follow from the fact that mania or dementia be shown, that there may not be reason or capacity for business on some subjects. In determining the ability of the alleged insane person to execute any particular act, the inquiry should first be, what degree of mental capacity is essential to the proper execution of the act in question ; and then whether such capacity was possessed at the time by the party. It is evident that a very different degree of capacity is required for the execution of a complicated contract, and a single transaction of a simple character, like the purchase or sale of a lot.

" The act done in the case at bar was the execution of a power of attorney to sell three lots in San Francisco. The act required no greater exercise of reason than is essential to the valid execution of a will of real property; and the authorities which determine the degree of capacity essential in such cases may properly be relied upon as furnishing the proper rule in this case. And those authorities concur, especially the later authorities, substantially in this: that it is only necessary to the validity of the will that the testator had sufficient mind and memory to understand the business upon which he was engaged, and the effect of the act he was doing. 'He must,' in the language of Judge Washington, in Harrison vs. Rowan (3 Wash. Cir. Ct., 585), 'have a sound and disposing mind and memory. In other words, he ought to be capable of making his will, with an understanding of the nature of the business in which he is engaged—a recollection of the property he means to dispose of—of the persons who are the objects of his bounty, and the manner in which it is to be distributed between them. It is not necessary that he should view his will with the eye of a lawyer, and comprehend its provisions in their legal form. It is sufficient if he has such a mind and memory as will enable him to understand the elements of which it is composed—the distribution of his property in its simple forms. It is the business of the testator to dictate the purposes of his mind, and of the scrivener to express them in legal form.'

"It is true, as stated by counsel, that the authorities generally go to the extent that it requires less intelligence and reason to make a will than to execute a contract; but for the execution of an act of a simple character, not involving complicated details, and provisions, the rule laid down by Judge Washington is sufficiently stringent.

"According to that rule, it was material to the valid execution of the power in this case, that Hall should at the time have possessed sufficient mind and memory to understand the nature of the business he was engaged in, to know the character and location of the property, and the object and effect of the act he was doing; in other words, it was essential that he should recollect that he was the owner of the property mentioned; that such property was situated in the city of San Francisco, and that the instrument conferred authority for the sale of the same.

"In considering this case, it is to be remembered that the law presumes that every adult man is sane, and possessed of the absolute right to sell and dispose of his property in whatever way he may choose—his will in every case standing as the reason of his conduct. Whoever denies his sanity must establish the position; the burden of proof rests upon the party who alleges the mental derangement. And if, as in the present case, the validity of a particular act is assailed, the assailant must establish that at the time the act was done the insanity existed. Testimony as to previous or subsequent insanity will not answer, unless the insanity be shown to be habitual—that is, such as is in its nature continuous and chronic. The fact of the existence of a prior or subsequent lunacy, except where it is habitual, does not suffice to change the burden of proof. The case is, however, otherwise when such habitual insanity is shown to have existed—then the presumption is that the party was insane at the time and the burden of proof rests with those who allege the party's competency.

"Again, in considering whether a particular act assailed for the alleged insanity of the party was valid or not, regard must be had, in the absence of direct testimony on the point, to all the attending circumstances—the reasonableness of the act in itself, and its approval by the family and relatives of the party. The reasonableness of the act, and the approval of the family and relatives will not render the act valid, if the party were at the time insane, but they are circumstances tending to show that the party was not at the time incompetent, and that his family and relatives did not so regard and treat him.

"In this case it appears that the lot in controversy was at the time in the adverse possession of others, and that the Supreme Court of the State had decided that Alcalde grants conferred no title. A sale of his interest, if anything could be obtained for it, under the circumstances, would seem to have been a judicious and a wise step.

"The only testimony which relates directly to the time of the execution of the power is that of Broadhead, the witness to the instrument, and the officer before whom it was acknowledged. It was the duty of this officer to satisfy himself of the competency of Hall before attesting the instrument. As said by the Supreme Court of Pennsylvania in Werstlee vs. Custer (10 Penn., 503), 'No honest man will subscribe as a witness to a will, or any other instrument executed by an insane man, an imbecile, an idiot, or a person manifestly incompetent for any reason to perform, with legal effect, the act in question. A duty attaches to the witness to satisfy himself of the competency of the party before he lends his name to attest the act. Like the magistrate who takes the acknowledgment of a deed, he is to be reasonably assured of the facts he undertakes to verify, else he makes himself instrumental in a fraud upon the public. And, therefore, the legal presumption, always favorable to competency, is greatly strengthened by the fact of attestation by witnesses.'

"Such is the general effect of the attestation of a witness and officer, but whether the attestation in the present case, under the peculiar circumstances in which it was made, can add anything to the legal presumption of competency may well be doubted. It is a circumstance worthy of consideration, whether the Commissioner should have gone to the asylum to take the acknowledgment of an inmate of the institution, with whom he had no previous acquaintance, without information from the officers of the institution, that the patient at the time was in possession of sufficient reason to understand the business, which it was proposed he should execute.

"Broadhead testifies that he went to the Frankford Asylum to take the acknowledgment of Hall, with whom he was not previously acquainted; that he read the power to Hall, and handed it to him to read, and asked him if he understood it; that Hall replied 'perfectly,' or words to that effect, and that the property was valuable, and that he wanted it sold for the benefit of his wife and children. The Commissioner also testifies that he could not have believed Hall was on all subjects of sound mind from the simple fact that he was an inmate of the asylum, but that as to the power of attorney Hall was clear as to what he was giving; that there was nothing in his appearance which led the Commissioner to suppose he was insane, and from the fact that he stated that he wanted the property to be sold, the Commissioner was led to believe he had a lucid interval. The witness adds that he would not have permitted Hall to execute the instrument, and he would not himself have taken the acknowledgment, unless Hall had been of sufficient mind, memory, judgment, and understanding to execute such a paper.

"Aside from the peculiar circumstances under which the Commissioner acted, there is one fact in his testimony, which should be considered by you as throwing possibly some light on the condition of Hall's mind at the time, somewhat in conflict with the Commissioner's own opinion. He states that Hall at first wrote something besides his signature to the instrument. The instrument itself shows that there has been an erasure of something near the signature. The Commissioner states, as his impression, that Hall wrote some other name than his own. This is at least a singular circumstance, if, as stated by the Commissioner, he had heard the instrument read and perfectly understood its purport.

" We will now briefly refer to the testimony produced by the plaintiffs to show the general insanity of Hall at the time he executed the power in question. If he was then insane, and his insanity was general, the instrument was a nullity, and no title could be transferred under it. In that case the plaintiffs are entitled to a verdict. It matters not, if such were the case, what consideration may have been paid to the attorney, or with what good faith the parties may have purchased. The instrument in such case is no more to be regarded as the act of John Hall than if he was dead at the time of its execution."

The Judge then commented at length upon the testimony and submitted the case. The jury found a verdict for the plaintiffs and judgment was entered in their favor. Afterwards the case was taken to the Supreme Court of the United States, where the judgment was affirmed. It is reported under the title of Dexter vs. Hall (15 Wall., 9).

Montgomery vs. Bevans.

In the preceding case an account is given of the pueblo of San Francisco, existing on the acquisition of California, its claim to the use of four square leagues of land, and the power exercised by its Alcaldes to make grants of portions of such lands to individuals for building, cultivation, and other purposes.

On the 1st of December, 1846, a grant was made of a fifty-vara lot, that is, a lot of one hundred and thirty-seven and a half feet square, within the limits of San Francisco, to John E. Montgomery, by Alcalde Bartlett, of that place. Subsequently—in February, 1847—a grant for the same premises was made to Andrew J. Grayson by Alcalde Bryant, of the town.

The question presented to the Court for decision was, whether the first grant ever took effect, and that depends upon the further question whether, at the time that it was made, the grantee was living. On the 15th of November preceding he left the United States vessel-of-war, the Portsmouth, then lying in the harbor of San Francisco, in a launch, with others, and was never afterwards heard from. He was never married and left no will, and by the law of California the father takes the estate of a child dying intestate.

This suit was brought by the father to recover the premises, and was tried by the Court without the intervention of a jury, by stipulation of the parties, in August, 1871. In his opinion deciding the case, Judge Field said as follows:

"The testimony of the plaintiff which proves the delivery of the grant, also proves the death of the grantee, or rather proves that he has not been heard from since the fifteenth of November, 1846, and the law presumes the death of a person who has not been heard from for the period of seven years. The plaintiff claims the premises as the heir of the grantee, and relies upon the presumption of law as to the grantee's death to establish his case. And at the same time he relies upon what he insists is a presumption of law of equal force, that the grantee having been shown to be alive on the 15th of November, 1846, continued alive until the lapse of seven years, when the presumption of death arose. The counsel for the defendants, on the other hand, contend that there is no presumption of the continuance of life during this period of seven years, and that the plaintiff asserting that the grantee was alive on the 1st day of December, 1846, as he must do to give efficacy to the grant of the Alcalde, is bound to prove the fact, and failing to do so his claim of title falls to the ground. The argument upon which this position is based is substantially this: The presumption of death arises from the lapse of time since the party has been heard from; for it is considered extraordinary if he was alive that he should not be heard of during this period. Now, if he is to be presumed to be alive up to the last day but one of the seven years, there is nothing extraordinary in his not having been heard of on the last day, and the previous lapse of time during which he was not heard of becomes immaterial by reason of the assumption that he was living so lately. Language similar to this is found in the opinion of the Exchequer Chamber in the case of Knight vs. Nepean (2 Mees. and Wels., 895), and hence counsel argue that there is no presumption in favor of the continuance of life during the penumbra, or death period, of seven years, for if such presumption prevailed for one day after disappearance proved, it would necessarily prevail for six years and 364 days, and the whole basis upon which the presumption of death rests would become absurd. The cases of Doe vs. Nepean, decided by the Court of King's Bench, of Knight vs. Nepean, mentioned above, decided by the Exchequer Chamber, and the case of In re Phené Trusts, recently decided by the Court of Appeal in Chancery in England, are cited in support of this position.

" In Doe vs. Nepean (5 Barn. and Adolph, 86) the lessor of the plaintiff claimed the premises in controversy by title accruing on the death of one Matthew Knight, who left England for America in 1806 and was not heard of after 1807. The action was brought in 1832, and the question at the trial was whether the action was barred by the statute, which limited the entry of a person into lands to twenty years after title accrued. It was admitted that Knight must be presumed to have died, more than seven years having elapsed since he was heard of, and if that presumption were referable to the time when the last intelligence was received of him, 1807, the action was brought too late ; but if it arose only when seven years had elapsed from the receipt of such intelligence the action was in time. The judge before whom the case was tried was of opinion that the presumption of death only arose at the expiration of the period of seven years, or in other words, that the presumption of life continued until that time, and directed a verdict for the plaintiff, with leave to the defendant to move for a non-suit. After argument upon the motion the Court of the King's Bench held that the lessor of the plaintiff who gave no other evidence of Knight's death than his absence, failed to establish that his death took place within twenty years before the action was brought. Mr. Chief Justice Denman, in giving the opinion of the Court, observed that though absence of a person for seven years without being heard of naturally led the mind to believe he was dead, and therefore was sufficient to warrant a presumption of fact that he was dead at the end of that period, it raised no inference as to the exact time of his death, and still less that death took place at the end of seven years.

" In the case of Knight vs. Nepean, which was another action of ejectment for the same premises, the same question was considered by the Exchequer Chamber (2 Mees. & Wells., 805), and after elaborate argument, the doctrine laid down in Doe vs. Nepean was approved, the Court observing in its opinion that when nothing is heard of a person for seven years, it is matter of complete uncertainty at what point of time in those seven years he died, and that of all the points of time, the last day is the most improbable and inconsistent with the ground of presuming the fact of death. And yet, in the opinion both of the King's Bench, in Doe vs. Nepean, and of the Exchequer Chamber, in this case, it is stated that the law presumes that a person once shown to be alive continues so until the contrary be shown, and that for this reason the onus of establishing the death of Knight rested upon the lessor of the plaintiff. The presumption of the continuance of life, thus stated, is inconsistent with the conclusions reached in both cases. If the presumption of life exists until death is shown, it is difficult to perceive why it should not continue, when death is not shown, until the period is reached at which the law has fixed as the commencement of a different presumption. Clearly there is no rule or principle which can limit its continuance at any period within the seven years, if it be admitted to exist at all.

"In the case of Phené Trusts (Law Rep., 5, Chan. Appeals, 139) the Court of Appeal in Chancery held, after elaborate consideration, that the time at which a person died within the seven years was not a matter of presumption, but of proof; also, that there was no presumption in favor of the continuance of life after the disappearance of the party, and that the onus of proving the death of the party at any particular time within the seven years, or that he survived any particular time within that period, lay upon the person who claimed a right resting upon the establishment of either of these facts.

"In that case it appeared that one Francis Phené had died in January, 1861, having by his will bequeathed the residue of his estate to his nephews and nieces in equal shares. Nicholas Phené Mill was one of his nephews, and the share to which he would have been entitled, if living, was paid into Court, because it was uncertain whether he survived the testator. In 1869 letters of administration were granted to his brother, who presented a petition for the payment of the fund to him. It appeared in evidence that he left his parents' home in England and went to America in August, 1853, and was last heard of in June, 1860. Vice-Chancellor James, to whom the petition was presented, granted its prayer, holding in deference to three previous decisions of Vice-Chancellor Kindersly and one of Vice-Chancellor Malins, that the deceased must be presumed to have survived the testator, upon the general doctrine that continuance of life once shown to exist is presumed until death is proved, or at least for a reasonable period after disappearance; but as he dissented from the decisions, he directed the fund to be retained in Court until the respondents had an opportunity to bring the matter before the Court of Appeal.

"The decision of Vice-Chancellor Kindersly proceeded upon the presumption of the continuance of life for a reasonable period after the party is shown to have been in existence; but Vice-Chancellor Malins extended the presumption of the continuance of life to the expiration of the seven years. In re Phené Trusts (Law Rep., 4, Eq. Cases, 416) the doctrine held by these judges was overruled, and if the opinion of the Court of Appeal contains a correct exposition of the law of England, and we are bound to presume that it does in the absence of any decision of the House of Lords on the subject, that law supports the position of the counsel of the defendants in this case, that the onus rests on the plaintiff of showing that John E. Montgomery, who disappeared on the 15th of November, 1846, and of whom no intelligence has since been received, was alive on the 1st day of December, 1846, when the grant of the Alcalde was made.

"But the law as thus declared in England is different from the law which obtains in this country, so far as it relates to the presumption of the continuance of life. Here, as in England, the law presumes that a person who has not been heard of for seven years is dead, but here the law, differing in this respect from the law of England, presumes that a party once shown to be alive continues alive until his death is proved, or the rule of law applies by which such death is presumed to have occurred, that is, at the end of seven years. And this presumption of life is received, in the absence of any countervailing testimony, as conclusive of the fact, establishing it for the purposes of determining the rights of parties as fully as the most positive proof. The only exception to the operation of this presumption is when it conflicts with the presumption of innocence, in which case the latter prevails.

"This rule is much more convenient in its application, and works greater justice than the doctrine which obtains in England, according to the decision in Phené Trusts, that the existence of life at any particular time within the seven years, when the fact becomes material, must be affirmatively proved. In numerous cases such proof can never be made, and property must often remain undistributed, or be distributed between the contestants, not according to any settled principles, but according as one or the other happens to be the moving party in Court. Take this case by way of illustration: A man goes to sea on the first of January, 1860, and is never heard of again; his father makes his will and dies on the first of July of the same year, leaving to him a portion of his property, and the residue to a distant relative. If persons claiming under the missing man apply for the legacy to him, they must fail, for they cannot prove that he survived the testator. On the other hand, if the residuary legatee applies for the property on the ground that the legacy to the missing man has lapsed, he must fail, for he cannot prove that the missing man died before the testator; and the proof of his death in such case would be essential to the establishment of the applicant's right.

"Nor is this rule, as to the presumption of the continuance of life up to the end of the seven years, justly subject to the criticism of counsel, that it renders absurd the whole basis on which the presumption of death rests. There must be some period when the presumption of the continuance of life ceases and the presumption of death supervenes; and as in all cases where the existence of a presumption arising from the lapse of time is limited by a fixed period, it is difficult to assign any valid reason why one presumption should cease at the particular time designated, rather than at some other period, and a different presumption arise, except that it is important that some time when the change takes place should be permanently established.

"It would be difficult to assign any other reason than this for the presumption, which obtains in some States, that a debt is paid, upon which no action has been brought, after the lapse of six years; and that it is unpaid up to the last hour of the sixth year. The presumption of payment arising from the lapse of time without action, it might be said with equal propriety, as in the present case with respect to the presumption of life to the end of the seventh year, that if the presumption of non-payment extends up to the end of the sixth year, it renders absurd the whole basis upon which the presumption of payment rests. So it would be difficult to give any sufficient reason for admitting in evidence a deed thirty years old without other proof of its execution than what is apparent on its face, and at the same time refusing admission to a deed except upon full proof of its execution, which has existed thirty years less one day— except that it is important that the period should be fixed on which the presumption arises which supersedes the necessity of direct proof.

"But it is unnecessary to pursue the subject further. I am of opinion that the plaintiff could rely, in the first instance, upon the presumption of law as to the continuance of life to establish the fact that John E. Montgomery was alive on the 1st day of December, 1846, when the grant of the Alcalde was issued. This leaves the plaintiff with a *prima facie* case for recovery.

"We turn now to the consideration of the affirmative positions of the defendants. They contend that the evidence in the case rebuts the presumption of the continuance of life, and warrants the inference that the alleged grantee died previous to the 1st of December, 1846, and that the action is barred by the statute of limitations.

"It appears from the evidence that about the middle of November, 1846, a launch from the United States sloop-of-war *Warren*, a vessel then lying in the harbor of San Francisco, and, with the *Portsmouth*, under the command of Captain Montgomery, sailed from the harbor with ten seamen and two officers for Sutter's Fort on the Sacramento River. The two sons of Captain Montgomery were on the launch—William H. Montgomery, a midshipman and the Sailing Master on the sloop *Warren*, had command of it. John E. Montgomery, who was clerk of Captain Montgomery on board the *Portsmouth*, accompanied his brother. It was understood at the time on board the *Warren* that the launch was sent with money to pay troops of the United States. Sutter's Fort is distant from the harbor of San Francisco about 120 miles, and the voyage between the two places is often made in a single day. An ordinary voyage from San Francisco to the Fort and back would not occupy over four or five days. The launch in this case was propelled both by sails and by oars. From the time it sailed no intelligence has ever been received of it, or of either of the officers, or of any of the men who accompanied it.

About ten days after its departure Capt. Montgomery became uneasy at its absence and sent out several boats in search of his sons and the men who sailed with them, and these boats were kept on the search for about two weeks, but no trace could be found of the launch or men. Of their fate, absolute ignorance has existed to this day, now nearly a quarter of a century since their disappearance. Captain Montgomery himself left the port of San Francisco with the *Portsmouth* on the 5th or 6th of December following.

" Now it appears to me that there are only two inferences which can be drawn from these facts, when considered with reference to the character and positions of the men and officers: One is, that they died during the period within which they should have returned to San Francisco; the other is that they deserted from the service. The latter inference cannot be entertained for several reasons : First, desertion is the highest, and with cowardice, the basest of offences which can be committed by men in the naval service; it has never, it is believed, been charged upon a naval officer of the United States. It can never, therefore, be accepted as an explanation of any act of his, except upon the clearest proof. Second, if the case had been one only of desertion, and not death, it is highly improbable that no intelligence should have been received of any of the men during the long period which has since elapsed. Besides, with respect to the sons of Captain Montgomery, the natural effect of relationship must have led them to break the silence of years, and to seek communication with their father.

" The theory of desertion would require us to believe that officers and men conspired to commit the basest of crimes, besides larceny of the public funds in their custody, and that for nearly a quarter of a century they have not only kept to themselves the secret of their crime, but have so secluded themselves, twelve in number, from observation that no intelligence respecting any of them has reached the public.

" If desertion cannot be received as a reasonable explanation of their conduct, then death must be inferred. Death is the only fact which reconciles their conduct with the presumption of innocence, and with the ordinary conduct which officers and men of the navy pursue while in the public service. It is the sole fact which satisfactorily explains, according to the common experience and knowledge of men, which are proper grounds for judgment, the failure of the officers and men to return to San Francisco, and the absolute silence of the world since respecting them.

" My mind is thus led irresistibly from the evidence to the conclusion, that the officers and crew on board the launch perished on the voyage to Sacramento, within a few days after their departure from San Francisco. They probably perished in the bay of San Pablo, or the bay of Suisun. If the accident which occasioned their death had occurred in the Sacramento River, it is probable that some of the men would have succeeded, from the narrowness of the stream, in reaching the shore; and probably some trace of the launch would have been discovered.

"Finding, as I do, that John E. Montgomery died before the 1st of December, 1846, the conclusion follows that the grant of Alcalde Bartlett, intended for him, was inoperative to pass the title,

" A grant to a person deceased is void. The instrument must be issued to a person in being, or it will be as invalid as if made to a fictitious party. The position of the plaintiff's counsel that, if the grantee were dead at the date of the grant, his heir-at-law took the title, is not tenable. The case of Landes vs. Brant,* cited in support of this position is an authority against it. In that case Clamorgan, the patentee, had died in 1814, and the patent issued in 1845. The Supreme Court said, that according to the common law the patent was void for want of a grantee, but that the defect was cured by the act of Congress of May 20th, 1836, declaring: ' That in all cases where patents for public lands have been or may hereafter be issued, in pursuance of any law of the United States to a person who had died, or who shall hereafter die, before the date of such patent, the title to the land designated therein shall enure to and become vested in the heirs, devisees, and assigns of such deceased patentee, as if the patent had issued to the deceased person during life.', This act, of course, has no application to grants issued by Alcaldes in the Pueblo of San Francisco, whose authority never extended to the alienation of any public lands, but only to lands belonging to the pueblo."

The Judge, also, in this case considered at length the effect of the statute of limitations upon the right of the plaintiff, and still more elaborately upon a subsequent motion for a new trial.

The judgment entered was for the defendant.

UNITED STATES VS. FLINT.—UNITED STATES VS. THROCKMORTON.—UNITED STATES VS. CARPENTIER.

When California was acquired by the United States a very large portion of it, particularly that portion situated in the valleys, which was fitted for agricultural and grazing purposes, had been alienated by grants of the former government of Mexico. It was the policy of that government to encourage the settlement of the country, and for that purpose land was readily granted to settlers, in large quantities, upon their application. By the treaty of cession with Mexico the United States stipulated for the protection of all rights of property of the inhabitants of the ceded country. To carry out this stipulation the act of Congress of March 3, 1851, to settle private land claims in California was passed. The long and tedious proceedings which the holders of such grants were required by it, and subsequent acts, to take, in order to secure a recognition of their claims and the patent of the United States, are set forth in the opinion af Judge Field which is given below. It occupied, in the majority of cases, several years of labor, accompanied in the meantime with anxiety and constant conflict with intruders and squatters. When such patents were finally issued, it was hoped and believed that peace and quiet were secured to the possessors in the enjoyment of the land patented, but this proved to be a delusion. The land plunderers immediately commenced making indiscriminate charges of fraud, perjury, and subornation of perjury against the patentees, and of bribery against all or most of the officers of the government, through whose agency the patentees' title had been examined and established. In some instances their clamors were of sufficient potency to obtain from the Attorney-General of the United States authority to use his name in proceedings by the government for the cancellation of the patents as having been fraudulently obtained. The most notable of these cases were those designated at the head of this chapter. They were heard in the Circuit Court by Judges Field, Sawyer, and Hoffman, in February, 1876. Elaborate opinions were given in them by Judges Field and Hoffman, the former confining himself especially to the case of the United States vs. Flint, and the latter to that of the United States vs. Carpentier. The following is the opinion of Judge Field:

"The case of the United States vs. Flint is a suit in equity, the main object of which is to set aside and annul the decree of the District Court of the Southern District of California, confirming the claim of Teodocio Yorba to the Rancho Lomas de Santiago, situated in the county of Los Angeles, in this State, and to recall and cancel the patent issued thereon by the United States. It is brought by the District Attorney for California, and purports to be on behalf of the United States.

" It appears, from the allegations of the bill, and the record to which the bill refers, that, in October, 1852, the claimant—who has since deceased—presented to the Board of Land Commissioners, created under the act of Congress of March 3d, 1851, to ascertain and settle private land claims in California, a petition setting forth his claim to the rancho in question, and stating that the same was granted to him in May, 1846, by the Governor of the Department; that the grant had been approved by the Departmental Assembly; that juridical possession of the land had been delivered to him by competent authority, and its boundaries defined, and that he was then, and had been previously in its peaceable occupation.

" With the petition, and as part thereof, the claimant presented copies of the grant and act of juridical possession, accompanied by a translation of the same, and prayed that the grant be adjudged valid, and confirmed to him. The Board of Commissioners considered the claim thus presented, and took the depositions of several witnesses in support of it, and in August, 1854, rendered a decree adjudging it to be valid, and directing its confirmation. In November, 1855, a petition was filed on behalf of the United States, in the District Court for the Southern District of California, for a review of the decision, alleging that the claim confirmed was invalid, and the decision of the Commissioners erroneous; that the allegations of the claimant in his petition were unsupported by sufficient proof; and denying that he had any right or title to the land confirmed, or to any part of it. The claimant answered this petition, joining issue upon its allegations, and the Court took jurisdiction of the case, heard it anew, and, in December, 1856, rendered its decree, affirming the decision of the Commissioners, and re-adjudged the claim to be valid. An appeal from this decree to the Supreme Court of the United States was allowed, but the Attorney-General, after some months' deliberation, gave notice that the appeal would not be prosecuted, and thereupon the District Court, upon the consent of the District Attorney, vacated the order allowing the appeal, and gave the claimant leave to proceed upon its decree as a final decree in the case. A survey of the land was subsequently made under the direction of the Surveyor-General of the United States for California, and approved by that officer, and in February, 1868, a patent was issued to the claimant.

" It thus appears that, after a contest for nearly sixteen years before officers and tribunals of the United States, the claimant obtained a patent from the government—an instrument designed to give to its holder security and protection in the enjoyment of the property covered by its terms. All the defendants acquired their interest in the land after the decree of confirmation, and two of them after the patent was issued.

" Nineteen years after the final decree was thus rendered, and eight years after the patent was issued, the present bill was filed. And as grounds for setting aside and annulling the decree, and recalling and cancelling the patent, the District Attorney alleges, upon information and belief: 1st. That the grant and act of juridical possession were made subsequent to the acquisition of the country in 1846, and were fraudulently antedated, and that this appears on the face of the original papers on file in the Spanish archives in the custody of the Surveyor-General of the United States; that the claimant fraudulently omitted to exhibit a complete record of the proceedings and only presented extracts from them, and by this suppression the Law Agent of the United States was misled, the United States deprived of all opportunity to contest the confirmation, and the Land Commission and Court were deceived into a confirmation of the claim; and 2d. That previous to the issue of the alleged grant, and as early as 1840, the claimant had obtained from the Mexican nation a grant of eleven leagues, situated in the counties of Sacramento, San Joaquin, and Amador, which was subsequently confirmed by the Supreme Court of the United States; that, by the laws of Mexico, a grant for more than eleven leagues could not be made to the same person, and that the claimant was, therefore, disqualified from receiving any other grant, and that the existence of this prior grant was fraudulently concealed from the Law Agent of the United States, the Land Commission, and the District Court.

"The District Attorney also alleges in the bill, upon information and belief, that the approved survey is not in conformity with the boundaries given in the diseño, or map accompanying the grant and the act of juridical possession, but embraces a much greater quantity, and was made upon the fraudulent instigation and procurement of three of the defendants. The District Attorney therefore prays that, in case he fail to obtain the annulment of the decree, and the recall and cancellation of the patent, the boundaries of the tract confirmed may be re-established and fixed in accordance with the views stated by him as to the location intended by the grant and act of juridical possession.

"The first inquiry, which naturally arises upon the perusal of this bill, is as to what jurisdiction this Court has to interfere with and review the determinations of the Land Commission and District Court upon the validity of claims to land derived from Mexican or Spanish authorities, and of the Land Department in approving the surveys of the claims confirmed. The questions submitted to the Commission and the District Court were not within the ordinary cognizance of a Court of Law, or a Court of Equity. They related to the obligations devolving upon our government from the concessions of the former government to its inhabitants. How far these concessions should be respected and how far enforced were the matters to be considered; and in their determination the tribunals were to be governed by the stipulations of the treaty, the law of nations, the laws, usage, and customs of the former government, the principles of equity and the decisions of the Supreme Court, so far as they were applicable.

"By the transfer of California from Mexico to the United States, the rights of private property of the inhabitants were not affected. They remained as under the former government. The public property of Mexico and sovereignty over the country alone passed to the United States. This was in accordance with the rule of public law, which is recognized by all civilized nations, when territory is ceded by one State to another. The obligation, therefore, to protect private rights of property devolved upon the United States without any formal declaration to that effect. But, in recognition of this obligation, Mexico obtained from the United States, in the treaty of cession, an express stipulation for such protection. And the term property, as applied to lands and as used in the treaty, comprehends every species of title, perfect or imperfect; 'it embraces,' says Chief Justice Marshall, 'those rights which are executory as well as those which are executed.' The United States, therefore, took California bound by the established principles of public law, and by express stipulation of the treaty, to protect all private rights of property of the inhabitants. The obligation rested for its fulfillment in the good faith of the government, and required legislative action. It could, therefore, only be discharged in such manner, and at such times and upon such conditions, as Congress might in its discretion direct. In its discharge, such action was required as would enable the inhabitants to assert and maintain their rights to their property in the Courts of the country as fully and absolutely as though their titles were derived directly from the United States. Where the titles were imperfect, and such was the condition of nearly all the titles held in the country, further action, by way of confirmation or release from the new government, was essential. With respect to all such titles, and indeed, with respect to all matters dependent upon executory engagements of the government, the ordinary Courts of the United States, whether of Law or Equity, were entirely powerless; they were without jurisdiction, and utterly incompetent to deal with them.

" By the act of March 3d, 1851, the legislative department prescribed the mode in which the provisions of the treaty should be carried out, and the obligations of the government to the former inhabitants discharged, so far as their rights respected the territory acquired ; and thus provided the means of separating their property from the public domain. That act created a Commission of three persons, to be appointed by the President, by and with the advice and consent of the Senate, for the express purpose of ascertaining and settling private land claims in the State. It gave a secretary to the Commission, skilled in the Spanish and English languages, to act as interpreter and to keep a record of its proceedings. It provided an agent, learned in the law and skilled in those languages, to superintend the interests of the United States, and it was made his duty to attend the meetings of the Commissioners, to collect testimony on behalf the United States, and to be present on all occasions when the claimant, in any case, took depositions. To the Commission, every person claiming lands in California, by virtue of any right or title derived from the Spanish or Mexican government, was required, on pain of forfeiting his land, to present his claim, together with the documentary evidence and testimony upon which he relied in its support. The Com-

23

missioners while sitting as a board, and at their chambers, were authorized to administer oaths and take depositions in any case pending before
them. The testimony was to be reduced to writing, and recorded in
books provided for that purpose. The Commissioners were obliged to
hear every case and decide upon the validity of the claim, and, within
thirty days after their decision, to certify the same, with the reasons on
which it was founded, to the District Attorney of the district. The act
provided also for a review of the decision of the Commissioners, upon petition of the claimant or the District Attorney, setting forth the grounds
upon which the validity or invalidity of the claim was asserted. To the
petition an answer was required from the contestant, whether claimant or
the United States. Subsequently, in August, 1852, the act was changed
in this particular, and when a decision was rendered by the Commissioners they were required to prepare two certified transcripts of their proceedings and decision, and of the papers and evidence upon which the
same were founded—one of which was to be transmitted to the Attorney-General, and the other filed with the clerk of the District Court, and
this filing operated as an appeal on behalf of the party against whom the
decision was rendered. In case the decision was against the United
States, the Attorney-General, within six months after receiving the transcript, was required to cause a notice to be filed with the clerk that the
appeal would be prosecuted, or it was to be regarded as dismissed.

" Upon the review by the District Court upon the petition or appeal,
not merely the evidence before the Commissioners was considered, but
further evidence could be taken by either the claimant or the government; so that, in fact, the whole matter was heard anew, as upon an original proceeding. From its decision, an appeal lay to the Supreme Court
of the United States.

" As thus seen, the most ample powers were vested in the Commissioners and the District Court to inquire into the merits of every claim ; and
they were not restricted in their deliberations by any narrow rules of
procedure or technical rules of evidence, but could take into consideration the principles of public law and of equity in their broadest sense.
When the claim was finally confirmed, the act provided for its survey
and location, and the issue of a patent to the claimant. The decrees and
the patents were intended to be final and conclusive of the rights of the
parties, as between them and the United States. The act, in declaring
that they should only be conclusive between the United States and the
claimants, did, in fact, declare that as between them they should have
that character.

" Here, then, we have a special tribunal, established for the express
purpose of ascertaining and passing upon private claims to land derived
from Spanish or Mexican authorities, clothed with ample powers to investigate the subject and determine the validity of every claim, and the
propriety of its recognition by the government, capable as any Court
could possibly be made of detecting frauds connected with the claim,

and whose first inquiry in every case was necessarily as to the authenticity and genuineness of the documents upon which the claim was founded.

"We have a special jurisdiction of a like nature in the District Court to review the decision made by the Commission, and investigate anew the claim. We have principles prescribed for the government of both Commission and Court in these cases, and of the Supreme Court, upon appeal from their decisions, not applicable in ordinary proceedings, either at law or in equity. And, as slready stated, every person claiming land in the State was required to present his claim for investigation. The onerous duty thus thrown upon him was relieved of its oppressive character by the accompanying assurance, that, when his claim was adjudged valid, the adjudication should be final and conclusive.

"On principle, such adjudications cannot be reviewed or defeated by a Court of Equity, upon any suggestion that the Commissioners and Court misapprehended the law, or were mistaken as to the evidence before them, even if that consisted of fabricated papers supported by perjured testimony. The very questions presented by the present bill were necessarily involved in the proceeding before the Commissioners and the District Court, and the credibility of the testimony offered was a matter considered by them. Whether the grant produced by the claimant was genuine, and the claim resting thereon was entitled to confirmation, were the points at issue. The bill avers that the alleged grant was not genuine because it was ante-dated. But the genuineness of the document was the matter *sub judice*, and could not hava been established, and the claim based upon it affirmed, except by evidence satisfactory to the Commission and Court, that it was made at the time stated.

"It is to no purpose in such case to invoke the doctrine that fraud vitiates all transactions, even the most solemn, and that a Court of Equity will set aside or enjoin the enforcement of the most formal judgments when obtained by fraud. The doctrine of equity in this respect is not questioned; it is a doctrine of the highest value in the administration of justice, and its assertion in proper cases is essential to any remedial system adequate to the necessities of society. But it cannot be invoked to reopen a case in which the same matter has been once tried, or so put in issue between the parties that it might have been tried. The judgment rendered in such a case is itself the highest evidence that the alleged fraud did not exist, and estops the parties from asserting the contrary. It is afterwards mere assumption to say that the fraud was perpetrated. The judgment has settled the matter otherwise; it is *res judicata*.

"The frauds for which Courts of Equity will interfere to set aside or stay the enforcement of a judgment of a Court having jurisdiction of the subject-matter and the parties, must consist of extrinsic collateral acts not involved in the consideration of the merits. They must be acts by which the successful party has prevented his adversary from presenting the merits of his case, or by which the jurisdiction of the Court has been imposed upon.

"All litigants are equally entitled to justice from the tribunals of the country; they have equally a right to an impartial judge; they can claim equal opportunities of producing their testimony and presenting their case, and they can equally have the advocacy of counsel. Whenever one party by any contrivance prevents his adversary from having this equality with him before the Courts, he commits a fraud upon public justice, which, resulting in private injury, may be the ground of equitable relief against the judgment recovered. Thus if, through his instrumentality, the witnesses of his adversary be forcibly detained from the Court, or bribed to disobey its subpœna, or the testimony of his adversary be secreted or purloined, or if the citation to him be given under such circumstances as to defeat its purpose, a fraud is committed, for which relief will be granted by a Court of Equity, if it produce injury to the innocent party. Any conduct of the kind mentioned would tend to prevent a fair trial on the merits, and thus to deprive the innocent party of his rights. So, if a judge sit when disqualified from interest or consanguinity; if the litigation be collusive; if the parties be fictitious; if real parties affected are falsely stated to be before the Court, the judgment recovered may be set aside, or its enforcement restrained, for in all these cases there would be the want of the judicial impartiality or the actual litigation which is essential to a valid judicial determination. To every such case the words of the jurist would be applicable: *Fabula non judicium, hoc est; in scena, non in foro, res agitur.*

"The credibility of testimony given in a case, bearing upon the issue, is not an extrinsic collateral act, but is a matter involved in the consideration of the merits; and the introduction of false testimony, known or shown to be so, does not affect the validity of the judgment rendered. In every litigated case where the interests involved are large, there is generally conflicting evidence. Witnesses looking at the same transaction from different stand-points, give different accounts of it. The statements of some are unconsciously affected by their wishes, hopes, or prejudices. Some, from defective recollection, will blend what they themselves saw or heard with what they have received from the narration of others. Uncertainty as to the truth in a contested case will thus arise from the imperfection of human testimony. In addition to this source of uncertainty may be added the possibility of the perjury of witnesses, and the fabrication of documents. The cupidity of some and the corruption of others may lead to the use of these culpable means of gaining a cause. But every litigant enters upon the trial of a cause, knowing not merely the uncertainty of human testimony when honestly given, but that, if he has an unscrupulous antagonist, he may have to encounter frauds of this character. He takes the chances of establishing his case by opposing testimony, and by subjecting his opponent's witnesses to the scrutiny of a searching cross-examination. The case is not the less tried on its merits, and the judgment rendered is none the less conclusive, by reason of the false testimony produced. Thus, if an action be brought upon a promissory note, and issue be joined on its execution, and judgment go for the plaintiff, and there is no appeal, or if an appeal be taken, and the judgment be affirmed, the judgment is conclusive between the parties, although, in fact, the note may have been forged and the witnesses who proved its execution may have committed perjury in their testimony. The rules of evidence, the cross-examination of witnesses, and the fear of criminal prosecution with the production of counter testimony, constitute the only security afforded by law to litigants in such cases. A Court of Equity could not afterwards interfere upon an allegation of the forgery and false testimony, for that would be to reopen the case to a trial upon the execution of the note, which had already been *sub judice*, and passed into judgment.

"These views are in consonance with the adjudged cases. We have looked in vain through all those cited by the learned associate counsel in the Throckmorton Case for anything infringing upon them. In the Duchess of Kingston's Case the sentence of the Spiritual Court was held to be fraudulent and void, because obtained by collusion of the parties. And, in giving the opinion of the judges to the House of Lords, Chief Justice De Grey observed that, although a judgment was conclusive evidence upon the point involved, and could not be impeached from within, yet, like all other acts of the highest judicial authority, could be impeached from without, and that fraud was *an extrinsic collateral act* which vitiated the most solemn proceedings of Courts of Justice.

"In the Shedden Case (1 Macqueen, 535) the question was whether a judgment of the Court of Sessions of Scotland against the legitimacy of the plaintiff, affirmed by the House of Lords, could be attacked in another suit in the inferior Court, and treated as a nullity for collusive suppression of proof which would have established his parents' marriage. The House of Lords held that the judgment could be thus attacked, but that the allegations of fraud and collusion in the case were not sufficiently specific, pointed, and relevant to be admitted to proof. Opinions in the case were given by the Chancellor and two of the Law Lords, Brougham and St. Leonards. The judgment of the House of Lords, said Brougham, was to be 'dealt with in the inferior Court before which its merits were brought; that is to say, not the merits of the judgment, but the merits of the parties who had so fraudulently obtained it—the question being, was it a real judgment or not? For that is *the only question in such cases*, and that is the question in this case.'

"In Fermor's Case (2 Coke, 77) the tenant continued to pay rent to his landlord after he had levied a fine with proclamation to bar the inheritance, and thus kept the latter in ignorance of that proceeding. The tenant attempting, after the expiration of the lease, to hold the property on the ground that the right of the landlord was barred by the lapse of time allowed by statute to make an entry or bring his action after the fine, the Court, upon a bill filed for relief, held that he was not barred by reason of the deception practiced upon him. The payment of the rent was in fact a declaration by the tenant that his relation to the landlord had not changed, and operated as a fraud preventing the latter from asserting his rights.

"Great stress is placed by the learned associate counsel upon these last two cases, but it is evident, from the statement we have made, that the fraud alleged in both cases was an extrinsic collateral act which prevented the complaining party, in one instance, from having the merits of his case considered, and in the other instance, from taking proceedings for his protection. So in all the other cases, extrinsic collateral acts of fraud will be found to constitute the grounds upon which the Court has acted. And on principle it must be so, for if the merits of a case could be a second time examined by a new suit, upon a suggestion of false testimony, documentary or oral, in the first case, there would be no end to litigation. The greater the interests involved in a suit, the severer generally the contention ; and in the majority of such cases the recovery of judgment would be the occasion of a new suit to vacate it, or restrain its enforcement. If the present bill could be sustained upon the grounds alleged, and we should set aside the decree of the District Court, a new bill might years hence be filed to annul our judgment and reinstate the original decree, on the same grounds urged in this case, that fabricated papers and false testimony had been used before us, which eluded the scrutiny of the counsel and escaped our detection. Of course, under such a system of procedure, the settlement of land titles in this State would be postponed indefinitely, and the industries and improvements, which require for their growth the assured possession of land, would be greatly paralyzed.

" For the reasons stated, we are of opinion that there is no ground of fraud presented by the bill for the interference of a Court of Equity with the decree of confirmation rendered by the District Court. It is upon that ground alone that the bill proceeds. It is not a bill of review for new matter, discovered since the decree. A bill of that character can only be filed by leave of the Court ; and that cannot be obtained without a showing that the new matter could not have been used in the original cause, and could not previously have been ascertained by reasonable diligence. It does not lie where the decree in the original cause was obtained by consent, or where objections to the decree rendered were subsequently withdrawn and consent was given to its execution. And it can only be allowed by a court possessing the power, upon a review of the case, to determine the rights of the parties to the property, or in the matter involved, or, at least, authorized to remit the case to a tribunal having adequate jurisdiction for that purpose. The present bill was not filed upon leave ; and this Court possesses no power to determine the right of the claimant, upon any review of the case, to a confirmation of his claim, and the only tribunal to which such a determination could be remitted has long since ceased to exist.

" But there are other and equally potential grounds against the maintenance of the present suit. The Land Commission and the District

Court, though exercising a special jurisdiction, were invested with very large and extensive powers. They were not, as already stated, bound in their decisions to any strict rules of technical law, but could be governed by the principles of equity in their widest scope. The result of their inquiries was to guide the government in the discharge of its treaty obligations. Considerations, therefore, which could not be presented to ordinary tribunals, might very properly be regarded by them.

"After the determination of the Commissioners, if against the United States, the control of the proceedings was placed with the Attorney-General. It rested with him exclusively to determine whether the appeal from the Commissioners, taken by filing a copy of the transcript with the clerk of the District Court, should be prosecuted or dismissed. So also when an appeal was taken from the decree of the District Court, he could, in the same way, direct its prosecution or dismissal. Considerations of policy, as well as of strict right, might be deemed by him sufficient to control his action in this respect. In coming to a determination on the subject, he was not restricted to an examination of the transcript transmitted to him: he could look into the archives of the former government, the reports of officers previously appointed to examine into the subject of the land titles of the State, the records of the Land Department at Washington, and any correspondence existing between Mexico and the United States respecting the title. His power was unlimited, and the propriety or legality of his action in any case was not the subject of review by any tribunal whatever, and it could only be revoked by the appellate Court upon his own application.

"In the case of Yorba, the appeal from the decree of confirmation, rendered by the District Court, was dismissed upon notice of the Attorney-General that the appeal would not be prosecuted, and thereupon the decree became final. The decree was thus assented to by the highest legal officer of the government, specially charged with supervision over the subject. The validity of the decree, and of the grant upon which the claim of Yorba was founded, was thus forever put at rest. From that day it could never be successfully questioned in any form of procedure, or by any tribunal known to our laws. It was a closed question for all time.

"But this is not all. The defendants purchased their interests after the final decree. They are charged in the bill, it is true, generally, with notice of the alleged frauds of the claimant; but how, or where, or in what manner they had notice, is not averred. The vagueness of the allegation gives it only the weight of mere clamor. But, assuming that the defendants had sufficient notice to put them upon inquiry, they had at the same time notice of the decree, which was an adjudication—the highest possible evidence—that the alleged frauds had no actual existence, and that to this adjudication the government, through its Attorney-General, had consented. They had a right, therefore, to rely implicitly upon the decree, and rest in confidence upon the assurance of its finality, given by the only officer of the United States who could question it. They can, therefore, justly insist upon protection in the property purchased ; and no Court of Equity, under the circumstances, would lend its aid to the commission of so great a wrong as the destruction of their title.

" Where the District Attorney of this district obtains authority to institute in the name of the United States a suit for that purpose, we are not informed. There is no law of Congress which requires it or allows it; and we have sought in vain for the power of the Attorney-General to direct it. That officer can, it is true, institute or direct the institution of suits for the revocation or cancellation of patents of lands belonging to the United States, issued upon false or fraudulent representations to the executive officers of the Land Department, or upon their misconstruction of the law. He is the legal adviser of the heads of the executive departments, and if they are fraudulently imposed upon, or have mistaken the law, he can take the necessary legal proceedings to recall the results of their action. But that is a very different matter from instituting or directing proceedings to vacate or recall patents founded upon decrees of a Commission or Court exercising a special and exclusive jurisdiction over the subjects investigated, where the law declares that such decrees shall be final and conclusive between the parties, and to which decrees the Attorney-General in office at that time assented. Those decrees established the obligation of the United States to the claimants under the treaty, and if the 'legislative department, which authorized the proceedings before the Commission and Court, be satisfied with the result, it is difficult to see upon what pretence the Attorney-General can seek to disturb it. If the Attorney-General, by virtue of his office, possesses any such extraordinary power, as claimed in the case, to disregard the action of his predecessor, and to renew litigation at his pleasure respecting the titles of a whole people, upon a suggestion that false testimony may have been used in the original proceedings, the security which the holders of patents from the government issued upon such decrees have hitherto felt in their possessions, is unfounded and delusive. We must have further evidence than is presented to us before we can admit the existence of a power so liable to abuse, and so dangerous to the peace of the community.

" But if we admit that the Attorney-General is authorized to direct the institution of a suit like the present, in the name of the United States, and that the District Attorney has been thus directed, his power in this respect must be exercised in subordination to those rules of procedure and those principles of equity which govern private litigants seeking to avoid a previous judgment against them. The United States, by virtue of their sovereign character, may claim exemption from legal proceedings, but when they enter the Courts of the country as a litigant they waive this exemption, and stand on the same footing with private individuals. Unless otherwise provided by statute, the same rules as to the admissibility of evidence are then applied to them : the same strictness as to motions and appeals is enforced; they must move for a new trial or take an appeal within the same time and in like manner, and they are equally bound to act upon evidence within their reach. And, when they go into a Court of Equity, they must equally present a case by allegation and proof entitling them to equitable relief.

"Although, on grounds of wise public policy, no statute of limitations runs against the United States, and no laches in bringing a suit can be imputed to them, yet the facility with which the truth could originally have been shown by them if different from the finding made; the changed condition of the parties and of the property from lapse of time; the difficulty, from this cause, of meeting objections which might, perhaps, at the time have been readily explained; and the acquisition of interests by third parties upon faith of the decree, are elements which will always be considered by the Court in determining whether it be equitable to grant the relief prayed. All the attendant circumstances of each case will be weighed, that no wrong be done to the citizen, though the government be the suitor against him.

" The bill in the present case not only does not disclose, as already shown, any extrinsic collateral acts of fraud constituting grounds for equitable relief, but alleges that the ante-dating of the grant and act of juridical possession, which form the gravamen of complaint, appear on the face of the original documents on file in the archives in the custody of the Surveyor-General of the United States. If this be so, the Law Agent should have shown the fact by the production of the originals. He should have inspected original documents in all cases where copies alone were offered by the claimant, whether suspicions were excited or not as to their genuineness. The law of Mexico with respect to the alienation of her public lands was well known at the time. It had been the subject of reports to the government by agents employed to look into the grants of the former government, and of consideration and comment by the Courts in numerous instances. That law pointed out the proceedings required for the acquisition of titles of land from Mexico, and showed that a record of them was required to be kept. That record was in the possession of the United States, and should have been examined by the Law Agent of the government whenever any of its entries or documents were the foundation of a claim. He was appointed for the express purpose of looking after and protecting the interests of the United States. The allegation that the claimant was guilty of a fraudulent suppression in not producing all the documents in the archives respecting his title is puerile. He produced all that was necessary to present his claim, and if the Law Agent was not satisfied with them, he should have made his objection at the time. The archives were not in an ' unsearchable condition,' as alleged, until 1858, but even if they had been, the Law Agent could still have insisted upon the production of the originals for inspection.

"After the archives were arranged and the alleged ' unsearchable condition ' ceased, nearly eighteen years elapsed before the present bill was filed, and no excuse is offered for this delay. During these eighteen years, which constitute a period equivalent almost to a century in other countries, great changes in the condition and value of real property in the State have occurred. During this period, the original claimant, who might perhaps have explained the alleged alteration of dates, has deceased, and third parties have acquired his interests, and, it is said, have made valuable and expensive improvements upon the property. Courts of Equity will not entertain a suit to vacate a decree, even in case of palpable frauds, when there has been unnecessary delay in its institution, and the rights of third parties, as in this case, have intervened in reliance upon the decree. Considerations of public policy require prompt action in such cases, and if, by delay in acting, innocent parties have acquired interests, the Courts will turn a deaf ear to the complaining party. This is the doctrine of equity, irrespective of any statute of limitations, and irrespective of the character of the suitor. It is essential that this doctrine should be vigorously upheld for the repose of titles and the security of property.

"It only remains to notice the allegations of the bill with respect to a previous grant of eleven leagues, stated to have been obtained by the claimant from the Mexican nation in 1840, and the allegation that the approved survey of the claim confirmed was not in accordance with the map accompanying the grant, and the act of juridical possession.

"Whether the issue of a previous grant to the claimant for the quantity designated would have disqualified him from receiving a second grant, was a question of law, to be determined by the Commissioners and District Court; and any error committed in its determination could only be corrected on appeal. And the allegation of fraudulent concealment by the claimant of the existence of the prior grant is an idle one in the face of the fact that the Mexican law, of which the Court is bound to take notice, required a record of every grant to be kept, and that this record, with other public property, passed to the United States on the cession of the country. If there was any such grant as stated, so far from its existence being concealed by the claimant, the evidence of its existence was in the custody of the government, and its attention had been specially directed to the document by agents appointed to ascertain what grants had been made by the former government, who examined the records and reported a list of all grants found among them. Allegations thus in conflict with the public records and public history of the country need not be specially controverted any more than allegations at variance with the settled law. A fraudulent concealment by the claimant of a public record, never in his possession, but always in the keeping of the government, and open at all times to the inspection of the world, was a thing impossible. The bill might with as much propriety have alleged that the claimant concealed from the Court one of the public statutes of the country.

"As to the alleged error in the survey of the claim, it need only be observed that the whole subject of surveys upon confirmed grants, except as provided by the act of 1860, which did not embrace this case, was under the control of the Land Department, and was not subject to the supervision of the Courts. Whether the survey conforms to the claim confirmed or varies from it, is a matter with which the Courts have nothing to do; that belongs to a department whose action is not the subject of review by the judiciary in any case, however erroneous. The Courts can only examine into the correctness of a survey when, in a controversy between parties, it is alleged that the survey made infringes upon the prior rights of one of them; and can then look into it only so far as may be necessary to protect such rights. They cannot order a new survey or change that already made.

"It follows, from the views we have expressed, that the demurrer to the bill must be sustained; and as no amendment would reach the principal objection, namely, that the alleged frauds are not such extrinsic collateral acts as would justify the interference of equity with the decree of confirmation, the bill must be dismissed.

"The principal objection to the bill in this case applies with equal force to the bills in the Throckmorton and Carpentier Cases, and the demurrers in those cases will also be sustained and the bills dismissed. The allegation in the Throckmorton Case, that the defendant Howard had notice of the fabrication of the papers from the claimant, given in other proceedings before the Board, and other allegations imputing guilty knowledge to him and to the other defendants, are too vague and general to merit consideration, made as they are in a bill not verified and only upon information and belief. The District Attorney should at least have stated the sources of his information and the grounds of his belief, that the Court might see that the former was something better than idle rumor, and the latter something more than unfounded credulity.

"The defendant, Howard, has filed an answer denying under oath, generally and specifically, every charge against him, but by stipulation on the argument, he is to have the benefit of the decision upon the demurrer.

"As the questions presented in the several cases are of vast importance to the people of this State, the District Judge, whose great experience in the examination of land cases gives weight to his views, will read a concurring opinion with special reference to the Carpentier Case.

"Our judgment is, that the demurrers be sustained in the three cases, and the bills be dismissed; and it is so ordered."

In this opinion Judges Sawyer and Hoffman concurred. The cases were appealed to the Supreme Court of the United States, where the one against Throckmorton was argued and confirmed.—(8 Otto, 61.) The disposition of the other cases followed this decision and were confirmed without contest.

THE EUREKA CASE.

From the time gold was discovered in California, in 1848, until 1866—a period of eighteen years—there was no legislation by Congress for the sale of the mineral lands of the government. The value of property in mines on the public lands, with the machinery and mills constructed either for their development or the separation of the precious metals from the ores—of gold at first, and afterwards of silver also—can hardly be estimated. It amounted, including the mining property in Nevada and adjoining Territories, as well as in California, to several hundred millions of dollars. Until 1866 all this vast property was governed by the regulations and customs of miners as enforced and moulded by the Courts, and sanctioned by the legislation of the Pacific States and Territories. Upon them the miners relied with confidence for protection, and felt absolute security in their possessions. A more just and reasonable system for the development of a great industry was never devised by the wisest of legislators. In July, 1866, Congress passed an act entitled "An act granting the right of way to ditch and canal owners over public lands, and for other purposes," of which Senator Stewart, of Nevada, was the author. This act, in its first section, declared that the mineral lands of the public domain, both surveyed and unsurveyed, were free and open to exploration and occupation by citizens of the United States, and those who had declared their intention to become citizens, subject to such regulations as might be prescribed by law, and the local customs or rules of miners, in their several mining districts, so far as the same were not in conflict with the laws of the United States. In other sections provisions were made for acquiring the title of the United States *to claims in veins or lodes of quartz, or other rock in place, bearing gold, silver, cinnabar, or copper,* where the possessory right to such claims had been previously acquired under the customs or rules of miners, and upon which a certain amount in labor and improvements had been expended. Although the sections of the act of 1866, containing these provisions, were repealed by the act of May 10th, 1872, " To promote the development of the mining resources of the United States," the provisions themselves were in substance re-enacted in the repealing act. The object of the two acts, and also of the act of 1870, amending that of 1866, was not to interfere with the possessory rights of the miners acquired under their own regulations, but rather to secure them by the patent of the United States, and also to prescribe, by general law, the extent of ground which an individual claim might cover. Until 1857, the principal amount of mining was done on placer claims. These became, by that time, so fully worked out as to yield little remuneration to the laborer. More profitable mining, both for gold and silver, was found in veins or lodes of quartz, and mills for crushing quartz were consequently erected in mining districts in great numbers. Large deposits of gold were also found in the channels of old streams, buried under the hills, in some instances to the depth of over one hundred feet from the surface, and hydraulic machinery was employed to wash off the super-incumbent mass and separate the mineral.

Litigation followed the passage of the acts of Congress, in many cases. The meaning of the terms used had to be judicially defined and applied. Miners were not agreed as to what was intended by the terms " vein or lode " of quartz, or other rock in place, bearing gold or silver. The acts gave to the owner of claims on lodes a right to follow, within certain parallel lines, the metal found within them, and this right was of great importance and value and was the occasion of much controversy. A case from the Eureka Mining District, in the State of Nevada, between the Eureka Consolidated Mining Company and the Richmond Mining Company, brought the question as to the meaning of those terms before the Circuit Court for decision, at its July term in 1877. At the trial—which was had without the intervention of a jury—Judge Sawyer, and also Judge Hillyer of the Nevada District, occupied the bench with Judge Field. The case was tried, by stipulation of parties, at San Francisco. There were three principal questions in the case: 1st. Whether the mining ground in controversy was part of one vein or lode, within the meaning of those terms in the act of Congress; 2d. Whether the patents of the plaintiff were valid, notwithstanding the end lines of the locations patented were not parallel, as required by the act of 1872; and 3d. Whether the ground in dispute had been assigned to the plaintiff in a settlement made in June, 1873.

The Court gave an affirmative answer to these questions. Upon the first two, Judge Field, in delivering the opinion of the Court—first stating the case—said as follows :

"The premises in controversy are of great value, amounting by estimation to several hundred thousands of dollars, and the case has been prepared for trial with a care proportionate to this estimate of the value of the property ; and the trial has been conducted by counsel on both sides with eminent ability.

"Whatever could inform, instruct, or enlighten the Court has been presented by them. Practical miners have given us their testimony as to the location and working of the mine. Men of science have explained to us how it was probable that nature in her processes had deposited the mineral where it is found. Models of glass have made the hill, where the mining ground lies, transparent, so that we have been able to trace the course of the veins and see the chambers of ore found in its depths. For myself, after a somewhat extended judicial experience, covering now a period of nearly twenty years, I can say that I have seldom, if ever, seen a case involving the consideration of so many and varied particulars, more thoroughly prepared or more ably presented. And what has added a charm to the whole trial has been the conduct of counsel on both sides, who have appeared to assist each other in the development of the facts of the case, and have furnished an illustration of the truth that the highest courtesy is consistent with the most earnest contention.

"The mining ground which forms the subject of controversy is situated in a hill known as Ruby Hill, a spur of Prospect Mountain, distant about two miles from the town of Eureka in Nevada. Prospect Mountain is several miles in length, running in a northerly and southerly course. Adjoining its northerly end is this spur called Ruby Hill, which extends thence westerly, or in a southwesterly direction. Along and through this hill, for a distance slightly exceeding a mile, is a zone of limestone, in which, at different places throughout its length, and in various forms, mineral is found, this mineral appearing sometimes in a series or succession of ore bodies more or less closely connected, sometimes in apparently isolated chambers, and at other times in what would seem to be scattered grains. And our principal inquiry is to ascertain the character of this zone, in order to determine whether it is to be treated as constituting one lode, or as embracing several lodes, as that term is used in the acts of Congress of 1866 and 1872, under which the parties have acquired whatever rights they possess. In this inquiry the first thing to be settled is the meaning of the term in those acts. This meaning being settled, the physical characteristics and the distinguishing features of the zone will be considered.

"Those acts give no definition of the term. They use it always in connection with the term vein. The act of 1866 provided for the acquisition of a patent by any person or association of persons claiming 'a vein or lode of quartz, or other rock in place, bearing gold, silver, cinnabar, or copper.' The act of 1872 speaks of veins or lodes of quartz or other rock in place, bearing similar metals or ores. Any definition of the term should, therefore, be sufficiently broad to embrace deposits of the several metals or ores here mentioned. In the construction of statutes, general terms must receive that interpretation which will include all the instances enumerated as comprehended by them. The definition of a lode given by geologists is, that of a fissure in the earth's crust filled with mineral matter, or more accurately, as aggregations of mineral matter containing ores in fissures.—(See Von Cotta's Treatise on Ore Deposits, Prime's Translation, 26.) But miners used the term before geologists attempted to give it a definition. One of the witnesses in this case, Dr. Raymond, who for many years was in the service of the general government as Commissioner of Mining Statistics, and in that capacity had occasion to examine and report upon a large number of mines in the States of Nevada and California, and the Territories of Utah and Colorado, says that he has been accustomed as a mining engineer to attach very little importance to those cases of classification of deposits, which simply involve the referring of the subject back to verbal definitions in the books. The whole subject of the classification of mineral deposits, he states, to be one in which the interests of the miner have entirely overridden the reasonings of the chemists and geologists. 'The miners,' to use his language, 'made the definition first. As used by miners, before being defined by any authority, the term lode simply meant that formation by which the miner could be led or guided. It is an alteration of the verb lead; and whatever the miner could follow, expecting to find ore, was his lode. Some formation within which he could find ore, and out of which he could not expect to find ore, was his lode.' The term lodestar, guiding star, or north star, he adds, is of the same origin. Cinnabar is not found in any fissure of the earth's crust, or in any lode as defined by geologists, yet the acts of Congress speak, as already seen, of lodes of quartz, or rock in place, bearing cinnabar. Any definition of lode as there used, which did not embrace deposits of cinnabar, would be as defective as if it did not embrace deposits of gold or silver. The definition must apply to deposits of all the metals named, if it apply to a deposit of any one of them. Those acts were not drawn by geologists or for geologists; they were not framed in the interests of science, and consequently with scientific accuracy in the use of terms. They were framed for the protection of miners in the claims which they had located and developed, and should receive such a construction as will carry out this purpose. The use of the terms *vein* and *lode* in connection with each other in the act of 1866, and their use in connection with the term *ledge* in the act of 1872, would seem to indicate that it was the object of the legislator to avoid any limitation in the application of the acts, which a scientific definition of any one of these terms might impose.

"It is difficult to give any definition of the term as understood and used in the acts of Congress, which will not be subject to criticism. A fissure in the earth's crust—an opening in its rocks and strata made by some force of nature, in which the mineral is deposited, would seem to be essential to the definition of a lode in the judgment of geologists. But to the practical miner the fissure and its walls are only of importance as indicating the boundaries within which he may look for and reasonably expect to find the ore he seeks. A continuous body of mineralized rock lying within any other well-defined boundaries on the earth's surface and under it, would equally constitute in his eyes a lode. We are of opinion, therefore, that the term as used in the acts of Congress is applicable to any zone or belt of mineralized rock lying within boundaries clearly separating it from the neighboring rock. It includes, to use the language cited by counsel, all deposits of mineral matter found through a mineralized zone or belt coming from the same source, impressed with the same forms, and appearing to have been created by the same processes.

"Examining now, with this definition in mind, the features of the zone which separate and distinguish it from the surrounding country, we experience little difficulty in determining its character. We find that it is contained within clearly defined limits, and that it bears unmistakable marks of originating, in all its parts, under the influence of the same creative forces. It is bounded on the south side, for its whole length, at least so far as explorations have been made, by a wall of quartzite of several hundred feet in thickness; and on its north side, for a like extent, by a belt of clay, or shale, ranging in thickness from less than an inch to seventy or eighty feet. At the east end of the zone, in the Jackson mine, the quartzite and shale approach so closely as to be separated by a bare seam, less than an inch in width. From that point they diverge, until on the surface in the Eureka mine, they are about 500 feet apart, and on the surface in the Richmond mine, about 800 feet. The quartzite has a general dip to the north, at an angle of about 45 degrees, subject to some local variations, as the course changes. The clay or shale is more perpendicular, having a dip at an angle of about 80 degrees. At some depth under the surface these two boundaries of the limestone, descending at their respective angles, may come together. In some of the levels worked, they are now only from two to three hundred feet apart.

" The limestone found between these two limits—the wall of quartzite and the seam of clay or shale—has, at some period of the world's history, been subjected to some dynamic force of nature, by which it has been broken up, crushed, disintegrated, and fissured in all directions, so as to destroy, except in three or four places of a few feet each, so far as explorations show, all traces of stratification ; thus specially fitting it, according to the testimony of the men of science, to whom we have listened, for the reception of the mineral which, in ages past, came up from the depths below in solution, and was deposited in it. Evidence that the whole mass of limestone has been, at some period, lifted up and moved along the quartzite, is found in the marks of attrition engraved on the rock. This broken, crushed, and fissured condition pervades, to a greater or less extent, the whole body, showing that the same forces which operated upon a part, operated upon the whole, and at the same time. Wherever the quartzite is exposed the marks of attrition appear. Below the quartzite no one has penetrated. Above the shale the rock has not been thus broken and crushed. Stratification exists there. If in some isolated places there is found evidence of disturbance, that disturbance has not been sufficient to affect the stratification. The broken, crushed, and fissured condition of the limestone gives it a specific, individual character, by which it can be identified and separated from all other limestone in the vicinity.

"In this zone of limestone numerous caves or chambers are found, further distinguishing it from the neighboring rock. The limestone being broken and crushed up as stated, the water from above readily penetrated into it, and operating as a solvent, formed these caves and chambers. No similar cavities are found in the rock beyond the shale, its hard and unbroken character not permitting, or at least opposing such action from the water above.

"Oxide of iron is also found in numerous places throughout the zone, giving to the miner assurance that the metal he seeks is in its vicinity.

"This broken, crushed, and fissured condition of the limestone, the presence of the oxides of iron, the caves or chambers we have mentioned, with the wall of quartzite and seam of clay bounding it, give to the zone, in the eyes of the practical miner, an individuality, a oneness as complete as that which the most perfect lode in a geological sense ever possessed. Each of the characteristics named, though produced at a different period from the others, was undoubtedly caused by the same forces operating at the same time upon the whole body of the limestone.

" Throughout this zone of limestone, as we have already stated, mineral is found in numerous fissures of the rock. According to the opin-

24

ions of all the scientific men who have been examined, this mineral was brought up in solution from the depths of the earth below, and would, therefore, naturally be very irregularly deposited in the fissures of the crushed matter, as these fissures are in every variety of form and size, and would also find its way in minute particles in the loose material of the rock. The evidence shows that it is sufficiently diffused to justify giving to the limestone the general designation of mineralized matter—metal-bearing rock. The three scientific experts produced by the plaintiff, Mr. Keyes, Mr. Raymond, and Mr. Hunt, all of them of large experience and extensive attainments, and two of them of national reputation, have given it as their opinion, after examining the ground, that the zone of limestone between the quartzite and the shale constitutes one vein or lode, in the sense in which those terms are used by miners. Mr. Keyes, who for years was superintendent of the mine of the plaintiff, concludes a minute description of the character and developments of the ground, by stating that in his judgment, according to the customs of miners in this country and common sense, the whole of that space should be considered and accepted as a lead, lode, or ledge of metal-bearing rock in place.

" Dr. Raymond, after giving a like extended account of the character of the ground, and his opinion as to the causes of its formation, and stating with great minuteness the observations he had made, concludes by announcing as his judgment, after carefully weighing all that he had seen, that the deposit between the quartzite and the shale is to be considered as a single vein in the sense in which the word is used by miners—that is, as a single ore deposit of identical origin, age, and character throughout.

" Dr. Hunt, after stating the result of his examination of the ground and his theory as to the formation of the mine, gives his judgment as follows:

"' My conclusion is this: that this whole mass of rock is impregnated with ore; that although the great mass of ore stretches for a long distance above horizontally and along an incline down the foot-wall, as I have traced it, from this deposit you can also trace the ore into a succession of great cavities or bonanzas lying irregularly across the limestone, and into smaller caverns or chasms of the same sort; and that the whole mass of the limestone is irregularly impregnated with the ore. I use the word impregnation in the sense that it has penetrated here and there; little patches and stains, ore-vugs and caverns and spaces of all sizes and all shapes, irregularly disseminated through the mass. . . . I conclude, therefore, that this great mass of ore is, in the proper sense of the word, a great lode, or a great vein, in the sense in which the word is used by miners; and that practically the only way of utilizing this deposit, is to treat the whole of it as one great ore-bearing lode or mass of rock.'

" This conclusion as to the zone constituting one lode of rock bearing metal, it is true, is not adopted by the men of science produced as witnesses by the defendant, the Richmond Company. These latter gentlemen, like the others, have had a large experience in the examination of mines, and some of them have acquired a national reputation for their scientific attainments. No one questions their learning or ability, or the sincerity with which they have expressed their convictions. They agree with the plaintiff's witnesses as to the existence of the mineralized zone of limestone with an underlying quartzite and an overlying shale; as to the broken and crushed condition of the limestone, and substantially as to the origin of the metal and its deposition in the rock. In nearly all other respects they disagree. In their judgment the zone of limestone has no features of a lode. It has no continuous fissure, says Mr. King, to mark it as a lode. A lode, he adds, must have a foot-wall and a hanging-wall, and if it is broad, these must connect at both ends, and must connect downwards. Here there is no hanging-wall or foot-wall; the limestone only rests as a matter of stratigraphical fact on underlying quartzite and the shale overlies it. And distinguishing the structure at Ruby Hill from the Comstock Lode, the same witness says that the one is a series of sedimentary beds laid down in the ocean and turned up; the other is a fissure extending between two rocks.

"The other witnesses of the defendant, so far as they have expressed any opinion as to what constitutes a lode, have agreed with the views of Mr. King. It is impossible not to perceive that these gentlemen at all times carried in their minds the scientific definition of the term as given by geologists—that a lode is a fissure in the earth's crust filled with mineral matter—and disregarded the broader, though less scientific, definition of the miner, who applies the term to all zones or belts of metal-bearing rock lying within clearly marked boundaries. For the reasons already stated, we are of opinion that the acts of Congress use the term in the sense in which miners understand it.

"If the scientific definition of a lode, as given by geologists, could be accepted as the only proper one in this case, the theory of distinct veins existing in distinct fissures of the limestone, would be not only plausible, but reasonable; for that definition is not met by the conditions in which the Eureka mineralized zone appears. But as that definition cannot be accepted, and the zone presents the case of a lode as that term is understood by miners, the theory of separate veins, as distinct and disconnected bodies of ore, falls to the ground. It is, therefore, of little consequence what name is given to the bodies of ore in the limestone, whether they be called pipe veins, rake veins, or pipes of ore, or receive the new designation suggested by one of the witnesses, they are but parts of one greater deposit, which permeates, in a greater or less degree, with occasional intervening spaces of barren rock, the whole mass of limestone, from the Jackson mine to the Richmond, inclusive.

"The acts of Congress of 1866 and 1872 dealt with a practical necessity of miners; they were passed to protect locations on veins or lodes, as miners understood those terms. Instances without number exist where the meaning of words in a statute has been enlarged or restricted and qualified to carry out the intention of the Legislature. The inquiry, where any uncertainty exists, always is as to what the Legislature intended, and when that is ascertained it controls. In a recent case before the Supreme Court of the United States, singing birds were held not to be live animals, within the meaning of a revenue act of Congress.— (*Riche vs. Smgthe*, 13 Wall., 162.) And in a previous case, arising upon the construction of the Oregon Donation Act of Congress, the term, a single man, was held to include in its meaning an unmarried woman.— —(*Silver vs. Ladd*, 7 Wall., 219.) If any one will examine the two decisions, reported as they are in Wallace's Reports, he will find good reasons for both of them.

" Our judgment being that the limestone zone in Ruby Hill, in Eureka District, lying between the quartzite and the shale, constitutes, within the meaning of the acts of Congress, one lode of rock bearing metal, we proceed to consider the rights conveyed to the parties by their respective patents from the United States. All these patents are founded upon previous locations, taken up and improved according to the customs and rules of miners in the district. Each patent is evidence of a perfected right in the patentee to the claim conveyed, the initiatory step for the acquisition of which was the original location. If the date of such location be stated in the instrument, or appear from the record of its entry in the local land office, the patent will take effect by relation as of that date, so far as may be necessary to cut off all intervening claimants, unless the prior right of the patentee, by virtue of his earlier location, has been lost by a failure to contest the claim of the intervening claimant, as provided in the act of 1872.' As in the system established for the alienation of the public lands, the patent is the consummation of a series of acts, having for their object the acquisition of a title, the general rule is to give to it an operation by relation at the date of the initiatory step, so far as may be necessary to protect the patentee against subsequent claimants to the same property. As was said by the Supreme Court in the case of *Shepley vs. Cowan* (1 Otto, 338), where two parties are contending for the same property, the first in time, in the commencement of proceedings for the acquisition of the title, when the same are regularly followed up, is deemed to be the first in right.

" But this principle has been qualified in its application to patents of mining ground, by provisions in the act of 1872 for the settlement of adverse claims before the issue of the patent. Under that act, when one is seeking a patent for his mining location and gives proper notice of the fact as there prescribed, any other claimant of an unpatented location objecting to the patent of the claim, either on account of its extent or form, or because of asserted prior location, must come forward with his objections and present them, or he will afterwards be precluded from objecting to the issue of the patent. While, therefore, the general doctrine of relation applies to mining patents so as to cut off intervening claimants, if any there can be, deriving title from other sources, such perhaps as might arise from a subsequent location of school warrants or a subsequent purchase from the State, as in the case of *Heydenfeldt vs. Daney Gold Mining Company*, reported in the third of Otto, the doctrine cannot be applied so as to cut off the rights of the earlier patentee, under a later location where no opposition to that location was made under the statute. The silence of the first locator is, under the statute, a waiver of his priority.

"But from the view we take of the rights of the parties under their respective patents, and the locations upon which those patents were issued, the question of priority of location is of no practical consequence in the case.

"The plaintiff is the patentee of several locations on the Ruby Hill lode, but for the purpose of this action it is only necessary to refer to three of them—the patents for the Champion, the At Last, and the Lupita or Margaret claims. The first of these patents was issued in 1872, the second in 1876, and the third in 1877. Within the end lines of the locations, as patented in all these cases, when drawn down vertically through the lode, the property in controversy falls. Objection is taken to the validity of the last two patents, because the end lines of the surface locations patented are not parallel, as required by the act of 1872. But to this objection there are several obvious answers. In the first place, it does not appear upon what locations the patents were issued. They may have been, and probably were, issued upon locations made under the act of 1866, where such parallelism in the end lines of the surface locations was not required. The presumption of the law is, that the officers of the Executive Department, specially charged with the supervision of applications for mining patents, and the issue of such patents, did their duty ; and in an action of ejectment, mere surmises to the contrary will not be listened to. If, under any possible circumstances, a patent for a location without such parallelism may be valid, the law will presume that such circumstances existed. A patent of the United States for land, whether agricultural or mineral, is something upon which its holder can rely for peace and security in his possessions. In its potency it is ironclad against all mere speculative inferences. In the second place, the provision of the statute of 1872, requiring the lines of each claim to be parallel to each other, is merely directory, and no consequence is attached to a deviation from its direction. Its object is to secure parallel end lines drawn vertically down, and that was effected in these cases by taking the extreme points of the respective locations on the length of the lode. In the third place, the defect alleged does not concern the defendant, and no one but the government has the right to complain."

The Judge then proceeded to say that both the defendant and the plaintiff, by virtue of their respective patents, whether issued upon locations under the act of 1866, or under the act of 1872, were limited to veins or lodes lying within planes drawn vertically downward through the end lines of their respective locations, and that each took the ores found within those planes, at any depth in all veins or lodes, the apex or top of which lay within the surface lines of its locations; that the question of priority of location was of no practical importance in the case; that this question became important only where the lines of one patent overlapped the other; that here neither plaintiff nor defendant could pass outside of the end lines of its own location, whether they were made before or after those upon which the other party relied; and as the ground in dispute lay within planes drawn vertically downward through the end lines of the plaintiff's location, the conclusion was that the ground was the property of the plaintiff. Judgment was accordingly ordered in its favor. The same conclusion was reached by the Court upon the agreement of the parties of the 16th of June, 1873.

Judgment being entered for the plaintiff, an appeal was taken to the Supreme Court of the United States, and the judgment was there affirmed, the Court placing its decision upon the agreement of the parties. This agreement, however, could not have settled the controversy, unless the lines drawn on the surface mentioned in the agreement, cut through the whole extent of the mining property—that is, unless that property was a part of a lode as defined in the opinion of the Circuit Court. All lines dividing claims upon veins or lodes, must necessarily divide all that the location on the surface carries, and would not serve as a boundary between them, if such were not the case.—(13 Otto.)

The Pueblo Case.

In a preceding case the existence of a Mexican *pueblo*, or town, at the site of the present city of San Francisco— its claim to the use of four square leagues of land—the power of the Mexican Alcaldes to distribute these lands in small parcels to the inhabitants of the town for building, cultivation, and other uses, and the exercise of a similiar power by the Alcaldes appointed by our military and naval commanders after the conquest of the country—have been stated.—See p. 322.

As the Supreme Court of the United States said in Trenouth vs. San Francisco: " Upon the sudden increase of population at that place, following the discovery of gold, the Alcaldes were called upon for building-lots in great numbers, and those officers distributed them with a generous liberality usually attending the grant of other people's property. Numerous persons, however, arriving at the town were not disposed to recognize the authority in this respect of the American magistrates, and finding it less troublesome to appropriate what land they needed than to apply to the magistrates for it, they asserted that the land on which the pueblo was situated belonged to the United States, and, as evidence of the sincerity of their convictions, immediately proceeded to take as much of it for themselves as they could conveniently enclose and hold. Thus the town was soon filled with an active and restless population, making large and expensive improvements upon lands held in some instances under grants from the Alcaldes, and in others by the right of prior possession. Sometimes the same parcel was claimed by different parties; by one party as a settler, and by another as the holder of an Alcalde grant. Disputes both in and out of the Courts, the natural consequence of this difference in the origin of the titles of the claimants, were greatly increased in bitterness by the enormous value which in a short period the lands acquired."—(10 Otto, 251.)

After California was organized as a State, San Francisco was incorporated as a city by its Legislature, and municipal officers were elected to administer its government. As has happened in many other cases, the city contracted more debts than its revenues authorized, and did not always make suitable provision to meet its obligations as they matured. Numerous suits were consequently instituted against it and judgments recovered. Executions were issued upon these judgments and levied upon the land claimed by the city. Those who denied that the city possessed any title to the property, of course paid no attention to the sales; and property of immense value, covering in some instances hundreds of acres, was in consequence struck off at a mere nominal price. What tended to add to the confusion of titles was the different opinions entertained respecting them by the Supreme Court of the State at different times. The first bench of judges of the Court decided that San Francisco never was a pueblo, had no proprietary rights, and that the grants made by the Alcaldes appointed by the American officers after the conquest, conveyed no title. The successors of these judges decided just the reverse, and held that San Francisco was a pueblo, that it had proprietary rights to four square leagues, and that the change of flags worked no change in those rights or the power of her officers to make grants of the land. In the mean time the action of the city authorities increased this confusion. Asserting that there originally was a Mexican pueblo, and that the city of San Francisco had succeeded to its proprietary rights, she made a claim to the lands of the pueblo, as its successor, and when the Board of Land Commissioners was created by the act of Congress of March 3d, 1851, she presented the claim for confirmation. In December, 1854, the Board confirmed this claim for a portion of the four square leagues. Dissatisfied with the limitation of the claim, the city appealed from the decree of the Board to the District Court of the United States, where the case remained undecided until September, 1864—a period of nearly ten years. Pending this appeal, the city passed an ordinance, known in her history—from the name of its author—as the " Van Ness Ordinance," the object of which, as expressed in the title, was " for the settlement and quieting of the land titles in the city of San Francisco." It relinquished and granted all the right and claim of the city to land within the corporate limits, as defined by the charter of 1851—with certain exceptions—to parties in the actual possession thereof, by themselves or tenants, on or before the first of January, 1855, provided such possession was continued up to the time of the introduction of the ordinance into the Common Council, or if interrupted by an intruder or trespasser, had been or might be recovered by legal process. And it declared that for all the purposes contemplated by the ordinance, persons should be deemed possessors, who held titles to lands within those limits by virtue of a grant made by any ayuntamiento, town council, alcalde, or justice of the peace of the former pueblo, before the 7th of July, 1846, or by virtue of a grant subsequently made by those authorities, within certain limits of the city, previous to its incorporation by the State, provided the grant or a material portion of it had been recorded in a proper book of records in the control of the recorder of the county previous to April 3d, 1851. In March, 1858, the Legislature ratified and confirmed this ordinance. Its framers, however, being in doubt whether the city had any title to the lands claimed by her as successor of the Mexican pueblo, provided for the ultimate determination of the question either way; and directed, on the assumption that the land was public land, that an entry of it be made at the proper land office of the United States, and declared that whatever title might be acquired, either on a confirmation of the pueblo claim, or through the action of the land officers, should inure to the benefit of parties in possession, within the meaning of the ordinance.

As was to be expected, large numbers of suits were brought in the Courts, by the holders of the conflicting titles, to test their validity. These suits were carried to the Supreme Court of the State, where various decisions were rendered, not always consistent with each other, nor always meeting the entire approval of the profession, but generally holding that a Mexican pueblo, with an interest of some sort in the lands, had existed at the site of the city on the acquisition of the country, and that such lands, like other property of the city not used for public purposes, were vendible on execution. Finally a test case—Hart vs. Burnett—presenting the different titles for adjudication, found its way to that Court. It was there elaborately argued by able and learned counsel, and the whole law of Mexico upon the subject of pueblos, their organization, rights, and powers, the nature of their proprietary rights, the effect of the change of sovereignty, the powers of alcaldes in the disposition of municipal lands, and the effect of the Van Ness Ordinance, and the confirmatory act of the Legislature, were thoroughly and fully presented. The magnitude of the interests involved, the previous uncertainty in relation to the law, and the character and erudition of the counsel employed, attracted very general attention to the case.

In April, 1860, the opinion of the Court, prepared by Judge Baldwin and concurred in by Judge Field, was delivered. That opinion is remarkable for the exhaustive learning and research it exhibits upon the points discussed. The law was established with such precision and clearness that its doctrines have never since been successfully assailed; on the contrary, they have been repeatedly reaffirmed by the Supreme Court of the State and often recognized as sound by the Supreme Court of the United States. The Court held, among other things, that at the date of the conquest and cession of the country, San Francisco was a pueblo; that, as such, it had proprietary rights in certain lands which were held in trust for the public uses of the city and for its inhabitants, and were not subject to seizure and sale under execution; that such portions as were not set apart for public uses could be granted in lots to its inhabitants by its ayuntamiento, or alcaldes, or other officers succeeding to their powers; that the trusts upon which these lands were held were public and political in their nature, and as such had been, since the organization of the State, under the control of the Legislature; that the Van Ness Ordinance and the confirmatory act of the Legislature vested in the persons therein described a title to the lands mentioned, and that the city held the lands, not already disposed of by herself, unaffected by sheriff sales under executions against her.

By this decision the title of the city to her public squares, streets, sites for school-houses, city hall, engine-houses, and other public buildings belonging to the corporation, and other lots reserved by the ordinance for public uses, was confirmed and established; and all persons occupying lands, not thus reserved, were quieted in their possessions, so far as any claim of the city or State was concerned. Property of vast value, to be estimated only by millions, was thus secured to the city or to persons in possession.

In order to a complete settlement of the title, however, it was still necessary to obtain the action of the tribunals of the United States upon the claim made by the city as successor of the pueblo. As already stated, the appeal to the District Court from the decision of the Commissioners had not been acted upon.

By the 5th section of the act of Congress, entitled "An act to expedite the settlement of titles to lands in the State of California," passed July 1, 1864, all the right and title of the United States to land within the corporate limits of San Francisco—as defined by its charter of 1851, with certain exceptions — were relinquished and granted to the city and its successors for the uses and purposes specified in the Van Ness Ordinance.* Thus, whatever was essential to perfect the title to parties holding under that ordinance, and to the city, was completed. That section was drawn by Judge Field. The exceptions enumerated related to lands previously or then occupied by the United States for military, naval, and other purposes, or such parcels as might be subsequently

---

* 13 Stats. at Large, 333.

designated for that purpose by the President within a year after the return to the Land Office of an approved plat of the city limits. But the claim of the city—as successor of the pueblo—was for a much greater quantity than the land embraced within the charter limits of 1851, and, by the 4th section of the act mentioned, authority was given to transfer the case pending in the District Court to the Circuit Court of the United States. The case was accordingly transferred in September, 1864, and it was decided in October of that year.

In deciding the case Judge Field gave the following opinion :

" This case comes before this Court upon a transfer from the District Court under the act of Congress of July 1st, 1864, 'to expedite the settlement of titles to lands in the State of California.' It was in the District Court on appeal from the decree of the Board of Land Commissioners, created by the act of March 3d, 1851. It involves the consideration of the validity of the claim asserted by the city of San Francisco to a tract of land situated in the county of San Francisco, and embracing so much of the peninsula, upon which the city is located, as will contain an area of four square leagues.

" The city presented her petition to the Board of Land Commissioners in July, 1852, asserting in substance, among other things, that, in pursuance of the laws, usages, and customs of the government of Mexico, and the act of the Departmental Assembly of California of November, 1833, the Pueblo of San Francisco was created a municipal government, and became invested with all the rights, properties, and privileges of pueblos under the then existing laws, and with the proprietorship of the tract of land of four square leagues above described ; that the pueblo continued such municipality and proprietor until after the accession of the government of the United States, July 7th, 1846, and until the passage of the act of the Legislature of the State of California incorporating the city ; and that she thereupon succeeded to the property of the pueblo, and has a good and lawful claim to the same.

" In December, 1854, the Board of Commissioners confirmed the claim of the city to a portion of the four square leagues, and rejected the claim for the residue. The land to which the claim was confirmed was bounded by a line running near the Mission of Dolores, and known as the Vallejo Line. That line was adopted principally in reliance upon the genuineness and authenticity of the document described in the proceedings as the Zamorano document. The spuriousness of that document is now admitted by all parties. From the decree of the Board an appeal was taken by the filing of a transcript of the proceedings and decision with the clerk of the District Court. The appeal was by statute for the benefit of the party against whom the decision was rendered—in this case of both parties—of the United States, which controverted the entire claim, and of the city, which asserted a claim to a larger quantity of land—and both parties gave notice of their intention to prosecute the appeal. Afterwards, in February, 1857, the Attorney-General withdrew the appeal on the part of the United States, and in March following, upon the stipulation of the District Attorney, the District Court ordered that appeal to be dismissed, and gave leave to the city to proceed upon the decree of the Commission as upon a final decree. The case, therefore, remained in the District Court upon the appeal of the city alone, and that is its position here. But the proceeding in the District Court, being in the nature of an original suit, the prosecution of the appeal by either party keeps the whole issue open. 'The suit in the District Court,' said Mr. Justice Nelson in United States vs. Ritchie (17 How., 534), 'is to be regarded as an original proceeding—the removal of the transcript, papers, and evidence into it from the Board of Commissioners being but a mode of providing for the institution of the suit in that Court. The transfer, it is true, is called an appeal ; we must not, however, be misled by a name, but look to the substance and intent of the proceeding. The District Court is not confined to a mere re-examination of the case as heard and decided by the Board of Commissioners, but hears the case *de novo*, upon the papers and testimony which had been used before the Board, they being made evidence in the District Court ; and also upon such further evidence as either party may see fit to produce.'

" But though the whole issue is thus open, the dismissal of the appeal on the part of the United States may very properly be regarded as an assent by the government to the main facts upon which the claim of the city rests, namely : the existence of an organized pueblo at the site of the present city upon the acquisition of the country by the United States on the 7th of July, 1846 ; the possession by that pueblo of proprietary rights in certain lands, and the succession to such proprietary rights by the city of San Francisco. The District Attorney does not, therefore, deem it within the line of his duty to controvert these positions, but on the contrary admits them as facts in the case, contending only that the lands appertaining to the pueblo were subject, until by grant from the proper authorities they were vested in private proprietorship, to appropriation to public uses by the former government and, since· the acquisition of the country, by the United States. He, therefore, insists upon an exception from the confirmation to the city of the land heretofore reserved or occupied by the government for public uses ; and I do not understand that the counsel of the city objects to an exception of this character.

" It is unnecessary, therefore, to recite the historical evidence of the existence of a pueblo previous to, and at the date of, the acquisition of the country at the present site of the city of San Francisco, which is very fully presented in the elaborate opinion filed by the Commission on the rendition of its decision. Since that decision was made the question has been considered by the Supreme Court of the State; and in an opinion in which the whole subject is examined a similar conclusion is reached; and if anything were wanting in addition to the arguments thus furnished, it is found in the able and exhaustive brief of the counsel of the city. The documents of undoubted authenticity, to which the opinions and the brief of counsel refer, establish beyond controversy the fact that a pueblo of some kind, having an Ayuntamiento composed of Alcaldes, Regidores, and other municipal officers, existed as early as 1834; and that the pueblo continued in existence until, and subsequent to, the cession of the country. The action of the officers of the United States in the government of the city and the appointment or election of its magistrates after the conquest, both preceding and subsequent to the treaty of peace, proceeded upon the recognition of this fact; and the titles to property within the limits of the present city to the value of many millions rest upon a like recognition.

" The material question, therefore, for determination. as the case stands before this Court, relates to the extent of the lands in which the pueblo was interested. It is not pretended that such lands were ever marked off and surveyed by competent authority. It is admitted, as already stated, that the so-called Zamorano document, given in evidence, is spurious. The question presented must, therefore, be determined by reference to the laws of Mexico at the date of the conquest.

" As stated by the Commissioners in their opinion, there can be no doubt that by those laws, pueblos or towns, and their residents, were entitled to the use and enjoyment of certain lands within the prescribed limits immediately contiguous to and adjoining the town proper; that this right was common to the cities and towns of Spain from their first organization, and was incorporated by her colonies into their municipal system on this continent ; and that the same continued in Mexico, with but little variation, after her separation from the mother country. And there is as little doubt that by those laws a pueblo or town, when once established and officially recognized, became entitled, for its own use and the use of its inhabitants, to four square leagues of land. The compilation known as the *Recopilacion de Leyes de las Indias* contains several laws relating to this subject. The Sixth Law of Title Five, of Book Four, provides for the establishment of towns by contract with individuals, and upon compliance with the conditions of the contract, for the grant of four square leagues of land, to be laid off in a square or prolonged form, according to the character of the country.

" The opinion of the Assessor or legal adviser of the Vice Royalty of New Spain given to the Commandante General in October, 1785, upon the petition of certain settlers in California, for grants of tracts of land situated within the limits claimed by pueblos, recognizes this right of pueblos to have four square leagues assigned to them. His language is that the grants ' cannot nor ought to be made to them within the boundaries assigned to each pueblo, which, in conformity with the Law Six, Title Five, Liber Four of the Recopilacion, must be *four leagues of land* in a square or oblong body, according to the nature of the ground ; because the petition of the new settlers would tend to make them private owners of the forests, pastures, water, timber, wood, and other advantages of the lands which may be assigned, granted, and distributed to them, and to deprive their neighbors of these benefits. It is seen at once that their claim is entirely contrary to the directions of the forementioned laws, and the express provision in Art. 8 of the Instructions for Settlements (Poblaciones) in the Californias, according to which all the waters, pastures, wood, and timber, within the limits which in conformity to law may be allowed to each pueblo, must be for the common advantage—so that all the new settlers may enjoy and partake of them, maintaining thereon their cattle, and participating of the other benefits that may be produced.'

" But the royal instructions of November, 1789, for the establishment of the town of Pitic, in the province of Sonora, is conclusive as to the right of pueblos in California under the laws of Spain.

" The instructions were made applicable to all new towns that should be subsequently established within the general *comandancia*, which included the province of California. They gave minute directions for the formation and government of the new pueblos, and referring to the laws of the Indies already cited, declared that there should be granted to the towns four leagues of land in a square or prolonged form. They also provided for the distribution of building· and farming lots to settlers, the laying out of pasture lands and lands for the *propios*, the residue to constitute the *egidos* or commons for the use of the inhabitants.

" The general provisions of the laws of the Indies, to which these instructions and the opinion of the Assessor refer, continued in force in Mexico after her separation from Spain. They were recognized in the regulations of November, 1828, which were adopted to carry into effect the Colonization Law of 1824, and in the regulation of the Departmental Assembly of August, 1834, providing funds for towns and cities. They were referred to in numerous documents in the archives of the former government in the custody of the Surveyor-General. The report of Jimeno, for many years Secretary of the Government of California, found in the expediente of Doña Castro made in February, 1844, is cited by the Commissioners in their opinion as removing all doubt on this point. The report is as follows :

" ' MOST EXCELLENT GOVERNOR.—The title given to Doña Castro is drawn, subject to the conditions that were inserted in many other titles during the time of Gen. Figueroa, in which they subjected the parties to pay *censas* (taxes) if the land proved to belong to the *egidos* of the town.

" ' I understand that the town of Branciforte is to have for *egidos* of its population four square leagues, in conformity to the existing law of the

Recopilacion of the Indies, in volume the second, folios 88 to 149, in which it mentions that to the new towns that extent may be marked, to which effect it would be convenient that your Excellency should commission two persons deserving your confidence, in order that accompanied by the Judge of the Town, the measurement indicated may be made, and it may be declared for *egidos* of the town the four square leagues, leaving to the deliberation of your Excellency to free some of the grantees of the conditions to which they are subject. The supreme judgment of your Excellency may resolve as it may deem it convenient.

" ' MONTEREY, *February 8th*, 1844. MANUEL JIMENO.'

" The documents to which reference has been made are sufficient to establish the position that pueblos once formed and officially recognized as such, became by operation of the general laws entitled to have four square leagues of land assigned to them, for their use and the use of their inhabitants. It does not appear that formal grants were made to the new pueblos, though in some instances an officer was appointed to mark off the boundaries of the four square leagues, and to designate the uses to which particular tracts should be applied. But the right of the pueblos and their inhabitants to the use and enjoyment of the lands was not made dependent upon such measurement and designation.

" It follows from these views that the pueblo, which is admitted to have been regularly established at the site of San Francisco, on the seventh of July, 1846, was, as such pueblo, vested with the right to four square leagues of land, to be measured either in a square or prolonged form, according to the nature of the country, excepting from such tract such portions as had been previously dedicated to or reserved for public uses, or had become private property by grant from lawful authority.

" It is difficult to determine with precision the exact character of the right or title held by pueblos to the lands assigned to them. The government undoubtedly retained a right to control their use and disposition, and to appropriate them to public uses until they had been vested in private proprietorship. Numerous laws have been cited to show that the title remained absolutely in the government. The same laws were cited to the Supreme Court of this State when the subject was before that tribunal, and in relation to them the Court said: ' We see nothing in these laws opposed to the views we have already expressed, that the towns had such a right, title, and interest in these lands as to enable them to use and dispose of them in the manner authorized by law or by special orders, and consonant with the object of the endowment and trust. Undoubtedly the right of control remained in the sovereign, who might authorize or forbid any municipal or other officer to grant or dispose of such lands, even for the purpose of the endowment or trust. Such general right, with respect to a public corporation, exists in any sovereign State, and must, of course, have existed in the absolute monarchy of Spain, where the property of private corporations and individuals was to a great degree subject to the royal will and pleasure.'—(*Hart vs, Burnett*, 15 Cal.,

569.) And referring to objections to the theory of absolute title in the pueblo, and the questions which upon that view might be suggested, the Court said : ' There is but one sensible answer to these questions, and we think that answer is given in the laws themselves, and in the recorded proceedings of the officers who administered them, and who must be presumed to have interpreted them correctly. It is, that the lands assigned to pueblos, whether by general law regulating their limits to four leagues, or by special designation of boundaries, were not given to them in absolute property, with full right of disposition and alienation, but to be held by them in trust for the benefit of the entire community, with such powers of use, disposition, and alienation, as had been already or might afterwards be conferred for the due execution of such trusts, upon such pueblos, or upon their officers.'—(*Id.*, 573.) And this view, the Court adds, fully reconciles the apparently conflicting disposition of the laws and the commentaries of publicists respecting the relative rights of the Crown and the municipalities to which counsel had referred.

" In this view of the nature of the title of the pueblo and of the city, its successor, I fully concur; and I am of opinion that under the provisions of the act of March 3d, 1851, the city is entitled to a confirmation of her claim. I regret that the recent transfer of the case to the Circuit Court, and the great pressure of other engagements since, have prevented me from considering at greater length the interesting questions presented. To those who desire to extend their inquiries, the elaborate opinions to which I have made frequent reference, and the able brief of counsel will furnish ample materials.

" A decree will be entered confirming the claim of the City of San Francisco to a tract of land, situated in the county of San Francisco, and embracing so much of the peninsula upon which the city is located as will contain an area equal to four square leagues, as described in the petition. From the confirmation will be excepted such parcels of land within said tract as have been heretofore reserved or dedicated to public use by the United States, or have been by grant from lawful authority vested in private proprietorship. The confirmation will be in trust for the benefit of lot-holders under grants from the pueblo, town, or city ; and as to any residue, in trust for the use and benefit of all the inhabitants. A decree will be prepared by counsel in conformity with this opinion and submitted to the Court." *—(4 Sawyer, 559-67.)

---

* The following extract is from the opinion of the Supreme Court of the State, in Hart vs. Burnett, reported in 15 California Reports :

" On the third of November, 1834, the Territorial Deputation authorized the election of an Ayuntamiento, to reside at the Presidio of San Francisco, to be composed of an Alcalde, two Regidores or Councilmen, and a Sindico-Procurator. This Ayuntamiento, when organized, was to exercise the political functions pertaining to such office, and the Alcalde was also to perform the judicial functions which the laws conferred upon him. This decree was communicated to the Military Commandant by the Governor, on the fourth of November, 1834. An election was accordingly held on the seventh of December, 1834, at the Presidio of San Francisco, and the Ayunta-

A motion for a rehearing having been afterwards made, the decree entered was modified, and as finally settled was not entered until the 18th of May of the following year, 1865. By it the claim of the city, subject to certain reservations, was confirmed to the extent of four square leagues embracing the northern portion of the peninsula, upon which the city is situated, above ordinary high-water mark in 1846, and bounded on the north and east by the Bay of San Francisco; on the west by the Ocean, and on the south by a due east and west line so as to include the area designated. The title, so confirmed, was declared to be in trust for the benefit of lot-holders under grants from the pueblo, town, city, or other competent authority, and as to any residue, in trust for the use and benefit of the inhabitants of the city. From this decree appeals were taken to the Supreme Court, both by the city and the United States; by the latter from the whole decree, and by the former from so much as included the reservations in the estimate of the quantity of land confirmed. This appeal, in the ordinary course of the business of the Supreme Court, would not have been reached for two or

---

miento duly installed. A similar election was held on the thirteenth of December of the following year (1835), at the same place, which was then officially designated as the Pueblo of San Francisco. Other elections of the same character were subsequently held; and there are numerous official documents, of undisputed authenticity, which refer to the 'Ayuntamiento of San Francisco,' the 'Alcalde of San Francisco,' and to the 'Pueblo of San Francisco,' proving, as we think, beyond a doubt, that there was at that place, in 1834, 1835, 1836, and subsequently, a pueblo of some kind, with an Ayuntamiento composed of Alcaldes, Regidores, and other municipal officers. What were the rights of this municipality, and what the powers of its officers, and the extent of its territory and jurisdiction, we shall not now inquire. We here refer merely to the *fact* of the existence, at that time and at that place, of such an organization, whether corporate or incorporate. And that fact is proved by the official returns of elections, by the official acts of the Governor and of the Territorial or Departmental Legislature, by the official correspondence of government officers, and by the acts, proceedings, records, and correspondence of the officers of the pueblo itself. As a part of the evidence of this *fact*, we refer to the election returns of December 7th, 1834, December 13th, 1835, December 3d, 1837, and December 8th, 1838; to the Governor's letters of January 31st, 1835, October 26th, 1835, January 19th, 1836, January 17th, 1839, and November 14th, 1843; to the expediente of proceedings between May and November, 1835, with respect to certain persons obliged to serve as municipal officers of that pueblo; and to the official correspondence between the Alcaldes of that pueblo and the various officers of the Territorial or Departmental Government of California."—(15 Cal., 540.)

three years; and inasmuch as the decree of the Circuit Court was found to give very general satisfaction, and a desire was freely expressed that a final end of this litigation be arrived at on the basis of that decree, Judge Field prepared a bill, which was introduced and passed by the united assistance of the whole delegation in Congress from California and Nevada, quieting the title of the city to all lands embraced within the decree of confirmation. This act of Congress became a law on the 8th of March, 1866. By it all the right and title of the United States to the land embraced in the decree of the Circuit Court were relinquished and granted to the city, and its claim to the land was confirmed, subject to certain exceptions and reservations, and upon trust that all the lands not previously granted by the city, should be disposed of and conveyed by it to the parties in the bona-fide actual possession thereof, by themselves or tenants, on the passage of the act, in such quantities and upon such terms and conditions as the Legislature of the State might prescribe, except such parcels as might be reserved and set apart by ordinance of the city for public uses. Shortly afterwards the appeals to the Supreme Court were dismissed by stipulation of the parties, and the litigation over the source of title to the lands within the city was thus settled and closed. As has been adjudged by the Supreme Court of the United States, the title to the lands within the four square leagues rests upon the decree of the Circuit Court, and this confirmatory act of Congress.

In several cases in the Circuit Court and in the Supreme Court of the United States, in which the opinions were delivered by Judge Field, the positions settled by this decision, viz., the existence of a pueblo at the site of the city of San Francisco at the time the country was acquired by the United States; the possession by it of certain proprietary rights to land, and the succession to them of the present city, are either impliedly recognized or directly asserted. The following are the cases in the Circuit Court:

Grisar vs. McDowell (4 Sawyer, 599); United States vs. Hare (Ibid., 653); United States vs. Carr (3 Ibid., 481); and Tripp vs. Spring (5 Ibid., 219). The following are the cases in the Supreme Court: Townsend vs. Greely (5 Wall., 326); Grisar vs. McDowell (6 Ibid., 363); and Trenouth vs. San Francisco (10 Otto, 251).

The fifth section of the act of July 1, 1864, " to expedite the settlement of titles to lands in the State of California," mentioned above, is as follows :

"SEC. 5. *And be it further enacted*, That all the right and title of the United States to the lands within the corporate limits of the City of San Francisco, as defined in the act incorporating said city, passed by the Legislature of the State of California on the fifteenth of April, one thousand eight hundred and fifty one, are hereby relinquished and granted to the said city and its successors, for the uses and purposes specified in the ordinance of said city, ratified by an act of the Legislature of the said State, approved on the eleventh of March, eighteen hundred and fifty-eight, entitled ' An act concerning the City of San Francisco, and to ratify and confirm certain ordinances of the common council of said city,' there being excepted from this relinquishment and grant all sites or other parcels of lands which have been, or now are, occupied by the United States for military, or other public uses, [or such other sites or parcels as may hereafter be designated by the President of the United States, within one year after the rendition to the General Land Office, by the Surveyor-General, of an approved plat of the exterior limits of San Francisco, as recognized in this section, in connection with the lines of the public surveys: And provided, That the relinquishment and grant by this act shall in no manner intefere with or prejudice any bona-fide claims of others, whether asserted adversely under rights derived from Spain, Mexico, or the laws of the United States, nor preclude a judicial examination and adjustment thereof."]—(13 Stats. at Large, 333.)

The part included within brackets was inserted at the request of the Commissioner of the General Land Office. No map, such as is there mentioned, was ever sent to the General Land Office. The only map made was of the land subsequently confirmed to the city. Nor were any reservations ever made by the War Department.

This section was, as stated above, drawn by Judge Field, but the honor of securing its passage, with the rest of the act, is due to Senator Conness,

The act of March 8th, 1866, entitled "An act to quiet the title to certain lands within the corporate limits of the city of San Francisco," is as follows:

"*Be it enacted by the Senate and House of Representatives of the United States of America in Congress assembled,* That all the right and title of the United States to the land situated within the corporate limits of the city of San Francisco, in the State of California, confirmed to the city of San Francisco by the decree of the Circuit Court of the United States for the Northern District of California, entered on the eighteenth day of May, one thousand eight hundred and sixty-five, be, and the same are hereby, relinquished and granted to the said city of San Francisco and its successors, and the claim of the said city to said land is hereby confirmed, subject, however, to the reservations and exceptions designated in said decree, and upon the following trusts, namely: that all the said land, not heretofore granted to said city, shall be disposed of and conveyed by said city to parties in the bona fide actual possession thereof, by themselves or tenants, on the passage of this act, in such quantities and upon such terms and conditions as the Legislature of the State of California may prescribe, except such parcels thereof as may be reserved and set apart by ordinance of said city for public uses: *Provided, however,* That the relinquishment and grant by this act shall not interfere with or prejudice any valid adverse right or claim, if such exist, to said land or any part thereof, whether derived from Spain, Mexico, or the United States, or preclude a judicial examination and adjustment thereof. —(14 Stat. at Large, 4.)"

The bill for this act was, as stated above, also drawn by Judge Field. He gave it to Senator Conness, who took charge of it in the Senate, and through his influence it was passed by that body. In the House, Mr. McRuer took charge of it, and, with the aid of the rest of the State delegation, and of the delegation from Nevada, its passage there was secured.

The appeals to the Supreme Court of the United States from the decree in the Pueblo Case being dismissed after the passage of this act, as stated above, the municipal authorities proceeded, under its provisions, to set apart lands for school-houses, hospitals, court-house buildings, and other public purposes, and, through their exertions, seconded and encouraged by Mr. McCoppin, the very able and efficient Mayor of the city at that time, a park was laid out upon the Ocean and the Golden Gate, which is known as the Ocean Park, and which, in time, will be one of the finest parks in the world. But inasmuch as, in many cases, the ground taken for public purposes and for the park, was occupied by settlers or had been purchased by them, an assessment was levied by the city, with the approval of the Legislature, upon other lands conveyed to the occupants, as a condition of their receiving the deeds of the city, and the moneys obtained in this way were applied to compensate those whose lands had been thus appropriated.

The Chinese in California, and the Legislation of the State and of the City of San Francisco against them.

The presence of Chinese in California, and the constant immigration of them into the State, has created a great deal of irritation with its inhabitants of other races, and has led, not only to much inflammatory declamation, but to legislation—State and municipal—in conflict with the Constitution of the United States, and which, if it should be carried out, would involve the destruction of the most important powers of the General Government.

The Constitution vests in Congress the power to regulate commerce with foreign nations, and that includes the transportation of persons as well as goods. Congress alone can determine the conditions upon which foreigners shall be permitted to land and remain in the country. The State may, indeed, as a matter of self-preservation, exclude convicts, paupers, persons having contagious or incurable diseases, or likely to become a charge upon it. Whatever legislation is required for any thing further must proceed from Congress. Except in the cases mentioned, its power is absolute and exclusive. Yet the legislation, both of the State and of the city of San Francisco, against the Chinese, has been in direct disregard of this well-settled doctrine of constitutional law.

Again, the President and Senate of the United States are vested exclusively with the treaty-making power of the government. That power extends to all subjects of foreign commerce, to all forms of intercourse with foreign nations, and may prescribe the rights and privileges which shall be accorded to their citizens or subjects. By treaty, the conditions upon which foreigners shall be allowed to reside, do business, purchase and hold property in the country, may be designated. And the Constitution declares that " all treaties made or which shall be made under the authority of the United States, shall be the supreme law of the land." As will be seen hereafter, the legislation—State and municipal—of California, has been directly in the face of the express and positive stipulations of our treaties with China.

Again, the Fourteenth Amendment of the Constitution declares that no State shall deny to *any person* within its jurisdiction " the equal protection of the laws "—a provision which makes equality before the law the constitutional right of *every person* within the territory of the United States, from whatever country he may have come, or from whatever race he may have descended. Yet the legislation—State and municipal—of California against the Chinese has been in open and flagrant disregard of this command. So palpable has been this disregard that no just man in his senses could deny it.

For some centuries previously to the present one, the policy of China was to exclude intercourse with foreign nations, except for purposes of trade at a few designated ports. All entrance into the interior of the country, and even trading, except at the points designated, was strictly forbidden, and the law imposing the prohibition was rigorously enforced. Many attempts were made by European nations to induce the Chinese government to make treaties with them, but approaches of the kind were generally repelled, or the reception of ministers was allowed only on condition of performing such acts of humiliation as few nations would permit.

In August, 1842, as the result of the war between England and China, caused by the seizure by the Chinese government of opium imported in violation of its laws by the East India Company, a treaty was signed between them providing for "lasting peace and friendship between them," and also the payment by China to England of twenty-one millions of dollars.

Americans, ever since their independence, had carried on trade with China, and had at this time a factory at Canton. They had no trouble with the Chinese people or the government, and all that the Chinese government had yielded by compulsion to the English, it freely granted to them by a treaty made July 13th, 1844, negotiated on behalf of the United States by our minister, Caleb Cushing. This treaty was ratified in December of the following year. It opens by stating that "The United States of America and the Ta Tsing Empire, desiring to establish firm, lasting, and sincere friendship between the two nations, have resolved to fix, in a manner clear and positive, by means of a treaty or general convention of peace, amity, and commerce, the rules which shall in future be mutually observed in the intercourse of their respective countries."

And it declares, in its first article, that "there shall be a perfect, permanent, and universal peace, and a sincere and cordial amity between the United States of America, on the one part, and the Ta Tsing Empire, on the other part, and between their people, respectively, without exception of persons or places." And, in article nineteen, that "all citizens of the United States in China, peaceably attending to their affairs, being placed on a common footing of amity and good-will with subjects of China, shall receive and enjoy, for themselves and everything appertaining to them, the special protection of the local authorities of government, who shall defend them from all insult or injury of any sort on the part of the Chinese. If their dwellings or property be threatened or attacked by mobs, incendiaries, or other violent or lawless persons, the local officers, on requisition of the consul, will immediately despatch a military force to disperse the rioters, and will apprehend the guilty individuals and punish them with the utmost rigor of the law."

There is, throughout this treaty, an unusual and studied warmth of expression, and its thirty-four articles are all in favor of Americans. There is not one securing any special right or advantage to China, and no complaint has been made that a single article has ever been violated.

The peace between England and China, following the enforced treaty between those two countries, was not real. There were continued riots at Canton, and in May, 1847, British ships-of-war captured some Chinese forts; and in 1856 the two nations were in open war. President Buchanan sent Hon. William B. Reed, of Philadelphia, to watch the course of events, and to act the part of mediator and peace-maker when opportunity should offer. He endeavored, in vain, to persuade the Chinese officials to yield to the demands of England. But in the midst of the troubles with that country, and on the 18th of June, 1858, a new treaty was signed between the United States and China. In it the Chinese government reiterated, in equally strong language, their cordial regard and appreciation of the United States. In its first paragraph it declares that "there shall be, as there have always been, peace and friendship between the United States of America and the Ta Tsing Empire, and between their people, respectively. They shall not insult or oppress each other for any trifling cause, so as to produce an estrangement between them; and if any other nation should act unjustly or oppressively, the United States will exert their good offices, on being informed of the case, to bring about an amicable arrangement of the question, thus showing their friendly feelings."—(12 Stats. at Large, 1,023.)

In article eleven it declares that "all citizens of the United States of American in China, peaceably attending to their affairs, being placed on a common footing of amity and good-will with subjects of China, shall receive and enjoy for themselves and everything appertaining to them, the protection of the local authorities of government, who shall defend them from all insult or injury of any sort. If their dwellings or property be threatened or attacked by mobs, incendiaries, or other violent or lawless persons, the local officers, on requisition of the consul, shall immediately despatch a military force to disperse the rioters, apprehend the guilty individuals, and punish them with the utmost rigor of the law."

And in article twenty-nine, protection is given to Christians teaching and following the principles of their religion. It is as follows: "The principles of the Christian religion, as professed by the Protestant and Roman Catholic Churches, are recognized as teaching men to do good, and to do to others as they would have others do to them. Hereafter those who quietly profess and teach these doctrines shall not be harassed nor persecuted on account of their faith. Any person, whether citizen of the United States or Chinese convert, who, according to these tenets, peaceably teaches and practices the principles of Christianity, shall in no case be interfered with or molested."

It is seldom that the annals of diplomacy exhibit such a manifestation of trust and friendship.

In 1868 Hon. Anson Burlingame came to the United States at the head of a mission from China. It is still fresh in the recollection of all, with what enthusiasm this mission was received, how its members were entertained and banqueted on their arrival at San Francisco, and how some of the leading men of the State rejoiced at what they believed to be the opening of intercourse between the two countries, which would be immensely beneficial to the United States, and particularly to California.

In July, 1868, through this mission, additional articles to the treaty of 1858 were concluded and signed. Of these articles the 5th, 6th, and 7th are as follows:

"ARTICLE 5. The United States of America and the Emperor of China cordially recognize the inherent and inalienable right of man to change his home and allegiance, and also the mutual advantage of the free migration and emigration of their citizens and subjects, respectively, from the one country to the other, for purposes of curiosity, of trade, or as permanent residents. The high contracting parties, therefore, join in reprobating any other than an entirely voluntary emigration for these purposes. They consequently agree to pass laws making it a penal offence for a citizen of the United States or Chinese subjects to take Chinese subjects either to the United States or to any other foreign country, or for a Chinese subject or citizen of the United States to take citizens of the United States to China or to any other foreign country, without their free and voluntary consent respectively.

" ARTICLE 6. Citizens of the United States, visiting or residing in China, shall enjoy the same privileges, immunities, or exemptions in respect to travel or residence, as may there be enjoyed by the citizens or subjects of the most favored nation, and reciprocally Chinese subjects, visiting or residing in the United States, shall enjoy the same privileges, immunities, and exemptions in respect to travel or residence, as may there be enjoyed by the citizens or subjects of the most favored nation. But nothing herein contained shall be held to confer naturalization upon citizens of the United States in China, nor upon the subjects of China in the United States.

" ARTICLE 7. Citizens of the United States shall enjoy all the privileges of the public educational institutions under the control of the government of China; and, reciprocally, Chinese subjects shall enjoy all the privileges of the public educational institutions under the control of the government of the United States which are enjoyed in the respective countries by the citizens or subjects of the most favored nation. The citizens of the United States may freely establish and maintain schools within the Empire of China, at those places where foreigners are by treaty permitted to reside ; and, reciprocally, Chinese subjects may enjoy the same privileges and immunities in the United States."

With these treaties—with these strong expressions of friendship and pledges of protection to the people of the two countries—by each to the people of the other country—the legislation of California, and also of the city of San Francisco, has been almost constantly in conflict.

On the 25th of April, 1855, the Legislature of the State passed an act entitled "An act to discourage immigration to this State of persons who cannot become citizens thereof," which imposed a tax of fifty dollars upon every person arriving in the State who was incompetent to become a citizen. This was directed especially at the Chinese, as they, with a very few exceptions, were the only persons coming to this country, who, under our laws, could not become naturalized. This act was declared unconstitutional by the Supreme Court of the State in People vs. Downer (7 Cal., 169).

On the 26th of April, 1858, an act was passed entitled "An act to prevent the further immigration of Chinese or Mongolians to this State," which absolutely forbade their landing in California, under a penalty of from four hundred to six hundred dollars, and imprisonment. This, also, was held to be unconstitutional and was never enforced.

On the 26th of April, 1862, was passed "An act to protect free, white labor against competition with Chinese coolie labor, and discourage the immigration of the Chinese into the State of California," which imposed on each Chinese, male or female, a monthly capitation tax of two dollars and a half. This act was declared unconstitutional by the Supreme Court of the State in Lin Sing vs. Washburn (20 Cal., 534).

In the year 1872, the Legislature adopted a series of codes, embracing the whole body of the law of the State. One of these was entitled " The Political Code " of the State, and a chapter, under the title of " General Police " of the State, contains provisions relating to immigration. Some of the sections of the chapter were amended in 1874. They required the master of a vessel arriving at any port of the State, bringing passengers from any place out of the State, to make a written report to the Commissioner of Immigration at such port, stating, amongst other things, the name, place of birth, last residence, age, and occupation of all passengers who were not citizens of the United States, and whether any of the passengers, thus reported, " are lunatic, idiotic, deaf, dumb, blind, crippled, or infirm and not accompanied by any relative able to support them, or lewd or abandoned women." One section, as amended in 1874, required " the Commissioner of Immigration ' to satisfy himself whether or not any passenger who shall arrive in this State by vessels from any foreign port or place (who is not a citizen of the United States), is lunatic, idiotic, deaf, dumb, blind, crippled or infirm, and is not accompanied by relatives who are able and willing to support him, or is likely to become permanently a public charge, or has been a pauper in any other country, or is, from sickness or disease, existing either at the time of sailing from the port of departure, or at the time of his arrival in this State, a public charge, or likely to become so, or is a convicted criminal, or a lewd or debauched woman;' and then declare that ' no person who shall belong to either class, or who possesses any of the infirmities or vices specified herein, shall be permitted to land in this State, unless the master, owner, or consignee of said vessel shall give a joint and several bond to the people of the State of California, in the penal sum of five hundred dollars, in gold coin of the United States, conditioned to indemnify and save harmless every county, city and county, town and city of this State against all costs and expenses which may be by them necessarily incurred for the relief, support, medical care, or any expense whatever, resulting from the infirmities or vices herein referred to, of the persons named in said bonds, within two years from the date of said bonds; . . . and if the master, owner, or consignee of said vessel shall fail or refuse to execute the bond herein required to be executed, they are required to retain such persons on board of said vessel until said vessel shall leave the port, and then convey said passengers from this State; and if said master, owner, or consignee shall fail or refuse to perform the duty and service last herein enjoined, or shall permit said passengers to escape from said vessel and land in this State, they shall forfeit to the State the sum of five hundred dollars, in gold coin of the United States, for each passenger so escaped, to be recovered by suit at law.' "

Under the provisions of this section the case of Ah Fong, a Chinese woman, came before the Circuit Court on writ of *habeas corpus*.

The case was as follows: The petitioner, a subject of the Emperor of China, arrived at the port of San Francisco as a passenger on board the American steamship " Japan," owned by the Pacific Mail Steamship Company, under the command, as master, of J. H. Freeman, in August, 1874. On the arrival of the steamship she was boarded by the Commissioner of Immigration of California, who proceeded, under the provisions of the above statute, to examine into the character of the petitioner and of other alien passengers. Upon such examination the Commissioner found, and so declared, that the petitioner and twenty-one other persons, also subjects of the Empire of China, arriving as passengers by the same steamship, were lewd and debauched women. He thereupon prohibited the master of the steamship from landing the women, unless he or the owner or consignee of the vessel gave the bonds required by the statute. Neither of the parties designated would consent to give the required bonds, and the women were consequently detained by the master on board of the steamship. They thereupon applied for a writ of *habeas corpus* to a District Court of the State, to inquire into the cause of their detention, alleging in their petition its illegality, on the ground that the statute under which they were held was in contravention of the treaty between the United States and the Empire of China, and in conflict with the Constitution of the United States, and denying, also, that they were either lewd or debauched women. The District

Court granted the application and heard the petitioners, and after the hearing, remanded them back to the charge of the master of the steamship, holding that the statute of California was neither in violation of the treaty or the Constitution, and that the evidence presented justified the finding of the Commissioner, that the petitioners were lewd and debauched women. The petitioners thereupon applied to the Chief Justice of the State for another writ of *habeas corpus*, alleging the illegality of their restraint, on grounds similar to those taken in the petition to the District Court, and also alleging that they were, since the order of the District Court remanding them to the custody of the master of the steamship, about to be forcibly returned to China against their will and consent. They therefore prayed that with the writ of *habeas corpus* a warrant might issue to the Sheriff of the city and county of San Francisco to take them into his custody. The Chief Justice granted the writ, returnable before the Supreme Court of the State, and at the same time issued a warrant commanding the Coroner of the city and county to take the parties into his custody.

Under this warrant the parties were taken into the custody of the Coroner and brought before the Court, which sustained the ruling of the District Court, and denied the application of the parties to be discharged. It further directed that the Coroner should return the parties to the master or owner or consignee of the steamship *Japan*, on board of the steamship, and required such master, owner, or consignee to retain the parties on board of the steamship until she should leave the port of San Francisco, and then to carry them beyond the State.

Its order also provided, that in case the steamship *Japan* was not in the port of San Francisco, the Coroner should retain the parties in his possession until the arrival in port of the steamship, and then enforce the order returning the parties to the vessel, or retain the parties until the further direction of the Court.

The petitioner was one of the women thus held by the Coroner, and she invoked the aid of the Circuit Court to be released from her restraint, alleging, as in the other applications, that the restraint was illegal, that the statute which is supposed to authorize it was in contravention of the treaty with China and the Constitution of the United States, and averring that she was not within either of the classes designated in the statute. It further appeared from the special traverse to the return of the Coroner, and was admitted by counsel, that since the judgment of the Supreme Court, the steamship *Japan* had sailed from the port of San Francisco, and would not probably return under three months, and that Freeman had been discharged from the service of the steamship company, and was no longer master of the *Japan*.

The case was heard in the Circuit Court by Judge Field, assisted by Judges Sawyer and Hoffman.

There was no evidence presented to the Court that the women were lewd or abandoned women, except that the Commissioner of Immigration had so concluded, and it was stated that he came to such conclusion from their general appearance and the particular sleeves they wore as part of their dress. It was not pretended or suggested that the Commissioner had taken any testimony upon the subject, or had any information whatever, except from personal observation of them, to govern his action in the matter ; and, in point of fact, two of the women were wives of persons at the time in the employment of Mr. William C. Ralston, the cashier of the Bank of California, at his residence at Belmont. He so stated to the presiding judge, and offered his affidavit to that effect, with that of his servants.

There is no doubt that a State, in the interest of decency and morality, may exclude from its borders lewd and abandoned women who persist in following prostitution, but in every government which makes any pretence of affording security against wanton accusation, some evidence of such

purpose should be produced more than the mere guess or
inference of a Commissioner of Immigration, from personal inspection of the parties whilst walking over the
deck of a vessel. The law of California in this case (as
will be seen) confounded all distinctions, and opened the
door to the greatest oppression and cruelty. In deciding
the case, after stating the provisions of the section quoted,
Judge Field gave the following opinion:

" In re Ah Fong.·

" The decision of the District Court, and of the Supreme Court of the
State, although entitled to great respect and consideration.from the acknowledged ability and learning of their judges, is not binding upon this
Court. The petitioner being an alien, and a subject of a country having
treaty relations with the government of the United States, has a right
to invoke the aid of the federal tribunals for her protection, when her
rights, guaranteed by the treaty, or the Constitution, or any law of Congress, are in any respect invaded ; and·is, of course, entitled to a hearing
upon any allegation in proper form that her rights are thus invaded.
" I proceed, therefore, to the consideration of the questions presented,
notwithstanding the adjudications of the State tribunals."

Here the Judge quoted the provisions of the section
given above, and continued as follows :

" The provisions of this section are of a very extraordinary character.
They make no distinction between the deaf, the dumb, the blind, the
crippled, and the infirm, who are poor and dependent, and those who
are able to support themselves and are in possession of wealth and all its
appliances. If they are not accompanied by relatives, both able and
willing to support them, they are prohibited from landing within the
State, unless a specified bond is given, not by them or such competent
sureties as they may obtain, but by the owner, master, or consignee of
the vessel. Neither do the provisions of the statute make any distinction between a present pauper, and one who has been a pauper, but has
ceased to be such. If the emigrant has ever been within that unfortnate
class, notwithstanding he may have at the time ample means at his command, he must obtain the designated bond or be excluded from the
State. They subject also to the same condition, and possible exclusion,
the passenger whose sickness or disease has been contracted on the passage, as well as the passenger who was sick or diseased on his departure
from the foreign port. It matters not that the sickness may have been
produced by exertions for the safety of the ship or passengers, or by at-
tentions to their wants or health. If he is likely on his arrival to be-

26

come a public charge, he must obtain the bond designated, or be denied a landing within the State. Nor does the statute make any distinction between the criminal convicted for a misdemeanor, or a felony, or for an offence *malum in se*, or one political in its character. The condemned patriot, escaping from his prison and fleeing to our shores, stands under the law upon the same footing with the common felon who is a fugitive from justice. Nor is there any difference made between the woman, whose lewdness consists in private unlawful indulgence, and the woman who publicly prostitutes her person for hire, or between the woman debauched by intemperance in food or drink, or debauched by the loss of her chastity.

"A statute thus sweeping in its terms, confounding by general designation persons widely variant in character, is not entitled to any very high commendation. If it can be sustained as the exercise of the police power of the State as to any persons brought within any of the classes designated, it must be sustained as to all the persons of such class. That is to say, if it can be sustained when applied to the infirm, who is poor and dependent, when unaccompanied by his relatives, able and willing to support him, it must be sustained when applied to the infirm, who is surrounded by wealth and its attendants, if he is thus unaccompanied. If it can be sustained when applied to a woman whose debauchery consists in the prostitution of her person, it must be sustained when applied to a woman whose debauchery consists in her intemperance in food and drink ; and even when applied to the repentant Magdalen, who has once yielded to temptation and lost her virtue. The Commissioner of Immigration is not empowered to make any distinction between persons of the same class ; and there is nothing on the face of the act which indicates that the Legislature intended that any distinction should be made.

"It is undoubtedly true that the police power of the State extends to all matters relating to the internal government of the State, and the administration of its laws, which have not been surrendered to the General Government, and embraces regulations affecting the health, good order, morals, peace, and safety of society. Under this power all sorts of restrictions and burdens may be imposed, having for their object the advancement of the welfare of the people of the State, and when these are not in conflict with established principles, or any constitutional prohibition, their validity cannot be questioned.

"It is equally true that the police power of the State may be exercised by precautionary measures against the increase of crime or pauperism, or the spread of infectious diseases from persons coming from other countries; that the State may entirely exclude convicts, lepers, and persons afflicted with incurable disease; may refuse admission to paupers, idiots, and lunatics and others. who from physical causes are likely to become a charge upon the public, until security is afforded that they will not become such a charge; and may isolate the temporarily diseased until the danger of contagion is gone. The legality of precautionary measures of this kind has never been doubted. The right of the State in this respect has its foundation, as observed by Mr. Justice Grier in the Passenger Cases, in the sacred law of self-defence, which no power granted to Congress can restrain or annul.

"But the extent of the power of the State to exclude a foreigner from its territory is limited by the right in which it had its origin, the right of self-defence. Whatever outside of the legitimate exercise of this right affects the intercourse of foreigners with our people, their immigration to this country and residence therein, is exclusively within the jurisdiction of the General Government, and is not subject to State control or interference. To that government the treaty-making power is confided; also the power to regulate commerce with foreign nations, which includes intercourse with them as well as traffic; also the power to prescribe the conditions of migration or importation of persons, and rules of naturalization; whilst the States are forbidden to enter into any treaty, alliance, or confederation with other nations.

"I am aware that the right of the State to exclude from its limits any persons whom it may deem dangerous or injurious to the interests and welfare of its citizens, has been asserted by eminent judges of the Supreme Court of the United States. Mr. Chief Justice Taney maintained the existence of this right in his dissenting opinion in the Passenger Cases, and asserted that the power had been recognized in previous decisions of the Court. The language of the opinion in the case of the City of New York vs. Miln (11 Peters, 141) would seem to sustain this doctrine. But neither in the Passenger Cases nor in the case of the City of New York vs. Miln, did the decision of the Court require any consideration of the power of exclusion which the State possessed; and all that was said by the eminent judges in those cases upon that subject, was argumentative and not necessary and authoritative.

"But independent of this consideration, we cannot shut our eyes to the fact that much which was formerly said upon the power of the State in this respect, grew out of the necessity which the Southern States, in which the institution of slavery existed, felt of excluding free negroes from their limits. As in some States negroes were citizens, the right to exclude them from the Slave States could only be maintained by the assertion of a power to exclude all persons whom they might deem dangerous or injurious to their interests. But at this day no such power would be asserted, or if asserted, allowed in any Federal Court. And the most serious consequences affecting the relations of the nation with other countries might, and undoubtedly would, follow from any attempt at its exercise. Its maintenance would enable any State to involve the nation in war, however disposed to peace the people at large might be.

"Where the evil apprehended by the State from the ingress of foreigners is that such foreigners will disregard the laws of the State, and thus be injurious to its peace, the remedy lies in the more vigorous enforcement of the laws, not in the exclusion of the parties. Gambling is considered by most States to be injurious to the morals of their people, and is made a public offence. It would hardly be considered as a legitimate exercise of the police power of the States to prevent a foreigner who had been a gambler in his own country from landing in ours. If, after landing, he pursues his former occupation, fine him, and, if he persists in it, imprison him, and the evil will be remedied. In some States the manufacture and sale of spirituous and intoxicating liquors are forbidden and punished as a misdemeanor. If the foreigner coming to our shores is a manufacturer or dealer in such liquors, it would be deemed an illegitimate exercise of the police power to exclude him, on account of his calling, from the State. The remedy against any apprehended manufacture and sale would lie in such case in the enforcement of the penal laws of the State. So if lewd women, or lewd men, even if the latter be of that baser sort, who, when Paul preached at Thessalonica, set all the city in an uproar, (Acts xvii., verse 5,) land on our shores, the remedy against any subsequent lewd conduct on their part must be found in good laws, or good municipal regulations and a vigorous police.

" It is evident that if the possible violation of the laws of the State by an emigrant, or the supposed immorality of his past life or profession, where that immorality has not already resulted in a conviction for a felony, is to determine his right to land and to reside in the State, or to pass through into other and interior States, a door will be opened to all sorts of oppression. The doctrine now asserted by counsel for the Commissioner of Immigration, if maintained, would certainly be invoked, and at no distant day, when other parties, besides low and despised Chinese women, are the subjects of its application, and would then be seen to be a grievous departure from principle.

" I am aware of the very general feeling prevailing in this State against the Chinese, and in opposition to the extension of any encouragement to their immigration hither. It is felt that the dissimilarity in physical characteristics, in language, in manners, religion, and habits, will always prevent any possible assimilation of them with our people. Admitting that there is ground for this feeling, it does not justify any legislation for their exclusion, which might not be adopted against the inhabitants of the most favored nations of the Caucasian race, and of Christain faith. If their further immigration is to be stopped, recourse must be had to the Federal Government, where the whole power over this subject lies. The State cannot exclude them arbitrarily, nor accomplish the same end by attributing to them a possible violation of its municipal laws. It is certainly desirable that all lewdness, especially when it takes the form of prostitution, should be suppressed, and that the most stringent measures to accomplish that end should be adopted. But I have little respect for that discriminating virtue which is shocked when a frail child of China is landed on our shores, and yet allows the bedizened and painted harlot of other countries to parade our streets and open her hells in broad day, without molestation and without censure,

" By the 5th article of the treaty between the United States and China, adopted on the 28th of July, 1868, the United States and the Emperor of China recognize the inherent and inalienable right of man to change his home and allegiance, and also the mutual advantage of the free migration and emigration of their citizens and subjects respectively from the one country to the other, for purposes of curiosity, of trade, or as permanent residents. The 6th article declares that citizens of the United States visiting or residing in China shall enjoy the same privileges, immunities, or exemptions in respect to travel or residence as may there be enjoyed by citizens or subjects of the most favored nation. And, reciprocally, that Chinese subjects visiting or residing in the United States shall enjoy the same privileges, immunities, and exemptions in respect to travel or residence as may there be enjoyed by citizens or subjects of the most favored nation.

" The only limitation upon the free ingress into the United States and egress from them of subjects of China is the limitation which is applied to citizens or subjects of the most favored nation ; and as the General Government has not seen fit to attach any limitation to the ingress of subjects of those nations, none can be applied to the subjects of China. And the power of exclusion by the State, as we have already said, extends only to convicts, lepers and persons incurably diseased, and to paupers and persons who, from physical causes, are likely to become a public charge. The detention of the petitioner is, therefore, unlawful under the treaty.

" But there is another view of this case equally conclusive for the discharge of the petitioner, which is founded upon the legislation of Congress since the adoption of the Fourteenth Amendment. That amendment in its first section designates who are citizens of the United States, and then declares that no State shall make or enforce any law which abridges their privileges and immunities. It also enacts that no State shall deprive *any person* (dropping the distinctive designation of citizens) of life, liberty, or property without due process of law ; nor deny to *any person* the equal protection of the laws. The great fundamental rights of all citizens are thus secured against any State deprivation, and all persons, whether native or foreign, high or low, are, whilst within the jurisdiction of the United States, entitled to the equal protection of the laws. Discriminating and partial legislation, favoring particular persons, or against particular persons of the same class, is now prohibited. Equality of privilege is the constitutional right of all citizens, and equality of protection is the constitutional right of all persons. And equality of protection implies not only equal accessibility to the Courts for the prevention or redress of wrongs and the enforcement of rights, but equal exemption, with others of the same class, from all charges and burdens of every kind. Within these limits the power of the State exists, as it did previously to the adoption of the amendment, over all matters of internal police. And within these limits the act of Congress of May 31st, 1870, restricts the action of the State with respect to foreigners immigrating to our country.

'No tax or charge,' says the act, 'shall be imposed or enforced by any State upon any person immigrating thereto from a foreign country which is not equally imposed or enforced upon every person immigrating to such State from any other foreign country, and any law of any State in conflict with this provision is hereby declared null and void.'—(16 Statutes at Large, 144.)

" By the term *charge*, as here used, is meant any onerous condition, it being the evident intention of the act to prevent any such condition from being imposed upon any person immigrating to the country, which is not equally imposed upon all other immigrants, at least upon all others of the same class. It was passed under and accords with the spirit of the Fourteenth Amendment. A condition which makes the right of the immigrant to land depend upon the execution of a bond by a third party, not under his control and whom he cannot constrain by any legal proceedings, and whose execution of the bond can only be obtained upon such terms as he may exact, is as onerous as any charge which can well be imposed, and must, if valid, generally lead, as in the present case, to the exclusion of the immigrant.

" The statute of California, which we have been considering, imposes this onerous condition upon persons of particular classes on their arrival in the ports of the State by vessel, but leaves all other foreigners of the same classes entering the State in any other way, by land from the British possessions or Mexico, or over the plains by railway, exempt from any charge. The statute is, therefore, in direct conflict with the act of Congress.

" It follows from the views thus expressed, that the petitioner must be discharged from further restraint of her liberty ; and it is so ordered."

The other twenty persons of the twenty-one were also discharged immediately upon the rendition of this decision. Of the twenty-two who had been before the Supreme Court of the State, one did not apply to the Circuit Court, but appealed from the decision refusing her discharge to the Supreme Court of the United States. Her case came before that Court under the title of Chy Lung vs. Freeman, and was decided at the October Term in 1875.—(2 Otto, 276.)

The judgment of the Supreme Court of the State was unanimously reversed, accompanied with indignant condemnation of the statute of California.

Said Mr. Justice Miller, speaking for the Court:

" It is hardly possible to conceive a statute more skillfully framed, to place in the hands of a single man the power to prevent entirely vessels engaged in a foreign trade, say with China, from carrying passengers, or to compel them to submit to systematic extortion of the grossest kind.

"The Commissioner has but to go aboard a vessel filled with passengers ignorant of our language and our laws, and without trial or hearing or evidence, but from the external appearances of persons with whose former habits he is unfamiliar, to point with his finger to twenty, as in this case, or a hundred if he chooses, and say to the master, these are idiots, these are paupers, these are convicted criminals, and these are lewd women, and these others are debauched women. I have here a hundred blank forms of bonds, printed. I require you to fill me up and sign each of these for $500 in gold, and that you furnish me two hundred different men, residents of this State, and of sufficient means, as sureties on these bonds. I charge you five dollars in each case for preparing the bond and swearing your sureties, and I charge you seventy-five cents each for examining these passengers, and all others you have on board. If you don't do this you are forbidden to land your passengers under a heavy penalty.

"But I have the power to commute with you for all this for any sum I may choose to take in cash. I am open to an offer, but you must remember that twenty per cent. of all I can get out of you goes into my own pocket, and the remainder into the treasury of California. . . . . .

"Individual foreigners, however distinguished at home for their social, their literary, or their political character, are helpless in the presence of this potent Commissioner. Such a person may offer to furnish any amount of surety on his own bond, or deposit any sum of money, but the law of California takes no note of him. It is the master, owner, or consignee of the vessel alone whose bond can be accepted. And so a silly, an obstinate, or a wicked Commissioner, may bring disgrace upon the whole country, the enmity of a powerful nation, or the loss of an equally powerful friend.

"While the occurrence of the hypothetical case just stated may be highly improbable, we venture the assertion that if citizens of our own government were treated by any foreign nation as subjects of the Emperor of China have been actually treated under this law, no Administration could withstand the call for a demand on such government for redress.

"Or, if this plaintiff and her twenty companions had been subjects of the Queen of Great Britain, can any one doubt that this matter would have been the subject of international inquiry, if not of a direct claim for redress? Upon whom would such a claim be made? Not upon the State of California, for by our Constitution she can hold no exterior relations with other nations. It would be made upon the government of the United States. If that government should get into a difficulty which would lead to war or to suspension of intercourse, would California alone suffer, or all the Union? If we should conclude that a pecuniary indemnity was proper as a satisfaction for the injury, would California pay it, or the Federal Government? If that government has forbidden the States to hold negotiations with any foreign nations, or to declare war, and has taken the whole subject of these relations upon herself, has the Constitution, which provides for this, done so foolish a thing as to leave it in the power of the States to pass laws whose enforcement renders the General Government liable to just reclamations which it must answer, while it does not prohibit to the States the acts for which it is held responsible?

"The Constitution of the United States is no such instrument. The passage of laws which concern the admission of citizens and subjects of foreign nations to our shores belongs to Congress and not to the States. It has the power to regulate commerce with foreign nations; the responsibility for the character of those regulations and the manner of their execution belongs solely to the National Government. If it be otherwise, a single State can at her pleasure embroil us in disastrous quarrels with other nations.

"We are not called upon by this statute to decide for or against the right of a State, in the absence of legislation by Congress, to protect herself by necessary and proper laws against paupers and convicted criminals from abroad, nor to lay down the definite limit of such right, if it exist. Such a right can only arise from a vital necessity for its exercise, and cannot be carried beyond the scope of that necessity. When a State statute, limited to provisions necessary and appropriate to that object alone, shall in a proper controversy come before us, it will be time enough to decide that question. The statute of California goes so far beyond what is necessary or even appropriate for this purpose, as to be wholly without any sound definition of the right under which it is supposed to be justified. . . . .

"The money when paid does not go to any fund for the benefit of immigrants, but is paid into the general treasury of the State and devoted to the use of all her indigent citizens. The blind, or the deaf, or the dumb passenger is subject to contribution, whether he be a rich man or a pauper. The patriot seeking our shores, after an unsuccessful struggle against despotism in Europe or Asia, may be kept out because there his resistance has been adjudged a crime. The woman whose error has been repaired by a happy marriage and numerous children, and whose loving husband brings her with his wealth to a new home, may be told she must pay a round sum before she can land, because it is alleged that she was debauched by her husband before marriage. Whether a young woman's manners are such as to justify the Commissioner in calling her lewd may be made to depend on the sum she will pay for the privilege of landing in San Francisco.

"It is idle to pursue the criticism. In any view which we can take of this statute it is in conflict with the Constitution of the United States, and, therefore, void."

The legislation of the city of San Francisco against the Chinese has been equal to that of the State, and much more offensive in its character.

In July, 1870, an ordinance of the city and county was passed regulating lodging-houses. Section one required that every house, room, or apartment, except of prisons, occupied as a lodging, in which persons lived or slept, should contain within the walls of such house, room, or apartment, at least five hundred cubic feet of air for each adult person dwelling or sleeping therein; and that any owner or tenant of a house, room, or apartment, who should lodge or permit to be lodged in such room or apartment more than one person to every five hundred cubic feet of air, should be deemed guilty of a misdemeanor, and for every offence should be fined not less than ten nor more than five hundred dollars, or be imprisoned in the city prison not less than five days nor more than three months, or be punished both by such fine and imprisonment. The ordinance also imposed the same penalty on each occupant of any such room or apartment.

In May, 1873, a large number of Chinese in San Francisco were arrested under this ordinance, and a fine of ten dollars inflicted on each of them. The parties fined in most cases preferred to go to jail rather than to pay the fine. By a law of the State an imprisonment for one day works a discharge of a fine to the amount of two dollars. Of this action of the Chinese, the *Evening Bulletin*, a leading journal of San Francisco, thus speaks in its edition of May 22, 1873:

" CHINESE OBSTINACY.

" The Mongols have determined upon the policy of worrying the authorities in their attempt to enforce the ordinance prohibiting the unwholesome crowding of lodging-houses, in the hope of rendering the effort futile.

" The large gang brought up and fined on Tuesday, with the re-inforcements to-day, have completely filled the prison accommodations. And if the crusade is continued, the cattle pound, or some other spacious enclosure, will have to be utilized for their confinement. A few were inclined to pay the fines imposed, but were prevented from doing so by the commands of the leading men in the Chinese quarter, who declared, in substance, that they would make the city sick of prosecuting and maintaining Chinamen in prison, under this ordinance."

There was a good deal of difficulty in enforcing the ordinance, on account of the number of Chinese who violated it, and their omission to pay the fines imposed. They were arrested in great numbers, and packed in cells where they had not 100 feet of cubic air to the person. They over-crowded the jails, and it was thought necessary by the authorities of the city to adopt a policy which would compel them to pay their fines and at the same time prevent the immigration of others of their countrymen. Accordingly, on the 25th May, 1873, three ordinances were introduced in the Board, having this object in view.

One of the ordinances provided that every male person imprisoned in the county jail, in pursuance of a judgment or conviction of the Police Court of the city and county, should, immediately upon his arrival at the jail, have the hair of his head cut or clipped to a uniform length of one inch from the scalp. Another of the ordinances provided that no person should remove or cause to be removed, from any cemetery or grave-yard within the limits of the city and county, the remains of any deceased person or persons there placed or disposed, without the written permit of the coroner of the city and county. The third of the ordinances imposed a license-tax of fifteen dollars a quarter upon keepers of laundries or laundry offices, or wash-houses, who employed no vehicle drawn by animal power.

Of two of these ordinances the *Evening Bulletin* of May 27, 1873, said as follows :

"It is generally known . . . . . that to deprive a Chinaman of his queue is to humiliate him as deeply as is possible.

"It is also very generally known, that the bones of no Chinaman are permitted to remain in a foreign land, and that all Chinese, before leaving their country, feel assured that, after death, no matter where they die, their bones will be taken back to mingle with their native sod.

"So strict are all Chinese on these two points, that it is believed, if they were prevented from wearing their tails here, and if after death their bones were denied transportation to their native land, the immigration of this superstitious people would be effectually stopped, and a reflux commence from our shores to the Flowery Kingdom."

And in its edition of June 2d, 1873, the *Bulletin* had the following article upon one of the ordinances:

"THE SUPERVISORS ON HAIR CUTTING.

"The Board of Supervisors have passed to print an ordinance requiring the cropping of the hair of every person who is serving a term in the jail under a criminal conviction. *The ordinance, while it nominally makes no discrimination as to race or condition, is aimed specially at the Chinese.* The enforcement of the sanitary ordinance against the over-crowding of Chinese is just, and ought to be certain. But it should be enforced lawfully. The Chinese go to jail, in most cases, rather than pay the fine. The readiness to be fed and lodged for a week or more, at the public expense, extracts all the real penalty there is in the sanitary law. Five hundred or a thousand Chinese going willingly to jail, and rather liking the opportunity for free board and lodging, quite superior to their own miserable accommodations, presents a new phase of the question. The judgment has no penalty. The Chinese who offend against the ordinance refuse to pay the fine, but go to jail and board it out. The Supervisors, casting about for some means of relief, have hit upon the plan of cropping the hair. White criminals would care nothing about this, and the ordinance would probably never be enforced against them. The loss of a pigtail is a great calamity to the Chinese. It is his national badge of honor. If it is cut off, he is maimed. He will not venture home without it, and becomes a fixture from very necessity. The sanitary regulations enforced in this way is a kind of boomerang, which comes back with telling effect."

The queue-cutting ordinance and the laundry ordinance were both passed, but they were both vetoed by Mayor Alford of the city, and his action received the general approval of the Press of the State and of the country generally. In his message vetoing the Queue Ordinance he stated that its manifest motive was to inflict upon the persons of Chinese convicted of misdemeanors a punishment which, in their estimation, was shameful and degrading, and that, in his judgment, minor offences which do not belong to the class of crimes called infamous should not be punished by penalties, which inflicted disgrace upon the person of the offender.

On the 3d of April, 1876, the Legislature of the State passed an act entitled " An act concerning lodging-houses and sleeping-apartments within the limits of incorporated cities," in which it provided that any person or persons found sleeping or lodging, or hired or used for the purpose of sleeping, any room or apartment which contained less than five hundred cubic feet of space in the clear, every such person, so keeping such room or apartment, should be deemed guilty of a misdemeanor and should be punished by a fine of not less than ten nor more than fifty dollars, or by both fine and imprisonment. In June afterwards, the Board of Supervisors of the city and county of San Francisco, took up and passed anew the old vetoed queue-cutting ordinance. It was introduced by Supervisor Gibbs, who stated that it was necessary to resort to this mode of treatment to compel the payment of the fines imposed upon the Chinese, and for that purpose it was passed by a vote of ten to two, and approved by the then mayor. It was believed that the dread of the loss of his queue would compel every Chinaman to pay the fine rather than to go to jail.

Under this ordinance, a Chinaman, by the name of Ah Kow, was sentenced to pay a fine of ten dollars, and in default to be imprisoned in the county jail. Failing to pay his fine, he was arrested, and on being taken to the jail the Sheriff cut off his queue.

For this treatment he sued the Sheriff, setting forth his conviction under the act of the Legislature, and the treatment to which he was subjected, and the injury and suffering he had endured, and asked damages. To this complaint the Sheriff answered justifying his act under the ordinance of the city. To this answer the plaintiff demurred. The particulars of the complaint and answer are more fully stated in the opinion delivered by Judge Field in overruling the demurrer, which is as follows :

"Ah Kow vs. Noonan.

" The plaintiff is a subject of the Emperor of China, and the present action is brought to recover damages for his alleged maltreatment by the defendant, a citizen of the State of California and the Sheriff of the city and county of San Francisco. The maltreatment consisted in having wantonly and maliciously cut off the queue of the plaintiff, a queue being worn by all Chinamen, and its deprivation being regarded by them as degrading and as entailing future suffering.

"It appears that in April, 1876, the Legislature of California passed an act ' concerning lodging-houses and sleeping-apartments within the limits of incorporated cities,' declaring, among other things, that any person found sleeping or lodging in a room or an apartment containing less than five hundred cubic feet of space in the clear for each person occupying it, should be deemed guilty of a misdemeanor, and on conviction thereof be punished by a fine of not less than ten or more than fifty dollars, or imprisonment in the county jail, or by both such fine and imprisonment.* Under this act the plaintiff, in April, 1876, was convicted and sentenced to pay a fine of ten dollars, or in default of such payment to be imprisoned five days in the county jail. Failing to pay the fine, he was imprisoned. The defendant, as sheriff of the city and county, had charge of the jail, and during the imprisonment of the plaintiff cut off his queue, as alleged. The complainant avers, that it is the custom of Chinamen to shave the hair from the front of the head and to wear the remainder of it braided into a queue; that the deprivation of the queue is regarded by them as a mark of disgrace, and is attended, according to their religious faith, with misfortune and suffering after death; that the defendant knew of this custom and religious faith of the Chinese, and knew also that the plaintiff venerated the custom and held the faith ;† yet, in disregard of his rights, inflicted the injury complained of; and that the plaintiff has, in consequence of it, suffered great mental anguish, been disgraced in the eyes of his friends and relatives, and ostracised from association with his countrymen; and that hence he has been damaged to the amount of $10,000.

"Two defences to the action are set up by the defendant; the second one being a justification of his conduct under an ordinance of the city and county of San Francisco. It is upon the sufficiency of the latter defence that the case is before us. The ordinance referred to was passed on the 14th day of June, 1876, and it declares that every male person imprisoned in the county jail, under the judgment of any Court having jurisdiction in criminal cases in the city and county, shall immediately upon his arrival at the jail have the hair of his head 'cut or clipped to an uniform length of one inch from the scalp thereof,' and it is made the duty of the sheriff to have this provision enforced. Under this ordinance the defendant cut off the queue of the plaintiff.

---

* Session Laws of 1875–6, p. 759.

† It has been suggested that this averment of the complaint is not in point of fact strictly accurate; and that, according to the belief of the Chinamen, the loss of the queue is only *evidence* of previous bad character, and as such *may* affect his future condition, not necessarily. It is not perceived that this statement, if correct, alters in any respect the argument of the opinion. The loss of his queue is the cause of reproach and degradation to him.

" The validity of this ordinance is denied by the plaintiff on two grounds: 1st, that it exceeds the authority of the Board of Supervisors, the body in which the legislative power of the city and county is vested; and 2d, that it is special legislation imposing a degrading and cruel punishment upon a class of persons who are entitled, alike with all other persons within the jurisdiction of the United States, to the equal protection of the laws. We are of the opinion that both of these positions are well taken.

" The Board of Supervisors is limited in its authority by the act consolidating the government of the city and county. It can do nothing unless warrant be found for it there, or in a subsequent statute of the State. As with all other municipal bodies, its charter—here the Consolidation Act—is the source and measure of its powers. In looking at this charter, we see that the powers of the Board, and the subjects upon which they are to operate, are all specified. The Board has no general powers, and its special power to determine the fines, forfeitures, and penalties which may be incurred, is limited to two classes of cases: 1st, breaches of regulations established by itself; and 2d, violations of provisions of the Consolidation Act, where no penalty is provided by law. It can impose no penalty in any other case; and when a penalty other than that of fine or forfeiture is imposed, it must, by the terms of the act, be in the form of imprisonment. It can take no other form. 'No penalty to be imposed,' is the language used, 'shall exceed the amount of one thousand dollars, or six months imprisonment, or both.' The mode in which a penalty can be inflicted, and the extent of it, are thus limited in defining the power of the Board. In their place nothing else can be substituted. No one, for example, would pretend that the Board could, for any breach of a municipal regulation or any violation of the Consolidation Act, declare that a man should be deprived of his right to vote, or to testify, or to sit on a jury, or that he should be punished with stripes, or be ducked in a pond, or be paraded through the streets, or be seated in a pillory, or have his ears cropped, or his head shaved.

" The cutting off the hair of every male person within an inch of his scalp, on his arrival at the jail, was not intended and cannot be maintained as a measure of discipline or as a sanitary regulation. The act by itself has no tendency to promote discipline, and can only be a measure of health in exceptional cases. Had the ordinance contemplated a mere sanitary regulation, it would have been limited to such cases and made applicable to females as well as to males, and to persons awaiting trial as well as to persons under conviction. The close cutting of the hair which is practiced upon inmates of the State Penitentiary, like dressing them in striped clothing, is partly to distinguish them from others, and thus prevent their escape, and facilitate their recapture. They are measures of precaution, as well as parts of a general system of treatment prescribed by the Directors of the Penitentiary under the authority of the State, for parties convicted of and imprisoned for felonies. Nothing of the kind is prescribed or would be tolerated with respect to persons confined in a county jail for simple misdemeanors, most of which are not of a very grave character. For the discipline or detention of the plaintiff in this case, who had the option of paying a fine of ten dollars, or of being imprisoned for five days, no such clipping of the hair was required. It was done to add to the severity of his punishment.

"But even if the proceeding could be regarded as a measure of discipline, or as a sanitary regulation, the conclusion would not help the defendant, for the Board of Supervisors had no authority to prescribe the discipline to which persons convicted under the laws of the State should be subjected, or to determine what special sanitary regulations should be enforced with respect to their persons. That is a matter which the Legislature had not seen fit to intrust to the wisdom and judgment of that body. It is to the Board of Health of the city and county that a general supervision of all matters appertaining to the sanitary condition of the county jail is confided; and only in exceptional cases would the preservation of the health of the institution require the cutting of the hair of any of its inmates within an inch of his scalp.* The claim, however, put forth, that the measure was prescribed as one of health, is notoriously a mere pretence. A treatment to which disgrace is attached, and which is not adopted as a means of security against the escape of the prisoner, but merely to aggravate the severity of his confinement, can only be regarded as a punishment additional to that fixed by the sentence. If adopted in consequence of the sentence, it is punishment in addition to that imposed by the Court; if adopted without regard to the sentence, it is wanton cruelty.

"In the present case the plaintiff was not convicted of any breach of a municipal regulation, nor of violating any provision of the consolidation act. The punishment which the Supervisors undertook to add to the fine imposed by the Court was without semblance of authority. The Legislature had not conferred upon them the right to change or add to the punishments which it deemed sufficient for offences; nor had it bestowed upon them the right to impose in any case a punishment of the character inflicted in this case. They could no more direct that the queue of the plaintiff should be cut off than that the punishments mentioned should be inflicted. Nor could they order the hair of any one, Mongolian or other person, to be clipped within an inch of his scalp. That measure was beyond their power.

"The second objection to the ordinance in question is equally conclusive. It is special legislation, on the part of the Supervisors, against a class of persons who, under the Constitution and laws of the United States, are entitled to the equal protection of the laws. The ordinance was intended only for the Chinese in San Francisco. This was avowed by the Supervisors on its passage, and was so understood by every one.

*Act of April 4, 1870; Session Laws of 1869-70, p. 717.

The ordinance is known in the community as the 'Queue Ordinance,' being so designated from its purpose to reach the queues of the Chinese, and it is not enforced against any other persons. The reason advanced for its adoption, and now urged for its continuance, is that only the dread of the loss of his queue will induce a Chinaman to pay his fine. That is to say, in order to enforce the payment of a fine imposed upon him, it is necessary that torture should be superadded to imprisonment. Then, it is said, the Chinaman will not accept the alternative, which the law allows, of working out his fine by imprisonment, and the State or county will be saved the expense of keeping him during his imprisonment. Probably the bastinado, or the knout, or the thumbscrew, or the rack, would accomplish the same end; and no doubt the Chinaman would prefer either of these modes of torture to that which entails upon him disgrace among his countrymen and carries with it the constant dread of misfortune and suffering after death. It is not creditable to the humanity and civilization of our people, much less to their Christianity, that an ordinance of this character was possible.

" The class character of this legislation is none the less manifest because of the general terms in which it is expressed. The statements of Supervisors in debate on the passage of the ordinance, cannot, it is true, be resorted to for the purpose of explaining the meaning of the terms used; but they can be resorted to for the purpose of ascertaining the general object of the legislation proposed, and the mischiefs sought to be remedied. Besides, we cannot shut our eyes to matters of public notoriety and general cognizance. When we take our seats on the bench we are not struck with blindness, and forbidden to know as judges what we see as men; and where an ordinance, though general in its terms, only operates upon a special race, sect, or class, it being universally understood that it is to be enforced only against that race, sect, or class, we may justly conclude that it was the intention of the body adopting it that it should only have such operation, and treat it accordingly. We may take notice of the limitation given to the general terms of an ordinance by its practical construction as a fact in its history, as we do in some cases that a law has practically become obsolete. If this were not so, the most important provisions of the Constitution, intended for the security of personal rights, would, by the general terms of an enactment, often be evaded and practically annulled.—(*Brown vs. Piper*, 1 Otto, 42; *Ohio Live Ins. and Trust Company vs. Debolt*, 16 How., 435; *Scott vs. Sandford*, 19 Id., 407.) The complaint in this case shows that the ordinance acts with special severity upon Chinese prisoners, inflicting upon them suffering altogether disproportionate to what would be endured by other prisoners if enforced against them. Upon the Chinese prisoners its enforcement operates as 'a cruel and unusual punishment.'

" Many illustrations might be given where ordinances, general in their terms, would operate only upon a special class, or upon a class with exceptional severity, and thus incur the odium and be subject to the legal objection of intended hostile legislation against them. We have, for instance, in our community, a large number of Jews. They are a highly intellectual race, and are generally obedient to the laws of the country. But, as is well known, they have peculiar opinions with respect to the use of certain articles of food, which they cannot be forced to disregard without extreme pain and suffering. They look, for example, upon the eating of pork with loathing. It is an offence against their religion, and is associated in their minds with uncleanness and impurity. Now, if they should, in some quarter of the city, overcrowd their dwellings, and thus become amenable, like the Chinese, to the act concerning lodging-houses and sleeping-apartments, an ordinance of the Supervisors requiring that all prisoners confined in the county jail should be fed on pork, would be seen by every one to be leveled at them ; and, notwithstanding its general terms, would be regarded as a special law in its purpose and operation.

"During various periods of English history, legislation, general in its character, has often been enacted with the avowed purpose of imposing special burdens and restrictions upon Catholics; but that legislation has since been regarded as not less odious and obnoxious to animadversion than if the persons at whom it was aimed had been particularly designated.

"But, in our country, hostile and discriminating legislation by a State against persons of any class, sect, creed, or nation, in whatever form it may be expressed, is forbidden by the Fourteenth Amendment of the Constitution. That amendment in its first section declares who are citizens of the United States, and then enacts that no State shall make or enforce any law which shall abridge their privileges and immunities. It further declares that no State shall deprive *any person* (dropping the distinctive term citizen) of life, liberty, or property, without due process of law, nor deny to *any person* the equal protection of the laws. This inhibition upon the State applies to all the instrumentalities and agencies employed in the administration of its government; to its executive, legislative, and judicial departments; and to the subordinate legislative bodies of counties and cities. And the equality of protection thus assured to every one whilst within the United States, from whatever country he may have come, or of whatever race or color he may be, implies not only that the Courts of the country shall be open to him on the same terms as to all others, for the security of his person or property, the prevention or redress of wrongs, and the enforcement of contracts; but that no charges or burdens shall be laid upon him which are not equally borne by others, and that in the administration of criminal justice he shall suffer for his offences no greater or different punishment.

"Since the adoption of the Fourteenth Amendment, Congress has legislated for the purpose of carrying out its provisions in accordance with these views. The Revised Statutes, re-enacting provisions of law passed in 1870, declare that 'all persons within the jurisdiction of the United

States shall have the same right in every State and Territory to make and enforce contracts, to sue, be parties, give evidence, and to the full and equal benefit of all laws and proceedings for the security of persons and property, as is enjoyed by white citizens, and shall be subject to like punishment, pains, penalties, taxes, licenses, and exactions of every kind, and to *no other.*'—(Sec. 1,977.) They also declare, that 'every person who, under color of any statute, ordinance, regulation, custom, or usage of any State or Territory, subjects, or causes to be subjected, any citizen of the United States, or *other person* within the jurisdiction thereof, to the deprivation of any rights, privileges, or immunities secured by the Constitution and laws, shall be liable to the party injured in an action at law, suit in equity, or other proper proceeding for redress.'—(Sec. 1,979.)

" It is certainly something in which a citizen of the United States may feel a generous pride that the government of his country extends protection to all persons within its jurisdiction ; and that every blow aimed at any of them, however humble, come from what quarter it may, is ' caught upon the broad shield of our blessed Constitution and our equal laws.' *

" We are aware of the general feeling—amounting to positive hostility—prevailing in California against the Chinese, which would prevent their further immigration hither, and expel from the State those already here. Their dissimilarity in physical characteristics, in language, manners, and religion, would seem, from past experience, to prevent the possibility of their assimilation with our people. And thoughtful persons, looking at the millions which crowd the opposite shores of the Pacific, and the possibility at no distant day of their pouring over in vast hordes among us, giving rise to fierce antagonisms of race, hope that some way may be devised to prevent their further immigration. We feel the force and importance of these considerations ; but the remedy for the apprehended evil is to be sought from the General Government, where, except in certain special cases, all power over the subject lies. To that government belong exclusively the treaty-making power, and the power to regulate commerce with foreign nations, which includes intercourse as well as traffic, and, with the exceptions presently mentioned, the power to prescribe the conditions of immigration or importation of persons. The State in these particulars, with those exceptions, is powerless, and nothing is gained by the attempted assertion of a control which can never be admitted. The State may exclude from its limits paupers and convicts of other countries, persons incurably diseased, and others likely to become a burden upon its resources. It may, perhaps, also exclude persons whose presence would be dangerous to its established institutions. But there its power ends. Whatever is done by way of exclusion beyond this must come from the General Government. That goverment alone can determine what aliens shall be permitted to land within the United

* Judge Black's argument in the Fossat Case, 2 Wallace, p. 703.

States, and upon what conditions they shall be permitted to remain; whether they shall be restricted in business transactions to such as appertain to foreign commerce, as is practically the case with our people in China; or whether they shall be allowed to engage in all pursuits equally with citizens. For restrictions necessary or desirable in these matters, the appeal must be made to the General Government; and it is not believed that the appeal will ultimately be disregarded. Be that as it may, nothing can be accomplished in that direction by hostile and spiteful legislation on the part of the State, or of its municipal bodies, like the ordinance in question—legislation which is unworthy of a brave and manly people. Against such legislation it will always be the duty of the judiciary to declare and enforce the paramount law of the nation.

"The plaintiff must have judgment on the demurrer to the defendant's plea of justification, and it is so ordered."

This decision raised a storm of abuse against its author. It seemed as though, for the time, reason had fled from the minds of the people of the State. It was not enough for them that the Judge was equally opposed to the immigration of Chinese, believing, as he did, that it was not wise that persons should be encouraged to come to the country who, by their habits, religion, language, and manners, could not assimilate readily with our people; that the presence of such a class would necessarily engender enmities and conflicts, disturbing to the peace and injurious to the prosperity of the country. They wanted him to disregard the Constitution of the United States and the provisions of the treaty with China, and hold that the State was supreme in all matters affecting the Chinese. It is enough to say that the Judge would have deserved the reproach of all good men had he listened to such wild and senseless clamor.

During the same year a new Constitution for the State had been adopted. The members of the Convention, who framed it, had been elected under the excitement existing at the time against the Chinese, and they seemed to think that all obstacles to the hostile legislation would be removed if authority for it was expressed in the organic law. Accordingly, the instrument adopted is filled with clauses leveled against the people of the hated race, showing a determination to exclude them from the State at all hazards, without regard to treaty stipulations with their country or inhibitions of the Constitution of the United States. Provisions of various kinds are found in it, exhibiting ignorance of the plainest doctrines of political economy as well as of public and constitutional law. Hostility to capital and to the Chinese appears to have been the ruling principle of the Convention, and the exclusion of both from the State its object—of the former by onerous taxation, and of the latter by cutting off the means of livelihood. The Nineteenth Article contained the following provision :

" Section 2. No corporation now existing, or hereafter formed under the laws of this State, shall after the adoption of this Constitution employ *directly* or *indirectly*, in any capacity, any Chinese or Mongolians. The Legislature shall pass such laws as may be necessary to enforce this provision.

" Section 3. No Chinese shall be employed on any State, county, municipal, or other public work, except in punishment for crime.

" Section 4. The presence of foreigners ineligible to become citizens of the United States is declared to be dangerous to the well-being of this State, and the Legislature shall discourage their immigration by all the means within its power." . . . .

Under this article the first Legislature which assembled under the new Constitution added to the penal code of the State the following sections:

" 178. Any officer, director, manager, member, stockholder, clerk, agent, servant, attorney, employé, assignee, or contractor of any corporation now existing, or hereafter formed under the laws of this State, who shall employ, in any manner or capacity, upon any work or business of such corporation, any Chinese or Mongolian, is guilty of a misdemeanor, and is punishable by a fine of not less than one hundred nor more than one thousand dollars, or by imprisonment in the county jail of not less than fifty nor more than five hundred days, or by both such fine and imprisonment; *Provided*, That no director of a corporation shall be deemed guilty under this section who refuses to assent to such employment, and has such dissent recorded in the minutes of the board of directors.

" 1· Every person who, having been convicted of violating the provisions of this section, commits any subsequent violation thereof after such conviction, is punishable as follows:

" 2. For each subsequent conviction such person shall be fined not less than five hundred nor more than five thousand dollars, or by imprisonment not less than two hundred and fifty days nor more than two years, or by both such fine and imprisonment.

" 179. Any corporation now existing, or hereafter formed under the laws of this State, that shall employ, directly or indirectly, in any capacity, any Chinese or Mongolian, shall be guilty of a misdemeanor, and upon conviction thereof shall for the first offence be fined not less than five hundred nor more than five thousand dollars, and upon the second conviction shall, in addition to said penalty, forfeit its charter and franchise, and all its corporate rights and privileges, and it shall be the duty of the Attorney-General to take the necessary steps to enforce such forfeiture."

As this law went into effect immediately, some corporations dissolved, others resisted its enforcement. The president of one of them—the Sulphur Bank Quicksilver Mining Company, organized under the laws of the State—was arrested and held to answer before a State Court, upon a complaint setting forth the offence of employing in the business of the corporation certain Chinese citizens of the Mongolian race. He thereupon sued out a writ of habeas corpus in the Circuit Court of the United States. That Court, Sawyer, the Circuit Judge, and Hoffman, the District Judge, sitting, held the law invalid, and discharged him from arrest. Both of the judges delivered very elaborate and able opinions. They showed by clear and unanswerable reasoning, that the law in question was in conflict with the treaty with China and the Fourteenth Amendment of the Constitution; that the privileges and immunities pledged to the Chinese by the treaty, guaranteed to them the right to labor, and to pursue any lawful business equally with the subjects of the most favored nation; and that the power. to repeal and amend acts of incorporation, reserved to the Legislature by the Constitution of the State, did not authorize it to require corporations to exclude from employment persons who were thus protected by treaty stipulations. As said by Judge Hoffman, if the provisions of the law were enforced, a bank or a railroad company would " lose the right to employ a Chinese interpreter to enable it to communicate with Chinese with whom it does business. A hospital association would be unable to employ a Chinese servant to make known, or to minister to, the wants of a Chinese patient, and even a society for the conversion of the heathen would not be allowed to employ a Chinese convert to interpret the gospel to Chinese neophytes."

The judge was of opinion that the legislation, under the guise of amendment or alteration, was merely an attempt to drive the Chinese from the State by preventing them from laboring for their livelihood, and he thought that no enumeration would " be attempted, of the privileges, immunities, and exemptions of the most favored nation, or even of man in civilized society, which would exclude the right to labor for a living."

" It is as inviolable," he added, " as the right of property, for property is the offspring of labor. It is as sacred as the right to life, for life is taken if the means whereby we live be taken. Had the labor of the Irish or Germans been similarly proscribed, the legislation would have encountered a storm of just indignation. The right of persons of those or other nationalities, to support themselves by their labor, stands on no other or higher ground than of the Chinese. The latter have even the additional advantage afforded by the express and solemn pledge of the Nation."

The judge concluded his opinion by observing, what was generally felt to be true, " that the unrestricted immigration of the Chinese to this country is a great and growing evil. That it presses with much severity on the laboring classes, and that if allowed to continue in numbers bearing any considerable proportion to that of the teeming population of the Chinese Empire, it will be a menace to our peace and even to our civilization, is an opinion entertained by most thoughtful persons. The demand, therefore, that the treaty shall be rescinded or modified is reasonable and legitimate."* " But," he added, " while that treaty exists, the Chinese have the same rights of immigration and residence as are possessed by any other foreigners. Those rights it is the duty of Courts to maintain and of the Government to enforce."

The opinion of Judge Sawyer was equally clear and emphatic in its condemnation of the law of the State. Both opinions will appear in 6th Sawyer's Reports under the title of the case, " In Re Tiburcio Parrott, on Habeas Corpus."

Nothing could better exhibit the unreasonable character of the legislation of the State than the illustration above given. It was the offspring of ignorance, and of a spitefulness which always over-leaps its mark and defeats itself.

OTHER CASES IN THE CIRCUIT COURT.

A great many other cases of interest have been decided by the Circuit Court whilst Judge Field presided, but only a few of them have been reported. In much the larger number merely an oral opinion has been given by him, briefly recapitulating the grounds of the decision. Of the reported cases, other than those from which the quotations above are made, the following may be named as the most important :

Central Pacific Railroad Co. vs. Dyer, 1 Sawyer, 643.
Cole Silver Mining Co. vs. Virginia & Gold Hill Mining Co., 1 Ibid., 685.
Galpin vs. Page, 3 Ibid., 93.
Patterson vs. Tatum, 3 Ibid., 164.

---

* The treaty with China has since been modified, so as to admit of legislation by Congress restricting the immigration of Chinese to this country. The power which Congress always possessed can now be exercised without a breach of the treaty.

Leroy vs. Jamison, 3 Ibid., 370.
Leroy vs. Wright, 4 Ibid., 530.
Norton vs. Meador, 4 Ibid., 603.
Gray vs. Lammore, 4 Ibid., 638.
United States vs. Hare, 4 Ibid., 653.
Nicholson Pavement Co. vs. Hatch, 4 Ibid., 692.
Grisar vs. McDowell, 4 Ibid., 597.
Gimmy vs. Culverson, 5 Ibid., 605.
The Ship Harriman, 5 Ibid., 611.
United States vs. Outerbridge, 5 Ibid., 620.
In Re Frank McCoppin, 5 Ibid., 630.

THE ELECTORAL COMMISSION OF 1877. *

Any notice of the judicial labors of Justice Field would be incomplete which failed to include his action as a member of the Electoral Commission created for counting the Presidential vote of 1876. Although the history of that memorable tribunal, and the circumstances which led to its creation, are probably familiar to most readers, it may not be amiss briefly to recapitulate them.

On the morning of the Presidential election held November 7th, 1876, it was announced and generally conceded that Samuel J. Tilden, the Democratic candidate, had secured a majority of the Electoral College. The total number of electors composing it was 369, of whom 203 favorable to him, and 166 favorable to the Republican candidate, Rutherford B. Hayes, had received a majority of the popular vote of their States. In the number for Mr. Tilden, however, were included four electors from Florida, eight from Louisiana, and seven from South Carolina. If these nineteen votes could be taken from Mr. Tilden's column and added to that of Mr. Hayes, the latter would have a majority of one. Some of the leaders of the Republican party, therefore, determined to originate a contest in these States, for which peculiar facilities were

---

* This article was prepared by John T. Doyle, Esq., of San Francisco, a distinguished member of the Bar of California. In the note on page 259, there is a mistake in designating the Commission as of 1876. It was created by the act of Congress approved January 29th, 1877.

afforded by the fact that in them the canvassing of the votes and declaration of the result were confided to " returning boards," a majority of whose members were not only of the same party, but were political adventurers, wholly without character. On the other hand, among the electors chosen in the States, which had been fairly carried by the Republicans, there were several who, by holding a Federal office, or otherwise, were ineligible for the position. So that the slenderness of the majority for Mr. Hayes (even supposing his partisans successful in their effort to count for him the votes of the returning-board States) rendered it necessary for them to retain also the votes of all these ineligible electors. The Democrats, therefore, in turn, contested the election of the latter.

When the movements of the Republican leaders first intimated a design to attempt to count the votes of the returning-board States for their candidate, in the face of notorious popular majorities, people refused to credit the suggestion. The rumors on the subject were, by most persons, regarded as merely sensational, and intended at most to effect some other purpose. But when President Grant invited a large number of prominent Republicans to visit those States, and act as voluntary Supervisors of the count; when these gentlemen, all pronounced partisans of the Republican candidate, took upon themselves this supervision, and in carrying it out refused to act in concert with a committee of citizens equally distinguished, chosen by their opponents; and when they, with a single exception, gave their countenance and sanction to flagrant violations of the local law by the returning boards, it became too clear to doubt that an attempt was to be made to overrule the popular vote, and by means of fraudulent devices, to confer the Presidency on a candidate who had been defeated at the polls. The success of such a scheme did indeed at first appear incredible, and most persons looked forward to seeing justice attained by the ordinary processes. But meantime the returning boards went on, and, after various preliminary violations of law, proceeded by methods now conceded by their own partisans to be wholly illegal and indefensible, to consummate the crime of certifying the election of all the defeated candidates.

The electors actually chosen, but counted out by this process, however, met and voted as required by law, and transmitted certificates of their votes to the President of the Senate in Washington, in proper form. In the Republican States where the Democrats claimed the defeat of particular electors on the ground of ineligibility, proceedings were also taken to question their votes, and thus the final count of the electoral vote and the ascertainment of the result of the election presented a series of judicial questions, the determination of each one of which vitally affected the result. If every question were decided in favor of the Republicans they had the Presidency by a majority of one electoral vote. The decision of a single point against them was fatal to their pretensions.

What tribunal was to decide these tremendous issues? *Quis tantas componere lites?*

The constitutional provision on the subject was extremely meagre. "*The President of the Senate shall, in 'presence of the Senate and House of Representatives, open 'all the certificates, and the votes shall then be counted.*" And there was no statute nor even a joint rule of the two Houses providing how the count was to be made or how any disputed question which arose on it should be determined. The Republicans put forward the claim that the President of the Senate alone had the power to determine what were and what were not the genuine electoral votes, and so, practically, to judge the whole question. The other side contended that the two Houses of Congress were to count, and that, therefore, the assent of both was necessary to the recognition of each vote claimed. The whole country became excited on the question, and the newspapers teemed with discussions of it. The records of all previous Presidential counts were ransacked and every precedent quoted; but none could be claimed as decisive, for the contest itself was without precedent.

The House of Representatives was Democratic both numerically and on a count by States. On a failure to elect by the Colleges it would, undoubtedly, have chosen Mr. Tilden. But the Congress was to expire and the House be dissolved on the fourth of March, and the new House, though similarly constituted, would not assemble until the following December. Meantime the Senate and all the Executive Departments, which were permanent bodies, were in the hands of the Republicans, and the Senate would doubtless elect, and the Executive Departments recognize, Mr. Hayes. The outgoing President was expected to do all in his power to confirm the claim by inducting him into office and turning over to him all the machinery of the Executive Government. He would thus become President *de facto* with a claimant *de jure* opposed, and no tribunal to decide between them, no law applicable to the case, and to all appearances no appeal possible except to the sword.

People stood aghast at the magnitude of the peril before them. Treason in its worst form, not only to the Republic, but to all Republican government, menaced the very life of the Nation. The public excitement became intense; rage and indignation took possession of men's minds, and projects for resisting fraud by violence, and of arming large bodies of men to march on Washington and insist on a fair count by the two Houses of Congress, were freely canvassed. The President, on the other hand, concentrated a military force at the Capital, and civil war in its worst form seemed imminent;—not section against section, nor State against State, but neighbor against neighbor, throughout every State, county, and village in the land.

Under these circumstances a Joint Committee of the Senate and House of Representatives devised, and on January 29th, 1877, Congress passed a bill creating a commission of fifteen members,—five Senators, five Representatives, and five Judges of the Supreme Court,—to whose adjudication the whole subject was committed. Justice Field was selected as one of the last-named members.*

It is not deemed necessary to detail the particulars of the points of contest in each of the cases submitted. They can be sufficiently gathered from the extracts which we make from his opinions.

The Florida Case.

The frauds practiced in Florida consisted in substituting, for the returns of certain counties regularly made up by the proper officers in conformity with the votes legally cast, other returns subsequently prepared by different officers, in which a sufficient number of the votes were thrown out to change the result in the State. A statement of the proceedings in one of the counties—Baker County—will show how the frauds were perpetrated.

By the laws of the State, the counties were divided into polling precincts, and the votes of those precincts were to be returned to the county clerk, at the county seats, where they were to be canvassed; and the county canvassers were to certify the result to the State canvassers. The county canvassers were, by law, the county judge, the county clerk, (or clerk of the circuit court of the county,)

---

* Justice Field had always expressed the opinion that it was the duty of the two Houses of Congress to meet in joint convention and count the votes, and if they could not agree upon the votes to be received, so as to be able to declare who were elected President and Vice-President, the duty would then devolve upon the House of Representatives to elect the President, and upon the Senate to elect the Vice-President. He did not, therefore, believe in the necessity of any commission, but was willing to act as one of its members, not doubting, for a moment, that it would go behind the certificates issued by the Governors of the disputed States, and determine, not who had received them, for that was apparent on their face, but who were entitled, as electors, to receive them.

and a justice of the peace, to be called in by them for their assistance. In case either the judge or clerk was absent, or could not attend, the sheriff of the county was to be called in his place. The law provided that the canvass by the county canvassers should be on the sixth day after the election, or sooner, if the returns were all received.

In Baker County there were but four precincts, and the returns were all received in three days. On the 10th of November the county clerk, considering that the returns were in, and that further delay in the canvass might be embarrassing, requested the county judge to join in the canvass. The county judge refused. The clerk then asked the sheriff, but he declined. The clerk then called to his assistance a justice of the peace, and made the canvass, which was a correct one. But it so happened that the county judge, on the same day—the 10th—issued a notice to the county clerk, and to a justice of the peace, to attend him at the county seat on the 13th, for the purpose of making the count. On that day and at the hour named, the county clerk and the justice of the peace, thus requested, attended. The county judge, however, absented himself. He was invited and urged to go on with the canvass, but he declined to attend. The sheriff was then applied to, and he refused. Thereupon the county clerk and a justice of the peace recanvassed the votes, giving the same result as in the first canvass, and so certified the same to the State canvassers, stating in their certificate the reasons why neither the county judge nor the sheriff was present. The office of the clerk was then closed for the day. On the evening of that day, the same county judge and the same sheriff, taking to their assistance a justice of the peace who had been commissioned on the 10th by the Governor, and who had never acted before, entered the office surreptitiously, opened a drawer and took out the returns, threw aside two precincts, and certified the two remaining, and sent the certificate to the State canvassers. This was done without any evidence whatever of any illegality or irregularity in the election in either of those precincts. The deposition of the sheriff, on the subject, was taken; and he testified that no evidence was before them; that one person had stated that he had been prevented at one of the precincts from voting, but gave no proof of it; and as to the other precinct, they merely believed that some illegal votes had been given, but of that no proof was offered to them.

When the State canvassers met they amended the canvass by counting the returns from all the precincts, thus making the certificate conform to the actual vote cast. But they eliminated from the returns of other counties a sufficient number to equal what was thus returned by the true certificate of Baker County, and enough to give the State to the Hayes electors. At that time Stearns and Drew were candidates for the office of governor of the State, and Drew contested the legality of this action, so far as he was concerned. The Supreme Court of the State, before which the question was carried, held that the canvassers had no right to eliminate the votes from the other counties; that their duty was ministerial, which was to count the votes properly returned. The result gave Drew the office of governor. The State canvassers, seeing this result, recalled their amendment of the Baker County canvass, and adopted the false certificate as returned with the two precincts omitted. This was done, as without it the convass showed a majority for the electors of Mr. Tilden.

The action of the Courts and of the Legislature of the State, to correct the fraud thus perpetrated by the canvassers, will appear in the argument, given below, of Justice Field.

When the original certificate was before the Commission for examination, it was contended that Congress had no right to go behind it and count the votes of the electors actually chosen, and upon this question Justice Field said as follows:

" MR. PRESIDENT: . . . .

" The main question submitted to us, the one to which all other inquiries are subordinate, is, whom has the State of Florida appointed as
electors to cast her vote for President and Vice-President ? The Electoral
Act, under which we are sitting, makes it our duty to decide ' how many
and what persons were *duly appointed* electors ' in that State.

" The Constitution declares that each State shall appoint electors ' in
such manner as the Legislature thereof may direct.' It fixes the number to be appointed, which is to be equal to the whole number of Senators and Representatives to which the State may be entitled in Congress. It declares who shall not be appointed; that is, no Senator or
Representative, or person holding an office of trust or profit under the
United States. With the exception of these provisions as to the number of electors and the ineligibility of certain persons, the power of choice
on the part of the State is unrestricted. The manner of appointment is
left entirely to its Legislature.

" What, then, was the manner of appointment directed by the Legislature of Florida ? This is manifestly a proper subject for our inquiry,
for if another and different manner from that directed by the Legislature
has been followed in the appointment of persons as electors, such persons
are not ' duly appointed ' in the State, and we must so decide. Any substantial departure from the manner prescribed must necessarily vitiate
the whole proceeding, If, for example, the appointment of electors
should be made by the Governor of a State, when its Legislature had directed that they should be chosen by the qualified voters at a general
election, the appointment would be clearly invalid and have to be rejected. So, too, if the Legislature should prescribe that the appointment
should be made by a majority of the votes cast at such election, and the
canvassers, or other officers of election, should declare as elected those
who had received only a plurality or a minority of the votes, or the
votes of a portion only of the State, the declaration would be equally invalid as not conforming to the legislative direction; and the appointment of the parties thus declared elected could only be treated as a
nullity.

" In inquiring whether the manner prescribed by the State has been
followed, we do not trench upon any authority of the State, or question
in any respect her absolute right over the subject, but, on the contrary,
we seek only to give effect to her will and ascertain the appointment she
has actually made.

" What, then, was the manner directed by the Legislature of Florida ?
It was by popular election. It was by the choice of a majority of the
qualified voters of the State. When their votes were cast on the 7th of
November, the electors were appointed, and all that remained was to ascertain and declare the result. The appointment was then completed,
and could not afterward be changed. What subsequently was required
of the officers of election and canvassing-boards was an authentic declaration of the result."

Justice Field then proceeded to show that the duty of the State canvassers of Florida was ministerial and not judicial—so decided by the Supreme Court of the State, quoting from its opinion to that effect; that it was their duty to certify the result shown by the returns from the county canvassers; and that, according to such returns, the certificates of the State board should have been given to the Tilden electors, and not to the Hayes electors. And, as to the objection taken, that the certificates issued by the Governor of the State to the Hayes electors, upon the result found by the board of canvassers, was the only evidence which the Commission could receive of the appointment of electors, he said as follows:

"The Constitution does not prescribe the evidence which shall be received of the appointment. That only provides for the voting of the electors, and the transmission by them of a list of the persons voted for, to the seat of government, directed to the President of the Senate. Congress has, therefore, enacted that the Governor shall issue a certified list of the electors to them before the time fixed for their meeting. The language of the act is that 'It shall be the duty of the executive of each State to cause three lists of the names of the electors of such State to be made and certified, and to be delivered to the electors of such State on or before the day on which they are required by the previous section to meet.'—(Revised Statutes, sec. 136.)

"There is nothing in this act which declares that the certificate thus issued shall be conclusive of the appointment. It does not say that the evidence thus furnished is indispensable, or that other evidence of the appointment may not be received. Its only object was simply to provide convenient evidence of the appointment for the consideration of the two Houses of Congress when called upon to count the votes. It was not its purpose to control their judgment in deciding between different sets of papers purporting to contain the votes of the State. A compliance with the act is not obligatory upon the executive of the State. He is not in that respect subject to the control of Congress. He could not be compelled to give the certificate, nor could he be subject to any punishment for refusal to act in the matter. And certainly, when Congress can furnish no means to control the action of a State officer, it cannot render his action either indispensable or conclusive of the rights of the State. Instances may be readily imagined where, from accident, disability, or sickness of the Governor, the certified lists could not be obtained, or be obtained and delivered in time, or, if obtained, might be lost or destroyed before delivery. In such cases would there be no remedy? Would the

State in such cases lose its vote? Surely, no one will seriously contend for such a result. Suppose, further, that the Governor, by mistake* or fraud, should deliver certified lists in favor of persons not appointed electors; for instance, to persons who had not received a majority of the votes cast for those officers, (the persons having such majority of votes being eligible to the office under the Constitution;) would it be pretended that the will of the State should be thwarted through the force of his certificate? I feel confident that no lawyer in the country would hold that the truth could not be shown in such case against the face of the certificate; and I will never believe in the possibility of this Commission so holding until I see its decision to that effect.

"The truth is, a certificate is only *prima-facie* evidence of the fact certified. Indeed, I venture to assert, without fear of successful contradiction, that in the absence of positive law declaring its effect to be otherwise, a certificate of any officer to a fact is never held conclusive on any question between third parties; it is always open to rebuttal. There are, indeed, cases where a party who had been induced to act upon the certificate of a fact may insist that the truth of the certificate shall not be denied to his injury, but those cases proceed upon the doctrine of estoppel, which has no application here. The fact here to be ascertained is, who have been duly appointed electors of the State of Florida, not who have the certificates of appointment. It is the election, and not the certificate, which gives the right to the office. The certificate being only evidence, can be overcome by any evidence which is in its nature superior. And this is equally true of the certificate issued under the law of the State as of the certificate issued under the act of Congress. And it is equally true of the certificate of the board of canvassers. Those officers exercised mere ministerial functions; they possessed no judicial power; their determination had none of the characteristics or conclusiveness of a judicial proceeding; it has been so decided by the Supreme Court of the State. And yet, in the opinion of the distinguished Commissioner from Indiana, [Senator Morton,] and some other Commissioners from the Senate and House appear to concur with him, the determination of those canvassers, as expressed by their certificate, is more sacred and binding than the judgment of the highest court of the land, incapable of successful attack on any ground whatever.

"I put, yesterday, to these gentlemen this question: Supposing the canvassers had made a mistake in addition in footing up the returns, a mistake that changed the result of the election, and acting upon the supposed correctness of the addition they had issued a certificate to persons as electors who were not in fact chosen, and such persons had met and voted for President and Vice-President and transmitted the certificate of their votes to Washington; and afterwards, before the vote was counted by the two Houses of Congress, the mistake was discovered—was there no remedy? The gentlemen answered that there was none; that whatever mistakes of the kind may have been committed must be corrected before the vote was cast by the electors or they could not be corrected at all. If this be sound doctrine, then it follows that by a clerical mistake in arithmetical computation a person may be placed in the Chief Magistracy of the nation against the will of the people, and the two Houses of Congress are powerless to prevent the wrong.

" But the gentlemen do not stop here. I put the further question to them : Supposing the canvassers were bribed to alter the returns, and thus change the result, or they had entered into a conspiracy to commit a fraud of this kind, and in pursuance of the bribery or conspiracy they did in fact tamper with and alter the returns, and declare as elected persons not chosen by the voters, and such persons had voted and transmitted their vote to the President of the Senate, but before the vote was counted the fraud was detected and exposed—was there no remedy ? The gentlemen answered, as before, that there was none ; that whatever fraud may have existed must be proceeded against and its success defeated before the electors voted ; that whatever related to their action was then a closed book. If this be sound doctrine, it is the only instance in the world where fraud becomes enshrined and sanctified behind a certificate of its authors. It is elementary knowledge that fraud vitiates all proceedings, even the most solemn ; that no form of words, no amount of ceremony, and no solemnity of procedure can shield it from exposure and protect its structure from assault and destruction. The doctrine asserted here would not be applied to uphold the pettiest business transaction, and I can never believe that the Commission will give to it any greater weight in a transaction affecting the Chief Magistracy of the nation.

" But the gentlemen do not stop here. I put the further question to them : Supposing the canvassers were coerced by physical force, by pistols presented to their heads, to certify to the election of persons not chosen by the people, and the persons thus declared elected cast the vote of the State—was there no remedy ? and the answer was the same as that given before. For any wrong, mistake, fraud, or coercion in the action of the canvassers, say these gentlemen, the remedy must be applied before the electors have voted ; the work of the electors is done when they have acted, and there is no power under existing law by which the wrong can be subsequently righted.

" The canvass of the votes in Florida was not completed until the morning of the day of the meeting of the Electoral College, and within a few hours afterwards its vote was cast. To have corrected any mistake or fraud during these hours, by any proceeding known to the law, would have been impossible. The position of these gentlemen is, therefore, that there is no remedy, however great the mistake or crime committed. If this be sound doctrine, if the representatives in Congress of forty-two millions of people possess no power to protect the country from the installation of a Chief Magistrate through mistake, fraud, or force, we are the only self-governing people in the world held in hopeless bondage at the mercy of political jugglers and tricksters.

" This doctrine, which seems to me to be as unsound in law as it is shocking in morals, is supported upon the notion that if we are permitted to look behind the certificate of the Governor, and of the canvassing-board upon which that certificate is founded, we shall open the door to an investigation which may not be brought to a close before the fourth of March. The argument is that as the new President is to be installed on that day, and the votes of the Electoral Colleges are to be counted in February, all inquiry as to the truth of that certificate is forbidden, because it may be impracticable to carry the inquiry to a termination in time for the installation. This position was taken by counsel before the Commission, and presented in every possible form, and was repeated yesterday by Commissioners Hoar and Garfield, and dwelt upon by them as though it were conclusive of the question. The argument amounts only to this, that the difficulty of exposing in time a mistake or fraud of the canvassing-board is a sufficient reason for not attempting the exposure at all, and for quietly submitting to the consequent perpetration of a monstrous wrong.

" It is true that the machinery for the election of President, devised by the framers of the Twelfth Amendment to the Constitution, contemplates the induction of the successful candidate into office on the 4th of March, and that the office shall not on that day be either vacant or disputed. I admit, therefore, to the fullest extent claimed by gentlemen, that no proceedings can be permitted which will postpone the counting of the votes so as to prevent a declaration within that period of the person elected, or a reference of the election to the House of Representatives. But this limitation of time, so far from being a reason for submitting to a mistake or to a fraud, is a reason for immediate action to correct the one and expose the other. Whatever is done to overthrow the *prima-facie* evidence presented by the certificate of the Governor must be commenced, carried forward, and completed, so that the result of the proceeding can be considered by the two Houses of Congress when the certificates are opened in their presence and the votes are counted. The countervailing evidence must be presented in some authentic form, like the judgment of a competent tribunal, or the legislative declaration of a State, or the finding of an appropriate committee approved by the House appointing it; and then it will constitute a basis for the action of the Houses without delaying their proceedings. If, for example, the certificate of the Governor were forged, or designated as electors persons for whom no votes were cast, the fact, if it were desired to ask the action of the two Houses upon it in counting the vote, should be presented in such a conclusive form as to be the subject of consideration as a fact found. If an investigation is then required to establish the fact alleged, I admit that the proceeding cannot be had, *except by permission of the two Houses*, by reason of the delay it would occasion. The two Houses cannot be required to stop the count to take testimony and investigate the truth of mere allegations; but if the fact of forgery or falsity has already been found by competent authority, and the finding is laid before the two Houses, the finding would not only be a proper subject of consideration by them, but it would be their manifest duty to act upon the finding, in order that the nation might not be defrauded in its choice of a Chief Magistrate.

" In the view which I take of this subject there would be no great delay in the counting of the electoral votes if Congress were permitted to look behind the action of the Governor or of the canvassing-board; for the facts to be brought to the attention of the two Houses would have to be presented in the manner indicated before they could be received and acted upon, unless the two Houses should consent that testimony be taken at the time. If the fact alleged could be readily established without seriously delaying the count, it is not probable that testimony upon the subject would be refused. For example, testimony would hardly be refused as to the ineligibility of an elector, or the constitution of a canvassing-board, or the condition of a State as under military rule at the time of the election. But where the fact alleged is one of conflicting evidence, and is not susceptible of proof within reasonable limits, then, I think, the fact must be presented properly authenticated, as I have stated.

" Evidence in this form, impeaching the correctness of the certificate of the Governor and canvassing-board, can be furnished by the State or by either House of Congress; by the State, which is interested that it shall not be defrauded of its vote in the election; and by either House of Congress, which is interested that the forty-two millions of people composing the nation shall not be deprived of the President of their choice.

" In this case the State of Florida has furnished evidence in an authentic form and conclusive in its character, that the Hayes electors were never appointed and that the certificate of the Governor and of the canvassing-board in that respect is false; and that the Tilden electors were duly appointed. It has furnished the declaration of its Legislature in a statute affirming such to be the fact, and it has furnished a judicial determination of its Courts to the same effect.

" Soon after the canvass of the State board was closed, and its certificate of the result was filed, Mr. Drew, who had been a candidate for the office of governor at the same election, against Stearns, the incumbent, and had been declared defeated by the action of the canvassers in excluding votes for him, instituted proceedings by mandamus in the Supreme Court of the State to compel the canvassers to count the votes given, as shown by the returns. In his petition for the writ he averred that, according to the returns received at the office of the Secretary of State, and on file there, a majority of the votes for the office of governor were cast for him; and charged against the canvassers the same disregard of the law of the State which is alleged against them in the count for the electors. Indeed, their action affected equally the candidates for governor and for electors. The canvassers appeared to the writ, and pro-- ceedings were conducted to a judgment on the merits. The Supreme Court adjudged that the canvassers had no authority to exclude the votes, by which exclusion alone Stearns had been declared elected, and directed them to restore the votes. In obedience to this judgment they restored the excluded votes, and certified a majority for Drew, who went into office and has ever since been the accepted Governor of the State. It was the exclusion of the same votes for electors that enabled the canvassers to declare the Hayes electors chosen. In deciding this case the court gave a construction to the statute under which the canvassers acted, and delivered the opinion from which I have already quoted.

"As soon as it was known that the canvassers had certified to the election of the Hayes electors, the Tilden electors filed an information in the nature of a *quo warranto* against them in one of the Circuit Courts of the State, to determine the validity of their respective claims to the office of electors. This proceeding was commenced upon the day on which the canvass was completed, and process was served on the Hayes electors before they had cast their votes. The Circuit Court had jurisdiction of the proceeding by the constitution of the State, the eighth section of which provides in terms that the Circuit Court and the judges thereof shall have power to issue writs of *quo warranto*. In the information the Tilden electors alleged that they were lawfully elected to the office of electors, and that the Hayes electors were not thus elected, but were usurpers. The Hayes electors appeared to the writ, and, first upon demurrer, and afterwards upon an investigation of the facts, their right to act as electors was determined. And it was adjudged that the Hayes electors were never appointed, and were never entitled to assume and exercise the functions of that office, and were usurpers; but that the Tilden electors were duly appointed at the election on the 7th of November, and were entitled on the 6th of December to receive certificates of election, and on that day and ever since to exercise the powers and perform the duties of that office. It matters not that this judgment was not reached until after the Hayes electors had voted ; it was an adjudication by a competent court upon the validity of their title as electors at the time they assumed to cast the vote of the State. That judgment remains in full force ; the appeal from it neither suspends its operation nor affects its validity.* It is certainly entitled to great, if not conclusive, weight upon the subject before us, especially when considered in connection with the action of the Legislature of the State. That action seems to me to be conclusive of the case.

" After the Supreme Court in the Drew proceeding had given a construc- tion to the election law, and decided that the canvassers had disregarded its plain provisions, exercised judicial functions which they never pos- sessed, and unlawfully rejected votes, the Legislature took steps to have

---

* The judgment was subsequently affirmed by the Supreme Court.

their count corrected with respect to the electors, as it had been with respect to the governor. And on the 17th of January last it passed 'An act to provide for a recanvass according to the laws of the State of Florida, as interpreted by the Supreme Court, of the votes for electors of President and Vice-President cast at the election held November 7, 1876.' This act required that the Secretary of State, the Attorney-General, and the Comptroller of Public Accounts, or any two of them, together with any other member of the Cabinet who might be designated by them, should meet forthwith at the office of the Secretary, pursuant to a notice from him, and form a board of State canvassers, and proceed to canvass the returns of election of electors of President and Vice-President held on the 7th of November, and determine and declare who were elected and appointed electors at that election, as shown by the returns on file. The act directed the canvassers to follow the construction of the law given by the Supreme Court defining the powers and duties of state canvassers. It directed that their certificate of the result should be recorded in the office of the Secretary of State, and a copy be published in one or more newspapers printed at the seat of government. The canvassers accordingly met and made the canvass directed, and certified that the Tilden electors, naming them, had received a majority of the votes and were duly elected.

"Subsequent to this, and on the 26th of January, the Legislature passed another act in relation to the Tilden electors. That act recited, among other things, that—

"'Whereas the board of state canvassers constituted under the act approved February 27, 1872, did interpret the laws of this State defining the powers and duties of the said board in such manner as to give them power to exclude certain regular returns, and did in fact under such interpretation exclude certain of such regular returns, which said interpretation has been adjudged by the Supreme Court to be erroneous and illegal;

"'And whereas the late Governor, Marcellus L. Stearns, by reason of said illegal action and erroneous and illegal canvass of the said board of State canvassers, did erroneously cause to be made and certified lists of the names of electors of this State, containing the names of said Charles H. Pearce, Frederick C. Humphreys, William H. Holden, and Thomas W. Long—

"The Hayes electors—

and did deliver such lists to said persons, when in fact the said persons had not received the highest number of votes, and, on a canvass conducted according to the rules prescribed and adjudged as legal by the Supreme Court, were not appointed as electors, or entitled to receive such lists from the Governor, but Robert Bullock, Robert B. Hilton, Wilkinson Call, and James E. Yonge—

"The Tilden electors—

were duly appointed electors, and were entitled to have their names compose the lists made and certified by the Governor, and to have such lists delivered to them:

"'Now, therefore, the people of the State of Florida, represented in Senate and Assembly, do enact, &c.'

"The act then proceeded to declare that the Tilden electors, naming them, were on the 7th of November duly chosen and appointed by and on behalf of the State of Florida in such manner as the Legislature thereof had directed, and were from that day entitled to exercise all the powers and duties of the office of electors and had full power and authority on the 6th of December, 1876, to vote as such electors for President and Vice-President, and to certify and transmit their votes as provided by law. The statute then ratified, confirmed, and declared as valid, to all intents and purposes, the acts of such electors. It also authorized and directed the Governor to make and certify in due form and under the seal of the State 'three lists of the names of the electors, and to transmit the same, with an authentic copy of the act, to the President of the Senate, and declared that such lists and certificates should be as valid and effectual to authenticate in behalf of the State the appointment of such electors by the State as if they had been made and delivered on or before the 6th of December, 1876, and had been transmitted immediately thereafter, and that the lists and certificates containing the names of the Hayes electors were illegal and void. The act further authorized and directed the Governor to cause three other lists of the names of the Tilden electors to be made and certified and forthwith delivered to them, and required those electors to meet at the Capitol of the State and to make and sign three additional certificates of the votes given by them on the 6th of December, to each of which should be annexed one of the lists of the electors furnished by the Governor, and that one of the certificates should be transmitted by messenger, and one by mail, to the President of the Senate, and the third delivered to the judge of the district, as required by law.

"Pursuant to this act, the Governor of the State made and certified three lists of the Tilden electors and delivered the same to them, and the said electors assembled and certified that they had met on the 6th day of December at the Capitol and given their votes as electors for President and Vice-President by distinct ballots, the votes for President being for Mr. Tilden, and the votes for Vice-President being for Mr. Hendricks, and signed three certificates of their action, which were forwarded as required by law. The certificates were accompanied by the certified lists of the Governor, by a certified copy of the two acts of the State, and by a certified copy of the returns on file in the office of the Secretary of State, with a tabulated statement annexed showing the result of the votes. The third certificate, which is before us, embraces all these proceedings.

"Here, then, we have the highest possible evidence of the action of the State of Florida. The two sets of electors both conformed to every requirement of the law in their proceedings. One set, the Hayes electors, have the certificate of Governor Stearns of their election, based upon a certificate of the canvassing-board, which in its nature is mere *prima-facie* evidence; the other set, the Tilden electors, have an adjudication of a State Court of competent jurisdiction, that they alone were the legally-appointed electors. They have the authoritative declaration of the Legislature of the State that they alone were entitled to act as electors and vote for President on the 6th of December; and they have a certificate of Governor Drew. based upon a recanvass of the votes, that they were duly appointed. And accompanying this evidence they have a certified copy of the returns, showing that they received a majority of the votes cast at the election.

"Under these circumstances can it be possible that there is any serious question as to which of the two sets of electors was *duly appointed?* As the Legislature was alone authorized to determine the manner in which the electors should be appointed, it could furnish in its own way evidence of their acts as agents of the State, whatever may be the power of Congress for its convenience in requiring a certificate of the Governor. Were this transaction one that involved merely questions of property, instead of a matter of great public and political interest, I do not think there is a lawyer on this Commission who could hesitate a moment as to the conclusive character of the evidence in favor of the Tilden electors.

" In addition to this action of the State, Congress has moved in the matter, and very properly so; for the entire people are interested in the election of their Chief Magistrate. No other officer can exercise so great an influence for good or for evil upon the whole country. He is not only the Commander-in-Chief of our Army and Navy, but he is the executor of our laws, the organ of intercourse with foreign nations, the bestower of offices of honor and trust, and is charged with the duty of maintaining and defending the Constitution. Of all the obligations resting upon the representatives of the people none is greater than that of seeing that no one takes that high office with a defective and tainted title. Acting upon this obligation, the House of Representatives early in the session, when it was rumored that irregular and fraudulent proceedings had characterized the election in some of the States, and in Florida among others, appointed committees of investigation to ascertain the facts and report who in truth had been appointed electors by those States. One of these committees proceeded to Florida, and took there a large amount of testimony on the subject, which it has returned to the House with its conclusions as to the result. This committee has reported that the Tilden electors were duly appointed, concurring in that respect with the action of the State tribunals and the State Legislature. Their report and its conclusions, if adopted by the House, would undoubtedly have a controlling influence upon its action in counting the vote of the State, if this Commission had not been created, and for that reason they should be received, and if not accepted as final, at least be considered by us.*

---

* " The committee presented to the House their report on the 31st of January, in which they declared that the evidence was perfectly conclusive that the State of Florida had cast her vote for the Tilden electors,

"We are invested with all the powers of the two Houses of Congress to ascertain and decide what persons were 'duly appointed' electors of Florida. By the law which has governed legislative bodies from their earliest existence, matters upon which they may be called to act can be investigated by committees appointed for that purpose. And either House may receive the testimony taken by its committee and proceed upon that, or accept the finding of its committee as its judgment, and act upon that as conclusive. And not until now has it ever been questioned that the power of each House to take testimony in that way was not as extensive as the subjects upon which it could act. One of the gentlemen on this Commission [Mr. Edmunds] introduced into the Senate during the present session resolutions for the appointment of committees to inquire into the matters which we are now considering, and Senators Morton and Frelinghuysen voted for them. One of the resolutions authorized the committees to inquire, among other things, 'whether the appointment of electors, or those claiming to be such, in any of the States has been made by force, fraud, or other means otherwise than in conformity with the Constitution and laws of the United States and the laws of the respective States;' and in compliance with the resolutions the committees have passed weeks in their investigations. It certainly provokes surprise and comment to hear these gentlemen now deny that either House of Congress has any power to go behind the certificate of the Governor and that of the canvassing-board of the State, and to inquire into the matters for which those committees were appointed.

"It is said that the Hayes electors were *de facto* officers, and, therefore, that their action is to be deemed valid until they are adjudged usurpers. But they were no more *de facto* officers than the Tilden electors. Both sets of electors acted at the same time and in the same building. The doctrine that the validity of the acts of *de facto* officers cannot be collaterally assailed, and that they are binding until the officers are ousted, is usually applied where there is a continuing office, and then

---

and they closed with recommending the passage of the following resolution:

"'*Resolved*, That at the election held on November 7th, A. D. 1876, in the State of Florida, Wilkinson Call, J. E. Yonge, R. B. Hilton, and Robert Bullock were fairly and duly chosen as Presidential electors, and that this is shown by the face of the returns, and fully substantiated by the evidence of the actual votes cast; and that the said electors having, on the first Wednesday of December, A. D. 1876, cast their votes for Samuel J. Tilden for President and for Thomas A. Hendricks for Vice-President, they are the legal votes of the State of Florida, and must be counted as such.'

"This resolution was subsequently adopted by the House by a vote of 142 yeas to 82 nays.

"The Subcommittee on Privileges and Elections of the Senate also made an investigation of the Florida case, and a report which was adverse in its conclusions to those of the House committee, but the report was never adopted by the Senate."

only on grounds of public policy. Private individuals are not called upon, and in most cases are not permitted, to inquire into the title of persons clothed with the insignia of public office and in apparent possession of its powers and functions. They are required, for the due order and peace of society, to respect the acts of such officers, and yield obedience to their authority, until in some regular mode provided by law their title is determined and they are ousted. As a consequence of the respect and obedience thus given, private individuals can claim, in all that concerns themselves and the public, for the acts of such officers, the same efficacy as though the officers were rightfully clothed with authority. The doctrine may be applied even to a single act of an officer where the office is a continuing one, but it may be doubted whether it is applicable to the case of a person simply charged with the performance of a single act. In such performance it would seem that the person could properly be regarded only as the official agent of the State, and if, therefore, he was without authority, his act would be void. If the doctrine is ever applicable to such a case, it cannot be applied, where the act performed has not accomplished its purpose before the want of right in the officer to do the act in question is determined. None of the reasons upon which the doctrine rests, of policy, convenience, or protection to private parties, has any application to a case of this kind. It does not seem, therefore, to me that there is any force in the position."

Justice Field concluded his argument as follows :

"Mr. President, I desire that this Commission should succeed and give by its judgment peace to the country. But such a result can only be attained by disposing of the questions submitted to us on their merits. It cannot be attained by a resort to technical subtleties and ingenious devices to avoid looking at the evidence. It is our duty to ascertain if possible the truth, and decide who were in fact duly appointed electors in Florida, not merely who had received certificates of such appointment. That State has spoken to us through her courts, through her legislature and through her executive, and has told us in no ambiguous terms what was her will and whom she had appointed to express it. If we shut our ears to her utterances, and closing our eyes to the evidence decide this case upon the mere inspection of the certificates of the Governor and canvassing-board, we shall abdicate our powers, defeat the demands of justice, and disappoint the just expectations of the people. The country may submit to the result, but it will never cease to regard our action as unjust in itself, and as calculated to sap the foundations of public morality."

The Commission by a vote of eight to seven—each member voting according to his party predilections—came to the amazing conclusion—and so decided—that it was " *not competent under the Constitution and the law, as it existed*

*at the date of the passage of the said act [creating the Electoral
Commission] to go into evidence aliunde the papers opened by
the President of the Senate, in the presence of the two Houses,
to prove that other persons than those regularly certified to by
the Governor of the State of Florida in, and according to the
determination and declaration of their appointment by the board
of State canvassers of said State, prior to the time required for
the performance of their duties, had been appointed electors, or,
by counter proof, to show that they had not, and that all proceedings of the Courts, or acts of the Legislature or of the Executive
of Florida subsequent to the casting of the votes of the electors
on the prescribed day, are inadmissible for any such purpose."*

This decision gave the vote of Florida to Mr. Hayes for
President, and to Mr. Wheeler for Vice-President.

THE LOUISIANA CASE.

In the Louisiana case the frauds committed by its returning-board were astounding. The number of votes
cast in the State for the Tilden electors, taking the first
name on the list as representing all, was 83,723, but the
certificate of the returning-board put them at 70,508,
turning Mr. Tilden's majority of more than thirteen thousand into a majority for Mr. Hayes. This reduction was
made by throwing out more than 13,000 votes of legal
voters, which had been cast for Mr. Tilden. More than
10,000 of these were thrown out upon the assumed authority of a statute of Louisiana which, in terms, gave
the board power to throw out votes, upon examination
and deliberation, "whenever, from any poll or voting-
place, there should be received the statement of any supervisor of registration or commissioner of election, in form,
as required by section 26 of this act, on *affidavit of three
or more citizens,* of any riot, tumult, acts of violence, intimidation, armed disturbance, bribery, or corrupt influences, which prevented, or tended to prevent, a fair,

free, and peaceable vote of all qualified electors entitled to vote at such poll or voting-place."

The only ground upon which a vote could have been thrown out, for intimidation or other corrupt influence, as thus seen, was the statement of a supervisor of registration or commissioner of election, founded upon the affidavits of three citizens. The statements and affidavits upon which the returning-board pretended to justify its action, were alleged by counsel to be forged and fabricated by persons acting under its direction and with its knowledge; and proof of this allegation was ready to be produced, but the Commission held it inadmissible.

Mr. Abbott, a member of the Commission, offered the following resolution:

"*Resolved*, That evidence is admissible that *the statements and affidavits* purporting to have been made and forwarded to said returning-board in pursuance of the provisions of section 26 of the election law of 1872, alleging riot, tumult, intimidation, and violence, at or near certain polls, and in certain parishes, *were* falsely fabricated and *forged* by certain disreputable persons *under the direction* and with the knowledge *of said returning-board*, and that said returning-board, knowing said statements and affidavits to be false and forged, and that none of the said statements or affidavits were made in the manner or form or within the time required by law, did knowingly, willfully, and fraudulently fail and refuse to canvass or compile more than 10,000 votes lawfully cast, as is shown by the statements of votes of the commissioners of election."

This offer the Commission rejected by a vote of 8 to 7.

The principles enunciated in his opinion in the Florida case, governed Justice Field's action, also, in that of Louisiana. In both of the cases he gave his vote in favor of the candidates of his party, and unquestionably in favor of truth and justice. The Commission by the same vote— 8 to 7—came to a result similar to that reached in the Florida case, as to the conclusive character of the certificates issued by the Governor of the State upon the determination of the returning-board.

Two of the persons certified to have been chosen as electors held, at the time of the election, offices of profit under the United States—one being Surveyor-General for the District of Louisiana, and the other being Commissioner of the Circuit Court of the United States for that District. But the Commission held, by a like vote of 8 to 7, that it was "*not competent to prove that any of said persons so appointed electors as aforesaid* [by the determination of the returning-board, as certified by the Governor] *held an office of trust and profit under the United States at the time when they were appointed, or that they were ineligible under the laws of the State, or any other matter offered to be proved aliunde the said certificates and papers.*" This was held in the face of the constitutional provision declaring " *that no Senator or Representative, or person holding an office of trust or profit under the United States, shall be appointed an elector.*"— (Art. II, sec. 1.)

This decision gave the vote of Louisiana to Mr. Hayes for President and to Mr. Wheeler for Vice-President.

THE OREGON CASE.

In the Oregon case the Democratic managers claimed the election of one of their electors on the ground of the constitutional ineligibility of his opponent. Justice Field was unable to go with them. The case, in brief, was this: Watts, one of the Hayes electors, was constitutionally ineligible, as he held at the time of the election an office of profit under the United States; and it was claimed by the Democrats that Cronin, who stood highest on the poll of the opposite side, was, therefore, legally chosen. The Governor of Oregon took this view of the case and certified the election of two Republican electors and one Democratic elector. The Republicans, however, claimed that Watts' ineligibility created a vacancy in the office which his associates could fill, and he having resigned both his electorship and the Federal office which rendered him ineligible to it, was elected by his colleagues on the ticket to fill the supposed vacancy thus created. Justice Field was of opinion that the clause of the Constitution declaring the ineligibility was absolute and self-operative, but declined to admit either of the conflicting consequences claimed from it, regarding the case as simply a failure to elect. He said:

"MR. PRESIDENT: . . . . .

"It appears that Odell, Watts, and Cartwright received at the election in Oregon, in November last, a higher number of votes for electors of President and Vice-President than the candidates against them. Odell and Cartwright were accordingly elected; of that there is no question. Watts would also have been elected had he been at the time eligible to the office. He was then and for some time afterward a postmaster at La Fayette, in the State. The office he held was one of trust and profit under the United States; it imposed trusts, and was one to which a pecuniary compensation was attached. He was, therefore, ineligible to the office of an elector; he was at the time incapable of being appointed to that office. Such is the language of the Constitution, which declares that 'No Senator or Representative, or person holding an office of trust or profit under the United States, shall be appointed an elector.' The prohibition here made is unqualified and absolute. All the power of appointment possessed by the State comes from the Constitution. The office of elector is created by that instrument. Her power of selection is, therefore, necessarily limited by its terms; and from her choice the class designated is excluded. The object of the exclusion was to prevent the use of the patronage of the Government to prolong the official life of those in power.

"The clause in question is one that operates by its own force. Like the prohibition against passing an *ex post facto* law, or a bill of attainder, or a law impairing the obligation of contracts, it executes itself; it requires no legislation to carry it into effect. As applied to Watts, it must be read as if his name were inserted in the text, and was as follows: 'The State of Oregon shall appoint, in such manner as the Legislature thereof may direct, a number of electors equal to the whole number of Senators and Representatives to which the State may be entitled in the Congress; but Watts shall not be appointed one of them.' The power to appoint him not existing in the State, the votes cast for him availed nothing; he was incapable of receiving them. He was not, therefore, appointed the third elector.

"The provision of the Constitution excluding from the choice of the State as electors certain classes of officers is very different from those provisions which create a mere personal disqualification to hold particular offices. Thus the clause declaring that 'No person *shall be* a Representative who shall not have attained to the age of twenty-five years,' and the clause that ' No person *shall be* a Senator who shall not have attained to the age of thirty years,' do not forbid an election of persons thus disqualified ; they only prohibit them from holding the office so long as the disqualification exists. They can take the office whenever that ceases. But with respect to electors the case is different. There is an incapacity on the part of the State to appoint as electors certain classes of officers. This distinction between ineligibility to an office and disqualification to hold the office is well marked. The one has reference to the time of election or appointment; the other to the time of taking possession of the office. The ineligibility existing at the date of the election is incurable afterwards; the disqualification to hold may be removed at any time before induction into office. If, therefore, at the time of the election persons are within the classes designated, their appointment is impossible. The Constitution prohibits it, and unless the probibition is to be frittered away whenever conflicting with the wishes of political partisans, it should be enforced equally with the provision fixing the number of electors. One clause of the same section cannot be disregarded any more than the other, and surely the appointment of a greater number of electors than the State was entitled to have would be a vain proceeding.

"The ineligibility of Watts was a fact known to the Governor. He had held the office of postmaster for years, and was in its possession and exercise at the time of the election. This was a fact of public notoriety, and was not denied by any one. It was asserted by parties who protested against the issue of a certificate of election to him, and it was abundantly proved. Besides this, the rule of law is that, whenever the ineligibility of a candidate arises from his holding a public office within the State, the people are chargeable with notice of the fact. The Governor is, of course, bound by the Constitution, and whenever the performance of a duty devolved upon him is affected by the existence of public offices under the United States, he may take notice officially of such offices and ascertain who are their incumbents. This is a doctrine which I had not supposed open to question. But I find that I am mistaken; and I am told by some gentlemen on this Commission that it was not competent for the Governor to consider the question of the ineligibility of the candidate, though made known to him in every possible way ; and that its determination involved the exercise of judicial functions, with which he was not invested. The general position advanced by them is that the duty of the Governor, as a commissioning officer, is to issue his certificate of election to any one who may obtain, according to the determination of the canvassers, the highest number of votes, however ineligible the person, and however imperative the prohibition may be against his taking the office.

"To test this doctrine I put this question to these gentlemen : Supposing the law declared that only white persons should be eligible to an office, and the highest number of votes, according to the canvassers, should be cast for a colored man, would the Governor be bound to issue a commission to him? The gentlemen answered that he would be thus bound; that the Governor could not in such case decide the question of the colored man's ineligibility. Mr. Senator Thurman put this further question: Supposing the law of the State declared that only males should be elected to an office, and the highest number of votes were cast, according to the report of the canvassers, for a female, would the Governor be bound to issue a commission to her? The gentlemen replied, as before, that he would be thus bound; that the Governor could not determine the ineligibility of the party on the ground of her sex. There is something refreshing in these days of sham and pretence to find men who will thus accept the logic of their principles, to whatever result they may lead.

"A different doctrine, I think, prevails in this country. Every department of government, when called upon to apply a provision of the Constitution, must, in the first instance, pass upon its construction and determine the extent of its obligation. A just man empowered to issue a certificate of election will, it is true, hesitate to decide on the question of the ineligibility of a candidate, where there is any serious doubt on the subject, and for that reason to refuse his certificate. He will in such a case leave the matter to the determination of the judicial tribunals. But where there is no doubt on the subject, and the language of the Constitution forbidding the appointment is clear and imperative, he cannot, without violating his oath of office, disregard its mandate.

" The law is laid down in numerous adjudications in conformity with these views. In the case of the State of Missouri on the relation of Bartley against the Governor, which is cited by counsel, (39 Missouri, 399,) the doctrine for which I contend is stated with great clearness and precision. There a mandamus was prayed against the Governor to compel him to issue a commission to the relator as one of the justices of the County Court. The Supreme Court refused the writ on the ground that the issuing of a commission was the exercise of political power, and not a mere ministerial act. After reciting that by the Constitution the duty devolved upon the Governor to commission all officers not otherwise provided by law, the Court said:

" ' The Governor is bound to see that the laws are faithfully executed, and he has taken an oath to support the Constitution. In the correct and legitimate performance of his duty he must inevitably have a discretion in regard to granting commissions; for should a person be elected or appointed who was constitutionally ineligible to hold any office of profit or trust, would the executive be bound to commission him when his ineligibility was clearly and positively proven? If he is denied the exercise of any discretion in such case, he is made the violator of the Constitution, not its guardian. Of what avail then is his oath of office? Or, if he has positive and satisfactory evidence that no election has been held in a county, shall he be required to violate the law and issue a commission to a person not elected, because a clerk has certified to the election? In granting a commission the Governor may go behind the certificate to

29

determine whether an applicant is entitled to receive a commission or not, where the objection to the right of the applicant to receive it rests upon the ground that a constitutional prohibition is interposed.'

"In Gulick against New, also cited by counsel, (14 Indiana, 93,) the Supreme Court of Indiana used language substantially to the same effect, holding that the Governor, who was authorized to commission officers, might determine, even against the decision of a board of canvassers, whether an applicant was entitled to receive a commission or not, where the objection to his right to receive it rested upon a constitutional prohibition.

"Other adjudications might be cited, but I believe these express the law as recognized generally throughout the country.* The question then arises, Watts being ineligible, whether the person receiving the next highest number of votes, he being eligible, was elected. Governor Grover held that such person was elected and issued a certificate of election to him. In his action in this respect he followed the rule which obtains in England, where, if the voters having knowledge of the ineligibility of a candidate persist in voting for him, their votes are considered as thrown away, and the eligible candidate receiving the next highest number of votes is declared elected. There are numerous decisions by courts of the highest character in this country to the same effect. They have been cited to us by counsel in their elaborate arguments, and

---

"* In the debate which took place in the Senate on the 16th of December, 1876, on the electoral vote of Oregon, Senator Thurman replied to some remarks of Senator Morton upon the action of Governor Grover, as follows:

"'The Senator from Indiana says that the question whether Watts was eligible or not was a judicial question, and that the sole duty of the Governor was a ministerial duty, that he had no judicial function whatever, that it was, therefore, his duty simply to certify to the person who received the highest number of votes. He states that in the most absolute manner. If his statement be correct, then, if, instead of voting for Watts, the voters who cast their votes for him had voted for Queen Victoria, it would have been the duty of the Governor to issue a certificate of election to Her Majesty the Queen that she was chosen elector of President and Vice-President for the State of Oregon. . . . . It is very true in Oregon, as in every State in the Union and in the Federal Government, that there is a department of government which is called the judiciary, and another department called the executive, and another the legislative, and the constitutions endeavor to partition out the great powers of government between these three departments; but does it follow from that, that no power to judge in any case can be devolved either upon the legislative department or upon the executive department of the government or an executive officer? We could not get along with the government one day on such an idea as that. The judicial power which the Governor of Oregon cannot exercise, which the Legislature cannot exercise; the judicial power that Congress cannot exercise, that the President cannot exercise, is the power of deciding litigated cases that arise in jurisprudence, and is a wholly different thing from the exercise of that quasi-judical power which executive officers are called upon every day to exercise and which they must exercise.'

in view of them an honorable and conscientious man might well have acted as the Governor did. But I do not yield my assent to them; they are not in harmony with the spirit of our system of elections. The theory of our institutions is that the majority must govern; and their will can only be carried out by giving the offices to those for whom they have voted. In accordance with this view, the weight of judicial opinion in this country is, that votes given for an ineligible candidate are merely ineffectual to elect him, and that they are not to be thrown out as blanks, and the election given to the eligible candidate having the next highest number of votes. It is fairer and more just to thus limit the operation of votes for an ineligible candidate than to give them, as said in the California case, 'the effect of disappointing the popular will and electing to office a man whose pretensions the people had designed to reject.'—(Saunders vs. Haynes, 13 California, 154.)

" I cannot, therefore, vote that Cronin, the candidate having the next highest number of votes to Watts, 'was duly appointed' an elector of the State at the election in November. As there was, in my opinion, a failure to appoint a third elector, the question arises whether a vacancy was thus produced which the other electors could fill. In a general sense, an office may be said to be vacant when it is not filled, though this condition arise from non-election, or the death, resignation, or removal of an incumbent. Cases have been cited before us where the term 'vacancy' is used in both these senses. But the question for us to decide is whether there was a vacancy within the meaning of the legislation of Congress. That legislation distinguishes between cases of non-election and cases of vacancy, evidently treating the latter as only occurring after the office has once been filled. I refer to sections 133 and 134 of the Revised Statutes, which are as follows:

" 'SEC. 133. Each State may by law provide for the filling of any vacancies which may occur in its College of Electors, when such college meets to give its electoral vote.

" 'SEC. 134. Whenever any State has held an election for the purpose of choosing electors, and has failed to make a choice on the day prescribed by law, the electors may be appointed on a subsequent day in such manner as the Legislature of such State may direct.'

" Under this legislation the State of Oregon has provided for filling vacancies in its Electoral College, treating, as does Congress, a vacancy as arising only after the office has once been filled. Its code of general laws declares when vacancies in any office shall be deemed to have occurred, as follows:

" ' Every office shall become vacant on the occurring of either of the following events before the expiration of the term of such office:

" ' 1. The death of the incumbent;

" ' 2. His resignation;

" ' 3. His removal;

" ' 4. His ceasing to be an inhabitant of the district, county, town, or village for which he shall have been elected or appointed, or within which the duties of his office are required to be discharged;

"'5. His conviction of an infamous crime, or of any offence involving a violation of his oath;

"'6. His refusal or neglect to take his oath of office, or to give or renew his official bond, or to deposit such oath or bond within the time prescribed by law;

"'7. The decision of a competent tribunal declaring void his election or appointment.'—(*General Laws of Oregon*, page 576, section 48.)

"On the subject of vacancies in the Electoral College, the same code of general laws provides that when the electors convene—

"'If there shall be any vacancy in the office of an elector, occasioned by death, refusal to act, neglect to attend, or otherwise, the electors present shall immediately proceed to fill, by *viva voce* and plurality of votes, such vacancy in the Electoral College.'—(*General Laws of Orygon*, page 578, section 59.)

"It seems evident from these provisions that there could be no vacancy in the office of elector unless the office had once been filled. The events upon the occurrence of which the statute declares that a vacancy shall occur in any office, all imply the existence of a previous incumbent.

"The word 'otherwise,' used with respect to a vacancy in the Electoral College, does not enlarge the scope of that term. The code having enumerated under one title the events upon which a vacancy may arise, including death, resignation, and other causes, proceeds to declare, under another title of the same chapter, that when a vacancy occurs in the office of elector by death, refusal to act, or *otherwise*, meaning thereby any other cause which would remove an incumbent, the electors present may fill the vacancy. As here there never had been an incumbent, there could be no vacancy, in the sense of the statute, by death or *otherwise*.

"The two electors, Odell and Cartwright, undertook to appoint Watts as the third elector, upon the assumption that he had resigned the office, and that a vacancy was thereby created. But inasmuch as he had never been elected, he had nothing to resign. The case was not one of a vacancy, but of a failure to elect; and the Legislature of the State had made no provision for a subsequent election in case of such failure, as it might have done under the legislation of Congress."

It followed from these views that there were only two electors duly appointed by Oregon, and that, therefore, only two electoral votes from that State could be counted.

Justice Field offered before the Commission three resolutions embodying the views thus expressed, but they were all rejected by a vote of eight to seven; and by that vote the Commission held: "*That though the evidence showed that Watts was a postmaster at the time of his election, that fact was rendered immaterial by his resignation both as postmaster and elector and his subsequent appointment to fill the vacancy made by the Electoral College.*"

Three votes, instead of two, from Oregon, were, therefore, counted for Mr. Hayes as President and for Mr. Wheeler as Vice-President.

THE SOUTH CAROLINA CASE.

The principal objections to the count of the electoral vote of South Carolina were, that there had been no registration of persons entitled to vote, as required by the constitution of the State; that the General Government, without authority of law, had stationed, prior to and during the election, in various parts of the State, at or near the polling places, detachments of the army of the United States, by whose presence the free exercise of the right of suffrage was prevented, and a fair election became impossible; and that over a thousand deputy marshals had been stationed at the polling places, who, by their arbitrary and illegal action, in obedience to the Department of Justice, had so interfered with the exercise of the right of suffrage that a fair election was impossible.

On the hearing before the Commission proof was ready to be produced to establish these objections, but the Commission ruled it inadmissible.

Justice Field offered the following resolutions:

"*Resolved*, That evidence is admissible to show that prior to and during the election on the 7th day of November, 1876, in the State of South Carolina, there were unlawfully stationed in various parts of the State, at or near the polling places, detachments of the troops of the army of the United States, by whose presence and interference qualified voters of the State were deprived of the right of suffrage, and a free choice by the people of Presidential electors was prevented.

"*Resolved*, That evidence is admissible to show that at the election on the 7th day of November, 1876, in South Carolina, there were stationed at the several polling places deputy marshals of the United States exceeding one thousand in number, by whose unlawful action and interference, under orders from the Department of Justice, qualified voters of the State were deprived of the right of suffrage, and a free choice by the people of Presidential electors was prevented."

These were rejected by a vote of eight to seven; and the Commission resolved by a like vote, as follows:

"That it is not competent for the two Houses of Congress when assembled to count the votes for President and Vice-President, by taking evidence, to inquire into the regularity of the action of the President of the United States in sending a military force into any State for the preservation of order or the suppression of insurrection and domestic violence, in order by such proof to lay a ground for rejecting the electoral vote of said State;" and, also, that there existed "no power in this Commission, as there exists none in the two Houses of Congress, in counting the electoral vote, to inquire into the circumstances under which the primary vote for electors was given."

The vote of South Carolina was accordingly cast for Mr. Hayes as President and for Mr. Wheeler as Vice-President.

The votes of the four States of Florida, Louisiana, Oregon, and South Carolina being all counted for these gentlemen under the rulings of the Commission, they were declared by Congress elected by a majority of one vote.

The general disappointment throughout the country at the action of the Commission was well expressed in the following article from the *Public Ledger and Daily Transcript*, of Philadelphia, of February 19th, 1877, which appeared whilst the Commission was in session, but after its decision on the Florida and Louisiana cases. That paper, though not a partisan journal, has always been of strong Republican proclivities :

"COUNTING THE ELECTORAL VOTE.

"There is reason for the strong dissatisfaction expressed concerning the course of the majority of the Electoral Commission. There is just cause for complaint, not because they have awarded the votes of Florida and Louisiana to Governor Hayes, but because of their persistent refusal to inquire into the truth of the certificates which covered those votes. Thus far their inquiries and their decisions, when reduced to plain terms, amount to nothing more than this: that Stearns was Governor of Florida on the 6th of December last, and that Kellogg was *de facto* Governor of Louisiana on the same date. It did not require the creation of a high and extraordinary Commission like that now in session to inquire into and decide historical facts like these. They were beyond dispute, and were not disputed. The Commission was created, under circumstances of the utmost solemnity, to inquire and decide whether such certificates as those given by Stearns and Kellogg did actually certify to the truth, and whether the electors named in those certificates were in truth and in law the electors who received majorities of the lawful votes of Florida and Louisiana. This the majority of the Commission have continuously refused to do, and taking their stand on bare technicalities, have abdicated the very jurisdiction and action they were brought into existence to exercise. Without the belief that they would exercise it, the Commission could have had no existence. It was that belief that made the appointment of the Commission a possibility, and caused its appointment to be hailed with welcome and confidence throughout the United States.

" This is said with profound regret. It is mortifying to be obliged to say it in the columns of a journal which was among the foremost in aiding to create the Commission, and which, in fact, sketched its outlines long before the law took shape anywhere else. We certainly understood that the Commission was to inquire into the *very truth and right* of the disputed votes in Florida and Louisiana, and that the decision of the Commission was to be given upon the *merits* after that inquiry, and not upon bald technicalities. The law gives to the Commission all the powers possessed in the premises by the two Houses of Congress, and to take into view such evidence as might be competent and pertinent. This portion of the law certainly means something; it means precisely what it says, and was universally understood to mean that the Commission were to inquire whether the papers from Florida and Louisiana, purporting to be votes, are in fact votes or false pretences, but the majority of the Commission have treated that part of the law as if it means nothing, by refusing to make that inquiry.

" This tribunal was, from the outset, trusted with the patriotic hopes and honored with the fullest confidence of three-fourths of the people of the United States, in the belief that the solemn circumstances attending the necessity and the act that brought it into being, would cause all its members (with possibly three exceptions) to rise above all party considerations in the discharge of their momentous duty. In the light of this antecedent hope and confidence, and in view of the votes written on the record of the Commission, it is pitiable to observe that every important question thus far submitted to the Commission has divided the Commissioners, eight to seven, on strict party lines, accordingly as the decision would help the case of Governor Hayes, or hurt the case of Governor Tilden. It was not believed by fairminded, intelligent men that such a division could come about. The outside adherents of each party mutually charge this as a discredit on the opposing members of the Commission. The zealous Democrats reproach the Republicans with these partisan votes of the eight Republican Commissioners; and the zealous Republicans retort by pointing to the partisan votes of the seven Democrats on the Commission. This is about what might be expected from that kind of discussion. But that which will live in history and in the minds of the vast majority of the public is this: that the seven voted to look into the evidence, voted to take testimony, and voted to let in light, so as to get at the truth; and that the eight voted all the time to turn away from evidence, to shut out the light, and so to close the door upon all effort to find the truth. The seven voted in a way to promote the great object for which the Commission was created; the eight voted in a way to make the Commission utterly useless for the principal purpose for which it has any reason for being in existence at all. The Senator, the Judge, the Presidential aspirant, the party that supposes the eyes of the American people can be closed to this vital aspect of the matter is making a signal and perilous mistake. The American people know what is honorable, fair, manly, and just; and their ultimate decisions always show that they not only know, but that they act upon their knowledge."

APPENDIX.

THE UNCONSTITUTIONALITY OF TEST OATHS FOR PAST CONDUCT.

THE OPINIONS OF THE SUPREME COURT OF
THE UNITED STATES

IN

CUMMINGS vs. THE STATE OF MISSOURI

AND IN

EX–PARTE GARLAND.

SUPREME COURT OF THE UNITED STATES.

JOHN A. CUMMINGS, Plaintiff in Error,

vs.

THE STATE OF MISSOURI.

Mr. Justice FIELD delivered the opinion of the Court.[*]

This case comes before us on a writ of error to the Supreme Court of Missouri, and involves a consideration of the test oath imposed by the constitution of that State. The plaintiff in error is a priest of the Roman Catholic Church, and was indicted and convicted in one of the Circuit Courts of the State of the crime of teaching and preaching as a priest and minister of that religious denomination without having first taken the oath, and was sentenced to pay a fine of five hundred dollars, and to be committed to jail until the same was paid. On appeal to the Supreme Court of the State the judgment was affirmed.

The oath prescribed by the constitution, divided into its separate parts, embraces more than thirty distinct affirmations or tests. Some of the acts, against which it is directed, constitute offences of the highest grade, to which, upon conviction, heavy penalties are attached. Some of the acts have never been classed as offences in the laws of any State; and some of the acts, under many circumstances, would not even be blameworthy. It requires the affiant to deny not only that he has ever " been in armed hostility to the United States, or to the lawful authorities thereof," but, among other things, that he has ever, " by act or word," manifested his adherence to the cause of the enemies of the United States, foreign or domestic, or his *desire* for their triumph over the arms of the United States, or his *sympathy* with those engaged in rebellion, or has ever *harbored* or *aided any person* engaged in guerrilla warfare against the loyal inhabitants of the United States, or has ever *entered* or *left* the State for the purpose of avoiding enrollment or draft in the military service of the United States; or, to escape the performance of duty in the

---

[*] Delivered at the December Term, 1866, and reported in 4th Wallace, Sup. Ct. Reports, 316.

militia of the United States, has ever indicated, *in any terms*, his *disaffection* to the government of the United States in its contest with the rebellion.

Every person who is unable to take this oath is declared incapable of holding, in the State, " any office of honor, trust, or profit under its authority, or of being an officer, councilman, director, or trustee, or other manager of any corporation, public or private, now existing or hereafter established by its authority, or of acting as a professor or teacher in any educational institution, or in any common or other school, or of holding any real estate or other property in trust for the use of any church, religious society, or congregation."

And every person holding, at the time the constitution takes effect, any of the offices, trusts, or positions mentioned, is required within sixty days thereafter to take the oath ; and, if he fail to comply with this requirement, it is declared that his office, trust, or position shall *ipso facto* become vacant.

No person, after the expiration of the sixty days, is permitted, without taking the oath, " to practice as an attorney or counsellor-at-law, nor after that period can any person be competent, as a bishop, priest, deacon, minister, elder, or other clergyman, of any religious persuasion, sect, or denomination, to teach, or preach, or solemnize marriages."

Fine and imprisonment are prescribed as a punishment for holding or exercising any of " the offices, positions, trusts, professions, or functions " specified, without having taken the oath; and false swearing or affirmation in taking it is declared to be perjury, punishable by imprisonment in the penitentiary.

The oath thus required is, for its severity, without any precedent that we can discover. In the first place, it is retrospective; it embraces all the past from this day; and, if taken years hence, it will also cover all the intervening period. In its retrospective feature we believe it is peculiar to this country. In England and France there have been test oaths, but they were always limited to an affirmation of present belief, or present disposition towards the government, and were never exacted with reference to particular instances of past misconduct. In the second place, the oath is directed not merely against overt and visible acts of hostility to the government, but is intended to reach words, desires, and sympathies also. And, in the third place, it allows no distinction between acts springing from malignant enmity and acts which may have been prompted by charity, or affection, or relationship. If one has expressed sympathy with any who were drawn into the rebellion, even if the recipients of that sympathy were connected by the closest ties of blood, he is as unable to subscribe to the oath as the most active and the most cruel of the rebels, and is equally debarred from the offices of honor or trust, and the positions and employments specified.

But, as it was observed by the learned counsel who appeared on behalf of the State of Missouri, this Court cannot decide the case upon the justice or hardship of these provisions. Its duty is to determine whether they are in conflict with the Constitution of the United States. On behalf of Missouri, it is urged that they only prescribe a qualification for holding certain offices, and practicing certain callings, and that it is, therefore, within the power of the State to adopt them. On the other hand, it is contended that they are in conflict with the Constitution which forbids any State to pass a bill of attainder or an *ex post facto* law.

We admit the propositions of the counsel of Missouri, that the States which existed previous to the adoption of the Federal Constitution possessed originally all the attributes of sovereignty; that they still retain those attributes, except as they have been surrendered by the formation of the Constitution, and the amendments thereto; that the new States, upon their admission into the Union, became invested with equal rights, and were thereafter subject only to similar restrictions, and that among the rights reserved to the States is the right of each State to determine the qualifications for office, and the conditions upon which its citizens may exercise their various callings and pursuits within its jurisdiction.

These are general propositions and involve principles of the highest moment. But it by no means follows that under the form of creating a qualification or attaching a condition, the States can in effect inflict a punishment for a past act which was not punishable at the time it was committed. The question is not as to the existence of the power of the State over matters of internal police, but whether that power has been made in the present case an instrument for the infliction of punishment against the inhibition of the Constitution.

Qualifications relate to the fitness or capacity of the party for a particular pursuit or profession. Webster defines the term to mean " any natural endowment or any acquirement which fits a person for a place, office, or employment, or enables him to sustain any character with success." It is evident from the nature of the pursuits and professions of the parties, placed under disabilities by the constitution of Missouri, that many of the acts, from the taint of which they must purge themselves, have no possible relation to their fitness for those pursuits and professions. There can be no connection between the fact that Mr. Cummings entered or left the State of Missouri to avoid enrollment or draft in the military service of the United States and his fitness to teach the doctrines or administer the sacraments of his church; nor can a fact of this kind, or the expression of words of sympathy with some of the persons drawn into the rebellion, constitute any evidence of the unfitness of the attorney or counsellor to practice his profession, or of the professor to teach the ordinary branches of education, or of the want of business knowledge or business capacity in the manager of a corporation, or in any director or trustee. It is manifest upon the simple statement of many of the acts and of the professions and pursuits, that there is no such relation between them as to render a denial of the commission of the acts at all appropriate as a condition of allowing the exercise of the

professions and pursuits. The oath could not, therefore, have been required as a means of ascertaining whether parties were qualified or not
for their respective callings or the trusts with which they were charged.
It was required in order to reach the person, not the calling. It was exacted, not from any notion that the several acts designated indicated unfitness for the callings, but because it was thought that the several acts
deserved punishment, and that for many of them there was no way to
inflict punishment except by depriving the parties, who had committed
them, of some of the rights and privileges of the citizen.

The disabilities created by the constitution of Missouri must be regarded as penalties; they constitute punishment. We do not agree with
the counsel of Missouri that "to punish one is to deprive him of life,
liberty, or property, and that to take from him anything less than these
is no punishment at all." The learned counsel does not use these terms,
life, liberty, and property, as comprehending every right known to the law.
He does not include under liberty freedom from outrage on the feelings
as well as restraints on the person. He does not include under property
those estates which one may acquire in professions, though they are often
the source of the highest emoluments and honors. The deprivation of
any rights, civil or political, previously enjoyed, may be punishment,
the circumstances attending and the causes of the deprivation determining this fact. Disqualification from office may be punishment, as in
cases of conviction upon impeachment. Disqualification from the pursuits of a lawful avocation, or from positions of trust, or from the privilege of appearing in the courts, or acting as an executor, administrator,
or guardian, may also and often has been, imposed as punishment. By
statutes 9 and 10 William III., chap. 32, if any person educated in or
having made a profession of the Christian religion, did, " by writing, printing, teaching, or advised speaking," deny the truth of the religion, or the
divine authority of the Scriptures, he was for the first offence rendered
incapable to hold any office or place of trust; and for the second he was
rendered incapable of bringing any action, being guardian, executor, legatee, or purchaser of lands, besides being subjected to three years imprisonment without bail.*

By statute 1 George I., chap. 13, contempts against the King's title, arising from refusing or neglecting to take certain prescribed oaths, and yet
acting in an office or place of trust for which they were required, were
punished by incapacity to hold any public office; to prosecute any suit;
to be guardian or executor; to take any legacy or deed of gift; and to
vote at any election for members of Parliament: and the offender was
also subject to a forfeiture of five hundred pounds to any one who would
sue for the same.†

" Some punishments," says Blackstone, " consist in exile or banishment
by abjuration of the realm or transportation; others in loss of liberty

* 4 Blackstone, 44.　　　† Ibid., 124.

by perpetual or temporary imprisonment. Some extend to confiscation by forfeiture of lands or movables, or both, or of the profits of lands for life; others induce a disability of holding offices or employments, being heirs, executors, and the like." *

In France deprivation or suspension of civil rights, or of some of them, and among these of the right of voting, of eligibility to office, or of taking part in family councils, of being guardian or trustee, of bearing arms, and of teaching or being employed in a school or seminary of learning, are punishments prescribed by her code.

The theory upon which our political institutions rest is, that all men have certain inalienable rights; that among these are life, liberty, and the pursuit of happiness; and that in the pursuit of happiness all avocations, all honors, all positions are alike open to every one, and that in the protection of these rights all are equal before the law. Any deprivation or suspension of any of these rights for past conduct is punishment, and can be in no otherwise defined.

Punishment not being, therefore, restricted, as contended by counsel, to the deprivation of life, liberty, or property, but also embracing deprivation or suspension of political or civil rights, and the disabilities prescribed by the provisions of the Missouri constitution, being in effect punishment, we proceed to consider whether there is any inhibition in the Constitution of the United States against their enforcement.

The counsel for Missouri closed his argument in this case by presenting a striking picture of the struggle for ascendency in that State during the recent rebellion, between the friends and enemies of the Union, and of the fierce passions which that struggle aroused. It was in the midst of the struggle that the present constitution was framed, although it was not adopted by the people until the war had closed. It would have been strange, therefore, had it not exhibited in its provisions some traces of the excitement amidst which the convention held its deliberations.

It was against the excited action of the States under such influences as these that the framers of the Federal Constitution intended to guard. In Fletcher vs. Peck,† Mr. Chief Justice Marshall, speaking of such action, uses this language: "Whatever respect might have been felt for the State sovereignties, it is not to be disguised that the framers of the Constitution viewed with some apprehension the violent acts which might grow out of the feelings of the moment; and that the people of the United States, in adopting that instrument, have manifested a determination to shield themselves and their property from the effects of those sudden and strong passions to which men are exposed. The restrictions on the legislative power of the States are obviously founded in this sentiment; and the Constitution of the United States contains what may be deemed a bill of rights for the people of each State."

"'No State shall pass any bill of attainder, *ex post facto* law, or law impairing the obligation of contracts.'"

---

* 4 Vol., 377. † 6 Cranch, 137.

A bill of attainder is a legislative act which inflicts punishment without a judicial trial. If the punishment be less than death the act is termed a bill of pains and penalties. Within the meaning of the Constitution, bills of attainder include bills of pains and penalties. In these cases the legislative body, in addition to its legitimate functions exercises the powers and office of a judge; it assumes, in the language of the textbooks, judicial magistracy; it pronounces upon the guilt of the party without any of the forms or safeguards of trial; it determines the sufficiency of the proofs produced, whether conformable to the rules of evidence or otherwise; and it fixes the degree of punishment in accordance with its own notions of the enormity of the offence.

" Bills of this sort," says Mr. Justice Story, " have been most usually passed in England in times of rebellion or gross subserviency to the Crown, or of violent political excitements; periods, in which all nations are most liable (as well the free as the enslaved) to forget their duties, and to trample upon the rights and liberties of others."*

These bills are generally directed against individuals by name, but they may be directed against a whole class. The bill against the Earl of Kildare and others, passed in the reign of Henry VIII.,† enacted that " all such persons which be or heretofore have been comforters, abettors, partakers, confederates, or adherents unto the said " late earl, and certain other parties who were named, " in his or their false or traitorous acts and purposes, shall in likewise stand, and be attainted, adjudged, and convicted of high treason;" and that "the same attainder, judgment, and conviction against the said comforters, abettors, partakers, confederates, and adherents, shall be as strong and effectual in the law against them, and every of them, as though they and every of them had been specially, singularly, and particularly named by their proper names and surnames in the said act."

These bills may inflict punishment absolutely, or may inflict it conditionally.

The bill against the Earl of Clarendon, passed in the reign of Charles the Second, enacted that the earl should suffer perpetual exile, and be forever banished from the realm; and that if he returned, or was found in England, or in any other of the King's domains after the first of February, 1667, he should suffer the pains and penalties of treason; with the proviso, however, that if he surrendered himself before the said first day of February for trial, the penalties and disabilities declared should be void and of no effect.‡

" A British Act of Parliament," to cite the language of the Supreme Court of Kentucky, " might declare, that if certain individuals, or a class of individuals, failed to do a given act by a named day, they should be deemed to be, and treated as convicted felons or traitors. Such an act

---

* Commentaries on the Constitution, § 1, 344.
† 28 Henry VIII., Chap. 18, 3 Stats. of the Realm, 694.
‡ Printed in 6 Howell's State Trials, p. 391.

comes precisely within the definition of a bill of attainder, and the English courts would enforce it without indictment or trial by jury." *

If the clauses of the second article of the constitution of Missouri, to which we have referred, had in terms declared that Mr. Cummings was guilty, or should be held guilty, of having been in armed hostility to the United States, or of having entered that State to avoid being enrolled or drafted into the military service of the United States, and, therefore, should be deprived of the right to preach as a priest of the Catholic Church, or to teach in any institution of learning, there could be no question that the clauses would constitute a bill of attainder within the meaning of the Federal Constitution. If these clauses, instead of mentioning his name, had declared that all priests and clergymen within the State of Missouri were guilty of these acts, or should be held guilty of them, and hence be subjected to the like deprivation, the clauses would be equally open to objection. And further, if these clauses had declared that all such priests and clergymen should be so held guilty, and be thus deprived, provided they did not, by a day designated, do certain specified acts, they would be no less within the inhibition of the Federal Constitution.

In all these cases there would be the legislative enactment creating the deprivation without any of the ordinary forms and guards provided for the security of the citizen in the administration of justice by the established tribunals.

The results which would follow from clauses of the character mentioned do follow from the clauses actually adopted. The difference between the last case supposed and the case actually presented is one of form only, and not of substance. The existing clauses presume the guilt of the priests and clergymen, and adjudge the deprivation of their right to preach or teach unless the presumption be first removed by their expurgatory oath; in other words, they assume the guilt and adjudge the punishment conditionally. The clauses supposed differ only in that they declare the guilt instead of assuming it. The deprivation is effected with equal certainty in the one case as it would be in the other, but not with equal directness. The purpose of the law-maker in the case supposed would be openly avowed; in the case existing it is only disguised. The legal result must be the same, for what cannot be done directly cannot be done indirectly. The Constitution deals with substance, not shadows. Its inhibition was leveled at the thing, not the name. It intended that the rights of the citizen should be secure against deprivation for past conduct by legislative enactment, under any form, however disguised. If the inhibition can be evaded by the form of the enactment, its insertion in the fundamental law was a vain and futile proceeding.

We proceed to consider the second clause of what Mr. Chief Justice Marshall terms a bill of rights for the people of each State; the clause which inhibits the passage of an *ex post facto* law.

---

* Gaines vs. Buford, 1 Dana, 510.

By an *ex post facto* law is meant one which imposes a punishment for an act which was not punishable at the time it was committed ; or imposes additional punishment to that then prescribed ; or changes the rules of evidence by which less or different testimony is sufficient to convict than was then required.

In Fletcher vs. Peck, Mr. Chief Justice Marshall defined an *ex post facto* law to be one "which renders an act punishable in a manner in which it was not punishable when it was committed." "Such a law," said that eminent judge, "may inflict penalties on the person, or may inflict pecuniary penalties which swell the public treasury. The Legislature is then prohibited from passing a law by which a man's estate, or any part of it, shall be seized for a crime, which was not declared by some previous law to render him liable to that punishment. Why, then, should violence be done to the natural meaning of words for the purpose of leaving to the Legislature the power of seizing for public use the estate of an individual, in the form of a law annulling the title by which he holds the estate ? The Court can perceive no sufficient grounds for making this distinction. This rescinding act would have the effect of an *ex post facto* law. It forfeits the estate of Fletcher for a crime not committed by himself, but by those from whom he purchased. This cannot be effected in the form of an *ex post facto* law, or bill of attainder; why, then, is it allowable in the form of a law annulling the original grant?"

The act to which reference is here made was one passed by the State of Georgia, rescinding a previous act, under which lands had been granted. The rescinding act, annulling the title of the grantees, did not, in terms, define any crimes, or inflict any punishment, or direct any judicial proceedings ; yet, inasmuch as the Legislature was forbidden from passing any law by which a man's estate could be seized for a crime, which was not declared such by some previous law rendering him liable to that punishment, the Chief Justice was of opinion that the rescinding act had the effect of an *ex post facto* law, and was within the constitutional prohibition.

The clauses in the Missouri constitution, which are the subject of consideration, do not, in terms, define any crimes, or declare that any punishment shall be inflicted, but they produce the same result upon the parties, against whom they are directed, as though the crimes were defined and the punishment was declared. They assume that there are persons in Missouri who are guilty of some of the acts designated. They would have no meaning in the constitution were not such the fact. They are aimed at past acts, and not future acts. They were intended especially to operate upon parties who, in some form or manner, by action or words, directly or indirectly, had aided or countenanced the rebellion, or sympathized with parties engaged in the rebellion, or had endeavored to escape the proper responsibilities and duties of a citizen in time of war ; and they were intended to operate by depriving such persons of the right to hold certain offices and trusts, and to pursue their ordinary and regular avocations. This deprivation is punishment; nor is it any less so because a way is opened for escape from it by the expurgatory oath. The framers of the constitution of Missouri knew at the time that whole classes of individuals would be unable to take the oath prescribed. To them there is no escape provided; to them the deprivation was intended to be, and is, absolute and perpetual. To make the enjoyment of a right dependent upon an impossible condition is equivalent to an absolute denial of the right under any condition, and such denial, enforced for a past act, is nothing less than punishment imposed for that act. It is a misapplication of terms to call it anything else.

Now, some of the acts to which the expurgatory oath is directed, were not offences at the time they were committed. It was no offence against any law to enter or leave the State of Missouri for the purpose of avoiding enrollment or draft in the military service of the United States, however much the evasion of such service might be the subject of moral censure. Clauses which prescribe a penalty for an act of this nature, are within the terms of the definition of an *ex post facto* law; "they impose a punishment for an act not punishable at the time it was committed."

Some of the acts at which the oath is directed constituted high offences at the time they were committed, to which, upon conviction, fine and imprisonment, or other heavy penalties were attached. The clauses which provide a further penalty for these acts are also within the definition of an *ex post facto* law; "they impose additional punishment to that prescribed when the act was committed."

And this is not all. The clauses in question subvert the presumptions of innocence, and alter the rules of evidence, which heretofore, under the universally recognized principles of the common law, have been supposed to be fundamental and unchangeable. They assume that the parties are guilty; they call upon the parties to establish their innocence; and they declare that such innocence can be shown only in one way; by an inquisition, in the form of an expurgatory oath, into the consciences of the parties.

The objectionable character of these clauses will be more apparent if we put them into the ordinary form of a legislative act. Thus, if instead of the general provisions in the constitution the convention had provided as follows: Be it enacted, that all persons who have been in armed hostility to the United States shall, upon conviction thereof, not only be punished as the laws provided at the time the offences charged were committed, but shall also be thereafter rendered incapable of holding any of the offices, trusts, and positions, and of exercising any of the pursuits mentioned in the second article of the constitution of Missouri; no one would have any doubt of the nature of the enactment. It would be an *ex post facto* law, and void; for it would add a new punishment for an old offence. So, too, if the convention had passed an enactment of a similar kind with reference to those acts which did not constitute offences. Thus, had it provided as follows: Be it enacted, that all persons who have heretofore, at any time, entered or left the State of Missouri, with intent to avoid enrollment or draft in the military service of the United States, shall, upon conviction thereof, be forever rendered incapable of holding any office of honor, trust, or profit in the State, or of teaching in any seminary of learning, or of preaching as a minister of the Gospel of any denomination, or of exercising any of the professions or pursuits mentioned in the second article of the constitution; there would be no question of the character of the enactment. It would be an *ex post facto* law, because it would impose a punishment for an act not punishable at the time it was committed.

The provisions of the constitution of Missouri accomplish precisely what enactments like those supposed would have accomplished. They impose the same penalty, without the formality of a judicial trial and conviction; for the parties embraced by the supposed enactments would be incapable of taking the oath prescribed; to them its requirement would be an impossible condition. Now, as the State, had she attempted the course supposed, would have failed, it must follow that any other mode producing the same result must equally fail. The provisions of the Federal Constitution, intended to secure the liberty of the citizen, cannot be evaded by the form in which the power of the State is exerted. If this were not so, if that which cannot be accomplished by means looking directly to the end, can be accomplished by indirect means, the inhibition may be evaded at pleasure. No kind of oppression can be named, against which the framers of the Constitution intended to guard, which may not be effected. Take the case supposed by counsel; that of a man tried for treason and acquitted, or if convicted, pardoned; the Legislature may nevertheless enact that, if the person thus acquitted or pardoned does not take an oath, that he never has committed the acts charged against him, he shall not be permitted to hold any office of honor, or trust, or profit, or pursue any avocation in the State. Take the case before us; the constitution of Missouri, as we have seen, excludes, on failure to take the oath prescribed by it, a large class of persons within her borders from numerous positions and pursuits; it would have been equally within the power of the State to have extended the exclusion so as to deprive the parties, who are unable to take the oath, from any avocation whatever in the State. Take still another case; suppose that, in the progress of events, persons now in the minority in the State, should obtain the ascendency, and secure the control of the government; nothing could prevent, if the constitutional prohibition can be evaded, the enactment of a provision requiring every person, as a condition of holding any position of honor or trust, or of pursuing any avocation in the State, to take an oath that he had never advocated or advised or supported the imposition of the present expurgatory oath. Under this form of legislation the most flagrant invasion of private rights, in periods of excitement, may be enacted, and individuals, even whole classes, may be deprived of political and civil rights.

A question arose in New York, soon after the Treaty of Peace in 1783, upon a statute of that State, which involved a discussion of the nature and character of these expurgatory oaths, when used as a means of inflicting punishment for past conduct. The subject was regarded as so important, and the requirement of the oath such a violation of the fundamental principles of civil liberty, and the rights of the citizen, that it engaged the attention of eminent lawyers and distinguished statesmen of the time, and among others of Alexander Hamilton. We will cite some passages of a paper left by him on the subject, in which, with his characteristic fullness and ability, he examines the oath, and demonstrates that it is not only a mode of inflicting punishment, but a mode in violation of all the constitutional guaranties, secured by the Revolution, of the rights and liberties of the people.

"If we examine it," (the measure requiring the oath,) said this great lawyer, "with an unprejudiced eye, we must acknowledge, not only that it was an evasion of the treaty, but a subversion of one great principle of social security, to wit: that every man shall be presumed innocent until he is proved guilty. This was to invert the order of things; and, instead of obliging the State to prove the guilt, in order to inflict the penalty, it was to oblige the citizen to establish his own innocence to avoid the penalty. It was to excite scruples in the honest and conscientious, and to hold out a bribe to perjury. . . . . It was a mode of inquiry who had committed any of those crimes to which the penalty of disqualification was annexed, with this aggravation, that it deprived the citizen of the benefit of that advantage, which he would have enjoyed by leaving, as in all other cases, the burthen of the proof upon the prosecutor.

"To place this matter in a still clearer light, let it be supposed that instead of the mode of indictment and trial by jury the Legislature was to declare that every citizen, who did not swear he had never adhered to the King of Great Britain, should incur all the penalties which our treason laws prescribe. Would this not be a palpable evasion of the treaty, and a direct infringement of the Constitution? The principle is the same in both cases, with only this difference in the consequences;— that in the instance already acted upon the citizen forfeits a part of his rights; in the one supposed he would forfeit the whole. The degree of punishment is all that distinguishes the cases. In either, justly considered, it is substituting a new and arbitrary mode of prosecution to that ancient and highly-esteemed one recognized by the laws and the constitution of the State. I mean the trial by jury.

"Let us not forget that the Constitution declares that trial by jury, in all cases in which it has been formerly used, should remain inviolate forever, and that the Legislature should at no time erect any new jurisdiction which should not proceed according to the course of the common law. Nothing can be more repugnant to the true genius of the common law than such an inquisition as has been mentioned into the consciences of men. . . . . . . If any oath with retrospect to past conduct were to be made the condition on which individuals, who have resided within the British lines, should hold their estates, we should immediately see that this proceeding would be tyrannical, and a violation of the treaty; and yet, when the same mode is employed to divest that right, which ought to be deemed still more sacred, many of us are so infatuated as to overlook the mischief.

"To say that the persons who will be affected by it have previously forfeited that right, and that therefore nothing is taken away from them, is a begging of the question. How do we know who are the persons in this situation? If it be answered, this is the mode taken to ascertain it, the objection returns, 'tis an improper mode, because it puts the most essential interests of the citizen upon a worse footing than we should be willing to tolerate where inferior interests were concerned, and because, to elude the treaty, it substitutes for the established and legal mode of investigating crimes and inflicting forfeitures, one that is unknown to the Constitution, and repugnant to the genius of our law."

Similar views have frequently been expressed by the judiciary in cases involving analogous questions. They are presented with great force in the matter of Dorsey,* but we do not deem it necessary to pursue the subject further.

The judgment of the Supreme Court of Missouri must be reversed, and the cause remanded, with directions to enter a judgment reversing the judgment of the Circuit Court, and directing that Court to discharge the defendant from imprisonment, and suffer him to depart without day. And it is so ordered.

---

* 7 Porter's Reports, 294.

SUPREME COURT OF THE UNITED STATES.

EX-PARTE GARLAND.

Mr. Justice FIELD delivered the opinion of the Court.*

On the 2d of July, 1862, Congress passed an act prescribing an oath to be taken by every person elected or appointed to any office of honor or profit under the Government of the United States, either in the civil, military, or naval departments of the public service, except the President, before entering upon the duties of his office, and before being entitled to its salary or other emoluments. On the 24th of January, 1865, Congress, by a supplementary act, extended its provisions so as to embrace attorneys and counsellors of the Courts of the United States. This latter act provides that after its passage no person shall be admitted as an attorney and counsellor to the bar of the Supreme Court, and, after the 4th of March, 1865, to the bar of any Circuit or District Court of the United States, or of the Court of Claims, or be allowed to appear and be heard by virtue of any previous admission, or any special power of attorney, unless he shall have first taken and subscribed the oath prescribed by the act of July 2d, 1862. It also provides that the oath shall be preserved among the files of the Court, and if any person take it falsely he shall be guilty of perjury, and, upon conviction, shall be subject to the pains and penalties of that offence.

At the December Term, 1860, the petitioner was admitted as an attorney and counsellor of this Court, and took and subscribed the oath then required. By the second rule, as it then existed, it was only requisite to the admission of attorneys and counsellors of this Court that they should have been such officers for three previous years in the highest Courts of the States to which they respectively belonged, and that their private and professional character should appear to be fair.

In March, 1865, this rule was changed by the addition of a clause requiring the administration of the oath in conformity with the act of Congress.

In May, 1861, the State of Arkansas, of which the petitioner was a citizen, passed an ordinance of secession which purported to withdraw the

---

* Delivered at the December Term, 1866, and reported in 4th Wallace, Supreme Court Reports, 374.

State from the Union, and afterwards, in the same year, by another ordinance, attached herself to the so-called Confederate States, and by act of the Congress of that Confederacy was received as one of its members.

The petitioner followed the State and was one of her representatives, first in the lower house and afterwards in the Senate, of the Congress of that Confederacy, and was a member of the Senate at the time of the surrender of the Confederate forces to the armies of the United States.

In July, 1865, he received from the President of the United States a full pardon for all offences committed by his participation, direct or implied, in the Rebellion. He now produces his pardon and asks permission to continue to practice as an attorney and counsellor of the Court without taking the oath required by the act of January 24th, 1865, and the rule of the Court, which he is unable to take by reason of the offices he held under the Confederate Government. He rests his application principally upon two grounds :

1st. That the act of January 24th, 1865, so far as it affects his status in the Court, is unconstitutional and void ; and,

2d. That, if the act be constitutional, he is released from compliance with its provisions by the pardon of the President.

The oath prescribed by the act is as follows :

1st. That the deponent has never voluntarily borne arms against the United States since he has been a citizen thereof;

2d. That he has not voluntarily given aid, countenance, counsel, or encouragement to persons engaged in armed hostility thereto;

3d. That he has never sought, accepted, or attempted to exercise the functions of any office whatsoever, under any authority, or pretended authority, in hostility to the United States ;

4th. That he has not yielded a voluntary support to any pretended government, authority, power, or constitution within the United States, hostile or inimical thereto ; and,

5th. That he will support and defend the Constitution of the United States against all enemies, foreign and domestic, and will bear true faith and allegiance to the same.

This last clause is promissory only, and requires no consideration. The questions presented for our determination arise from the other clauses. These all relate to past acts. Some of these acts constituted, when they were committed, offences against the criminal laws of the country ; others may, or may not, have been offences, according to the circumstances under which they were committed and the motives of the parties. The first clause covers one form of the crime of treason, and the deponent must declare that he has not been guilty of this crime, not only during the war of the Rebellion, but during any period of his life since he has been a citizen. The second clause goes beyond the limits of treason and embraces not only the giving of aid and encouragement of a treasonable nature to a public enemy, but also the giving of assistance of any kind to persons engaged in armed hostility to the United States. The third clause applies to the seeking, acceptance, or exercise, not only of offices created for the purpose of more effectually carrying on hostilities, but also of any of those offices which are required in every community, whether in peace or war, for the administration of justice and the preservation of order. The fourth clause not only includes those who gave a cordial and active support to the hostile government, but also those who yielded a reluctant obedience to the existing order, established without their co-operation.

The statute is directed against parties who have offended in any of the particulars embraced by these clauses. And its object is to exclude them from the profession of the law, or at least from its practice in the Courts of the United States. As the oath prescribed cannot be taken by these parties, the act, as against them, operates as a legislative decree of perpetual exclusion. And exclusion from any of the professions or any of the ordinary avocations of life for past conduct can be regarded in no other light than as punishment for such conduct. The exaction of the oath is the mode provided for ascertaining the parties upon whom the act is intended to operate, and instead of lessening, increases its objectionable character. All enactments of this kind partake of the nature of bills of pains and penalties, and are subject to the constitutional inhibition against the passage of bills of attainder, under which general designation they are included.

In the exclusion which the statute adjudges, it imposes a punishment for some of the acts specified, which were not punishable at the time they were committed; and for other of the acts it adds a new punishment to that before prescribed, and it is thus brought within the further inhibition of the Constitution against the passage of an *ex post facto* law. In the case of Cummings against The State of Missouri, just decided, we have had occasion to consider at length the meaning of a bill of attainder and of an *ex post facto* law in the clause of the Constitution forbidding their passage by the States, and it is unnecessary to repeat here what we there said. A like prohibition is contained in the Constitution against enactments of this kind by Congress; and the argument presented in that case against certain clauses of the constitution of Missouri is equally applicable to the act of Congress under consideration in this case.*

---

* " Suppose the act to have been mandatory to the Courts, to call upon all the members of their bar to answer on oath whether they had borne arms against the United States since they became citizens; whether they had voluntarily given aid, counsel, countenance, or encouragement to persons engaged in hostilities to the United States; whether they had sought or performed the functions of any office, under any authority, or pretended authority, in hostility to the United States; or had yielded a voluntary support to any pretended authority or government within the United States, or inimical thereto, and upon the failure of any one to answer such interrogations, and all elucidating interrogations, or to answer satisfactorily, it should be their duty to erase the name of such re-

The profession of an attorney and counsellor is not like an office created by an act of Congress, which depends for its continuance, its powers,
and its emoluments upon the will of its creator, and the possession of
which may be burdened with any conditions not prohibited by the Constitution. Attorneys and counsellors are not officers of the United States ;
they are not elected nor appointed in the manner prescribed by the Constitution for the election and appointment of such officers. They are officers of the Court, admitted as such by its order, upon evidence of their
possessing sufficient legal learning and fair private character. It has
been the general practice in this country to obtain this evidence by an
examination of the parties. In this Court the fact of the admission of
such officers in the highest Court of the States to which they respectively
belong, for three years preceding their application, is regarded as sufficient evidence of the possession of the requisite legal learning, and the
statement of counsel, moving their admission, sufficient evidence that
their private and professional character is fair. The order of admission

---

cusant attorney from the rolls. . . . And suppose in such case the
Attorney-General were asked whether, since he had been a citizen of the
United States, he had borne arms against the United States ? The Attorney-General would be informed that he might answer or not; but if
he failed to answer he would lose his faculty of appearing in Court. If
he answered in the affirmative he would forfeit his place, and if he answered falsely he would be liable to indictment. . . . . He must
have answered : 'May it please your Honors, the Constitution of the
United States declares that "no person SHALL BE HELD TO ANSWER FOR
A CAPITAL OR OTHER INFAMOUS OFFENCE, unless on the presentment of
a grand jury ; that no person shall be convicted of treason unless on the
testimony of two witnesses to the same overt act, or confession in open
court; and that no person shall be compelled in any criminal case to be
a witness against himself." The act of bearing arms against the United
States is an overt act of treason by a citizen thereof. The demand upon
a whole profession—a profession of which I am a member—to perform a
ceremony that violates the Constitution is an indignity. I fulfill my
oath of office to support this Constitution by declining to answer the
question. I submit this answer to the conscience of the Court.' I feel
satisfied that no Supreme Court would have insisted on the answer. . .
" Let us suppose that the act had enumerated by name all the members
of the bar of the different Courts of the United States, and had enacted
that each and all of those must be prohibited from entering the Courts
until they had made oath that they had not, in the course of their lives,
violated any one of the TEN commandments. Some of these commandments do not enter into the statute laws of the United States ; and others
are not, perhaps, the subject of legislative action in any of the United
States. Every one of the existing members of the legal profession would
probably find himself in a condition not to answer to his own satisfaction
such interrogatories to himself as the law would elicit.
" Jeremy Taylor, in his exposition of those commandments—not a
strained construction of them—shows that they include nearly all of the
social, civil, and personal obligations of men. I am wholly unable to
find any arguments in favor of my professional brethren to avoid the issue
of such a test, that are not equally applicable to the act of January, 1865."
—CAMPBELL.

is the judgment of the Court that the parties possess the requisite quali‑
fications as attorneys and counsellors, and are entitled to appear as such
and conduct causes therein. From its entry the parties become officers
of the Court, and are responsible to it for professional misconduct. They
hold their office during good behavior, and can only be deprived of it
for misconduct ascertained and declared by the judgment of the Court,
after opportunity to be heard has been afforded.* Their admission or
their exclusion is not the exercise of a mere ministerial power. It is the
exercise of judicial power, and has been so held in numerous cases. It
was so held by the Court of Appeals of New York in the matter of the
application of Cooper for admission.† "Attorneys and counsellors," said
that Court, "are not only officers of the Court, but officers whose duties
relate almost exclusively to proceedings of a judicial nature. And hence
their appointment may, with propriety, be intrusted to the Courts, and
the latter, in performing this duty, may very justly be considered as en‑
gaged in the exercise of their appropriate judicial functions."

In *Ex-parte Secombe*,‡ a *mandamus* to the Supreme Court of the Terri‑
tory of Minnesota to vacate an order removing an attorney and counsellor
was denied by this Court, on the ground that the removal was a judicial
act. "We are not aware of any case," said the Court, "where a *mandamus* was issued to an inferior tribunal, commanding it to reverse or
annul its decision, where the decision was in its nature a judicial act, and
within the scope of its jurisdiction and discretion." And in the same

---

* "It is a fundamental principle in jurisprudence that no man shall be
deprived of his right without citation and an opportunity of being heard.
In the jurisprudence of the Romans—the magistrates of mankind—it
was a rule that no judgment should be given before citation. A Roman
governor, in a remote and despised province—a governor weak, faithless,
and corrupt—in the case of the great Apostle, has made this principle a
home word in the mouths of all Christians. Festus informed Agrippa
that he had answered to the Jews: 'It is not the manner of the Romans
to deliver any man to die, before that he which is accused have the ac‑
cusers face to face, and have license to answer for himself concerning the
crime laid against him.'—(Acts, chap. 25, v. 16.) This sentence is a part
of the Constitution of the United States, with more generality than it
was necessary for Festus to state."—CAMPBELL.

In Ex-parte Robinson, decided at the October Term, 1873, (19 Wall.,
512-'13,) the Court held that before a judgment disbarring an attorney
was rendered, he should have notice of the grounds of complaint against
him and ample opportunity of explanation and defence, and that this
was a rule of natural justice which should be equally followed when pro‑
ceedings are taken to deprive him of his right to practice his profession,
as when they are taken to reach his real or personal property; observing
that the principle that there must be citation before hearing, and hearing
or opportunity of being heard before judgment, was essential to the se‑
curity of all private rights, and without its observance no one would be
safe from oppression wherever power may be lodged.—(See *Ex-parte* Hey‑
fron, 7 Howard, Mississippi, 127; People vs. Turner, 1 Cal., 148; Beene vs.
The State, 22 Ark., 157; and Fletcher vs. Daingerfield, 20 California, 430.)

† 22 New York, 81.   ‡ 19 Howard, 9.

case the Court observed that " it has been well settled by the rules and practice of Common-law Courts, that it rests exclusively with the Courts to determine who is qualified to become one of its officers, as an attorney and counsellor, and for what cause he ought to be removed."*

The attorney and counsellor being, by the solemn judicial act of the Court, clothed with his office, does not hold it as a matter of grace and favor. The right which it confers upon him to appear for suitors, and to argue causes, is something more than a mere indulgence, revocable at the pleasure of the Court, or at the command of the Legislature. It is a right of which he can only be deprived by the judgment of the Court for moral or professional delinquency.

The Legislature may undoubtedly prescribe qualifications for the office, to which he must conform, as it may, where it has exclusive jurisdiction, prescribe qualifications for the pursuit of any of the ordinary avocations of life. The question in this case is not as to the power of Congress to prescribe qualifications, but whether that power has been exercised as a means for the infliction of punishment against the prohibition of the Constitution. That this result cannot be effected indirectly by a State under the form of creating qualifications we have held, in the case of *Cummings vs. The State of Missouri*, and the reasoning by which that conclusion was reached applies equally to similar action on the part of Congress.

This view is strengthened by a consideration of the effect of the pardon produced by the petitioner, and the nature of the pardoning power of the President.

The Constitution provides that the President "shall have power to grant reprieves and pardons for offences against the United States, except in cases of impeachment."†

The power thus conferred is unlimited, with the exception stated. It extends to every offence known to the law, and may be exercised at any time after its commission, either before legal proceedings are taken or during their pendency, or after conviction and judgment. This power of the President is not subject to legislative control. Congress can neither limit the effect of his pardon nor exclude from its exercise any class of offenders. The benign prerogative of mercy reposed in him cannot be fettered by any legislative restrictions.

Such being the case, the inquiry arises as to the effect and operation of a pardon, and on this point all the authorities concur. A pardon reaches both the punishment prescribed for the offence and the guilt of the offender; and when the pardon is full, it releases the punishment and

---

* But when the Court below exceeds its jurisdiction, and disbars an attorney for an alleged contempt committed in its presence or before another Court, mandamus will lie from the Supreme Court to restore him to his office. So held in Ex-parte Bradley, 7 Wallace, and in Ex-parte Robinson—*Supra*.

† Article II., § 2.

blots out of existence the guilt, so that in the eye of the law the offender is as innocent as if he had never committed the offence. If granted before conviction, it prevents any of the penalties and disabilities consequent upon conviction from attaching; if granted after conviction, it removes the penalties and disabilities, and restores him to all his civil rights; it makes him, as it were, a new man, and gives him a new credit and capacity.

There is only this limitation to its operation: it does not restore offices forfeited, or property or interests vested in others in consequence of the conviction and judgment.*

The pardon produced by the petitioner is a full pardon " for all offences by him committed, arising from participation, direct or implied, in the Rebellion," and is subject to certain conditions which have been complied with. The effect of this pardon is to relieve the petitioner from all penalties and disabilities attached to the offence of treason, committed by his participation in the Rebellion. So far as that offence is concerned, he is thus placed beyond the reach of punishment of any kind. But to exclude him, by reason of that offence, from continuing in the enjoyment of a previously acquired right, is to enforce a punishment for that offence notwithstanding the pardon. If such exclusion can be effected by the exaction of an expurgatory oath covering the offence, the pardon may be avoided, and that accomplished indirectly which cannot be reached by direct legislation. It is not within the constitutional power of Congress thus to inflict punishment beyond the reach of executive clemency. From the petitioner, therefore, the oath required by the act of January 24th, 1865, could not be exacted, even if that act were not subject to any other objection than the one thus stated.

---

* 4 Blackstone's Commentaries, 402; 6 Bacon's Abridgment, tit. Pardon; Hawkins, book 2, c. 37, §§ 34 and 54.

In Carlisle vs. The United States, decided at the December Term, 1872, in speaking of the effect of the proclamation of pardon and amnesty, made by the President on the 25th of December, 1868, upon the rights of certain parties, who had given aid and comfort to the Rebellion, and who were claimants before the Court of Claims of the proceeds of cotton seized by the officers of the United States and turned over to the agents of the Treasury Department, the Court said: " Assuming that they [the claimants] are within the terms of the proclamation, the pardon and amnesty granted relieve them from the legal consequences of their participation in the Rebellion, and from the necessity of proving that they had not thus participated, which otherwise would have been indispensable to a recovery. It is true, the pardon and amnesty do not and cannot alter the fact that aid and comfort were given by the claimants, *but they forever close the eyes of the Court to the perception of that fact as an element in its judgment, no rights of third parties having intervened.*"

" There has been some difference of opinion among the members of the Court as to cases covered by the pardon of the President, but there has been none as to the effect and operation of a pardon in cases where it applies. All have agreed that the pardon not merely releases the offender from the punishment prescribed for the offence, but that it obliterates in legal contemplation the offence itself."—(16 Wallace, 151.)

It follows, from the views expressed, that the prayer of the petitioner must be granted.*

The case of R. H. Marr is similar, in its main features, to that of the petitioner, and his petition must also be granted.

And the amendment of the second rule of the Court which requires the oath prescribed by the act of January 24th, 1865, to be taken by attorneys and counsellors, having been unadvisedly adopted, must he rescinded.

And it is so ordered.†

---

* The President granted to Garland "a full *pardon* and *amnesty* for all offences by him committed arising from participation, direct or implied, in the Rebellion." The term amnesty is not found in the Constitution, but is generally used to denote the clemency which is extended to a class of persons or to a whole community. Pardon is the generic term, and includes every species of executive clemency, individual, general, conditional, and absolute.—(See The Federalist, No. 74; U. S. vs. Wilson, 7 Peters, 150; Ex-parte Wells, 18 How., 315.)

† In the decision of these two cases, Cummings vs. The State of Missouri, and Ex-parte Garland, Justices Wayne, Nelson, Grier, Clifford, and Field concurred. Chief Justice Chase, and Justices Swayne, Miller, and Davis dissented. Subsequently the Chief Justice expressed his concurrence in the opinion of the majority; and the decision was followed by the entire Court, with the exception of Mr. Justice Bradley, in the case of Pierce vs. Carskadon, decided at the December Term, 1872.—(16 Wallace, 234.)

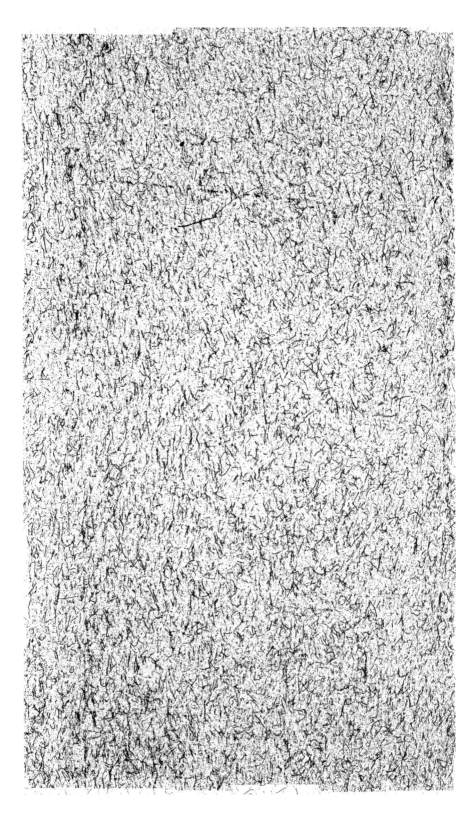

Lightning Source UK Ltd.
Milton Keynes UK
UKHW022358020119
334667UK00009B/1386/P